Handbook of Financial Risk Management

Wiley Handbooks in
FINANCIAL ENGINEERING AND ECONOMETRICS

Advisory Editor
Ruey S. Tsay
The University of Chicago Booth School of Business, USA

A complete list of the titles in this series appears at the end of this volume.

Handbook of Financial Risk Management

Simulations and Case Studies

N.H. Chan
H.Y. Wong
The Chinese University of Hong Kong

WILEY

Copyright © 2013 by John Wiley & Sons, Inc. All rights reserved.

Published by John Wiley & Sons, Inc., Hoboken, New Jersey.
Published simultaneously in Canada.

No part of this publication may be reproduced, stored in a retrieval system, or transmitted in any form or by any means, electronic, mechanical, photocopying, recording, scanning, or otherwise, except as permitted under Section 107 or 108 of the 1976 United States Copyright Act, without either the prior written permission of the Publisher, or authorization through payment of the appropriate per-copy fee to the Copyright Clearance Center, Inc., 222 Rosewood Drive, Danvers, MA 01923, (978) 750-8400, fax (978) 750-4470, or on the web at www.copyright.com. Requests to the Publisher for permission should be addressed to the Permissions Department, John Wiley & Sons, Inc., 111 River Street, Hoboken, NJ 07030, (201) 748-6011, fax (201) 748-6008, or online at http://www.wiley.com/go/permission.

Limit of Liability/Disclaimer of Warranty: While the publisher and author have used their best efforts in preparing this book, they make no representations or warranties with respect to the accuracy or completeness of the contents of this book and specifically disclaim any implied warranties of merchantability or fitness for a particular purpose. No warranty may be created or extended by sales representatives or written sales materials. The advice and strategies contained herein may not be suitable for your situation. You should consult with a professional where appropriate. Neither the publisher nor author shall be liable for any loss of profit or any other commercial damages, including but not limited to special, incidental, consequential, or other damages.

For general information on our other products and services or for technical support, please contact our Customer Care Department within the United States at (800) 762-2974, outside the United States at (317) 572-3993 or fax (317) 572-4002.

Wiley also publishes its books in a variety of electronic formats. Some content that appears in print may not be available in electronic books. For more information about Wiley products, visit our web site at www.wiley.com.

Library of Congress Cataloging-in-Publication Data:

Chan, Ngai Hang.
 Handbook of financial risk management: simulations and case studies / Ngai Hang Chan, Department of Statistics, The Chinese University of Hong Kong, Shatin, Hong Kong, Hoi Ying Wong, Department of Statistics, The Chinese University of Hong Kong, Shatin, Hong Kong.
   pages cm
 Includes bibliographical references and index.
 ISBN 978-0-470-64715-8 (cloth)
 1. Finance–Simulation methods. 2. Risk management–Simulation methods. I. Wong, Hoi Ying, 1974- II. Title.
 HG173.C4695 2013
 332.64'50113–dc23
                                                                                    2013001309

Printed in the United States of America

10 9 8 7 6 5 4 3 2 1

Contents

Preface xi

1 An Introduction to Excel VBA 1

    1.1   How to Start Excel VBA / 1
           1.1.1   Introduction / 1
           1.1.2   Visual Basic Editor / 2
           1.1.3   The Macro Recorder / 3
           1.1.4   Insert a Command Button / 5
    1.2   VBA Programming Fundamentals / 8
           1.2.1   Declaration of Variables / 8
           1.2.2   Types of Variables / 9
           1.2.3   Multivariable Declaration / 10
           1.2.4   Declaration of Constants / 10
           1.2.5   Operators / 11
           1.2.6   User-Defined Data Types / 11
           1.2.7   Arrays and Matrices / 13
           1.2.8   Data Input and Output / 14
           1.2.9   Conditional Statements / 14
           1.2.10 Loops / 16

1.3 Linking VBA to C++ / 18
1.4 Sub Procedures and Function Procedures / 19
   1.4.1 VBA Built-In Functions / 22
   1.4.2 Multiple Linear Regression / 23
1.5 Random Number Generation / 25
   1.5.1 Inverse Transform / 25
   1.5.2 Acceptance–Rejection Method / 26
1.6 List of Functions Defined in the Book / 28
   1.6.1 Constants / 28
   1.6.2 Types / 28
   1.6.3 General Functions / 28
   1.6.4 Asset Path Simulation Functions / 30
   1.6.5 Other Functions / 32
   1.6.6 Remarks / 32

2 Background 33

2.1 A Brief Review of Martingales and Itô's Calculus / 34
   2.1.1 Martingales / 34
   2.1.2 Brownian Motion / 35
   2.1.3 Itô's Process and Itô's Lemma / 39
   2.1.4 Discretization Methods / 41
   2.1.5 The Black–Scholes Equation and Risk-Neutral Valuation / 43
   2.1.6 Change of Measures / 47
2.2 Volatility / 50
2.3 Mark to Market and Calibration / 53
   2.3.1 Marking to Market / 53
   2.3.2 Calculation of MTM Values / 54
   2.3.3 Calibration / 55
2.4 Variance Reduction Techniques / 55
   2.4.1 A Brief Review of Variance Reduction Techniques / 55
   2.4.2 Pricing a Call Option / 68

3 Structured Products 71

3.1 When Is Simulation Unnecessary? / 72
   3.1.1 Portfolio Replication Pricing / 72
   3.1.2 Equity-Linked Notes / 72
3.2 Simulation of Black–Scholes Model and European Options / 73

3.3 American Options / 79
    3.3.1 Empirical Martingale Correction / 87
3.4 Range Accrual Notes / 89
    3.4.1 Possible Design and Sample Term Sheet / 89
    3.4.2 Closed-Form Solution for European RAN Under Black–Scholes Model / 89
    3.4.3 Callable and American Features / 91
3.5 FX Accumulator: The Case of Citic Pacific LTD / 95
    3.5.1 Event Playback / 95
    3.5.2 Structure of an Accumulator / 97
    3.5.3 Accumulator Valuation / 97
    3.5.4 Sensitivity Analysis / 103
3.6 Life Insurance Contracts / 105
    3.6.1 Introduction / 105
    3.6.2 Typical Contract Structures / 105
    3.6.3 Simulation Algorithms / 107
3.7 Multi-Asset Instruments / 108
    3.7.1 Multi-Asset Range Accrual Equity-Linked Notes / 112
    3.7.2 Currency-Translated Products / 116

4 Volatility Modeling 121

4.1 Local Volatility Models: Simulation and Binomial Tree / 122
    4.1.1 Calibration of Local Volatility Function and Dupire Equation / 123
    4.1.2 Implied Binomial Tree / 130
4.2 The Heston Stochastic Volatility Model / 135
    4.2.1 The Heston Model and Option Pricing / 136
    4.2.2 Model Calibration and Implementation / 138
    4.2.3 Calibration to European Options: Differential Evolution / 139
4.3 Simulation of Exotic Option Prices under Heston Model / 143
    4.3.1 Heston Stochastic Volatility Model Simulation Methods: Quadratic–Exponential Discretization Scheme / 143
    4.3.2 QE Discretization Scheme for $\widehat{V}(t)$ / 145
    4.3.3 QE Discretization Scheme for $\widehat{S}(t)$ / 146
    4.3.4 Performance Analysis of the QE Scheme / 148
    4.3.5 CITIC Case Study Revisited / 150
4.4 The GARCH Option Pricing Model / 156
    4.4.1 Estimation of Model Parameters / 157

viii CONTENTS

      4.4.2 Identification of the Risk-Neutral Process / 161
      4.4.3 Pricing Exotics / 163
  4.5 Jump-Diffusion Model / 164
      4.5.1 Simulation of Asset Price Paths and Product Valuation / 167
      4.5.2 Estimation of Jump-Diffusion / 171

5 Fixed-Income Derivatives I: Short-Rate Models   177

  5.1 Yield Curve Building / 179
      5.1.1 Building the Forward Rate Curve / 192
  5.2 The Hull–White Model / 194
      5.2.1 Calibration of the Hull–White Model / 197
  5.3 Pricing Interest Rate Products Using the Direction Simulation Approach / 204
      5.3.1 Target Redemption Notes / 206
      5.3.2 Interest Rate Range Accrual Notes / 207
  5.4 Pricing Interest Rate Products Using the Trinomial Tree Approach / 209
      5.4.1 Bond Price / 214
      5.4.2 Generalized Hull–White Model: The Tree Approach / 214
      5.4.3 Simulation Using the Trinomial Tree / 215
      5.4.4 Pricing Target Redemption Notes / 216
      5.4.5 Pricing Interest Rate Range Accrual Notes / 216

6 Fixed-Income Derivatives II: LIBOR Market Models   217

  6.1 LIBOR Market Models / 219
      6.1.1 Pricing Formula for Caplets/Caps / 222
      6.1.2 Swaption Formula / 224
  6.2 Calibration to Caps and Swaptions / 227
  6.3 Simulation Across Different Forward Measures / 241
  6.4 Bermudan Swaptions in a Three-Factor Model / 249
  6.5 Epilogue / 252

7 Credit Derivatives and Counterparty Credit Risk   255

  7.1 Structural Models of Credit Risk / 256
      7.1.1 The Merton Model / 256
      7.1.2 First Passage Time Model / 259
  7.2 The Vasicek Single-Factor Model / 260
      7.2.1 Credit Portfolio Management / 261
      7.2.2 Pricing Collateralized Debt Obligations / 266

7.3 Copula Approach to Credit Derivative Pricing / 272
    7.3.1 Basic Concepts of Copulas / 273
    7.3.2 The Gaussian Copula and t-Copula / 274
    7.3.3 Modeling Joint Default Times with Copulas / 278
    7.3.4 Pricing Basket Default Swaps / 280
7.4 Counterparty Credit Risk / 286
    7.4.1 Exposure in Trading Derivatives with a Counterparty / 287
    7.4.2 Counterparty-Level Exposure / 288
    7.4.3 Collateral Modeling for Margined Portfolios / 289
    7.4.4 Credit Value Adjustment / 290
    7.4.5 Independence of Probability of Default and Exposure / 291
    7.4.6 Modeling Right-Way and Wrong-Way Risks / 298

8 Value-at-Risk and Related Risk Measures   303

8.1 Value-at-Risk / 304
8.2 Parametric VaR / 305
    8.2.1 Two-Asset Case / 306
    8.2.2 Heavy-Tailed Distribution / 307
    8.2.3 Holding Period Adjustment / 312
    8.2.4 Portfolio VaR / 312
8.3 Delta-Normal Approximation / 314
    8.3.1 Option VaR / 314
    8.3.2 Fixed-Income VaR / 316
8.4 Delta–Gamma Approximation / 317
    8.4.1 Option VaR / 317
    8.4.2 Fixed-Income VaR / 318
8.5 VaR Simulation Methods / 319
    8.5.1 Historical Simulation / 319
    8.5.2 Advantages and Disadvantages / 322
    8.5.3 Monte Carlo Simulation / 323
    8.5.4 Gibbs Sampling and Multivariate Normal Distribution / 327
    8.5.5 Advantages and Disadvantages / 331
8.6 VaR-Related Risk Measures / 332
    8.6.1 Conditional Value-at-Risk / 333
    8.6.2 CVaR Distribution / 335
    8.6.3 Marginal, Incremental, and Component VaRs / 335
    8.6.4 VaR and CVaR in Local Volatility Models / 337

- 8.7 VaR Back-Testing / 339
  - 8.7.1 Back-Testing of VaR Models / 340

9 The Greeks   **343**

- 9.1 Black–Scholes Greeks / 346
- 9.2 Greeks in a Binomial Tree / 348
- 9.3 Finite Difference Approximation / 350
- 9.4 Likelihood Ratio Method / 355
- 9.5 Pathwise Derivative Estimates / 360
  - 9.5.1 Application to European Options / 360
  - 9.5.2 Application to Multi-Asset Derivatives / 365
  - 9.5.3 Application to Interest Rate Derivatives in LIBOR Market Model / 367
  - 9.5.4 Problem with the Adjoint Method / 373
- 9.6 Greek Calculation with Discontinuous Payoffs / 374
  - 9.6.1 Functional Approximation for Digital Options / 374
  - 9.6.2 Vibrato Method for Digital Options / 376
  - 9.6.3 Multivariate Generalization / 379

Appendix   **381**

References   **401**

Author Index   **405**

Subject Index   **407**

Preface

The sub-prime crisis of 2008 demonstrated that widely adopted risk management instruments, such as CDS, CDO, and CDO^2, can be amplifiers instead of mitigators of risk. Headlines such as "Did a mathematical formula really blow up Wall Street?" and "Living on the edge" became the norm. What really happened in 2008? The answer and verdict are yet to be found.

The deadly combination of bad prices, overconfidence in mathematical models, and non-transparency of market makers, reinforced by an overlay of scientific respectability for questionable models, ultimately resulted in a global financial tsunami. Does this mark the death of the "quants?" Not yet. Financial crises come and go. Some carry on over the short term, others (such as that of 2008) over the long term. These crises have not stopped financial institutions from creating and trading new derivative products, in the same way that sicknesses have not stopped medical developments. Modern financial markets would be too simple without derivatives; after all, derivative products are useful devices for reducing and hedging risks. Moreover, strong competition among financial institutions requires derivatives to offer extra profits. Against such a background, how market practitioners evaluate derivative products in an effective and transparent manner is a key issue. The market clearly requires quantitative skills, meaning, quants are here to stay.

Contrary to the opinion that demand for quantitative skills in the pro-crisis era would decrease due to the collapse of large-scale investment banks, demand in the commercial banking and risk management sectors has actually increased. In the past, major investment banks (i-banks) have been market makers of over-the-counter (OTC) derivative products. The creation, valuation, and risk management of OTC derivatives are collectively offered by a handful of i-banks, which usually employ quantitative professionals to perform such tasks. These highly educated talents are usually known as "quants" in the financial industry. Before the crisis, regional banks had no particular interest in hiring quants because they did not have large-risk exposure in the OTC market. They engaged in the OTC derivatives market mainly through "back-to-back" deals in which regional banks purchased OTC product portfolios for their clients upon request. These portfolios were packaged by i-banks, and contracts were established between the i-banks and the clients. The regional banks acted as intermediary agents and earned commissions from such deals. Neither the clients nor the regional banks anticipated the bankruptcy of i-banks. When Lehman went down in 2008, followed by a number of other institutions, both the regional banks and their clients were suddenly exposed to an unprecedented scale of loss they had never anticipated. To make matters worse, some regional banks faced litigation due to the unclear or non-transparent explanations of the risks embedded in many of the derivative products. Many of these banks had to settle lawsuits out of court and pay off huge losses. As a result, the share prices of these banks dipped more than 50%, and many have not yet recovered. The post-crisis regulations have since required financial institutions to report their investment risks when embracing back-to-back deals. This partly explains the surge in demand for quantitative risk managers in the regional banking industry.

Like other major financial markets, Hong Kong also witnessed the rapid growth of this demand based on the number of student applications made to quantitative-oriented financial programs. Students were eager to acquire practical quantitative risk management skills for their daily work. Although there are excellent textbooks on modern financial theory and mathematical finance, many of these books are either too elementary or too abstract and cannot bridge the gap between theory and application. When we were invited to contribute a volume to this handbook series back in 2008, we planned to write a book that offered practical computational examples using real datasets. If anything is to be learned from the 2008 calamity, it is that it offered a tremendous amount of information and data to illustrate many of the computational issues encountered in modern finance, albeit in a very painful and costly manner. In light of the gain-maximization rationale on Wall Street that drives financial practitioners ever closer to their ethical boundaries, the market needs practitioners to be scientifically critical, socially honest, and adherent to the highest ethical standards to resist temptation. With this in mind, the worked examples in this book comprise real financial products in the OTC market. Using data taken from the sub-prime credit crisis period, the pros and cons of different models are demonstrated. Case studies are provided to illustrate the discrepancies arising from different models for the same product. Many examples take the form of questions raised by students and practitioners alike when faced with a particular scenario while pricing certain financial instruments.

What follows is a brief synopsis of each chapter of this book. Modern financial products can hardly be modeled by pencil and paper alone, as they require large-scale computations. Although there is a multitude of possible software choices, we use Excel VBA in this book due to its wide applicability. Readers are not assumed to have a strong background in VBA, but some exposure to computer programming would be helpful. An introduction to VBA is given in Chapter 1.

Although this book consists of many worked numerical examples, readers have to incorporate theoretical notions, such as martingale theory, change of measure, and stochastic differential equations (SDE), with practical implementations to remain scientifically critical. To this end, a brief introduction to some basic theoretical constructs is given in Chapter 2. Although this chapter is technical in nature, it is not intended to provide a comprehensive theoretical background. For example, the technical conditions for the existence of a strong, unique SDE solution are not given in this chapter. Many excellent texts have been written on the subject, and readers are encouraged to consult them for more detailed information. The main purpose of this chapter is to offer a concise and useful introduction to some of the most important theoretical issues in modern finance. After making their way through Chapter 2, readers will garner an appreciation for the celebrated Ito's formula and the change of measure techniques, both of which are useful devices in designing simulation strategies.

Chapter 3 demonstrates the simulation of structured products using the Black–Scholes model and reviews their pricing and decomposition. Examples, including an FX accumulator (which caused CITIC Pacific to suffer a huge loss during the 2008 crisis), are used throughout the book.

Practitioners are well aware of the inadequacy of the Black–Scholes model. For example, it fails to capture the "implied volatility smiles" observed in the market. There are several alternative models to capture implied volatility smiles. Chapter 4 collectively refers to these models as volatility modeling. As no (simple) framework exists to unify these models, they are presented one by one to illustrate their similarities and discrepancies. Different models serve different purposes. For financial products contingent on an index, practitioners prefer a model that replicates the observed market option prices. In turn, the replication relies on the calibration of model parameters by minimizing the difference between model and market prices. Popular models of this kind include the local and stochastic volatility models. For financial products contingent on individual stocks that have limited or no traded options, the selected model can only be fitted using the historical prices of the underlying stock. In such cases, we have to estimate the underlying parameters statistically. One popular model in this approach is the GARCH option-pricing model. The jump-diffusion model is also useful, but its estimation requires the use of Bayesian methods. We examine the pricing of an accumulator using these models in Chapter 4.

Interest rate instruments are perhaps more important than equity derivatives in today's market. Chapters 5 and 6 detail the interest rate models and their implementations. Chapter 5 deals with the short-rate model, which is useful for fixed-income derivatives on a single interest rate, such as the 3-month rate. In practice, many regional banks lack the in-house software required to build yield curves and instead rely on the yield curves provided by data vendors. However, when the regional bank acquires a proprietary dataset of fixed-income prices, it may not be able to purchase the yield curve from external vendors, and yield curve building poses a hurdle for further analysis. With this in mind, Chapter 5 introduces several yield curve building models, and computer codes are also provided. Implementation of the Hull–White short-rate model that incorporates the super-calibration into the yield curve information is also discussed in this chapter.

Complicated interest rate derivatives involve several interest rates in their pay-off functions. Typical examples are options related to swap rate, which is a combination of interest rates with different tenors. The market usually uses the LIBOR market model in this situation. Chapter 6 demonstrates the LIBOR application with worked examples. In addition to fitting the yield curve, the LIBOR market model views the prices of caps, floors, and swaptions in the OTC market as the data input to calibrate its parameters. The prices and risks of complicated interest rate products are then evaluated using the simulation technique. Such a simulation requires the change of measure technique, which is introduced in Chapter 2.

Credit risk and credit derivatives are discussed in Chapter 7. One of the most intriguing concepts in finance is how to use a copula to value multi-asset credit derivatives such as CDOs. A numerical demonstration of the copula approach is given in this chapter to illustrate the pros and cons of modeling credit correlation risk. Post-crisis regulations require banks to report the counter-party risks of OTC products by adjusting the market values to reflect the credit risk. Such an adjustment can be used to determine the amount required in the margin account to guarantee smooth transactions. The difference between the adjusted and non-adjusted prices of the market value is known as the credit value adjustment (CVA). For regulatory purposes, risk managers are obviously interested in the CVA. Computational examples of and codes for computing CVA are offered in Chapter 7.

After the prices are computed, the next step is to report the risk through a single quantity, such as the value at risk (VaR), on a daily basis. Although VaR is not a completely satisfactory risk measure, it has long been a standard benchmark for summarizing risk in the industry. Chapter 8 provides some worked examples for computing the VaR of derivative positions.

When computing VaR, one faces the challenge of unstable Greek estimations. Because Greeks are partial derivatives of the value of a portfolio with respect to risk factors, they have to be calculated via simulation. Chapter 9 examines this issue by introducing several improved simulation strategies for Greeks in a high-dimensional setting. Computer codes can be downloaded from the following website. http://www.sta.cuhk.edu.hk/Book/HBS/.

This book would not have been possible without the help from students and research assistants alike. In particular, we would like to thank the generations of students who have taken courses on risk management with derivatives concepts (RMSC4007) and risk measures (RMSC5003) for their stimulating discussions, project presentations, penetrating questions, sharing of computer codes, and suggestions on model implementation. We are also grateful to our research assistants/associates for their data collection, programming, and refinement. They include Sau Lung Chan, Kelvin Hui, Brian Ling, Hon Yip Ng, Tsz Him Soo, Tsz Ki Tang, Tsz Wang Tang, Siu Fung Wong, Ben Yiu, and Rong Zhou. We would also like to thank Mr. Steve Quigley, Ms. Sari Friedman, and Ms. Jacqueline Palmieri, all of Wiley, for their professional editorial assistance. Of course, without the invitation and encouragement from Professor Ruey Tsay of the University of Chicago, this volume would not have been written. We gratefully acknowledge the financial support received from the General Research Fund of the Research Grant Council of Hong Kong during the preparation of this volume. Last, but not least, we would like to thank our families for their understanding and encouragement while writing this book. In particular, we would like to thank our wives, Pat Chao and Mei Choi Chiu, whose contributions to this book went far beyond the capacity of meticulous proofreaders. Any remaining errors are our sole responsibility.

N.H. CHAN
H.Y. WONG

Shatin, Hong Kong
January 2013

1

An Introduction to Excel VBA

Excel VBA is probably the most commonly used computational tool in financial institutions, particularly when a new model is tested at a preliminary stage within a division. Many traders use Excel VBA to compute their trading strategies. Some data providers allow users to update information in real time using the Excel format. Excel VBA thus allows traders and risk managers to implement their solutions conveniently in real time.

1.1 HOW TO START EXCEL VBA

1.1.1 Introduction

VBA stands for Visual Basic for Application. It is a programming language that enhances the applicability of MS Excel by enabling the users to instruct Excel to perform tasks automatically. As most of the programs in this book are written in VBA, a brief introduction to VBA is provided in this opening chapter. Although we do not assume that readers have prior programming knowledge, programming experience in other languages would be helpful. For readers already familiar with VBA, this chapter serves as a refresher and quick reference. A list of the functions defined throughout the book can be found at the end of the chapter. These functions not only improve readability and traceability but also simplify the programs. For a more thorough understanding of Excel VBA, readers are referred to other books

---

Handbook of Financial Risk Management: Simulations and Case Studies, First Edition. N.H. Chan and H.Y. Wong.
© 2013 John Wiley & Sons, Inc. Published 2013 by John Wiley & Sons, Inc.

2   AN INTRODUCTION TO EXCEL VBA

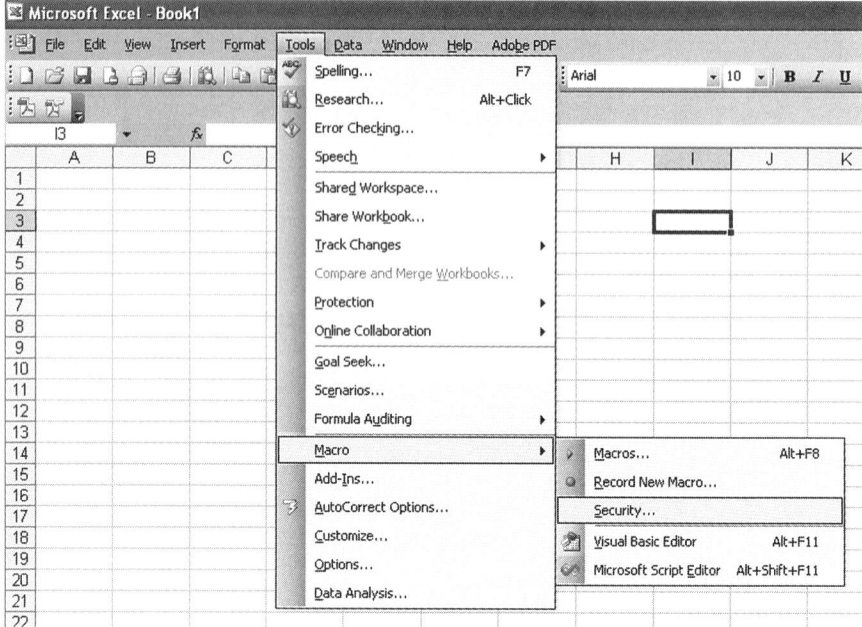

Figure 1.1 Set security level.

specializing in the matter. We believe, however, that this chapter is sufficient to allow a beginner to learn and execute the codes within the book.

MS Excel 2003 is used for illustration in this book. If readers are using another version of Excel, then they may find some minor differences. Nevertheless, if this is the first time for a reader to use Excel VBA, then set the macro security level to Medium or Low and restart Excel to enable the macros:

Click [Tools] → [Macro] → [Security] → [Medium] or [Low] (Fig. 1.1).

MS Excel 2007 users should click the Options button to enable the macros.

1.1.2 Visual Basic Editor

VBE, which stands for Visual Basics Editor, is the environment in which macros are created, modified and managed. Macros (VBA procedures) are the code components that automate repetitive Excel tasks. A macro consists of codes that start with the keyword *Sub* or *Function* and end with the keywords *End Sub* or *End Function*. These codes are known as *Sub* and *Function* procedures. A module contains one or more macros, and a project contains one or more modules. A macro developed in VBE

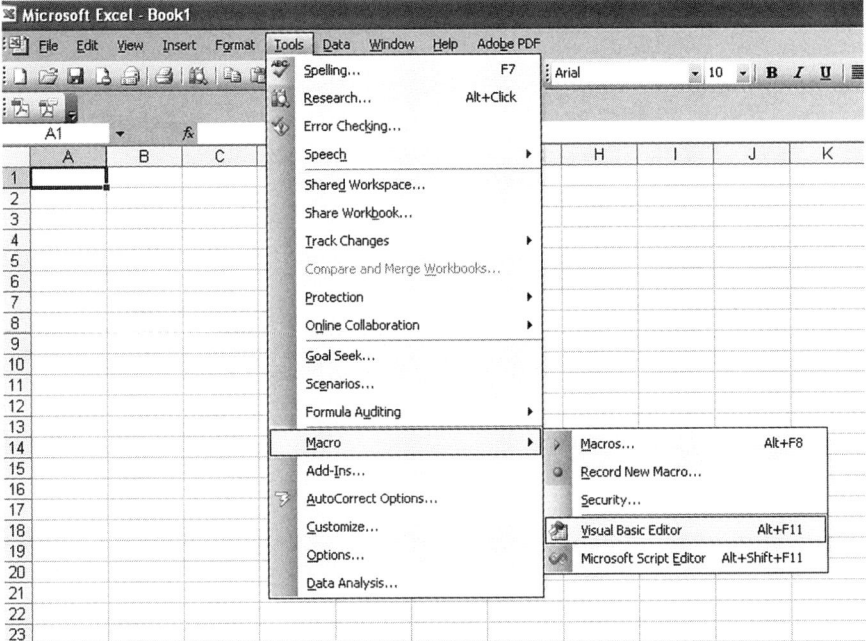

Figure 1.2 Open VBE.

becomes part of a workbook and is saved at the same time that the workbook is saved. To open and edit macros in VBE, follow the procedure below.

1. Open VBE: Click [Tools] → [Macro] → [Visual Basic Editor] or press Alt + F11 (Fig. 1.2).
2. Insert module: In the project window on the left of the VBE, right-click one of the worksheets → [Insert] → [Module] (Fig. 1.3).
3. Edit in VBE: Type the codes in the code window.
4. Execute the program: In VBE, click [Run] → [Run Sub] and choose the macro to be compiled. Equivalently, in Excel, click [Tools] → [Macro] → [Macro] and choose the macro to be compiled.

1.1.3 The Macro Recorder

Excel offers a macro recorder that records the actions of the mouse and/or keyboard and translates them into VBA codes, thus allowing the designated actions to be repeated by running the macro again. Although the macro recorder is sometimes useful, it is unable to generate codes that perform looping, assign variables, or execute conditional statements, which are fundamental components in simulation. In

4 AN INTRODUCTION TO EXCEL VBA

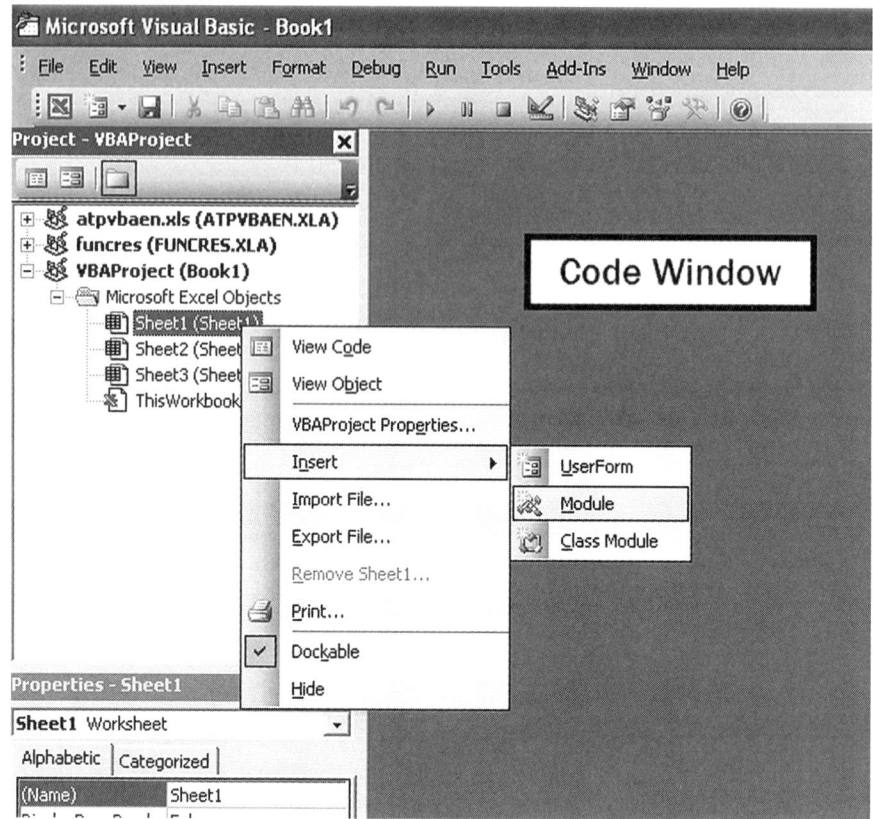

Figure 1.3 Insert modules.

addition, the codes that are generated depend on certain specific settings. To record a macro, follow the procedure below.

1. Open the macro recorder: Click [Tools] → [Macro] → [Record New Macro].
2. Type the macro name and click OK. Note that the name should begin with a letter and contain no spaces or special characters (Fig. 1.4).
3. Perform all of the actions to be recorded. Here, type "Hello" in cell A1.
4. Stop the macro recorder: Click [Stop recording macro] button.

Note that when a macro is recorded, MS Excel automatically inserts a VBA module to keep the recorded codes. To execute the recorded macros or other macros, click [Tools] → [Macro] → [Macros] or Alt + F8 in Excel. Then, select the designated macro to implement and click [Run] (Fig. 1.5). To view the codes in the recorded macro, open VBE and double-click the newly added module (Fig. 1.6).

HOW TO START EXCEL VBA 5

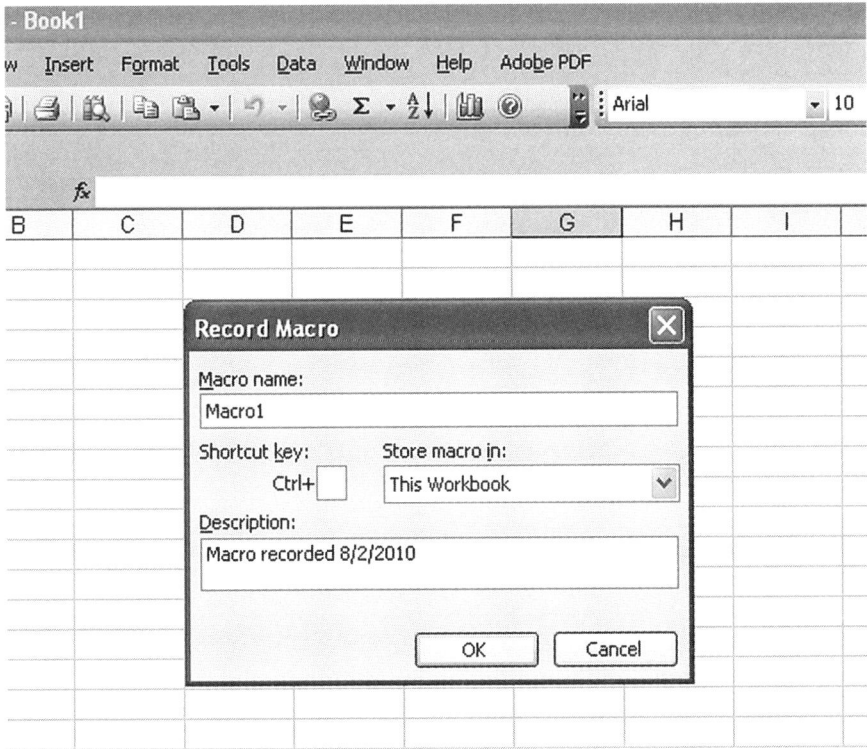

Figure 1.4 Name a macro.

Figure 1.6 shows that the recorded macro is a complete *Sub* procedure. The lines beginning with the symbol ' are not executed as they are program *comments*. A comment can be added to the code by preceding it with the symbol ' or by using the keyword *Rem* at the beginning of a line.

1.1.4 Insert a Command Button

Instead of having to remember a shortcut key or choosing a macro from a list, it is more convenient to add a command button to the worksheet to invoke the macro directly. To insert a command button, follow the following procedure.

1. Click [View] → [Toolbars] → [Visual Basic] (Fig. 1.7).
2. Click Control Toolbox.
3. Click Command Button and put it in the Excel worksheet (Fig. 1.8).
4. Edit the macro: Double-click the command button.

To use a *Sub* in the module, type *call* [name of the *Sub*] inside the macro of the command button. The common button can also be edited by clicking *Design Mode*

6 AN INTRODUCTION TO EXCEL VBA

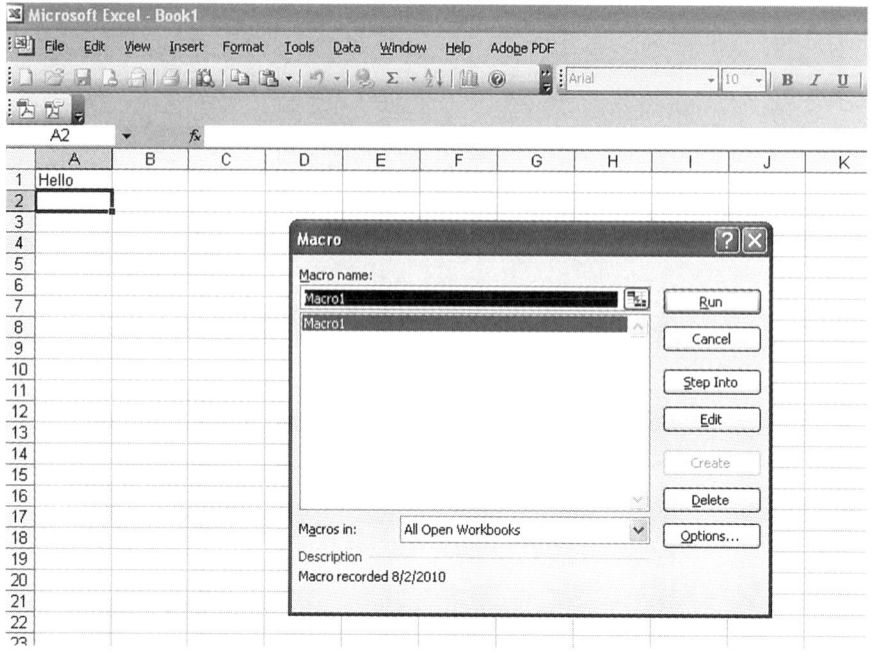

Figure 1.5 Run a macro.

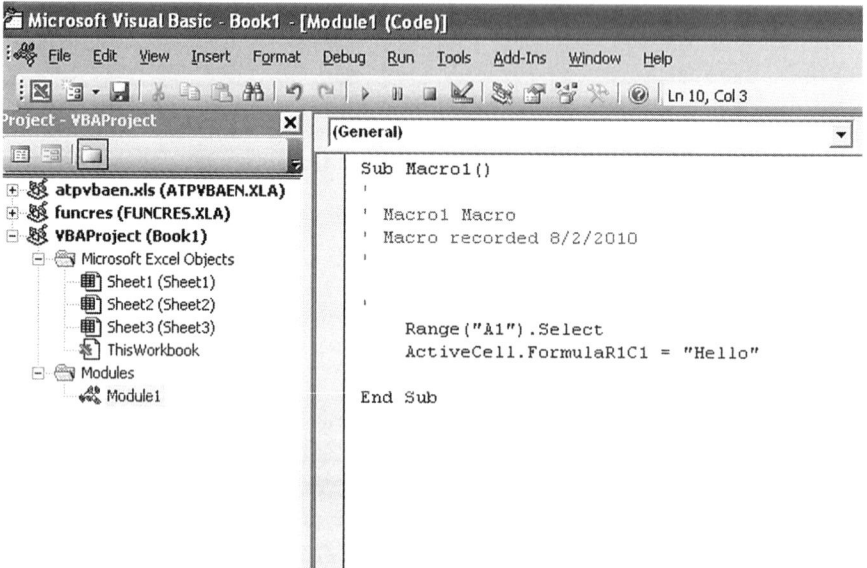

Figure 1.6 View the codes.

HOW TO START EXCEL VBA   7

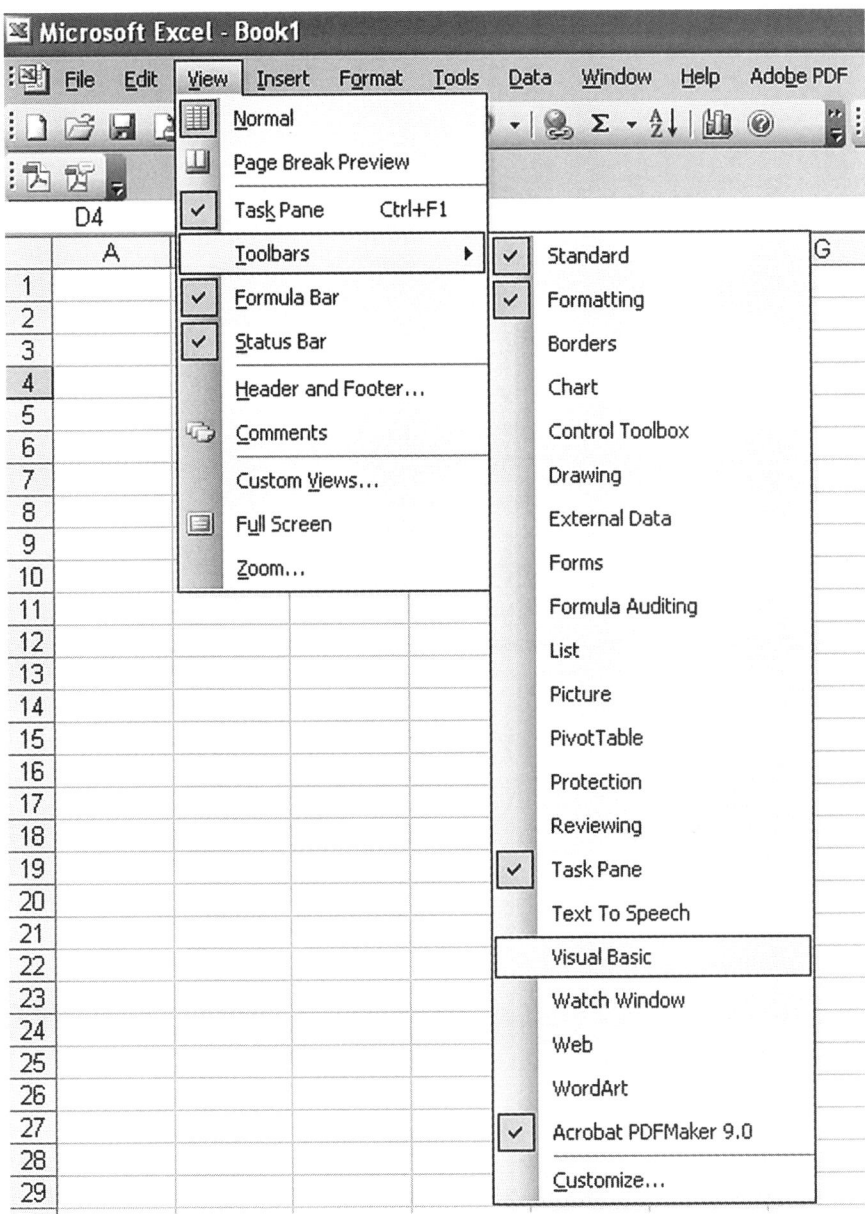

Figure 1.7   Insert command button 1.

8 AN INTRODUCTION TO EXCEL VBA

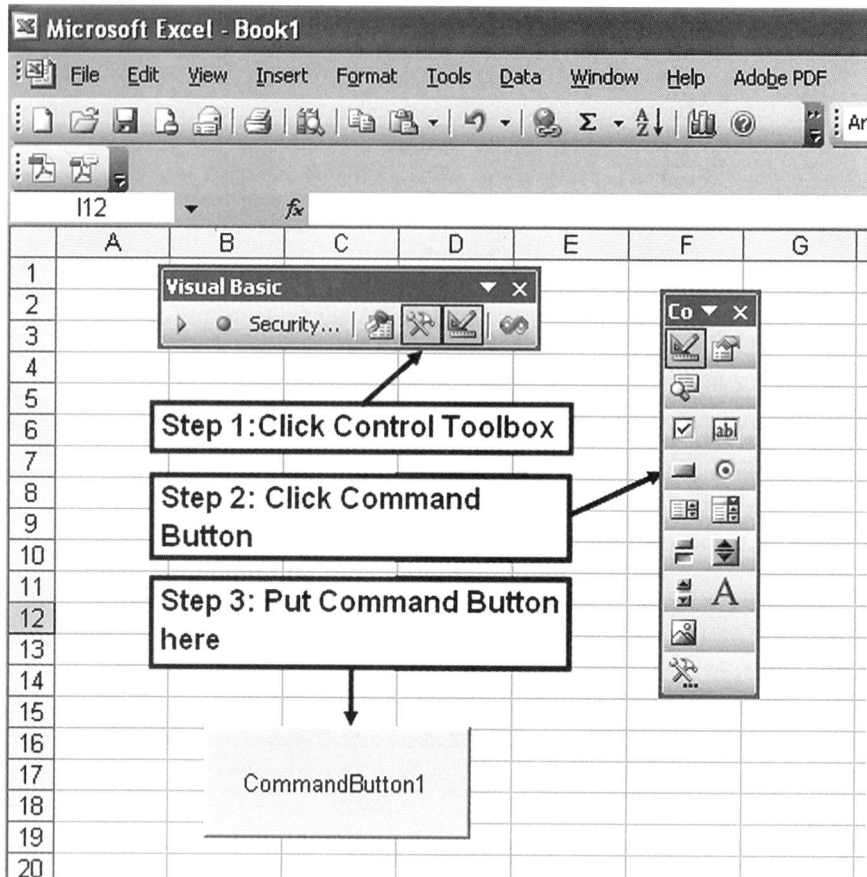

Figure 1.8 Insert command button 2.

in the Visual Basic Control Toolbox, which also contains other useful buttons, such as those for recording a macro and opening VBE.

1.2 VBA PROGRAMMING FUNDAMENTALS

1.2.1 Declaration of Variables

In programming, a *variable* is the name for a place in computer memory in which values or objects are stored. To declare a variable in VBA, use the following statement.

Dim varname [As vartype],

where *varname* is the variable name and *vartype* is the variable type. A variable name must begin with a letter and contain only numeric and letter characters and underscores. Moreover, the variable name should not be a VBA reserved word, such as Sub, Function, End, For, Optional, New, Next, Nothing, Integer, or String. It is also important to note that VBA does not distinguish between cases.

Different from other programming languages, specifying the variable type [As vartype] is optional. Other languages require the programmer to define explicitly the data type of each variable used. Although optional in VBA, if the data type is not explicitly specified, then execution is slower and memory is used less efficiently.

1.2.2 Types of Variables

Every variable has a type specifying the type of values it stores. Variables can be classified into four basic types: string data type, date data type, numeric data type, and variant data type. The string data type is used to store a sequence of characters, and the date data type can store dates and times separately or simultaneously. The types that are used most frequently in this book are the numeric and variant data types.

There are several numeric data types in VBA, the details of which are listed in Table 1.1. In general, a user should choose the data type that employs the smallest number of bytes to enhance program efficiency. Doing so may make a big difference in the computational time needed for simulation.

The variant data type is the most flexible data type in VBA. It stores both numeric and non-numeric values. VBA will try to convert a variant variable to the data type, which is able to store the input data. As noted, [As vartype] is optional, and the default variable type will be *Variant*.

In addition to normal data, a variant type variable can also store three special types of values: error code, Empty (which indicates that the variable is empty, and is not equal to 0, False, an empty string, or another value), and Null (which means that the variable has not been assigned memory, and is not equal to 0, False, an empty string, Empty, or another value).

TABLE 1.1 Numeric Data Type

Type	Shorthand	Range	Description
Byte		0 to 255	Unsigned, integer number
Boolean		True(-1) or False(0)	Truth value
Integer	%	$-32,768$ to $32,767$	Signed integer number
Long	&	$-2,147,483,648$ to $2,147,483,647$	Signed integer number
Single	!	$\pm 3.402823E38$ to $\pm 1.401298E-45$	Signed single-precision floating-point number
Double	#	$\pm 1.79769313486231E308$ to $\pm 4.94065645841247E-324$	Signed double-precision floating-point number
Decimal		$\pm 7.922819251426433759E28$ with no decimal point and $\pm 7.922816251426433759354$ with 28 digits behind the decimal point	Cannot be directly declared in VBA; requires the use of a variant data type

Here are some examples of variable declaration statements:

```
Dim a As integer
Dim b 'the type will be variant

Dim c As string
c = "It is a string"

Dim Today As Date
Today = #4/7/2011# 'defined using month/day/year format

Dim Noon As Date
Noon = #12:00:00#
```

1.2.3 Multivariable Declaration

To declare several variables, use the following statement.

```
Dim a As Integer, b As Integer, c As Integer
```

Different from other programming languages, attention must be paid to the following case.

```
Dim a, b, c As Integer
```

If the *Dim* statement is declared as above, then *a* and *b* will be declared as variant types. In this case, the following shorthand can be employed to ensure the cleanliness and readability of the program.

```
Dim a#, b#, c As Double
```

1.2.4 Declaration of Constants

Constants can be declared using a *Const* statement, of which the following are examples.

```
Const interest_rate as Integer = 0.05
Const dividend_yield = 0.03 'without declaring the constant
type
Const option_type as String = "Call"
```

VBA also defines many intrinsic constants that are used in *Sub* and *Function* procedures.

TABLE 1.2 VBA Logical Operators

Operator	What it does
Not	Performs a logical negation on an expression
And	Performs a logical conjunction on two expressions
Or	Performs a logical disjunction on two expressions
Xor	Performs a logical exclusion on two expressions
Eqv	Performs a logical equivalence on two expressions
Imp	Performs a logical implication on two expressions

1.2.5 Operators

This subsection introduces assignment operators, mathematical operators, comparative operators, and logical operators.

The equal sign (=) is an assignment operator and is usually used to assign the value of an expression to a variable or a constant. An expression is a combination of keywords, operators, variables, and constants that yields a string, number, or object. For example,

```
x = 4 * 3
x = x * 5
```

The result of x is 60.

Familiar mathematical operators include *addition*(+), *multiplication*(*), *division*(/), *subtraction*(−), and *exponentiation*(^).

VBA also supports the comparative operators used in Excel formulas: *equal to* (=), *greater than* (>), *less than* (<), *greater than or equal to* (>=), *less than or equal to* (<=), and *not equal to* (<>).

Table 1.2 presents the logical operators and their uses in VBA.

1.2.6 User-Defined Data Types

Users may sometimes wish to employ a more complex data type to store data. VBA provides the *Type* statement, which allows the creation of a custom data type or a user-defined data type (UDT). The syntax for creating a UDT is

```
[Private|Public] Type typename
    [elementname As vartype]
    [elementname As vartype]
    ...
End Type
```

[Private | Public]: (Optional) It is *public* by default, and indicates whether this UDT can be declared in all modules. If it is declared to be *private*, then the

UDT can be declared only in the same module as that in which the UDT is defined.

typename: (Required) This is the name of the UDT and follows standard variable naming conventions.

elementname: (Required) This is the name of the elements within a UDT and also follows standard variable naming conventions.

vartype: (Required) Unlike the declaration of ordinary variables, the elements within a UDT must be given a data type, which can be any of the aforementioned variable types (including *Variant*) or a UDT.

Declaring a UDT is the same as declaring another built-in variable type. To reference the sub-elements of the UDT, use the period (.) operator. Finally, the UDT should be defined at the top of the module before any procedures, as illustrated in the following example.

Example 1.1 *The following code defines a nested UDT which stores the name and coordinates of a point.*

```
Type Coordinate
     x As Double
     y As Double
End Type

Type Point
     name As String
     c As Coordinate
End Type

Sub UDTEx1()
    'Declare p1 as UDT Point
    Dim p1 as Point

    'Assigning the values
    p1.name = "A"
    p1.c.x = 2.5
    p1.c.y = 3

    'Print out the values to spreadsheet
    Cells(1, 1) = p1.name
    Cells(2, 1) = p1.c.x
    Cells(3, 1) = p1.c.y
End Sub
```

1.2.7 Arrays and Matrices

An array is a collection of variables of the same type that have a common name. An array allows access to the variables through the index number, thereby providing a way to loop through and process a collection of variables of the same type easily.

The following statement declares a one-dimensional (1D) array.

```
Dim varname(LowerIndex to UpperIndex) As vartype
```

In this way, a user can access variables with varname(LowerIndex), varname(LowerIndex +1), ..., varname(UpperIndex). If he or she specifies only the upper index, that is,

```
Dim varname(UpperIndex) As vartype,
```

then VBA will assume that 0 is the lower index.

The following statement declares a multidimensional array.

```
Dim varname(LowerIndex1 to UpperIndex1, LowerIndex2 to _
UpperIndex2,...,LowerIndexN to UpperIndexN) As vartype
```

For example, to create an array to store the scores of 20 students on three tests, declare:

```
Dim Score(1 to 20, 1 to 3) As Double
```

Here, Score(10, 2) stores the mark of the tenth student on the second test.

Note that both the lower and upper indices must be a constant or a number. If the user wants to employ a variable in the index, then he or she should use a *dynamic array* which has no preset number of elements. The following statement declares a dynamic array.

```
Dim varname() As vartype
```

Before a dynamic array is used, the *ReDim* statement should be employed to specify the number of elements in the array. For example,

```
ReDim varname(LowerIndex to UpperIndex)
```

In this case, the LowerIndex and UpperIndex can be a variable or a constant. In VBA, a matrix is essentially a two-dimensional (2D) array, and a column or row vector is a 1D array. A matrix is an important tool in risk management and finance, as it deals with high dimensional problems. For example, it can be used in multiple linear regression. To declare a matrix of size $m \times n$ containing real numbers, use the following statement.

```
Dim matrixmn() As Double
ReDim matrixmn(1 To m, 1 To n)
```

In the next subsection, we discuss functions related to matrix manipulation.

1.2.8 Data Input and Output

One advantage of Excel VBA is that it allows the VBE and the worksheet to be linked together, affording the user the ability to read and print out the data in the worksheet and execute programs written in VBE. The following statements are usually used for input and output, respectively.

```
'Read in data
Var = Cells(i, j)

'Print out data
Cells(i, j) = Var,
```

where i and j denote the row and column number of a cell, respectively. For example, to print out the score of the sixth student on the last test in cell A2 on the worksheet, write:

```
Cells(1, 2) = Score(6, 3)
```

1.2.9 Conditional Statements

When the program needs to follow different instructions in different cases, we use conditional statements. The two main conditional statements in VBA are *If-Then-Else* statements and *Select-Case* statements.

If-Then-Else Statements

There are two forms of *If-then-else* statements: single-lined and multi-lined. Only one statement can be inserted in the single-lined form whereas several can be inserted in the multi-lined form. With the use of Else statement, the extraneous conditions are not evaluated when an Else statement is used, which improves efficiency. The syntax of the two forms is as follows.

```
'the Else clause is optional
If [condition] Then [statement] (Else [elseStatement])
'... represents other more statements can be included
'these Else clauses are also optional
If [condition] Then
    [statement]
    ...
ElseIf [elseif condition1] Then
    [Statement]
    ...
ElseIf [elseif condition2] Then
    [Statement]
    ...
Else
    [Statement]
    ...
End If
```

In the conditional part of the statement, the users need to specify an expression that can be evaluated as True or False. Use the comparative operators and logical operators discussed in Section 1.2.5.

Select-Case Statements

Select-Case statements are useful for choosing among three or more options and are good alternative to If-Then-Else statements. The syntax for *Select-Case* is as follows.

```
Select Case [testexpression]
  Case expressionlist-n
     [instructions-n]
     ...
  Case expressionlist-n
     [instructions-n]
     ...
  Case Else
     [default_instructions]
     ...
End Select
```

The most common *expressionlist-n* is one of the following.

0 to 20
1, 7
Is >= 10

Example 1.2 *Suppose that the scores of 20 students on three tests have already been stored in the array Score(1 to 20, 1 to 3). Write a Sub ensuring that once the student ID and test number are entered into cells B1 and B2, respectively, the program will determine whether the student has passed the test (i.e., achieved a score equal to or higher than 60) and output the result to cell B3.*

The corresponding codes for the *If-Then-Else* statement are:

```
StudentID = Cells(1, 2)
TestNo = Cells(2, 2)

If Score(StudentID, TestNo) >= 60 Then
    Cells(3, 2) = "Pass"
Else
    Cells(3, 2) = "Fail"
End If
```

The corresponding codes for the *Select-Case* statement are:

```
StudentID = Cells(1, 2)
TestNo = Cells(2, 2)

Select Case Score(StudentID, TestNo)
    Case Is >= 60
      Cells(3, 2) = "Pass"
    Case Else
      Cells(3, 2) = "Fail"
End Select
```

1.2.10 Loops

The main purpose of using loops is to allow VBA to perform certain tasks several times. *For-Next* loops and *Do* loops are widely used in VBA programming, with the former, in particular, frequently used in simulations. The syntax for a *For-Next* loop is:

```
For counter = startValue To endValue [Step nStep]
    [statements]
    [Exit For]
    [statements]
Next counter
```

If the *Step nStep* part is omitted, then the counter will increase by 1 each time. We can set *nStep* to be *n* and the counter will then increase by *n* each time.

Example 1.3 *Suppose that the scores of 20 students on three tests have already been displayed in the Range of A1:C20 in the worksheet. To store the scores into the array Score(1 to 20, 1 to 3), we use the following For-Next statement.*

```
Sub LoopEx1()
    Dim Score(1 To 3, 1 To 20) As Double
    For i = 1 To 20
        For j = 1 To 3
            Score(i, j) = Cells(i, j)
        Next j
    Next i
End Sub
```

For a *Do* loop, the syntax is

```
Do [do_condition]
    [statements]
    [Exit Do]
    [statements]
Loop [loop_condition]
```

Although both *do_condition* and *loop_condition* are optional, only one of them can be used for a *Do* loop. If both are omitted, then the user must specify a condition and call `Exit Do` to end the loop. Otherwise, the program will not terminate. The syntax is the same for *do_condition* and *loop_condition*.

`While|Until condition`

For *While*, the loop continues as long as *condition* is *True*. For *Until*, the loop breaks once *condition* becomes *True*. If *While* is used, then the loop is also called the *Do While* loop; if *Until* is used, then it is called the *Do Until* loop. The use of *While* or *Until* depends solely on the programmer's preference, as the same task can always be performed either way. However, putting the condition after *Do* or *Loop* depends on the situation, because if it is put after *Loop*, then the loop is repeated at least once. The following example prints 1 to 10 in cells A1 to A10 using different methods.

Example 1.4 *Use five different methods to print 1 to 10 in cells A1 to A10.*

```
'For Loop
For i = 1 to 10
    Cells(i, 1) = i
Next i

'Do Loop Method 1
i = 1
Do while i <= 10
   Cells(i, 1) = i
   i = i + 1
Loop

'Do Loop Method 2
i = 1
Do Until i > 10
   Cells(i, 1) = i
   i = i + 1
Loop

'Do Loop Method 3
i = 1
Do
    Cells(i , 1) = i
    i = i + 1
Loop while i <= 10

'Do Loop  Method 4
i = 1
```

18 AN INTRODUCTION TO EXCEL VBA

```
Do
    Cells(i, 1) = i
    i = i + 1
Loop until i > 10
```

1.3 LINKING VBA TO C++

Even though C++ was developed back in the 1970s, many programmers still use it today because it is a high-level general-purpose programming language. As many procedures, functions, and algorithms are still developed in the C++ platform, it is important to link VBA to C++. In this section, we link VBA to C++ through .dll (dynamic-link library) by using Visual Studio and calling the functions from VBA. For further details, please refer to *Ch1.3_simplemath.xls*. To build .dll via Visual Studio:

1. Open Visual Studio and select [New Project].
2. Choose [Win32 Project] and enter a name for the project (for example, SimpleMath).
3. In Application Setting, choose [DLL] and select [Empty project]. Click [Finish].
4. Choose [Add New Item] to add new .cpp file. Enter a name (for example, main).
5. Add another item with .def suffix (for example, export.def).
6. In main.cpp, enter the corresponding C++ code for a user-defined function. For example,

   ```
   double minus(double x, double y){
       return x - y;}
   ```

7. In export.def, enter the following code.

   ```
   LIBRARY SimpleMath
   EXPORTS
   minus
   ```

8. Right-click the project file [SimpleMath] in Solution Explorer and choose [Properties].
9. Click [Configuration Properties] → [C/C++] → [Advanced].
10. Choose [__ stdcall(/Gz)] in [Calling Convention].
11. Click [Configuration Properties] → [Linker] → [Input].
12. Choose [.\export.def] in [Calling Convention]. Click [OK].
13. Build the project OR Click [F7].
14. A .dll file (e.g., SimpleMath.dll) is created in the project directory.

To establish linking with VBA:

1. Place the .dll file and .xls file in the same directory.
2. Open VBA editor, and enter the following code in the module.

   ```
   Private Declare Function SetCurrentDirectoryA Lib "kernel32"_
   (ByVal lpPathName As String) As Long
   Private Declare Function minus Lib "simplemath.dll" _
   (ByVal a As Double, ByVal b As Double) As Double

   Function test(a As Double, b As Double) As Double
        SetCurrentDirectoryA Application.ActiveWorkbook.Path
        test = minus(a, b)
   End Function
   ```

3. The function "test" can be called up in Excel Worksheet and VBA.

1.4 SUB PROCEDURES AND FUNCTION PROCEDURES

Writing a program in a systematic manner may necessitate the separation of a large program into smaller pieces that can be reused and managed easily. In VBA, a *procedure* is basically a unit of computer code that performs certain tasks. There are two types of procedures: a *Sub* procedure and a *Function* procedure. A *Sub* procedure performs tasks but does not return values, whereas a *Function* procedure does return a value.

The syntax that defines a *Sub* procedure is

```
[Private|Public] [Static] Sub name ([arglist])
     [statements]
End Sub
```

- *Private|Public*: (Optional) The *Sub* is *Public* by default if *public* or *private* is omitted. *Public* indicates that the *Sub* is accessible by other *Sub*s or *Function*s in all modules, whereas *Private* indicates that the *Sub* is accessible only to the *Sub*s and *Function*s in the same modules.
- *Static*: (Optional) *Static* indicates that all local variables of the *Sub* are preserved at the end of the *Sub*. If *Static* is omitted, then the values of the local variables will be reset each time the *Sub* ends. See Example 1.5 for an illustration.
- *name*: (Required) This is the identifier of the *Sub* and follows standard variable naming conventions. The *name* must be unique; it cannot be the same as the identifier of other *Sub*s, *Function*s, classes, etc.
- *arglist*: (Optional) This is a list of variables representing parameters that are passed to the *Sub* when it is called. Multiple variables are separated by commas. If the

procedure uses no arguments, then a set of empty parentheses is required. See Examples 1.6 and 1.7 for an illustration.

statements: (Optional) This refers to any group of statements to be executed within the *Sub*.

Example 1.5 *The following Sub SubEx1 adds one to the variable x each time it is called and writes the value of x into cell A1.*

```
Static Sub SubEx1()
    Dim x as integer
    x = x + 1
    Cells(1, 1) = x
End Sub
```

As the previous value of x is preserved each time *Sub SubEx1* is called, cell A1 adds one instead of always printing 1, as in the case of *Static* being omitted. The same effect can be accomplished with the following code.

```
Sub SubEx1()
    Static x as integer
    x = x + 1
    Cells(1, 1) = x
End Sub
```

Example 1.6 *The following procedure for* SubEx2 *calculates* var1 + var2 *and outputs the result in cell A1.*

```
Sub SubEx2(var1, var2)
    Cells(1, 1) = var1 + var2
End Sub
```

To call the *Sub*, use one of the two following statements, in which x, y can also be replaced with other constants or variables.

```
Call SubEx2(x, y)
SubEx2 x, y
```

Instead of simply specifying the name of the parameters, each parameter in *arglist* can be specified by the following syntax.

```
[Optional] [ByRef|ByVal] varname [As vartype] [= defaultvalue]
```

Optional: (Optional) This indicates that the parameter is optional and will take *defaultvalue* as its value if it is omitted when the *Sub* is called.

By Ref | By Val: (Optional) The parameter is passed to *ByRef* by default. *ByRef* and *ByVal* indicate whether the parameter is passed by address or by value. When calling with *ByRef*, the parameter's memory address is passed to the procedure, and any changes of the parameter value in the procedure cause changes to the original parameter. For *ByVal*, in contrast, a copy of the value of the parameter is passed and so the original parameter is not affected. See Example 1.7 for an illustration.

varname: (Required) This is the identifier of the parameters.

vartype: (Optional) The variable type is *Variant* by default. It is the variable type of the parameter that has been passed, and can be any of the variable types or a UDT. If the variable passed when calling the *Sub* does not match, then the error message "ByRef/ByVal argument type mismatch" is shown.

defaultvalue: (Optional) This is the value that the parameter takes when the parameter is not specified and the *Sub* is called.

Example 1.7 *The following codes demonstrate the difference between ByRef and ByVal.*

```
Sub SubEx3_Run()
    Dim x as integer, y as integer
    x = 1
    y = 1
    Call SubEx3(x, y)
    Cells(1, 1) = x
    Cells(2, 1) = y
End Sub

Sub SubEx3(ByRef var1 as integer, ByVal var2 as integer)
    var1 = var1 + 1
    var2 = var2 + 1
End Sub
```

The foregoing codes can be copied to a module with *SubEx3_Run*, then run. Cell A1 shows 2, as the change in the value of *var1* in *SubEx3* actually changes the value of *x*. Cell A2 shows 1, as the change in the value of *var2* in *SubEx3* does not affect the value of *y*.

VBA also allows the user to create a *Sub* to take an arbitrary number of parameters using *ParamArray*. When using *ParamArray*, the parameters can be passed only by reference and declared as the *Variant* type. They will be stored in an array with the parameter's name. To declare such a *Sub*, use

```
Sub SubEx4(ParamArray var())
    [statements]
End Sub
```

Although a *Function* returns a value, whereas a *Sub* does not, a *Function* can also be used in formulas in the Excel spreadsheet as a user-defined function. The syntax that defines a *Function* is

```
[Private|Public] [Static] Function name ([arglist, ...])
    [as vartype] [statements]
End Sub
```

22 AN INTRODUCTION TO EXCEL VBA

For *Private|Public*, *Static*, *name*, and *arglist* a *Function* is identical to *Sub*. The only difference between the declaration of a *Function* and a *Sub* is that the user may want to define the return type *vartype* of the *Function*. The return type is *Variant* by default if it is omitted. To return a value for a *Function*, the user needs to store that value in a variable with a name identical to the given function name. See Example 1.8 for an illustration. To call a *Function*, use one of the following statements.

```
Call FuncName(x, y)
FuncName x, y
z = FuncName(x, y)
```

Note that the first two are identical because *Sub* is used. For the third, the return value will be stored in z.

As *Sub* cannot return a value, we may need to use global variables or pass the variables by reference to accomplish certain tasks. Example 1.8 calculates $var1 + var2$ and outputs the result into cell A1, which is analogous to Example 1.6 using *Function*.

Example 1.8 *The following code is to calculate $2 + 3$ by calling Function FuncEx4 and output result 5 into cell A1.*

```
Sub SubEx4()
    Cells(1, 1) = FuncEx4(2, 3)
End Sub

Function FuncEx4(var1 as integer, var2 as integer) as integer
    FuncEx4 = var1 + var2
End Function
```

1.4.1 VBA Built-In Functions

VBA has a variety of built-in functions that can simplify calculations and operations. For a complete list of VBA functions, please refer to the VBA Help system. In VBE, one can type VBA to display a list of VBA functions. Table 1.3 presents some commonly used VBA built-in mathematical functions and their return values in descriptive and mathematical forms.

Example 1.9 *The following code calculates $sin(e^2)$ and outputs the result into cell A1.*

```
Sub expsquare()
    cells(1, 1) = sin(exp(2))
End Sub
```

TABLE 1.3 Common Built-In Mathematical Functions in VBA

Function	Return value	Math expression
Abs(x)	Absolute value of the x	$\|x\|$
Atn(x)	Arc-tangent of x in radians	$\tan^{-1} x$
Cos(x)	Cosine of x	$\cos x$
Exp(x)	Exponential of x	e^x
Int(x)	The integral part of x	$[x]$
Log(x)	Natural logarithm of x	$\ln x$
Round($x[, dp]$)	x rounded to dp decimal place dp is 0 by default if omitted	
Sgn(x)	Number indicates the sign of x -1 for $x < 0$, 0 for $x = 0$, 1 for $x > 0$	$\|x\|/x$
Sin(x)	Sine of x	$\sin x$
Sqr(x)	Square root of x	$\sqrt{x}$
Tan(x)	Tangent of x	$\tan x$

Remarks If the number is negative, then the function *Int* returns the first negative integer that is less than or equal to the number. For example, $Int(-8.3)$ will return -9. If a user wishes to return the first negative integer that is greater than or equal to the number, then he or she should use $Fix(-8.3)$, which will return -8.

Excel VBA also allows users to employ the worksheet functions of Excel, for example, *Average* and *Stdev*. To call the worksheet functions, use one of the following commands.

```
Application.FunctionName([arglist])
WorksheetFunction.FunctionName([arglist])
Application.WorksheetFunction.FunctionName([arglist])
```

For example, to calculate $\sin^{-1}(0.5)$, which is not provided in VBA's built-in function library but is included in Excel, we can use

```
x = Application.Asin(0.5),
```

which will return the value 0.5236 ($\approx \pi/6$) and be stored in x. Note that not all of Excel's worksheet functions can be used in VBA. For example, worksheet functions that have an equivalent VBA function, for example, sqrt and sin cannot be used. For a complete list of Excel's worksheet functions, please refer to Excel Help.

1.4.2 Multiple Linear Regression

A useful function for finding the ordinary least squares (OLS) estimate after defining a function in VBA and using the worksheet functions in Excel is given here. Recall that the general form of a multiple linear regression is given by

$$E[Y|X] = \beta_0 + \beta_1 x_1 + \cdots + \beta_p x_p,$$
$$Var(Y|X) = \sigma^2 I_n.$$

In matrix notation, it is written as

$$Y = X\beta + e,$$

where

$$Y = \begin{pmatrix} y_1 \\ \vdots \\ y_n \end{pmatrix}, \ X = \begin{pmatrix} 1 & x_{11} & \cdots & x_{1p} \\ \vdots & \vdots & \vdots & \vdots \\ 1 & x_{n1} & \cdots & x_{np} \end{pmatrix}, \ e = \begin{pmatrix} e_1 \\ \vdots \\ e_n \end{pmatrix}, \ \beta = \begin{pmatrix} \beta_0 \\ \vdots \\ \beta_p \end{pmatrix}.$$

Also,

$$E[e] = \mathbf{0} \text{ and } Var(e) = \sigma^2 I_n.$$

The OLS estimate is given by

$$\hat{\beta} = (X^T X)^{-1} X^T Y.$$

Example 1.10 *Write a function with matrices X, Y as the parameters which returns an array containing the OLS estimate with $array(i) = \beta_i$ for $i = 0, \ldots, p$.*

```
'Ordinary Least Squares

Public Function OLS(x As Variant, y As Variant) As Variant
Dim Beta As Variant
Dim i As Integer

With Application
  Beta = .MMult(.MInverse(.MMult(.Transpose(x), x)),
        .MMult(.Transpose(x), y))
End With

ReDim res(0 To UBound(Beta) - 1) As Double
For i = 0 To UBound(res)
    res(i) = Beta(i + 1, 1)
Next i

OLS = res
End Function
```

Specifically, Table 1.4 provides a list of worksheet functions and VBA built-in functions used in the OLS function.

TABLE 1.4 Functions Used in the OLS Function

Function	Nature	Return value
MMult (x, y)	Worksheet function	Returns the product of x and y
MInverse (x)	Worksheet function	Returns the inverse of x
Transpose (x)	Worksheet function	Returns the transpose of x
UBound (x)	VBA built-in function	Returns the largest subscript for an array x

1.5 RANDOM NUMBER GENERATION

Monte Carlo simulation requires the use of random numbers. VBA provides a built-in function, *rnd()*, that generates a sequence of pseudo-random numbers. Although they are pseudo-random by nature, they are sufficiently random for general applications in the sense that they satisfy certain characteristics.

The built-in function *rnd()* returns a uniform random number between 0 and 1, and the syntax is:

```
Randomize
x = Rnd()
```

See Table 1.5 for a complete description of *Randomize* and *Rnd*.

Simulation always involves the generation of random variables. In this section, the two main approaches to generating random variables are introduced: inverse transform and the acceptance–rejection method.

1.5.1 Inverse Transform

The inverse transform method makes use of the cumulative density function $F(x)$ of a random variable X. It is simple and easily implemented, but is limited to those random variables that have an analytic form for its cumulative density function.

TABLE 1.5 Description for the Random Number Generator

Procedure/Function	Description
Randomize([x])	The randomize statement is used to initialize the random number generator with an optional argument x as the seed. The system time is used as the seed if x is omitted. If randomize is not used, then the Rnd function (with no arguments) uses the same number as a seed the first time it is called, and thereafter uses the last generated number as a seed value
Rnd([x])	Return the next random number in the sequence if x is omitted. If x is not omitted, then Rnd([x]) returns the same number using x as the seed if $x < 0$; returns the most recent generated number if $x = 0$; and returns the next random number if $x > 0$

TABLE 1.6 Examples of Random Variable Generation Using Inverse Transform

Type	Description
Exponential with mean λ	$X = -\lambda \log(Rnd())$
Normal	$X = Application.NormSInv(Rnd())$

The algorithm of inverse transform is as follows.

1. Generate a standard uniform random variable $Y = U(0, 1)$.
2. The required random variable is given by $X = F^{-1}(Y)$.

Table 1.6 presents examples of random variable generation using inverse transform.

1.5.2 Acceptance–Rejection Method

The acceptance–rejection method was proposed to address some of the limitations of inverse transform. In this method, suppose that Y with density function g can be simulated easily. Use Y as a basis to simulate $X \sim F$ by first generating Y from g and then accepting the value with probability $f(Y)/(cg(Y))$. More specifically, let c be such that

$$\frac{f(y)}{g(y)} \leq c \text{ for all } y.$$

Note that g should have tails heavier than those of the target distribution. The algorithm of the acceptance–rejection method is as follows.

1. Generate Y from density g.
2. Generate $U \sim U(0, 1)$.
3. If $U \leq f(Y)/(cg(Y))$, then set $X = Y$.
4. Otherwise, return to step 1.

Example 1.11 *Student-t distribution is similar to normal distribution except that it has heavier tails. This feature is very useful in calculating Value at Risk. However, inverse transform is not possible for t distribution, and so the acceptance–rejection method is used. Simulation of a t distribution with two degrees of freedom is illustrated here. A double exponential with mean 1 is used as the proposed distribution.*

First find the maximum value of $f(y)/g(y)$ via differentiation, and c is found to be equal to 1.046267 (the maximum occurs at $y = 1$). The corresponding code for the acceptance–rejection method is:

```
Sub tdist()
Dim c As Double, p As Double
Dim Y As Double, X As Double, U1 As Double, U2 As Double
```

```
c = 2 * Exp(1) / ((2 + 1 ^ 2) ^ (3 / 2))

Do
'Generate exp(1)
Y = -Log(Rnd())

'Test if Y is accepted or rejected
U1 = Rnd()
p = 2 * Exp(Y) / (c * ((2 + Y ^ 2) ^ (3 / 2)))
Loop Until (U1 < p)
X = Y

'Generate the negative part of the distribution
U2 = Rnd()
If U2 < 0.5 Then
    X = -X
End If

End Sub
```

Generating normal random variables in an efficient way is very important in the simulation of asset prices. Inverse transform in Excel is not efficient as it is computationally intensive. A more efficient method of generating normal random variables is the Box–Muller transform, which states that if U_1 and U_2 are independent random variables that are uniformly distributed in the interval (0, 1], then

$$Z_0 = \sqrt{-2 \log U_1} \cos(2\pi U_2)$$
$$Z_1 = \sqrt{-2 \log U_1} \sin(2\pi U_2)$$

are independent standard normal random variables. The Box–Muller transform is coded in the following function *rGauss*.

```
Public Function rGauss() As Double
    Static store As Boolean, z As Double
        If store = True Then
            store = False
            rGauss = z
        Else
            z = Sqr(-2 * Log(1 - Rnd())) * Cos(Pi2 * Rnd())
            rGauss = z * Tan(Pi2 * Rnd(0))
            store = True
        End If
End Function
```

1.6 LIST OF FUNCTIONS DEFINED IN THE BOOK

To simplify the codes in the application programs, we have defined a number of constants, UDTs, and functions. This section briefly explains each of the constants, UDTs, and functions used in this book. For details of the code, please refer to the Excel files.

1.6.1 Constants

The following are the constants defined in the book.
xCall = 1
xPut = 2
xStraddle = 3

1.6.2 Types

Type BS_PathType
Type Garch_PathType
Type JD_PathType
Type Heston_PathType

1.6.3 General Functions

rGauss()
Parameters: none
Result: Returns a $\mathcal{N}(0, 1)$ random variable

rCGauss(LArray as Variant)
Parameters: LArray is the lower triangular matrix of the variance–covariance matrix of a vector of multivariate normal random variables
Result: Returns an array of normal random variables with LArray as the lower triangular matrix of the variance–covariance matrix

rGamma(alpha as Long, beta as Double)
Parameters: alpha is the shape parameter and beta is the scale parameter (where mean = alpha ∗ beta)
Result: Returns a Gamma(alpha, beta) random variable

rInvGamma(alpha as Long, beta as Double)
Parameters: alpha is the shape parameter and beta is the scale parameter
Result: Returns an InverseGamma(alpha, beta) random variable

rBeta(alpha as Long, beta as Long)
Parameters: alpha is the shape parameter and beta is the scale parameter
Result: Returns an Beta(alpha, beta) random variable

BS(S0 as Double, K as Double, rf as Double, q as Double, sigma as Double, T as Double, optionType as Integer)
Parameters: S0 is the initial stock price, K is the strike price, rf is the constant risk-free interest rate, q is the dividend yield, sigma is the volatility, T is the time to maturity in year, and optionType can be xCall, xPut, or xStraddle
Result: Returns the close-form solution of the option price for Black–Scholes formula

Max(Val1 as Double, Val2 as Double, optional Val3)
Parameters: Val1 is the first number, Val2 is the second number, and Val3 is optional
Result: Returns the maximum of the two (three) numbers

Min(Val1 as Double, Val2 as Double, optional Val3)
Parameters: Val1 is the first number, Val2 is the second number, and Val3 is optional
Result: Returns the minimum of the two (three) numbers

OLS(X as Variant, Y as Variant)
Parameters: X is the predictor matrix and Y is the response matrix
Result: Returns an array (base 0) of the least squares estimate for predictor X and response Y

Sort(sortArray as Variant, Optional lIndex as Long = −1, Optional rIndex as Long = −1)
Parameters: sortArray is the array you would like to sort
Result: The array inputted is sorted by the *Quicksort* algorithm
Remarks: This is in fact a *Sub* procedure, not a *Function* procedure

CDecom(VCMatrix as Variant)
Parameters: VCMatrix is a symmetric matrix
Result: Returns the lower triangular matrix of a symmetric matrix VCMatrix after Cholesky decomposition

Percentile(valArray as Variant, quantile as Double)
Parameters: valArray is the array for which you would like to find out a certain percentile
Result: Returns the percentile of valArray
Remarks: valArray need not be sorted before using this function

Average(valArray as Variant)
Parameters: valArray is the array for which you want to find the average of its elements
Result: Returns the average of valArray's elements

netDays(bDay as Date, eDay as Date)
Parameters: bDay is the beginning date and eDay is the ending date
Result: Returns the number of business days between bDay and eDay (measuring from the end of bDay to the end of eDay)

ND(z as Double)
Parameters: z
Result: Returns the density function of N(0, 1) at z

NCD(z as Double)
Parameters: z
Result: Returns the cumulative distribution function (CDF) of N(0, 1) at z

BS_Vega(ByVal S0 as Double, ByVal K as Double, ByVal rf as Double, ByVal q as Double, ByVal sigma as Double, ByVal T as Double)
Parameters: S0 is the initial stock price, K is the strike price, rf is the constant risk-free interest rate, q is the dividend yield, sigma is the volatility, and T is the time to maturity in years
Result: Returns the vega of the option under the Black-Scholes model

ImpVol(ByVal Price as Double, ByVal S0 as Double, ByVal K as Double, ByVal rf as Double, ByVal q as Double, ByVal T as Double, ByVal optionType as Integer)
Parameters: Price is the current market price, S0 is the initial stock price, K is the strike price, rf is the constant risk-free interest rate, q is the dividend yield, T is the time to maturity in years, and optionType can be xCall, xPut, or xStraddle
Result: Returns the implied volatility of the option under the Black-Scholes model

1.6.4 Asset Path Simulation Functions

BS_Path(A as BS_PathType)
Parameters: A is a user-defined data type (UDT) variable. Hence, the user has to specify parameters of the Black-Scholes model. An example can be found on page 74–75
Result: Returns a 2D array of asset path S(0 to m, 1 to n)

BS_CPath(A() as BS_PathType, VCMatrix as Variant)
Parameters: A is the UDT and VCMatrix is the variance-covariance matrix of the multi-asset Black-Scholes model. Chapter 3.7 presents an example
Result: Returns a 3D array of asset path S(0 to m, 1 to n, 1 to nAsset) according to the variance-covariance matrix VCMatrix. rf, m, n, dt, T will be read in A(1) only, and so other A(i) can be left empty with these parameters

Garch_Path(A as Garch_PathType)
Parameters: A is the UDT for the GARCH model. An illustrative example is given in Chapter 4.4 and Ch4.4_HSBC_RAN_GARCH(1,1).xls.
Result: Returns a 2D array of asset path S(0 to m, 1 to n) under GARCH

JD_Path(A as JD_PathType, Optional CalculateDrift as Boolean = True)
Parameters: A is an UDT. If Calculate Drift is set as False, then the drift specified in A will be used; otherwise, the risk-neutral drift will be used. An example using this function is given in Chapter 4.5
Result: Returns a 2D array of asset path S(0 to m, 1 to n) under the Jump–diffusion model with method 1.

JDExp_Path(A as JD_PathType, Optional CalculateDrift as Boolean = True)
Parameters: A is an UDT. If Calculate Drift is set as False, then the drift specified in A will be used; otherwise, the risk-neutral drift will be used. An example using this function is given in Chapter 4.5
Result: Returns a 2D array of asset path S(0 to m, 1 to n) under the Jump–diffusion model with method 2; if CalculateDrift is set as False, then the drift specified in A will be used; otherwise, the risk-neutral drift will be used

HestonVol_Path(A as Heston_PathType)
Parameters: A is an UDT for the Heston model. An example using this function is given in Chapter 4.3
Result: Returns a 2D array of asset path S(0 to m, 1 to n) under Heston, with moment matching

HestonVolQE_Path(A as Heston_PathType)
Parameters: A is an UDT for the Heston model. An example using this function is given in Chapter 4.3
Result: Returns a 2D array of asset path S(0 to m, 1 to n) under Heston, with the QE scheme

EO_Payoff(S as variant, K as double, optionType as Integer, optional m as long = −1)
Parameters: S is the stock price, K is the strike price, optionType is the type of options of either xCall, xPut, or xStraddle. Please refer to Example 3.1 on page 78
Result: Returns an array of the terminal payoff of the vanilla European option expiring at step m given the price path S

AO_Payoff(S as Variant, rf as Double, dt as Double, K as Double, optionType as Integer, optional m as long = −1)
Parameters: S is the stock price; rf is the interest rate; dt is the time step size; K is the strike price, optionType can be xCall, xPut, or xStraddle. Please refer to Example 3.2 on page 85
Result: Returns an array of the terminal payoff of a vanilla American option expiring at step m

EMartingale(S as Variant, rf as Double, q as Double, dt as Double)
Parameters: S is the original asset price path, rf is the risk-free rate, q is the dividend yield, and dt is the interval of each step

Result: Returns a 2D array of the asset price path after empirical martingale correction

1.6.5 Other Functions

ShowStatus(nStep as Long, tStep as Long, sStep as Integer)
Result: Show nStep/tStep in the status bar for each sStep; it can be disabled by setting HideStatus = True

ResetStatus
Parameters: None
Result: Reset the status bar

1.6.6 Remarks

Option Explicit

To force the declaration of all variables used, include the following as the first instruction in the VBA module.

Option Explicit

This statement causes the program to stop whenever VBA encounters a variable name that has not been declared. The variable must then be declared before proceeding.

2

Background

This chapter sets out the background for readers in three parts. The first part reviews the concept of stochastic calculus for derivatives pricing theory. We start with Black and Scholes' (1973) argument for formulating a risk-free portfolio for an option and its underlying asset through hedging. The consequences of hedging bring us to risk-neutral valuation, which asserts that a derivative price can be obtained by computing an expectation under a martingale (risk-neutral) probability measure rather than a data-generating (physical) probability measure. Hence, we need to introduce the martingale notion in advance. Risk-neutral valuation essentially requires a "revision" of the stochastic process of the underlying asset price for the purposes of derivative pricing. It turns out that two practical approaches are possible for identifying this "revised" process. They are as follows.

1. Estimate the model parameters from the historical prices of the underlying asset and then transform the model to the risk-neutral process by utilizing certain martingale properties.
2. Bypass the estimation from historical data, but directly calibrate the model parameters to fit current market prices or observations.

The first approach is useful for an underlying asset with very thin derivatives transactions. The market prices of the associated options are not reliable or may not even be available. The stochastic model can only fit the historical data. For instance, if a bank wants to issue a new option on a stock for which there is no option market,

Handbook of Financial Risk Management: Simulations and Case Studies, First Edition. N.H. Chan and H.Y. Wong.
© 2013 John Wiley & Sons, Inc. Published 2013 by John Wiley & Sons, Inc.

then it has to resort to estimating a presumed stochastic model. A typical approach is to fit the historical time series of the stock returns with a GARCH model originated by Engle (1982). To value options, this model should be adjusted by certain martingale conditions prior to option valuation. Valuation involves simulation of the asset price paths using the adjusted process.

The second approach is more common and is closely related to the notion of mark-to-market practice. Essentially, it is relative pricing. When a bank issues a new structured product (a tailor-made derivative for a bank client), its price is revised to be consistent with the price of similar derivatives in the market. Therefore, the bank calibrates the presumed stochastic model to the option prices on the asset underlying the new structured product and then simulates the asset price paths according to this calibrated model. In this way the structured product is inferred by the prices of other similar derivative securities.

Hence, the second part of this chapter introduces the notions of mark-to-market and calibration. The typical practice is to mark against market option prices, which, however, are quoted by their implied volatility. To better understand the prevailing market practice, it is indispensable that we define different types of volatilities and spell out the differences among them.

The final part of the chapter reviews a number of variance reduction techniques. Once a model has been either estimated or calibrated, valuation usually relies on simulation, which is the main focus of this book. However, the computational efficiency of simulation can be improved in a number of ways. The classical means is through variance reduction techniques.

2.1 A BRIEF REVIEW OF MARTINGALES AND ITÔ'S CALCULUS

The concepts of martingales and Itô's calculus are fundamental to the development of derivatives pricing theory and Monte Carlo simulation in financial risk management. The theoretical details are omitted here because they can be found in many standard references, for example, Bjork (2009), Mikosch (1998), Karataz and Shreve (1991), Shreve (2004), and Chan and Wong (2006). We present only the most important results, and readers who are familiar with these concepts may wish to browse this subsection quickly.

2.1.1 Martingales

A stochastic process $X \triangleq \{X_t : t \in \mathcal{T}\}$ is a collection of real-valued random variables indexed by t; that is, for any $t \in \mathcal{T}$, X_t is a random variable that follows a certain distribution. The index t is usually regarded as the time at which the stochastic process is observed. If t takes a countable number of values, for example, $\mathcal{T} = \{1, 2, 3, \ldots\}$, then X is called a discrete-time stochastic process. If t takes a continuum of values, for example, $\mathcal{T} = [0, T]$ for some $T > 0$, then X is called a continuous-time stochastic process.

Definition 2.1 *A stochastic process $X = \{X(n) : n = 1, 2, \ldots\}$ is called a discrete martingale if it satisfies, for any $n = 1, 2, \ldots$,*

$$E[|X(n)|] < \infty,$$
$$E[X(n)|X(i), i = 1, \ldots, n-1] = X(n-1).$$

Similarly, a stochastic process $X = \{X(t) : t \in [0, T]\}$, where $T \geq 0$, is called a continuous martingale if it satisfies, for any $t \in [0, T]$,

$$E[|X(t)|] < \infty,$$
$$E[X(t)|X(u), 0 \leq u \leq s] = X(s), \text{ for } s \leq t.$$

In Definition 2.1, it is sometimes inconvenient to write down the conditional sets $\{X(i), i = 1, \ldots, n-1\}$ repeatedly in discrete time or $\{X(u), 0 \leq u \leq s\}$ in continuous time to represent the information on process X accumulated up to time s (or $n-1$ in the case of discrete time). For convenience, we thus employ the standard notation: $\mathcal{F}_s^X = \{X(u), 0 \leq u \leq s\}$. Also, the equality about conditional expectation is supposed to hold almost surely. In this way, the martingale property can be written as

$$E[|X(t)|] < \infty, E[X(t)|\mathcal{F}_s^X] = X(s), \text{ for } s \leq t.$$

The notion of martingales, which is related to the concept of arbitrage opportunity, plays an important role in the modern theory of contingent claim pricing. An arbitrage opportunity is any trading strategy that starts with zero cost and has a positive probability of returning a profit in the future. It is usually assumed that an asset price model should not admit an arbitrage strategy; otherwise, it would be possible to make unlimited profits with zero initial wealth, which is unreasonable and unrealistic. The first fundamental theorem of asset pricing states that an asset pricing model admits no arbitrage opportunities if and only if there exists a risk-neutral probability measure (equivalent to the physical probability measure) under which the discounted asset price is a martingale, thus contributing to the notion of risk-neutral pricing. In simple terms, the price of a contingent claim can be obtained by first changing the return of the underlying asset to the risk-free interest rate and then taking the conditional expectation on the terminal value of the claim.

2.1.2 Brownian Motion

The application of simulation techniques to asset pricing and risk management is crucially reliant on the assumption of the evolution of the asset pricing process. Throughout the history of quantitative finance, Brownian motion has constituted a fundamental building block and is the most popular model of asset pricing process. Therefore, the basic properties of Brownian motion are briefly noted here.

Definition 2.2 (Brownian motion) *A standard Brownian motion $W(t)$ is a continuous-time stochastic process that satisfies the following properties.*

1. $W(0) = 0$ with probability one.
2. For $s, t \geq 0$, $W(s+t) - W(s)$ is a normally distributed random variable with mean 0 and variance t; that is, $W(s+t) - W(s) \sim \mathcal{N}(0, t)$.
3. For all $0 = t_0 < t_1 < \ldots < t_m$, the increments $W(t_1) - W(t_0)$, $W(t_2) - W(t_1)$, $\ldots$, $W(t_m) - W(t_{m-1})$ are independent.

The last two properties can be summarized as the Brownian motion having stationary independent increments. These properties lead to certain other properties which include but are not restricted to the following examples.

Example 2.1 (The martingale property of Brownian motion) *A Brownian motion $W(t)$ is a martingale.*

Let $0 \leq s \leq t$ be given. Then,

$$E[W(t)|W(s)]$$
$$= E[W(t) - W(s) + W(s)|W(s)]$$
$$= E[W(t) - W(s)|W(s)] + E[W(s)|W(s)]$$
$$= E[W(t) - W(s)] + W(s) (\text{as} W(t) - W(s) \text{ is independent of } W(s))$$
$$= W(s) (\text{as } W(t) - W(s) \text{ has mean } 0).$$

Example 2.2 (The Markov property of a Brownian motion) *It follows from the independent increment property that a Brownian motion is always a Markov process.*

Example 2.3 (Exponential martingale) *The process $\exp\left(-\frac{1}{2}\sigma^2 t + \sigma W(t)\right)$, where $t \geq 0$, is a martingale.*

Let $0 \leq s \leq t$ be given. Then,

$$E\left[\exp\left(-\frac{1}{2}\sigma^2 t + \sigma W(t)\right)\Big|W(s)\right]$$
$$= \exp\left(-\frac{1}{2}\sigma^2 t + \sigma W(s)\right) E\left[\exp\left(\sigma(W(t) - W(s))\right)\Big|W(s)\right]$$
$$= \exp\left(-\frac{1}{2}\sigma^2 t + \sigma W(s)\right) E\left[\exp\left(\sigma\sqrt{t-s}X\right)\right],$$

where X is a standard normal random variable

$$= \exp\left(-\frac{1}{2}\sigma^2 t + \sigma W(s)\right) \exp\left(\frac{1}{2}\sigma^2(t-s)\right)$$
$$= \exp\left(-\frac{1}{2}\sigma^2 s + \sigma W(s)\right).$$

We very often encounter expressions such as $dW(t) dW(t) = dt$, $dW(t) dt = 0$, and $dt \, dt = 0$, which can be derived from the concept of quadratic variation. The quadratic variation of a function $f(t)$ on $[0, T]$ is defined as

$$[f, f](T) \triangleq \lim_{\|\Pi\| \to 0} \sum_{j=0}^{n-1} [f(t_{j+1}) - f(t_j)]^2,$$

where $\Pi = \{t_0, t_1, \ldots, t_n\}$ and $0 = t_0 < t_1 < \ldots < t_n = T$, and $\|\Pi\| = \max_{j=0,1,\ldots,n-1}(t_{j+1} - t_j)$. For Brownian motion, $[W, W](T) = T$ with probability one. Let $QV = \sum_{j=0}^{n-1}(W(t_{j+1}) - W(t_j))^2$ and consider the mean and variance of the random variable QV. Then

$$\mathrm{E}[QV] = \sum_{j=0}^{n-1} \mathrm{E}\left[\left(W(t_{j+1}) - W(t_j)\right)^2\right]$$

$$= \sum_{j=0}^{n-1} \mathrm{Var}(W(t_{j+1}) - W(t_j))$$

$$= \sum_{j=0}^{n-1}(t_{j+1} - t_j)$$

$$= T,$$

and

$\mathrm{Var}(QV)$

$$= \sum_{j=0}^{n-1} \mathrm{Var}\left((W(t_{j+1}) - W(t_j))^2\right)$$

$$= \sum_{j=0}^{n-1} \mathrm{E}\left[\left((W(t_{j+1}) - W(t_j))^2 - (t_{j+1} - t_j)\right)^2\right]$$

$$= \sum_{j=0}^{n-1} \mathrm{E}\left[\left(W(t_{j+1}) - W(t_j)\right)^4 - 2(t_{j+1} - t_j)\left(W(t_{j+1}) - W(t_j)\right)^2 + (t_{j+1} - t_j)^2\right]$$

$$= \sum_{j=0}^{n-1}\left[3(t_{j+1} - t_j)^2 - 2(t_{j+1} - t_j)^2 + (t_{j+1} - t_j)^2\right]$$

$$= 2\sum_{j=0}^{n-1}(t_{j+1} - t_j)^2$$

$$\leq 2\sum_{j=0}^{n-1} \|\Pi\|(t_{j+1} - t_j)$$

$$= 2\|\Pi\|T.$$

Therefore, $\lim_{\|\Pi\| \to 0} \text{Var}(QV) = 0$. In conclusion, $\lim_{\|\Pi\| \to 0} QV = T$.
To show that $dW(t)\,dt = 0$, compute the cross-variation of $W(t)$ with t:

$$\lim_{\|\Pi\| \to 0} \sum_{j=0}^{n-1} \Big(W(t_{j+1}) - W(t_j)\Big)(t_{j+1} - t_j)$$

$$\leq \lim_{\|\Pi\| \to 0} \max_{k=0,\ldots,n-1} \Big(W(t_{j+1}) - W(t_j)\Big) \sum_{j=0}^{n-1}(t_{j+1} - t_j)$$

$$= T \lim_{\|\Pi\| \to 0} \max_{k=0,\ldots,n-1} \Big(W(t_{j+1}) - W(t_j)\Big)$$

$$= 0 \text{ (as } W \text{ is continuous, } \lim_{\|\Pi\| \to 0} \max_{k=0,\ldots,n-1}$$

$(W(t_{j+1}) - W(t_j))) = 0$.

Finally, to show that $dt\,dt = 0$, compute the quadratic variation of t:

$$\lim_{\|\Pi\| \to 0} \sum_{j=0}^{n-1}(t_{j+1} - t_j)^2$$

$$\leq \lim_{\|\Pi\| \to 0} \max_{k=0,\ldots,n-1}(t_{j+1} - t_j) \sum_{j=0}^{n-1}(t_{j+1} - t_j)$$

$$= T \lim_{\|\Pi\| \to 0} \|\Pi\|$$

$$= 0.$$

Because some contingent claims may involve more than one asset, one Brownian motion is needed for each asset. The definition of one-dimensional (1D) Brownian motion can easily be extended to multidimensional Brownian motion.

Definition 2.3 (Multidimensional Brownian motion) *A d-dimensional Brownian motion $\mathbf{W}(t)$ is a continuous-time stochastic process*

$$\mathbf{W}(t) = (W_1(t), \ldots, W_d(t))$$

that satisfies the following properties.

1. For $i = 1, \ldots, d$, W_i is a scalar Brownian motion.
2. For $i \neq j$, $W_i(t)$ and $W_j(t)$ are independent, that is, $\text{E}[W_i(t)\,W_j(t)] = 0$.

Correlations between Brownian motions can be introduced by a suitable linear transformation of the multidimensional Brownian motion. The details are discussed in the next chapter.

2.1.3 Itô's Process and Itô's Lemma

The idea of Brownian motion can be generalized as follows. Consider a process X that satisfies the following *stochastic differential equation (SDE)*.

$$dX(t) = \mu \, dt + \sigma \, dW(t), \qquad (2.1)$$

where μ and σ are constants, and $W(t)$ is the Brownian motion. Indeed, Equation 2.1 is the short hand version of

$$X(t) = \mu t + \sigma W(t). \qquad (2.2)$$

Equation 2.1 gives some basic idea of simulation. A natural extension of this SDE (Eq. 2.1; or, equivalently, Eq. 2.2) is to allow parameters μ and σ to depend on time t, which leads to the following definition.

Definition 2.4 *An Itô process is a stochastic process that is the solution to the following SDE.*

$$dX(t) = \mu(t, X(t)) \, dt + \sigma(t, X(t)) \, dW(t), \qquad (2.3)$$

or, equivalently,

$$X(t) = \int_0^t \mu(s, X(s)) \, ds + \int_0^t \sigma(s, X(s)) \, dW(s). \qquad (2.4)$$

In this equation, $\mu(t, x)$ is known as the drift function and $\sigma(t, x)$ as the volatility function. Restrictions must be imposed on these two functions to guarantee the existence of the solution to the SDE (Eq. 2.4). Assume drift and volatility to be "nice" functions to ensure that the existence of the solution is guaranteed. Obviously, the foregoing definition is not restricted to the 1D case, as it can be easily generalized to the multidimensional case. Several important properties concerning the Itô process are given as follows. The integral (Eq. 2.4) satisfies

$$E\left[X^2(t)\right] = E\left[\int_0^t \sigma^2(s, X(s)) \, ds\right],$$

and

$$[X, X](t) = \int_0^t \sigma^2(s, X(s)) \, ds, \text{ or } dX(t) \, dX(t) = \sigma^2(t, X(t)) \, dt.$$

Although similar, the former property renders computation of the expectation convenient, whereas the latter results in the second-order term involving "dt" in Itô's calculus, which is different from ordinary differential calculus. Finally, the integral (Eq. 2.4) with $\mu(t, x) \equiv 0$ is a martingale.

Given some function $f(t, x)$ and an Itô process $X(t)$, $f(t, X(t))$ is another stochastic process. A question concerning $f(t, X(t))$ is what is its dynamics? Itô's lemma shows that $f(t, X(t))$ is also an Itô process.

Theorem 2.1 (Itô's lemma) *Let $X(t)$ be an Itô process satisfying* (Eq. 2.3), *and let $f(t, x)$ be a function for which the partial derivatives $\frac{\partial}{\partial t} f(t, x)$, $\frac{\partial}{\partial x} f(t, x)$, and $\frac{\partial^2}{\partial x^2} f(t, x)$ are continuous. Then, for any $t \geq 0$,*

$$df(t, X(t))$$
$$= \left(\frac{\partial}{\partial t} f(t, X(t)) + \mu(t, X(t)) \frac{\partial}{\partial x} f(t, X(t)) + \frac{1}{2} \sigma^2(t, X(t)) \frac{\partial^2}{\partial x^2} f(t, X(t)) \right) dt$$
$$+ \sigma(t, X(t)) \frac{\partial}{\partial x} f(t, X(t)) \, dW(t), \qquad (2.5)$$

or, equivalently,

$$f(t, X(t)) - f(0, X(0))$$
$$= \int_0^t \left(\frac{\partial}{\partial s} f(s, X(s)) + \mu(s, X(s)) \frac{\partial}{\partial x} f(s, X(s)) + \frac{1}{2} \sigma^2(s, X(s)) \frac{\partial^2}{\partial x^2} f(s, X(s)) \right) ds$$
$$+ \int_0^t \sigma(s, X(s)) \frac{\partial}{\partial x} f(s, X(s)) \, dW(s). \qquad (2.6)$$

An equivalent but simple-to-remember version of Itô's lemma is the following.

$$df(t, X(t)) = \frac{\partial}{\partial t} f(t, X(t)) \, dt + \frac{\partial}{\partial x} f(t, X(t)) \, dX(t) + \frac{1}{2} \frac{\partial^2}{\partial x^2} f(t, X(t)) \, dX(t) \, dX(t).$$
$$(2.7)$$

Consider the following examples which are related to our applications.

Example 2.4 *Suppose that $X(t)$ satisfies the geometric Brownian motion (GBM) equation*

$$dX(t) = \mu X(t) \, dt + \sigma X(t) \, dW(t).$$

Compute the dynamics of $\log X(t)$. First, consider the function $f(t, x) = \log x$ and let $\mu(t, x) = \mu x$ and $\sigma(t, x) = \sigma x$. Then, $\frac{\partial f}{\partial t} = 0$, $\frac{\partial f}{\partial x} = \frac{1}{x}$, and $\frac{\partial^2 f}{\partial x^2} = -\frac{1}{x^2}$. By Itô's lemma (Eq. 2.5),

$$d \log X(t) = \left(\mu - \frac{\sigma^2}{2} \right) dt + \sigma \, dW(t);$$

that is,
$$X(t) = X(0)\exp\left(\left(\mu - \frac{\sigma^2}{2}\right)t + \sigma W(t)\right),$$

which is the basis for simulating the asset pricing process in the Black–Scholes (BS) model.

Example 2.5 Find the solution to the SDE
$$dX(t) = \mu X(t)\,dt + \sigma\,dW(t).$$

Consider the function $f(t, x) = e^{-\mu t}x$ and let $\mu(t, x) = \mu x$ and $\sigma(t, x) = \sigma$. Then, $\frac{\partial f}{\partial t} = -\mu e^{-\mu t}x$, $\frac{\partial f}{\partial x} = e^{-\mu t}$ and $\frac{\partial^2 f}{\partial x^2} = 0$. By Itô's lemma (Eq. 2.5),

$$d(e^{-\mu t}X(t)) = (-\mu e^{-\mu t}X(t) + \mu X(t)e^{-\mu t})\,dt + \sigma e^{-\mu t}\,dW(t)$$
$$= \sigma e^{-\mu t}\,dW(t);$$

that is,
$$X(t) = e^{-\mu t}X(0) + \sigma \int_0^t e^{\mu(t-s)}\,dW(s).$$

Example 2.6 Suppose that $X(t)$ satisfies the SDE
$$dX(t) = \mu X(t)\,dt + \sigma\,dW(t).$$

Compute the dynamics of $X^2(t)$. First, consider the function $f(t, x) = x^2$ and let $\mu(t, x) = \mu x$, and $\sigma(t, x) = \sigma$. Then, $\frac{\partial f}{\partial t} = 0$, $\frac{\partial f}{\partial x} = 2x$, and $\frac{\partial^2 f}{\partial x^2} = 2$. By Itô's lemma (Eq. 2.5),

$$dX^2(t) = (2\mu X^2(t) + \sigma^2)\,dt + 2\sigma X(t)\,dW(t).$$

For suitable parameter values, $X(t) \geq 0$ for any t. Set $Y(t) = X^2(t)$ and then
$$dY(t) = (\sigma^2 + 2\mu Y(t))\,dt + 2\sigma\sqrt{Y(t)}\,dW(t),$$

which is known as a square-root process or a CIR process. This process is frequently used to model the stochastic variance of an asset price.

2.1.4 Discretization Methods

In the BS model, once the closed-form solution of the underlying asset price has been obtained, that is, $S(t) = S(0)\exp\left(\left(\mu - \frac{\sigma^2}{2}\right)t + \sigma W(t)\right)$, the asset price paths can be simulated directly by simulating the standard normal random variables. In other words, the SDE $dS(t) = \mu S(t)\,dt + \sigma S(t)\,dW(t)$ plays no role in simulation, but represents the solution to the asset price. In more complicated models, such as local volatility and stochastic volatility models, the asset price paths cannot be obtained simply by simulating the standard normal random variables; otherwise, the simulated paths may deviate considerably from the true distribution. Instead, the asset price paths must be simulated on the basis of discrete approximations of the continuous solution to the system of the model's SDEs. To this end, the *Euler scheme* and *Milstein scheme* are introduced. The former is a direct discretization of the SDE and the latter leads to a higher order of accuracy.

Given an Itô process X on $[0, T]$ that satisfies the SDE,

$$dX(t) = a(X(t))\,dt + b(X(t))\,dW(t),$$

with deterministic initial value $X(0)$, where $a(x)$ and $b(x)$ are deterministic functions, and $W(t)$ is a Brownian motion. Now, let $\widehat{X}(t)$ be an approximation to $X(t)$ at time t. The Euler scheme of approximation on a time grid $0 = t_0 < t_1 < \ldots < t_n$ is defined by $\widehat{X}(t_0) = X(0)$, and, for $i = 0, 1, \ldots, m-1$,

$$\widehat{X}(t_{i+1}) = \widehat{X}(t_i) + a(\widehat{X}(t_i))(t_{i+1} - t_i) + b(\widehat{X}(t_i))\sqrt{t_{i+1} - t_i}\,Z_{i+1},$$

where $Z_1, Z_2, \ldots, Z_m$ are independent standard normal random variables. Once the functions $a(x)$ and $b(x)$ are known, implementation is achieved by generating independent standard normal random variables.

From this expression, the Euler discretization scheme expands the drift term up to $O(t_{i+1} - t_i)$ but the diffusion term up to $O(\sqrt{t_{i+1} - t_i})$ (recall that $dW(t)\,dW(t) = dt$ with probability one). To improve discretization accuracy, the Milstein scheme makes use of Itô's lemma to improve the accuracy of the approximation by adding the second-order term. Recall that the foregoing SDE is equivalent to

$$X(t+h) = X(t) + \int_t^{t+h} a(X(s))\,ds + \int_t^{t+h} b(X(s))\,dW(s).$$

The drift term is approximated as in the Euler scheme

$$\int_t^{t+h} a(X(s))\,ds \approx a(X(t))h.$$

For better approximation of the diffusion term, use Itô's lemma to expand $b(X(t))$

$$db(X(t)) = \mu_b(X(t))\,dt + \sigma_b(X(t))\,dW(t),$$

where $\mu_b(x) = a(x)\frac{\partial b(x)}{\partial x} + \frac{1}{2}b^2(x)\frac{\partial^2 b(x)}{\partial x^2}$ and $\sigma_b(x) = b(x)\frac{\partial b(x)}{\partial x}$. Applying the Euler scheme to approximate $b(X(t))$ and discarding the higher order terms, for $t \leq s \leq$

$t + h$, we have

$$b(X(s)) \approx b(X(t)) + \sigma_b(X(t))(W(s) - W(t)).$$

Then,

$$\int_t^{t+h} b(X(s)) \, dW(s)$$

$$\approx \int_t^{t+h} (b(X(t)) + \sigma_b(X(t))(W(s) - W(t))) \, dW(s)$$

$$= b(X(t))(W(t+h) - W(t)) + \sigma_b(X(t)) \int_t^{t+h} (W(s) - W(t)) \, dW(s)$$

$$= b(X(t))(W(t+h) - W(t)) + \frac{1}{2}\sigma_b(X(t))((W(t+h) - W(t))^2 - h).$$

Finally, the Euler scheme is refined as

$$X(t+h) \approx X(t) + a(X(t))h + b(X(t))(W(t+h) - W(t))$$
$$+ \frac{1}{2}\sigma_b(X(t))((W(t+h) - W(t))^2 - h).$$

The simulation algorithm is written as

$$\widehat{X}(t_{i+1}) = \widehat{X}(t_i) + a(\widehat{X}(t_i))(t_{i+1} - t_i)$$
$$+ b(\widehat{X}(t_i))Z_{i+1} + \frac{1}{2}\sigma_b(\widehat{X}(t_i))(t_{i+1} - t_i)((Z_{i+1})^2 - 1).$$

Further information about the Euler and Milstein schemes can be found in Kloeden and Platen (2010), Milstein (1995), and the seminal treatise of Jacod and Protter (2011).

2.1.5 The Black–Scholes Equation and Risk-Neutral Valuation

The application of Itô's calculus in finance can be effectively illustrated in the derivation of the celebrated BS equation. Suppose that in a frictionless market, an option writer sells a call option and simultaneously holds a portfolio to *perfectly hedge* the payoff of the call option, that is, the payoff of the call option is financed completely by the proceeds of portfolio liquidation. Now, at any time $t < T$, the portfolio value is $V(t)$ with $\Delta(t)$ shares of the underlying stock, $S(t)$, whose price process follows the GBM:

$$dS(t) = \mu S(t) \, dt + \sigma S(t) \, dW(t). \tag{2.8}$$

This stochastic process for the underlying asset is defined under the physical probability measure, $\mathbb{P}$, because parameters μ and σ are estimated with the historical prices of $S(t)$. Therefore, the standard Brownian motion $W(t)$ satisfies the conditions in Definition 2.2 under probability measure $\mathbb{P}$. More specifically, we need to understand that $E^{\mathbb{P}}[W(s+t) - W(s)] = 0$ and $E^{\mathbb{P}}[(W(s+t) - W(s))^2] = t$, where the expectation is defined through historical data fitting.

The remainder of the portfolio, $V(t) - \Delta(t)S(t)$, is invested in a risk-free money market account with constant interest rate r. In the next instant dt, the change in portfolio value comprises the change in the value of the stock position, $\Delta(t) dS(t)$, and the change in the value of the money market account position, $r(V(t) - \Delta(t)S(t)) dt$. Therefore, the value of the portfolio evolves as

$$dV(t) = \Delta(t) dS(t) + r(V(t) - \Delta(t)S(t)) dt$$
$$= \Delta(t)(\mu S(t) dt + \sigma S(t) dW(t)) + r(V(t) - \Delta(t)S(t)) dt$$
$$= rV(t) dt + \Delta(t)(\mu - r)S(t) dt + \Delta(t)\sigma S(t) dW(t). \quad (2.9)$$

Consider a European call option that pays $(S(T) - K)^+$ at time T. Suppose that the value of this call option at time t is $c(t, S(t))$. By Itô's lemma (Eq. 2.5),

$$dc(t, S(t)) = \left(\frac{\partial}{\partial t}c(t, S(t)) + \mu S(t)\frac{\partial}{\partial S}c(t, S(t)) + \frac{1}{2}\sigma^2 S^2(t)\frac{\partial^2}{\partial S^2}c(t, S(t))\right) dt$$
$$+ \sigma S(t)\frac{\partial}{\partial S}c(t, S(t)) dW(t). \quad (2.10)$$

Now, to hedge the payoff of the call option at time T, the hedging portfolio starts with initial capital $V(0)$ and invests in the underlying stock and the money market account dynamically such that for each time $t \in [0, T]$, $V(t) = c(t, S(t))$. This process is called replication, and V is known as a replicating portfolio. It occurs if for all $t \in [0, T)$,

$$dV(t) = dc(t, S(t)),$$

and

$$V(T) = c(T, S) = (S - K)^+.$$

Matching the coefficients of dt and $dW(t)$ in Equations 2.9 and 2.10, we have

$$\Delta(t) = \frac{\partial}{\partial S}c(t, S),$$

and

$$\frac{\partial}{\partial t}c(t, S) + \mu S\frac{\partial}{\partial S}c(t, S) + \frac{1}{2}\sigma^2 S^2\frac{\partial^2}{\partial S^2}c(t, S) = rV(t) + \Delta(t)(\mu - r)S,$$

which, after putting $V(t) = c(t, S)$, substituting $\Delta(t) = \frac{\partial}{\partial S} c(t, S)$, and canceling the terms involving μ, is equivalent to

$$\frac{\partial}{\partial t} c(t, S) + rS\frac{\partial}{\partial S} c(t, S) + \frac{1}{2}\sigma^2 S^2 \frac{\partial^2}{\partial S^2} c(t, S) = rc(t, S), \; c(T, S) = \max(S - K, 0),$$

which is the BS equation.

The BS equation generates two important insights. The first is the concept of risk-neutral pricing. As the BS equation does not involve the drift, μ, of the underlying asset price, the option pricing formula should be independent of the drift. Therefore, individual preferences regarding the performance or trend of a particular asset price do not affect the current price of the option on that asset. The second insight is that we are able to derive a price representation of a European option with any payoff function from the equation; that is, the price of a contingent claim with maturity can be obtained by first changing the drift rate of the asset to the risk-free interest rate and then taking the conditional expectation on the terminal value (which is a random variable) of the claim. Mathematically, consider a stochastic process X that satisfies

$$dX(t) = rX(t)\,dt + \sigma X(t)\,dW^*(t), \; X(0) = S(0), \qquad (2.11)$$

where W^* is the standard Brownian motion under a certain sense of the probability measure. Let us call it probability measure $\mathbb{Q}$ for the moment. Then, $c(0, S) = c(0, X)$. Consider the process $c(t, X(t))$ derived from $X(t)$. By Itô's lemma (Eq. 2.5),

$$dc(t, X(t)) = \left(\frac{\partial}{\partial t} c(t, X(t)) + rX(t)\frac{\partial}{\partial X} c(t, X(t)) + \frac{1}{2}\sigma^2 X^2(t)\frac{\partial^2}{\partial X^2} c(t, X(t))\right) dt$$

$$+ \sigma X(t)\frac{\partial}{\partial X} c(t, X(t))\,dW^*(t).$$

The BS equation stipulates that the coefficient of dt is identical to $rc(t, X(t))$, thereby resulting in

$$dc(t, X(t)) = rc(t, X(t))\,dt + \sigma X(t)\frac{\partial}{\partial X} c(t, X(t))\,dW^*(t).$$

Consider the discounted asset price $e^{-rt} c(t, X(t))$. Then

$$d(e^{-rt} c(t, X(t))) = \sigma e^{-rt} X(t) \frac{\partial}{\partial X} c(t, X(t))\,dW^*(t),$$

or, equivalently,

$$e^{-rT} c(T, X(T)) - c(0, X(0)) = \sigma \int_0^T e^{-rt} X(t) \frac{\partial}{\partial X} c(t, X(t))\,dW^*(t).$$

Because the right-hand side is a martingale, the discounted asset price is now a martingale. Taking the expectation conditional on $\mathcal{F}_0^X$ on both sides, we have

$$E^{\mathbb{Q}}[e^{-rT}c(T, X(T))|\mathcal{F}_0^X] - c(0, X(0)) = 0,$$

which implies that

$$c(0, S(0)) = E^{\mathbb{Q}}[e^{-rT}c(T, X(T))|\mathcal{F}_0^X], \qquad (2.12)$$

where the expectation is taken with respect to the random variable $X(T)$, which is driven by the standard Brownian motion defined in the sense of $\mathbb{Q}$. Probability measure $\mathbb{Q}$ is then called the *risk-neutral probability*, the associated expectation the *risk-neutral expectation*, and process X the *risk-neutral asset dynamics*. To avoid confusion, the "risk-neutral dynamics of S" is generally used to represent X.

Remarks

1. Because of the independent increment property of the standard Brownian motion,

$$c(0, S(0)) = E^{\mathbb{Q}}[e^{-rT}c(T, X(T))|\mathcal{F}_0^X] = E^{\mathbb{Q}}[e^{-rT}c(T, X(T))|X_0 = S(0)].$$

2. The expectation representation of a European option price in Equation 2.12 is called the risk-neutral valuation formula. In general, it asserts that

$$e^{-rt}V(t, S(t)) = E^{\mathbb{Q}}[e^{-rT}V(T, X(T))|\mathcal{F}_0^X]$$

for any contingent claim (or European-style derivative securities), $V(t, S(t))$. It is clear that the quantity $e^{-rt}V(t, S(t))$ is a martingale in the sense of $\mathbb{Q}$, and hence is a $\mathbb{Q}$-martingale.

3. As the discounted derivative price at time $t > 0$ is a martingale under $\mathbb{Q}$, probability measure $\mathbb{Q}$ is also known as a martingale measure that is equivalent to $\mathbb{P}$.

Comparing Equations 2.8 and 2.11, we observe that these two processes resemble each other except for the drift term and their driving standard Brownian motions. In fact, both processes describe the evolution of the stock price using a different sense of Brownian motion. If we force them to be equal to each other, then it is easy to deduce that

$$W^*(t) + \left(\frac{\mu - r}{\sigma}\right)t = W(t), \quad \text{or} \quad dW^*(t) + \left(\frac{\mu - r}{\sigma}\right)dt = dW(t). \qquad (2.13)$$

In other words, we shift only the mean of the Brownian motion by a factor $\left(\frac{\mu-r}{\sigma}\right)t$, where $\frac{\mu-r}{\sigma}$ is known as the market price of risk in finance and reflects the trade-off between excess return $\mu - r$ and risk σ.

2.1.6 Change of Measures

After establishing the connection between $W(t)$ and $W^*(t)$ in Equation 2.13, here we further clarify the relationship between $\mathbb{P}$ and $\mathbb{Q}$. Suppose that we want to evaluate expectation $\mathrm{E}^{\mathbb{Q}}[h(W(T))]$, where W is the $\mathbb{P}$-standard Brownian motion. By Equation 2.13, we have

$$\mathrm{E}^{\mathbb{Q}}[h(W(T))] = \mathrm{E}^{\mathbb{Q}}\left[h\left(W^*(T) + \left(\frac{\mu-r}{\sigma}\right)T\right)\right]. \quad (2.14)$$

As $W^*(T) \sim \mathcal{N}(0, T)$ under $\mathbb{Q}$, we have

$$\mathrm{E}^{\mathbb{Q}}\left[h\left(W^*(T) + \left(\frac{\mu-r}{\sigma}\right)T\right)\right] = \int_{-\infty}^{\infty} \frac{h\left(x + \left(\frac{\mu-r}{\sigma}\right)T\right)}{\sqrt{2\pi T}} \exp\left[-\frac{x^2}{2T}\right] dx. \quad (2.15)$$

Taking the transformation of the variable $y = x + \left(\frac{\mu-r}{\sigma}\right)T$, we have

$$\mathrm{E}^{\mathbb{Q}}\left[h\left(W^*(T) + \left(\frac{\mu-r}{\sigma}\right)T\right)\right] = \int_{-\infty}^{\infty} \frac{h(y)}{\sqrt{2\pi T}} \exp\left[-\frac{\left(y - \left(\frac{\mu-r}{\sigma}\right)T\right)^2}{2T}\right] dy$$

$$= \int_{-\infty}^{\infty} e^{-\frac{1}{2}\left(\frac{\mu-r}{\sigma}\right)^2 T + \left(\frac{\mu-r}{\sigma}\right)y} \frac{h(y)}{\sqrt{2\pi T}} \exp\left[-\frac{y^2}{2T}\right] dy$$

$$= \mathrm{E}^{\mathbb{P}}\left[e^{-\frac{1}{2}\left(\frac{\mu-r}{\sigma}\right)^2 T + \left(\frac{\mu-r}{\sigma}\right)W(T)} h(W(T))\right]. \quad (2.16)$$

The last equality of Equation 2.16 holds because x in Equation 2.15 plays the role of $W^*(T)$ and hence y plays the role of $W(T)$. In the second line of Equation 2.16, the probability density function (PDF) of $W(T)$ is the standard normal density function such that the calculation is transformed into an expectation problem using $\mathbb{P}$. From Equation 2.16, we learn that a $\mathbb{Q}$-expectation can be converted into an equivalent $\mathbb{P}$-expectation by multiplying an exponential factor with the function $h(\cdot)$. This factor is a $\mathbb{P}$-exponential martingale and constitutes the key change in the probability measure.

More specifically, consider the cumulative distribution functions (CDFs) using the two probability measures: $\mathbb{P}(W(T) < y)$ and $\mathbb{Q}(W^*(T) < x)$. Using the distributional properties of $W(T)$ and $W^*(T)$ under their respective probability measures, we calculate

$$d\mathbb{P}(W(T) < y) = \frac{\exp\left[-\frac{y^2}{2T}\right]}{\sqrt{2\pi T}} dy \quad \text{and} \quad d\mathbb{Q}(W^*(T) < x) = \frac{\exp\left[-\frac{x^2}{2T}\right]}{\sqrt{2\pi T}} dx.$$

Hence,

$$E^{\mathbb{Q}}[h(W(T))] = \int h \, d\mathbb{Q} = \int h \frac{d\mathbb{Q}}{d\mathbb{P}} \, d\mathbb{P} = E^{\mathbb{P}}\left[\frac{d\mathbb{Q}}{d\mathbb{P}} h(W(T))\right].$$

Comparing the foregoing to Equation 2.16, we deduce that

$$\frac{d\mathbb{Q}}{d\mathbb{P}} = \exp\left[-\frac{1}{2}\left(\frac{\mu-r}{\sigma}\right)^2 T + \left(\frac{\mu-r}{\sigma}\right) W(T)\right].$$

The differentiation of measures on the left-hand side is known as Radon–Nikodym derivatives. In the context of real analysis, see Chapter 7 of Rudin (1987); and in that of probability theory, see Chapter 4 of Durrett (1996). The right-hand side gives an explicit expression for our particular example.

In fact, there is a more general theorem for the change of measures:

Theorem 2.2 (Girsanov's theorem) *Let $\theta(t, W(t))$ be a deterministic function of t and $W(t)$, where W is the standard Brownian motion under $\mathbb{P}$ such that*

$$E^{\mathbb{P}}\left[\exp\left(\frac{1}{2}\int_0^T |\theta(t, W(t))|^2 \, dt\right)\right] < \infty.$$

Then we have the following.

1. $\eta_T = \exp\left[-\frac{1}{2}\int_0^T \theta(t, W(t))^2 \, dt + \int_0^T \theta(t, W(t)) dW(t)\right]$ *is an exponential martingale.*

2. *There is an equivalent probability measure $\mathbb{Q}$ such that*

$$\frac{d\mathbb{Q}}{d\mathbb{P}} = \eta_T \text{ and } E^{\mathbb{Q}}[h(W(T))] = E^{\mathbb{P}}[\eta_T h(W(T))].$$

3. *The standard Brownian motion W^* in $\mathbb{Q}$ can be defined through W such that*

$$dW^*(t) = dW(t) - \theta(t, W(t)) \, dt.$$

As the proof of this theorem is rather technical, interested readers may refer to Oksendal (2003). However, we demonstrate the theorem's use in the BS formula for European call options in the proof of the following theorem.

Theorem 2.3 (Black–Scholes [BS] formula) *Consider a European call option with terminal payoff $\max(S_T - K, 0)$, where the underlying stock price follows the BS model (Eq. 2.8). Suppose that the instantaneous interest rate is a constant r, and the stock has constant volatility σ. Then the call option price is given by*

$$c(t, S) = S\Psi(d_1) - Ke^{-r(T-t)}\Psi(d_2),$$

where $\Psi(x)$ is the CDF of a standard normal random variable and

$$d_1 = d_2 + \sigma\sqrt{T-t}, d_2 = \frac{\log\frac{S}{K} + (r - \frac{\sigma^2}{2})(T-t)}{\sigma\sqrt{T-t}}.$$

Proof: By the risk-neutral valuation formula (Eq. 2.12),

$$c_{BS}(t, S) = e^{-r(T-t)}\mathrm{E}^{\mathbb{Q}}[\max(S_T - K, 0)]$$
$$= e^{-r(T-t)}\left[\mathrm{E}^{\mathbb{Q}}\left[S_T 1_{\{S_T > K\}}\right] - K\mathbb{Q}(S_T > K)\right].$$

Under $\mathbb{Q}$, the stock process is given by Equation 2.11. Solving Equation 2.11 by Itô's lemma yields

$$S_T = S e^{(r-\frac{\sigma^2}{2})(T-t) + \sigma(W^*(T) - W^*(t))},$$

by which the event $\{S_T > K\}$ is recognized as equivalent to $\{W^*(T) - W^*(t) > -d_2\sqrt{T-t}\}$. Therefore,

$$\mathbb{Q}(S_T > K) = \mathbb{Q}(W^*(T) - W^*(t) > -d_2\sqrt{T-t}).$$

As zero mean normal distributions are symmetric at zero and $W^*(T) - W^*(t) \sim \mathcal{N}(0, T-t)$ under $\mathbb{Q}$, we have

$$\mathbb{Q}(S_T > K) = \Psi(d_2).$$

The challenge lies in the calculation of $\mathrm{E}^{\mathbb{Q}}\left[S_T 1_{\{S_T > K\}}\right]$. We employ the change of measure technique to overcome the difficulty. By substituting the expression of S_T in the expectation, we have

$$\mathrm{E}^{\mathbb{Q}}\left[S_T 1_{\{S_T > K\}}\right] = e^{r(T-t)} S \mathrm{E}^{\mathbb{Q}}\left[e^{-\frac{\sigma^2}{2}(T-t) + \sigma(W^*(T) - W^*(t))} 1_{\{S_T > K\}}\right]$$
$$= e^{r(T-t)} S \mathrm{E}^{\mathbb{Q}}\left[e^{-\frac{1}{2}\int_t^T \sigma^2 d\tau + \int_t^T \sigma\, dW^*(\tau)} 1_{\{S_T > K\}}\right]. \quad (2.17)$$

Girsanov's theorem with $\theta(t, W^*(t)) \equiv \sigma$ allows us to define a measure $\widehat{\mathbb{Q}}$, such that

$$\frac{d\widehat{\mathbb{Q}}}{d\mathbb{Q}} = \exp\left[-\frac{1}{2}\int_t^T \sigma^2 d\tau + \int_t^T \sigma\, dW^*(\tau)\right],$$
$$\mathrm{E}^{\mathbb{Q}}\left[S_T 1_{\{S_T > K\}}\right] = e^{r(T-t)} S \widehat{\mathbb{Q}}(S_T > K)$$
$$= e^{r(T-t)} S \widehat{\mathbb{Q}}(W^*(T) - W^*(t) > -d_2\sqrt{T-t}). \quad (2.18)$$

In addition, the $\widehat{\mathbb{Q}}$-standard Brownian motion, $\widehat{W}$, can be defined through the following shift.

$$\widehat{W}(T) - \widehat{W}(t) = (W^*(T) - W^*(t)) - \sigma(T-t).$$

Hence,

$$\widehat{\mathbb{Q}}(W^*(T) - W^*(t) > -d_2\sqrt{T-t}) = \widehat{\mathbb{Q}}(\widehat{W}(T) - \widehat{W}(t) > -d_1\sqrt{T-t}),$$

and the result follows.

2.2 VOLATILITY

Risk-neutral valuation shows that European option prices are deterministic functions of the observed underlying stock price $S(t)$, observed interest rate r, and unobserved volatility σ. The BS formula is a clear example of a European call option. Hence, it is crucial for traders to estimate σ in order to value an option. In the BS model (Eq. 2.8), volatility σ is a measure of the uncertainty of an asset's return. It can be defined as the standard deviation of the logarithmic return. To see this, apply Ito's lemma to $\log S(t)$ with respect to Equation. 2.8:

$$d\log S(t) = \left(\mu - \frac{\sigma^2}{2}\right) dt + \sigma\, dW(t) \Rightarrow \log \frac{S(t+\Delta t)}{S(t)}$$
$$= \left(\mu - \frac{\sigma^2}{2}\right) \Delta t + \sigma(W(t+\Delta t) - W(t)),$$

where Δt is the sampling frequency. Hence, the difference in log prices (the logarithmic return) follows the normal distribution with variance $\sigma^2 \Delta t$. We do not mention the mean because it will be replaced by $r - \sigma^2/2$ in the valuation process.

Volatility is measured on an annualized basis because interest rates and other financial parameters are quoted on an annualized basis. Therefore, if the sampling period Δt of the logarithmic return is 1 year, then it refers to annualized volatility. In general, for any sampling period of T years,

$$\sigma_T = \sigma_{\text{annualized}} \sqrt{T}.$$

For example, if there are 252 trading days in a year and volatility is primarily estimated on a daily basis, then annualized volatility is projected from daily volatility using the square-root rule in the market:

$$\sigma_{\text{annualized}} = \frac{\sigma_{\text{daily}}}{\sqrt{\frac{1}{252}}} = \sigma_{\text{daily}} \sqrt{252}.$$

The estimated volatility $\sigma_{\text{annualized}}$ is plugged into the BS formula to compute the call price if the trader believes in the BS model. However, there are alternatives to understanding and estimating volatility in financial markets.

1. **Historical volatility**
   Historical volatility is estimated on the basis of historical data. Given a sample of $n + 1$ stock prices, it can be estimated by the sample standard deviation s:

   $$s = \sqrt{\frac{1}{n-1} \sum_{i=1}^{n} (x_i - \bar{x})^2},$$

   where $x_i = \log \frac{S_i}{S_{i-1}}$ is the logarithmic return. The estimate of annualized volatility $\hat{\sigma}$ is

   $$\hat{\sigma} = \frac{s}{\sqrt{T}},$$

   where T is the length of each period. When daily stock prices are used, T is set to the reciprocal of the trading days in a year such as $1/252$. However, the number of trading days varies across different asset classes. The assumption of 252 trading days per year may be appropriate for the equity market, but not for the foreign exchange (FX) and interest rate markets. The FX markets open almost every day of the year, including holidays. The number of trading days defined in a particular contract refers to the date count convention specified in that contract. In this book, we use 252 trading days per year solely for illustration.

   Historical volatility has a number of limitations. For example, the analyst has to select the historical data window for estimation purposes such as 1 month, 3 months, or 1 year. Different windows may lead to quite different estimates. The analyst must also specify the sampling frequency: weekly, daily, or tick-to-tick. High frequency data pose additional technical difficulties. Finally, as there is plenty of empirical evidence against the use of the BS model for asset price dynamics, the historical volatility may contain insufficient information to describe the dispersion of asset returns.

2. **Implied volatility**
   Although the BS model is known to be inadequate for modeling asset dynamics, the BS formula is the benchmark by which option traders communicate with one another. Traders like to summarize the information contained in an option using the notion of implied volatility, which is the volatility implied by the market price of options using the BS model. Let $c_M(K, T)$ be the market price of a call with strike K and maturity T. Its implied volatility, σ_{imp}, is the solution to the following equation.

   $$c_M(K, T) = c_{BS}(S, K, T | \sigma = \sigma_{imp}),$$

where the BS formula is given in Theorem 18. As the BS formula is a strictly increasing function of σ, the implied volatility is the unique solution to the foregoing equation.

There is no analytical solution for implied volatility, but numerical root-finding methods are required to solve the non linear equation. In practice, traders quote the implied volatility rather than the option price itself. They then substitute the implied volatility into the BS formula to produce the option price. When a trader wants to issue a new call option, he or she may estimate its implied volatility from the implied volatilities of similar contracts using interpolation. The option price is then obtained by substituting the estimated implied volatility into the BS formula.

3. **Volatility smile and surface**

    The BS model assumes constant volatility. Although traders use the BS formula in their daily work, they do not assume the volatility to be constant. A more practical approach is to plot the implied volatilities against the strike prices for options in the same underlying stock, revealing a convex shape. For a put option, the implied volatility curve is usually downward sloping and skewed up on the right-hand side, a pattern commonly known as the *volatility smile*. A related concept is the term structure of volatility, which is a plot of implied volatility against maturity. Combining the volatility smile and term structure of volatility, a two-dimensional (2D) surface known as the *volatility surface* is obtained. Sophisticated traders interpolate discrete samples of implied volatilities to form a continuous implied volatility surface that infers option prices for all strikes and maturities. Figure 2.1 depicts a typical volatility surface in an FX option market.

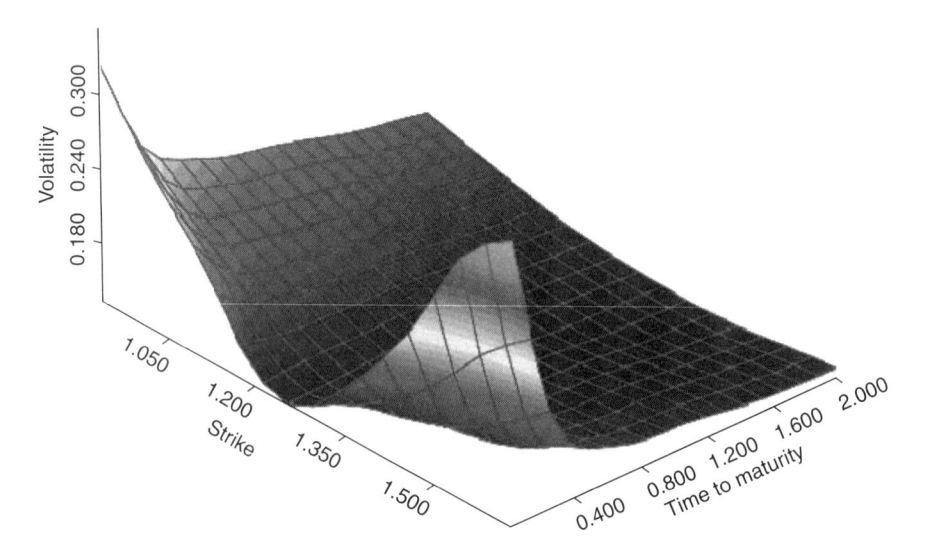

Figure 2.1 EURUSD option volatility surface.

4. **Volatility clustering**
   When there are limited option transactions, derivatives valuation is unable to benchmark against the option market using implied volatilities. In such a situation, traders may resort to historical estimates of volatility. However, they usually observe a volatility clustering effects, that is, large moves tend to be followed by large moves and small moves by small moves. Consequently, the constant volatility assumption in the BS model needs to be relaxed, which has led to the use of the GARCH model in derivative pricing. Empirical analysis shows that the GARCH(1,1) model can successfully model volatility clustering. Additional details of the GARCH option pricing model are provided in Chapter 4.

5. **Local volatility and stochastic volatility**
   There are models that employ local volatility and stochastic volatility instead of assuming volatility to be constant. Local volatility views volatility as a deterministic function of time and asset price. For instance, the local volatility model uses an SDE of the form

$$dS(t) = \mu S(t)\,dt + \sigma(t, S(t))S(t)\,dW(t),$$

where $\sigma(t, S(t))$ is the local volatility function. Stochastic volatility sees volatility as driven by a stochastic process that differs from Brownian motion W. Details of these models, including their estimation and simulation, are provided in Chapter 4.

2.3 MARK TO MARKET AND CALIBRATION

2.3.1 Marking to Market

Marking to market (MTM) usually refers to an accounting rule by which assets are reported at their current market values, although the term has slightly different meaning in security trading and risk management. When holding derivatives or other securities, a trader is usually more interested in their market value than their acquisition price. The daily revaluation of a security to reflect its current market price is known as MTM. MTM can make us aware of the risk exposure of our portfolio. Take a futures contract as an example. To reduce counterparty risks, MTM is performed at the end of each trading day to determine whether the balance of the investor's margin account fulfills margin requirements. If the balance of the margin account falls below the maintenance margin, then the investor will receive a margin call to deposit funds to the initial margin level. Otherwise, the broker will close out the position.

Banks perform MTM daily to monitor their market risk exposure and the credit exposure between the bank and its clients. If the direct quoting of the market price is not possible, then the MTM values of outstanding financial derivatives can be calculated via portfolio replication and internal pricing models. On the one hand, these values can be used to measure treasury limit usage, report such risk measures as the Value at Risk (VaR) of the portfolio and prepare profit–loss (P/L) statements. On the other, they can be employed to measure the counterparty risk in a derivative contract. One of the measures in credit exposure is the replacement cost, which can be calculated using MTM values. It is the amount that the bank will have to pay to replace the contract if the counterparty defaults. MTM values also allow the bank to check the reasonableness of a counterparty's credit support annex (CSA) report, in the case that a margin call is required as a result of a large discrepancy in MTM values between the two parties.

2.3.2 Calculation of MTM Values

In practice, market participants do not wish to perform tedious calculations to obtain MTM values for their financial products. Portfolio replication is a more typical method of calculating these values. Ideally, a financial product can be decomposed into a portfolio of liquidly traded products, whose market price can be observed directly. The products corresponding to MTM values can then be obtained by summing each of the individual MTM values. This method can potentially save considerable time. For example, certain types of equity-linked notes (ELN) can be regarded as a combination of the put option of the underlying asset and bonds. By calculating the value of the put option and the bonds using current market data, the MTM value of the ELN can be obtained. Details of portfolio replication and ELN are provided in Chapter 3.

However, certain products or derivatives may lack a comparable market counterpart or may be illiquid. In this case, the investor may rely on some of the proprietary financial models offered by such financial service providers as Bloomberg, Reuters, or FINCAD, or employ internal pricing models to calculate the MTM values. However, internal pricing models must be calibrated prior to use to minimize pricing error. Investors can also make use of the implied volatility surface of liquidly traded options to calculate the MTM values of options with different strike prices and maturities that are not traded in the market. Take ELN as an example. The put option embedded in an ELN may be untradable, meaning that the bank must interpolate the implied volatility surface from the put option market to infer the implied volatility of the embedded put as its MTM value.

The MTM procedures can be summarized as follows.

1. For generic products, such as vanilla options, swaps, and forward, the MTM values are the market quotes from the respective trading parties.
2. For non-generic products, market quotes are usually unavailable. If portfolio replication is possible, then these products can be decomposed into a portfolio of generic components for which MTM values can easily be obtained (either from market quotes or proprietary financial models). The MTM value of a

non-generic product is simply the sum of the MTM values of its individual generic components.
3. If the decomposition of a non-generic product is not possible, then an internal pricing model is needed for valuation. However, model calibration and validation should be conducted before the pricing of any non-generic products.

2.3.3 Calibration

Model calibration is the process of obtaining implied model parameters from market data. Numerous financial models for derivatives pricing have been developed in academe over the past 30 years to capture and predict the movement of financial market variables. Advances in technology and computational methods mean newly developed models are increasingly sophisticated. These models are usually expressed in terms of different parameters, which should be accurately determined before their adoption in derivatives pricing. Note that a change in the value of a parameter can greatly affect the price of a product. Accordingly, model calibration has become a very important pricing component, and many feasible calibration methods have been developed. In general, a practical model calibration method determines the optimal values of input parameters to minimize the difference between the prices calculated by the model and actual market prices. In other words, the aim is to minimize

$$\sum_{i=1}^{N}(V_i - M_i)^2,$$

where the V_i's are the model-calculated values of the products and the M_i's are their actual market prices.

Special attention should be paid to the differences between parameter estimation and model calibration as the underlying concepts are completely different. Parameter estimation involves such statistical estimates as maximum likelihood estimation which requires knowledge of historical data. Although model calibration involves parameter determination, it requires no statistical estimation. In addition, instead of historical data, it makes use of the current market prices of many products. Model calibration is performed extensively in later chapters.

2.4 VARIANCE REDUCTION TECHNIQUES

2.4.1 A Brief Review of Variance Reduction Techniques

Here we provide a brief review of some of the most commonly used variance reduction techniques, namely, antithetic variables, control variates, stratification, and importance sampling. These techniques are then illustrated via an option pricing example. Further details can be found in Chan and Wong (2006) and the references therein.

2.4.1.1 Antithetic Variables

Antithetic variables can best be illustrated by considering a special example. Suppose that we want to estimate $\theta = E[X]$ by generating two outputs, X_1 and X_2, such that $E[X_1] = E[X_2] = \theta$ and $Var(X_1) = Var(X_2) = \sigma^2$. Then

$$E\left[\frac{1}{2}(X_1 + X_2)\right] = \theta,$$

and

$$\begin{aligned}
Var\left(\frac{1}{2}(X_1 + X_2)\right) &= \frac{1}{4}\Big(Var(X_1) + Var(X_2) + 2Cov(X_1, X_2)\Big) \\
&= \frac{1}{2}\sigma^2 + \frac{1}{2}Cov(X_1, X_2) \\
&\leq \frac{1}{2}\sigma^2, \text{ if } Cov(X_1, X_2) \leq 0.
\end{aligned}$$

Note that when X_1 and X_2 are independent, $Var(\frac{X_1+X_2}{2}) = \frac{\sigma^2}{2}$. Thus, the foregoing inequality asserts that if X_1 and X_2 are negatively correlated then the variance of their sample mean is less than if they were independent.

How are negatively correlated random numbers generated? Suppose that m independent uniform random numbers, $U_1, \ldots, U_m$, are generated. Then $V_1 = 1 - U_1, \ldots, V_m = 1 - U_m$ are also n independent uniform random numbers, with the property that (U_i, V_i) are negatively correlated, for $i = 1, \ldots, m$. If $X_1 = h(U_1, \ldots, U_m)$, then $X_2 = h(V_1, \ldots, V_m)$ must have the same distribution as X_1. It turns out that if h is a monotonically increasing or decreasing function in each of its arguments, then X_1 and X_2 will be negatively correlated. Thus, after generating $U_1, \ldots, U_m$ to compute X_1, rather than generate another new independent set of U_i's to compute X_2, we compute X_2 by $X_2 = h(V_1, \ldots, V_m)$. Accordingly, $\frac{X_1+X_2}{2}$ should have a smaller variance.

Generating antithetic variables for a normal distribution is straightforward. Suppose that $X_i \sim \mathcal{N}(\mu, \sigma^2)$, then, $Y_i = 2\mu - X_i$ also has the same distribution as X_i, and X_i and Y_i are negatively correlated.

In general, we generate $X_i = F^{-1}(U_i)$ using the inverse transform method, where F is the CDF of the random variable X. Let $Y_i = F^{-1}(V_i)$. Because F is monotonically increasing, so is F^{-1}, and hence X_i and Y_i are negatively correlated. Both $X_1, \ldots, X_n$ and $Y_1, \ldots, Y_n$ generated in this way are independent and identically distributed (i.i.d.) sequences with CDF F, but are negatively correlated. The sequence Y_i is called the sequence of antithetic variables.

More generally, if we want to compute $E[H(X)]$ for some function H then standard Monte Carlo simulation suggests the use of $\frac{1}{n}\sum_{i=1}^{n} H(X_i)$. Then an antithetic estimator of E[H(X)] is given by

$$\widehat{H}_{AN} = \frac{1}{2n} \sum_{i=1}^{n} (H(X_i) + H(Y_i)),$$

where Y_i is a sequence of antithetic variables. To see how variance reduction is achieved using this antithetic estimator, let $\mathrm{Var}(H(X)) = \sigma^2$ and $\mathrm{Corr}(H(X), H(Y)) = \rho$. Consider

$$\mathrm{Var}(\widehat{H}_{AN}) = \frac{1}{4n^2} \sum_{i=1}^{n} \Big(\mathrm{Var}(H(X_i)) + \mathrm{Var}(H(Y_i)) + 2\mathrm{Cov}(H(X_i), H(Y_i))\Big)$$

$$= \frac{1}{4n^2}(2n\sigma^2 + 2n\rho\sigma^2)$$

$$= \frac{\sigma^2}{2n}(1 + \rho).$$

Note that when $H(X)$ and $H(Y)$ are uncorrelated ($\rho = 0$), the variance is reduced by a factor of 2, which is equivalent to doubling the simulation size. If in contrast, $\rho = -1$, then the variance is reduced to zero. As long as ρ is negative, a certain degree of variance reduction can be achieved. An obvious question in view of this observation is why not choose Y such that $\rho = -1$? Doing so may be difficult as ρ represents the correlation between $H(X)$ and $H(Y)$. In the case of $H(X) = X$, $\widehat{H}_{AN}$ is reduced to a constant, which is the perfect scenario. In view of these caveats, antithetic variables Y are usually chosen such that ρ is negative, but not necessarily equal to -1. When H is linear, as in the case of $H(X) = X$, the antithetic variable works best. In general, the more linear H is, the more effective the antithetic variable.

Example 2.7 *To price a European call option on stock S with strike price K and maturity K, whose risk-neutral dynamics are given by $dS(t) = rS(t)\,dt + \sigma S(t)\,dW(t)$, with $S(0) = S_0$, where r is the risk-free rate, $\sigma > 0$, and $W(t)$ is a standard Brownian motion. In the previous subsection, the solution to the foregoing SDE is given by*

$$S(T) = S_0 \exp\Big((r - \frac{\sigma^2}{2})T + \sigma W(T)\Big).$$

The payoff of the European option is $\max\{S(T) - K, 0\}$, which is a monotonic function of $S(T)$. $S(T)$ is also a monotonic function of $W(T)$. We can therefore apply the antithetic variable method to achieve variance reduction in estimating the option price. Now, if $Z_i \sim \mathcal{N}(0, 1)$ for $i = 1, \ldots, n$, which is a sequence of random numbers, then $Y_i = -Z_i$ is a sequence of antithetic variables. The original stock price paths can be simulated by, for $i = 1, \ldots, n$,

$$S_i(T) = S_0 \exp\left((r - \frac{\sigma^2}{2})T + \sigma\sqrt{T}Z_i\right),$$

and the antithetic stock price paths are generated by, for $i = 1, \ldots, n$,

$$S_i^{AN}(T) = S_0 \exp\left((r - \frac{\sigma^2}{2})T - \sigma\sqrt{T}Z_i\right).$$

Therefore, the estimated price of the European call option is given by

$$e^{-rT} \frac{1}{2n} \sum_{i=1}^{n} \left(\max\{S_i(T) - K, 0\} + \max\{S_i^{AN}(T) - K, 0\}\right).$$

2.4.1.2 Control Variates The control variate concept is simple. Suppose that we wish to estimate $\theta = E[X]$ from simulated data. Also suppose that for some other variable Y, the mean $\mu_Y = E[Y]$ is known. Then, for any given constant c, the quantity

$$X_{CV} = X + c(Y - \mu_Y)$$

is also an unbiased estimator of θ, as $E[X_{CV}] = \theta$. Presumably, if the constant c is chosen wisely, then a certain degree of variance reduction can be achieved. How can we achieve this reduction? In other words, what is a good choice for c? To answer this question, first consider the variance in the new estimator X_{CV}. Call it σ_{CV}^2:

$$\sigma_{CV}^2 = \text{Var}(X + c(Y - \mu_Y)) = \text{Var}(X) + c^2\text{Var}(Y) + 2c\text{Cov}(X, Y).$$

The objective is to find c such that σ_{CV}^2 is minimized. Differentiating the preceding expression with respect to c and setting the resulting derivative to zero yields

$$2c\text{Var}(Y) + 2\text{Cov}(X, Y) = 0.$$

Solving for such a c, $c^* = -\text{Cov}(X, Y)/\text{Var}(Y)$ is the value of c that minimizes σ_{CV}^2. For such a c^*,

$$\sigma_{c^*}^2 = \text{Var}(X) - \frac{(\text{Cov}(X, Y))^2}{\text{Var}(Y)}.$$

The variable Y used in this way is known as a control variate for simulation estimator X. Recall that $\text{Corr}(X, Y) = \text{Cov}(X, Y)/\sqrt{\text{Var}(X)\text{Var}(Y)}$. Therefore,

$$\sigma_{c^*}^2 = \text{Var}(X)(1 - \text{Corr}^2(X, Y)).$$

Hence, as long as $\text{Corr}(X, Y) \neq 0$ some form of variance reduction is achieved. In practice, such quantities as $\sigma_Y^2 = \text{Var}(Y)$ and $\text{Cov}(X, Y)$ are usually unavailable, and must be estimated from simulations based on sample values. For example, let $\overline{X} = \sum_{i=1}^{n} X_i/n$ and $\overline{Y} = \sum_{i=1}^{n} Y_i/n$. Then

$$\widehat{\text{Cov}}(X, Y) = \frac{1}{n-1} \sum_{i=1}^{n} (X_i - \overline{X})(Y_i - \overline{Y})$$

$$\widehat{\sigma}_Y^2 = \frac{1}{n-1} \sum_{i=1}^{n} (Y_i - \overline{Y})^2$$

$$\widehat{c}^* = -\frac{\widehat{\text{Cov}}(X, Y)}{\widehat{\sigma}_Y^2}.$$

Suppose that we employ $\overline{X}$ obtained from simulation to estimate θ. Then the control variate is $\overline{Y}$ and the control variate estimator is

$$\overline{X} + c(\overline{Y} - \mu_Y),$$

with variance

$$\frac{1}{n}\left(\text{Var}(X) - \frac{(\text{Cov}(X, Y))^2}{\text{Var}(Y)}\right) = \frac{\sigma_X^2}{n}(1 - \rho^2).$$

Equivalently, we can employ a simple linear regression equation,

$$X = a + bY + e,$$

to estimate c^*. In fact, it can easily be shown that the least squares estimate of b, $\widehat{b} = -\widehat{c}^*$. In such a case, the control variate estimator is given by

$$\overline{X} + c^*(\overline{Y} - \mu_Y) = \overline{X} - \widehat{b}(\overline{Y} - \mu_Y) = \widehat{a} + \widehat{b}\mu_Y,$$

where $\widehat{a} = \overline{X} - \widehat{b}\overline{Y}$ is the least squares estimate of a. In other words, the control variate estimate is equal to the estimated regression equation evaluated at point μ_Y.

Note that there is a very simple geometric interpretation. First, observe that the estimated regression line

$$\widehat{X} = \widehat{a} + \widehat{b}Y$$
$$= \overline{X} + \widehat{b}(Y - \overline{Y}).$$

Thus, this line passes through the point $(\overline{Y}, \overline{X})$. Second, observe that

$$\widehat{X}_{\text{CV}} = \widehat{a} + \widehat{b}\mu_Y = \overline{X} - \widehat{b}(\overline{Y} - \mu_Y).$$

Suppose that $\overline{Y} < \mu_Y$, that is, the simulation run underestimates μ_Y, and that X and Y are positively correlated. It is likely in this case that $\overline{X}$ would underestimate $E[X] = \theta$. Hence, we need to adjust the estimator upward, as indicated by the fact that $\widehat{b} = -\widehat{c}^* > 0$. The additional amount by which it needs to be adjusted upward is equal to $-\widehat{b}(\overline{Y} - \mu_Y)$, which is governed by the linear equation.

Finally, $\widehat{\sigma}^2$, the regression estimate of σ^2, is the estimate of $\text{Var}(X - \widehat{b}Y) = \text{Var}(X + \widehat{c}^*Y)$. To see this, recall that

$$\widehat{\sigma}^2 = \frac{1}{n} \sum_{i=1}^{n} \widehat{e}_i^2$$

$$= \frac{1}{n} \sum_{i=1}^{n} (X_i - \widehat{a} - \widehat{b}Y_i)^2$$

$$= \frac{1}{n} \sum_{i=1}^{n} \left(X_i - (\overline{X} - \widehat{b}\overline{Y}) - \widehat{b}Y_i \right)^2$$

$$= \frac{1}{n} \sum_{i=1}^{n} \left((X_i - \overline{X}) + \widehat{b}(Y_i - \overline{Y}) \right)^2$$

$$= \frac{1}{n} \sum_{i=1}^{n} \left((X_i - \overline{X})^2 - \widehat{b}^2 (Y_i - \overline{Y})^2 \right)$$

$$= \widehat{\text{Var}}(X) - \widehat{b}^2 \widehat{\text{Var}}(Y)$$

$$= \widehat{\text{Var}}(X - \widehat{b}Y).$$

The last equality follows from the standard expansion of the variance estimate. It follows that the estimated variance of the control variate estimator $\overline{X} + \widehat{c}^*(\overline{Y} - \mu_Y)$ is $\widehat{\sigma}^2/n$.

In general, if more than one control variate is desired, then the outputs of the multiple linear regression model given by

$$X = a + \sum_{i=1}^{k} b_i Y_i + e$$

can be used. In this case, the least squares estimates of a and b_is, $\widehat{a}$ and $\widehat{b}_i$s, can easily be shown to satisfy $\widehat{c}_i^* = -\widehat{b}_i$, for $i = 1, \ldots, k$. Furthermore, the control variate estimate is given by

$$\overline{X} + \sum_{i=1}^{k} c_i(\overline{Y}_i - \mu_{Y_i}) = \widehat{a} + \sum_{i=1}^{k} \widehat{b}_i \mu_{Y_i},$$

where $E[Y_i] = \mu_{Y_i}$, for $i = 1, \ldots, k$. In other words, the control variate estimate is equal to the estimated multiple regression line evaluated at the point $(\mu_{Y_1}, \ldots, \mu_{Y_k})$.

By the same token, the variance in the control variate estimate is given by $\widehat{\sigma}^2/n$, where $\widehat{\sigma}^2$ is the regression estimate of σ^2.

Example 2.8 *Consider the pricing of the European call option in the previous example using a control variate.*

Use the terminal asset price $S(T)$ as the control variate. The control variate estimator is given by

$$C^{CV} = C + c^*(S(T) - E[S(T)]).$$

Recall that $S(T) = S_0 \exp\left((r - \tfrac{1}{2}\sigma^2)T + \sigma\sqrt{T}Z\right)$. It can easily be deduced that

$$E[S(T)] = S_0 e^{rT},$$
$$\text{Var}(S(T)) = S_0^2 e^{2rT}(e^{\sigma^2 T} - 1).$$

The algorithm is as follows.

1. Simulate N_1 independent standard normal random variables Z_i, where $i = 1, \ldots, N_1$.
2. Compute the terminal stock price by $S_i(T) = S_0 \exp((r - \tfrac{1}{2}\sigma^2)T + \sigma\sqrt{T}Z_i)$ and the option payoff by $C_i = e^{-rT}\max\{S_i(T) - K, 0\}$, where $i = 1, \ldots, N_1$.
3. Compute $E[S(T)]$ as $S_0 e^{rT}$ or estimate it by $\sum_{i=1}^{N_1} S_i(T)/N_1$.
4. Compute $\text{Var}(S(T))$ as $S_0^2 e^{2rT}(e^{\sigma^2 T} - 1)$ or estimate it by $\sum_{i=1}^{N_1}(S_i(T) - \overline{S(T)})^2/(N_1 - 1)$.
5. Estimate the covariance by $\widehat{\text{Cov}}(S(T), C) = \frac{1}{N_1-1}\sum_{i=1}^{N_1}(S_i(T) - \overline{S(T)})(C_i - \overline{C})$, where $\overline{C} = \sum_{i=1}^{N_1} C_i/N_1$ and $\overline{S(T)} = \sum_{i=1}^{N_1} S_i(T)/N_1$.
6. Repeat the simulations of $S(T)$ and C by means of the control variate.
7. Simulate other N_2 independent standard normal random variables Z_i, where $i = 1, \ldots, N_2$ and compute the terminal stock price and option payoff as before.
8. Compute $C_i^{CV} = C_i + c^*(S_i(T) - E[S(T)])$ for $i = 1, \ldots, N_2$, where $c^* = -\frac{\widehat{\text{Cov}}(S(T),C)}{\text{Var}(S(T))}$ is computed from the preceding step.
9. Calculate the control variate estimator by $\widehat{C^{CV}} = \frac{1}{N_2}\sum_{i=1}^{N_2} C_i^{CV}$.
10. Complete the simulation by evaluating the standard error of $\widehat{C^{CV}}$.

2.4.1.3 Stratified Sampling
The idea behind stratification lies in the observation that a population may be heterogeneous but comprise a variety of homogeneous subgroups (such as those made up of a particular gender, race, or socioeconomic status). If we wish to learn about the entire population, then we could take a random sample from that population. It would be more efficient, however, to take small

samples from each subgroup and combine the estimates in each according to the fraction of the population it represents. Because it is possible to learn the opinions of a homogeneous subgroup using a relatively small sample size, the stratified sampling procedure is more efficient.

In general, to estimate $E[X]$, where X depends on a random variable S that takes one of the values in $\{1, \ldots, k\}$ with known probabilities, the stratification technique is run with k groups, with the ith group having $S = i$. Let $\overline{X}_i$ be the average values of X in those runs having $S = i$, and then estimate $E[X] = \sum_{i=1}^{k} E[X|S = i] \Pr(S = i)$ by

$$\sum_{i=1}^{k} \overline{X}_i \Pr(S = i).$$

This technique is known as stratified sampling.

To illustrate further, suppose that we want to estimate $E[g(U)] = \int_0^1 g(x)dx$. Consider two estimators based on a sample of $2n$ runs. The first is the standard method,

$$\widehat{g} = \frac{1}{2n} \sum_{i=1}^{2n} g(U_i).$$

Note that $E[\widehat{g}] = E[g(U)]$, and

$$\mathrm{Var}(\widehat{g}) = \frac{1}{4n^2} \sum_{i=1}^{2n} \mathrm{Var}(g(U_i)) = \frac{1}{2n} \left(\int_0^1 g^2(x)\,dx - \left(\int_0^1 g(x)\,dx \right)^2 \right).$$

We can also write

$$E[g(U)] = \int_0^{\frac{1}{2}} g(x)\,dx + \int_{\frac{1}{2}}^1 g(x)\,dx.$$

Instead of selecting the U's from $[0, 1]$, select the first n U's from $[0, 1/2]$ and the remaining n U's from $[1/2, 1]$ to construct a new estimator

$$\widehat{g}_s = \frac{1}{2n} \left(\sum_{i=1}^{n} g\left(\frac{U_i}{2}\right) + \sum_{i=1}^{n} g\left(\frac{U_i + 1}{2}\right) \right).$$

It can easily be seen that if $U \sim U(0, 1)$, then $V = a + (b - a)U$ is distributed as $U(a, b)$. In addition, $U/2 \sim U(0, 1/2)$ and $(U + 1)/2 \sim U(1/2, 1)$. To compute the variance in the new estimator, consider

$$\mathrm{Var}(\widehat{g}_s) = \frac{1}{4n^2} \left[\sum_{i=1}^{n} \mathrm{Var}\left(g\left(\frac{U_i}{2}\right) \right) + \mathrm{Var}\left(g\left(\frac{U_i + 1}{2}\right) \right) \right].$$

Direct computations show that if $U_i \sim U(0, 1)$, then

$$\operatorname{Var}\left(g\left(\frac{U_i}{2}\right)\right) = 2\int_0^{\frac{1}{2}} g^2(x)\,dx - 4m_1^2,$$

$$\operatorname{Var}\left(g\left(\frac{U_i+1}{2}\right)\right) = 2\int_{\frac{1}{2}}^{1} g^2(x)\,dx - 4m_2^2,$$

where $m_1 = \int_0^{1/2} g(x)\,dx$ and $m_2 = \int_{1/2}^{1} g(x)\,dx$. Now, we have

$$\operatorname{Var}\left(g\left(\frac{U_i}{2}\right)\right) + \operatorname{Var}\left(g\left(\frac{U_i+1}{2}\right)\right) = 2\int_0^1 g^2(x)\,dx - 4(m_1^2 + m_2^2).$$

Consequently,

$$\operatorname{Var}(\widehat{g_s}) = \frac{1}{2n}\left(\int_0^1 g^2(x)\,dx - 2(m_1^2 + m_2^2)\right).$$

Note that

$$(m_1 + m_2)^2 + (m_1 - m_2)^2 = 2(m_1^2 + m_2^2).$$

Therefore,

$$\operatorname{Var}(\widehat{g_s}) = \frac{1}{2n}\left(\int_0^1 g^2(x)\,dx - (m_1 + m_2)^2 - (m_1 - m_2)^2\right)$$

$$= \operatorname{Var}(\widehat{g}) - \frac{1}{2n}(m_1 - m_2)^2.$$

Because the second term above is always non-negative, stratification reduces the variance by an amount equal to this term. The larger the difference in m_1 and m_2, the greater the reduction in variance. In general, if more strata are introduced then greater reduction will be achieved. This result can be generalized to the multi-strata case, but we omit the mathematical details here.

Stratified sampling is also very useful for drawing random samples from designated ranges. For example, to sample $Z_1, \ldots, Z_{100}$ from a standard normal distribution, the standard technique is to partition the whole real line $(-\infty, \infty)$ into a number of bins and then sample Z's from these bins randomly. It is inevitable that some bins will have more samples than others and those near the tails may have no samples at all. A random sample drawn in this way thus under-represents the tails. Although this may not be a serious issue in general, it may have a severe effect when the tail is the quantity of interest, such as in the case of the simulation of VaR. To ensure that the bins are regularly represented, we can generate the Z's as follows. Let

$$V_i = \frac{1}{100}\Big(U_i + (i-1)\Big), \text{ for } i = 1, \ldots, 100,$$

where $U_i \sim U(0, 1)$. By the uniform distribution property, $V_i \sim U(\frac{i-1}{100}, \frac{i}{100})$. Now, let $Z_i = \Psi^{-1}(V_i)$. Then, Z_i falls between the $(i-1)$th and ith percentiles of a standard normal distribution. For example, if $i = 1$, then $V = U/100 \sim U(0, 1/100)$ such that $Z = \Psi^{-1}(V)$ falls between $\Psi^{-1}(0) = -\infty$ and $\Psi^{-1}(0.01)$, that is, the zeroth and first percentiles of a standard normal distribution.

This method gives equal weight to each of the 100 equiprobable strata. Of course, the number 100 can be replaced with any number that is desirable. The price paid in stratification is the Z's loss of independence, which complicates the statistical inference for simulation results.

The following examples illustrate the application of stratified sampling to the pricing of a European option.

Example 2.9 *Similar to the situation in the European call option pricing example, here we simulate the terminal prices $S_1(T), \ldots, S_n(T)$ and employ the standard technique (instead of the antithetic variable method) to compute the estimate of the price of a European call option as*

$$e^{-rT} \frac{1}{n} \sum_{i=1}^{n} \max\{S_i(T) - K, 0\}.$$

In this standard simulation, the normal random variables are sampled arbitrarily over the whole real line. We can improve the efficiency by introducing stratification:

1. *Partition $(-\infty, \infty)$ into B strata or bins.*
2. *Set $V_i = \frac{1}{B}(U_i + (i-1))$, for $i = 1, \ldots, B$, and generate the desired number of random samples, say, N_B, of the V's in the ith bin.*
3. *Apply $\Psi^{-1}(V_i)$ to obtain the desired normal random numbers from each bin and calculate $\overline{C}_i$ for each bin.*
4. *Average the $\overline{C}_i$ over the total number of bins to get an overall estimate, $\overline{C}$.*
5. *Calculate the standard error.*

Regular stratification places equal weight on each of the B bins. Such allocation may not be ideal, as it may be preferable to have the sample sizes directly related to the variability of the target function over the bin. To illustrate this point, consider the payoff of a European call option again.

Example 2.10 *Note that if $S(T) < K$, then the payoff of the call option is zero. Recall that*

$$S(T) = S_0 \exp\Big((r - \frac{\sigma^2}{2})T + \sigma\sqrt{T}Z\Big).$$

Therefore, $S(T) < K$ if and only if $S_0 \exp\left((r - \frac{\sigma^2}{2})T + \sigma\sqrt{T}Z\right) < K$, that is,

$$Z < L \triangleq \frac{\log(K/S_0) - (r - \frac{1}{2}\sigma^2)T}{\sigma\sqrt{T}}.$$

Every simulated $Z < L$ is wasted as it simply returns a value of 0. We need to concentrate on the interval $[L, \infty)$. The goal is achieved as follows.

1. Determine the CDF of a normal distribution Y restricted on $[L, \infty)$. It can be shown that Y has a CDF of

$$F(y) = \frac{\Psi(y) - \Psi(L)}{1 - \Psi(L)}.$$

2. Use the inverse transform method to generate Y. Consider the inverse transformation of F, that is, solve for y such that $y = F^{-1}(x)$. Writing it out, $x = F(y) = \frac{\Psi(y) - \Psi(L)}{1 - \Psi(L)}$, such that

$$y = \Psi^{-1}(x(1 - \Psi(L)) + \Psi(L)).$$

Now, generate $U \sim U(0, 1)$ and evaluate

$$Y = \Psi^{-1}(U(1 - \Psi(L)) + \Psi(L)).$$

3. Plug the generated Y into the simulation step of the call option payoff and complete the analysis. Note that when evaluating the new estimator for the payoff, one needs to multiply the factor $1 - \Psi(L)$, that is,

$$C^* = (1 - \Psi(L))\overline{C},$$

where $\overline{C}$ is the average of the simulated payoffs using the truncated normal random variables.

The stratification technique is generally applied to bins in which the variability of the integrand is greatest. Here, we focus the entire sample on the case of $S(T) > K$.

2.4.1.4 Importance Sampling The idea underpinning importance sampling is similar to that for the acceptance–rejection method discussed in the previous subsection. The main idea is to approximate in places in which the quantity of interest carries the most information, hence "importance sampling."

Suppose that we are interested in estimating

$$\theta = E[h(X)] = \int h(x)f(x)\,dx,$$

where $X = (X_1, \ldots, X_n)$ denotes an n-dimensional random vector with a joint PDF, $f(x) = f(x_1, \ldots, x_n)$. Suppose that direct simulation of the random vector is inefficient such that computing $h(X)$ is infeasible. This inefficiency may be due to difficulties encountered in simulating X, the variance in $h(X)$ being too great, or a combination of the two.

Suppose that there exists another density $g(x)$, which is easy to simulate and satisfies the condition that $f(x) = 0$ whenever $g(x) = 0$. Then, θ can be estimated by

$$\theta = \mathrm{E}[h(X)]$$
$$= \int \frac{h(x)f(x)}{g(x)} g(x)\, dx$$
$$= \mathrm{E}_g\left[\frac{h(X)f(X)}{g(X)}\right],$$

where the notation E_g denotes the expectation of random vector X taken under density g. It follows that θ can be estimated by generating X with density g and then using it as the estimator of the average of the values of $h(X)f(X)/g(X)$. In other words, we construct a Monte Carlo estimator of $\theta = \mathrm{E}[h(X)]$ by first computing the i.i.d. random vectors X_i with PDF $g(X)$ and then using the estimator

$$\widehat{\theta} = \frac{1}{n}\sum_{i=1}^n \frac{h(X_i)f(X_i)}{g(X_i)}.$$

If the density $g(x)$ can be chosen to ensure that the random variable $\frac{h(X)f(X)}{g(X)}$ has a small degree of variance, then this approach is known as the importance sampling approach, and it can result in an efficient estimator of θ.

To see how it works, note that the ratio of $f(X)/g(X)$ represents the likelihood ratio of obtaining X with respective densities of f and g. If X is distributed according to g, then $f(X)$ is small relative to $g(X)$. Therefore, when X is simulated according to g, the likelihood ratio of $f(X)/g(X)$ is usually small in comparison to 1. It can also be seen that

$$\mathrm{E}_g\left[\frac{f(X)}{g(X)}\right] = \int \frac{f(x)}{g(x)} g(x)\, dx = \int f(x)\, dx = 1.$$

Thus, even though the likelihood ratio of $f(X)/g(X)$ is smaller than 1, its mean is equal to 1, which suggests that it occasionally takes large values and results in a large degree of variance.

To render the variance of $h(X)f(X)/g(X)$ small, we must arrange for the density g such that the values of X for which $f(X)/g(X)$ is large are precisely those for which $h(X)$ is small, thus ensuring that the ratio of $h(X)f(X)/g(X)$ remains small. Because importance sampling sometimes requires h to be small, it works best when estimating a small probability.

How is the function g generally chosen? It requires the notion of tilted density. Let $M_X(t) = \mathrm{E}[e^{tX}]$ represent the moment-generating function of a random variable X with density f. Then density function

$$f_t(x) \triangleq \frac{e^{tx} f(x)}{M_X(t)}$$

is called the tilted density of a given f, where $-\infty < t < \infty$. Note from this definition that a random variable with density f_t tends to be larger than the one with density f when $t > 0$ and smaller when $t < 0$.

In many instances, what is of interest is the sum of independent random variables. In such cases, the joint density $f(\boldsymbol{x})$ of $\boldsymbol{x} = (x_1, \ldots, x_n)$ can be written as the product of the marginals f_i of x_i such that

$$f(\boldsymbol{x}) = f_1(x_1) \cdots f_n(x_n).$$

In this situation, it is often useful to generate the X_i according to their tilted densities with a common t.

Another application of importance sampling is the estimation of tail probabilities (recall that importance sampling works best with a small probability). Suppose that we are interested in estimating $\Pr(X > a)$, where X has PDF f and a is a given constant. Let $\mathbf{1}_{\{X > a\}} = 1$ if $X > a$, and 0 otherwise. Then

$$\begin{aligned}
\Pr(X > a) &= \mathrm{E}_f[\mathbf{1}_{\{X>a\}}] \\
&= \mathrm{E}_g\left[\mathbf{1}_{\{X>a\}} \frac{f(X)}{g(X)}\right] \\
&= \mathrm{E}_g\left[\mathbf{1}_{\{X>a\}} \frac{f(X)}{g(X)} \bigg| X > a\right] \Pr(X > a) \\
&\quad + \mathrm{E}_g\left[\mathbf{1}_{\{X>a\}} \frac{f(X)}{g(X)} \bigg| X \leq a\right] \Pr(X \leq a) \\
&= \mathrm{E}_g\left[\mathbf{1}_{\{X>a\}} \frac{f(X)}{g(X)} \bigg| X > a\right] \Pr(X > a).
\end{aligned}$$

Take $g(x) = \lambda e^{-\lambda x}$, where $x > 0$, as an exponential density with parameter λ. Then the foregoing derivation shows that

$$\Pr(X > a) = \mathrm{E}_g[e^{\lambda x} f(X) | X > a] \frac{e^{-\lambda a}}{\lambda}.$$

Using the memoryless property, that is, $\Pr(X > s + t | X > s) = \Pr(X > t)$, of the exponential distribution, it can easily be seen that the conditional distribution of an exponential distribution conditioned on $\{X > a\}$ has the same distribution as $a + X$.

Therefore,

$$\Pr(X > a) = \frac{e^{-\lambda a}}{\lambda} E_g[e^{\lambda(X+a)} f(X+a)]$$

$$= \frac{1}{\lambda} E_g[e^{\lambda X} f(X+a)].$$

We can now estimate θ by generating $X_1, \ldots, X_n$ according to an exponential distribution with parameter λ using

$$\hat{\theta} = \frac{1}{\lambda} \frac{1}{n} \sum_{i=1}^{n} e^{\lambda X_i} f(X_i + a).$$

Example 2.11 *Reconsider the simulation of a European call option price using the importance sampling technique. Evaluate the value of a deep out-of-money ($S_0 \ll K$) European call option with a short maturity T.*

Many sampling paths result in $S(T) \leq K$ and give zero values. These samples are wasted. A possible way of dealing with this problem is to increase the values of Z_i by sampling them from a distribution with a large mean and a large degree of variance. Sample $\tilde{Z}_i$ from $\mathcal{N}(\frac{m}{\sigma\sqrt{T}}, s^2)$ such that

$$\sigma\sqrt{T}\tilde{Z}_i \sim \mathcal{N}(m, \sigma^2 T s^2).$$

Note that $\tilde{Z}_i$ can be written as

$$\tilde{Z}_i = \frac{m}{\sigma\sqrt{T}} + sZ_i, \text{ where } Z_i \sim \mathcal{N}(0, 1).$$

The importance sampling estimator is then given by

$$C^I = e^{-rT} \frac{1}{N} \sum_{i=1}^{N} \max\left\{ S_0 \exp\left((r - \frac{\sigma^2}{2})T + \sigma\sqrt{T}\tilde{Z}_i\right), 0 \right\} R(\tilde{Z}_i),$$

where

$$R(\tilde{Z}_i) = \frac{\frac{1}{\sqrt{2\pi}} \exp\left(-\frac{1}{2}\tilde{Z}_i^2\right)}{\frac{1}{\sqrt{2\pi}s} \exp\left(-\frac{1}{2s^2}(\tilde{Z}_i - \frac{m}{\sigma\sqrt{T}})^2\right)}.$$

2.4.2 Pricing a Call Option

The following example demonstrates the use of antithetic variables, control variates, and stratified sampling by valuing a standard European call option under the BS

TABLE 2.1 Simulation Results for a Call Option Using Variance Reduction Techniques

Method	Average simulated price	Standard deviation of simulated price
Normal simulation	4.932844845	0.362843551
Antithetic variables	4.977191984	0.149962208
Control variates	4.934841586	0.119927058
Stratified sampling (Bin = 5)	4.953226605	0.016694595
Closed-form solution	4.952225138	–

model, with $S(0) = 50$, $K = 48$, $r = 3\%$, $\sigma = 25\%$, and $T = 0.5$ year. For each variance reduction technique, 10,000 sample paths are used. The average simulated option price and standard deviation are computed by repeating the simulation 30 times. The results are presented in Table 2.1.

All of the variance reduction methods used here are able to achieve a certain degree of variance reduction. With the antithetic method of drawing random numbers, the standard deviation decreases by 58.67%. Employing the terminal asset value as a control variate for valuation, the standard deviation decreases by 66.9%. We could add more correlated variables to achieve further variance reduction, but choosing new correlated variables may be difficult, and the simulation time increases considerably when the number of control variates increases. Stratified sampling achieves the best variance reduction, as evidenced by the 95.3% decrease in the

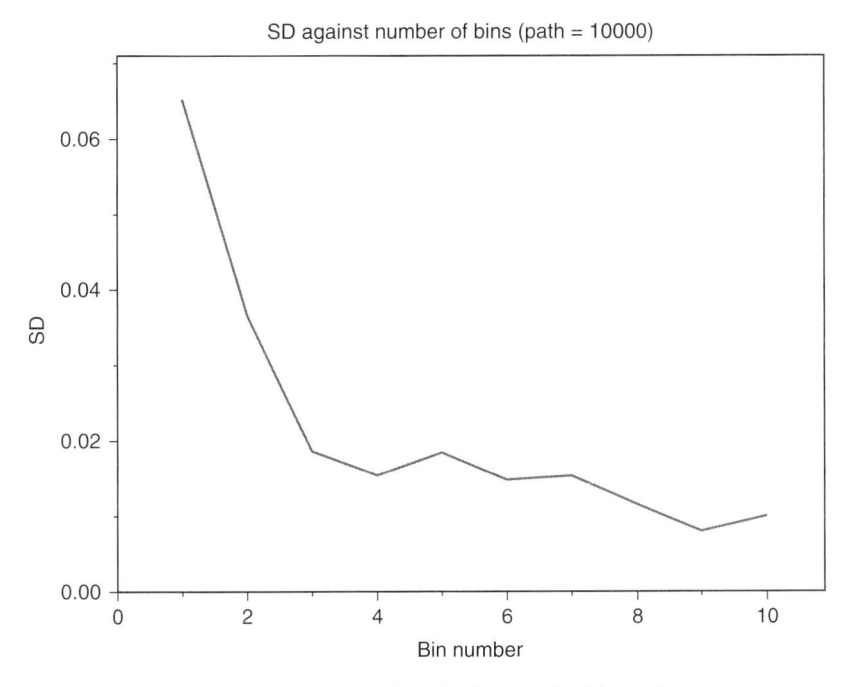

Figure 2.2 Standard deviation of estimate against bin numbers.

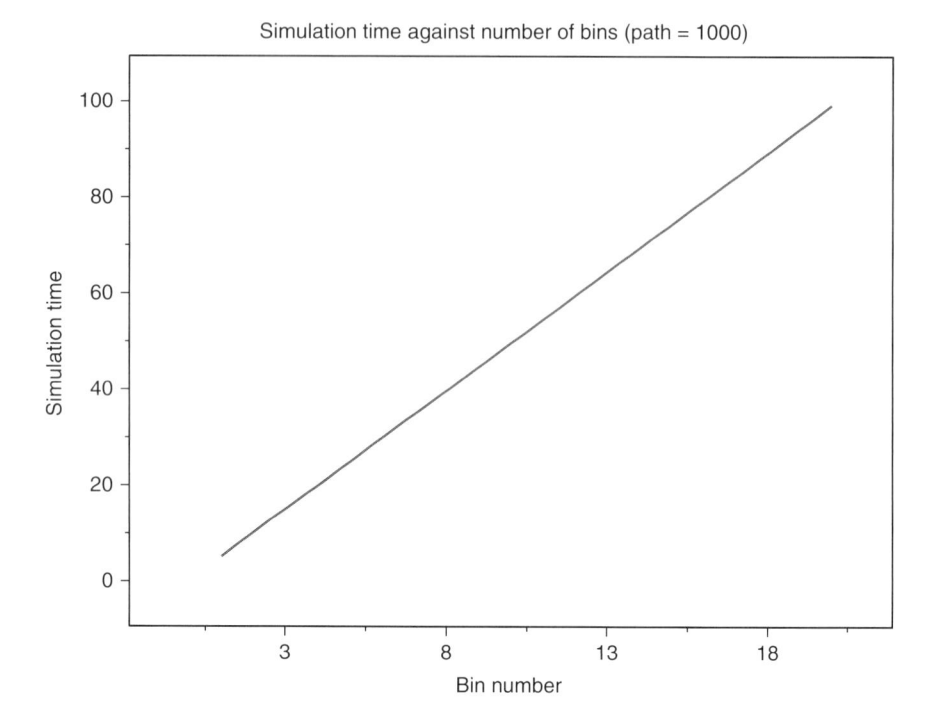

Figure 2.3 Simulation time against bin numbers.

standard deviation. Special attention should be paid to the number of bins chosen. Theoretically, increasing the number of bins can result in better variance reduction performance (see Fig. 2.2). However, the computation time increases linearly when the number of bins increases (see Fig. 2.3). For further details, please refer to Ch2.2_Stratified_Sampling_Graphs.xls.

3

Structured Products

A structured product is a prepackaged investment strategy that is based on derivatives. The value of a structured product is contingent upon the movement of its underlying stocks, indices, commodities, interest rates, credits, and/or other financial variables. Hence, a structured product is itself a derivative security and simply an alternative term for a nonstandard derivative.

When a bank issues a structured product, regulations require it to report the product's price and risk level on a daily basis. Its price should be marked to the market. Simulation is not a must in such valuation, and a number of interpolation techniques are often employed to do the job. However, simulation becomes indispensable in the calculation of risk, which should take into account possible future scenarios.

We first employ equity-linked notes (ELN) as an example to show the circumstances under which simulation is unnecessary. Certain practical methods can produce the price in seconds. We then discuss the limitation of these methods in reporting risk and show how simulation comes into play. Throughout the process, we also introduce practical simulation techniques for handling ELN with special additional features, such as callability, early redemption, and accrual interest. These simulation techniques are then applied to other types of structured products. Typical examples include the FX accumulator, which almost ruined Citic Pacific LTD in 2008, participating policy contracts, which are popular in some European life insurance packages, and multi-asset instruments, which are popular in Asian markets.

Handbook of Financial Risk Management: Simulations and Case Studies, First Edition. N.H. Chan and H.Y. Wong.
© 2013 John Wiley & Sons, Inc. Published 2013 by John Wiley & Sons, Inc.

3.1 WHEN IS SIMULATION UNNECESSARY?

Valuation via simulation may be unnecessary if closed-form solutions are available or if the structured product can be replicated. When another numerical method, such as the finite difference method or tree approach, is applicable, simulation may also be unnecessary either. However, for problems involving higher dimensions, simulation is usually necessary and may be the only means of valuation possible. Without simulation, the most popular valuation method is to replicate the product payoff using available quotes.

3.1.1 Portfolio Replication Pricing

Pricing a structured product by means of portfolio replication involves formation of a portfolio of products that has the same payoff as the structured product at all times. Because these products have the same payoff at all times, they also have the same value. The value of a structured product is simply the sum of the values of its components.

3.1.2 Equity-Linked Notes

We illustrate the portfolio replication procedure with an example of a real ELN that was traded in 2008. As its name implies, an ELN is a financial instrument that has much in common with a deposit note. The main difference between an ELN and a standard note is that the former's return is determined by the value of the underlying equity or equity index, such that it is "equity-linked." An ELN can serve as a yield-enhancement device or a hedging vehicle.

The term sheet of this particular ELN contract can be found in the appendix. For purposes of illustration, we first assume trigger event provisions to be excluded and that the contract will not be redeemed prematurely by the issuer. In other words, we consider a European-style ELN in which all cash payments are settled on the terminal date of the contract and there is no intermediate accrual interest (coupon). Later in the chapter, we discuss these neglected issues. The underlying equity in this example is HSBC Holdings Plc., and the coupon rate is fixed at 1.3333% for each of the three periods. Note that in a more general case, the coupon rate may depend on how many days (or weeks or some other period of time) the stock price is at or above a prescribed barrier price. The barrier price is the stock price above which interest is accrued. At maturity, if the price of HSBC stock is at or above the strike price, then the issuer redeems the note by paying the denomination. Otherwise, there is physical delivery of the equity with a number of shares equal to D/K, where D denotes the denomination and K denotes the strike price. Hence, the payoff to the holder at maturity is

$$\Pi_T = \begin{cases} C + \frac{D}{K}K, & \text{if } S_T \geq K, \\ C + \frac{D}{K}S_T, & \text{otherwise,} \end{cases}$$

$$= C + \frac{D}{K}\min\{K, S_T\}.$$

The payoff can also be written as

$$\Pi_T = (C+D) - \frac{D}{K}\max\{K-S_T, 0\},$$

where C denotes the total number of coupons. Thus, the payoff function of the note is a combination of a long position on bonds and short position on the put option on the equity. The note holder is selling a put option. Therefore, this ELN can be replicated by investing cash in bonds with a corresponding maturity and short-selling $\frac{D}{K}$ put options on an equity with a corresponding maturity, strike price, and underlying equity. In practice, we may be unable to find bonds and put options with the same terms as those of the ELN, in which case proxies are used. For instance, the bond price is estimated from an interpolation of the yield curve. The yield curve fitting procedure is detailed in Chapter 5. The implied volatility of an embedded put option can be interpolated from the implied volatility surface (see Chapter 4).

However, risk managers may be interested in the worst-case scenario associated with such a product before setting the trading limit or determining the capital reserve for risk management purposes. Simulation is required to determine the possible losses by calculating such risk measures as value-at-risk (VaR). In addition, when an ELN involves barrier provisions and allows early redemption, as does the real product shown in the appendix, portfolio replication is impossible. Simulation thus helps in understanding the price of the product after calibrating the model to market prices.

3.2 SIMULATION OF BLACK–SCHOLES MODEL AND EUROPEAN OPTIONS

Before discussing the simulation of more sophisticated models, we begin with the Black–Scholes (BS) model and demonstrate simulation with European options, including an ELN with barrier provisions and early redemption. Under the BS model, the asset price $S(t)$ is assumed to follow a geometric Brownian motion (GBM) with drift parameter μ and volatility parameter σ; that is, the asset dynamics are given by

$$\frac{dS(t)}{S(t)} = \mu\,dt + \sigma\,dW(t),$$

where μ represents the annualized expected return on the asset, σ represents the annualized volatility of the asset, and W is $\mathbb{P}$-standard Brownian motion. Both μ and σ are assumed to be constants. In the physical world, μ and σ can be estimated from historical data. For the valuation of derivatives in the risk-neutral world, the drift is the annualized rate of return of a risk-free asset, that is, risk-free rate r. If the asset pays a continuous annualized dividend yield q, then the asset dynamics in the risk-neutral world become

$$\frac{dS(t)}{S(t)} = (r-q)\,dt + \sigma\,dW^*(t),$$

or

$$dS(t) = (r - q)S(t)\,dt + \sigma S(t)\,dW^*(t), \qquad (3.1)$$

where W^* is $\mathbb{Q}$-standard Brownian motion.

Equation 3.1 provides a way of simulating the asset price path from time 0 to time T. Consider a partition of the interval $[0, T]$ with m subintervals of equal length, $\Delta t = T/m$. From Equation 3.1, an approximation from step j to $j + 1$ (write $S_j = S(t_j)$, $t_j = j\frac{T}{m}$) is given by

$$S_{j+1} = S_j + (r - q)S_j \Delta t + \sigma S_j \sqrt{\Delta t}\, Z_j, \qquad (3.2)$$

for $j = 0, \ldots, m - 1$, where the Z_j's are independent standard normal random variables. By setting S_0 as the initial asset price and iterating the equation m times, the terminal asset price S_m is obtained, and $\{S_0, S_1, \ldots, S_m\}$ is the asset path from time 0 to T. To generate n asset paths, we repeat this procedure n times (using different random numbers).

In VBA, an asset following GBM with n paths and m steps can be simulated easily. The following is a sample VBA code for a user-defined function, $BS\_DPath(A)$.

```
'Generating asset paths following GBM using discretization
'with an UDT BS_PathType as the parameter of the function
Public Function BS_DPath(A As BS_PathType) As Variant
Dim i As Long, j As Long
Dim dt As Double
ReDim S(0 To A.m, 1 To A.n) As Double
dt = A.T / A.m
'main part
For j = 1 To A.n
  S(0, j) = A.S0
  For i = 1 To A.m
    S(i, j) = S(i - 1, j) + (A.rf - A.q)*S(i - 1, j)*dt _
            + A.sigma*S(i - 1, j)*Sqr(dt)*rGauss()
  Next i
Next j

BS_DPath = S
End Function
```

In the foregoing, A is a user-defined data type (UDT) variable with the following VBA code.

```
'An UDT that stores the details of an asset
'that is required in simulation
```

```
'where the asset is assumed to follow the BS dynamics
Type BS_PathType
  S0 As Double    'inital asset price
  q As Double     'annualized dividend yield
  sigma As Double 'annualized volatility
  rf As Double    'risk-free rate
  T As Double     'peroid length
  dt As Double    'length of each subinterval/step
  m As Long       'no of subintervals/steps in the period
  n As Long       'no of paths
End Type
```

The use of a UDT variable can facilitate the parameter passing between a *Function* and a *Sub*, thus rendering the program more user-friendly and structured. Also note that the function *rGauss* is used to generate a standard normal variable.

Simulation using Equation 3.2 produces very nice results when Δt is small (or m is large). Different terminal asset prices are simulated using different numbers of steps m, with $S_0 = 50$, $r = 10\%$, $q = 2\%$, $\sigma = 40\%$, $T = 1$, and $n = 10,000$. Table 3.1 presents the simulation results and errors in comparison with closed-form solution 54.164 calculated by $E^Q[S_T|S_0] = S_0 e^{(r-q)T}$. The mean and standard deviation of the estimate are computed using 1000 simulations, and the error is calculated using the mean of the estimate and the closed-form value.

As shown in the Percentage error column of Table 3.1, increasing the number of steps decreases the error because of the more accurate discrete approximation of the stock price by Equation 3.2. The estimation is already very good when $\Delta t = 1/100$. Increasing the number of steps dose increase the computation time, however. Decreasing the number of steps m (or increasing Δt) actually underestimates the terminal asset price. To see this, increase T while keeping $m = 1$, such that $\Delta t = T$. The results are presented in Table 3.2. The mean, standard derivation, and error are calculated using 1000 simulations, as before.

In fact, discretization error can be avoided in this relatively simple stochastic process. Itô's lemma gives us

$$d \log S(t) = \left(r - \frac{\sigma^2}{2}\right) dt + \sigma \, dW^*(t),$$

$$S(t) = S(0) \exp\left[\left(r - \frac{\sigma^2}{2}\right) t + \sigma \sqrt{t} Z\right], \tag{3.3}$$

TABLE 3.1 Simulation Results Using Equation 3.2 with Different m

m	Mean	Standard deviation	Percentage error	Computation time (s)
1	54.004	0.1995	0.295%	0.008
10	54.148	0.2260	0.030%	0.064
100	54.162	0.2086	0.006%	0.574
250	54.168	0.2190	0.009%	1.461

TABLE 3.2 Simulation Results Using Equation 3.2 with Different T

T	$S_0 e^{(r-q)T}$	Mean	Standard deviation	Error	Percentage error
1	54.1644	53.993	0.1987	−0.171	−0.31%
2	58.6755	57.998	0.2778	−0.677	−1.15%
5	74.5912	70.011	0.4458	−4.581	−6.14%
10	111.277	89.970	0.6398	−21.307	−19.15%

where Z is a standard normal random variable. Equation 3.3 thus provides us with a much faster method for the exact simulation of an asset price. The corresponding VBA code for generating terminal asset prices becomes

```
S = S0 * Exp((rf - simga^2/2) * T + sigma * Sqr(T) * rGauss())
```

For path-dependent-type options such as American and Asian options, we require the entire asset path for valuation. Then the "exact" simulation can be used m times, such that, from t_j to t_{j+1},

$$S_{j+1} = S_j \exp\left(\left(\mu - \frac{\sigma^2}{2}\right)\Delta t + \sigma\sqrt{\Delta t}Z_j\right). \tag{3.4}$$

To simulate Equation 3.4, replace Equation 3.2 with Equation 3.4 in the VBA code in the function BS_DPath. This method can avoid discretization error. The corresponding VBA code is as follows.

```
Public Function BS_Path(A As BS_PathType) As Variant
Dim i As Long, j As Long
Dim dt As Double
ReDim S(0 To A.m, 1 To A.n) As Double
dt = A.t / A.m
For j = 1 To A.n
  S(0, j) = A.S0
  For i = 1 To A.m
    S(i, j) = S(i-1, j)*Exp((A.rf - A.q - A.sigma^2/2)*dt _
          + A.sigma * Sqr(dt) * rGauss())
  Next i
Next j
BS_Path = S
End Function
```

Table 3.3 presents the simulation results under the same conditions as those in Table 3.1. It can be seen that discretization error is barely observed for exact simulation. Figure 3.1 illustrates several simulated asset price paths with different numbers of subintervals m.

SIMULATION OF BLACK–SCHOLES MODEL AND EUROPEAN OPTIONS   77

TABLE 3.3 Simulation Results Using Equation 3.4 with Different *m*

m	Mean	Standard deviation	Percentage error	Computation time (s)
1	54.160	0.2222	0.009%	0.010
10	54.164	0.2280	0.001%	0.089
100	54.165	0.2104	0.002%	0.834
250	54.168	0.2136	0.007%	2.079

We can also employ Equation 3.3 to simulate the asset price using discretization. The corresponding approximation from step j to step $j+1$ is given by

$$\log S_{j+1} = \log S_j + \left(r - \frac{\sigma^2}{2}\right)\Delta t + \sigma\sqrt{\Delta t}\, Z_j.$$

The corresponding VBA code is:

```
Application.Ln(S(i, j)) = Application.Ln(S(i - 1, j)) + _
    (rf + sigma ^ 2 / 2) * dt + sigma * Sqr(dt) * rGauss()
```

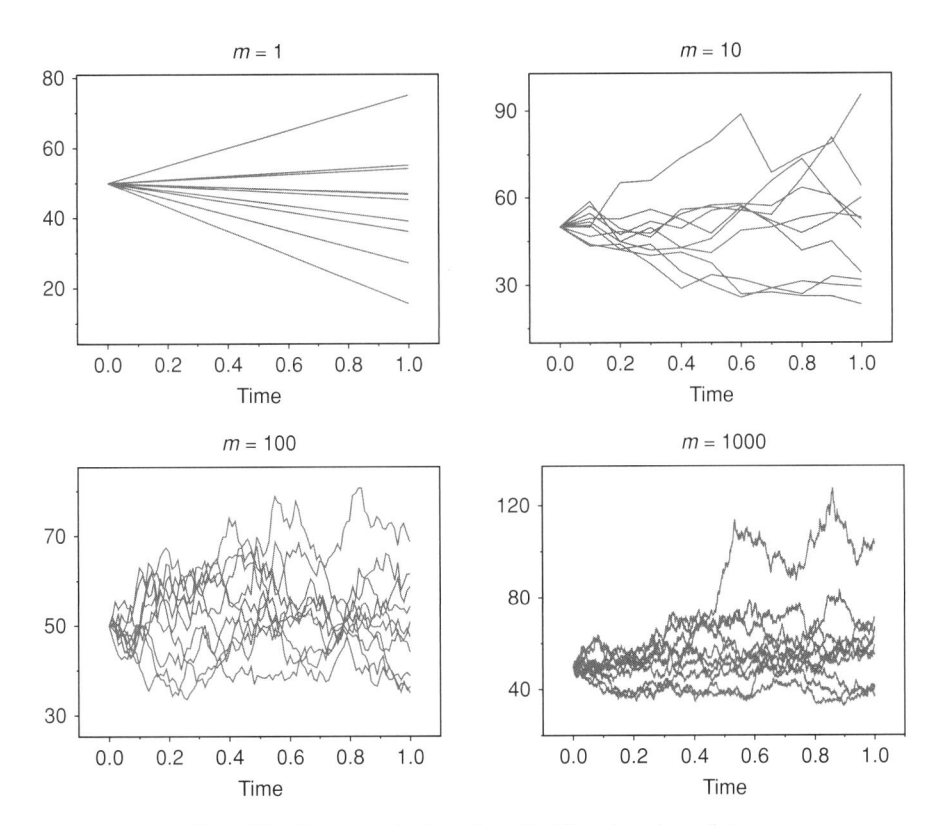

Figure 3.1 Sample asset price paths with different numbers of steps.

Finally, the following example illustrates the pricing of a European option using simulation.

Example 3.1 With $S_0 = 50$, $r = 10\%$, $q = 2\%$, $\sigma = 40\%$, $T = 1$, $m = 1$, $n = 50,000$, and $K = 50$, calculate the price of the European call and put option using simulation.

Now, suppose that having simulated the asset price path, the only task remaining is to evaluate the payoff. For a European call option, the terminal payoff for the jth path is $\max\{S_{m,j} - K, 0\}$. The price of a European call option, c, is estimated as

$$c \simeq \frac{1}{n} \sum_{j=1}^{n} e^{-rT} \max\{S_{m,j} - K, 0\}.$$

Similarly, the price of the European put option, p, is estimated as

$$p \simeq \frac{1}{n} \sum_{j=1}^{n} e^{-rT} \max\{K - S_{m,j}, 0\}.$$

A function that calculates the payoff with an array of asset price paths can be written in terms of the parameters, as follows.

```
Public Function EO_Payoff(S As Variant, ByVal K _
As Double, ByVal optionType As Integer, _ Optional ByVal m _
As Long = -1) As Variant
  Dim j As Long
  ReDim payoff(1 To UBound(S, 2)) As Double
  If m = -1 Then m = UBound(S, 1)

  Select Case optionType
    Case xCall
    For j = 1 To UBound(S, 2)
      payoff(j) = Max(S(m, j) - K, 0)
    Next
    Case xPut
      For j = 1 To UBound(S, 2)
        payoff(j) = Max(K - S(m, j), 0)
      Next
    Case xStraddle
      For j = 1 To UBound(S, 2)
        payoff(j) = Max(S(m, j) - K, K - S(m, j))
      Next
  End Select

  EO_Payoff = payoff
End Function
```

This function will return an array of payoffs. The VBA code for calculating the price using this function is:

```
'Simulate the path
S = BS_Path(A)

'Calculate the terminal payoff
Payoff = EO_Payoff(S, K, optionType)
Cells(2, 5) = Exp(-A.rf * A.t) * Average(Payoff)
```

For further details, please refer to Ch3.2_European_Option_with_EMS.xls.

Remark This code can easily be modified to cope with other types of options such as a European ELN and straddle. A long position in a straddle means a combination of long positions in a call option and put option on the same underlying asset, strike price, and time-to-maturity. By modifying the payoff function *EO_Payoff* in the program, other types of options can be calculated easily. For path-dependent options, such as the barrier provision in a realistic ELN, we can set $m = 252$ to handle the case of daily monitoring.

The simulated prices of the European call and put options are 9.508 and 5.723, respectively, whereas those calculated by the BS formulas are 9.501 and 5.733, respectively. The BS formulas with current stock price S, strike price K, time t, risk-free rate r, dividend yield q, volatility σ, and maturity T are

$$c(S, K, t, r, q, \sigma, T) = Se^{-q(T-t)}\Psi(d_1) - Ke^{-r(T-t)}\Psi(d_2),$$
$$p(S, K, t, r, q, \sigma, T) = Ke^{-r(T-t)}\Psi(-d_2) - Se^{-q(T-t)}\Psi(-d_1),$$

where Ψ is the cumulative distribution function (CDF) of a standard normal random variable, and

$$d_1 = \frac{\log \frac{S}{K} + \left(r - q + \frac{\sigma^2}{2}\right)(T-t)}{\sigma\sqrt{T-t}},$$
$$d_2 = d_1 - \sigma\sqrt{T-t}.$$

We can see that in both cases, the simulated prices are very close to the theoretical prices. Therefore, simulation does a good job of estimating the price of the European option in our example.

3.3 AMERICAN OPTIONS

Another feature found in a realistic ELN is early redemption, that is, the holder's right to terminate the contract prematurely. In finance, the early redemption feature refers to an American-style contracts. American options give holders the right of early exercise, a very common feature in financial markets. Although simulation can be employed to generate stock price paths, we need some way to determine whether it is optimal to exercise the option at each time step, a task that renders the valuation of an American option highly challenging.

In this section, we introduce the use of the backward stochastic dynamic programming approach together with the least squares approach introduced by Longstaff and Schwartz (2001). With these two approaches, the computation time needed to value an American option can be greatly reduced. Moreno and Navas (2003) and Stentoft (2004) reported the numerical performance of this approach.

As an ELN is embedded with a put option, we consider a fictitious in-the-money put option that gives the holder the right of immediate exercise at $t = 0$ or, alternatively, the right of exercise at maturity at $t = T$. At $t = 0$, the holder must decide whether to exercise the option immediately or continue. In deciding, he or she needs to compare the immediate exercise payoff with the expected discounted payoff of continuation, given the asset price at $t = 0$. Therefore, the value of this option at $t = 0$, $V(0)$, is the maximum between the immediate payoff and expected discounted payoff at $t = T$, $V(T)$, that is,

$$V(0) = \max\{K - S(0), \mathrm{E}[e^{-rT}V(T)|S(0)]\},$$

where $V(T) = \max\{K - S(T), 0\}$ and the expectation is taken under $\mathbb{Q}$. To simplify the notation, we suppress the superscript $\mathbb{Q}$.

Now, extend this idea to an American option that can be exercised at each time point $t_1, \ldots, t_m$ and matures at $t = t_m$, where $\Delta t = t_i - t_{i-1}$, which is an approximation of an American option with a continuous exercise right. Denote the value of this American option at time t_i by $V(t_i)$ for $i = 0, \ldots, m$ and $t_0 = 0$. Then, from the foregoing argument, we have

$$V(t_m) = \max\{K - S(t_m), 0\},$$
$$V(t_{m-1}) = \max\{K - S(t_{m-1}), \mathrm{E}[e^{-r\Delta t}V(t_m)|S(t_{m-1})]\}.$$
$$\vdots$$

In general,

$$V(t_{i-1}) = \max\{K - S(t_{i-1}), \mathrm{E}[e^{-r\Delta t}V(t_i)|S(t_{i-1})]\} \text{ for } i = 2, \ldots, m,$$

with the terminal condition

$$V(t_m) = \max\{K - S(t_m), 0\}.$$

This recurrence relation allows the value of an American option $V(0)$ to be computed.

It would be very time-consuming to compute $\mathrm{E}[e^{-r\Delta t}V(t_i)|S(t_{i-1})]$ by simulation again. Here, we employ the least squares approach, which uses a least squares regression to estimate the value of $\mathrm{E}[e^{-r\Delta t}V(t_i)|S(t_{i-1})]$. One of the choices is the quadratic conditional function

$$\mathrm{E}[e^{-r\Delta t}V(t_i)|S(t_{i-1})] = a + bS(t_{i-1}) + cS(t_{i-1})^2. \qquad (3.5)$$

In this approach, n asset price paths, each of them with m subintervals, are generated. We then work backward from $t = t_m$. At each t_i, for $i = 2, \ldots, m$, we regress $e^{-r\Delta t}V_j(t_i)$ on $S_j(t_{i-1})$ with a quadratic polynomial using every in-the-money path $S_j(t_{i-1})$ to obtain estimate $\widehat{E}[e^{-r\Delta t}V(t_i)|S(t_{i-1})]$. Then, we compare estimate $\widehat{E}[e^{-r\Delta t}V(t_i)|S(t_{i-1})]$ with the immediate exercise payoff, $K - S(t_{i-1})$. Therefore, the decision rule becomes

$$V(t_{i-1}) = \begin{cases} K - S(t_{i-1}) & \text{if } \max\{K - S(t_{i-1}), 0\} \geq f_{i-1}(S(t_{i-1})), \\ e^{-r\Delta t}V(t_i) & \text{otherwise,} \end{cases}$$

where $f_{i-1}(S(t_{i-1})) = \widehat{E}[e^{-r\Delta t}V(t_i)|S(t_{i-1})]$.

By repeating this procedure from $i = m$ to $i = 2$ and for $j = 1, \ldots, n$, we obtain $V_j(t_1)$ for every asset price path $j = 1, \ldots, n$. Then, $V_j(t_0)$ is equal to the discounted value of $V_j(t_1)$, and the estimated price of an American option is the average of $V_j(t_0)$:

$$V(t_0) \simeq \frac{1}{n} \sum_{i=1}^{n} e^{-r\Delta t} V_j(t_0).$$

Remark In Equation 3.5, only in-the-money paths are used in least squares estimation, as they are sensitive to immediate exercise.

To familiarize readers with the least squares approach, we illustrate the calculation using the following numerical example.

Example 3.2 *Let $S_0 = 50$, $r = 4\%$, and $\sigma = 40\%$. Compute the value of an American put option with strike price $K = 52$ and maturity $T = 1$. For simplicity, assume that the option can be exercised only at $t = 1/3, 2/3$, and 1.*

Use the formula $S(t + \Delta t) = S(t)\exp((r - \sigma^2/2)\Delta t + \sigma \Delta W^*(t))$ to generate asset prices at exercise time points $t = 1/3, 2/3, 1$. We include only 10 sample paths for illustration purposes. In practice, many more sample paths should be used. Table 3.4 gives the 10 sample paths. The terminal payoffs corresponding to each path, $V(1)$, are presented in the last column of Table 3.4.

In Table 3.5, only in-the-money paths 2, 7, 8, 9, and 10 are used for regression. The quadratic conditional function

$$\mathrm{E}[e^{-r\Delta t}V(1)|S(2/3)] = a + bS(2/3) + cS(2/3)^2$$

TABLE 3.4 Sample Paths and Payoffs at Maturity

Path	S(0)	S(1/3)	S(2/3)	S(1)	$V(1) = \max\{K - S(1), 0\}$
1	50	63.785	57.794	60.727	0
2	50	36.627	51.035	46.085	5.915
3	50	62.100	69.384	52.948	0
4	50	60.628	66.708	61.437	0
5	50	44.679	53.568	40.742	11.258
6	50	67.858	81.914	65.260	0
7	50	55.199	42.031	74.688	0
8	50	33.900	30.104	27.914	24.086
9	50	36.216	30.358	29.878	22.122
10	50	68.742	44.205	44.247	7.753

gives us

$$f_2(S(2/3)) = \widehat{E}[e^{-r\Delta t}V(1)|S(2/3)] = 185.441 - 8.115 S(2/3) + 0.090 S(2/3)^2.$$

We then calculate the estimated continuation value based on $f_2(S(2/3))$, which determines the exercise policy at $t = 2/3$; see Table 3.6. The option is exercised only if the immediate exercise value is greater than the estimated continuation value. $V(2/3)$ is determined by

$$V(2/3) = \begin{cases} K - S(2/3), & \text{if } \max\{K - S(2/3), 0\} \geq f_2(S(2/3)), \\ e^{-\Delta t} V(1), & \text{otherwise.} \end{cases}$$

At $t = 1/3$, paths 2, 5, 8, and 9 in Table 3.7 are in-the-money and are used for the following regression.

$$E[e^{-r\Delta t}V(2/3)|S(1/3)] = a + bS(1/3) + cS(1/3)^2.$$

TABLE 3.5 Exercise Values and Estimated Continuation Values at $t = 2/3$

Path	S(2/3)	Continuation value $e^{-r\Delta t}V(1)$	Exercise value $\max\{K - S(2/3), 0\}$	Estimated continuation value $\widehat{E}[e^{-r\Delta t}V(1)|S(2/3)]$
1	57.794	0	0	—
2	51.035	5.837	0.965	6.564
3	69.384	0	0	—
4	66.708	0	0	—
5	53.568	11.109	0	—
6	81.914	0	0	—
7	42.031	0	9.969	3.939
8	30.104	23.767	21.896	23.012
9	30.358	21.829	21.642	22.338
10	44.205	7.651	7.795	3.231

TABLE 3.6 Optimal Exercise Policy at $t = 2/3$

Path	Continuation value $e^{-r\Delta t}V(1)$	Exercise value $\max\{K - S(2/3), 0\}$	Estimated continuation value $f_2(S(2/3))$	Exercise	$V(2/3)$
1	0	0	—	No	0
2	5.837	0.965	6.564	No	5.837
3	0	0	—	No	0
4	0	0	—	No	0
5	11.109	0	—	No	11.109
6	0	0	—	No	0
7	0	9.969	3.939	Yes	9.969
8	23.767	21.896	23.012	No	23.767
9	21.829	21.642	22.338	No	21.829
10	7.651	7.795	3.231	Yes	7.795

This time,

$$f_1(S(1/3)) = 244.130 - 12.721 S(1/3) + 0.166 S(1/3)^2,$$

which determines the exercise policy at $t = 1/3$ (see Table 3.8). Once again, $V(1/3)$ is determined by

$$V(1/3) = \begin{cases} K - S(1/3), & \text{if } \max\{K - S(1/3), 0\} \geq f_1(S(1/3)), \\ e^{-\Delta t} V(2/3), & \text{otherwise.} \end{cases}$$

Finally, we discount $V_j(1/3)$ by $e^{-r\Delta t}$ to obtain $V_j(0)$, and compute the average of $V_j(0)$ to get the estimated American put option price. In this example, the estimated American price is 8.200, as shown in Table 3.9, which is higher than the European option price of 8.11.

TABLE 3.7 Exercise Values and Estimated Continuation Values at $t = 1/3$

Path	$S(1/3)$	Continuation value $e^{-r\Delta t}V(2/3)$	Exercise value $\max\{K - S(1/3), 0\}$	Estimated continuation value $\widehat{E}[e^{-r\Delta t}V(2/3)|S(1/3)]$
1	63.785	0	0	—
2	36.627	5.760	15.373	12.533
3	62.100	0	0	—
4	60.628	0	0	—
5	44.679	10.961	7.321	10.878
6	67.858	0	0	—
7	55.199	9.837	0	—
8	33.900	23.452	18.100	24.351
9	36.216	21.540	15.784	13.951
10	68.742	7.692	0	—

TABLE 3.8 Optimal Exercise Policy at $t = 1/3$

Path	Continuation value $e^{-r\Delta t}V(2/3)$	Exercise value $\max\{K - S(1/3), 0\}$	Estimated continuation value $f_1(S(1/3))$	Exercise	$V(1/3)$
1	0	0	—	No	0
2	5.760	15.373	12.533	Yes	15.373
3	0	0	—	No	0
4	0	0	—	No	0
5	10.961	7.321	10.878	No	8.307
6	0	0	—	No	0
7	9.837	0	—	No	9.837
8	23.452	18.100	24.351	No	23.452
9	21.540	15.784	13.951	Yes	15.784
10	7.692	0	—	No	7.692

To summarize, the steps in valuing an American option are as follows.

1. Generate n stock price paths, each of which has m subintervals.
2. Calculate the terminal payoff $V_j(t_m)$ of each stock price path.
3. Regress $e^{-r\Delta t}V(t_i)$ on $S(t_{i-1})$ using a quadratic conditional function.
4. If $\max\{K - S(t_{i-1}), 0\} \geq \widehat{E}[e^{-r\Delta t}V(t_i)|S(t_{i-1})]$, then set $V_j(t_{i-1}) = K - S(t_{i-1})$. Otherwise, set $V_j(t_{i-1}) = e^{-r\Delta t}V(t_i)$.
5. Repeat Steps 3 and 4 from $i = m$ to $i = 2$.
6. Discount $V_j(t_1)$ at the risk-free rate to obtain $V_j(0)$, and average $V_j(0)$ to obtain $V(0)$.

The VBA code for computing an American option price is as follows.

```
'Simulate the path
S = BS_Path(A)
```

TABLE 3.9 Estimated American Put Price

Path	$V(1/3)$	$V(0) = e^{-r\Delta t}V(1/3)$
1	0	0
2	15.373	15.169
3	0	0
4	0	0
5	8.307	10.816
6	0	0
7	9.837	9.707
8	23.452	23.141
9	15.784	15.575
10	7.692	7.590
		Average = 8.200

```
'Calculate the terminal payoff
Payoff = AO_Payoff(S, A.rf, A.dt, K, optionType)
Price = Exp(-A.rf * A.t) * Average(Payoff)
```

For further details, please refer to Ch3.3_American_Option_with_EMS.xls. Note that *AO_Payoff* is a user-defined function for calculating the "payoff at maturity." When it is used to calculate the price of a vanilla American option, the average of the payoff calculated from *AO_Payoff* must be discounted using the risk-free rate.

```
Public Function AO_Payoff(S As Variant, ByVal rf As
Double, ByVal dt As Double, _ ByVal K As Double, ByVal
optionType As Integer, Optional ByVal m As Long = -1)
    Dim i As Long, j As Long
    Dim n As Long
    Dim cntITM As Long
    Dim x As Variant 'predictor
    Dim y As Variant 'response
    Dim Beta As Variant
    Dim exeValue As Double
    If m = -1 Then m = UBound(S, 1)
    n = UBound(S, 2)
    ReDim optionVal(0 To m, 1 To n) As Double
    ReDim Payoff(1 To n)

    'Calculate the value of the option at maturity
    For j = 1 To n
        Select Case optionType
            Case xCall
                optionVal(m, j) = Max(S(m, j) - K, 0)
            Case xPut
                optionVal(m, j) = Max(K - S(m, j), 0)
            Case xStraddle
                optionVal(m, j) = Max(S(m, j) - K, K - S(m, j))
        End Select
    Next

    For i = m - 1 To 1 Step -1
        'Counting in the money path
        cntITM = 0
        For j = 1 To n
            Select Case optionType
                Case xCall
                    optionVal(i, j) = Max(S(i, j) - K, 0)
```

```
                    Case xPut
                        optionVal(i, j) = Max(K - S(i, j), 0)
                    Case xStraddle
                        optionVal(i, j = Max(S(i, j) - K, K - S(i, j))
                End Select
                If optionVal(i, j) > 0 Then cntITM = cntITM + 1
            Next
            
            If cntITM > 2 Then
                'create matrix for regression
                ReDim x(1 To cntITM, 1 To 3)
                ReDim y(1 To cntITM, 1 To 1)
                cntITM = 0
                For j = 1 To n
                    If optionVal(i, j) > 0 Then
                        cntITM = cntITM + 1
                        y(cntITM, 1) = Exp(-rf * dt) _
                                        * optionVal(i + 1, j)
                        x(cntITM, 1) = 1
                        x(cntITM, 2) = S(i, j)
                        x(cntITM, 3) = S(i, j) ^ 2
                    End If
                Next
                
                Beta = OLS(x, y)
            End If
            
            'determine if early exercise is preferred
            For j = 1 To n
                If optionVal(i, j) <= 0 Or optionVal(i, j) <= _
                    Beta(0) + Beta(1) * _ S(i, j) + Beta(2) _
                    * S(i, j) ^ 2 Then
                        optionVal(i, j) = Exp(-rf * dt) * optionVal(i + 1, j)
                End If
            Next
        Next
        
        For j = 1 To n
            optionVal(0, j) = Exp(-rf * dt) * optionVal(1, j)
            Payoff(j) = Exp(rf * dt * m) * optionVal(0, j)
        Next
        
        AO_Payoff = Payoff
End Function
```

3.3.1 Empirical Martingale Correction

To improve simulation quality, we can employ a simple correction method called empirical martingale simulation (EMS), which was introduced by Duan and Simonato (1998). The risk-neutral valuation formula gives us the martingale property for any stochastic models:

$$E^Q\left[e^{-rt} S(t) \mid S_0\right] = S_0.$$

Unfortunately, this martingale property fails to hold exactly in simulation due to discretization and sampling errors. Duan and Simonato (1998) showed that EMS can be used to achieve a certain level of variance reduction. This method is particularly useful in the valuation of path-dependent derivatives, although it can also be used with the other variance reduction techniques described in Chapter 2. For our original n stock price paths with m subintervals $S_j(t_i)$ each, empirical martingale correction goes as follows. First, set

$$S_j^*(t_0) = S_j(t_0) = S_0.$$

At each time point $t_1, \ldots, t_m$, calculate

$$Z_j(t_i) = S_j^*(t_{i-1}) \frac{S_j(t_i)}{S_j(t_{i-1})}, \quad \text{for } j = 1, \ldots, n,$$

$$Z_0(t_i) = \frac{1}{n} e^{-rt_i} \sum_{j=1}^{n} Z_j(t_i).$$

Then, the corrected jth stock price at time t_i is given by

$$S_j^*(t_i) = S_0 \frac{Z_j(t_i)}{Z_0(t_i)}.$$

It can be shown that after correction, the new stock price paths $S_j^*(t_i)$ at each time t_i satisfy

$$E^Q[e^{-rt_i} S_j^*(t_i) \mid S_0] = S_0.$$

The following is the corresponding VBA code for a function that employs EMS (this function can be found in the function library).

```
Function EMartingale(S, rf as double, q as double,
                    dt as double)
    Dim i As Long, j As Long, An As Long, Am As Integer
    Dim Z0 As Double
```

88 STRUCTURED PRODUCTS

```
    An = UBound(S, 2)
    Am = UBound(S, 1)
    ReDim zS(1 To An) As Double
    ReDim eS(0 To Am, 1 To An) As Double

    For j = 1 To An
        eS(0, j) = S(0, j)
    Next j

    For i = 1 To Am
        'Calculate the discounted sample average
        For j = 1 To An
            zS(j) = eS(i - 1, j) * S(i, j) / S(i - 1, j)
        Next j
        Z0 = Exp(-(rf - q) * dt * i) * Average(zS)

        'Correct the sample path at time i
        For j = 1 To An
            eS(i, j) = eS(0, j) * zS(j) / Z0
        Next j
    Next i

    EMartingale = eS
End Function
```

Incorporating EMS in the valuation of an American option price requires the addition of just one step using the foregoing function *EMartingale*.

1. Generate *n* stock price paths with *m* subintervals each.
2. Employ empirical martingale correction with S to S^*.
3. Continue the original Steps 2 to 6 with S^*.

The corresponding VBA code is as follows.

```
'Simulate the path
S = BS_Path(A)
eS = EMartingale(S, A.rf, A.q, A.dt)

'Calculate the terminate payoff
Payoff = AO_Payoff(eS, A.rf, A.dt, K, optionType)
Price = Exp(-A.rf * A.t) * Average(Payoff)
```

For further details, please refer to Ch3.3_American_Option_with_EMS.xls.

3.4 RANGE ACCRUAL NOTES

3.4.1 Possible Design and Sample Term Sheet

A range accrual note (RAN) pays a fixed rate each day if a chosen reference variable falls within a predefined corridor at a specified time; otherwise, no interest rate is paid on that day. The reference variable could be a stock price, index value, FX rate, bond yield, or reference portfolio value. Different types of RANs are liquidly traded in the over-the-counter (OTC) market.

The ELN discussed in Section 1 pays a constant coupon C, which is independent of the performance of the underlying stock. In certain circumstances, the ELN is embedded with a RAN such that the coupon payment is contingent upon a reference rate. Consider a situation in which the coupon rate accumulates each day that the closing price of HSBC is greater than or equal to the barrier price B. If the barrier price is not zero, then each day there is a binary option expiring with a strike price equal to B. Note that the term sheet of the ELN presented in the appendix does not involve barrier price B.

3.4.2 Closed-Form Solution for European RAN Under Black–Scholes Model

To simplify our discussion, assume that trigger events (say, a callable feature) and early redemption do not occur. As noted in Section 3.1, this ELN can be interpreted as a combination of zero-coupon bonds (CBs) and a put option on the stock HSBC Holdings Plc. Recall that the holder's payoff function at maturity is

$$ELN(T) = (C + D) - \frac{D}{K} \max\{K - S(T), 0\},$$

where D stands for the note denomination and C for the total fixed coupon payment. However, we consider that the total coupon payment, C, is no longer a constant, but rather a variable coupon depending on the performance of the underlying stock, such that the coupon paid in each year is proportional to the number of days that the underlying stock price remains above B. In such a situation, the present value of the coupon is given by

$$C_{\text{Discounted}} = \sum_{i=1}^{3} C_i e^{-r t_{N_i}}, \tag{3.6}$$

$$C_i = \frac{C}{N_i - N_{i-1}} \sum_{j=N_{i-1}}^{N_i} 1_{\{S(t_j) \geq B\}}, \tag{3.7}$$

where C is the maximum coupon rate, C_i is the realized coupon rate at t_{N_i}, N_i is the total number of trading days in i years, and $N_0 = 0$. Therefore, such an ELN can be decomposed into the sum of a RAN, a CB zero-coupon bond and a short position in a put. The present value of this ELN is given by

$$ELN = C \sum_{i=1}^{3} \frac{e^{-r t_{N_i}}}{N_i - N_{i-1}} \sum_{j=N_{i-1}}^{N_i} \mathbb{Q}(S(t_j) \geq B) + D e^{-rT} - \frac{D}{K} p(S, K, r, q, \sigma, T). \tag{3.8}$$

Under the BS model,

$$S(t_j) \geq B \text{ iff } W^*(t_j) \geq \frac{\log \frac{B}{S} - \left(r - q - \frac{\sigma^2}{2}\right) t_j}{\sigma}.$$

Hence,

$$\mathbb{Q}(S(t_j) \geq B) = \Psi\left(\frac{\log \frac{S}{B} + \left(r - q - \frac{\sigma^2}{2}\right) t_j}{\sigma \sqrt{t_j}}\right).$$

Substituting this into Equation 3.8, we obtain the following closed-form solution.

$$ELN = C \sum_{i=1}^{3} \frac{e^{-rt_{N_i}}}{N_i - N_{i-1}} \sum_{j=N_{i-1}}^{N_i} \Psi(d_j^B)$$

$$+ De^{-rT} - \frac{D}{K} K e^{-r(T-t)} \Psi(-d_2) - S e^{-q(T-t)} \Psi(-d_1), \quad (3.9)$$

where

$$d_1 = \frac{\log \frac{S}{K} + (r - q + \frac{\sigma^2}{2})T}{\sigma \sqrt{T}}, \; d_2 = d_1 - \sigma \sqrt{T},$$

$$d_j^B = \frac{\log \frac{S}{B} + (r - q - \frac{\sigma^2}{2}) t_j}{\sigma \sqrt{t_j}}.$$

In practice, a trader may infer the price of an embedded RAN by interpolating the RANs on the same underlying stock in the OTC market. In doing so, he or she needs three separate interpolations in the yield curve, implied volatility surface, and OTC RAN prices.

With the closed-form solution, the analytical price of the note on September 25, 2008 (the issue date), is calculated as 93,502.77, with $S_0 = 123.8$, $r = 3.40\%$, $q = 3.00\%$, $\sigma = 46.74\%$, $T = 0.4762$, and $K = 112.4535$.

In Section 4, we showed how to simulate the price of standard options when the dynamics of the stock price follow the BS model. VBA functions *BS_Path* and *EO_Payoff* can be used to simulate the price of this note, with only statement-length modification.

```
Dim S As Variant            'paths of stock price
Dim payoff As Variant       'payoff of each sample path
Dim price As Double         'price of the note
```

```
S = BS_Path(A)
payoff = EO_Payoff(S, K, xPut)
price = (D - D / K * Average(payoff))
          * Exp(-A.rf * A.t) + sumcoupon
'sumcoupond is the total discounted coupon value
```

For further details, refer to Ch3.4_Range_Accrual_Notes_(Plain).xls.

This example demonstrates that a structured product can be priced once it is decomposed into simpler products. Even when such decomposition is not possible, simulation can still help. In this case, the payoffs at maturity are to be simulated, discounted at the risk-free rate, and then added back to the discounted coupons. The procedure is as follows.

1. Simulate n stock price paths.
2. Calculate $\text{Payoff}^{(i)} = \frac{D}{K} \min\{S_T, K\}$.
3. Calculate $C_{\text{Discounted}}$ by Equation 3.6.
4. $\text{Price} = C_{\text{Discounted}} + \frac{e^{-r(T-t)}}{n} \sum_{i=1}^{n} \text{Payoff}^{(i)}$.

The corresponding VBA codes are as follows.

```
'Step1: Generate n stock price paths
S = BS_Path(A)

'Step2: calculate the payoffs
For j = 1 To A.n
  payoff(j) = D / K * Min(S(A.m, j), K)
Next j

'Step4: calculate the price
Price = Average(payoff) * Exp(-A.rf * A.t) + sumcoupon
'sumcoupond is the total discounted coupon value
```

For further details, refer to Ch3.4_Range_Accrual_Notes_(Plain).xls.

For $n = 50,000$, the simulated price is 93,495.68, which deviates little from the closed-form price. As the RAN requires that principal of HK$100,000 be put into the account when the contract is entered into, an expected payoff of 93,584.4364 shows that this contract may not be a good choice for investors.

3.4.3 Callable and American Features

ELN and RAN become complicated instruments when they include callable features and/or early redemption rights.

92 STRUCTURED PRODUCTS

3.4.3.1 Callable ELN A callable feature refers to the issuer's right to call back and terminate the product in face of a particular trigger event. A call provision is usually specified in the contract. A closed-form solution can no longer be derived when there is a callable feature because the ELN has become a path-dependent structured product. However, the simulation approach is still applicable. When the call provision is a barrier provision, it is known as an auto-call feature, and the valuation is less complicated.

According to the term sheet of the ELN in the appendix, there are three prices that can affect the payoff of the note. Barrier price B is used to decide whether or not the coupon rate should accumulate. As B happens to be zero in this note, the coupon rate is fixed at 1.3333% for each period. The trigger price TG checks whether the condition of the trigger event is satisfied on period end dates other than the final valuation date. Once the stock price at closing time on these specific dates exceeds the trigger price, the trigger event is deemed to have occurred, and the contract terminates immediately. The issuer then redeems the note by paying the denomination and the relevant coupon amount. This feature is known as auto-call. Strike price K is used to calculate the payoff when the note reaches maturity. For simplicity, assume that payments of all kinds are settled immediately. The payoff for each sample path is calculated as follows.

1. On the last trading day of period 1, compute the fixed coupon for period 1, where Coupon $= D * cr$ with $cr = 1.3333\%$.
2. On the same day, check whether the closing price has exceeded the trigger price TG. If yes, then compute the payoff of the trigger event as Payoff $= D +$ Total coupon, which concludes one sample path. Otherwise, continue.
3. Repeat Steps 1 and 2 for period 2.
4. Repeat Step 1 for period 3.
5. At maturity, compute the payoff as Payoff $= \frac{D}{K} \min\{S(T), K\} +$ Total coupon.

Note that both coupons and payoffs should be discounted to their present value (this procedure is omitted in the foregoing algorithm). The price can be obtained by averaging the discounted total coupons and payoff.

To improve the flexibility and accuracy of the simulation program, an array

$$td(0 \ To \ Application.Count(Range \ "H:H"))$$

is declared to record the cumulative trading days by the end of each observation period. The payment schedule, which lists the trading days of each period, is typed into an Excel spreadsheet before the simulation is performed to allow td to read in the data from the spreadsheet. *Number of steps* in the spreadsheet must be changed to *total cumulative days*. If any modification is made to the payment schedule, then only the spreadsheet needs to be adjusted; the program is kept unchanged.

Based on this algorithm, part of the corresponding VBA code is as follows.

```
Public Function RAN_Price(S As Variant, rf As Double,
dt As Double, D As Double, _ CR As Double, K As Double,
B As Double, TG As Double, td As Variant) As Variant

For j = 1 To n
  curPeriod = 1
  coupon = 0
  nBarrier = 0
  For i = 0 To m
    If S(i, j) > B Then nBarrier = nBarrier + 1
      If i = td(curPeriod) Then
        If curPeriod = 1 Then nBarrier = td(1)
        coupon = coupon + Exp(-rf * i * dt) * D * CR *
        nBarrier / _ (td(curPeriod) - td(curPeriod - 1))
        If i = m Then Exit For
        If S(i, j) >= TG Then
          Price(j) = D * Exp(-rf * i * dt)
          GoTo ContractEnd
        End If
      curPeriod = curPeriod + 1
      nBarrier = 0
    End If
  Next i
  Price(j) = Exp(-rf * m * dt) * D / K * Min(S(m, j), K)
ContractEnd:
  Price(j) = Price(j) + coupon
Next j
```

The corresponding *Sub* procedure is

```
S = BS_Path(A)
S = EMartingale(S, A.rf, A.q, A.dt)
Price = RAN_Price(S, A.rf, A.dt, D, CR, K, B, TG, td)
Cells(18, 2) = Average(Price)
```

For further details, please refer to Ch3.4_Range_Accrual_Notes_(Callable).xls.

Remark This function is more general as it allows B to be non-zero.

If the process is repeated 50,000 times, then the price of the callable note with $B = 0$ is simulated to be 94,768.45, which is a little higher than the previous price without a trigger event. The reason for this discrepancy is that rather than selling a standard put option to the issuer, the holder of a callable-RAN is short-selling an up-and-out put option with a knock-out price equal to the trigger price. As an option with a knock-out feature is cheaper than a standard option, the value of a RAN with a callable feature should be higher. With a lower trigger price, the value of a callable RAN is even higher because it is easier for it to be knocked out with a lower trigger price.

3.4.3.2 American ELN In an American ELN, upon occurrence of an issuer tax event and/or change in law and/or hedging disruption and/or increased cost of hedging, the issuer may redeem the entire note. In other words, the issuer has an early redemption right, or surrender right from the holder's perspective. To make a product more attractive, an early redemption right is sometimes given to the holder rather than the issuer. The holder can then exercise the note at any time he or she wishes by paying a premium when it is issued. In this case, we can treat the contract as an American-style ELN and employ the least squares approach to calculate the premium.

In this example, assume that the redemption right is given to the holder and use the same term sheet as that without a trigger event. Also assume the early redemption amount to be the full denomination. Based on the existing function *AO_Payoff*, which is used to price an American option, we make the following modifications.

1. The terminal payoff of each stock price path should agree with the term sheet, which is calculated as

$$payoff_T = coupon + \frac{D}{K} \min\{K, S_T\} - De^{r(T-t)}.$$

2. The coupon should be adjusted for different periods when calculating the option value because if the note is exercised before maturity, then subsequent coupons are lost.
3. All of the stock price paths should be used in the least squares regression.

With the same parameters as those in the European ELN example, the price of the American ELN is 102,337. The difference between the two (by simulation) is 8777, which is exactly the premium that the holder needs to pay in advance. The VBA codes are omitted here. For details, please refer to Ch3.4_Range_Accrual_Notes_(Callable).xls.

3.4.3.3 Early Redemption Request: Calculation of the Early Redemption Fee It is also possible that the client may wish to redeem the note before maturity even though the contract is not initially an American-style option. In this case, the issuer can still allow the client to exercise the contract early based on comparison between the client's account value and the remaining value of the note. The account value can be directly calculated as the sum of the denominations and total coupons received in the previous period, whereas the remaining value of the RAN can be obtained through simulation. There are two possible situations:

1. RAN value > Account value
   In this situation, the holder expects to receive more from the note than he or she would gain from exercising it now. From the issuer's point of view, he or she is willing to let the client redeem the contract upon request. The client's payoff will be the exact account value.
2. RAN value < Account value
   The issuer can still allow the client to terminate the contract by charging an early redemption premium, such that the client's payoff becomes

$$\begin{aligned} \text{Payoff} &= \text{Account value} + \text{Premium} \\ &= \text{Account value} + (\text{ELN} - \text{Account value}) \\ &= \text{ELN}. \end{aligned}$$

3.5 FX ACCUMULATOR: THE CASE OF CITIC PACIFIC LTD

Accumulators are popular derivatives in Asia, particularly in Hong Kong, although people in Hong Kong became more nervous about accumulators after their severe impact on CITIC Pacific LTD during the subprime mortgage crisis. When pronounced with a strong Hong Kong accent, the name "accumulator" in English sounds like "I will kill you later," an interesting nickname for a product whose risk is realized only after it is held for a long time. Hong Kong's painful experience with such derivatives as accumulators and Lehman Brother's mini-bonds (a subprime credit-linked bond) has reshaped its retail banking industry, which is now more aware of the risks contained within derivative products. In the following, we employ the BS model to illustrate the valuation and risk of an FX accumulator. Later chapters reinvestigate this product using more sophisticated models.

3.5.1 Event Playback

On October 20, 2008, CITIC Pacific LTD, a Hong Kong-listed company, issued a profit warning to its shareholders announcing that it had realized an aggregate loss of HK$807.7 million on a series of leveraged foreign exchange forward contracts. Moreover, the mark-to-market (MTM) loss on these outstanding contracts was deemed to be HK$14.7 billion, according to the valuation of relevant banks. CITIC Pacific's stock price plunged by 55% to HK$6.52 following the announcement.

Given the increased demand for iron and steel in mainland China, CITIC Pacific began to invest in an iron ore mine located in Western Australia in 2006. In the next 2 years, the AUD–USD exchange rate soared from about 0.75 to 0.9 (see Fig. 3.2), as Australia's central bank kept raising the interest rate to curtail inflation. CITIC Pacific was very likely to suffer a loss because of the appreciation of the AUD against the

96 STRUCTURED PRODUCTS

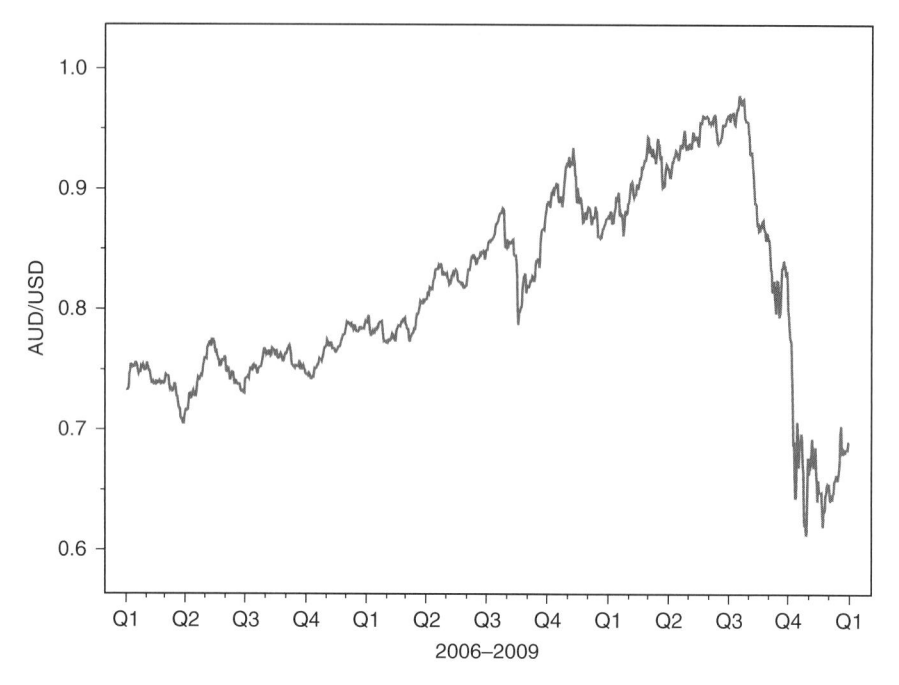

Figure 3.2 Historical AUD–USD exchange rate.

USD. To minimize the currency exposure of its Australian iron ore mining project, in July 2005, when the exchange rate was around 0.95, the company entered into several leveraged foreign exchange contracts to hedge against the exchange rate risk. According to these contracts, the company had to purchase Australian dollars (AUD) at a predetermined exchange rate on a series of settlement dates.

However, the AUD–USD exchange rate did not continue to rise as predicted. Following the financial crisis of 2008, the commodity market collapsed, and the price of iron fell rapidly. The AUD–USD exchange rate fell to 0.6345 on October 10, 2008. To fulfil the obligations of its leveraged foreign exchange contracts, CITIC Pacific had to buy AUD at a predetermined price that was much higher than the market price. The next section provides a brief introduction to the structure of one of these leveraged foreign exchange contracts, the AUD target redemption forward contract, followed by analysis of this product to see how it caused the firm to suffer a catastrophic loss.

Remark In an FX quotation, FOR-DOM represents the number of units of a domestic currency needed to buy one unit of a foreign currency. For FX quotations in the United States, the U.S. dollar is normally quoted as the foreign currency (or base currency) except for the Euro, AUD, British pound, and New Zealand dollar. For example, we would write AUD–USD.

3.5.2 Structure of an Accumulator

In the aforementioned announcement, CITIC Pacific disclosed that it had entered into four types of foreign exchange derivatives: an AUD target redemption forward contract, AUD daily accrual contract, dual-currency (AUD and EUR) target redemption forward contract, and an RMB target redemption forward contract. Of these contracts, the AUD target redemption forward contract accounted for the largest proportion in terms of both quantity and value. A target redemption forward contract is also known as a Knock-Out Discounted Accumulator, which was very popular with private banks in 2007.

A typical Knock-Out Discounted Accumulator requires the investor to purchase certain amounts of an underlying asset from the issuer at a predetermined strike price on a series of settlement dates. Obviously, the investor will make a profit from the contract when the market price is higher than the strike price and suffer a loss otherwise, as in a forward contract. However, the maximum profit usually has an upper limit due to the existence of a target profit or barrier price. A target profit is set to ensure that when the cumulative profit exceeds a predetermined target profit, the settlement amounts are paid by the issuer and the remaining transactions are terminated. The barrier price works in the same way except that the knock-out event is deemed to occur when the underlying asset price hits the barrier price on any date during the knock-out-event observation period. It is obvious that setting a target profit or barrier price is to the issuer's advantage. The underlying asset can be any financial product, most commonly a stock. In this case, the underlying asset is the exchange rate.

In effect, the holder of a target redemption forward contract has bought a series of up-and-out call options and sold a series of up-and-out put options to the issuer, with the maximum profit capped by the target. To make the contract appear more profitable to the holder, an accumulator is usually structured in such a way that the current market price is higher than the strike price.

3.5.3 Accumulator Valuation

For illustration purposes, we choose one of the 16 AUD target redemption forward contracts that CITIC Pacific entered into. According to published information, the company agreed to purchase AUD against delivery of USD at a strike rate of 0.7975. The purchase amount was AUD 8 million when the exchange rate on the settlement date was higher than the strike rate and AUD 20 million when it was lower. The target profit was set at AUD 1.5 million. (The barrier rate was 1.0, and the contract would end if the exchange rate on any day during the contract hit the barrier rate.) We assume that the contract took effect on July 15, 2008 (the contract starting date), and matured on September 30, 2010, for a total of 24 settlement dates. The periodic settlement dates are set as the last trading day of each month for simplicity.

Based on this information, we employ Monte Carlo simulation to determine the fair price of this accumulator. As the underlying asset is the FX rate and a foreign currency is analogous to a stock paying a known dividend yield, we adopt the the following BS model to simulate the path of foreign exchange rate $F(t)$.

$$dF(t) = (r_d - r_f)F(t)\,dt + \sigma F(t)\,dW^*(t), \qquad (3.10)$$

where r_d is the risk-free rate in the domestic country, r_f is the risk-free rate in the foreign country, and σ is the volatility of the exchange rate. The exchange rate path following the foregoing stochastic model can easily be generated from the existing function *BS_Path* by setting the risk-free rate at r_d and the dividend yield at r_f.

To better explicate the FX dynamics in Equation 3.10 and the associated FX-related derivatives, we develop a no-arbitrage condition for FX-related derivatives. It is easy to confuse the two interest rates involved in FX derivatives, namely, domestic rate r_d and foreign rate r_f in which case one might wonder which should be used for risk-neutral pricing. In fact, there are two risk-neutral probability measures, $\mathbb{Q}^d$ and $\mathbb{Q}^f$, corresponding to r_d and r_f, respectively.

Let $F(t)$ be the foreign-over-domestic FX rate quoted in the domestic currency and $S(t)$ be the price of a foreign asset quoted in the foreign currency. Therefore, $1/F(t)$ is traded in the foreign currency. Consider a foreign derivative with payoff function $\Phi(1/F(T), S(T)) = V(F(T), S(T))$. Using this foreign derivative, a domestic agent can issue a domestic derivative with terminal payoff $F(T)V(F(T), S(T))$. Then, the following result holds.

Theorem 3.1 *If there is no arbitrage opportunity, then*

$$e^{-r_d(T-t)} E^{\mathbb{Q}^d}\left[F(T)V(F(T), S(T))\right] = F(t)e^{-r_f(T-t)} E^{\mathbb{Q}^f}\left[V(F(T), S(T))\right].$$

Proof: By risk-neutral valuation, the present foreign value of the foreign derivative is given by

$$e^{-r_f(T-t)} E^{\mathbb{Q}^f}\left[V(F(T), S(T))\right],$$

whereas the present domestic value of the domestic derivative is given by

$$e^{-r_d(T-t)} E^{\mathbb{Q}^d}\left[F(T)V(F(T), S(T))\right].$$

A domestic investor interested in a foreign derivative has two investment opportunities. He or she can either purchase the foreign derivative right away with domestic value

$$F(t)e^{-r_f(T-t)} E^{\mathbb{Q}^f}\left[V(F(T), S(T))\right]$$

or do so through a domestic agent by engaging in a domestic derivative contract. As the two opportunities share the same domestic payoff, $F(T)V(F(T), S(T))$, their present domestic value should be the same. Otherwise, the investor can buy low and sell high. The difference is the arbitrage profit.

Using Theorem 3.1, we can deduce Equation 3.10 if the FX rate follows the BS model under $\mathbb{P}$. Consider $V(F(T), S(T)) = 1$. In other words, the foreign derivative is simply the foreign CB zero-coupon bond. Then Theorem 3.1 implies the well-known interest rate parity for the FX rate, which states that

$$E^{\mathbb{Q}^d}[F(T)|F(t)] = F(t)e^{(r_d - r_f)(T-t)}, \text{ for } t \leq T.$$

This sets up a martingale condition for the $\mathbb{Q}^d$ process of F.

Under $\mathbb{P}$, the FX rate is assumed to be

$$dF(t) = \mu F(t) dt + \sigma F(t) dW(t).$$

By Itô's lemma,

$$F(T) = F(t) \exp\left[\left(\mu - \frac{\sigma^2}{2}\right)(T-t) + \sigma(W(T) - W(t))\right].$$

It is easy to calculate

$$E^{\mathbb{P}}[F(T)|F(t)] = F(t)e^{\mu(T-t)}, \text{ for } t \leq T.$$

To match the martingale condition, we require the drift of F under $\mathbb{Q}^d$ to be $r_d - r_f$, which implies that

$$W^*(t) = W(t) - \left(\frac{\mu - r_d + r_f}{\sigma}\right)t.$$

The Girsanov theorem can help us to characterize the change of measure.

By replacing μ with $r_d - r_f$, we obtain the domestic risk-neutral dynamics for F, as in Equation 3.10. We then base our simulation on Equation 3.10 to compute the FX accumulator in the domestic currency or in U.S. dollars. Note that the Hong Kong dollar is pegged to the U.S. dollar, and thus the HKD–USD FX rate is (almost) fixed. Accordingly, many derivatives in Hong Kong are quoted in U.S. dollars. For such products, including the FX accumulator under study, we use the U.S. risk-neutral measure.

3.5.3.1 Without a Knock-Out Feature Without a knock-out feature (i.e., no target redemption or barrier price), the FX accumulator is a portfolio that longs a series of in-the-money call options and shorts a series of out-of-the-money put options, with the ratio of call options to put options being 8 : 20. Therefore, using portfolio replication, the price of an accumulator can easily be calculated by calculating the corresponding calls and puts. The result for October 16, 2008, is US$76.62 million. However, on the date on which CITIC Pacific entered into this contract, the price of the accumulator was US$5.23 million, which means that the MTM loss was already US$5.23 million when the company signed the the contract.

3.5.3.2 With Target Redemption
The price of an accumulator with target redemption has no closed-form solution, although simulation can easily determine its fair price. The procedure is as follows.

1. Generate n exchange rate paths with m subintervals each, where m is the total number of trading days.
2. For each period's ending date, if exchange rate $F(T_i) \geq$ strike rate K, then the discounted payoff for that period is $8e^{-rT_i \Delta t}(F_{T_i} - K)$. Otherwise, the discounted payoff is $20e^{-rT_i \Delta t}(F_{T_i} - K)$, where T_i denotes the cumulative trading days from "today" to the period i ending date and Δt denotes the reciprocal of the number of trading days in a year.
3. For each period's ending date, if the total payoff (non-discounted) > target profit, then the path is finished.
4. Repeat Steps 2 and 3 for all periods, and sum the discounted and non-discounted payoffs.
5. Repeat Steps 2 and 4 n times to obtain n discounted payoffs.
6. The price of the accumulator is the average of the discounted payoffs.

Remark In Step 1, if there are y periods, then we can simply generate y subintervals. However, for simplicity, we employ the previously developed function, which will generate more subintervals. However, for the knock-out event when the exchange rate hits the barrier rate, we are required to generate the exchange rate each day.

Part of the corresponding VBA code for the valuation is as follows.

```
'simulate the paths of exchange rate
FX = BS_Path(F)
'Employ the empirical martingale correction
FX = EMartingale(FX, F.rf, F.q, F.dt)

'the following calculate the DISCOUNTED payoff of the
    Accumulator
For i = 1 To F.n 'the i path
  sum = 0 'to store the total discounted payoff
  nsum = 0 'to store the total payoff
  For j = 1 To UBound(td) 'the array td stores the cumulative
trading days
    If FX(td(j), i) >= K Then
        'need to buy AUD 8 million
        sum = sum + (FX(td(j), i) - K) * 8 *
            Exp(-F.rf * td(j) * F.dt)
        nsum = nsum + (FX(td(j), i) - K) * 8
    Else
        'need to buy AUD 20 million
        sum = sum + (FX(td(j), i) - K) * 20 *
            Exp(-F.rf * td(j) * F.dt)
```

```
      nsum = nsum + (FX(td(j), i) - K) * 20
    End If
    'STEP 3 'Knock-out event occurs when the target
    profit is met
    If nsum > TG Then
      GoTo ContractEnd
    End If
  Next j
  ContractEnd:
  payoff(i) = sum
Next i

Price = Average(payoff) 'price without barrier
```

3.5.3.3 With Target Redemption and Barrier Rate In the case that the knock-out event is deemed to have occurred when the exchange rate hit the barrier rate, a small modification is needed for valuation. We need to check whether the exchange rate on each day exceeds the barrier rate. If it does, then the contract is terminated. The accumulator is then similar to a portfolio of up-and-out European options with target redemption. The corresponding VBA code for calculating the discounted payoff is as follows.

```
'simulate the paths of exchange rate
FX = BS_Path(F)
'Employ the empirical martingale correction
FX = EMartingale(FX, F.rf, F.q, F.dt)

For i = 1 To F.n
  sum = 0 'to store the total discounted payoff
  nsum = 0 'to store the total payoff
  count = 1
  For j = 1 To td(UBound(td))
    If FX(j, i) > B Then
      GoTo ContractEnd
    ElseIf j = td(count) Then
      If FX(j, i) >= K Then
        'need to buy AUD 8 million
        sum = sum + (FX(j, i) - K) * 8 *
            Exp(-F.rf * j * F.dt)
        nsum = nsum + (FX(j, i) - K) * 8
      Else
        'need to buy AUD 20 million
        sum = sum + (FX(j, i) - K) * 20 *
            Exp(-F.rf * j * F.dt)
        nsum = nsum + (FX(j, i) - K) * 20
```

```
      End If
      'STEP 3 'Knock-out event occurs when the target
              profit is met
      If nsum > TG Then
        GoTo ContractEnd
      End If
      count = count + 1
    End If
  Next j
  ContractEnd:
  payoff(i) = sum
Next i
Price = Average(payoff)
```

Suppose that today is October 16, 2008, and the spot FX rate is 0.6929. Using 30-day historical volatility $\sigma = 49.89\%$, $r_d = 0.0469$, $r_f = 0.0637$, and $dt = 1/252$, the simulated price of the accumulator with target redemption alone is US$83.099 million, and that with both target redemption and barrier rate is US$82.431 million. However, 30-day historical volatility is not the only choice for σ, and some prefer to use the average implied volatility of at-the-money (ATM) options. If we substitute ATM volatility $\sigma = 61.85\%$ into the program, then we obtain a simulated price US$88.629 million. In this case, the ATM volatility is greater than its historical counterpart and leads to a more severe MTM loss. Later in this chapter, we demonstrate that volatility and the simulated price are negatively correlated.

Historical volatility is calculated from recent historical exchange rates, whereas implied volatility is obtained from the option price rather than the exchange rate, and therefore reflects the market view of future volatility. It is difficult to tell which is correct or which should be used in valuation simulation, as both make sense. In Chapter 4, we revisit this example with more complicated volatility models, in which volatility is no longer treated as a constant.

Another issue that deserves attention is the choice of time increment dt. Similar to the day count convention in the bond market, people have different ideas of how many days there are in a year when performing derivative valuation. We usually assume 252 trading days and 360 calendar days in a year. If we use $dt = 1/360$ instead of $1/252$, then the simulated price changes to US$82.933 million. As we can see from the dynamics,

$$dF(t) = (r_d - r_f)F(t)\,dt + \sigma F(t)\,dW(t),$$

the diffusion term of $F(t)$, $\sigma F(t) dW(t)$, grows smaller when dt changes from $1/252$ to $1/360$ and all else remains the same, which is consistent with the fact that volatility is usually much greater when the market is open. When dt changes from $1/252$ to $1/360$, volatility is diluted, and the expected price will be higher according to the negative relationship between volatility and price.

TABLE 3.10 Effect of Risk-Free Rates on Valuation

r_d	r_f	Simulated price
0.03	0.02	−80.102
0.02	0.02	−82.338
0.02	0.03	−83.475

In addition to volatility and the time increment, the risk-free rates are other parameters that are difficult to select. Risk-free rates can be spotted from the zero-coupon yield curves or calculated from the price of the forward contracts available in the market. However, yield curves vary among banks due to different construction methods, and the risk-free rates implied by various forward or future contracts are not always the same. If we refer to financial data servers, then we may be confused about which to use. Relative to volatility and the time increment, however, the risk-free rate selection has few significant effects on the simulation results. To see this clearly, we select a number of possible combinations of (r_d, r_f) and obtain the results presented in Table 3.10. The dynamics, $dF(t) = (r_d - r_f)F(t)\,dt + \sigma F(t)\,dW(t)$, also show that volatility plays a more important role than the drift term. Instead of spending time improving the accuracy of estimated risk-free rate attainment, it is better to perform simulation based on a more reliable range of risk-free rates.

3.5.4 Sensitivity Analysis

After simulating the price of the accumulator, we modify our program to examine the sensitivity of that price to a small change in the underlying parameters such as volatility and the initial exchange rate. Sensitivity analysis helps us measure the risks and potential rewards of derivatives.

Figure 3.3 shows that the price goes in the opposite direction to volatility. As previously noted, this accumulator is equivalent to holding a series of up-and-out call options and selling up-and-out put options to the issuer with maturities the same as the settlement dates. When volatility increases, the value of long position in call options increases but the short position in put options decreases. The exchange rate by that time was 0.6929, which was far below the strike rate. Consequently, the benefits that result from deep out-of-the-money call options cannot compensate the losses accrued from in-the-money put options, because the ratio of call options to put options was 8 : 20 at that time. Therefore, an accumulator may not be a good choice for investors who expect market volatility to increase.

Figure 3.4 illustrates the relationship between price and the initial FX rate. With a higher initial exchange rate, the future exchange rate is likely to remain at a higher level, thereby generating more profit for the holder and resulting in a higher price for the accumulator. Figures 3.3 and 3.4 together show that no matter how small the volatility or how high the initial exchange rate, the price of the accumulator rarely rises above zero. Accordingly, although the exchange rate on July 16, 2008, was 0.9693, which seemed to offer a good deal to investors, the contract that CITIC Pacific entered into was not favorable for the firm just 3 months later. Our simulation results show

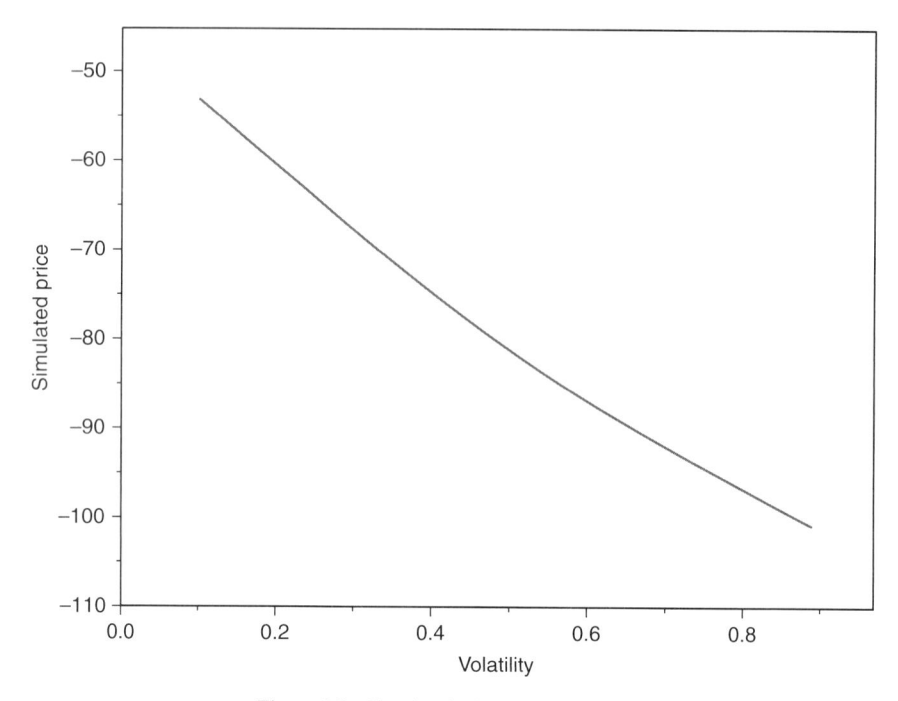

Figure 3.3 Simulated price against volatility.

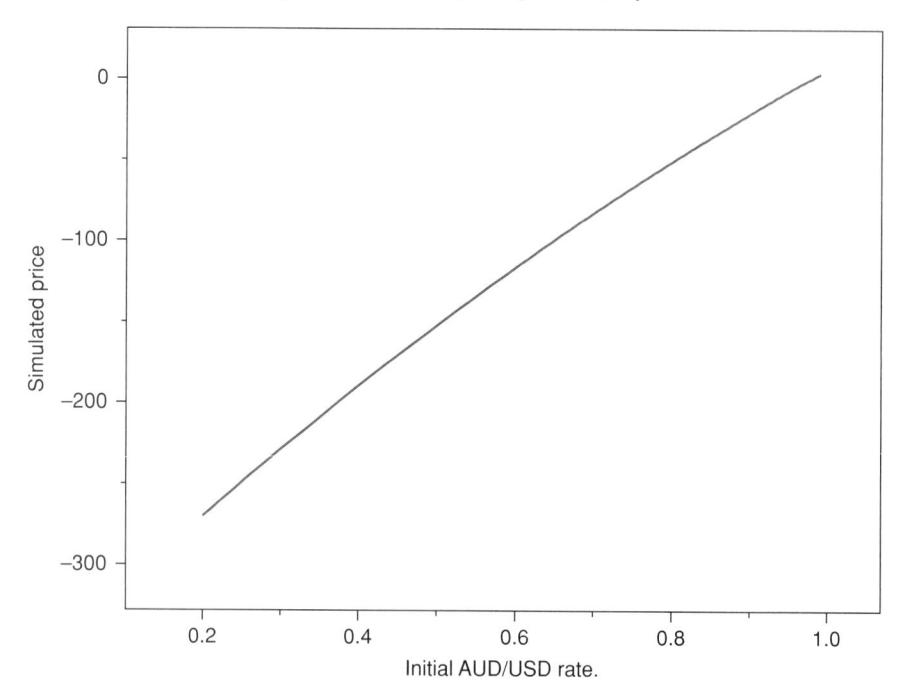

Figure 3.4 Simulated price against initial exchange rate on October 16, 2008.

the aptness of the product's nickname "I will kill you later." In fact, the simulated fair price on July 16, 2008, was US$11.107 million (calculated using the same parameters as before except for the initial exchange rate which was set to 0.9693).

As noted, CITIC Pacific's original objective in purchasing foreign exchange derivatives was to hedge against its exposure to the AUD. Our analysis suggests that accumulators are not good instruments for hedging as their structure is far from fair. The issuer would have to pay CITIC Pacific US$11.107 million for the accumulator in question to be fair to both parties. However, in reality, it entered into the contract without paying anything to CITIC. Also, the accumulator is somewhat equivalent to long calls and short puts. If CITIC Pacific had wanted to limit its losses as due to the rise of the AUD, then it should have held some call options. However, buying an accumulator shorts puts. Although these puts can help reduce the cost of longing calls, it also increases the company's exposure to downside risks. To make matters worse, the upside gain from the accumulator was limited by both the profit target and the barrier rate. Options, forwards, or swaps would have been better instruments for CITIC Pacific. CITIC Pacific was overhedged in any case, as the maximum deliverable amount under the AUD accumulator was AUD9.05 billion, whereas the actual AUD requirement for operational expenditures was only AUD1.6 billion. For further details, please refer to the spreadsheets Ch3.5_Citic_FX_Accumulator_with_Barrier.xls and Ch3.5_Citic_FX_Accumulator_without_Barrier.xls that are downloadable through the web: "http://www.sta.cuhk.edu.hk/hywong".

3.6 LIFE INSURANCE CONTRACTS

3.6.1 Introduction

Participating life policies are investment contracts that are associated with life insurance benefits that specify a benchmark return, a guaranteed annual minimum rate of return, and the distribution of the surplus annual return in excess of that guaranteed return between the insurer and the policy holder. In recently years, these contracts constitute the majority of the life insurance policies traded in the United States, Canada, Japan, and EU member states. Regulatory authorities have increased their monitoring of insurance companies' exposure to the market, credit, and persistence risks induced by participating contracts. For instance, in the United Kingdom, insurers are required to establish realistic balance sheets designed to capture the cost of guarantees and smoothing on a market-consistent basis, to ensure that their provisions are more responsive to changes in the market value of the backing assets of with-profit funds. Hence, implementation of adequate, consistent, and objective models of backing asset behavior and calculation of realistic liabilities have become necessary.

3.6.2 Typical Contract Structures

At the beginning of the contract, the insured party pays a single-sum premium, P_0, to purchase from the insurer a participating policy that expires in T years. The insurance company then invests the funds received in the financial market and acquires portfolio A. The policy's reserve, $P(t)$, where $t < T$, receives interest, which is specified by the guaranteed benefit plus the reversionary bonus according to a smoothing mechanism that depends on each year's market return until contract expiration.

Consider a smoothing mechanism in which the level of its smoothed policy reserve at time t is determined by a linear combination of the unsmoothed value of the reserve at time t and its smoothed value at time $(t-1)$ (see Needleman and Roff, 1995). Note that the linear smoothing scheme is not unique, and other schemes such as arithmetic averaging can also be used. Thus, the policy reserve is defined as

$$P(t) = \alpha P'(t) + (1-\alpha)P(t-1), \alpha \in (0,1), \qquad (3.11)$$
$$P(0) = P_0,$$

where $P'(t)$ is the unsmoothed asset value such that

$$P'(0) = P_0,$$
$$P'(t) = P'(t-1)(1 + r_p(t)),$$
$$r_p(t) = \max\{r_G, \beta r_A\}.$$

Here, r_G and $\beta \in (0,1)$ are the guaranteed rate and the participation rate, respectively, and r_A is the backing asset's annual rate of return, which can be written as

$$r_A = \frac{A(t) - A(t-1)}{A(t-1)}.$$

If death occurs at time t, where $t < T$, then the company returns the remaining policy reserve to the insured, that is,

$$C(t) = P(t-1).$$

Otherwise, at the contract termination date, a bonus payment, $\gamma R(T)$, is given to the insured in addition to the guaranteed amount, which is defined as the extra surplus, $R(T) = \max\{A(T) - P(T), 0\}$, earned by the backing asset. Here γ is the bonus participation rate in the company's surplus declared near contract maturity. To summarize, the insured's payoff at maturity if no death occurs is given by

$$C(T) = \begin{cases} A(T), & \text{if } A(T) < R(T), \\ P(T) + \gamma R(T), & \text{otherwise.} \end{cases} \qquad (3.12)$$

From the terminal payoff and definition of $P(t)$, it is not difficult to see that the value of this type of contract is highly path-dependent. Although the asset process is a GBM, obtaining a closed-form pricing formula is impossible. Thus, simulation is the only solution to the valuation of this contract.

3.6.3 Simulation Algorithms

Because participating contracts are life insurance contracts, mortality risk needs to be included in the valuation process. Let x be the age of the insured, and $T(x)$ be his or her remaining life span at age x. Suppose that the mortality table for a given year can be obtained. From the last column of this table, we obtain the expected future life span, $e(x)$, of an individual of a given sex at age x. For simplicity, we can assume that $T(x)$ follows a certain distribution. Consider a $T(x)$ that is exponentially distributed with mean θ; the cumulative distribution of $T(x) \sim \text{Exp}(\theta)$ is

$$F_{T(x)}(t) = 1 - e^{-\frac{t}{\theta}}.$$

By inverse transform, the remaining future life span t of a given individual of age x can be generated when parameter θ_x is specified such that

$$t = -\theta_x \log(1 - U), \text{ where } U \sim U(0,1).$$

For illustration purposes, we assume that $T(x) \sim \exp(\theta_x)$ and parameter θ_x is specified by the expected future life span of an individual of age x and a given sex, $e(x)$, obtained from the aforementioned mortality table.

Suppose that the asset price process follows GBM under the risk-neutral measure, that is,

$$\frac{dA(t)}{A(t)} = r\,dt + \sigma\,dW_A(t), \tag{3.13}$$

where r is the risk-free rate and σ is the volatility of the asset. The value of the contract can be computed as follows.

1. Specify θ_x from the mortality table, using the client's age and sex.
2. For each path j, generate $t = T(x) \sim \exp(\theta_x)$, which is the stopping time (in years) of the contract. Round t to the next integer.
3. For each step i (year), simulate a new asset value according to Equation 3.13.
4. If step $i = t$, then the payoff of path j is $C(j) = P(j-1)$ discounted by factor e^{-ri}; otherwise, compute $P(j)$ according to Equation 3.11.
5. If step $i = T$, then the payoff of path j is given by Equation 3.12, discounted by e^{-rT}.
6. Repeat Steps 2 to 5 j times.
7. The value of the contract is given by $\frac{1}{j}\sum_{l=1}^{j} C(l)$.

Example 3.3 *Suppose that we need to price a participating life contract of the simplest structure using the foregoing algorithm. Tables 3.11 and 3.12 list the parameter inputs. A total of 500,000 sample paths are generated, and empirical martingale correction is applied. The simulation is repeated 30 times, and the average price and standard deviation are shown in Table 3.13.*

108 STRUCTURED PRODUCTS

TABLE 3.11 Information of the Participating Policy Client

Age	30
Sex	Male
Retirement age	65

TABLE 3.12 Participating Policy Parameters and Underlying Asset Price Process

P_0	100
A_0	100
r	0.05
q	0
σ	0.2
α	0.5
β	0.7
γ	0.01
r_G	0.025

3.7 MULTI-ASSET INSTRUMENTS

There are numerous financial products whose payoffs depend on more than one underlying asset. Basket options, exchange options, and quanto options (options that involve a foreign asset and the FX rate) are typical examples of such multi-asset options. In addition, structured products may also have several underlying assets. The main difficulty in dealing with these multi-asset instruments lies in the generation of their stock price paths.

Consider the case of two assets, S_1 and S_2. Suppose that their risk-neutral dynamics follow multidimensional GBM, that is,

$$dS_i(t) = rS_i(t)\,dt + \sigma_i S_i(t)\,dW_i^*(t), \text{ for } i = 1, 2,$$

where

$$E^Q[dW_1^*(t)\,dW_2^*(t)] = \rho\,dt.$$

By Itô's lemma and the normality of Brownian motion,

$$S_i(T) = S_i(0)\exp\left((r - \frac{\sigma_i^2}{2})T + \sigma_i\sqrt{T}X_i\right), \text{ for } i = 1, 2,$$

TABLE 3.13 Simulation Results

Average price	71.516
Standard deviation	0.0337

where X_1 and X_2 are standard normal random variables with correlation coefficient ρ. Therefore, the problem becomes one of generating a pair of X_1 and X_2:

$$X = \begin{pmatrix} X_1 \\ X_2 \end{pmatrix} \sim \mathcal{N}\left(\begin{pmatrix} 0 \\ 0 \end{pmatrix}, \begin{pmatrix} 1 & \rho \\ \rho & 1 \end{pmatrix}\right).$$

To generate this pair of correlated normal random variables X_1 and X_2, we first decompose X_1 and X_2 into two uncorrelated random normal variables, Z_1 and Z_2, through the linear transformation:

$$Z_1 = X_1,$$
$$Z_2 = \frac{X_2 - \rho X_1}{\sqrt{1-\rho^2}}.$$

Thus, X_1 and X_2 can be generated using two independent normal random variables, Z_1 and Z_2, through the following formula.

$$X_1 = Z_1,$$
$$X_2 = \rho Z_1 + \sqrt{1-\rho^2} Z_2.$$

We can check that $X_1 \sim \mathcal{N}(0,1)$, $X_2 \sim \mathcal{N}(0,1)$, and $\text{Cov}(X_1, X_2) = \text{Corr}(X_1, X_2) = \rho$. If n assets are involved, then a multivariate normal random vector has to be generated. In general, if $X = (X_1, \ldots, X_n)^T$ follows a multivariate normal distribution, then

$$X \sim \mathcal{N}(\boldsymbol{\mu}, \Sigma),$$

where $\boldsymbol{\mu} = \text{E}[X] = (\mu_1, \ldots, \mu_n)^T$ is the mean vector and $\Sigma = \text{Var}(X) = \left[\text{Cov}(X_i, X_j)\right]_{i,j=1,\ldots,n}$ is the variance–covariance matrix. Similar to the bivariate normal case, we first decompose the X_i's into n uncorrelated normal random variables and use independent normal random variables to generate X_i's. To do so, we employ Cholesky decomposition for Σ. Because Σ is a positive semi-definite matrix (i.e., $\boldsymbol{v}^T \Sigma \boldsymbol{v} \geq 0$ for all real vectors $\boldsymbol{v}$), there exists a lower triangular matrix L such that $\Sigma = LL^T$. Cholesky decomposition is an algorithm that obtains this lower triangular matrix L.

Given the matrix L, a random vector $X \sim \mathcal{N}(\boldsymbol{\mu}, \Sigma)$ can be generated by

$$X = \boldsymbol{\mu} + LZ, \text{ where } Z \sim \mathcal{N}(\mathbf{0}, I),$$

where I is the identity matrix of suitable dimensions.

For $n \times n$ matrices $\Sigma = [a_{ij}]$ and $L = [l_{ij}]$, the Cholesky decomposition algorithm works as follows.

1. Set $l_{11} = \sqrt{a_{11}}$.
2. For $j = 2, \ldots, n$, set $l_{j1} = a_{j1}/l_{11}$.
3. For $i = 2, \ldots, n - 1$, perform Steps 4 and 5.
4. Set $l_{ii} = \left[a_{ii} - \sum_{k=1}^{i-1} l_{ik}^2\right]^{1/2}$.
5. For $j = i + 1, \ldots, n$, set $l_{ji} = \frac{1}{l_{ii}}\left[a_{ji} - \sum_{k=1}^{i-1} l_{jk}l_{ik}\right]$.
6. Set $l_{nn} = \left[a_{nn} - \sum_{k=1}^{n-1} l_{nk}^2\right]^{1/2}$.

The following *CDecom* function returns the lower triangular matrix of a symmetric matrix *VCMatrix* following Cholesky decomposition. The algorithm is implemented with the following VBA codes.

```
Public Function CDecom(VCMatrix As Variant) As Variant
  ReDim LArray(1 To UBound(VCMatrix), 1 To UBound(VCMatrix)) _
        As Double
  Dim i As Integer, j As Integer, l As Integer, n As Integer
  n = UBound(VCMatrix)

  LArray(1, 1) = Sqr(VCMatrix(1, 1))
  For j = 2 To n
    LArray(j, 1) = VCMatrix(j, 1) / LArray(1, 1)
  Next j
  For i = 2 To n - 1
    For l = 1 To i - 1
      LArray(i, i) = LArray(i, i) - LArray(i, l) ^ 2
    Next l
    LArray(i, i) = Sqr(VCMatrix(i, i) + LArray(i, i))
    For j = i + 1 To n
      For l = 1 To i - 1
        LArray(j, i) = LArray(j, i) - LArray(j, l) _
                       * LArray(i, l)
      Next l
      LArray(j, i) = (VCMatrix(j, i) + LArray(j, i)) / _
                     LArray(i, i)
    Next j
  Next i
  For l = 1 To n - 1
    LArray(n, n) = LArray(n, n) - LArray(n, l) ^ 2
  Next l
  LArray(n, n) = Sqr(VCMatrix(n, n) + LArray(n, n))

  CDecom = LArray
End Function
```

Function *rCGauss* is used to generate X more conveniently. The corresponding VBA code is as follows.

```
Public Function rCGauss(LArray As Variant) As Variant
  Dim nRV As Integer
  nRV = UBound(LArray)
  Dim i As Integer, j As Integer
  ReDim rNV(1 To nRV) As Double
  ReDim tmpRV(1 To nRV)

  For i = 1 To nRV
    tmpRV(i) = rGauss()
    For j = 1 To i
      rNV(i) = rNV(i) + LArray(i, j) * tmpRV(j)
    Next j
  Next i

  rCGauss = rNV
End Function
```

This function returns an array of $\mathcal{N}(\mathbf{0}, \mathbf{LL}^T)$ random variables, where *LArray* is the lower triangular matrix $\mathbf{L}$ of the variance–covariance matrix.

Consider the following risk-neutral asset dynamics for n assets with correlated Brownian motions.

$$dS_i(t) = r S_i(t)\,dt + \sigma_i S_i(t)\,dW_i^*(t), \text{ for } i = 1, \ldots, n,$$

where

$$\mathrm{E}^{\mathbb{Q}}[dW_i^*(t)\,dW_j^*(t)] = \rho_{ij}\,dt,$$

or, equivalently,

$$S_i(T) = S_i(0)\exp\left(\left(r - \frac{\sigma_i^2}{2}\right)T + \sigma_i\sqrt{T}X_i\right), \text{ for } i = 1, \ldots, n,$$

where $X \sim \mathcal{N}(\mathbf{0}, \Sigma)$ and $\mathbf{0} = (0 \cdot 0)^T$, and Σ is the same as the correlation matrix because $\text{Var}(X_i) = 1$. The n assets' paths can be generated by the following function.

```
Public Function BS_CPath(A() As BS_PathType, CorrMatrix As
      Variant) As Variant
  Dim i As Long, j As Long
  Dim nAsset As Integer, l As Integer
  Dim LArray As Variant
  Dim cRV As Variant

  nAsset = UBound(CorrMatrix) 'VCMatrix(1 to nAsset, 1 to nAsset)
```

```
    LArray = CDecom(CorrMatrix)

    ReDim S(0 To A(1).m, 1 To A(1).n, 1 To nAsset) As Double

    For j = 1 To A(1).n
        For l = 1 To nAsset
            S(0, j, l) = A(l).S0
        Next
    Next

    For i = 1 To A(1).m
        For j = 1 To A(1).n
            cRV = rCGauss(LArray)
            For l = 1 To nAsset
                S(i, j, l) = S(i - 1, j, l) * Exp((A(1).rf -
                A(1).q - A(1).sigma _ ^2 / 2) * A(1).dt +
                Sqr(A(1).dt) * A(1).sigma * cRV(l))
            Next
        Next
        ShowStatus i, A(1).m, 1
    Next

    ResetStatus
    BS_CPath = S
End Function
```

We should input Σ as the *CorrMatrix*. This function returns a three-dimensional array of asset paths S(0 to m, 1 to n, 1 to $nAsset$) according to the correlation matrix, which can be used to price path-dependent multi-asset products. Here m represents the number of steps and n the number of paths.

3.7.1 Multi-Asset Range Accrual Equity-Linked Notes

In this section, we demonstrate the pricing of an existing multi-asset structured product using the aforementioned methods. The product inquisition is a 2-Year HKD 34.00% (annualized basis) Periodic Daily Knock-Out Variable Maturity Range Accrual-Equity-Linked Note. Details of the terms and structure of this RAN can be found in the term sheet in the appendix. To streamline our presentation, we summarize the structure and payoff here.

This RAN is linked to the stock prices of China Communications Construction Company Limited (01800.HK) and Datang International Power Generation Company (00991.HK). Its structure is described in its term sheet as follows.

> 2-Year HKD 34.0% (annualized basis) Periodic Daily Knock-Out Variable Maturity Range Accrual–Equity–Linked Note with 5.67% Fixed Coupon after the

First 2 Months and Variable Coupon Payable 2 Months Thereafter, Subject to Mandatory Early Redemption Provision.

We define the following before proceeding.

S_i^j: Stock price of the jth asset at step (day) i; and S_0^j refers to the initial share price of the jth asset for $j = 1, 2$.

D: Denomination of the note. For this note, $D = 50,000$.

F: Accrual factor, which is used to determine the coupon amount. For this note, $F = \frac{34.0\%}{6} = 5.6667\%$.

K: Conversion price factor and lower range band factor. The conversion price is used to determine the redemption amount at maturity, and the lower range band is used to determine the coupon amount. The conversion price and lower range band for the jth asset is $K S_0^j$, where, for this note, $K = 80\%$.

C: Callable price factor. The callable price is used to determine whether a mandatory early redemption event has occurred. The callable price for the jth asset is $C S_0^j$, where, for this note, $C = 92\%$.

B_1: The starting date of the periodic fixed coupon period.

E_1: The termination date of the periodic fixed coupon period.

B_x: The starting date of the xth periodic variable coupon period. It is equivalent to $S\,dt_x$ in the term sheet. For this note, there are 11 variable coupon periods, and hence $x = 2, \ldots, 12$.

E_x: The termination date of the xth periodic variable coupon period. It is equivalent to $E\,dt_x$ in the term sheet, and hence $x = 2, \ldots, 12$.

n_x: The number of business days in the xth periodic variable coupon period (from B_x to the earlier of E_x and M, if any) on which the closing prices of both shares are greater than or equal to their respective lower range bands, that is, $S_i^1 \geq K S_0^1$ and $S_i^2 \geq K S_0^2$, $i > E_1$ and $x = 2, \ldots, 12$.

N_x: The number of business days in the xth periodic variable coupon period; $x = 2, \ldots, 12$.

$S_i^* = \min\{\frac{S_i^1}{S_0^1}, \frac{S_i^2}{S_0^2}\}$.

M: Mandatory early redemption date, which is the date on which the note is called back. This date is triggered when $S_i^* \geq C$ for $E_1 \leq i < E_{12}$ or, equivalently, when both share prices are equal to or greater than their respective callable prices on or after E_1 and before E_{12}, that is, $S_i^1 \geq C S_0^1$ and $S_i^2 \geq C S_0^2$ for $E_1 \leq i < E_{12}$.

B_x and E_x are expressed as the number of trading days from $B_1 = 1$, and Δt represents the length of a trading day in a given year. In this contract, all payments are made five business days after each payment determination date. For simplicity, assume that payments are made immediately after each payment determination date.

The payment determination dates are essentially the end dates E_x. With the forgoing notations, the structure of this note is as follows.

1. Receive coupon payment $D \times F$ on date E_1 ($x = 1$).
2. If $S_{E_1}^1 \geq CS_0^1$ and $S_{E_1}^2 \geq CS_0^2$, then receive denomination D, and the contract ends.
3. Go to the next period ($x = x + 1$).
4. If $S_i^1 \geq CS_0^1$ and $S_i^2 \geq CS_0^2$ for $B_x \leq i \leq E_x$ if $x = 2, \ldots, 11$, or if $S_i^1 \geq CS_0^1$ and $S_i^2 \geq CS_0^2$ for $B_{12} \leq i < E_{12}$, then mandatory early redemption occurs. Receive coupon payment $D \times \frac{n_x}{N_x} \times F$ plus denomination D, and the contract ends. Otherwise, the contract continues; go to Step 5.
5. Receive coupon payment $D \times \frac{n_x}{N_x} \times F$ on date E_x. If $x < 12$, then go back to Step 3. Otherwise, go to the next step to calculate the payoff at maturity.
6. At maturity, if the share prices of both assets are equal to or greater than their conversion prices, that is, $S_i^1 \geq KS_0^1$ and $S_i^2 \geq KS_0^2$, then receive denomination D. Otherwise, receive $\min\{\frac{D}{KS_0^1}S_{E_{12}}^1, \frac{D}{KS_0^2}S_{E_{12}}^2\}$.

Using S_i^*, the note's structure can be restated as follows.

1. Receive coupon payment $D \times F$ on date E_1 ($x = 1$).
2. If $S_{E_1}^* \geq C$, then receive denomination D, and the contract ends.
3. Go to the next period ($x = x + 1$).
4. If $S_i^* \geq C$ for $B_x \leq i \leq E_x$ if $x = 2, \ldots$, 11 or if $S_i^* \geq C$ for $B_{12} \leq i < E_{12}$, then mandatory early redemption occurs. Receive coupon payment $D \times \frac{n_x}{N_x} \times F$ plus denomination D, and the contract ends. Otherwise, the contract continues; go to Step 5.
5. Receive coupon payment $D \times \frac{n_x}{N_x} \times F$ on date E_x. If $x < 12$, then go back to Step 3. Otherwise, go to the next step to calculate the payoff at maturity.
6. At maturity, receive $D \min\{\frac{S_{E_{12}}^*}{K}, 1\}$.

The price of this note can be calculated using the following steps.

1. Set Coupon $= e^{-rE_1\Delta t} DF$.
2. Set $S_{E_1}^* = \min\{\frac{S_{E_1}^1}{S_0^1}, \frac{S_{E_1}^2}{S_0^2}\}$.
3. If $S_{E_1}^* \geq C$, then set $P = e^{-rE_1\Delta t} D$, and go to Step 13. Otherwise, continue.
4. Set $i = E_1 + 1$, $x = 2$.
5. Set $S_i^* = \min\{\frac{S_i^1}{S_0^1}, \frac{S_i^2}{S_0^2}\}$.
6. If $S_i^* \geq K$, then set $n_x = n_x + 1$.
7. If $S_i^* \geq C$, then set Coupon $=$ Coupon $+ e^{-ri\Delta t} \frac{n_x}{E_x - E_{x-1}} DF$ and $P = e^{-ri\Delta t} D$, and go to Step 13. Otherwise, continue.

8. If $i = E_x$, then set Coupon = Coupon + $e^{-rE_x \Delta t} \frac{n_x}{E_x - E_{x-1}} DF$, $x := x + 1$.
9. Set $i = i + 1$ and repeat Steps 5 to 8 until $i = E_{12}$ (i.e., do not repeat the steps when i = E_{12}).
10. Set $S^*_{E_{12}} = \min \left\{ \frac{S^1_{E_{12}}}{S^1_0}, \frac{S^2_{E_{12}}}{S^2_0} \right\}$.
11. If $S^*_{E_{12}} \geq K$, then set $n_{12} = n_{12} + 1$.
12. Set Coupon = Coupon + $e^{-rE_{12}\Delta t} \frac{n_{12}}{E_{12}-E_{11}} DF$.
13. Set $P = e^{-rE_{12}\Delta t} D \min \left\{ \frac{S^*_{E_{12}}}{K}, 1 \right\}$.
14. Price = P + Coupon (in terms of the present value at t_0).

With the payoff function at the ready, we can begin to estimate the parameters needed to generate the asset paths using the historical share prices of China Communications Construction (Asset 1, denoted by subscript 1) and Datang International Power Generation (Asset 2, denoted by subscript 2) from December 15, 2006, to September 20, 2007. With $S^1_0 = 18.4$, $S^2_0 = 7.8$, $r = 4.6\%$, $q_1 = 0.05\%$, $q_2 = 2.32\%$, $\sigma_1 = 44.33\%$, $\sigma_2 = 60.43\%$, $\rho = 0.3907$, and $n = 30,000$, the simulated price of this structured note on September 20, 2007, is 47,593.75.

The corresponding VBA code is as follows.

```
For j = 1 To n
  'step 1
  coupon = Exp(-rf * td(1) * dt) * D * F
  'step 2
  Snl = Min(S(td(1), j, 1) / S(0, j, 1), S(td(1), j, 2) /
        S(0, j, 2))
  'step 3
  If Snl >= C Then
    price(j) = Exp(-rf * td(1) * dt) * D
    GoTo ContractEnd
  End If
  'step 4
  cP = 2

  For i = td(1) + 1 To m - 1
    'step 5
    Snl = Min(S(i, j, 1) / S(0, j, 1), S(i, j, 2) / S(0, j, 2))
    'step 6
    If Snl >= K Then nBarrier = nBarrier + 1
    'step 7
    If Snl >= C And i < m Then
      coupon = coupon + Exp(-rf * i * dt) * D * F *
               nBarrier / (td(cP) - td(cP - 1))
      price(j) = Exp(-rf * i * dt) * D
```

```
        GoTo ContractEnd
    End If
    'step 8
    If i = td(cP) Then
        coupon = coupon + Exp(-rf * i * dt) * D * F *
                 nBarrier / (td(cP) - td(cP - 1))
        nBarrier = 0
        cP = cP + 1
    End If
  Next i
  'step 10
  Snl = Min(S(m, j, 1) / S(0, j, 1), S(m, j, 2) / S(0, j, 2))
  'step 11
  If Snl >= K Then nBarrier = nBarrier + 1
  'step 12
  cP = 12
  coupon = coupon + Exp(-rf * i * dt) * D * F *
           nBarrier / (td(cP) - td(cP - 1))
  'step 13
  price(j) = Exp(-rf * m * dt) * D * Min(Snl / K, 1)
  ContractEnd:
  price(j) = price(j) + coupon
Next j
```

For further details, please refer to Ch3.7_Multi_Assets_RAN.xls.

3.7.2 Currency-Translated Products

Currency-translated (or quanto) structured products are contingent claims whose payoff is determined by a financial price or index in a foreign currency, but whose actual payout is made in the domestic currency. Confusion arises in the pricing of quanto products because an appropriate risk-neutral measure must be selected. Should it be the domestic or foreign risk-neural measure? More precisely, what domestic and foreign interest rates should be placed in the asset dynamics? The answer is very simple. The risk-neutral measure should be that corresponding to the contract's settlement currency, in other words, the domestic risk-neutral measure. However, Theorem 25 links the domestic and foreign risk-neutral valuations, and thus one can always transform the valuation from one risk-neutral measure to the other.

We consider a vanilla RAN contingent upon a foreign index as our example. Let the foreign index value be $S(t)$ at time t. If the index falls between L and H on a particular date, where $L < H$, then the RAN holder receives accrual interest in the domestic currency on that date. Further suppose that this RAN has a maturity of 1 year and that all cash transactions will be settled on the maturity date in the domestic currency. Then, for a $100 initial deposit, the RAN has a payoff of

$$RAN(T=1) = 100 \times \left(1 + \frac{c}{252} \sum_{j=1}^{252} 1_{\{L \leq S(t_j) \leq H\}}\right),$$

where c is the maximum accrual interest received by the RAN holder and 252 is the number of trading days in the year. Hence, by risk-neutral valuation, the present value of this RAN reads

$$RAN(0) = 100 e^{-r_d} \left[1 + \frac{c}{252} \sum_{j=1}^{252} \mathbb{Q}^d(L \leq S(t_j) \leq H)\right],$$

where r_d is the domestic instantaneous interest rate and $\mathbb{Q}^d$ is the domestic risk-neutral measure.

This RAN appears to be a single-asset structured product, but its valuation incurs multi-asset pricing analysis because the contribution of the FX rate must be taken into account. As a foreign financial variable, the foreign risk-neutral dynamic for $S(t)$ is clear. If we assume that $S(t)$ follows the BS model, then its foreign risk-neutral dynamic is

$$dS(t) = r_f S(t) dt + \sigma S(t) d\widehat{W}_S(t), \text{ which implies } S(T)$$
$$= S(t) e^{\left(r_f - \frac{\sigma_S^2}{2}\right)(T-t) + \sigma(\widehat{W}_S(T) - \widehat{W}_S(t))}, \quad (3.14)$$

where r_f is the foreign instantaneous interest rate, $\widehat{W}_S(t)$ is the $\mathbb{Q}^f$-standard Brownian motion driving index $S(t)$, and $\mathbb{Q}^f$ is the foreign risk-neutral measure. However, domestic risk-neutral valuation requires that we compute the expectation using the $\mathbb{Q}^d$ dynamics of $S(t)$.

Under $\mathbb{Q}^d$, in Section 3.5, we derived the risk-neutral dynamics of the FX rate as

$$dF(t) = (r_d - r_f) F(t) dt + \sigma_F F(t) dW^*(t).$$

To derive the $\mathbb{Q}^d$ dynamics for $S(t)$, we first substitute $V(F(T), S(T)) = 1/F(T)$ into Theorem 3.1. By this theorem, we have

$$\frac{1}{F(t)} e^{-(r_f - r_d)(T-t)} = \mathrm{E}^{\mathbb{Q}^f} \left[\frac{1}{F(T)}\right].$$

In other words, the DOM-FOR FX rate $1/F(t)$ has $\mathbb{Q}^f$ dynamics

$$d\left(\frac{1}{F(t)}\right) = (r_f - r_d) \left(\frac{1}{F(t)}\right) dt + \sigma_F \left(\frac{1}{F(t)}\right) d\widehat{W}(t).$$

Hence,

$$\frac{1}{F(T)} = \frac{1}{F(t)} e^{\left(r_f - r_d - \frac{\sigma_F^2}{2}\right)(T-t) + \sigma_F(\widehat{W}(T) - \widehat{W}(t))}. \tag{3.15}$$

Assume that the correlation coefficient between the returns of $F(t)$ and $S(t)$ is ρ. Then, that between the returns of $1/F(t)$ and $S(t)$ should be $-\rho$ because $F(t)$ and $1/F(t)$ must go in opposite directions. Hence, we have $\mathrm{E}^{\mathbb{Q}^f}[d\widehat{W}_S(t) d\widehat{W}(t)] = -\rho\, dt$.

Next, substitute $V(F(T), S(T)) = S(T)/F(T)$ into Theorem 3.1. By this theorem, we have

$$\mathrm{E}^{\mathbb{Q}^d}[S(T)] = F(t) e^{-(r_f - r_d)(T-t)} \mathrm{E}^{\mathbb{Q}^f}\left[\frac{1}{F(T)} \times S(T)\right].$$

Substituting Equations 3.14 and 3.15 into the right-hand side yields

$$\mathrm{E}^{\mathbb{Q}^d}[S(T)] = S(t) e^{r_f(T-t)} e^{-\frac{1}{2}(\sigma_F^2 + \sigma^2)(T-t)} \mathrm{E}^{\mathbb{Q}^f}$$
$$\left[\exp\left(\sigma(\widehat{W}_S(T) - \widehat{W}_S(t)) + \sigma_F(\widehat{W}(T) - \widehat{W}(t))\right)\right].$$

The sum of the two normal random variables is also a normal random variable, and

1. $\mathrm{E}^{\mathbb{Q}^f}\left[\sigma(\widehat{W}_S(T) - \widehat{W}_S(t)) + \sigma_F(\widehat{W}(T) - \widehat{W}(t))\right] = 0$;
2. $\mathrm{E}^{\mathbb{Q}^f}\left[(\sigma(\widehat{W}_S(T) - \widehat{W}_S(t)) + \sigma_F(\widehat{W}(T) - \widehat{W}(t)))^2\right]$
$= \left(\sigma^2 - 2\rho\sigma\sigma_F + \sigma_F^2\right)(T-t).$

Using the moment-generating function of a normal random variable, it is clear that

$$\mathrm{E}^{\mathbb{Q}^d}[S(T)] = S(t) e^{(r_f - \rho\sigma\sigma_F)(T-t)}.$$

Hence, the $\mathbb{Q}^d$ dynamics of $S(t)$ are deduced as

$$\frac{dS(t)}{S(t)} = (r_f - \rho\sigma\sigma_F)\, dt + \sigma\, dW_S^*(t) \text{ or } d\log S(t)$$
$$= (r_f - \rho\sigma\sigma_F - \sigma^2/2)\, dt + \sigma\, dW_S^*(t). \tag{3.16}$$

Simulation can be constructed on the basis of Equation 3.16.

For this foreign-index-linked vanilla RAN, a closed-form solution can also be derived using Equation 3.16. Probability

$$\mathbb{Q}^d(L \le S(t_j) \le H) = \mathbb{Q}^d(S(t_j) \le H) - \mathbb{Q}^d(S(t_j) < L)$$

can be expressed in terms of standard normal CDF Ψ. More specifically, event $\{S(t_j) \leq H\}$ is equivalent to $\{W_S^*(t_j) \leq -d_j^*(H)\sqrt{t_j}\}$, where

$$d_j^*(H) = \frac{\log \frac{S}{H} + (r_f - \rho\sigma\sigma_F - \sigma^2/2)t_j}{\sigma\sqrt{t_j}}.$$

Hence, the present value of the RAN is given by

$$RAN(0) = 100e^{-r_d}\left[1 + \frac{c}{252}\sum_{j=1}^{252}\left(\Psi(d_j^*(H)) - \Psi(d_j^*(L))\right)\right].$$

We recognize that this RAN is affected by the FX rate through its volatility, σ_F, and the correlation between the FX and the index returns, ρ, in addition to the dynamics of the foreign index.

In general, for a quanto-type structured product, simulation can be constructed using the joint dynamics of the FX rate and the foreign assets under the domestic risk-neutral measure. Simulation involving one foreign asset and the FX rate uses the stochastic differential equation (SDE):

$$d\log F(t) = (r_d - r_f - \frac{\sigma_F^2}{2})dt + \sigma_F\, dW^*(t),$$

$$d\log S(t) = (r_f - \rho\sigma\sigma_F - \frac{\sigma^2}{2})dt + \sigma\, dW_S^*(t),$$

$$E^{\mathbb{Q}^d}[dW^*(t)dW_S^*(t)] = \rho\, dt.$$

4

Volatility Modeling

The Black–Scholes (BS) model assumes constant volatility. However, most empirical studies strongly reject both this assumption and the normality assumption made by the BS model. To enhance the flexibility of the underlying asset dynamics to better fit market data, the constant volatility assumption must be relaxed and volatility is modeled as a deterministic function or even stochastic process. This chapter demonstrates applications of these more appropriate models.

We begin with a local volatility model that simply modifies the BS model by replacing constant volatility with a deterministic function of time and the underlying asset price. The function is then calibrated to the observed option data. Theoretic grounds for such calibration include the ability of the observed call and put option prices to deduce the risk-neutral distribution of the underlying asset price if the risk-neutral valuation is correct.

Theorem 4.1 *Assume that the risk-neutral valuation is correct. Suppose that we observe a spectrum of call option prices against strike prices $(c(S, K, T), K)$ with the same maturity date T. Then, the risk-neutral survival function of the underlying asset price at T is given by*

$$\mathbb{Q}(S_T > K) = -e^{rT} \frac{\partial c}{\partial K}.$$

If we further assume that the risk-neutral probability density function, $\varphi(S_T, T)$, exists, then

$$\varphi(S_T, T) = e^{rT} \frac{\partial^2 c}{\partial K^2}.$$

Handbook of Financial Risk Management: Simulations and Case Studies, First Edition. N.H. Chan and H.Y. Wong.
© 2013 John Wiley & Sons, Inc. Published 2013 by John Wiley & Sons, Inc.

Proof: By the foregoing risk-neutral valuation,

$$c(S, K, T) = e^{-rT} E^{\mathbb{Q}}[\max(S_T - K, 0)] = e^{-rT} \int_K^\infty (S_T - K) \, d\mathbb{Q}.$$

As we observe many call prices with a different K, we can draw a curve that represents the call option price as a function of K. In practice, this is done using interpolation methods. Differentiating a call with respect to K yields

$$\frac{\partial c}{\partial K} = -e^{-rT} \int_K^\infty d\mathbb{Q}.$$

If the probability density function exists, then differentiating the foregoing call gives the result for $\varphi(S_T, T)$.

In other words, if we observe numerous call and put option prices, then these prices are sufficient to allow us to estimate or imply the risk-neutral distribution of the underlying asset price without considering its history. However, the entire stochastic evolution of the underlying asset price remains unknown, and the valuation of path-dependent options and contracts is infeasible. Thus, practitioners modify this process to fit option prices to a local volatility model to allow them to simulate the paths of the underlying asset under $\mathbb{Q}$.

This local volatility model has several limitations. For example, it presumes volatility to be deterministic, a presumption that has also been rejected by empirical studies, as risk (volatility) can change randomly over time. From the practical perspective, traders have discovered that when a local volatility model is fit to an option price, it still exhibits a large degree of error in capturing the implied volatilities that are market quotes.

A local volatility model extension is to allow volatility to be driven by another stochastic variable. One difficulty with such stochastic volatility models, however, is that they increase the number of random variables and render simulation less efficient, although this is a minor issue given modern computing power.

4.1 LOCAL VOLATILITY MODELS: SIMULATION AND BINOMIAL TREE

As noted, in the BS world, volatility is assumed to be constant, and the stock price is assumed to evolve continuously. In practice, it is widely known that volatility is not in fact a constant, as reflected in the volatility smile and jumps in stock prices. In this section, we introduce the local volatility models that extend the BS model.

In a local volatility model, volatility $\sigma(S(t), t)$ is a deterministic function of stock price $S(t)$ and time t. The dynamics of a stock price in the physical world are given by

$$dS(t) = \mu S(t) \, dt + \sigma(S(t), t) S(t) \, dW(t). \tag{4.1}$$

The discrete approximation is

$$S_i = S_{i-1} + \mu S_{i-1} \Delta t + \sigma(S_{i-1}, t_i) S_{i-1} \sqrt{\Delta t} Z_i, \qquad (4.2)$$

where Z_i is a standard normal random variable. If the exact form of the local volatility function $\sigma(S(t), t)$ is known, then only slight modification is needed when the simulation is changed from the BS model to a local volatility model. We simply need to replace constant volatility σ in the BS simulation algorithm with function $\sigma(S_{i-1}, t_i)$, which represents the volatility of stock price S_{i-1} at time t_i. The corresponding VBA code is

```
S(i, j) = S(i - 1, j) + (A.rf - A.q) * S(i - 1, j) * dt _
 + LocalVol(S(i-1, j), i*dt) * S(i-1, j) * Sqr(dt) * rGauss()
```

A key advantage of local volatility models is that they preserve the BS hedging argument and the risk-neutral valuation. As the physical dynamic of $S(t)$ in Equation 4.1 contains only one stochastic factor, $W(t)$, the BS hedging procedure can be retained to produce an extended BS equation.

$$\frac{\partial}{\partial t} c(t, S) + rS \frac{\partial}{\partial S} c(t, S) + \frac{1}{2} \sigma(t, S)^2 S^2 \frac{\partial^2}{\partial S^2} c(t, S) = rc(t, S),$$
$$c(T, S) = \max(S - K, 0).$$

We can replace constant volatility in this BS equation directly with the local volatility function. Moreover, we can retain the risk-neutral valuation (Eq. 2.12), although the risk-neutral dynamics of S are revised to

$$dS(t) = rS(t)\,dt + \sigma(S(t), t)S(t)\,dW^*(t). \qquad (4.3)$$

4.1.1 Calibration of Local Volatility Function and Dupire Equation

Calibration of the local volatility function can be formulated using the Dupire (1994) equation. Suppose that we observe call option prices with different strikes maturities, that is, we have a sample of $(K, T, c(K, T))$, at the present time $t = 0$. We can interpolate and extrapolate the observed call prices to form a surface, and we therefore theoretically assume the function $c(K, T)$ to be known. Our goal is to extract the local volatility function, $\sigma(t, S(t))$, from function $c(K, T)$.

We are able to (numerically) obtain the differentials $\frac{\partial c}{\partial K}$, $\frac{\partial^2 c}{\partial K^2}$, and $\frac{\partial c}{\partial T}$ from function $c(K, T)$. The expressions for the first two differentials are presented in Theorem 4.1, and for the third differential, we have

$$\frac{\partial c}{\partial T} = \frac{\partial}{\partial T}\left[e^{-rT} \int_K^\infty (S_T - K)\varphi(S_T, T)\,dS_T \right]$$
$$= -rc + e^{-rT} \int_K^\infty (S_T - K) \frac{\partial \varphi(S_T, T)}{\partial T}\,dS_T.$$

The risk-neutral process (Eq. 4.3) confirms that this is a Markov process, and hence $\varphi(S_T, T)$ is the transition density function that satisfies the forward Kolmogorov equation (or Fokker–Plank equation):

$$\frac{\partial \varphi(S, T)}{\partial T} = -\frac{\partial}{\partial S}[rS\varphi(S, T)] + \frac{1}{2}\frac{\partial^2}{\partial S^2}[\sigma(t, S)^2 S^2 \varphi(S, T)].$$

Thus,

$$\frac{\partial c}{\partial T} + rc = e^{-rT} \int_K^\infty (S - K)\left[-\frac{\partial}{\partial S}[rS\varphi(S, T)] + \frac{1}{2}\frac{\partial^2}{\partial S^2}[\sigma(t, S)^2 S^2 \varphi(S, T)]\right] dS.$$

Integration by parts yields the Dupire equation:

$$\frac{\partial c}{\partial T} = -rK\frac{\partial c}{\partial K} + \frac{1}{2}K^2 \sigma(T, K)^2 \frac{\partial^2 c}{\partial K^2},$$

or

$$\sigma(K, T) = \sqrt{2\frac{\frac{\partial c}{\partial T} + rK\frac{\partial c}{\partial K}}{K^2 \frac{\partial^2 c}{\partial K^2}}}.$$

In practice, the local volatility is unknown and must be calibrated to the market prices of the option data. To demonstrate such calibration, we first employ a fictitious local volatility function

$$\sigma(S, t) = 0.1 + \left(\frac{S - 90}{100}\right)^2 t^{0.1}. \tag{4.4}$$

Note that this function captures two characteristics of the local volatility: that it is a decreasing function of the stock price and an increasing function of time. The shape of Equation 4.4 is illustrated in Figure 4.1.

The corresponding VBA code for the function *LocalVol* used in the simulation is as follows.

```
Public Function LocalVol (S As Double, t As Double)
  LocalVol = 0.1 + ((S - 90) / 100) ^ 2 * (t ^ 0.1)
End Function
```

With $S_0 = 50$, $r = 5\%$, $q = 0\%$, $n = 200,000$, and $dt = 1/360$, we can generate a call price surface using the stock price paths from Equation 4.2. The call prices and their corresponding true local volatilities are presented in Tables 4.1 and 4.2, respectively.

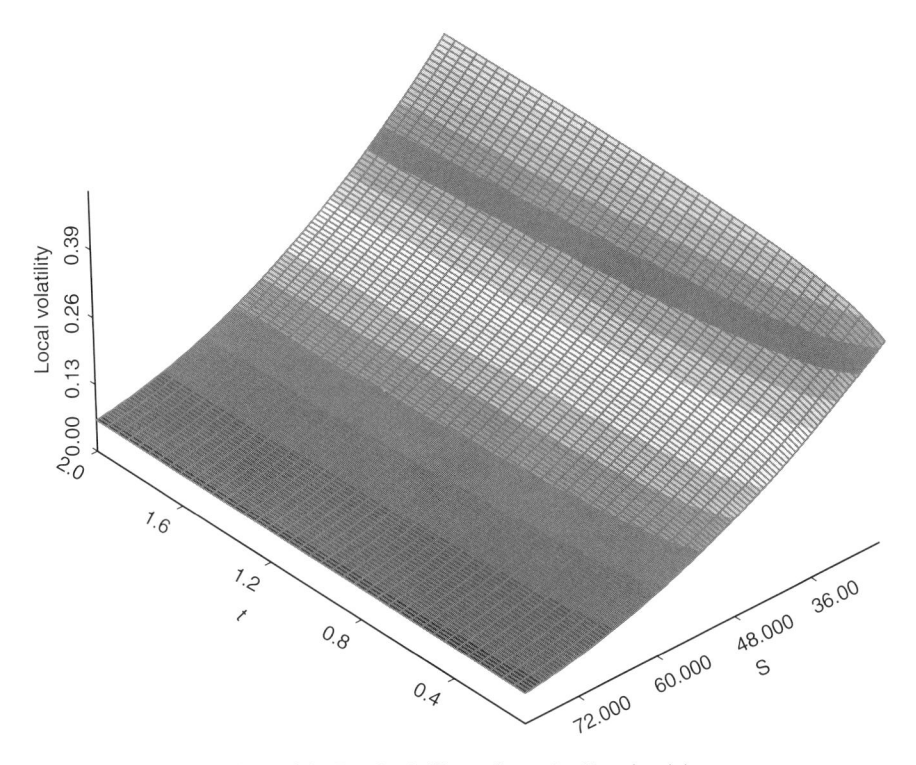

Figure 4.1 Local volatility surface using Equation 4.4.

TABLE 4.1 Generated Call Prices

Strike\Maturity	0.25	0.5	1	1.5	2
20	30.24844	30.49401	30.99557	31.54363	32.12791
30	20.37296	20.76163	21.68060	22.68283	23.68910
40	10.57732	11.38030	13.04635	14.56893	15.96776
50	2.57212	3.93215	6.07283	7.84000	9.39895
60	0.09283	0.54232	1.82616	3.16497	4.48168
70	0.00013	0.01510	0.26502	0.80525	1.53652
80	0.00000	0.00005	0.01248	0.10239	0.32781

TABLE 4.2 True Local Volatility

Strike\Maturity	0.25	0.5	1	1.5	2
20	0.52657	0.55719	0.59000	0.61028	0.62517
30	0.41340	0.43589	0.46000	0.47490	0.48584
40	0.31764	0.33326	0.35000	0.36034	0.36794
50	0.23929	0.24929	0.26000	0.26662	0.27148
60	0.17835	0.18397	0.19000	0.19372	0.19646
70	0.13482	0.13732	0.14000	0.14166	0.14287
80	0.10871	0.10933	0.11000	0.11041	0.11072

126   VOLATILITY MODELING

We employ two methods to calibrate the local volatility and compare the results with known values. The first method uses the Dupire (1994) equation,

$$\sigma(K,T) = \sqrt{2\frac{\frac{\partial c}{\partial T} + rK\frac{\partial c}{\partial K}}{K^2 \frac{\partial^2 c}{\partial K^2}}}, \quad (4.5)$$

where $c(K, t)$ is the price of a call with strike K and time-to-maturity T.

The second method is that proposed by Derman and Kani (1994), who approximate the implied volatility $\Sigma(K, t)$ as the average of local volatility $\sigma(K, t)$ and state the following relation.

$$\Sigma(K,T) \approx \frac{1}{K - S(0)} \int_{S(0)}^{K} \sigma(S,T)\,dS.$$

If the local volatility is restricted to being independent of t and to vary linearly with the price, that is,

$$\sigma(K,T) = \sigma_0 + \beta K, \quad (4.6)$$

then

$$\Sigma(K,T) \approx \sigma_0 + \frac{\beta}{2}(S(0) + K). \quad (4.7)$$

Substituting Equation 4.6 into Equation 4.7, after simplification, local volatility $\sigma(S, t)$ is approximated by

$$\sigma(K,T) \approx \Sigma(S(0),T) + 2(\Sigma(K,T) - \Sigma(S(0),T)). \quad (4.8)$$

We first test the second method with the call surface generated to check whether it is able to recover the local volatility surface. We convert the generated market option prices to the implied volatility surface. The converted values of the implied volatilities are listed in Table 4.3, in which the bicubic spline is used to smooth the surface and interpolate the implied local volatilities at different strikes and times-to-maturity. The

TABLE 4.3   Implied Volatility of the Generated Call Prices

Strike\Maturity	0.25	0.5	1	1.5	2
20	0.32507	0.36015	0.37983	0.39002	0.39593
30	0.29650	0.31198	0.32757	0.33427	0.33915
40	0.26039	0.27183	0.28336	0.28863	0.29262
50	0.22692	0.23559	0.24497	0.24982	0.25297
60	0.19719	0.20374	0.21174	0.21555	0.21851
70	0.17523	0.17692	0.18295	0.18593	0.18860
80	0.12918	0.15708	0.15893	0.16142	0.16416

TABLE 4.4 Local Volatilities Estimated with Method 2

Strike\Maturity	0.25	0.5	1	1.5	2
20	0.42321	0.48471	0.51469	0.53022	0.53889
30	0.36608	0.38837	0.41016	0.41871	0.42533
40	0.29386	0.30806	0.32176	0.32743	0.33227
50	0.22692	0.23559	0.24497	0.24982	0.25297
60	0.16746	0.17189	0.17851	0.18128	0.18404
70	0.12354	0.11825	0.12094	0.12203	0.12423
80	0.03143	0.07856	0.07289	0.07301	0.07535

calibrated local volatilities and their percentage errors at these nodes are presented in Tables 4.4 and 4.5. Figure 4.2 shows the percentage error of the calibrated local volatility surface from time 0 to time 2.25, and strike 5 to strike 95. For further details, please refer to

Ch4.2_Local_Volatility_Method_2.xls.

It can be seen from Figure 4.2 that Method 2 consistently underestimates the local volatility because the approximation assumes the linear relationship between local volatility and the stock price to be independent of time. If we instead employ a quadratic relationship between the two, then calibration of the local volatility remains quite good in the central region covered by the call option. We discuss the effect of underestimation later in the chapter. When the stock price is in the range of 30 to 70, the average error is about 10%. When it is below 20 or above 70, the quality of the estimate worsens, and when it is beyond call option coverage (below 20 or above 80), this method can even produce negative local volatility. However, the error varies very little over time.

We next employ Equation 4.5 to calibrate local volatility, for which we require differentials $\frac{\partial c}{\partial T}$, $\frac{\partial c}{\partial K}$, and $\frac{\partial^2 c}{\partial K^2}$. An intuitive way of proceeding is to use a bicubic spline to fit the call surface and then calculate these partial derivatives from the fitting result. Although a call price estimated via direct fitting is close to the simulated price, partial derivatives calculated in this way are numerically unstable. They render the estimation highly inaccurate and are unable to produce an estimate, as the products inside the square root are very often negative. Accordingly, rather than use the call price for the bicubic spline, we fit the implied volatility calculated from the call option

TABLE 4.5 Percentage Error in Local Volatility Estimation with Method 2

Strike\Maturity	0.25	0.5	1	1.5	2
20	−19.63%	−13.01%	−12.76%	−13.12%	−13.80%
30	−11.45%	−10.90%	−10.83%	−11.83%	−12.45%
40	−7.49%	−7.56%	−8.07%	−9.13%	−9.70%
50	−5.17%	−5.49%	−5.78%	−6.30%	−6.82%
60	−6.10%	−6.57%	−6.05%	−6.42%	−6.32%
70	−8.37%	−13.89%	−13.61%	−13.85%	−13.05%
80	−71.08%	−28.14%	−33.74%	−33.88%	−31.94%

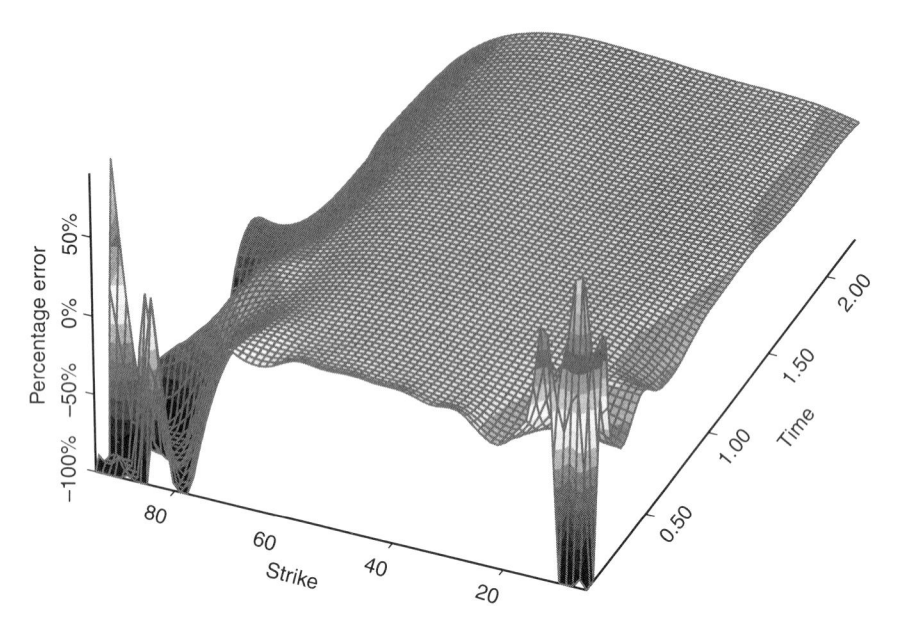

Figure 4.2 Percentage error in local volatility estimation with Method 2.

price and create an implied volatility surface. As there are no closed-form formulas for the partial derivatives in a local volatility model, we have to employ the finite difference method to approximate them, as follows.

$$\frac{\partial C}{\partial T} \approx \frac{C(K, T+h) - C(K, T-h)}{2h},$$

$$\frac{\partial C}{\partial K} \approx \frac{C(K+h, T) - C(K+h, T)}{2h},$$

$$\frac{\partial^2 C}{\partial K^2} \approx \frac{C(K+h, T) - 2C(K, T) + C(K-h, T)}{h^2}.$$

We use the implied volatility surface to calculate the call option prices in the BS formula to estimate the partial derivatives at the desired K and T. Tables 4.6 and 4.7

TABLE 4.6 Estimated Local Volatilities with Method 1

Strike\Maturity	0.25	0.5	1	1.5	2
20	0.42737	0.56095	0.55818	0.62484	0.64256
30	0.38206	0.43451	0.45678	0.47063	0.48749
40	0.31120	0.33655	0.34901	0.35763	0.37259
50	0.23766	0.25111	0.25876	0.26620	0.26913
60	0.17888	0.18558	0.19152	0.19288	0.19876
70	0.12592	0.13720	0.14204	0.13972	0.14369
80	0.06176	0.13240	0.09047	0.11324	0.10801

TABLE 4.7 Percentage Error in Estimated Local Volatilities with Method 1

Strike\Maturity	0.25	0.5	1	1.5	2
20	−18.84%	0.68%	−5.39%	2.39%	2.78%
30	−7.58%	−0.32%	−0.70%	−0.90%	0.34%
40	−2.03%	0.99%	−0.28%	−0.75%	1.26%
50	−0.68%	0.73%	−0.48%	−0.16%	−0.87%
60	0.29%	0.87%	0.80%	−0.43%	1.17%
70	−6.61%	−0.09%	1.46%	−1.36%	0.57%
80	−43.18%	21.10%	−17.75%	2.56%	−2.44%

list the estimated local volatilities and their percentage errors, and Figure 4.3 illustrates the percentage error of the estimated local volatility surface for time from 0 to 2.25 and the strike prices from 5 to 95. At $K = 20$ and $T = 0.5$, this method fails to produce an estimate.

Unlike Method 2, Equation 4.5 does not consistently underestimate local volatility, and it produces very nice estimates in the central region. It can be observed that when the price is between 20 and 80, the estimation is within a 5% error rate. In the central region, this method's performance is excellent, with error of only about 1%. Again, when the price is lower than 20 or higher than 80, estimate quality worsens, and the method sometimes fails to produce a real number as the value of the square root becomes negative. For more details, please refer to Ch4.2_Local_Volatility_Method_1.xls.

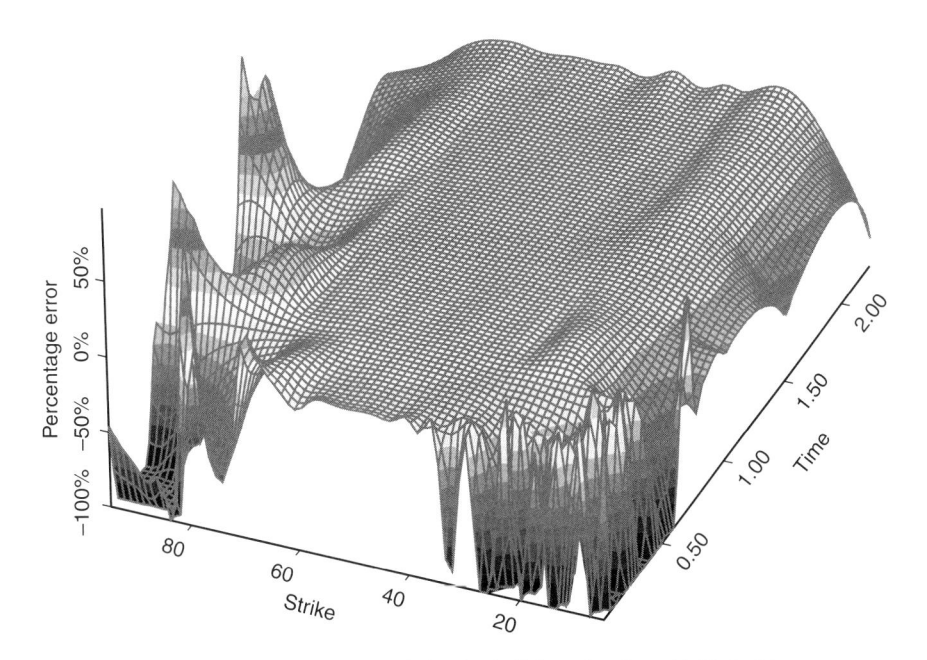

Figure 4.3 Percentage error in local volatilities estimation with Method 1.

For simulation, we need to handle the region in which calibration is imprecise. We employ the minimum (or maximum) value of the strike price from the option data when that price falls below (or above, respectively) the average strike price, which means that when the stock price falls below 20, we approximate its local volatility using the stock price 20. When the stock price rises above 80, we approximate its local volatility using a stock price of 80. If the equation fails to provide an estimate, then we assign a default value (20%) for simplicity.

For $S_0 = 50$, $r = 5\%$, $q = 0$, $K = 55$, $T = 1.75$, $dt = 1/360$, and $n = 20,000$, the simulated price of a call option using the local volatility estimated from Dupire's (1994) Equation is 5.92, which is close to the price (5.81) that is simulated under the actual local volatility function in Equation 4.4. In simulation, the stock price falls below 20 or rises above 80 about 230,000 times, accounting for around 1.8% of the total local volatilities estimated. Of the $10,000 \times 270 = 2,700,000$ estimation times, only about 0.5% fail to produce an estimate.

Recall that in Method 2, the simulated price was 5.63, which is lower than the simulated price using actual local volatility and Method 1. The degree of underestimation does not improve even when the number of paths is increased. Method 2 produces an estimation percentage error of about 3.1%, whereas Method 1's error rate is 1.9%. For more details, please refer to

Ch4.2_Local_Volatility_Simulation_European_Option.xls.

We also test the two methods for a call option with knock-out features. In this case, $S_0 = 50$, $r = 5\%$, $q = 0$, $K = 45$, $T = 1$, $dt = 1/360$, knock-out price $= 65$, and $n = 200,00$. The simulated price under actual local volatility is 4.08, and that using Method 1 is 4.02, which is about a 1.4% percentage error. Method 2 produces a simulated price of 4.40, which constitutes a nearly 7.8% percentage error. The simulated price is overestimated because the underestimation of local volatility means that the call option is knocked out less often. To correct the local volatility surface in Method 2, we first generate another call surface with local volatility estimated by Method 2 as shown in Figure 4.4. We then compare the local volatility estimated by the new call surface $\widehat{\sigma}_2(S, T)$ with the original estimation $\widehat{\sigma}_1(S, T)$ and set

$$\alpha(S, T) = \frac{\widehat{\sigma}_1(S, T)}{\widehat{\sigma}_2(S, T)},$$

$$\widehat{\sigma}(S, T) = \alpha(S, T)\widehat{\sigma}_1(S, T),$$

where $\widehat{\sigma}(S, T)$ is our corrected local volatility. Tables 4.8 and 4.9 list the corrected local volatilities and their percentage errors. We can see that the underestimation is somewhat rectified. The simulated price of this call option with knock-out features and corrected local volatility is 4.1, which is close to 4.08.

4.1.2 Implied Binomial Tree

Another method for capturing local volatility is the implied tree. Here, we demonstrate how to build an implied binomial tree with uniformly spaced levels that are Δt apart.

TABLE 4.8 Estimated Local Volatilities with Method 2 After Correction

Strike\Maturity	0.25	0.5	1	1.5	2
20	0.42119	0.55941	0.54732	0.58024	0.60149
30	0.48393	0.41423	0.43918	0.45299	0.46732
40	0.30207	0.32082	0.33987	0.34992	0.36102
50	0.22895	0.24450	0.25808	0.26470	0.27080
60	0.17602	0.18234	0.18976	0.19318	0.19710
70	0.11615	0.13415	0.13898	0.13836	0.14052
80	0.04847	0.20028	0.09996	0.11113	0.10863

TABLE 4.9 Percentage Errors in Estimated Local Volatilities with Method 2 After Correction

Strike\Maturity	0.25	0.5	1	1.5	2
20	−20.01%	0.40%	−7.23%	−4.92%	−3.79%
30	17.06%	−4.97%	−4.53%	−4.61%	−3.81%
40	−4.90%	−3.73%	−2.89%	−2.89%	−1.88%
50	−4.32%	−1.92%	−0.74%	−0.72%	−0.25%
60	−1.31%	−0.89%	−0.13%	−0.28%	0.33%
70	−13.85%	−2.31%	−0.73%	−2.33%	−1.65%
80	−55.41%	83.19%	−9.13%	0.65%	−1.88%

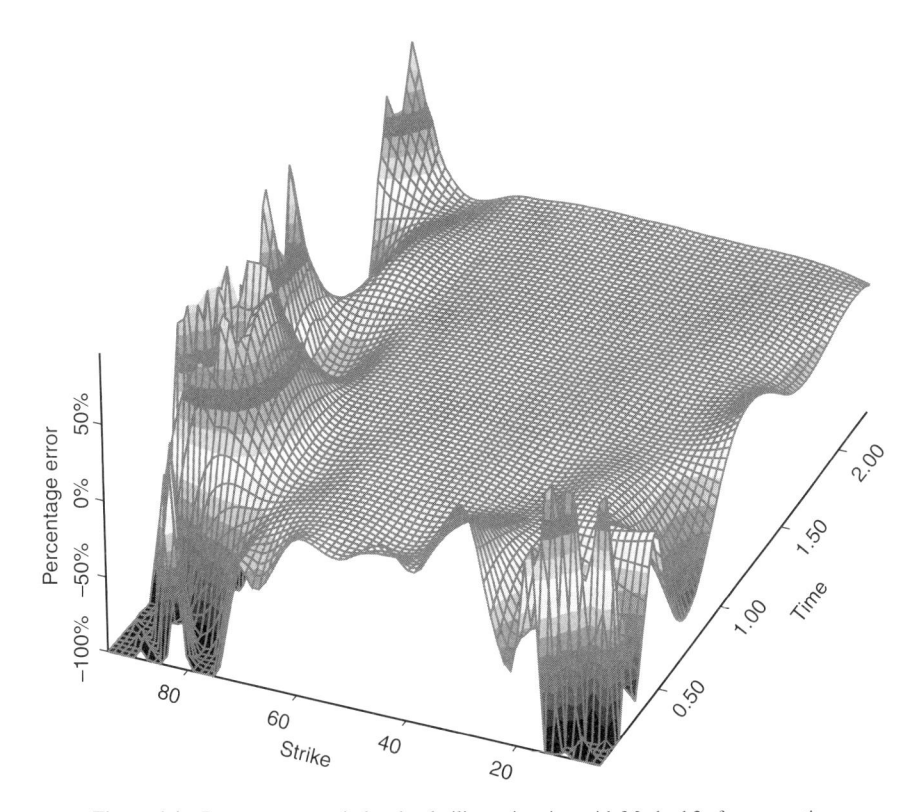

Figure 4.4 Percentage error in local volatility estimation with Method 2 after correction.

132 VOLATILITY MODELING

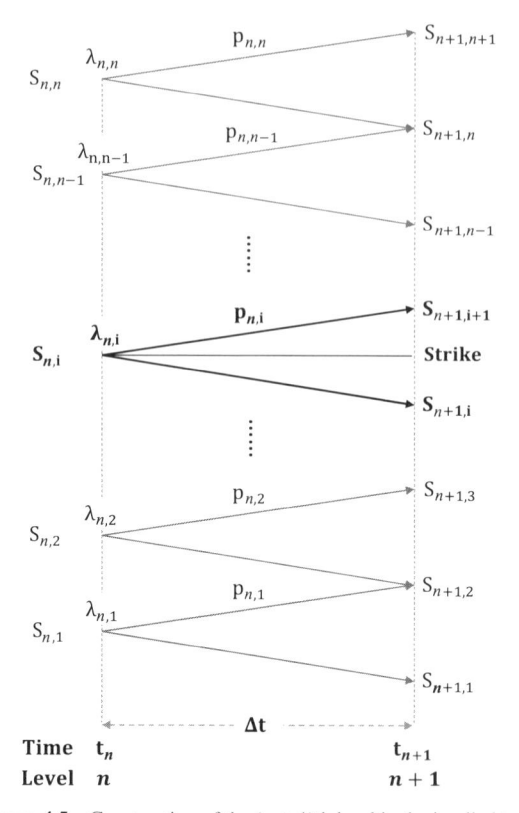

Figure 4.5 Construction of the $(n + 1)$th level in the implied tree.

In the following, r denotes the continuous risk-free rate, $S_{n,i}$ denotes the ith node of the stock price at level n, $p_{n,i}$ denotes the probability of going up from node $S_{n,i}$ to node $S_{n+1,i+1}$, $F_{n,i}$ denotes the one-period forward price corresponding to price $S_{n,i}$, and $\lambda_{n,i}$ denotes the probability of reaching node $S_{n,i}$ discounted by the risk-free rate. $\lambda_{n,i}$ is also called the Arrow–Debreu price. All $\lambda_{n,i}$ and $F_{n,i}$ at level n are known and can be calculated through the following relationship.

$$\lambda_{n,i} = e^{-r\Delta t}\left(p_{n-1,i-1}\lambda_{n-1,i-1} + (1 - p_{n-1,i})\lambda_{n-1,i}\right),$$
$$F_{n,j} = e^{r\Delta t} S_{n,i}.$$

At the nth step, all n nodes at the nth level are calculated, and the $n + 1$ nodes at the $(n + 1)$th level are implied by the nodes at the nth level. Figure 4.5 depicts the relationship between the notations at the nth step, where we begin to construct the $(n + 1)$th level of the implied binomial tree.

Denote today's market call price for a call struck at K and expiring at t by $C(K, t)$. Estimate the values of calls with a different K and t by interpolating the market data.

As before, we estimate the call price by fitting the implied volatility surface. The theoretical binomial value of a call struck at K and expiring at t_{n+1} is given by the sum of the discounted probability of reaching node $(n+1, j)$ multiplied by the call payoff over all nodes $(n+1, j)$ at the $(n+1)$th level, which relates the market value of a call struck at $S_{n,i}$ and expiring at t_{n+1} via

$$c(S_{n,i}, t_{n+1}) = \sum_{j=1}^{n} \lambda_{n+1,j+1} \max\{S_{n+1,j+1} - S_{n,i}, 0\}, \tag{4.9}$$

where

$$\lambda_{n+1,j+1} = e^{-r\Delta t}\left(p_{n,j}\lambda_{n,j} + (1 - p_{n,j+1})\lambda_{n,j+1}\right).$$

Note that node $S_{n,i}$ splits up and down nodes $S_{n+1,i+1}$ and $S_{n,i}$ at the next level, which ensures that only nodes above $S_{n,i}$ contribute to a call struck at $S_{n,i}$. Equation 4.9 becomes

$$c(S_{n,i}, t_{n+1}) = \sum_{j=i}^{n} \lambda_{n+1,j+1} \max\{S_{n+1,j+1} - S_{n,i}, 0\}. \tag{4.10}$$

As the implied tree is risk-neutral, the forward price $F_{n,i}$ of stock price $S_{n,i}$ at node (n, i) is its expected value one period later, which leads to the following equation.

$$F_{n,i} = p_{n,i} S_{n+1,i+1} + (1 - p_{n,i}) S_{n+1,i}. \tag{4.11}$$

Using Equation 4.11, Equation 4.10 can be simplified as

$$e^{r\Delta t} c(S_{n,i}, t_{n+1}) = \lambda_{n,i} p_{n,i} (S_{n+1,i+1} - S_{n,i}) + \Sigma, \tag{4.12}$$

where

$$\Sigma = \sum_{j=i+1}^{n} \lambda_{n,j}(F_{n,j} - S_{n,j}). \tag{4.13}$$

Solving Equations 4.11 and 4.12 simultaneously for $S_{n+1,i+1}$ and $p_{n,i}$ gives us

$$S_{n+1,i+1} = \frac{S_{n+1,i}\left(e^{r\Delta t}c(S_{n,i}, t_{n+1}) - \Sigma\right) - \lambda_{n,i}S_{n,i}(F_{n,i} - S_{n+1,i})}{\left(e^{r\Delta t}c(S_{n,i}, t_{n+1}) - \Sigma\right) - \lambda_{n,i}(F_{n,i} - S_{n+1,i})}, \tag{4.14}$$

and

$$p_{n,i} = \frac{F_{n,i} - S_{n+1,i}}{S_{n+1,i+1} - S_{n+1,i}}, \tag{4.15}$$

where Σ denotes the terms in Equation 4.13.

Using Equations 4.14 and 4.15, we find $S_{n+1,i+1}$ and $p_{n,i}$ iteratively for all nodes above central node $S_{n+1,ctr}$. Suppose that we are at step n, and there are $n+1$ nodes to fix at the $(n+1)$th level.

If n is even, then we choose $ctr = (n/2 + 1)$ and set $S_{n+1,ctr} = S_0$, where S_0 is today's spot price. Using Equation 4.14, we imply all nodes in the upper half of the tree at the $(n+1)$th level starting from node $S_{n+1,ctr+1}$ and proceeding one by one.

If n is odd, then we choose $ctr = (n+1)/2$ such that $S_{n+1,ctr}$ denotes the lower central node and $S_{n+1,ctr+1}$ denotes the upper central node at the $(n+1)$th level. In this case, we set $S_{n+1,ctr} = S_0^2 / S_{n+1,ctr+1}$, such that the logarithmic spacing between the two central nodes and today's spot price S_0 are equal. Substituting this relation into Equation 4.14 gives us

$$S_{n+1,ctr+1} = \frac{S_0 \left(e^{r\Delta t} c(S_0, t_{n+1}) + \lambda_{n,ctr} S_0 - \Sigma \right)}{\lambda_{n,ctr} F_{n,ctr} - e^{r\Delta t} c(S_0, t_{n+1}) + \Sigma},$$

$$S_{n+1,ctr} = \frac{S_0^2}{S_{n+1,ctr+1}}.$$

When the central nodes are fixed, we continue to fix the higher nodes, as before. This time, we imply the upper half of the tree starting from node $S_{n+1,ctr+2}$ until we reach the highest node at that level.

We can fix the nodes below the central node in a similar way using put prices. In the following, $P(K, t)$ denotes the put option price struck at K and expiring at t. The put price can be obtained from the estimated call option through put-call parity. The analogous formula that determines a lower nodes's price from that of an upper node is

$$S_{n+1,i} = \frac{S_{n+1,i+1}(e^{r\Delta t} P(S_{n,i}, t_{n+1}) - \Sigma) + \lambda_{n,i} S_{n,i}(F_{n,i} - S_{n+1,i+1})}{e^{r\Delta t} P(S_{n,i}, t_{n+1}) - \Sigma + \lambda_{n,i}(F_{n,i} - S_{n+1,i+1})},$$

where

$$\Sigma = \sum_{j=1}^{i-1} \lambda_{n,j}(S_{n,i} - F_{n,j}).$$

Repeating this process from node $S_{n+1,ctr-1}$, we imply every node in the lower half of the tree.

In Derman and Kani (1994), the problem of producing a transition probability greater than 1 or lower than 0 is resolved by replacing the stock price with the price that keeps the logarithmic spacing between the corresponding node at and its adjacent nodes the same level as before. However, their solution may still violate the inequality $F_{n,i} \leq S_{n+1,i+1} \leq F_{n,i+1}$ and indicate an arbitrage opportunity. To resolve this problem, we take the geometric average of the forwards by setting $S_{n+1,i+1} = e^{r\Delta t} \sqrt{S_{n,i} S_{n,i+1}}$ when the inequality is violated.

For the highest node, we check whether $F_{n,n} \leq S_{n+1,n+1}$. If this inequality is violated, then we replace price $S_{n+1,n+1}$ with $S_{n+1,n} \frac{S_{n,n}}{S_{n,n-1}}$, which keeps the logarithmic spacing between $S_{n+1,n+1}$ and $F_{n,n}$ at the same level as that between $S_{n+1,n}$ and $F_{n,n-1}$.

For the lowest node, we check whether $S_{n+1,1} \leq F_{n,1}$ and $S_{n+1,1} \geq 0$ because the stock price produced can be negative in some cases. If one of these two conditions is violated, then we set $S_{n+1,1} = S_{n+1,2} \frac{S_{n,1}}{S_{n,2}}$. For more details, please refer to Ch4.2_Implied_Binomial_Tree.xls.

4.2 THE HESTON STOCHASTIC VOLATILITY MODEL

As all market practitioners are aware, the BS model is seriously flawed. The model's implied volatilities for different strikes and times-to-maturity are not constant and therefore cannot capture the volatility smile observed in the market. An alternative to the local volatility models introduced in Section 4.1 is stochastic volatility models.

Under the physical probability measure $\mathbb{P}$, a general stochastic volatility model can be represented in a pair of stochastic differential equation (SDEs),

$$\frac{dS(t)}{S(t)} = \mu(t, S(t), V(t)) \, dt + \sqrt{V(t)} \, dW_S(t),$$

$$dV(t) = \mu_V(t, V(t)) \, dt + \sigma_V(t, V(t)) \, dW_V(t), \quad (4.16)$$

$$\mathbb{E}^{\mathbb{P}}[dW_S(t) \, dW_V(t)] = \rho \, dt,$$

where $\sigma_V(t, V(t))$ is a positive function and $V(t)$ is the non-negative variance process of the underlying asset for an appropriately chosen μ_V and σ_V. Typical parameterization assumes that $\mu(t, S(t), V(t)) = r + \lambda(t)\sqrt{V(t)}$ to ensure that the excess return of holding the asset is proportional to the asset's volatility. Parameter $\lambda(t)$ is essentially the market price of risk.

To identify a risk-neutral process corresponding to Equation 4.17, a $\mathbb{Q}$-standard Brownian motion driving the asset price is defined as

$$dW_S^*(t) = dW_S(t) + \lambda(t) \, dt.$$

As $\mathbb{E}^{\mathbb{P}}[dW_S(t) \, dW_V(t)] = \rho \, dt$, we employ the Cholesky decomposition to obtain

$$\begin{aligned} dW_V(t) &= \rho \, dW_S(t) + \sqrt{1 - \rho^2} \, dW^{\perp}(t) \\ &= \rho \, (dW_S^*(t) - \lambda(t) \, dt) + \sqrt{1 - \rho^2} \, dW^{\perp}(t) \\ &= \rho \, dW_S^*(t) + \sqrt{1 - \rho^2} \, dW^{\perp}(t) - \rho \lambda(t) \, dt \\ &= dW_V^*(t) - \rho \lambda(t) \, dt, \end{aligned}$$

where $W^{\perp}(t)$ is a standard Brownian motion that is independent of $W_S(t)$, and $W_V^*(t)$ is a $\mathbb{Q}$-standard Brownian motion. Putting these together forms a pair of SDEs for the $\mathbb{Q}$-dynamics of the asset:

$$\frac{dS(t)}{S(t)} = r\,dt + \sqrt{V(t)}\,dW_S^*(t),$$

$$dV(t) = [\mu_V(t, V(t)) - \rho\lambda(t)\sigma_V(t, V(t))]\,dt + \sigma_V(t, V(t))\,dW_V^*(t),$$

$$\mathrm{E}^{\mathbb{Q}}[dW_S^*(t)\,dW_V^*(t)] = \rho\,dt.$$

Often, the market price of risk is positive, and correlation coefficient ρ is negative. In such a situation, the risk-neutral volatility is higher than the physical volatility. The consequence is that the implied volatility is higher than the historical volatility for nearly at-the-money (ATM) options. When such a situation occurs, the difference between the implied volatility and the historical volatility refers to the volatility premium because call and put options are quoted at higher prices than their BS prices using historical volatility.

4.2.1 The Heston Model and Option Pricing

The Heston model (Heston, 1993) stands out in the class of stochastic volatility models for two simple reasons. First, its volatility process is non-negative and has a mean-reverting feature that can be observed in market data. Second, the Heston model features a closed-form solution for vanilla options that explains the volatility smile, allows market implementation, and provides a consistent framework for the valuation of exotic products. In terms of calibration, the Heston stochastic volatility model has the following two-dimensional SDE under $\mathbb{Q}$.

$$\frac{dS(t)}{S(t)} = r\,dt + \sqrt{V(t)}\,dW_S(t),$$

$$dV(t) = \kappa(\theta - V(t))\,dt + \epsilon\sqrt{V(t)}\,dW_V(t), \tag{4.17}$$

$$\mathrm{E}[dW_S(t)\,dW_V(t)] = \rho\,dt,$$

where κ is the mean-reverting rate of variance, θ is long-run average variance, ϵ is the volatility of the variance process, and $\rho \in [-1, 1]$ is the correlation between the stock price and variance processes.

Inspired by Theorem 4.1, the call option prices are closely related to the $\mathbb{Q}$-distribution of the underlying asset price. From standard probability theory, we also know that this distribution can be fully characterized by the characteristic function. Let $X_T = \log S_T$. The $\mathbb{Q}$-characteristic function for the log-asset value is defined as

$$\Phi(x, v, 0; \phi) = \mathrm{E}^{\mathbb{Q}}\left[e^{i\phi X_T}\,\big|\,X_0 = x, V_0 = v\right], \tag{4.18}$$

where $i = \sqrt{-1}$ is a complex number.

Theorem 4.2 *(Carr and Madan, 1999) If the $\mathbb{Q}$-characteristic function of the log-asset value is known to be $\Phi(\phi)$, then the dampened Fourier transform of the call* *option with respect to the log-strike is given by*

$$\int_{-\infty}^{\infty} e^{i\xi k} e^{\alpha k} c(e^k, T) \, dk = \frac{e^{-rT} \Phi(x, v, t; \phi = \xi - (\alpha + 1)i)}{\alpha^2 + \alpha - \xi^2 + i(2\alpha + 1)\xi},$$

where $\alpha > 0$ is a dampened parameter chosen to stabilize the Fourier inversion numerically and $k = \log K$. In other words, the call option price can be calculated through an inverse Fourier transform:

$$c(K, T) = e^{-rT} e^{-\alpha k} \mathcal{F}_{\xi,k}^{-1} \left\{ \frac{\Phi(x, v, 0; \phi = \xi - (\alpha + 1)i)}{\alpha^2 + \alpha - \xi^2 + i(2\alpha + 1)\xi} \right\},$$

where $\mathcal{F}_{\xi,k}^{-1}\{\cdot\}$ denotes the Fourier inversion operator.

Proof: By risk-neutral valuation, the call option price is given by

$$c(K, T) = \int_k^{\infty} (e^x - e^k) \varphi(x, T) \, dx,$$

where $\varphi(x, T)$ is the risk-neutral density function for the log-asset value, $x = \log S_T$ and $k = \log K$. Apply the Fourier transform with dampened parameter $\alpha > 0$ to the integral representation with respect to k. Then,

$$\int_{-\infty}^{\infty} e^{i\xi k} e^{\alpha k} c(e^k, T) \, dk = \int_{-\infty}^{\infty} e^{i\xi k} e^{-\alpha k} \int_k^{\infty} (e^x - e^k) \varphi(x, T) \, dx \, dk,$$

$$= \int_{-\infty}^{\infty} \int_{-\infty}^{x} e^{i\xi k} e^{\alpha k} (e^x - e^k) \varphi(x, T) \, dk \, dx,$$

$$= \int_{-\infty}^{\infty} \varphi(x, T) \int_{-\infty}^{x} e^{i\xi k} e^{\alpha k} (e^x - e^k) \, dk \, dx.$$

After integrating out the internal integration, the result follows by recognizing the definition of the characteristic function.

A clear advantage of the Heston model is that the characteristic function can be derived in a closed-form solution. It also enables the call option price to be computed very efficiently using Fast Fourier Transform (FFT) techniques. The characteristic function defined in Equation 4.18 resembles the valuation of a derivative whose payoff is $e^{i\phi X_T}$ and has no discounting factor e^{-rT}. By the BS equation on the aforementioned pair of SDE (Eq. 4.18), we obtain the partial differential equation (PDE) for the characteristic function as

$$\frac{\partial \Phi}{\partial t} + \left(r - \frac{v}{2}\right) \frac{\partial \Phi}{\partial x} + \kappa(\theta - v) \frac{\partial \Phi}{\partial v} + \frac{1}{2} v^2 \frac{\partial^2 \Phi}{\partial x^2} + \rho \epsilon v \frac{\partial^2 \Phi}{\partial x v} + \frac{1}{2} v \epsilon^2 \frac{\partial^2 \Phi}{\partial v^2} = 0,$$

$$\Phi(x, v, T) = e^i \phi x.$$

Heston (1993) discovered that the characteristic function should take an exponential affine form:

$$\Phi_H(x, v, t) = \exp[i\phi x + A(t, T)v + B(t, T)]. \tag{4.19}$$

Substituting it into the PDE deduces that

$$\dot{A} + (-\kappa\theta + i\phi\epsilon\rho)A + \frac{\epsilon^2}{2}A^2 - \frac{1}{2}(i\phi + \phi^2) = 0, A(T, T) = 0,$$

$$\dot{B} + ir\phi + \kappa\theta A = 0, B(T, T) = 0,$$

where $\dot{A}$ and $\dot{B}$ are the differentials of A and B with respect to t. The ordinary differential equations (ODEs) for A and B have well-known solutions:

$$A(t, T) = ir\phi(T - t) + \frac{\kappa\theta}{\epsilon^2}\left[(\kappa - i\phi\rho\epsilon + d)(T - t) - 2\log\left(\frac{1 - ge^{d(T-t)}}{1 - g}\right)\right],$$

$$B(t, T) = \left(\frac{\kappa - i\phi\rho\epsilon + d}{\epsilon^2}\right)\left(\frac{1 - e^{d(T-t)}}{1 - ge^{T-t}}\right), \tag{4.20}$$

$$g = \frac{\kappa - i\phi\rho\epsilon + d}{\kappa - i\phi\rho\epsilon - d},$$

$$d = \sqrt{(i\rho\epsilon\phi - \kappa)^2 + \epsilon^2(i\phi - \phi^2)}.$$

Hence, the Heston call pricing formula reads as follows.

$$c_H(S, V, t) = e^{-rT}e^{-\alpha k}\mathcal{F}_{\xi,k}^{-1}\left\{\frac{\Phi_H(\log S, V, t; \phi = \xi - (\alpha + 1)i)}{\alpha^2 + \alpha - \xi^2 + i(2\alpha + 1)\xi}\right\},$$

where Φ_H is obtained through Equations 4.19 and 4.21.

4.2.2 Model Calibration and Implementation

The efficient computational method using FFT proposed by Carr and Madan (1999) allows vanilla option prices to be efficiently computed under the Heston model, which renders parameter calibration easy and implementable. When the Heston model is used as an internal pricing model for mark-to-market (MTM) procedures, the model parameters must be updated daily on the basis of the market situation through calibration. Therefore, an efficient and effective calibration method must be employed to obtain accurate parameters that fully reflect market conditions. Incorrect calibration can lead to miscalculation of the bank's MTM position in turn possibly incurring huge losses and increase operational risk. In addition to accuracy, it is also important that the calibration method not be overly time-consuming, at it is the first procedure in daily MTM. If the process takes too long, then it will affect the bank's efficiency in daily valuation and risk-reporting.

The main objective of calibration is to obtain a set of model parameters that minimizes the sum of the squared difference between the market-observed option prices and the model option prices. Thus, a good calibration method must ensure that the calibrated parameters are located at the global minimum of the problem. Such optimization methods as the Levenberg–Marquardt and Downhill Simplex approaches could be used to calibrate the Heston model, although both algorithms tend to get stuck in local minima rather than the global minimum. Adaptive Simulated Annealing is another possibility, but it is very time-consuming. In this section, we introduce an efficient stochastic optimization method called differential evolution (DE) for calibrating the Heston model.

4.2.3 Calibration to European Options: Differential Evolution

DE is an evolutionary algorithm that finds the minimum of a cost function by evolving a family of solutions in parallel instead of using a single point in the parameter space. The probability of getting stuck in a local minimum is thus greatly reduced. The DE algorithm comprises four stages: selection of the population, mutation, crossover, and selection. (Note: The following notations are similar to those used in Vollrath and Wendland (2009).)

1. **Selection of the population**
   A family of parameter sets is generated randomly according to the parameter bounds. The size of this family (number of random parameter sets), denoted by NP, must be at least four to permit the independent selection of family vectors in the mutation process. Define a member of the population as

   $$P_i = (\alpha_1, \alpha_2, \ldots, \alpha_M),$$

   where $i = 1, \ldots, NP$ and M is the dimension of the problem.

2. **Mutation**
   This key step of the DE algorithm aims to mutate an individual of the population. A single individual, P_a, is chosen at random, and added to the difference between two other mutually independent individuals, P_b and P_c, selected at random and multiplied by scale factor F. That is,

   $$P'_i = P_a + F \cdot (P_b + P_c),$$
   $$P'_i = (\alpha'_1, \alpha'_2, \ldots, \alpha'_M),$$

   where $i = 1, \ldots, NP$.

   The foregoing process is repeated NP times and a new set of mutated population with size NP is generated. After mutation, it is common to find that the boundary conditions of some parameters are violated, in which case adjustments are necessary. A common practice is to set the parameter value as the midpoint of the original population parameter value and the violated boundary. Other adjustment methods can also be used.

3. **Crossover of mutated parameters into an individual**
At this point, we have a new population of mutated individuals with size NP, each containing mutated parameters. The crossover step now determines which mutated parameters will be accepted into the original population:

$$P_i'' = (\alpha_1'', \alpha_2'', \ldots, \alpha_M'').$$

P_i'' is a new individual containing a mixture of mutated and original parameters, and α_j'', for $j = 1, \ldots, M$, is given by

$$\alpha_j'' = \begin{cases} \alpha_j', & \text{if } U(0,1) \leq CR \text{ or } j = r, \\ \alpha_j, & \text{if } U(0,1) > CR \text{ or } j \neq r, \end{cases}$$

where α_j' is mutated from α_j, $CR \in [0, 1]$ is the crossover ratio, and r is a randomly selected index from $1, 2, \ldots, M$. The use of index r is to ensure that at least one mutated parameter will be accepted into the original population. This crossover process is repeated NP times, and a new population set is generated.

4. **Selection of individuals into the population for the next generation**
The final step of the algorithm computes the cost function of each individual in population P_i''. If the value computed is less than the original P_i cost value, then we retain P_i'' as the population for the next generation; otherwise, we discard it. The process is repeated NP times, which completes one generation of the algorithm. Steps 2 to 4 are repeated according to the maximum number of generations N or until the algorithm converges. The final solution is the parameter set with the lowest cost function value.

With the foregoing DE algorithm, we have now demonstrated the calibration of the Heston model. The volatility surface of the observed market option data is collected via Bloomberg application programming interface (API) and imported into Excel. The C++ platform is used for calibration to increase the computational speed. For further improvement, we simplify a method based on the Fourier-cosine series expansions in Fang and Oosterlee (2008), COS, to increase the computational speed for calculating the Heston option prices. The main objective here is to minimize the sum of the squared difference between the market and model prices. Each option datum is assigned a suitable weight via a weighting scheme based on its time-to-maturity. Mathematically, we have to find a set of parameters, denoted as Ω, such that

$$\min_{\Omega} \sum_{i=1}^{N} \left(w_i (c_{mkt}^i - c_H^i)^2 + \text{Penalty}^i \right),$$

TABLE 4.10 Parameter Bounds for the Heston Model

Parameter	Lower bound	Upper bound
κ	0	20
θ	0	1
V_0	0	1
ϵ	0	1
ρ	-1	1

where w_i is the assigned weight for option i, c_{mkt}^i is the market mid bid-ask price of option i, c_H^i is the Heston call price computed by FFT, and Penalty^i is the penalty function assigned to option i. Our implementation of the DE calibration applies the following two practical settings.

1. **Parameter bounds and model parameter constraint**
   In the Heston model, there are five parameters that require calibration: mean-reverting speed κ, long-term average variance θ, initial variance $V(0)$, the volatility of variance ϵ, and the correlation between the stock and variance ρ. Each parameter is randomly generated in the initial selection of the population according to its bounds. The bounds for each parameter are presented in Table 4.10.

   It is rather common in the mutation stage for some of the mutated parameters to violate their own bounds. One remedy is to set the mutated parameter at the midpoint of the original population parameter value and the violated bound, which is the strategy employed here.

   In addition, to reduce the possibility of generating negative variances in direct simulation, the constraint $2\kappa\theta > \epsilon^2$ has to be satisfied at the expense of a poorer fit. Relaxing this constraint would require a better simulation method. To add this constraint to the calibration, it is suggested that a penalty function be added to the cost function. The simplest approach is as follows. If the parameter vectors after mutation and crossover do not meet the condition $2\kappa\theta > \epsilon^2$, then a large penalty is assigned to this vector such that it will not be accepted into the new population for the next generation. This approach ensures that the ultimate parameter output is reasonable and can be used for further calculations and simulations.

2. **Strategy**
   The efficiency of the DE algorithm is largely dependent on the DE parameters that are input. Vollrath and Wendland (2009) suggest that the strategy with $NP = 15D$, where D is the dimensionality of the model parameter vector, $CR = 0.5$ and $F = 0.8$ works best for most minimization problems, including Heston model calibration. In addition, 400 generations are sufficient to allow the solution to converge in the Heston calibration problem. Calibration is complete in 5 min, which is not very efficient time-wise. In practice, some of the parameters are fixed in advance using values calibrated earlier, with only the remaining parameters re-calibrated in real time.

142 VOLATILITY MODELING

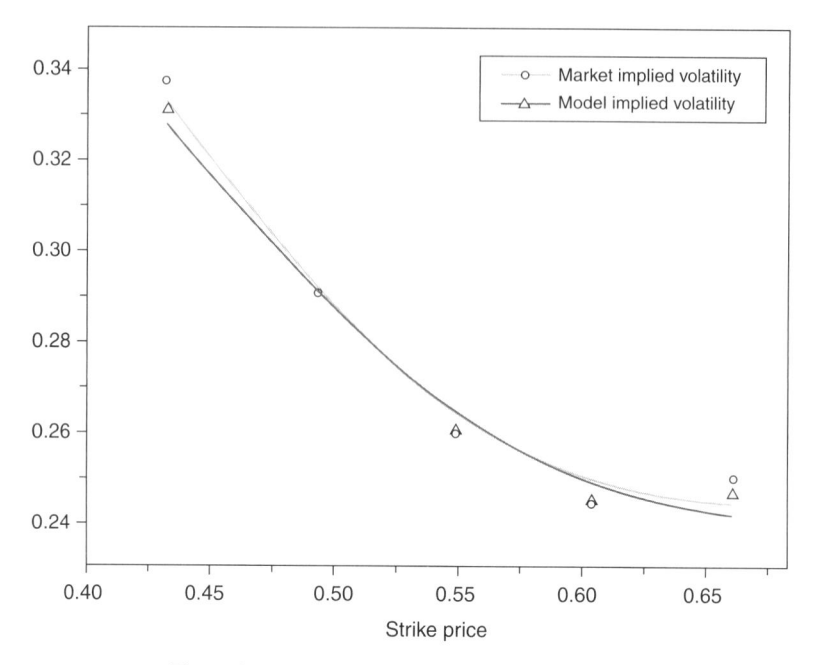

Figure 4.6 Volatility smiles before and after calibration.

For an illustration, see Figures 4.6, 4.7, and 4.8, which show the volatility smile and surface fitted by the DE algorithm with the model constraint added. It can be concluded that the DE algorithm consistently finds the global minimum of the problem. For further details, please refer to the Ch4.5 Calibration Interface folder.

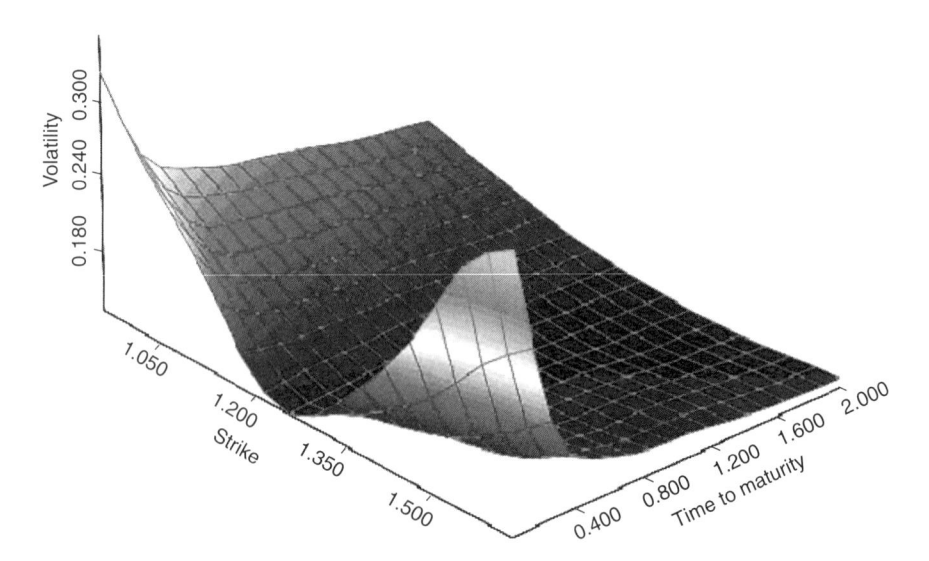

Figure 4.7 EURUSD option volatility surface.

4.3 SIMULATION OF EXOTIC OPTION PRICES UNDER HESTON MODEL

4.3.1 Heston Stochastic Volatility Model Simulation Methods: Quadratic–Exponential Discretization Scheme

Recall that, under the risk-neutral measure, the Heston stochastic volatility model is characterized by the following two-dimensional SDE.

$$\frac{dS(t)}{S(t)} = r\,dt + \sqrt{V(t)}\,dW_S(t),$$

$$dV(t) = \kappa(\theta - V(t))\,dt + \epsilon\sqrt{V(t)}\,dW_V(t),$$

$$E[dW_S(t)\,dW_V(t)] = \rho\,dt.$$

If $2\kappa\theta > \epsilon^2$ and $V(0) > 0$, then the variance process $V(t)$ is always positive and well-defined. Denote the discrete-time approximation of S and V by $\widehat{S}$ and $\widehat{V}$. After the log transform of $S(t)$, and using Itô's lemma, a Euler scheme for the path simulations is given by

$$\log \widehat{S}(t+\Delta) = \log \widehat{S}(t) + \left(r - \frac{\widehat{V}(t)}{2}\right)\Delta + \sqrt{\widehat{V}(t)}Z_S\sqrt{\Delta},$$

$$\widehat{V}(t+\Delta) = \widehat{V}(t) + \kappa(\theta - \widehat{V}(t))\Delta + \epsilon\sqrt{\widehat{V}(t)}Z_V\sqrt{\Delta},$$

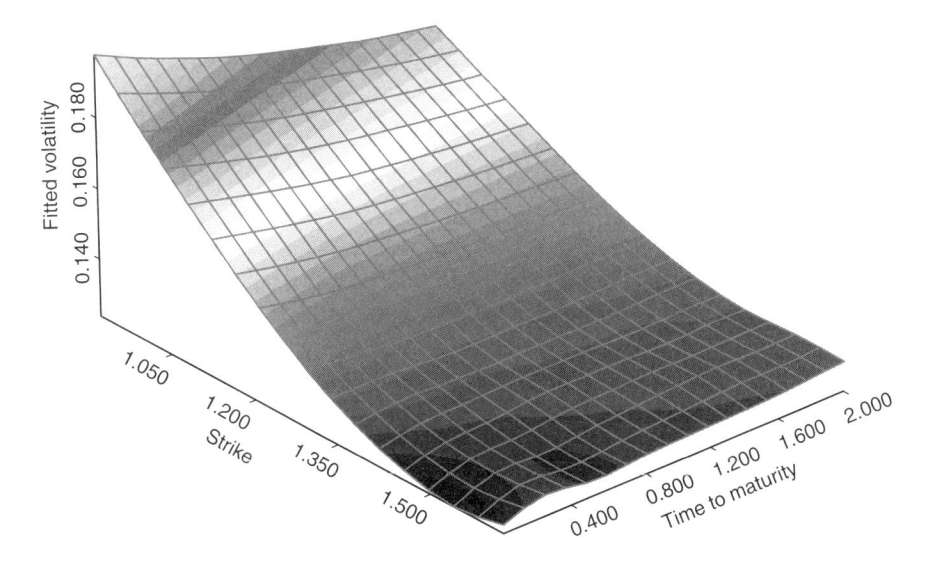

Figure 4.8 EURUSD fitted option volatilty surface.

where Z_S and Z_V are standard normal random variables with correlation ρ. By Cholesky decomposition, Z_S and Z_V are generated by

$$Z_S = \Psi^{-1}(U_1),$$
$$Z_V = \rho Z_X + \sqrt{1-\rho^2}\Psi^{-1}(U_2).$$

This Euler scheme suffers from the problem that negative variance can be generated with non-zero probability, even though the model constraint is satisfied. The problem usually occurs when $\widehat{V}(t)$ approaches zero and a large negative value of Z_V is drawn. As a result, the calculation of $\sqrt{\widehat{V}(t)}$ becomes impossible and the simulation process breaks down. Unconstrained calibration of the model often produces extreme parameters, which quickly halts the simulation. Even though the model constraint has been added into the calibration process, the calibrated parameters are usually quite extreme, $2\kappa\theta - \epsilon^2 \approx 0$ or $\epsilon > 0.75$, depending on the market situation, which increases the likelihood of negative variances in the simulation. Several remedies for resolving the problem have been proposed in the literature. See Lord, Koekkoek, and van Dijk (2008) for a comparison of the bias in different schemes. According to these authors, the scheme that produces the smallest degree of bias is the full truncation scheme that sets $\widehat{V}(t) := \max\{\widehat{V}(t), 0\}$.

Unfortunately, these remedies fail to reflect the true distribution of $V(t)$ when it approaches zero, and the bias increases when the number of time steps is large. Andersen (2008) proposes a quadratic-exponential (QE) discretization scheme that is shown to price out-of-money options accurately in comparison with the closed-form solution with extreme model parameters. The scheme works in the following way. For sufficiently large values of $\widehat{V}(t)$, it is known that $\widehat{V}(t+\Delta)$ is proportional to a non-central chi-square random variable with non-centrality parameter $\widehat{V}(t) \cdot n(t, t+\Delta)$, where n is independent of $\widehat{V}(t)$, and the distribution will converge to a normal distribution as the non-centrality parameter approaches infinity. Therefore, $\widehat{V}(t+\Delta)$ can be approximated by a normal variable using the quadratic sampling scheme

$$\widehat{V}(t+\Delta) = a(b+Z_V)^2,$$

where Z_V is a standard normal random variable, and a and b are constants determined by moment-matching at each time step. This moment-matching method fails when $\widehat{V}(t)$ approaches zero because $\widehat{V}(t+\Delta)$ can no longer be approximated by a standard normal random variable. For a small $\widehat{V}(t)$, the distribution of $\widehat{V}(t+\Delta)$ becomes proportional to an ordinary central chi-square distribution with $4\kappa\theta/\epsilon^2$ degrees of freedom. Thus, Andersen (2008) takes inspiration from this asymptotic density and models the density of $\widehat{V}(t+\Delta)$ according to the following exponential scheme.

$$\Pr(\widehat{V}(t+\Delta) \in [x, x+dx]) \approx \left(p\delta(0) + \beta(1-p)e^{-\beta x}\right)dx, x \geq 0,$$

where δ is the Dirac delta-function, and p and β are non-negative constants to be determined. The cumulative distribution function (CDF) can be determined easily, and inverse transform can be employed in the simulation if $\widehat{V}(t)$ approaches zero:

$$\Psi(x) = \Pr(\widehat{V}(t+\Delta) \leq x) = p + (1-p)(1 - e^{-\beta x}), x \geq 0,$$

$$\widehat{V}(t+\Delta) = \Psi^{-1}(U_V; p, \beta),$$

where U_V is a uniform random variable.

Note that the quadratic scheme can be moment-matched only for $\psi \leq 2$, whereas the exponential scheme can be moment-matched only for $\psi \geq 1$. As can be seen here, these domains of applicability overlap. Thus, a natural procedure is to introduce a critical level $\psi_c \in [1, 2]$ and use the quadratic scheme if $\psi \leq \psi_c$, and the exponential scheme otherwise. For practical use, Andersen (2008) suggests that $\psi = 1.5$ is sufficient for simulation accuracy.

4.3.2 QE Discretization Scheme for $\widehat{V}(t)$

The following variables are computed at every time step under the QE scheme.

$$m = \theta + (\widehat{V}(t) - \theta)e^{-\kappa\Delta},$$

$$s^2 = \frac{\widehat{V}(t)\epsilon^2 e^{-\kappa\Delta}}{\kappa}(1 - e^{-\kappa\Delta}) + \frac{\theta\epsilon^2}{2\kappa}(1 - e^{-\kappa\Delta})^2,$$

$$\psi = \frac{s^2}{m^2},$$

$$b = 2\psi^{-1} - 1 + \sqrt{2\psi^{-1}}\sqrt{2\psi^{-1} - 1} \geq 0,$$

$$a = \frac{m}{1+b^2},$$

$$p = \frac{\psi - 1}{\psi + 1},$$

$$\beta = \frac{1-p}{m} = \frac{2}{m(\psi+1)} > 0,$$

$$\Psi^{-1}(u; p, \beta) = \begin{cases} 0, & 0 \leq u \leq p, \\ \beta^{-1} \log \frac{1-p}{1-u}, & p < u \leq 1. \end{cases}$$

Definitions and proofs can be found in Andersen (2008). Using the foregoing formulas, the following algorithm shows how to compute $\widehat{V}(t+\Delta)$ under the QE scheme.

1. Given $\widehat{V}(t)$, compute m, s^2 and ψ.
2. Generate $U_V \sim U(0, 1)$, and set $\psi_C \in [1, 2]$.
3. If $\psi \leq \psi_c$, then compute a and b, and set $\widehat{V}(t+\Delta) = a(b + Z_V)^2$, where $Z_V = \Phi^{-1}(U_V)$. Otherwise, compute β and p, and then set $\widehat{V}(t+\Delta) = \Psi^{-1}(U_V; p; \beta)$.

4.3.3 QE Discretization Scheme for $\widehat{S}(t)$

To obtain a bias-free scheme for the asset price process, we need to obtain the explicit form of $\log \widehat{S}(t)$. Integrate the SDE of $V(t)$ to obtain

$$V(t+\Delta) = V(t) + \int_t^{t+\Delta} \kappa(\theta - V(u))\,du + \epsilon \int_t^{t+\Delta} \sqrt{V(u)}\,dW_V(u),$$

where $\int_t^{t+\Delta} \sqrt{V(u)}\,dW_V(u) = \epsilon^{-1}\left(V(t+\Delta) - V(t) - \kappa\theta\Delta + \kappa \int_t^{t+\Delta} V(u)\,du\right)$. Cholesky decomposition of $S(t)$ shows that

$$d\log S(t) = \left(r - \frac{V(t)}{2}\right)dt + \rho\sqrt{V(t)}\,dW_V(t) + \sqrt{1-\rho^2}\sqrt{V(t)}\,dW(t),$$

where W is a standard Brownian motion independent of W_V. Integrating both sides yields

$$\log S(t+\Delta) = \log S(t) + r\Delta + \frac{\rho}{\epsilon}(V(t+\Delta) - V(t) - \kappa\theta\Delta)$$

$$+ \left(\frac{\kappa\rho}{\epsilon} - \frac{1}{2}\right)\int_t^{t+\Delta} V(u)\,du + \sqrt{1-\rho^2}\int_t^{t+\Delta} \sqrt{V(u)}\,dW_V(u).$$

To discretize $S(t)$, we need to handle the integrals of $V(t)$. The first integral, $\int_t^{t+\Delta} V(u)\,du$, can be approximated as

$$\int_t^{t+\Delta} V(u)\,du \approx (\gamma_1 V(t) + \gamma_2 V(t+\Delta))\Delta,$$

for some constants γ_1 and γ_2. The simplest setting is the Euler scheme, where $\gamma_1 = 1$ and $\gamma_2 = 0$. Central discretization can also be used, where $\gamma_1 = \gamma_2 = \frac{1}{2}$.

Because W is independent of V, and conditional on $V(t)$ and $\int_t^{t+\Delta} V(u)\,du$, the second integral,

$$\int_t^{t+\Delta} \sqrt{V(u)}\,dW_V(u),$$

is a standard normal random variable with mean zero and variance $\int_t^{t+\Delta} V(u)\,du$. Therefore, with the foregoing approximation, the discretization scheme for $\log S(t)$ is

$\log \widehat{S}(t+\Delta)$

$$= \log \widehat{S} + r\Delta + \frac{\rho}{\epsilon}(\widehat{V}(t+\Delta) - \widehat{V}(t) - \kappa\theta\Delta) + \Delta\left(\frac{\kappa\rho}{\epsilon} - \frac{1}{2}\right)(\gamma_1 \widehat{V}(t) + \gamma_2 \widehat{V}(t+\Delta))$$

$$+ \sqrt{\Delta}\sqrt{1-\rho^2}\sqrt{\gamma_1 \widehat{V}(t) + \gamma_2 \widehat{V}(t+\Delta)} \cdot Z$$

$$= \log \widehat{S}(t) + r\Delta + K_0 + K_1 \widehat{V}(t) + K_2 \widehat{V}(t+\Delta) + \sqrt{K_3 \widehat{V}(t) + K_4 \widehat{V}(t+\Delta)} \cdot Z,$$

where Z is a standard normal random variable that is independent of $\widehat{V}$, and $K_0, \ldots, K_4$ are given by

$$K_0 = \frac{-\rho\kappa\theta}{\epsilon}\Delta,$$

$$K_1 = \gamma_1\Delta\left(\frac{\kappa\rho}{\epsilon} - \frac{1}{2}\right) - \frac{\rho}{\epsilon},$$

$$K_2 = \gamma_1\Delta\left(\frac{\kappa\rho}{\epsilon} - \frac{1}{2}\right) + \frac{\rho}{\epsilon},$$

$$K_3 = \gamma_1\Delta(1 - \rho^2),$$

$$K_4 = \gamma_2\Delta(1 - \rho^2),$$

γ_1 and γ_2 are predetermined constants, and $K_i, i = 0, \ldots, 4$ depend on different time steps in the simulation.

With the discretization schemes for $\widehat{V}(t)$ and $\widehat{S}(t)$, the algorithm for simulating stock prices under the Heston model using the QE scheme is as follows.

1. Choose γ_1 and γ_2 according to the user's preference.
2. Given $\widehat{V}(t)$, generate $\widehat{V}(t+\Delta)$ according to the discretization scheme of $\widehat{V}(t+\Delta)$.
3. Generate $U \sim U(0, 1)$, independent of all random numbers used in $\widehat{V}(t+\Delta)$.
4. Set $Z = \Psi^{-1}(U)$.
5. Given $\log \widehat{S}(t)$, $\widehat{V}(t)$, and $\widehat{V}(t+\Delta)$ computed from Step 2, calculate $\log \widehat{S}(t+\Delta)$.

The QE method can be implemented in VBA with the following code.

```
Public Function HestonQE_Path(a As Heston_PathType) As Variant

Dim i As Long, j As Long
Dim Phi_C As Double, P As Double, Beta As Double, a_2 As
    Double, b As Double
Dim Phi As Double, v As Double, V_Delta As Double
Dim m As Double, s_square As Double
Dim K0 As Double, K1 As Double, K2 As Double, K3 As Double,
    K4 As Double
Dim C1 As Double, C2 As Double
Dim ZV As Double, U As Double
ReDim S(0 To a.m, 1 To a.n) As Double

C1 = 0.5
C2 = 0.5
```

```
Phi_C = 1.5
For j = 1 To a.n
  S(0, j) = a.S0
  v = a.v0
  For i = 1 To a.m
    m = a.theta + (v - a.theta) * Exp(-a.kappa * a.dt)
    s_square = v * a.epsilon ^ 2 * Exp(-a.kappa * a.dt) *
      (1 - Exp(-a.kappa * a.dt)) _ / a.kappa + a.theta *
      a.epsilon ^ 2 * (1 - Exp(-a.kappa * a.dt)) ^ 2 / 2 / a.kappa
    Phi = s_square / m ^ 2
    ZV = rGauss
    U = Rnd()
    If Phi <= Phi_C Then
      b = Sqr(2 / Phi - 1 + Sqr(2 / Phi) * Sqr(2 / Phi - 1))
      a_2 = m / (1 + b ^ 2)
      V_Delta = a_2 * (b + ZV) ^ 2
    Else
      P = (Phi - 1) / (Phi + 1)
      Beta = 2 / (m * (Phi + 1))
      If U <= P Then
        V_Delta = 0
      Else
        V_Delta = Log((1 - P) / (1 - U)) / Beta
      End If
    End If
    K0 = -a.rho * a.kappa * a.theta * a.dt / a.epsilon
    K1 = C1 * a.dt * (a.kappa * a.rho / a.epsilon - 0.5) -
      a.rho / a.epsilon
    K2 = C2 * a.dt * (a.kappa * a.rho / a.epsilon - 0.5) +
      a.rho / a.epsilon
    K3 = C1 * a.dt * (1 - a.rho ^ 2)
    K4 = C2 * a.dt * (1 - a.rho ^ 2)
    S(i, j) = S(i - 1, j) * Exp((a.rf - a.q) * a.dt + K0 + K1 *
      v + K2 * V_Delta + Sqr(K3 * v + K4 * V_Delta) * rGauss)
    v = V_Delta
  Next i
Next j
HestonQE_Path = S
End Function
```

4.3.4 Performance Analysis of the QE Scheme

We investigate the pricing accuracy and performance of the simulation scheme defined under the QE approach by comparing it with the closed-form solution and truncated normal simulation scheme. In this performance analysis, standard European call

TABLE 4.11 Parameters for Different Simulation Cases

	Case 1	Case 2	Case 3	Case 4
κ	12	8	6	0.3
θ	0.04	0.04	0.04	0.04
V_0	0.025	0.025	0.025	0.025
ϵ	0.5	0.75	0.75	0.95
ρ	−0.97	−0.97	−0.97	−0.97
$2\kappa\theta - \epsilon^2$	0.71	0.0775	−0.0825	−0.8785

TABLE 4.12 Simulation Results for Case 1

Strike	Normal	SD(Normal)	QE	SD(QE)	Analytic
0.35	0.39847	0.00025	0.39856	0.00026	0.39848
0.45	0.32809	0.00033	0.32821	0.00033	0.32812
0.55	0.26506	0.00055	0.26553	0.00049	0.26518
0.65	0.21052	0.00067	0.21113	0.00078	0.21091
0.75	0.16519	0.00129	0.16620	0.00082	0.16550
0.85	0.12842	0.00121	0.12850	0.00033	0.12844

options are priced across different strikes, including in-the-money and out-of-the-money options, with the QE and truncated normal schemes. Benchmark closed-form solutions are also calculated to access the accuracy. The initial parameters are $S_0 = 0.67$, $r = 0.04$, $q = 0$, $T = 6$, $dt = 1/252$, and $n = 10,000$. The Heston parameters for the different cases are listed in Table 4.11. Empirical martingale correction and antithetic variables are used in both schemes for variance reduction. The simulation results are presented in Tables 4.12, 4.13, 4.14, and 4.15.

Note that the QE scheme outperforms the normal truncation scheme in all cases. It is also worth noting that the QE scheme maintains pricing accuracy even when the parameters are extreme (Case 4). In this circumstance, the normal truncation scheme fails completely, especially for out-of-the-money options. Therefore, it is strongly recommended that the QE scheme be used in the Monte Carlo valuation of exotic derivatives.

TABLE 4.13 Simulation Results for Case 2

Strike	Normal	SD(Normal)	QE	SD(QE)	Analytic
0.35	0.39995	0.00017	0.39970	0.00025	0.39968
0.45	0.33043	0.00041	0.32991	0.00038	0.32980
0.55	0.26797	0.00025	0.26702	0.00061	0.26670
0.65	0.21362	0.00045	0.21190	0.00090	0.21153
0.75	0.16662	0.00059	0.16496	0.00083	0.16471
0.85	0.12948	0.00071	0.12613	0.00086	0.12602

150   VOLATILITY MODELING

TABLE 4.14   Simulation Results for Case 3

Strike	Normal	SD(Normal)	QE	SD(QE)	Analytic
0.35	0.40052	0.00035	0.40037	0.00034	0.40032
0.45	0.33202	0.00027	0.33096	0.00021	0.33062
0.55	0.26871	0.00077	0.26715	0.00084	0.26734
0.65	0.21363	0.00101	0.21164	0.00072	0.21162
0.75	0.16803	0.00071	0.16389	0.00111	0.16396
0.85	0.12841	0.00144	0.12427	0.00092	0.12434

4.3.5   CITIC Case Study Revisited

Consider the CITIC case studied in Chapter 2. We investigated different payoff scenarios under the celebrated BS model. What if the Heston model were used instead? Would the loss incurred be larger than expected? In this section, we compare the results obtained with the Heston model with those produced by the BS model, and explain why the stochastic volatility model works better when dealing with the pricing and hedging of exotic derivatives.

4.3.5.1   Basic FX Market Quotes   In the FX market, exchange rates $F(t)$ are usually quoted as (Foreign–Domestic). Here, let USD–HKD be the exchange rate $F(t)$, with USD the foreign currency and HKD the domestic. If the USD–HKD rate = 7.75, then HK\$7.75 can be exchanged for US\$1. Note that "Domestic" does not refer to the location, but to the numeraire.

Under the risk-neutral measure, the foreign exchange rate $F(t)$ is assumed to follow the Heston model.

$$\frac{dF(t)}{F(t)} = (r_d - r_f)\,dt + \sqrt{V(t)}\,dW_F(t),$$

$$dV(t) = \kappa(\theta - V(t))\,dt + \epsilon\sqrt{V(t)}\,dW_V(t),$$

$$E^Q[dW_F(t)\,dW_V(t)] = \rho\,dt,$$

TABLE 4.15   Simulation Results for Case 4

Strike	Normal	SD(Normal)	QE	SD(QE)	Analytic
0.35	0.41578	0.00070	0.40219	0.00034	0.40187
0.45	0.34890	0.00098	0.32720	0.00047	0.32717
0.55	0.28442	0.00066	0.25434	0.00037	0.25361
0.65	0.22399	0.00128	0.18167	0.00073	0.18168
0.75	0.16679	0.00096	0.11275	0.00050	0.11201
0.85	0.11471	0.00105	0.04698	0.00069	0.04686

where r_d is the domestic risk-free rate, r_f is the foreign risk-free rate, κ is the mean-reverting rate of the variance, θ is the long-run average variance, ϵ is the volatility of the variance process, and $\rho \in [-1, 1]$ is the correlation between the exchange rate and variance processes.

Let $\widehat{F}(t, T) = F(t)e^{(r_d - r_f)(T-t)}$ be the forward price at time t with maturity T. Applying Itô's lemma on $\widehat{F}(t, T)$, we obtain the dynamics of $\widehat{F}(t, T)$ under the risk-neutral measure as follows.

$$\frac{d\widehat{F}(t, T)}{\widehat{F}(t, T)} = \sqrt{V(t)}\, dW_{\widehat{F}}(t),$$

$$dV(t) = \kappa(\theta - V(t))\, dt + \epsilon\sqrt{V(t)}\, dW_V(t),$$

$$\mathrm{E}^Q[dW_{\widehat{F}}(t)\, dW_V(t)] = \rho\, dt.$$

To avoid confusion and for ease of reporting, we set r_f as the USD interest rate in our computation of option prices. From Table 4.16, we can see that the use of different interest rates has little effect on the calibration results because option prices are not sensitive to interest rates. As the forward price of different maturities can be obtained from Bloomberg, we compute the option prices by replacing $F(t, T)$ with $\widehat{F}(t, T)$ and setting $r_d = r_f = 0$ in the closed-form solution under the Heston model, and then discounting the result by $e^{-r_d(T-t)}$.

$$\begin{aligned} c(t, T, F(t), r_d, r_f, K, \Omega) &= e^{-r_d(T-t)}\mathrm{E}^Q[\max\{F(T) - K, 0\}] \\ &= e^{-r_d(T-t)}\mathrm{E}^Q[\max\{\widehat{F}(t, T) - K, 0\}] \\ &= e^{-r_d(T-t)}c(t, T, \widehat{F}(t, T), r_d = 0, r_f = 0, K, \Omega), \end{aligned}$$

and

$$\widehat{F}(T, T) = F(T),$$

$$\Omega = \{\kappa, \theta, V_0, \epsilon, \rho\}.$$

TABLE 4.16 Calibration Results for AUD–USD Option on July 5, 2010, with Different Interest Rates

Parameter	6M USD deposit	USD yield rate
κ	1.36398	1.32475
θ	0.03855	0.03788
V_0	0.03284	0.03434
ϵ	0.32430	0.31679
ρ	−0.69729	−0.72704

4.3.5.2 Obtaining the Volatility Surface

In the FX market, options are quoted by deltas. The delta, Δ, of a standard European call with strike K, maturity T, and volatility σ can be given by

$$\Delta = e^{-r_f T} \Psi(d_1),$$

$$d_1 = \frac{\log \frac{\widehat{F}(t,T)}{K} + \frac{1}{2}\sigma^2 T}{\sigma \sqrt{T}}.$$

The FX option market is characterized by three volatility quotes up to relatively long maturities: ATM straddle, risk reversal (RR), and Vega-weighted butterfly (VWB). RR and VWB are quoted across different deltas, from 35Δ to 5Δ. With these quotes, we can construct the entire volatility surface.

The ATM straddle has 0Δ, where, for a given maturity, the strike price is chosen such that the call and put options have the same Δ but with different signs. Denote the ATM volatility for the expiry T by $\sigma_{\text{ATM}}(T)$. The following ATM strike $K_{\text{ATM}}(T)$ can be derived.

$$K_{\text{ATM}}(T) = F(0,T) e^{\frac{1}{2}\sigma_{\text{ATM}}(T)^2 T}. \tag{4.21}$$

RR is a structure in which the buyer buys a call and sells a put with symmetric deltas. RR is quoted as the difference between the two implied volatilities, σ_c and σ_p, plugging into the BS formula for the call option and put option, respectively. Let $\sigma_{\text{RR}}(T)$ be the implied volatility of the RR with time-to-maturity T. Then,

$$\sigma_{\text{RR}}(T) = \sigma_c(T) - \sigma_p(T). \tag{4.22}$$

The VWB is built by selling and buying a quantity of ATM straddles such that the resulting structure has a zero Vega. Let $\sigma_{\text{VWB}}(T)$ be the implied volatility of the VWB with time to maturity T. Then

$$\sigma_{\text{VWB}}(T) = \frac{\sigma_c(T) + \sigma_p(T)}{2} - \sigma_{\text{ATM}}(T). \tag{4.23}$$

For a given expiry T, the two implied volatilities across different deltas can be immediately identified by solving the linear system from Equations 4.21, 4.22, and 4.23.

$$\sigma_{35\Delta c}(T) = \sigma_{\text{ATM}}(T) + \sigma_{35\Delta \text{VWB}}(T) + 0.5 \sigma_{35\Delta \text{RR}}(T),$$

$$\sigma_{35\Delta p}(T) = \sigma_{\text{ATM}}(T) + \sigma_{35\Delta \text{VWB}}(T) - 0.5 \sigma_{35\Delta \text{RR}}(T).$$

The implied volatilities of 25Δ and 10Δ can be calculated similarly.

Once the implied volatilities are computed, their corresponding strikes can easily be calculated by

$$K_{35\Delta p}(T) = \widehat{F}(0,T) e^{-\alpha_{35} \sigma_{35\Delta p}(T) \sqrt{T} + 0.5 \sigma_{35\Delta p}(T)^2 T},$$

$$K_{35\Delta c}(T) = \widehat{F}(0,T) e^{\alpha_{35} \sigma_{35\Delta c}(T) \sqrt{T} + 0.5 \sigma_{35\Delta c}(T)^2 T},$$

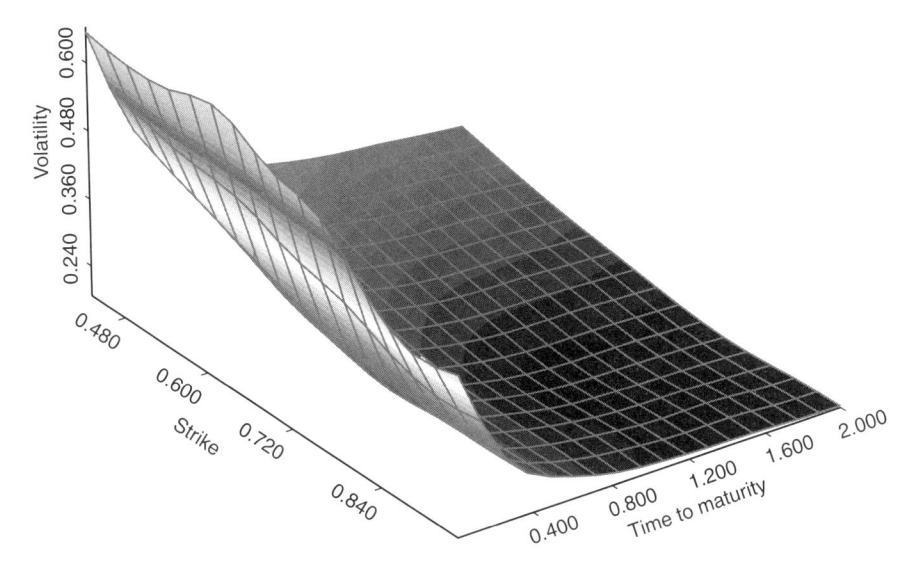

Figure 4.9 AUD–USD option volatility surface on October 16, 2008.

where $\alpha_{35} = -\Psi^{-1}(0.35e^{r_f T})$. Similarly, the strike prices for 25Δ and 10Δ can be computed using $\alpha_{25} = -\Psi^{-1}(0.25e^{r_f T})$ and $\alpha_{10} = -\Psi^{-1}(0.1e^{r_f T})$. For typical market parameters, $\alpha_j > 0$ and $K_{35\Delta p} < K_{\text{ATM}} < K_{35\Delta c}$, we can construct the entire implied volatility smile for all times-to-maturity T.

4.3.5.3 Case Study Revisited: MTM under Heston Model
As previously discussed, to price derivatives under the Heston model, it is necessary to infer the model parameters from the market-implied volatility surface. Suppose that we would like to price the CITIC AUD–USD FX accumulator for October 16, 2008, using the Heston model. The market-implied volatility surface data for that date is collected for calibration using DE. Figure 4.9 depicts the market volatility surface and Figure 4.10 the fitted volatility surface. Model constraint $2\kappa\theta > \epsilon^2$ can be added. Table 4.17 presents the calibration results with and without this model constraint, and it can be seen that they are quite similar; although in the absence of the constraint, the model's fit to market data is better, as shown by the lower value of the cost function. Note that without the model constraint, negative variance may easily be generated in Monte Carlo simulation if the standard Euler scheme is employed. It is advisable to use the QE method instead. For more details, please refer to the folder entitled Ch4.6_MTM_HestonQE.

Next, we conduct MTM evaluation of the FX accumulator for CITIC Pacific to determine the expected payoffs during the period from October 16 to 29, 2008. The implied volatility surface in Figure 4.9 is an inverted smile, which is not particularly abnormal in the FX option market. For a BS model in which few parameters are employed, only the interest rates and constant volatility are updated daily. For the local volatility and Heston models, however, calibration is required to obtain more

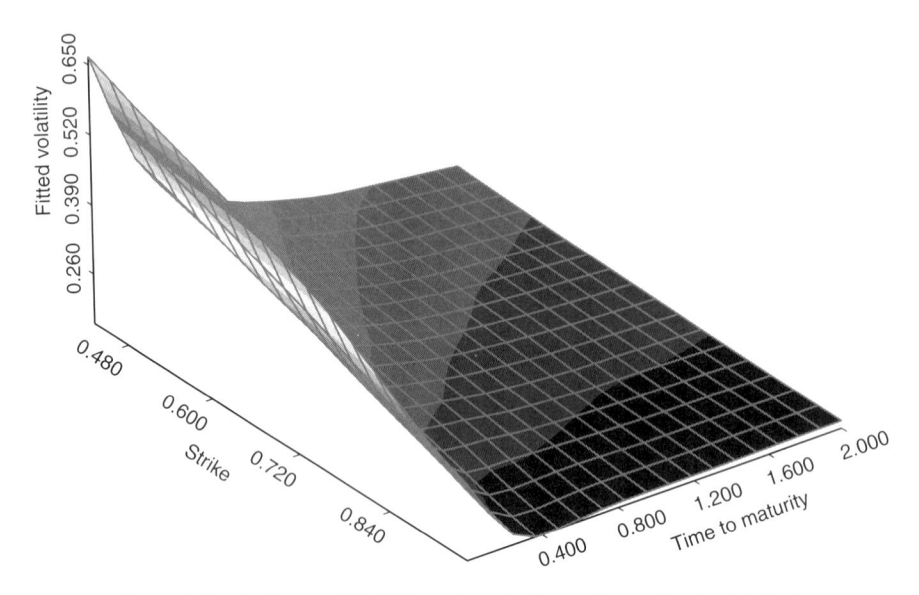

Figure 4.10 Calibrated AUD–USD option volatility surface on October 16, 2008.

accurate parameters. Repeating the simulation process for each trading day during the observation period, we obtain the following results.

It can be seen from Table 4.17 that the calibrated correlation coefficient is consistently equal to -1, which suggests a strong negative correlation between the asset's return and its volatility. This result also implies that the Heston stochastic volatility model behaves very similarly to a local volatility model. When the correlation coefficient is 1 or -1, the two Brownian motions in the Heston model are essentially the same. Thus, the volatility is a deterministic function of the asset value, and the model is reduced to a local volatility model. We can see that the Heston model is sufficiently general to embrace some of the local volatility models.

Table 4.18 presents the option prices generated by the different models. We can see that the BS model seems to overstate the losses from the accumulator, and the Heston and local volatility models produce a similar option price. Therefore, CITIC Pacific

TABLE 4.17 Results of Heston Model Calibration to AUD–USD Options on October 16, 2008, with and Without the Model Constraint

Parameter\Constraint	Yes	No
κ	12.68644716	11.37941545
θ	0.037710057	0.037596388
V_0	0.301166409	0.286968849
ϵ	0.978168333	1
ρ	-1	-1
$2\kappa\theta - \epsilon^2$	0.00000000129	-0.14435016
Lowest cost	0.0074227197	0.0070266384

TABLE 4.18 Simulated Payoffs of the Three Models After Marking-to-Market

Date	Exchange rate	BS model	Heston model	Local volatility model
10/16/2008	0.6749	−153.56	−120.41	−118.85
10/17/2008	0.6763	−151.88	−119.46	−118.54
10/20/2008	0.7003	−146.36	−108.69	−107.73
10/21/2008	0.6915	−150.71	−111.84	−112.33
10/22/2008	0.6688	−157.56	−126.73	−125.29
10/23/2008	0.6628	−159.74	−127.54	−127.68
10/24/2008	0.6178	−181.65	−152.32	−152.01
10/27/2008	0.6058	−184.16	−159.54	−158.75
10/28/2008	0.6187	−183.19	−153.53	−151.75
10/29/2008	0.6498	−170.87	−135.08	−133.44

LTD would most likely pay too much to settle the accumulator if the settlement fee were calculated using the BS model.

As shown in Figure 4.11, the trends of the expected payoffs with time are almost the same regardless of the model. However, the payoffs simulated by the local volatility and Heston models are always higher than that obtained from the BS model, primarily because the volatility measure differs among the models. The BS model uses 30-day historical volatility, whose horizon is much shorter than the maturity of the contract, thereby underestimating the payoff of the FX accumulator. This constitutes one of the disadvantages of the BS model. As the accumulator consists of a series of up-and-out options with different maturities, a single constant volatility leads to a biased simulation result. If we decompose the accumulator into several up-and-out options and perform simulation on them separately, then the bias is reduced. It is interesting that a single parameter can exert such a pronounced effect on the simulation results.

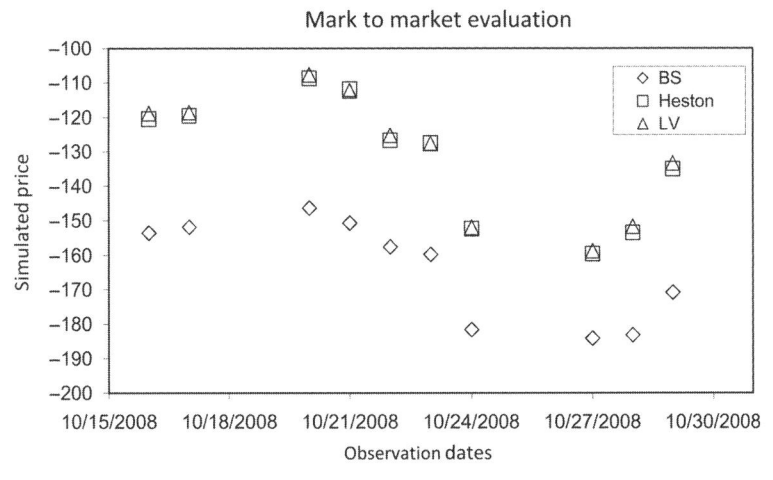

Figure 4.11 Simulated payoffs of the three models after marking to market.

4.4 THE GARCH OPTION PRICING MODEL

The local volatility and stochastic volatility models constitute practical approaches to financial engineering. However, both approaches require a large number of option data to calibrate the model parameters. When a bank wants to issue a structured product on an asset with no or very few options being traded in the market, calibration-based volatility models are not useful. Although the bank could attempt to filter the local volatility function or stochastic volatility model from the time series of asset returns, the computation involved is rather sophisticated and insufficiently efficient to support real-time trading.

The generalized autoregressive conditional heteroskedastic (GARCH) model is probably the most suitable alternative for valuing options in such a situation because of its tractability in allowing estimation using historical returns. In time-series analysis, volatility itself plays a fundamental role, being a measure of the intensity of random changes in an asset return; see Figure 4.12. Many derivatives are sensitive to volatility and correlation changes, and volatility modeling for forecasting, pricing, and hedging has become increasingly popular since 1990. For a discussion of the GARCH model, see Chan (2010).

The GARCH model expresses variance as a function of past returns and historical volatilities. The GARCH model was introduced by Engle (1982) and subsequently

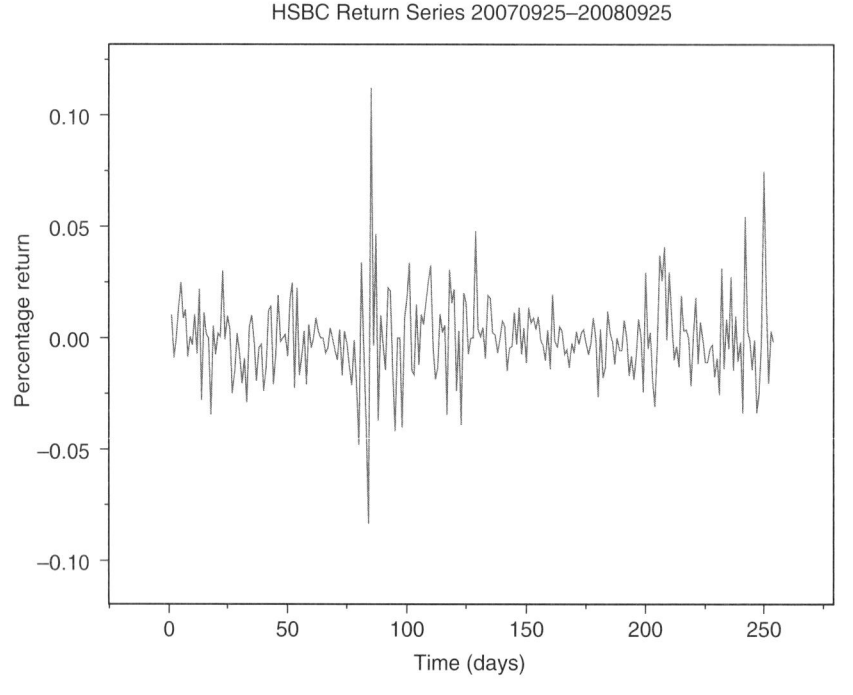

Figure 4.12 HSBC return time series.

generalized by Bollerslev (1986). Suppose that variance follows the GARCH(p, q) model:

$$R_t = \mu + \epsilon_t,$$

$$\sigma_t^2 = \alpha_0 + \sum_{i=1}^{q} \alpha_i \epsilon_{t-i}^2 + \sum_{i=1}^{p} \beta_i \sigma_{t-i}^2,$$

where R_t is the asset return at time t, μ is a constant, α_i and β_j are constant for $i = 1, \ldots, q$ and $j = 1, \ldots, p$. To ensure stationarity, it is required that $\sum_{i=1}^{q} \alpha_i + \sum_{i=1}^{p} \beta_i < 1$. In this model, we have to estimate the $p + q + 1$ parameters. The simplest GARCH class model is the GARCH(1,1) model, in which only three parameters require estimation. In fact, empirical analysis indicates that the GARCH(1,1) model can often be used to successfully model the volatility clustering observed in the market. The GARCH(1,1) model can be formally expressed as

$$R_t = \mu + \epsilon_t,$$

$$\sigma_t^2 = \omega + \alpha \epsilon_{t-1}^2 + \beta \sigma_{t-1}^2,$$

where $\omega = \gamma V_L$, V_L is the long-run average variance specifying the model's mean reversion level, $\gamma = 1 - \alpha - \beta$, and ϵ_{t-1}^2 is the squared return at $t - 1$. Note that, conditionally, $\epsilon_{t-1} \sim \mathcal{N}(0, \sigma_{t-1}^2)$. The model must satisfy constraint $\alpha + \beta < 1$ to ensure stationarity. Once the parameters (ω, α, β) are estimated, the entire term structure of volatility can be calculated. The model can be extended to combination with the asset process to price derivatives under risk-neutral measure $\mathbb{Q}$, which is discussed later in this chapter.

4.4.1 Estimation of Model Parameters

One of the main innovations of the GARCH model is that its parameters can be both estimated and checked using historical data. A set of parameters can be employed to compute volatility everyday over the sample period. If the fitted volatility fails to capture the observed volatility clusters, then new parameters are chosen. In the estimation problem, the parameters (ω, α, β) have to be estimated with the constraint that $\alpha + \beta + \gamma = 1$ via maximum likelihood estimation (MLE). The likelihood function of ϵ_t is

$$\prod_{t=1}^{n} \frac{1}{\sqrt{2\pi \sigma_t^2}} \exp\left(\frac{-\epsilon_t^2}{2\sigma_t^2}\right),$$

and the log-likelihood function of ϵ_t is

$$\frac{n}{2} \log 2\pi + \frac{1}{2} \sum_{t=1}^{n} \left(-\log \sigma_t^2 - \frac{\epsilon_t^2}{\sigma_t^2}\right).$$

158 VOLATILITY MODELING

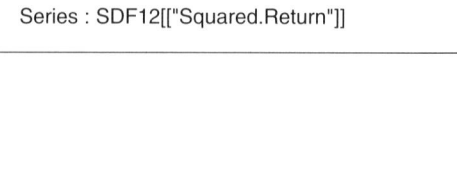

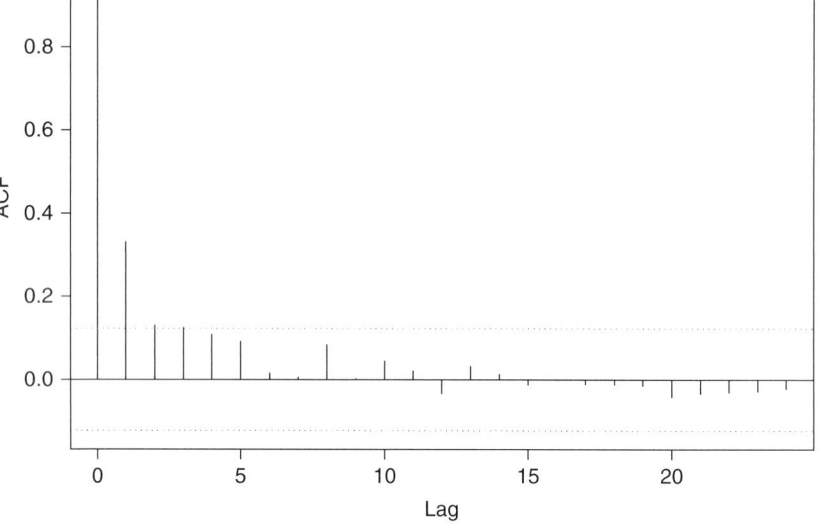

Figure 4.13 Autocorrelation function (ACF) plot of HSBC squared returns.

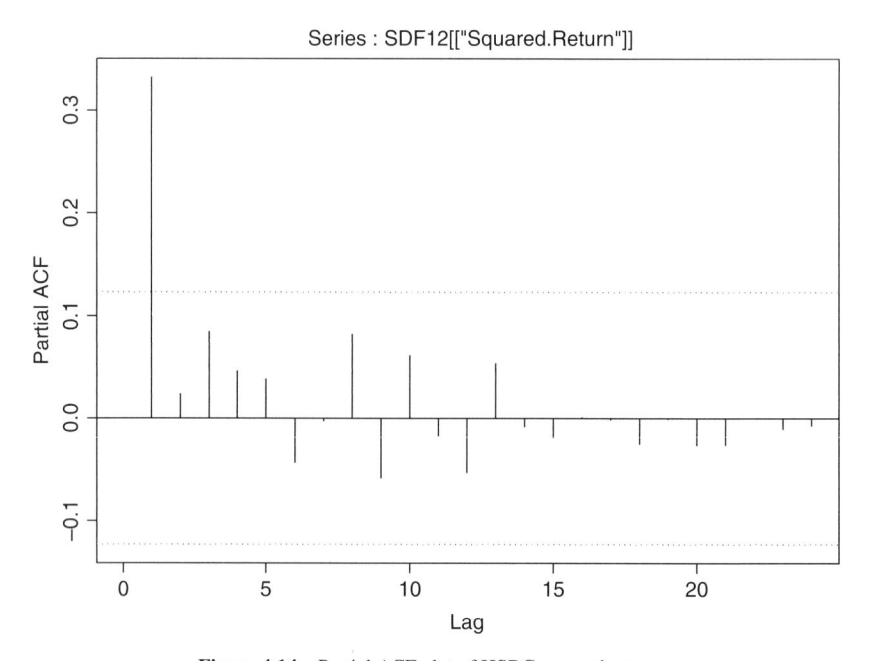

Figure 4.14 Partial ACF plot of HSBC squared returns.

TABLE 4.19 Results of GARCH(1,1) Model-Fitting for HSBC Return Series

ω	0.000015699
α	0.232639483
β	0.75159
σ_0^2	0.000876

Therefore, we have to choose the parameters such that the function

$$l(\omega, \alpha, \beta) = \sum_{t=1}^{n}\left(-\log \sigma_t^2 - \frac{\epsilon_t^2}{\sigma_t^2}\right)$$

is maximized. It is easy to see that the objective function is not quadratic, and thus iterative algorithms are required for maximization. In Excel, the built-in solver employs the gradient approach for optimization, and it can be applied to this MLE estimation problem. Other statistical packages, such as R and S-PLUS, would also be appropriate.

Example 4.1 *Suppose that we would like to fit a GARCH(1,1) model to HSBC's return series. Daily stock prices (adjusted close) from the 09/25/2007 to 09/25/2008 period are collected from Bloomberg. Percentage returns are computed as $R_t = (S_t - S_{t-1})/S_{t-1}$. The daily return series is fitted to the GARCH model using the Excel solver, and the output is presented in Table 4.19. Note that the parameters are estimated from daily data.*

Figures 4.13 and 4.14 are the autocorrelation plot and the partial autocorrelation plot of the HSBC squared return series, respectively. These graphs show that GARCH(1,1) seems reasonable to model the HSBC return series. The estimation procedure is sometimes highly unstable and sensitive to the initial values of ω, α, and β. Variance targeting can be applied so that only α and β have to be estimated. V_L can then be estimated by the sample variance of ϵ_t, and hence $\omega = V_L(1 - \alpha - \beta)$.

To check the adequacy of the model, it is often useful to check the standardized residuals. As $\epsilon_t \sim \mathcal{N}(0, \sigma_t^2)$, if GARCH(1,1) is correct, then the residual is $\epsilon_t/\sigma_t \sim \mathcal{N}(0, 1)$. A QQ-plot can be created to observe whether the standardized residuals are approximately normal. Furthermore, an important diagnostic test is to determine whether the standardized residuals are now free of volatility clusters. These pre- and post-tests show whether the model captures the observed historical patterns of volatility. The Ljung–Box test can also be employed to detect volatility clusters. Let γ_n be the nth autocorrelation of the T-squared returns. This test reveals whether the size of today's movement has any predictability for the size of the movement K days in the future. We define the Ljung–Box test statistics as

$$\text{LB} = T(T+2) \sum_{n=1}^{K} \frac{\gamma_n^2}{T-n}.$$

TABLE 4.20 Ljung–Box Test for the Squared Residuals of the GARCH(1,1) Model Fitted to HSBC Returns

	ϵ_t^2	ϵ_t^2/σ_t^2
LB test statistics	45.87965164	7.428528528
P-value	0.0000555641	0.944650091

The statistics are chi-square distributed with K degrees of freedom. At significance level α, the critical region for rejection of the null hypothesis that there is no autocorrelation ($H_0 : \gamma_K = 0$) is given by

$$\text{LB} > \chi^2_{1-\alpha, K},$$

where $\chi^2_{1-\alpha, K}$ is the 100αth percentile of the chi-square distribution with K degrees of freedom.

Example 4.2   *Consider the parameter estimation of the GARCH(1,1) model with respect to HSBC's return series, and examine the model performance. Let $K = 15$, Table 4.20 presents the result of the Ljung–Box test, and Figure 4.15 is a QQ-plot of the standardized residuals. The p-value of ϵ_t^2 is small, which shows that autocorrelations exist in ϵ_t^2. The p-value of ϵ_t^2/σ_t^2 however is large, which indicates that there is no autocorrelation in ϵ_t^2/σ_t^2. In conclusion, the autocorrelation of ϵ_t^2 is removed by the GARCH(1,1) model. Therefore, σ_t^2 is a good estimate of the variance rate. For further details, please refer to* Ch4.4_GARCH(1,1)_HSBC_Example.xls.

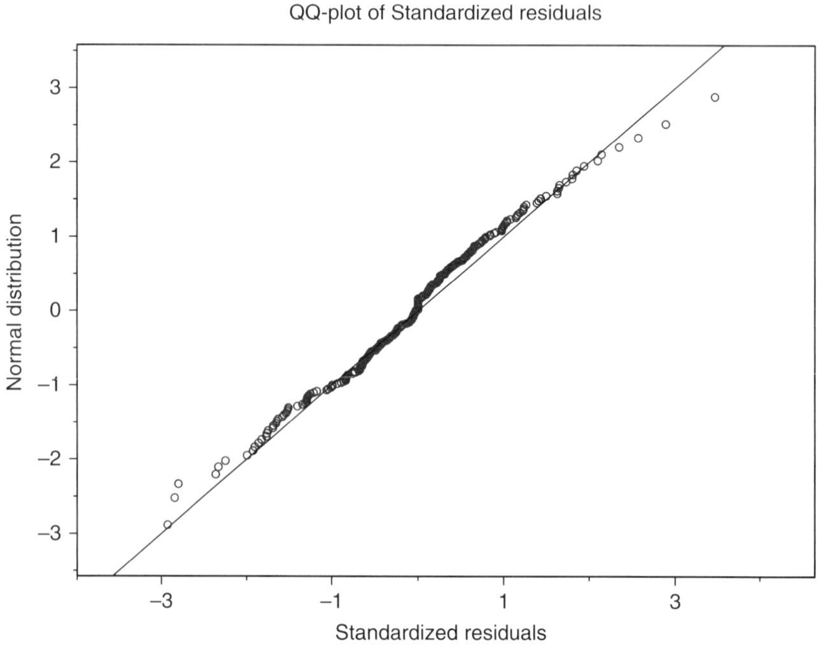

Figure 4.15 QQ-plot of standardized residuals of GARCH(1,1) model fitted to HSBC returns.

4.4.2 Identification of the Risk-Neutral Process

As noted, the GARCH model proposed by Bollerslev (1986) and its extensions have become popular tools for modeling financial time series in recent years. Duan (1995) utilizes the locally risk-neutral valuation relationship (LRNVR) to develop a GARCH option pricing model for derivatives, which he claims to have three distinctive features. First, the GARCH option price is a function of the risk premium embedded in the underlying asset, which agrees with the standard preference-free option pricing result. Second, the model is non-Markovian. Last but not least, the model can potentially explain some of the systematic biases associated with the BS model, such as the underpricing of out-of-the-money options, the options on low volatility securities, and short-maturity options and the smile-shaped implied volatility curve observed in a typical market.

Suppose that the log-stock prices follow the following GARCH(1,1) process under physical measure $\mathbb{P}$.

$$\log \frac{S_{t+1}}{S_t} = r + \lambda \sigma_{t+1} - \frac{1}{2}\sigma_{t+1}^2 + \sigma_{t+1}\epsilon_{t+1},$$

$$\sigma_{t+1}^2 = \omega + \alpha \epsilon_t^2 + \beta \sigma_t^2,$$

where ϵ_t, conditional on the information up to time t ($\mathcal{F}_t$), is a standard normal random variable, r is the constant continuously compounded one-period risk-free rate of return, and λ is the stock's constant unit risk premium. The estimation of this GARCH(1,1) model can employ MLE, and the likelihood function is given by

$$\prod_{t=1}^{n} \frac{1}{\sqrt{2\pi \sigma_t^2}} \exp\left[\frac{-\left(\log \frac{S_t}{S_{t-1}} - r + \lambda \sigma_t - \frac{1}{2}\sigma_t^2\right)^2}{2\sigma_t^2} \right].$$

The parameters $(\lambda, \omega, \alpha, \beta, \sigma_0)$ are estimated by maximizing the likelihood function.

To price derivatives under the risk-neutral measure, the conventional risk-neutral valuation relationship has to be generalized to accommodate the heteroskedasticity of the asset return process. A pricing measure $\mathbb{Q}$ is said to satisfy the LRNVR if it is mutually absolutely continuous with respect to physical measure $\mathbb{P}$. $\frac{S_{t+1}}{S_t}|\mathcal{F}_t$ is log-normally distributed under $\mathbb{Q}$:

$$\mathrm{E}^{\mathbb{Q}}\left[\frac{S_{t+1}}{S_t}\bigg|\mathcal{F}_t\right] = e^r,$$

and

$$\mathrm{Var}^{\mathbb{Q}}\left(\log \frac{S_{t+1}}{S_t}\bigg|\mathcal{F}_t\right) = \mathrm{Var}^{\mathbb{P}}\left(\log \frac{S_{t+1}}{S_t}\bigg|\mathcal{F}_t\right)$$

almost surely with respect to measure $\mathbb{P}$. The LRNVR implies that under pricing measure $\mathbb{Q}$,

$$\log \frac{S_{t+1}}{S_t} = r - \frac{\sigma_{t+1}^2}{2} + \sigma_{t+1}\xi_{t+1},$$

$$\sigma_{t+1}^2 = \omega + \alpha(\xi_t - \lambda\sigma_t)^2 + \beta\sigma_t^2,$$

where $\xi_{t+1} = \epsilon_{t+1} + \lambda$, conditional on $\mathcal{F}_t$, is a standard normal random variable under $\mathbb{Q}$.

It should be noted that no analytical solution is available for this problem, and the pricing of derivatives thus relies heavily on Monte Carlo simulation. Variance reduction techniques, such as empirical martingale simulation (EMS), should be used to ensure accuracy. To reduce the variance of the simulation, the same set of normal random variables should be used for each simulation. This method is called bumping, and the relevant VBA code is as follows.

```
Public Function bGauss(Optional Step As Integer = 1) As Double
    Static SGauss
    Static nStep As Long
    Dim i As Long

    If Step > 0 Then
        nStep = nStep + Step
        If nStep > UBound(SGauss) Then
            ReDim Preserve SGauss(1 To UBound(SGauss) + bufNumber)
            For i = UBound(SGauss) - bufNumber + 1 To UBound(SGauss)
                SGauss(i) = rGauss()
            Next i
        End If
        bGauss = SGauss(nStep)
        Exit Function
    ElseIf Step = 0 Then
        nStep = 0
    Else
        ReDim SGauss(1 To bufNumber) As Double
        Randomize
        For i = 1 To bufNumber
            SGauss(i) = rGauss()
        Next i
        nStep = 0
    End If
    bGauss = 1
End Function
```

For further variance reduction, the inclusion of other variance reduction techniques, such as empirical martingale correction or antithetic variables, is encouraged. In addition, a large number of paths should be used, and more subintervals should be included for accuracy.

Although the price of risk λ can be estimated from historical returns, some practitioners prefer to calibrate it to option prices, if there are any, even for a limited number of options in the market. Other parameters are estimated with the GARCH(1,1) model. Such ad hoc GARCH model practice combines calibration and estimation.

4.4.3 Pricing Exotics

After parameter estimation, we are ready to price exotic derivatives using the GARCH(1,1) model. Consider the callable ELN term sheet discussed in Chapter 3. Suppose that we would like to price this product using the GARCH(1,1) model. The HSBC historical return series from September 25, 2007, to September 25, 2008, is obtained from Bloomberg. This series is then used to infer the parameters (ω, α, β) using MLE. To find λ, we have to infer it from traded options. Thus, the traded option data for September 25, 2008, is collected for calibration. The choice of options to be fitted is not unique, and we opt to fit short-maturity ATM and near-ATM options. The parameters are listed in Table 4.21.

Using the parameters shown in Table 4.21, we simulate the price of the range accrual note (RAN) in Chapter 3 using the GARCH(1,1) model. Using the function CRAN_Payoff and repeating the simulation process 50,000 times, we obtain a simulated price of 94,826.4892. Compared to the BS price of 94,846.9387, the percentage difference is only 0.02%. By means of the formula

$$V_L = \frac{\omega}{1 - \alpha - \beta},$$

we obtain the long-term average variance in GARCH(1,1) on annual basis V_L, which is 50.09%, and thus close to the constant volatility (46.74%) used in the BS model. The prices obtained from the two models exhibit little difference. For more details, please refer to Ch4.4_HSBC_RAN_GARCH(1,1).xls.

TABLE 4.21 Parameters of the GARCH(1,1) Model Fitted to the Options Traded on September 25, 2008

ω	0.000015699
α	0.232639483
β	0.75159
σ_0^2	0.000876
λ	0.2187
S_0	122.5
r	0.034
q	0

164 VOLATILITY MODELING

4.5 JUMP-DIFFUSION MODEL

Both local and stochastic volatility models assume continuous sample paths for the underlying asset, thereby ignoring the possibility that the asset price could change abruptly in a very short period of time. Jump-diffusion models compensate for the weakness of volatility models.

Jump-diffusion models deserve a separate chapter, although some of the volatility model results are applicable to jump-diffusion models. Adding jumps to a diffusion model essentially affects the estimated volatility and is aimed at fitting the implied volatility smile. Thus, we decided to include these models in this chapter.

Under $\mathbb{P}$, a jump-diffusion model postulates that the asset price dynamics follow

$$dX(t) = \mu\, dt + \sigma\, dW(t) + Y\, dN(t), \qquad (4.24)$$

where $X(t) = \log S(t)$ is the logarithmic stock price, $W(t)$ is standard Brownian motion, $N(t)$ is a Poisson process with constant intensity λ, and Y is the random jump size with a moment-generating function. Processes $W(t)$ and $N(t)$ and the random jump size are independent for all t. The distribution of the jump size can be chosen to fit the empirical data.

For the purpose of derivative valuation, we have to find the risk-neutral jump-diffusion model corresponding to Equation 4.24, which can be expressed as

$$S(t) = S(0)\exp\left(\mu t + \sigma W(t) + \sum_{j=1}^{N(t)} Y_j\right).$$

Under $\mathbb{Q}$, the process of $S(t)$ should agree with the martingale condition:

$$\mathrm{E}^{\mathbb{Q}}[S(t)|\mathcal{F}_0] = S(0)e^{rt}.$$

As there are two stochastic processes driving $S(t)$, the risk-neutral probability is not unique. However, if the $\mathbb{Q}$ process for $S(t)$ is confined to a form similar to Equaton 4.24, then one way to specify $\mathbb{Q}$ is to shift only the Brownian motion. Hence, we assume the $\mathbb{Q}$-process for $S(t)$ to be

$$S(t) = S(0)\exp\left(\mu^* t + \sigma W^*(t) + \sum_{j=1}^{N(t)} Y_j\right).$$

Taking the $\mathbb{Q}$-expectation on both sides, we have

$$\mathrm{E}^{\mathbb{Q}}[S(t)] = S(0)\mathrm{E}^{\mathbb{Q}}\left[\exp\left(\mu^* t + \sigma W^*(t)\right)\right]\mathrm{E}^{\mathbb{Q}}\left[\exp\left(\sum_{j=1}^{N(t)} Y_j\right)\right]. \qquad (4.25)$$

The first part of Equation 4.25 is simply the moment-generating function of a normal random variable:

$$E^{\mathbb{Q}}\left[\exp\left(\mu^*t + \sigma W^*(t)\right)\right] = \exp\left(\mu^*t + \frac{1}{2}\sigma^2 t\right).$$

The second part is evaluated using the conditional expectation:

$$E^{\mathbb{Q}}\left[\exp\left(\sum_{j=1}^{N(t)} Y_j\right)\right] = E^{\mathbb{Q}}\left[E^{\mathbb{Q}}\left[\exp\left(\sum_{j=1}^{n} Y_j\right)\Bigg| N(t) = n\right]\right]$$

$$= E^{\mathbb{Q}}\left[E^{\mathbb{Q}}\left[\prod_{j=1}^{n} E^{\mathbb{Q}}[e^{Y_j}]\Bigg| N(t) = n\right]\right]$$

$$= E^{\mathbb{Q}}\left[\exp\left(mN(t)\right)\right]$$

$$= \exp\left(\lambda t(e^m - 1)\right),$$

where $m = \log E^{\mathbb{Q}}[e^Y]$, and the last line applies the moment-generating function of the Poisson distribution. The risk-neutral expected asset price becomes

$$E^{\mathbb{Q}}[S(t)] = S(0)\exp\left(\mu^*t + \frac{\sigma^2}{2}t\right)\exp\left(\lambda t(E^{\mathbb{Q}}[e^Y] - 1)\right).$$

By the martingale condition, $E^{\mathbb{Q}}[S(t)] = S(0)e^{rt}$, we deduce that

$$\mu^* = r - \frac{1}{2}\sigma^2 - \lambda\left(E[e^Y] - 1\right), \tag{4.26}$$

where the jump distribution is the same under both $\mathbb{P}$ and $\mathbb{Q}$.

Let $\Phi_J(\phi)$ be the $\mathbb{Q}$-characteristic function of $X(t)$ such that

$$\Phi_J(x, 0; \phi) = E^{\mathbb{Q}}\left[e^{i\phi X(t)}\Big| X(0) = x\right].$$

Then,

$$\Phi_J(x, 0; \phi) = \exp\left(i\phi x + i\phi\mu^*t - \frac{\sigma^2}{2}\phi t + \lambda t(E^{\mathbb{Q}}[e^{i\phi Y}] - 1)\right). \tag{4.27}$$

Once the characteristic function of Y is specified, the $\mathbb{Q}$-characteristic function for the log-asset value is known.

166 VOLATILITY MODELING

This characteristic function can then be used to obtain the option price using the Carr and Madan formula in Theorem 4.2 as

$$c_J(K,T) = e^{-rT} e^{-\alpha k} \mathcal{F}_{\xi,k}^{-1} \left\{ \frac{\Phi_J(x, 0; \phi = \xi - (\alpha+1)i)}{\alpha^2 + \alpha - \xi^2 + i(2\alpha+1)\xi} \right\}.$$

Observing the market call and put prices, we can calibrate the risk-neutral parameters by minimizing the difference between the market prices and the model prices:

$$\min_{\Omega} \sum_{i,j} |c_{market}(K_i, T_j) - c_J(K_i, T_j)|^p,$$

for some pre selected p norm. Minimization can be carried out using the DE procedure presented in Section 4.2.3.

If the jump size, Y, is normally distributed, then the call pricing formula can be further simplified to avoid inverse Fourier transform. Such a jump-diffusion was proposed by Merton (1976), and was the first to appear in the finance literature. More specifically, assume $Y \sim \mathcal{N}(\mu_Y, s^2)$.

Theorem 4.3 *Under Merton (1976) jump-diffusion model, the call option price is given by*

$$c_J(K,T) = e^{-rT} \sum_{n=0}^{\infty} \frac{e^{-\lambda T} (\lambda T)^{-n}}{n!} \left[S e^{\mu_n T} \Psi(d_1^n) - K \Psi(d_2^n) \right],$$

where

$$\mu_n = r - \frac{1}{2}\sigma^2 - \lambda \left(e^{\mu_Y + s^2/2} - 1 \right) + n \frac{\mu_Y}{T},$$

$$d_1^n = \frac{\log \frac{S}{K} + \mu_n T}{\sqrt{\sigma^2 T + ns^2}}, \quad d_2^n = d_1^n - \sqrt{\sigma^2 T + ns^2}.$$

Proof:

$$c_J(K,T) = e^{-rT} \mathrm{E}^{\mathbb{Q}} \left[\max \left(S e^{\mu^* T + \sigma W_T + \sum_{j=1}^{N(T)} Y_j} - K, 0 \right) \right]$$

$$= e^{-rT} \mathrm{E}^{\mathbb{Q}} \left[\mathrm{E}^{\mathbb{Q}} \left[\max \left(S e^{\mu^* T + \sigma W_T + \sum_{j=1}^{N(T)} Y_j} - K, 0 \right) \middle| N(T) = n \right] \right]$$

$$= e^{-rT} \mathrm{E}^{\mathbb{Q}} \left[\mathrm{E}^{\mathbb{Q}} \left[\max \left(S e^{\tilde{X}_n} - K, 0 \right) \middle| N(T) = n \right] \right],$$

where

$$\tilde{X}_n \sim \mathcal{N}(\mu_n T, \sigma^2 T + ns^2).$$

The internal expectation can be evaluated via the BS formula. Then the outer expectation can be expressed using the probability mass function of Poisson distribution. The result follows.

From Merton jump-diffusion model, we observe that the volatility, $\sqrt{\sigma^2 T + ns^2}$, depends on the number of jumps occurring prior to maturity. Hence, a jump-diffusion model randomizes volatility with Poisson shocks and is able to generate an implied volatility smile.

4.5.1 Simulation of Asset Price Paths and Product Valuation

To simulate asset price paths, recall Equation 4.24:

$$d \log S(t) = \mu \, dt + \sigma \, dW(t) + Y \, dN(t). \tag{4.28}$$

With a fixed Δt, let $S_j = S(j \Delta t)$ for some positive integer j. Discrete approximation to these dynamics (Eq. 4.28) is given by

$$\log S_j = \log S_{j-1} + \mu \Delta t + \sigma Z_j \sqrt{\Delta t} + Y_j \Delta N_j, \tag{4.29}$$

where the Z_j's are independent standard normal random variables. When Δt is sufficiently small, ΔN_j is either 1 with probability $\lambda \Delta t$ or 0 with probability $1 - \lambda \Delta t$, which enables us to simulate the asset price paths of the jump-diffusion model as follows.

1. Partition $[0, T]$ into m equal subintervals, where $\Delta t = T/m$.
2. Set $j = 1$.
3. Generate $U_j \sim U(0, 1)$.
4. Set $\log S_j = \begin{cases} \log S_{j-1} + \mu \Delta t + \sigma Z_j \sqrt{\Delta t}, & \text{if } U_j > \lambda \Delta t, \\ \log S_{j-1} + (\mu + k) \Delta t + Z_j \sqrt{\sigma \Delta t + s^2}, & \text{otherwise.} \end{cases}$
5. Set $j = j + 1$.
6. Repeat Steps 3 to 5 until $j > m$.

To simulate n paths, repeat the foregoing procedure n times. The corresponding VBA code is as follows.

```
Type JD_PathType
    S0 As Double
    mu As Double
    sigma As Double
    t As Double
    dt As Double
    m As Long
    n As Long
```

```
      lambda As Double
      j_mu As Double
      j_sigma As Double
    End Type

    Public Function JD_Path(A As JD_PathType) As Variant
      Dim i As Long, j As Long
      Dim mu As Double
      ReDim S(0 To A.m, 1 To A.n) As Double

      For j = 1 To A.n
        S(0, j) = Log(A.S0)
        For i = 1 To A.m
          If Rnd() > A.lambda * A.dt Then
            S(i, j) = S(i - 1, j) + A.mu * A.dt + A.sigma _
                      * Sqr(A.dt) * rGauss()
          Else
            S(i, j) = S(i - 1, j) + A.mu * A.dt + A.j_mu + _
                      Sqr(A.dt * A.sigma ^ 2 + A.j_sigma ^ 2) _
                      * rGauss()
          End If
        Next i
      Next j

      For j = 1 To A.n
        For i = 0 To A.m
          S(i, j) = Exp(S(i, j))
        Next i
      Next j

      JD_Path = S
    End Function
```

Instead of generating a uniform random variable to determine whether there is a jump at each step, we can also generate an exponential random variable to determine when there is a jump and simulate the jump at that step. As the sojourn time for the Poisson process follows an exponential distribution with mean λ, we simulate $W \sim \text{Exp}(\lambda)$ at the beginning of the simulation and calculate the step number of that jump. Then we simulate the jump amplitude at that step, after which we simulate the sojourn time of the next jump and the next jump amplitude. By the memoryless property of the exponential distribution, $W \sim \text{Exp}(\lambda)$. We repeat this process until the final step is reached. The simulation procedure proceeds as follows.

1. Partition $[0, T]$ into m equal subintervals, where $\Delta t = T/m$.
2. Set $j = 1, r = 1$.

… JUMP-DIFFUSION MODEL   169

3. Generate $W_r \sim \text{Exp}(\lambda)$ by $W_r = -\log(U_r)/\lambda$, where $U_r \sim \text{U}(0, 1)$.
4. Set nextJumpStep = Round-Up$((W_1 + \ldots + W_r)/\Delta t)$.
5. If $j = $ nextJumpStep, then set $\log S_j = \log S_{j-1} + k + sZ_j$, $r = r + 1$, and go back to Step 3.
6. Set $\log S_j = \log S_{j-1} + \mu \Delta t + \sigma \sqrt{\Delta t} Z_j$.
7. Set $j = j + 1$.
8. Repeat Steps 5 to 7 until $j > m$.

The corresponding VBA code is as follows.

```
Public Function JDExp_Path(A As JD_PathType) As Variant
  Dim i As Long, j As Long
  Dim expValue As Double, mu As Double
  Dim nextJumpTime As Double, nextJumpStep As Long
  ReDim S(0 To A.m, 1 To A.n) As Double

  For j = 1 To A.n
    S(0, j) = A.S0
    nextJumpTime = -(Log(1 - Rnd())) / A.lambda
    nextJumpStep = Round(nextJumpTime / A.dt + 0.5) 'To round up
    For i = 1 To A.m
      expValue = A.mu * A.dt + A.sigma * Sqr(A.dt) * rGauss()
CheckJump:
      If i = nextJumpStep Then
        expValue = expValue + (A.j_mu + A.j_sigma * rGauss())
        nextJumpTime = nextJumpTime - (Log(1 - Rnd())) / A.lambda
        nextJumpStep = Round(nextJumpTime / A.dt + 0.5) 'To round up
        GoTo CheckJump
      End If
      S(i, j) = S(i - 1, j) * Exp(expValue)
    Next i
  Next j

  JDExp_Path = S
End Function
```

We propose two methods. The first generates a single jump at a single step, whereas the second allows multiple jumps at a single step. When Δt is small, there is no difference between the two methods. However, when Δt is large, the first method always results in a large discretization error, whereas the second results in no such error. In addition, the latter method offers us a way to perform an exact simulation.

As a simple illustration, we simulate the price of a European call option and compare it with the value from the BS formula.

Example 4.3 With $S_0 = 50$, $r = 8\%$, $\sigma = 20\%$, $\lambda = 5$, $k = 0$, $s = 5\%$, $T = 0.5$, $dt = 1/250$, $n = 50{,}000$, and $K = 50$, simulate the call price with the two aforementioned methods using the following VBA code.

```
Dim A As JD_PathType
Dim S As Variant, Payoff As Variant
Dim Price1 As Double, Price2 as Double

rf = 0.08
A.S0 = 50
A.sigma = 0.2
A.lambda = 5
A.j_mu = 0
A.j_sigma = 0.05
A.t = 1
A.dt = 1 / 250
A.m = A.t / A.dt
A.n = 50000
A.mu = rf - 1 / 2 * A.sigma ^ 2 - A.lambda * _
       (Exp(A.j_mu + 1 / 2 * A.j_sigma ^ 2) - 1)
K = 50

'First Method
S = JD_Path(A)
Payoff = EO_Payoff(S, K, xCall)
Price1 = Exp(-rf * A.t) * Average(payoff)

'Second Method
S = JDExp_Path(A)
Payoff = EO_Payoff(S, K, xCall)
Price2 = Exp(-rf * A.t) * Average(payoff)
```

The BS price is 3.853. The simulated prices using the first and second methods are 4.234 and 4.237, respectively, thereby suggesting that the two methods agree. Now, change $dt = 0.5$ so that exact simulation is used to simulate the price again. The simulated prices using the first and second methods are now 4.011 and 4.234, respectively. In the first method, when Δt is large, the condition that ΔN_j is either 1 with probability $\lambda \Delta t$ or 0 with probability $1 - \lambda \Delta t$ no longer holds, which underestimates the number of jumps and thus the call price. In contrast, the second method allows for multiple jumps, and thus this issue does not affect the simulated price. For further details, please refer to Ch4.3_Jump_Diffusion_Simulation_Example.xls

Now, price the callable ELN in Section 2.3 using a jump-diffusion model. With $S_0 = 122.5$, $r = 3.40\%$, $q = 3.00\%$, $\sigma = 44.03\%$, $\lambda = 20.86$, $k = -0.28\%$, $s = 11.40\%$, $dt = 1/252$, and $n = 50{,}000$, the simulated price is 90,198.5. For more details, please refer to Ch4.3_Jump_Diffusion_RAN.xls. The parameters used in this numerical example are estimated in the next section using historical prices developed by HSBC. The physical process is transformed to a risk-neutral process by shifting the Brownian motion.

4.5.2 Estimation of Jump-Diffusion

Instead of calibrating the risk-neutral jump-diffusion model to option prices, we can also estimate a physical jump-diffusion model and then adjust the Brownian motion to produce risk-neutral asset dynamics. The latter approach is suitable for an underlying asset that has no (illiquid) option market. However, the MLE may not be possible for this jump-diffusion model due to subtle degeneracy in the likelihood function.

We therefore adopt a Bayesian framework for estimation. There are five parameters in the Merton jump-diffusion model, and their corresponding conditional conjugate priors are as follows.

In the physical jump-diffusion model (Eq. 4.24), we assume that the prior distribution of μ is a normal distribution, $\mu \sim \mathcal{N}(\theta, \tau^2)$, and the posterior can be derived as

$$\mu_{i+1} \sim \mathcal{N}(\theta_{i+1}, \tau_{i+1}^2), \qquad (4.30)$$

$$\theta_{i+1} = \frac{\tau^2 \sum_{j=1}^{n}(x_j - Y_j \Delta N_j) + \theta \sigma_i^2}{n\tau^2 + \sigma_i^2},$$

$$\tau_{i+1}^2 = \frac{\tau^2 \sigma_i^2}{n\tau^2 + \sigma_i^2}.$$

For σ^2, assume that $\sigma^2 \sim \mathrm{IG}(\alpha, \beta)$, which is the inverse Gaussian distribution, and the posterior is given by

$$\sigma_{i+1}^2 \sim \mathrm{IG}(\alpha_{i+1}, \beta_{i+1}), \qquad (4.31)$$

$$\alpha_{i+1} = \alpha + n/2,$$

$$\beta_{i+1} = \beta + \frac{\sum_{j=1}^{n}(x_j - \mu_i - Y_j \Delta N_j)^2}{2}.$$

In a short time period or sampling frequency, $\Delta N \sim \mathrm{Bin}(n, \lambda \Delta t)$. Hence, we select $\lambda \sim \mathrm{Beta}(a, b)$ such that the posterior is given by

$$\lambda_{i+1} \Delta t \sim \mathrm{Bin}(a_{i+1}, b_{i+1}), \qquad (4.32)$$

$$a_{i+1} = a + N_i,$$

$$b_{i+1} = b + n - N_i.$$

172 VOLATILITY MODELING

For k, assume that $k \sim \mathcal{N}(m, v^2)$, and the posterior is given by

$$k_{i+1} \sim \mathcal{N}(m_{i+1}, v_{i+1}^2),$$

$$m_{i+1} = \frac{v^2 \sum_{j=1}^{N} Y_j + m_i s_i^2}{N_i v^2 + s_i^2}, \qquad (4.33)$$

$$v_{i+1}^2 = \frac{v^2 s_i^2}{N_i v^2 + s_i^2}.$$

For s^2, assume that $s^2 \sim IG(p, q)$, and the posterior is given by

$$s_{i+1}^2 \sim IG(p_{i+1}, q_{i+1}),$$

$$p_{i+1} = p + N_i/2, \qquad (4.34)$$

$$q_{i+1} = q + \frac{\sum_{j=1}^{N_i}(Y_j - k_i)^2}{2}.$$

The posteriors are conditional distributions, given Y_j and ΔN_i, which are not observable. Therefore, at each time point, they should be simulated. Consider the two following conditional distributions.

$$X_j | \Delta N_j = 0 \sim \mathcal{N}(\mu, \sigma^2),$$
$$X_j | \Delta N_j = 1 \sim \mathcal{N}(\mu + k, \sigma^2 + s^2).$$

By Bayes' Theorem,

$$\Pr(\Delta N_j = 1 | x_j) = \frac{\Pr(x_j | \Delta N_j = 1)\lambda \Delta t}{\Pr(x_j | \Delta N_j = 1)\lambda \Delta t + \Pr(x_j | \Delta N_j = 0)(1 - \lambda \Delta t)},$$

$$\Pr(\Delta N_j = 0 | x_j) = 1 - \Pr(\Delta N_j = 1 | x_j).$$

The foregoing equations can be simplified to

$$\Pr(\Delta N_j = 1 | x_j) = \frac{C_1}{C_1 + \frac{1}{\sqrt{C_2}} \exp\left(-\frac{C_3}{2\sigma^2}\right)},$$

$$C_1 = \frac{\lambda \Delta t}{1 - \lambda \Delta t}, \qquad (4.35)$$

$$C_2 = \frac{\sigma^2}{\sigma^2 + s^2},$$

$$C_3 = (x_j - \mu)^2 - (x_j - \mu - k)^2 C_2.$$

After ΔN_j is simulated, jump size Y_j is simulated when $\Delta N_j = 1$. In such a case,

$$Y_j|x_j \sim \mathcal{N}(m_{y|x}, s_{y|x}^2),$$

$$m_{y|x} = \frac{(x_j - \mu)s^2 + k\sigma^2}{s^2 + \sigma^2}, \qquad (4.36)$$

$$s_{y|x}^2 = \frac{s^2\sigma^2}{s^2 + \sigma^2}.$$

With these equations, the Gibbs sampling procedure is as follows. For further details, please refer to Ch4.3_Gibbs_Sampling.xls.

1. Choose initial values of μ_0, σ_0^2, k_0, λ_0, and s_0^2, and set $i = 1$.
2. Sample $Y_{j,0}$ and $\Delta N_{j,0}$ using Equations 4.35 and 4.36 with the initial parameters.
3. Sample $\mu_j \sim p(\mu_j|\sigma_{j-1}^2, \lambda_{j-1}, k_{j-1}, s_{j-1}^2)$, as given in Equation 4.30.
4. Sample $\sigma_j^2 \sim p(\sigma_j^2|\mu_j, \lambda_{j-1}, k_{j-1}, s_{j-1}^2)$, as given in Equation 4.31.
5. Sample $\lambda_j \sim p(\lambda_j|\mu_j, \sigma_j^2, k_{j-1}, s_{j-1}^2)$, as given in Equation 4.32.
6. Sample $k_j \sim p(k_j|\mu_j, \sigma_j^2, \lambda_j, s_{j-1}^2)$, as given in Equation 4.33.
7. Sample $s_j^2 \sim p(s_j^2|\mu_j, \sigma_j^2, \lambda_j, k_j)$, as given in Equation 4.34.
8. Sample $\Delta N_{j,i} \sim p(\Delta N_{j,i}|\mu_j, \sigma_j^2, \lambda_j, k_j, s_j^2)$, as given in Equation 4.35, for $j = 1, \ldots, n$.
9. Sample $Y_{j,i} \sim p(Y_{j,i}|\mu_j, \sigma_j^2, \lambda_j, k_j, s_j^2)$, as given in Equation 4.36, for $\Delta N_{j,i} = 1$.
10. Set $i = i + 1$, and repeat Steps 3 to 9 until $i = M + M'$.
11. Average the last M' sets of parameters to obtain the estimate.

To test the algorithm, we first simulate the sample path under dynamics (Eq. 4.24) and then examine the convergence of the algorithm with an increasing burnt-in time. The simulation method is discussed in the next subsection. With $S(0) = 50$, $\mu = 8\%$, $\sigma = 20\%$, $\lambda = 15$, $k = 0\%$, $s = 10\%$, $T = 1$, $dt = 1/250$, and $M' = 50{,}000$, the simulated path represents the daily log-returns of a stock over a 1-year horizon. The Gibbs sampling results are presented in Table 4.22.

TABLE 4.22 Estimates Using Gibbs Sampling with an Increasing Burn-In Time

M	μ	σ	λ	k	s
50,000	7.99%	20.78%	11.40	0.85%	13.60%
100,000	8.04%	20.78%	11.42	0.84%	13.60%
200,000	8.06%	20.77%	11.43	0.84%	13.59%
500,000	8.08%	20.77%	11.44	0.84%	13.58%
1,000,000	8.10%	20.77%	11.45	0.83%	13.58%
2,000,000	8.10%	20.77%	11.45	0.83%	13.58%
3,000,000	8.10%	20.77%	11.45	0.83%	13.58%
4,000,000	8.10%	20.77%	11.45	0.83%	13.58%
5,000,000	8.09%	20.77%	11.45	0.83%	13.58%

TABLE 4.23 Performance of Gibbs Sampling

Trial	μ	σ	λ	k	s
1	15.84%	19.72%	21.55	2.46%	9.19%
2	21.60%	20.67%	15.03	−0.26%	10.68%
3	−6.84%	20.82%	15.87	0.87%	9.79%
4	47.95%	19.19%	13.41	0.41%	12.49%
5	−0.77%	21.50%	12.34	−2.46%	9.99%
6	16.03%	20.81%	16.53	−1.68%	10.36%
7	−2.42%	19.90%	19.88	1.76%	10.25%
8	17.14%	20.30%	14.31	0.87%	9.12%
9	−0.81%	20.12%	15.23	2.66%	7.23%
10	−13.31%	20.05%	14.45	0.66%	9.21%
True value	6.00%	20.00%	15.00	0.00%	10.00%
Mean	6.07%	20.01%	14.74	−0.04%	9.96%
Standard deviation	15.51%	0.74%	3.25	2.07%	1.44%

From Table 4.22, it can be seen that the estimates converge when $M = 1,000,000$. When $M = 2,000,000$, the estimates are already very close to the converged values. With the same setting, we simulate 250 sample paths, with each sample path replicating the daily log-returns of a stock over a 1-year horizon. Based on these 250 paths, we employ Gibbs sampling to estimate μ, σ, λ, k, and s, and then compare the results with the true values. In the Gibbs sampling, we choose $M = 200,000$ and $M' = 50,000$. As with $M = 200,000$, this sampling performs reasonably well. This result and the estimates of the first 10 sample paths are presented in Table 4.23, from which it can be seen that Gibbs sampling's performance is very good, as the estimates are very close to the true values.

After testing the algorithm with simulated data, we examine the jump-diffusion model empirically. In the previous section, we already used this model to price the callable ELN linked to the price of HSBC shares, as in Section 3.4. The parameters that we use are based on the Gibbs sampling of HSBC stock prices between 2003 and 2009.

Again, we first perform Gibbs sampling to get some idea of the estimates' convergence with an increasing burnt-in time. Table 4.24 presents the results with M

TABLE 4.24 Estimates for HSBC Using Gibbs Sampling with Increasing Burn-In Time

M	μ	σ	λ	k	s
50,000	−23.75%	44.25%	19.95	−0.35%	11.61%
100,000	−24.01%	44.21%	20.10	−0.33%	11.58%
200,000	−24.22%	44.17%	20.25	−0.32%	11.54%
500,000	−24.40%	44.13%	20.44	−0.31%	11.50%
1,000,000	−24.50%	44.10%	20.56	−0.30%	11.47%
2,000,000	−24.61%	44.07%	20.67	−0.29%	11.44%
3,000,000	−24.65%	44.06%	20.73	−0.29%	11.43%
4,000,000	−24.70%	44.05%	20.76	−0.29%	11.42%
5,000,000	−24.71%	44.04%	20.79	−0.29%	11.41%

TABLE 4.25 Estimation of Jump-Diffusion Model for HSBC

Year	μ	σ	λ	k	s
2003	35.48%	13.62%	6.54	0.01%	2.14%
2004	4.05%	12.84%	1.75	2.29%	0.71%
2005	5.97%	7.75%	7.91	−1.40%	0.43%
2006	15.15%	8.62%	25.53	−0.05%	1.56%
2007	2.99%	14.05%	9.99	−0.99%	1.72%
2008	−47.17%	29.15%	27.18	−0.37%	7.13%
2009	18.77%	37.50%	17.10	−0.19%	10.75%
Mean	5.03%	17.65%	13.71	−0.10%	3.49%
Standard deviation	25.65%	11.24%	9.78	1.18%	3.91%

ranging from 50,000 to 5,000,000 using HSBC stock prices from September 25, 2007, to September 24, 2008.

This table shows that $M = 200,000$ may not be sufficient for the estimates to converge, and so we choose $M = 2,000,000$ and estimate the parameters for HSBC stock prices between January 1, 2003, and December 31, 2009. The results are presented in Table 4.25. For further details, please refer to Ch4.3_HSBC_Gibbs_Sampling.xls.

5

Fixed-Income Derivatives I: Short-Rate Models

Fixed-income derivatives are derivative securities based on interest rates. In previous chapters, we assumed a constant interest rate because interest rate volatility is much smaller than the volatility of either stocks or the FX rate. Hence, ignoring the interest rate risk in equity derivatives would not cause a serious problem. However, interest rates must be considered as stochastic for fixed-income products.

Interest rate models are more complicated (or tedious) than equity models. In the latter, the stock price can be observed directly in the market, but interest rates are not really directly observable, they are extracted from the yield curve that is fit to liquidly traded fixed-income securities. In this sense, the interest rate is a concept rather than a tradable asset. Interest rate models should consider the entire yield curve rather than focus on the movement of a specific interest rate. For instance, the present value of a fixed-income derivative with 1-year maturity and based on the 3-month interest rate depends at the least on the current 3-month, 6-month, 9-month, and 1-year rates because the 6-month rate is related to the 3-month rate observed 3 months from today, the 9-month rate is related to the 3-month rate observed 6 months from today, and so on. More precisely, interest rate models should take the current term structure of the interest rate into account.

To illustrate the complications in the interest rate market, we start with an elementary example: coupon bonds (CBs). In a constant interest rate economy, a CB with a

---

Handbook of Financial Risk Management: Simulations and Case Studies, First Edition. N.H. Chan and H.Y. Wong.
© 2013 John Wiley & Sons, Inc. Published 2013 by John Wiley & Sons, Inc.

face value of $100 and annual coupon rate C has a present value of

$$\text{CB}(0) = 100 \left[\sum_{j=1}^{2n} \frac{C}{2} e^{-rT_j} + e^{-rT_{2n}} \right], \qquad (5.1)$$

where the CB matures in n years, the coupon is paid semi-annually, $T_j = j/2$, and r is the constant instantaneous interest rate. In practice, interest rates should vary across different times T_j. Therefore, the correct present value of the CB should be

$$\text{CB}(0) = 100 \left[\sum_{j=1}^{2n} \frac{C}{2} e^{-R(0,T_j)T_j} + e^{-R(0,T_{2n})T_{2n}} \right]. \qquad (5.2)$$

The curve $(t, R(0, t))$ is called the zero-coupon yield curve because the quantity $e^{-R(0,T_j)T_j}$ represents a CB paying $1 at T_j. In an elementary finance course, we would solve the constant interest rate from Equation 5.1. Such a pseudo-interest rate is called the yield-to-maturity.

How is the zero-coupon yield curve obtained in the market? In practice, it is calibrated using Equation 5.2 in a reverse-engineering manner. Take the U.S. treasury bond market as an example. There are many U.S. treasury bonds trading in the market, and their prices are accessible. In other words, CB prices are input in a calibration system that optimally fits the yield curve to observed data. The yield curve is the output of the calibration system.

The calibrated yield curve is the fundamental input for interest rate product pricing and interest rate risk management. In interest rate derivative pricing, the full yield curve at time t plays the same role as that of the observed single stock price at time t in equity option pricing. Therefore, the preprocess for such pricing involves building the yield curve to fit market bond prices. The general procedure for interest rate derivative pricing is depicted in Figure 5.1.

The idea behind this procedure is that because such structured products as interest rate range accrual notes (RAN) and target redemption notes (TRN) are not liquidly traded in the market, they should be priced using interest rate models whose

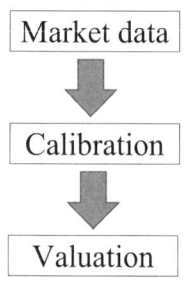

Figure 5.1 Interest rate product pricing procdure.

parameters are calibrated to market-traded instruments, such as bonds, forward rate agreements, swaps, and even such options as caps and swaptions, to reflect current market conditions. These calibrated models are then used to price, via closed-form solution, tree, or Monte Carlo simulation, structured products in a consistent manner.

In the flow chart in Figure 5.1, the market data step refers to the zero rates and forward rates extracted from the prices of treasury bonds (zero CBs and coupon-bearing bonds), which are usually regarded as risk-free bonds. Therefore, this chapter first introduces techniques for building continuous yield curves and forward rate curves from discrete rates, namely, the cubic spline interpolation of yield curves, the Nelson–Siegel model, and the cubic spline interpolation of the discount curve.

In the next step, given the zero rates and forward rates so constructed, we then calibrate the term structure models to interest rate derivatives to capture the interest rate volatilities. More specifically in this chapter, we calibrate the Hull–White short-rate model to the Black cap market volatilities using the closed-form formula for cap prices.

In the final step, the valuation of interest rate products is accomplished. Based on the calibrated Hull–White short-rate model, this chapter implements the trinomial tree and Monte Carlo simulation to price interest rate RAN and TRN.

5.1 YIELD CURVE BUILDING

In this section, three approaches to yield curve construction are introduced. A yield curve is the relation between the zero rate and time-to-maturity. The zero rate of a particular time to maturity is obtained from the price of a CB with the same time-to-maturity. More specifically, with the assumption of continuous compounding, zero rate $R(t, t_j)$ with maturity t_j is related to the price $P(t, t_j)$ of a CB (or discount bond) of the same maturity via the following equation.

$$P(t, t_j) = \exp\left(-R(t, t_j)(t_j - t)\right).$$

For simple compounding, the relationship is given by

$$P(t, t_j) = \frac{1}{1 + R(t, t_j)(t_j - t)}.$$

To simplify matters, we stick with the notion of a continuously compounding interest rate and consider the discount bond to follow an exponential function.

5.1.0.1 Cubic Spline Interpolation To begin, we assume an ideal situation in which some of the zero rates are observable and demonstrate the smoothing technique with cubic spline interpolation. Given n zero rates of n distinct maturities, we use the cubic spline to interpolate these rates to produce a continuous and smooth yield curve. Denote the jth maturity and zero rate pair by (t_j, R_j), where $j = 1, \ldots, n$.

Then $n-1$ cubic polynomials are used to produce a cubic spline, as follows.

$$R(0,t) = \begin{cases} \beta_{1,0} + \beta_{1,1}t + \beta_{1,2}t^2 + \beta_{1,3}t^3, & t \in [t_1, t_2], \\ \beta_{2,0} + \beta_{2,1}t + \beta_{2,2}t^2 + \beta_{2,3}t^3, & t \in [t_2, t_3], \\ \vdots & \vdots \\ \beta_{i,0} + \beta_{i,1}t + \beta_{i,2}t^2 + \beta_{i,3}t^3, & t \in [t_i, t_{i+1}], \\ \vdots & \vdots \\ \beta_{n-2,0} + \beta_{n-2,1}t + \beta_{n-2,2}t^2 + \beta_{n-2,3}t^3, & t \in [t_{n-2}, t_{n-1}], \\ \beta_{n-1,0} + \beta_{n-1,1}t + \beta_{n-1,2}t^2 + \beta_{n-1,3}t^3, & t \in [t_{n-1}, t_n]. \end{cases}$$

By restricting $R(0, t)$, such that it is continuous and twice-differentiable in t, these $n - 1$ equations can be simplified as

$$R(0, t) = a + b(t - t_1) + c(t - t_1)^2 + \sum_{k=1}^{n-1} d_k (t - t_k)_+^3,$$

where $a, b, c, d_1, \ldots, d_{n-1}$ are $n + 2$ unknowns, and $(t - t_k)_+ = \max\{t - t_k, 0\}$. Because there are only n discrete zero rates, two additional conditions are needed to solve this set of equations. If we choose $\lim_{t \downarrow t_1} R'(0, t) = c_1$ and $\lim_{t \uparrow t_n} R'(0, t) = c_2$ for given values c_1 and c_2, then it is called a clamped cubic spline. However, these two values are usually unknown, and thus we can use a natural cubic spline in which the remaining two conditions are given by $\lim_{t \downarrow t_1} R''(0, t) = \lim_{t \uparrow t_n}$ and $R''(0, t) = 0$. Now, there are $n + 2$ linear equations with $n + 2$ unknowns. Mathematically, the cubic spline equations can be written in matrix form as

$$\begin{pmatrix} R_1 \\ R_2 \\ \vdots \\ R_n \\ 0 \\ 0 \end{pmatrix} = \begin{pmatrix} 1 & t_1 - t_1 & (t_1 - t_1)^2 & (t_1 - t_1)_+^3 & (t_1 - t_2)_+^3 & \cdots & (t_1 - t_n)_+^3 \\ 1 & t_2 - t_1 & (t_2 - t_1)^2 & (t_2 - t_1)_+^3 & (t_2 - t_2)_+^3 & \cdots & (t_2 - t_n)_+^3 \\ \vdots & \vdots & \vdots & \vdots & \vdots & & \vdots \\ 1 & t_n - t_1 & (t_n - t_1)^2 & (t_n - t_1)_+^3 & (t_n - t_2)_+^3 & \cdots & (t_n - t_n)_+^3 \\ 0 & 0 & 2 & 0 & 0 & \cdots & 0 \\ 0 & 0 & 2 & 6(t_n - t_1) & 6(t_n - t_2) & \cdots & 6(t_n - t_n) \end{pmatrix} \begin{pmatrix} a \\ b \\ c \\ d_1 \\ \vdots \\ d_n \end{pmatrix},$$

which can be solved using the built-in *MInverse* function in Excel. The corresponding VBA code is as follows.

```
Public Function NSpline(xi As Variant, yi As Variant)
  As Variant
    Dim nPoints As Long
    Dim Output, X, Y, tOutput
    nPoints = UBound(xi)
    ReDim Output(1 To nPoints + 2, 1 To 2) As Double
    ReDim X(1 To nPoints + 2, 1 To nPoints + 2) As Double
    ReDim Y(1 To nPoints + 2, 1 To 1) As Double
```

```
    Dim i As Long, j As Long
    For i = 1 To nPoints
        X(i, 1) = 1
        X(i, 2) = xi(i) - xi(1)
        X(i, 3) = (xi(i) - xi(1)) ^ 2
        For j = 1 To i - 1
            X(i, 3 + j) = (xi(i) - xi(j)) ^ 3
        Next j
            Y(i, 1) = yi(i)
    Next i

    'Leftmost
    Y(nPoints + 1, 1) = 0
    X(nPoints + 1, 3) = 2
    'Rightmost
    Y(nPoints + 2, 1) = 0
    X(nPoints + 2, 3) = 2
    For j = 1 To nPoints - 1
        X(nPoints + 2, 3 + j) = 6 * (xi(nPoints) - xi(j))
    Next j

    With Application
        tOutput = .MMult(.MInverse(X), Y)
    End With

    For i = 1 To UBound(Output)
        Output(i, 1) = xi(Max(1, i - 3))
        Output(i, 2) = Round(tOutput(i, 1), 10)
    Next i
    Output(1, 1) = 0

    NSpline = Output
End Function
```

Table 5.1 lists the continuously compounding treasury yield rates on August 24, 2010, from the U.S. Department of the Treasury. These data can be used to build the yield curve using the cubic spline, as discussed. The resulting yield curve and corresponding discount factor are shown in Figure 5.2. For more details, please refer to Ch5.2_Natural_Spline_Interpolation.xls.

5.1.0.2 Building with functional form of the yield curve Although cubic spline interpolation is simple and straightforward, zero rates are not usually directly observable because zero-CBs may not be available for all maturities. However, coupon-bearing bonds may be available. In the following, we show how to build a yield curve from coupon-bearing bonds using a functional form of the yield curve. Of the many

182 FIXED-INCOME DERIVATIVES I: SHORT-RATE MODELS

TABLE 5.1 Treasury Yield Rates on August 24, 2010

Time to maturity	Yield rate (continuously compounding)
3 mos	0.14%
6 mos	0.19%
1 yr	0.25%
2 yrs	0.51%
3 yrs	0.75%
5 yrs	1.41%
7 yrs	2.02%
10 yrs	2.57%
30 yrs	3.63%

functional forms available, we use the Nelson–Siegel model as our example because the European Central Bank reports the Euro yield curve by offering Nelson–Siegel parameters. This model assumes that

$$R(0, t) = \beta_0 + \beta_1 \left(\frac{1 - e^{-t/\tau_1}}{t/\tau_1} \right) + \beta_2 \left(\frac{1 - e^{-t/\tau_1}}{t/\tau_1} - e^{-t/\tau_1} \right). \tag{5.3}$$

Note that β_0 is the limit of $R(0, t)$ for $t \to \infty$, and thus it is the long-term interest rate, and $\beta_0 + \beta_1$ is the limit of $R(0, t)$ for $t \to 0$, and thus it is the spot interest rate. Therefore, a natural constraint for the parameters is $\beta_0 \geq 0$ and $\beta_0 + \beta_1 \geq 0$.

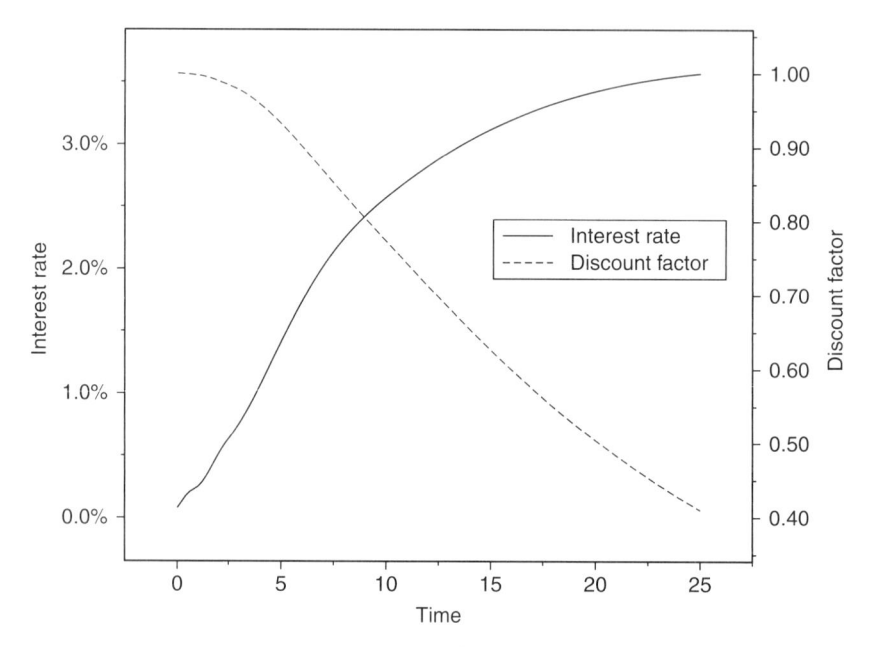

Figure 5.2 Fitted yield curve and discount factor using cubic spline interpolation on zero rates.

Suppose that there are N CBs. For $i = 1, \ldots, N$, the ith bond has the following specification.

- B_i: The dirty price of the bond.
- m_i: The remaining number of coupon payments.
- t_i^j: Coupon payment date, for $j = 1, \ldots, m_i$. t_i^1 is the date of the next coupon payment, and $t_i^{m_i}$ is both the maturity date and the date of the last coupon payment.
- δ_i: Time between each periodic coupon payment, $\delta_i = t_i^{j+1} - t_i^j$. For a bond that pays coupons semiannually, $\delta_i = 0.5$.
- P_i: The bond principal, which is assumed to be \$100 for all bonds.
- C_i: The amount of each coupon, which is equal to $\delta_i P_i \times$ Coupon Rate.

Because the market usually reports the clean price, we have to recover the dirty price of a bond by adding the accrued interest to its clean price, that is,

$$B_i = \text{Market-Quoted Clean Price} + C_i \frac{\delta_i - t_i^1}{\delta_i}.$$

Hereafter, unless otherwise specified, when we refer to a bond price, we are referring to its dirty price. With this specification, the theoretical price for the ith bond is

$$\widehat{B}_i(0) = \sum_{j=1}^{m_i} e^{-R(0, t_i^j) t_i^j} C_i + e^{-R(0, t_i^{m_i}) t_i^{m_i}} P_i.$$

The remaining task is to find the parameters $\beta_0, \beta_1, \beta_2, \tau_1$ that minimize $\sum_{i=1}^{N} w_i (\widehat{B}_i - B_i)^2$ and satisfy the constraints $\beta_0 \geq 0$ and $\beta_0 + \beta_1 \geq 0$, where w_i is the weight assigned to the ith bond. Possible choices of w_i include $w_i = 1/t_i^{m_i}$ (maturity of the ith bond) and $w_i = -\frac{1}{B_i} \frac{\partial B_i}{\partial \text{YTM}}$ (duration of the ith bond), where YTM is the yield-to-maturity of the bond. The YTM is the constant r in Equation 5.1 obtained from a rooting-finding technique. For the two constraints, we assign a very large penalty to the cost function when they are violated. Then we employ the DE algorithm with parameters identical to those in Section 4.2.3, that is, $NP = 15$, $D = 60$, $CR = 0.5$, and $F = 0.8$. The bounds of the parameters are specified in Table 5.2.

TABLE 5.2 Parameter Bounds

Parameter	Lower bound	Upper bound
β_0	0	0.5
β_1	-0.5	0.5
β_2	-0.5	0.5
τ_1	0.1	5

TABLE 5.3 The Original and Fitted Prices of U.S. Treasury CBs

Time to next payment	Payment frequency	Time to maturity	Coupon rate	Clean price	Dirty price	Fitted price	Percentage error
0.4356	2	0.4356	0.875%	100.30	100.35	100.3	0.06%
0.2644	2	0.7644	0.875%	100.48	100.69	100.66	0.03%
0.2658	2	1.2658	0.750%	100.50	100.68	100.75	0.07%
0.4342	2	1.9342	0.625%	100.31	100.35	100.46	0.10%
0.0192	2	2.0192	0.375%	99.78	99.96	100.07	0.11%
0.4753	2	2.9753	0.750%	100.16	100.17	100.16	0.01%
0.3534	2	3.3534	1.500%	102.34	102.56	102.46	0.10%
0.1000	2	3.6000	1.750%	103.08	103.78	103.7	0.07%
0.2685	2	4.2685	2.125%	104.19	104.68	104.67	0.01%
0.4342	2	4.9342	1.750%	102.06	102.18	102.07	0.10%
0.2274	2	5.2274	4.500%	115.91	117.13	116.82	0.26%
0.1027	2	5.6027	2.375%	104.36	105.30	105.44	0.13%
0.2712	2	6.2712	2.750%	105.86	106.49	106.74	0.23%
0.4370	2	6.9370	2.375%	102.97	103.12	103.22	0.10%
0.4822	2	7.4822	3.500%	110.53	110.59	110.4	0.18%
0.2260	2	7.7260	3.875%	113.09	114.16	114.03	0.11%
0.4822	2	8.4822	2.750%	103.98	104.03	103.98	0.05%
0.2260	2	8.7260	3.125%	106.50	107.36	107.55	0.18%
0.2301	2	9.2301	3.375%	108.00	108.91	109.28	0.34%
0.4808	2	9.9808	2.625%	101.19	101.24	101.06	0.18%
0.4932	2	25.4932	4.500%	117.58	117.61	117.64	0.02%
0.4959	2	26.4959	4.750%	122.28	122.30	122.09	0.18%
0.2397	2	26.7397	5.000%	126.97	128.27	127.9	0.29%
0.4959	2	27.4959	4.375%	115.19	115.21	115.26	0.05%
0.2397	2	27.7397	4.500%	117.47	118.64	118.7	0.05%
0.4959	2	28.4959	3.500%	98.98	99.00	98.83	0.17%
0.2397	2	28.7397	4.250%	112.44	113.54	113.91	0.32%
0.2438	2	29.2438	4.375%	114.67	115.79	116.23	0.38%
0.4945	2	29.9945	3.875%	105.75	105.77	105.5	0.26%

We collect the prices of 29 U.S. treasury CBs on August 24, 2010. Using the functional form Equation 5.3 and durations as weights, the estimated parameters are $\beta_0 = 0.0455$, $\beta_1 = -0.0410$, $\beta_2 = -0.0577$, and $\tau_1 = 2.0253$. The original and fitted prices of the treasury bonds are listed in Table 5.3. The average pricing error is 0.14%, and the maximum pricing error is 0.38%. The estimated yield curve and corresponding discount factor are shown in Figure 5.3. For further details, please refer to Ch5.2_Nelson-Siegel_Model.xls.

5.1.0.3 Cubic Spline Discount Function Rather than assume the yield curve follows a specific functional form, a standard approach is to regress to the discount function on a spline and then convert the discount function into a yield curve. This approach could be interpreted as a combination of two preceding methods. With the N bonds specified as before, we use n piecewise polynomials to approximate the

YIELD CURVE BUILDING   185

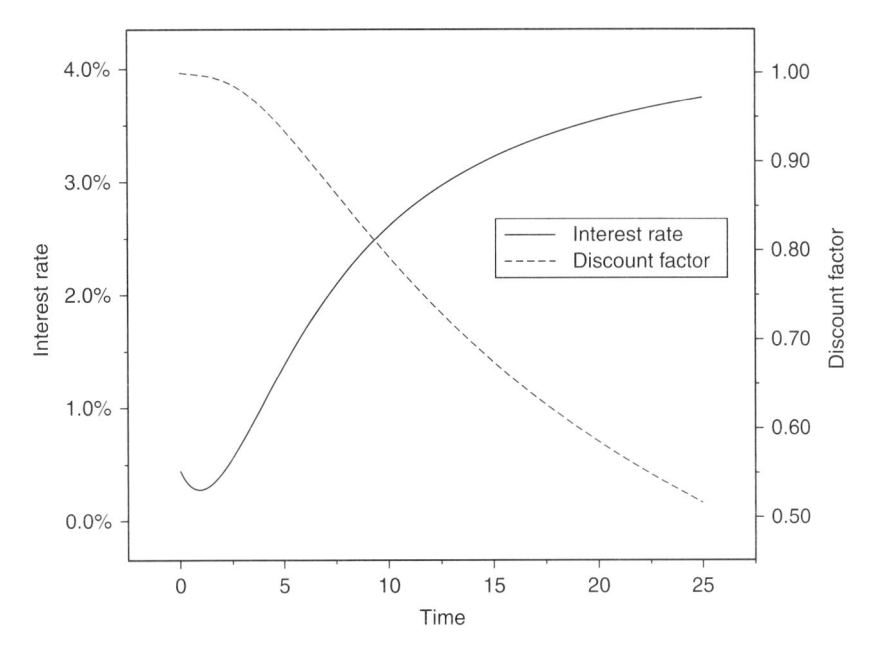

Figure 5.3   The fitted yield curve and discount factor using the Nelson–Siegel model.

discount function $P(0, t)$.

$$P(0, t) = \begin{cases} \beta_{1,0} + \beta_{1,1}t + \beta_{1,2}t^2 + \beta_{1,3}t^3, & t \in [t_1, t_2], \\ \beta_{2,0} + \beta_{2,1}t + \beta_{2,2}t^2 + \beta_{2,3}t^3, & t \in [t_2, t_3], \\ \vdots & \vdots \\ \beta_{i,0} + \beta_{i,1}t + \beta_{i,2}t^2 + \beta_{i,3}t^3, & t \in [t_i, t_{i+1}], \\ \vdots & \vdots \\ \beta_{n-1,0} + \beta_{n-1,1}t + \beta_{n-1,2}t^2 + \beta_{n-1,3}t^3, & t \in [t_{n-2}, t_{n-1}], \\ \beta_{n,0} + \beta_{n,1}t + \beta_{n,2}t^2 + \beta_{n,3}t^3, & t \in [t_{n-1}, t_n]. \end{cases}$$

As before, these n equations are reduced to

$$P(0, t) = a + bt + ct^2 + \sum_{k=1}^{n} d_k (t - t_k)_+^3, \tag{5.4}$$

where $a, b, c, d_1, \ldots, d_n$ are $n + 3$ unknowns. The t_j's are called knots with $t_1 = 0$. Because $D(0) = 1$ and $a = 1$, Equation 5.4 becomes

$$P(0, t) = 1 + bt + ct^2 + \sum_{k=1}^{n} d_k (t - t_k)_+^3. \tag{5.5}$$

Recall that the theoretical price of the ith bond is

$$B_i(0) = \sum_{j=1}^{m_i} P(0, t_i^j)C_i + P(0, t_i^{m_i})P_i. \tag{5.6}$$

Substitute Equation 5.5 into Equation 5.6, and we have

$$B_i(0) = C_i \sum_{j=1}^{m_i} \left(1 + bt_i^j + c(t_i^j)^2 + \sum_{k=1}^{n} d_k(t_i^j - t_k)_+^3\right)$$

$$+ \left(1 + bt_i^m + c(t_i^m)^2 + \sum_{k=1}^{n} d_k(t_i^m - t_k)_+^3\right) P_i$$

$$= (C_i m_i + P_i) + b \left(C_i \sum_{j=1}^{m_i} t_i^j + P_i t_i^{m_i}\right) + c \left(C_i \sum_{j=1}^{m_i} (t_i^j)^2 + P_i(t_i^{m_i})^2\right)$$

$$+ \sum_{k=1}^{n} \left[d_k \left(C_i \sum_{j=1}^{m_i} (t_i^j - t_k)_+^3 + P_i(t_i^{m_i} - t_k)_+^3 \right) \right]. \tag{5.7}$$

Define

$$y_i \triangleq B_i - C_i m_i - P_i,$$

$$x_{i,1} \triangleq C_i \sum_{j=1}^{m_i} t_i^j + P_i t_i^{m_i},$$

$$x_{i,2} \triangleq C_i \sum_{j=1}^{m_i} (t_i^j)^2 + P_i(t_i^{m_i})^2,$$

$$x_{i,k+2} \triangleq C_i \sum_{j=1}^{m_i} (t_i^j - t_k)_+^3 + P_i(t_i^{m_i} - t_k)_+^3, \text{ for } k = 1, \ldots, n.$$

For the ith bond, Equation 5.7 is expressed as

$$y_i = bx_{i,1} + cx_{i,2} + d_1 x_{i,3} + \cdots + d_n x_{i,n+2}.$$

Denote the matrix $(x_{ij})_{i=1,\ldots,N, j=1,\ldots,n+2}$ by X and the vector $(y_1 y_2 \cdots y_N)^T$ by Y. The least squares estimate $\beta^* = (b\, c\, d_1 \cdots d_n)^T$ is given by

$$\beta^* = (X^T X)^{-1} X^T Y.$$

As in the previous method, we assign a weight w_i to the ith bond. Denote the matrix $\{\omega_{ij}\}$ by Ω. Then,

$$\omega_{ij} = \begin{cases} w_i^2, & \text{if } i = j, \\ 0, & \text{otherwise.} \end{cases} \qquad (5.8)$$

For w_i^2, Vasicek and Fong (1982) suggest using the duration of the ith bond, although some practitioners prefer $w_i = t_i^{m_i}$ (the maturity of the ith bond). For this weighted least squares problem, $\boldsymbol{\beta}^*$ is now given by

$$\boldsymbol{\beta}^* = (X^T \Omega^{-1} X)^{-1} X^T \Omega^{-1} Y.$$

The inverse of $\Omega^{-1} = \{\omega'_{ij}\}$ is given by

$$\omega'_{ij} = \begin{cases} 1/w_i^2, & \text{if } i = j. \\ 0, & \text{otherwise.} \end{cases} \qquad (5.9)$$

It is advisable to compute Ω^{-1} using Equation 5.9, which is much more efficient than using Equation 5.8. The corresponding VBA code for this method is as follows.

```
Public Function RSpline(nxPmt, fqPmt, rmPmt, bYield, bPrice, _
    Knots, wType As Integer)
    Dim nKnots As Long, nBonds As Long
    Dim X, Y, Omega_inv
    Dim Ci As Double
    Dim tj As Double, tk As Double, tm As Double
    Dim i As Long, j As Long, ib As Long, kk As Long
    nBonds = UBound(nxPmt)
    nKnots = UBound(Knots)
    ReDim X(1 To nBonds, 1 To nKnots + 2) As Double
    ReDim Y(1 To nBonds, 1 To 1) As Double
    ReDim Omega_inv(1 To nBonds, 1 To nBonds) As Double

    For ib = 1 To nBonds
        Ci = bPrincipal * bYield(ib) * fqPmt(ib)
        Y(ib, 1) = bPrice(ib) - Ci * rmPmt(ib) - bPrincipal
        'Multply Ci later
        For j = 1 To rmPmt(ib)
            tj = nxPmt(ib) + fqPmt(ib) * (j - 1)
            X(ib, 1) = X(ib, 1) + tj
            X(ib, 2) = X(ib, 2) + tj ^ 2
            For kk = 1 To nKnots
                tk = Knots(kk)
                If tj < tk Then Exit For
```

188   FIXED-INCOME DERIVATIVES I: SHORT-RATE MODELS

```
                X(ib, kk + 2) = X(ib, kk + 2) + (tj - tk) ^ 3
            Next kk
        Next j

        'Ci and Pi*tm
        tm = nxPmt(ib) + fqPmt(ib) * (rmPmt(ib) - 1)
        X(ib, 1) = Ci * X(ib, 1) + bPrincipal * tm
        X(ib, 2) = Ci * X(ib, 2) + bPrincipal * tm ^ 2
        'x_i,k+2
        For kk = 1 To nKnots
            tk = Knots(kk)
            X(ib, kk + 2) = Ci * X(ib, kk + 2)
            If tm > tk Then
                X(ib, kk + 2) = X(ib, kk + 2) + bPrincipal _
                                * (tm - tk) ^ 3
            End If
        Next kk
Next ib

'For weights
If wType = 1 Then       'Equal Weight
    For ib = 1 To nBonds
        Omega_inv(ib, ib) = 1
    Next ib
ElseIf wType = 2 Then    '1/Maturity^2
    For ib = 1 To nBonds
        Omega_inv(ib, ib) = 1 / (nxPmt(ib) _
            + fqPmt(ib) * (rmPmt(ib) - 1)) ^ 2
    Next ib
Else
    For ib = 1 To nBonds
        Omega_inv(ib, ib) = 1 / Bond_dPdr(nxPmt(ib), _
            fqPmt(ib), rmPmt(ib), bYield(ib), bPrice(ib), 0.05, _
            0.00000001, 500) ^ 2
    Next ib
End If

'Weighted least squares
Dim XtOi, XtOiX_inv, beta
With Application
    XtOi = .MMult(Transpose(X), Omega_inv)
    XtOiX_inv = .MInverse(.MMult(XtOi, X))
    beta = .MMult(.MMult(XtOiX_inv, XtOi), Y)
End With
'Output the result
```

```
    Dim Output
    ReDim Output(1 To nKnots + 3, 1 To 2) As Double
    For i = 1 To UBound(beta, 1)
        Output(i + 1, 2) = beta(i, 1)
    Next i
    For i = 1 To nKnots
        Output(i + 3, 1) = Knots(i)
    Next i
    Output(1, 2) = 1
    RSpline = Output
End Function

'Calculate dPdr using Netwon's method for estimating r
Public Function Bond_dPdr(ByVal nxPmt0 As Double, _
  ByVal fqPmt0 As Double, _  ByVal rmPmt0 As Double, _
  ByVal bYield0 As Double, ByVal bPrice0 As Double, _
  Optional initGuess As Double = 0.05, _
  Optional tolerance As Double = 0.00001, _
  Optional maxItr As Long = 100)
    Dim rf As Double
    Dim bPrice1 As Double, dPdr As Double
    Dim exp_rtj As Double, Cj As Double, tj As Double
    Dim i As Long, j As Long
    rf = initGuess
    
    Cj = bPrincipal * bYield0 * fqPmt0
    For i = 1 To maxItr
        bPrice1 = 0
        dPdr = 0
        For j = 1 To rmPmt0
            tj = nxPmt0 + fqPmt0 * (j - 1)
            exp_rtj = Exp(-rf * tj)
            bPrice1 = bPrice1 + Cj * exp_rtj
            dPdr = dPdr + tj * Cj * exp_rtj
        Next j
        bPrice1 = bPrice1 + bPrincipal * exp_rtj
        dPdr = dPdr + tj * bPrincipal * exp_rtj
        rf = rf - (bPrice0 - bPrice1) / dPdr
        If Abs(bPrice0 - bPrice1) < tolerance Then Exit For
    Next i
    Bond_dPdr = -dPdr
End Function
```

For more details, please refer to Ch5.2_Regression_Spline_Discount_Function.xls.

190 FIXED-INCOME DERIVATIVES I: SHORT-RATE MODELS

TABLE 5.4 Original and Fitted Prices of Treasury CBs

Time to next payment	Payment frequency	Time to maturity	Coupon rate	Clean price	Dirty price	Fitted price	Percentage error
0.4356	2	0.4356	0.875%	100.30	100.35	100.34	0.01%
0.2644	2	0.7644	0.875%	100.48	100.69	100.69	0.00%
0.2658	2	1.2658	0.750%	100.50	100.68	100.75	0.07%
0.4342	2	1.9342	0.625%	100.31	100.35	100.42	0.07%
0.0192	2	2.0192	0.375%	99.78	99.96	100.03	0.07%
0.4753	2	2.9753	0.750%	100.16	100.17	100.09	0.08%
0.3534	2	3.3534	1.500%	102.34	102.56	102.39	0.17%
0.1000	2	3.6000	1.750%	103.08	103.78	103.64	0.13%
0.2685	2	4.2685	2.125%	104.19	104.68	104.65	0.03%
0.4342	2	4.9342	1.750%	102.06	102.18	102.1	0.08%
0.2274	2	5.2274	4.500%	115.91	117.13	116.87	0.23%
0.1027	2	5.6027	2.375%	104.36	105.30	105.51	0.19%
0.2712	2	6.2712	2.750%	105.86	106.49	106.83	0.32%
0.4370	2	6.9370	2.375%	102.97	103.12	103.32	0.19%
0.4822	2	7.4822	3.500%	110.53	110.59	110.47	0.11%
0.2260	2	7.7260	3.875%	113.09	114.16	114.09	0.06%
0.4822	2	8.4822	2.750%	103.98	104.03	103.97	0.06%
0.2260	2	8.7260	3.125%	106.50	107.36	107.5	0.14%
0.2301	2	9.2301	3.375%	108.00	108.91	109.18	0.25%
0.4808	2	9.9808	2.625%	101.19	101.24	100.88	0.35%
0.4932	2	25.4932	4.500%	117.58	117.61	117.84	0.19%
0.4959	2	26.4959	4.750%	122.28	122.30	122.17	0.11%
0.2397	2	26.7397	5.000%	126.97	128.27	127.96	0.24%
0.4959	2	27.4959	4.375%	115.19	115.21	115.23	0.02%
0.2397	2	27.7397	4.500%	117.47	118.64	118.65	0.01%
0.4959	2	28.4959	3.500%	98.98	99.00	98.74	0.26%
0.2397	2	28.7397	4.250%	112.44	113.54	113.83	0.25%
0.2438	2	29.2438	4.375%	114.67	115.79	116.18	0.34%
0.4945	2	29.9945	3.875%	105.75	105.77	105.55	0.21%

Finally, as $P(0, t)$ is the discount function, we convert it to the yield $R(0, t)$. For continuously compounding rates, the relationship between $R(0, t)$ and $P(0, t)$ is given by

$$R(0, t) = -\frac{1}{t} \log P(0, t).$$

We build the yield curve using the same set of data as in the previous method. The knots are set at $t = 0, 2, 10, 25$, and the weights are given by the durations of the bonds. The original and fitted prices of the Treasury bonds are presented in Table 5.4. The average pricing error is 0.15%, and the maximum pricing error is 0.35%. The estimated yield curve and corresponding discount factor are shown in Figure 5.4.

The yield curves with the three weighting schemes are depicted in Figure 5.5, although the human eye cannot distinguish among them. Figure 5.6 compares the

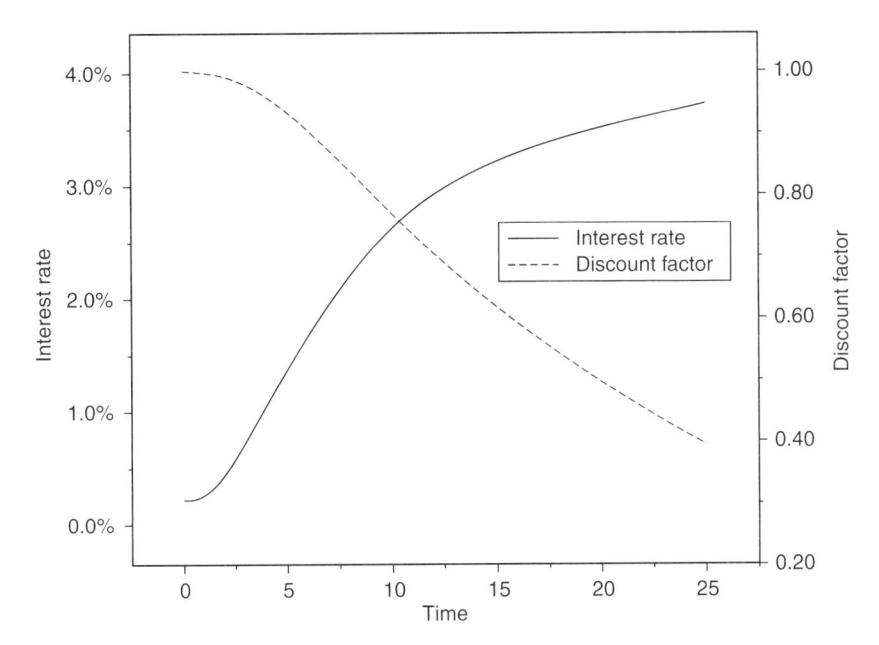

Figure 5.4 Fitted yield curve and discount factor using cubic spline interpolation on the discount factor.

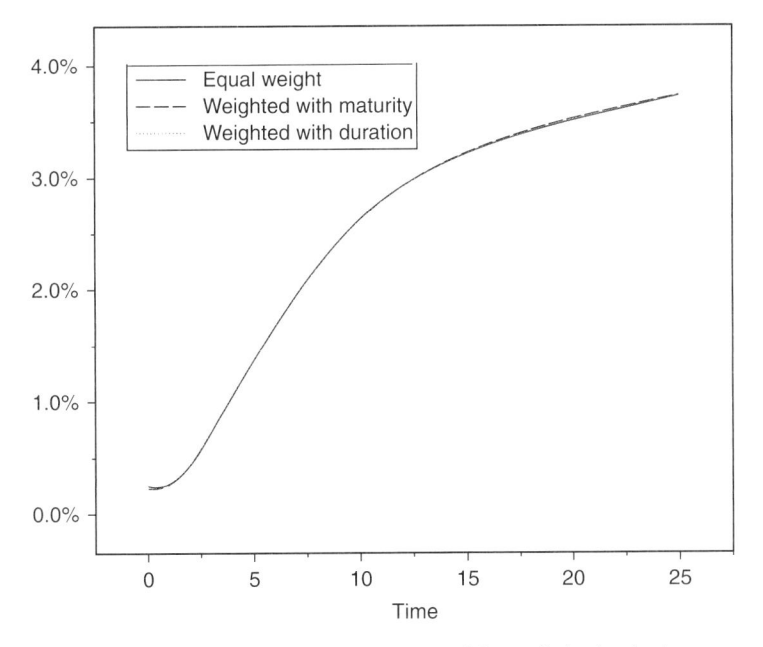

Figure 5.5 Yield curve built with different weights applied to bond prices.

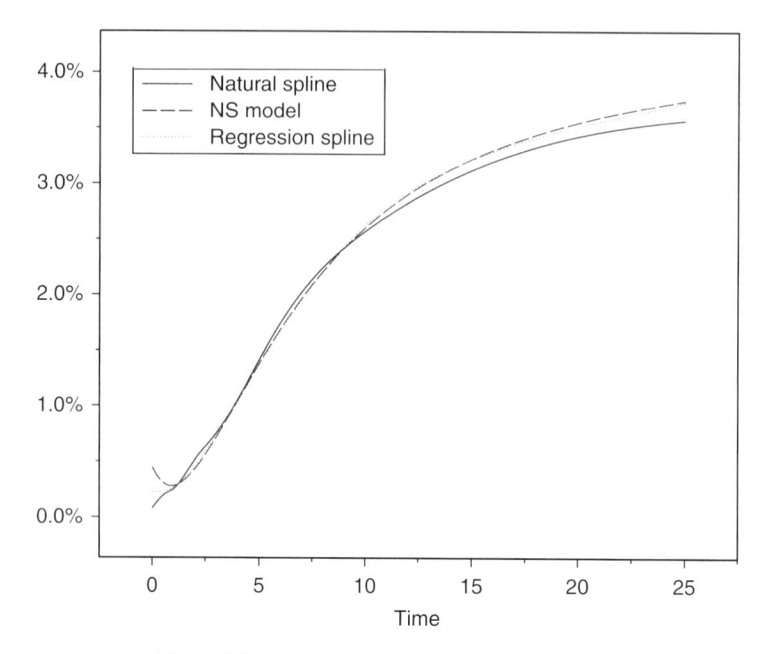

Figure 5.6 Yield curves built with different methods.

yield curves obtained from the cubic spline on rates, Nelson–Siegel model, and regression spline on prices. The three curves behave quite differently for short-term rates but are in general agreement for mediumterm rates. The Nelson–Siegel model and regression spline match each other except for extremely short-term rates. The natural spline on rates produces lower long-term rates.

5.1.1 Building the Forward Rate Curve

In contrast to the spot rate, the forward rate is a prediction of the future rate to borrow and lend. It can be calculated from the yield curve or the discount curve. For example, the rate to borrow money in 6 months' time with payment in 9 months' time is the 3-month forward rate for the 6th month, and the 3-month period is called the tenor of the forward rate. Denote the forward rate at time t for time t_i with tenor $\tau_i = t_{i+1} - t_i$ by $f(t, t_i, t_{i+1})$. When there is no chance of misunderstanding, the notation $f_i(t) = f(t, t_i, t_{i+1})$ is used. To extract the forward rate $f_i(t)$ from the discount function, we have

$$f_i(t) = \frac{1}{\tau_i}\left(\frac{P(t, t_i)}{P(t, t_{i+1})} - 1\right), \quad (5.10)$$

where $P(t, t_i)$ is the discount function (or the price of a CB with maturity t_i) for time t_i at time t. Suppose that the annually compounding yield curve $r(t, t_i)$ is given, and we wish to calculate the forward rate $f_i(t)$. Then,

$$P(t, t_i) = \frac{1}{1 + R(t, t_i)(t_i - t)}.$$

Therefore,

$$f_i(t) = \frac{1}{\tau_i} \left(\frac{1 + R(t, t_{i+1})(t_{i+1} - t)}{1 + R(t, t_i)(t_i - t)} - 1 \right),$$

where $R(t, t_i)$ is the annually compounding spot interest rate for time t_i at time t. Similarly, if $R(t, t_i)$ are continuously compounding spot interest rates, then

$$P(t, t_i) = e^{-R(t,t_i)(t_i - t)},$$

$$f_i(t) = \frac{1}{\tau_i} \left(e^{R(t,t_{i+1})(t_{i+1} - t) - R(t,t_i)(t_i - t)} - 1 \right).$$

Instead of calculating the discrete forward rate $f(t, t_i, t_{i+1})$, we obtain the instantaneous forward rate $F(t, t_i)$ for time t_i at time t by taking the limit $t_{i+1} \to t_i$ (or, equivalently, $\tau_i \to 0$) in Equation 5.10, that is,

$$F(t, t_i) = \lim_{\tau_i \to 0} \frac{P(t, t_i) - P(t, t_{i+1})}{\tau_i P(t, t_{i+1})}$$

$$= -\frac{1}{P(t, t_i)} \frac{\partial P(t, t_i)}{\partial t_i}.$$

If $R(t, t_i)$ is the continuously compounding spot interest rate, then

$$P(t, t_i) = e^{-R(t,t_i)(t_i - t)},$$

$$\frac{\partial P(t, t_i)}{\partial t_i} = -e^{-R(t,t_i)(t_i - t)} \left(R(t, t_i) + \frac{\partial R(t, t_i)}{\partial t_i}(t_i - t) \right),$$

$$F(t, t_i) = R(t, t_i) + \frac{\partial R(t, t_i)}{\partial t_i}(t_i - t).$$

The VBA code for extracting the forward rates (both discrete and instantaneous) with a yield curve constructed with regression splines is as follows.

```
'Forward Rate
Dim tau As Double
Dim t1 As Double, t2 As Double
Dim rt1 As Double, rt2 As Double
tau = Cells(4, 12) - Cells(3, 12)
nPoints = Application.Count(Range("L:L"))
Cells(3, 13).Resize(1000, 2).Clear
```

```
For i = 3 To nPoints + 2
    'Discrete
    t1 = Cells(i, 12)
    t2 = t1 + tau
    rt1 = Eval_Spline(t1)
    rt2 = Eval_Spline(t2)
    Cells(i, 13) = (Exp(rt2 * t2 - rt1 * t1) - 1) / tau
    Cells(i, 13).NumberFormatLocal = "0.00%"
    'Instantaneous
    Cells(i, 14) = rt1 + Eval_DSpline(t1) * t1
    Cells(i, 14).NumberFormatLocal = "0.00%"
Next i
```

The forward rate curves extracted from the yield curves used in the previous section with a tenor equal to 1 year are depicted in Figure 5.7, where tenor means $t_{j+1} - t_j$ are usually assumed to be constant. For further details, please refer to the three previously mentioned Excel files.

5.2 THE HULL–WHITE MODEL

To value interest rate derivatives, we begin with short-rate models and use the Hull–White approach in our implementation. The Hull–White model essentially combines

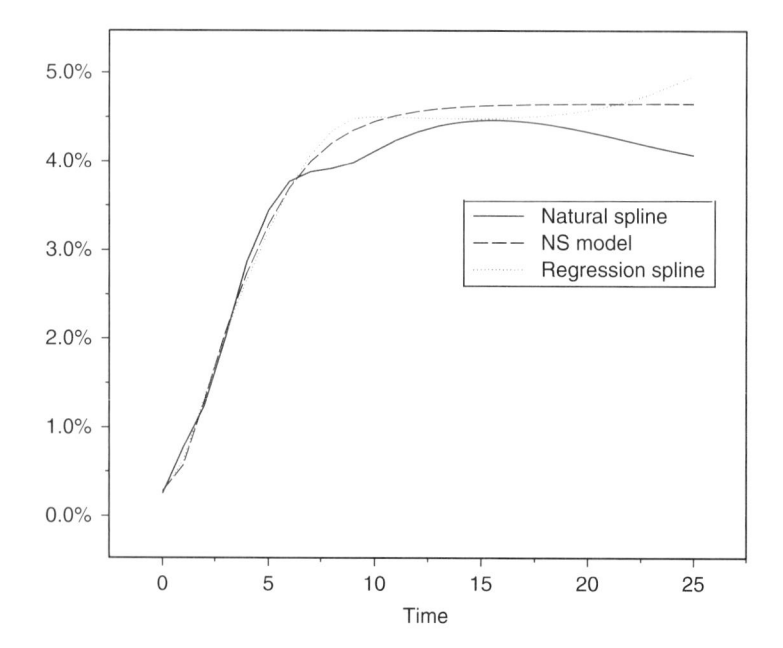

Figure 5.7 Forward-rate curves built with different methods.

the advantages of the Ho–Lee model (1986) and the Vasicek (1977) model. We demonstrate the use of the direct simulation approach and trinomial tree approach in pricing interest rate products.

The short rate at time t, denoted by $r(t)$, is the instantaneous risk-free interest rate at time t. Although it would be theoretically sound to model the short rate dynamics as the starting point, the short rate is not observed in the market. Theoretically, $R(0, t)$ tends to $r(t)$ when t goes to zero. Figure 5.6 shows that extremely short-term rates may be calibrated in an unstable manner, partly because of the trading noise or market microstructure noise associated with short-term bonds. Therefore, short rates are usually approximated as a short-term, but not very short-term rate, such as the 3-month rate. The proxy for a short rate sometimes depends on the product of concern. In this sense, the short rate is a concept rather than a market-observable element.

Theoretically, the price at time t of a default-free CB paying $1 at T has a present value of

$$P(t, T) = E^Q \left[\exp\left(-\int_t^T r(s)ds\right) \bigg| \mathcal{F}_t \right], \tag{5.11}$$

where the short rate $r(t)$ changes randomly over time. If the dynamics of $r(t)$ are given, then the bond price can be computed using Monte Carlo simulation or other appropriate means. In some cases, a closed-form formula for the CB price can be derived.

Let us focus on a particular one-factor, short-rate model proposed by Hull and White (1990, 1994a, b). In general, a one-factor, short-rate model assumes that the yield curve is driven by a single Brownian motion. The classical one-factor short-rate model follows Itô's process:

$$dr(t) = \mu(t, r(t))dt + \sigma(t, r(t))dW^*(t),$$

where $\mu(t, r)$ and $\sigma(t, r)$ are deterministic functions, and $W^*(t)$ is $\mathbb{Q}$-standard Brownian motion. In practice, the valuation of non-standard fixed-income products, such as interest rate RAN and convertibles, requires a short rate model to fit such market variables as bond prices and to produce a price that is consistent with the current market price; a sort of MTM concept.

The Hull–White model, or extended Vasicek model, assumes that

$$dr(t) = (\theta(t) - ar(t))dt + \sigma(t)dW^*(t), \tag{5.12}$$

where a is a positive constant known as the mean-reverting speed, $\theta(t)$ is a deterministic function of time capturing the yield curve information, and $\sigma(t)$ is a positive deterministic function of time, otherwise known as the volatility of the interest rate. Usually, $\theta(t)$ is determined by fitting the initial yield curve, and $\sigma(t)$ by fitting the implied volatility of caps, swaptions, or both, depending on the situation.

If we do not want to calibrate the volatility to the implied volatility of caps, then there is a way to estimate it using historical data. Suppose that we use the 3-month rate as a proxy for the short rate. Collect historical data on 3-month rates $\{r_0, \ldots, r_n\}$, where $r_j = r(j\Delta t)$ and r_n is the most recent interest rate. We assume an order 1 autoregressive model (AR(1)) for the interest rate:

$$r_j = \alpha + \beta r_{j-1} + \epsilon_j,$$

where $\epsilon_j \sim \mathcal{N}(0, s^2)$ independently. Using ordinary least squares estimates for α and β, the variance s^2 can be estimated as the sample variance of prediction errors: $\{\widehat{\epsilon}_j : \widehat{\epsilon}_j = r_j - \widehat{\alpha} - \widehat{\beta} r_{j-1}, j = 1, \ldots, n\}$. Hence, we have the following estimated AR(1) model.

$$r_j - r_{j-1} = \widehat{\alpha} + \left(\widehat{\beta} - 1\right) r_{j-1} + \epsilon_j,$$

which forms a stationary series if $|\widehat{\beta}| < 1$. Taking $\Delta t \to 0$, we have the following diffusion limit.

$$dr(t) = (\mu - ar(t))\, dt + \sigma\, dW(t), \qquad (5.13)$$

where $\mu \Delta t = \widehat{\alpha}$, $a\Delta t = 1 - \widehat{\beta}$, $\sigma^2 \Delta t = s^2$, and $W(t)$ is a $\mathbb{P}$-standard Brownian motion.

The $\mathbb{Q}$-process of $r(t)$ should satisfy Equation 5.11 for all $T > t$. We postulate that there exists a continuous function $\theta(t)$ such that

$$dW^*(t) = dW(t) + \left(\frac{\mu - \theta(t)}{\sigma}\right) dt,$$

where $W^*(t)$ is a $\mathbb{Q}$-standard Brownian motion, and this $\theta(t)$ ensures that Equation 5.11 is satisfied. Substituting $dW^*(t)$ into Equation 5.13 produces Equation 5.12.

More specifically, Hull and White (1994a) show that

$$\theta(t) = \frac{\partial}{\partial t} F^M(0, t) + a F^M(0, t) + \frac{\sigma^2}{2a}(1 - e^{-2at}), \qquad (5.14)$$

where $F^M(0, t)$ is the instantaneous market forward rate that satisfies

$$F^M(0, T) = -\frac{\partial}{\partial T} \log P^M(0, T) = -\frac{1}{P^M(0, T)} \frac{\partial}{\partial T} P^M(0, T),$$

where $P^M(t, T)$ is the price of the zero-CB at time t with maturity T. Because

$$\frac{\partial}{\partial T} F^M(0, T) = \frac{1}{P^M(0, T)^2} \left(\frac{\partial}{\partial T} P^M(0, T)\right)^2 - \frac{1}{P^M(0, T)} \frac{\partial^2}{\partial T^2} P^M(0, T),$$

$$(5.15)$$

the discounted bond price function $P^M(0, T)$ is assumed to be twice-differentiable in T.

Recall that we introduced a method of building the yield curve via spline regression and chose the form of the cubic polynomial to ensure that the discounted bond price curve was twice-differentiable, that is,

$$P^M(0, t) = 1 + bt + ct^2 + \sum_{k=1}^{n} d_k(t - t_k)_+^3, \qquad (5.16)$$

where $b, c, d_1, \ldots, d_k$ are the regression parameters and the t_k's are the knot points. The VBA code for calculating the second-order derivatives of the forward rate curve is as follows.

```
Public Function Eval_DDSpline(x_val As Double,
  Optional Coef As Variant) As Double
    Dim i As Long
    'For Worksheet use
    If IsMissing(Coef) Then Coef = SplineCoef
    Eval_DDSpline = 2 * Coef(3, 2)
    For i = 4 To UBound(Coef, 1)
        If Coef(i, 1) > x_val Then Exit For
        Eval_DDSpline = Eval_DDSpline + 6 * Coef(i, 2)
                        * (x_val - Coef(i, 1))
    Next i
End Function
```

The finite difference method can also be used to calculate the partial derivatives. Because the numerical differentiation has to be performed twice, however, it is inevitable that more errors will be present in the calculation.

Simulation of the interest rate $r(t)$ can be based on Equation 5.12 and 5.14, such that

$$r_{j+1} = r_j + [\theta(t_j) - ar_j]\Delta t + \sigma Z,$$

where $Z \sim \mathcal{N}(0, 1)$ and $\theta(t_j)$ takes values according to the market forward rate curve, as shown in Equation 5.14. This simulation is considered in greater depth later in the chapter.

5.2.1 Calibration of the Hull–White Model

Instead of using time series estimates of a and σ in the Hull–White model, market practitioners often calibrate them from interest rate options such as the cap and floor. Our goal is to search for the set of parameters a and σ that minimizes the differences between the model and market prices of options.

Calibration of the Hull–White model can be carried out conveniently when the closed-form formula of caplet prices is derived. There are two ways to compute the bond price: (1) derive the PDE for $P(t, T)$ by applying the Feynman–Kac formula to Equation 5.11 and 5.12, and then solve the PDE analytically and (2) calculate the expectation directly.

In Method 1, by the Feynman–Kac formula, the PDE for $P(t, T)$ satisfies

$$\frac{\partial P}{\partial t} + \frac{\sigma^2(t)}{2}\frac{\partial^2 P}{\partial r^2} + (\theta(t) - ar)\frac{\partial P}{\partial r} - rP = 0,$$

$$P(T, T) = 1. \tag{5.17}$$

Following Vasicek (1977), an initial guess is

$$P(t, T) = A(t, T)\exp(-r(t)B(t, T)),$$

where t is the time variable and T is considered to be a fixed parameter. To satisfy the condition that $P(T, T) = 1$, the terminal conditions $A(T, T) = 1$ and $B(T, T) = 0$ are imposed. Also, the partial derivatives (whose arguments are omitted for clarity) are

$$\frac{\partial P}{\partial r} = -BP,$$

$$\frac{\partial^2 P}{\partial r^2} = B^2 P,$$

$$\frac{\partial P}{\partial t} = \frac{\partial A}{\partial t}\frac{P}{A} - r\frac{\partial B}{\partial t}P.$$

Substituting the partial derivatives into Equation 5.17 and rearranging the terms, we have

$$\left(\frac{\dot{A}}{A} + \frac{\sigma^2(t)}{2}B^2 - \theta(t)B\right) + r(-\dot{B} + aB - 1) = 0.$$

For the foregoing equation to hold for all r, we must have

$$-\dot{B} + aB - 1 = 0, \text{ with } B(T, T) = 0,$$

$$\frac{\dot{A}}{A} + \frac{\sigma^2(t)}{2}B^2 - \theta(t)B = 0, \text{ with } A(T, T) = 1.$$

Solving these two ordinary differential equations (ODEs), we obtain

$$A(t, T) = \frac{P^M(0, T)}{P^M(0, t)}\exp\left(B(t, T)F^M(0, t) - \frac{\sigma^2}{4a}(1 - e^{-2at})B(t, T)^2\right) \text{ and}$$

$$B(t, T) = \frac{1}{a}\left(1 - e^{-a(T-t)}\right).$$

Note that the function $\theta(t)$ is absorbed by market bond prices $P^M(0, t)$ and the market instantaneous forward rates $F^M(0, t)$.

As $P(t, T) = A(t, T) \exp(-r(t)B(t, T))$, Itô's lemma shows that

$$dP(t, T) = \left(\frac{\partial P}{\partial t} + \frac{\sigma^2(t)}{2}\frac{\partial^2 P}{\partial r^2} + (\theta(t) - ar(t))\frac{\partial P}{\partial r}\right)(t, T)dt$$

$$+ \sigma(t)\frac{\partial P}{\partial r}(t, T)dW(t) \qquad (5.18)$$

$$= r(t)P(t, T)dt - \sigma(t)B(t, T)P(t, T)dW(t)$$

$$= r(t)P(t, T)dt + \sigma(t)B(t, T)P(t, T)d\widehat{W}(t),$$

where $\widehat{W}(t) \triangleq -W^*(t)$.

Consider a European call option on a CB, where the option's maturity is T and that of the CB is S, with $T \leq S$. Intuitively, as $P(t, T)$ evolves similarly to a GBM, as in Equation 5.18, the pricing formula for the call option on the bond should resemble the BS call option formula.

Theorem 5.1 *The Hull–White call option price on a CB is given by*

$$E^Q\left[e^{-\int_0^T r(s)ds} \max\{P(T, S) - K, 0\}\right]$$

$$= P(0, T)c_{BS}\left(\frac{P(0, S)}{P(0, T)}, K, 0, 0, 0, \Sigma(T, S), T\right),$$

where

$$\Sigma(T, S)^2 = \frac{1}{T}\int_0^T \sigma(u)^2(B(u, S) - B(u, T))^2 du,$$

and $c_{BS}(S, K, t, r, q, v, T)$ is the BS call option formula.

Proof: As $P(T, T) = 1$, the expectation can be written as

$$E^Q\left[e^{-\int_0^T r(s)ds} \max\{P(T, S) - K, 0\}\right]$$

$$= E^Q\left[e^{-\int_0^T r(s)ds} P(T, T)\max\left(\frac{P(T, S)}{P(T, T)} - K, 0\right)\right].$$

From Equation 5.18, we have

$$P(T, S) = P(0, S) \exp\left[\int_0^T r(t)\,dt - \frac{1}{2}\int_0^T (\sigma(t)B(t, S))^2\,dt \right.$$
$$\left. + \int_0^T \sigma(t)B(t, S)\,d\widehat{W}(t)\right]$$

for all $S \geq T$. Substituting this into the expectation yields

$$P(0, T)\mathrm{E}^{\mathbb{Q}}\left[e^{-\frac{1}{2}\int_0^T (\sigma(t)B(t,T))^2\,dt + \int_0^T \sigma(t)B(t,T)\,d\widehat{W}(t)} \max\left(\frac{P(T, S)}{P(T, T)} - K, 0\right)\right].$$

By Girsanov's Theorem, we define

$$\frac{d\mathbb{Q}^T}{d\mathbb{Q}} = e^{-\frac{1}{2}\int_0^T (\sigma(t)B(t,T))^2\,dt + \int_0^T \sigma(t)B(t,T)\,d\widehat{W}(t)}$$

and $\mathbb{Q}^T$-standard Brownian motion

$$d\widetilde{W}(t) = d\widehat{W}(t) - \sigma(t)B(t, T)\,dt.$$

The call on the CB becomes

$$P(0, T)\mathrm{E}^{\mathbb{Q}^T}$$
$$\left[\max\left(\frac{P(0, S)}{P(0, T)}e^{-\frac{1}{2}\int_0^T \sigma(u)^2(B(t,S)-B(t,T))^2\,dt + \int_0^T \sigma(t)(B(t,S)-B(t,T))\,d\widetilde{W}(t)} - K, 0\right)\right],$$

where the expectation resembles that of the BS call option with a current stock price of $\frac{P(0,S)}{P(0,T)}$, zero interest rate, and volatility of $\Sigma(T, S)$. Hence, the result follows.

Although CB options are seldom traded in the market, related products such as caps and caplets are liquidly traded. A caplet is a call option on a simple compounding interest rate, typically traded in the London Interbank Offered Rate (LIBOR) market, as LIBOR rates are quoted in a simple compounding manner. The CB is related to the LIBOR rate, $L(0, T)$, by the following formula.

$$P(0, T) = \frac{1}{1 + L(0, T)T}.$$

For a notional (or principal amount) N, a caplet holder has the right to exchange the LIBOR rate for a constant rate K at a future point in time. Therefore, the payoff is $N\tau_i \max\{L(T_{i-1}, T_i) - K, 0\}$, where N is the caplet's notional amount, and is determined at time T_{i-1} and made at time T_i, and $\tau_i = T_i - T_{i-1}$. Thus, the price of a caplet is given by

$$\text{Caplet}(T_i, K, N) = E^Q \left[e^{-\int_0^{T_i} r(s)ds} N \tau_i \max\{L(T_{i-1}, T_i) - K, 0\} \right].$$

Using the relation between the LIBOR rate and the bond, we have a caplet price of

$$E^Q \left[e^{-\int_0^{T_i} r(s)ds} N \tau_i \max \left\{ \frac{1}{\tau_i} \left(\frac{1}{P(T_{i-1}, T_i)} - 1 \right) - K, 0 \right\} \right]$$

$$= NE^Q \left[\frac{e^{-\int_0^{T_i} r(s)ds}}{P(T_{i-1}, T_i)} \max\{1 - (1 + K\tau_i) P(T_{i-1}, T_i), 0\} \right]$$

$$= NE^Q \left[\frac{e^{-\int_0^{T_{i-1}} r(s)ds}}{P(T_{i-1}, T_i)} E^Q \left[e^{-\int_{T_{i-1}}^{T_i} r(s)ds} \Big| \mathcal{F}_{T_{i-1}} \right] \max\{1 - (1 + K\tau_i) P(T_{i-1}, T_i), 0\} \right]$$

$$= N(1 + K\tau_i) E^Q \left[e^{-\int_0^{T_{i-1}} r(s)ds} \max \left\{ \frac{1}{1 + K\tau_i} - P(T_{i-1}, T_i), 0 \right\} \right]$$

$$= N' P(0, T_{i-1}) p_{BS} \left(\frac{P(0, T_i)}{P(0, T_{i-1})}, K', 0, 0, 0, \Sigma(T, S), T_{i-1} \right),$$

where $N' = N(1 + K\tau_i)$ and $K' = \frac{1}{1+K\tau_i}$, and $p_{BS}(S, K, t, r, q, v, T)$ is the BS put option formula. Here, the price of a caplet is related to the price of the put option of a CB. Therefore, a call on an interest rate is essentially equivalent to a put on a bond.

Remember that the market price of a caplet is usually quoted in terms of its Black volatility, v_{i-1}. More precisely, the LIBOR market usually prices a caplet as a call on the LIBOR rate and regards the LIBOR rate as log-normally distributed. To reduce confusion, the usual LIBOR market practice it to view the LIBOR rate as if it were an equity with a zero interest rate. Therefore, the call option on the LIBOR rate obeys the BS call option formula by inserting a zero interest rate therein. This BS formula incorporating a zero interest rate is referred to as the Black formula. Therefore, the quoted caplet price is

$$\text{Caplet}^{\text{market}}(T_i, K, N) = N P(0, T_i) c_{BS}(f_{i-1}(0), K, 0, 0, v_{i-1}, T_{i-1}),$$

where $f_{i-1}(0)$ is the current forward rate for $L(t_{i-1}, t_i)$, and v_{i-1} is the quoted Black volatility. Practitioners recognize that the Black formula is not necessarily accurate, but they use it simply for quotation purposes.

As noted, interest rate derivatives are structured in a relatively more complicated way than equity products. The standard options in an interest rate product are caps and floors. A cap is a portfolio of caplets with strike K. To price the caps in the

Hull–White model, we write

$$\text{Cap}(T_n, K, N) = \sum_{i=1}^{n} \text{Caplet}(T_i, K, N)$$

$$= N \sum_{i=1}^{n} \left(P(t, T_{i-1}) \Psi(-h_i + \sigma_p^i) - (1 + K\tau_i) P(t, T_i) \Psi(-h_i) \right),$$

(5.19)

where $\sigma(t)$ is assumed to be constant, and $\Psi(\cdot)$ is the cumulative distribution function of a standard normal random variable, and

$$\sigma_p^i = \sigma \sqrt{\frac{1 - e^{-2aT_{i-1}}}{2a}} B(T_{i-1}, T_i),$$

$$h_i = \frac{1}{\sigma_p^i} \log \frac{P(t, T_i)(1 + K\tau_i)}{P(t, T_i)} + \frac{\sigma_p^i}{2}.$$

A floor is a portfolio of floorlets, and a floorlet is a put option on the LIBOR. Hence, the price of a floor can be obtained by the put-call parity relation, as follows.

$$\text{Floor}(T_n, N, K) = N \sum_{i=1}^{n} \left((1 + K\tau_i) P(t, T_i) \Psi(h_i) - P(t, T_{i-1}) \Psi(h_i - \sigma_p^i) \right).$$

In practice, we can collect market quotes for Black volatilities from caps and floors. After substituting the quoted volatilities into the corresponding Black option formulas, we can then obtain the quoted prices of these options. Then the interest rate volatility can be backed out from the bond option formula, similar to the way we produced implied volatilities.

Returning to the problem of calibration, we illustrate only the results of the caplet data given in Table 5.5. All of these caplets have a strike rate of 0.1%, a nominal amount of $1, and are based on the LIBOR rate with maturity 0.25. We have to minimize the objective function with respect to a and σ, that is,

$$\min_{a, \sigma} \sum_{i=1}^{n} \left(\text{Caplet}^{\text{market}}(T_i, K) - \text{Caplet}^{\text{model}}(T_i, K) \right)^2.$$

(5.20)

Select the ranges of $a \in [0, 0.25]$ and $\sigma \in [0, 0.05]$, and calibrate the model using the built-in Excel Solver. The calibration procedure is as follows.

1. Set a pair of initial values for a and σ within the prescribed ranges.
2. Compute the market prices of the caplets using the Black volatilities and the Black formula.

TABLE 5.5 Caplet Data Used in Calibration of the One-Factor Hull–White Model

Caplet expiry date	Black caplet volatility
0.25	18.00%
0.50	18.25%
0.75	18.50%
1.00	18.75%
1.25	19.00%
1.50	19.25%
1.75	19.50%
2.00	19.75%
2.25	20.00%
2.50	20.25%
2.75	20.50%
3.00	20.75%

3. Compute the model prices of the caplets using parameters a and σ and the Hull–White formula.
4. Compute the objective function in Equation 5.20.
5. Use the Excel Solver to find the best fits of a and σ within the prescribed ranges.

In this example, the fitted values are $a = 0.1828128$ and $\sigma = 0.0003568$. The fitted prices of the caplets under the Black and Hull–White models are shown in Table 5.6. For more details, please refer to Ch5.3_Hull_White_Calibration, in which details of the calibration of the Hull–White model using DE can also be found.

TABLE 5.6 Caplet Prices Under the Black and Hull–White Models with Their Squared Differences

Caplet expiry date	Black caplet volatility	Black caplet price	Hull–White caplet price	Squared difference
0.25	18.00%	0.0311%	0.0335%	5.58E−10
0.50	18.25%	0.0369%	0.0425%	3.17E−09
0.75	18.50%	0.0492%	0.0581%	7.93E−09
1.00	18.75%	0.0679%	0.0801%	1.49E−08
1.25	19.00%	0.0932%	0.1087%	2.41E−08
1.50	19.25%	0.1249%	0.1438%	3.56E−08
1.75	19.50%	0.1631%	0.1854%	4.96E−08
2.00	19.75%	0.2078%	0.2321%	5.92E−08
2.25	20.00%	0.2548%	0.2785%	5.61E−08
2.50	20.25%	0.3000%	0.3230%	5.33E−08
2.75	20.50%	0.3433%	0.3658%	5.06E−08
3.00	20.75%	0.3848%	0.4068%	4.81E−08
			Sum	4.03E−07

5.3 PRICING INTEREST RATE PRODUCTS USING THE DIRECTION SIMULATION APPROACH

With Equations 5.12, 5.13, 5.14, 5.15, and 5.16 in the previous section, and given a yield curve, the short rate in the Hull–White model can be simulated directly by the following algorithm.

1. Initialize $r(0)$ as calculated from the yield curve.
2. Set $i = 0$.
3. Calculate $\theta(i)$ by Equation 5.14.
4. Calculate $r(i+1) = r(i) + (\theta(i) - ar(i))\Delta t + \sigma(i)\sqrt{\Delta t}\, Z_i$, where Z_i is a standard normal random variable.
5. Set $i = i + 1$, and repeat Steps 2 to 4 $M - 1$ times.
6. Repeat Steps 1 to 5 N times to generate N short-rate paths.

Note that the Hull–White model may generate negative interest rates during simulation, particularly for small initial values. Ad hoc procedures can be used, for example, taking the interest rate to be zero or its absolute value when it becomes negative. The negative value may also be retained, so that it is consistent with the bond price calculated from the discounted bond curve. The VBA code for simulation of the Hull–White model is as follows.

```
Public Function HW_path(t As Variant, f As Variant,
  Df As Variant, r0 As Double, _ a As Double, sigma As Double,
  N As Long) As Variant
    Dim M As Integer, i As Long, j As Long
    Dim dt As Double
    M = UBound(t)
    dt = t(1) - t(0)
    ReDim theta(0 To M) As Double
    ReDim r(0 To M, 1 To N) As Double
    For j = 1 To N
        r(0, j) = r0
        For i = 0 To M - 1
            theta(i) = Df(i) + a * f(i) + _
            sigma ^ 2 / 2 / a * (1 - Exp(-2 * a * i * dt))
            r(i + 1, j) = r(i, j) + (theta(i) - a * r(i, j))
              * dt + sigma * Sqr(dt) * rGauss()
            'Convention for r < 0, take r = 0
            'If r(i + 1, j) < 0 Then r(i + 1, j) = 0
            'Convention for r < 0, take r = 0
            'If r(i + 1, j) < 0 Then r(i + 1, j) =
            Abs(r(i + 1, j))
        Next i
```

```
    Next j

    HW_path = r
End Function
```

After the short-rate paths are generated from the Hull–White model, the values of bonds, RAN, TRN, and other interest rate derivatives can be calculated.

For example, the CB price can be simulated using Equation 5.11. The algorithm is as follows.

1. Simulate a sample path for $r(t)$ under the risk-neutral measure using the aforementioned simulation algorithm.
2. Perform numerical integration for the integral $\int_t^T r(s)\,ds$, and evaluate $\exp\left(-\int_t^T r(s)\,ds\right)$.
3. Repeat Steps 1 and 2 N times, and average the estimates.

The VBA code for computing the bond price via simulation is as follows.

```
Function intr(r As Variant, t0 As Double, t1 As Double,
    dt As Double) As Variant
    Dim i As Long, j As Long, N As Long
    N = UBound(r, 2)
    ReDim Sum(1 To N)
    For j = 1 To N
        Sum(j) = 0
        For i = Int(t0 / dt) To Int(t1 / dt) - 1
            Sum(j) = Sum(j) + r(i, j) * dt
        Next i
    Next j
    intr = Sum
End Function

Function Bond(intr As Variant) As Variant
    Dim N As Long, i As Long
    N = UBound(intr)
    ReDim Val(1 To N) As Double
    For i = 1 To N
        Val(i) = Exp(-intr(i))
    Next i
    Bond = Val
End Function
```

The price of a CB with $T = 10$ calculated from the discounted bond curve is 0.76899. For simulation of the Hull–White model, if $a = 0.1$, $\sigma = 0.01$, and $N = 10{,}000$, then the price is equal to 0.77013. If the convention that $r := 0$ for $r < 0$ is used, then the price is equal to 0.73688; if the convention that $r := -r$ for $r < 0$ is used, then the price is 0.73263. Thus, allowing a negative interest rate leads to a bond price that is consistent with the discounted bond curve. For further details, please refer to Ch5.4_Hull_White_MC_Bond.

5.3.1 Target Redemption Notes

A TRN provides a guaranteed coupon sum with the possibility of early termination. For interest-rate TRNs, if the reference interest rate satisfies certain conditions, then a coupon rate will be paid. Once the accumulated coupon reaches a given target, the note is terminated, and the principal and final coupon are paid to the holder. The risk faced by TRN investors is that their cash can be kept by the issuer for a very long time if the target is difficult to reach. In such a scenario, the holder loses the time value of money and liquidity.

Consider an 8-year TRN with denomination D. The first-year coupon rate is fixed at 4.0%. The coupon rates after the first year are calculated on the basis of the formula $\max\{3\% - L, 0\}$, where L is the spot LIBOR on the coupon date. The note will be terminated prematurely on the coupon date if the accumulated coupon rate reaches the target cap rate of 20%.

Let $P(t, T)$ be the price at time t of a unit-par CB with maturity date T. The relationship between the spot LIBOR $L(t, T)$ and price of CB $P(t, T)$ is given by

$$L(t, T) = \frac{1}{T - t}\left(\frac{1}{P(t, T)} - 1\right). \tag{5.21}$$

The algorithm for computing the price of this TRN proceeds as follows.

1. Set Accumulated coupon = First-year coupon(4%).
2. Calculate Value = Discount function × D × τ × First-year coupon.
3. Set $j = 2$.
4. Calculate the LIBOR L at time $j\tau$ by Equation 5.21.
5. Calculate Coupon = $\max\{3\% - L, 0\}$.
6. Accumulated coupon = Accumulated coupon + Coupon.
7. Value = Value + Discount function × τ × Coupon.
8. If Accumulated coupon > Target coupon, then exit loop.
9. Repeat Steps 4 to 8 for the number of payment times.
10. Value = Value + Discount function × D.

The corresponding VBA code is as follows.

```
Function HW_TRN(r As Variant, fcoupon As Double, _
    rcoupon As Double, TG As Double, _ term As Integer,
```

```
    tau As Double, D As Double, dt As Double) As Variant
      Dim N As Long, i As Long, j As Long, v As Long
      Dim yN As Double, tn As Double, tnp As Double,
      accoupon As Double, coupon As Double
      Dim TRNval() As Double
      Dim L As Double, P As Double

      N = UBound(r, 2)
      ReDim TRNval(1 To N) As Double
      For v = 1 To N
          accoupon = fcoupon * tau
          TRNval(v) = Eval_Spline(tau) * D * fcoupon * tau
          For j = 2 To term / tau
              tn = j * tau
              tnp = (j + 1) * tau
              P = Bond2(r, tn, tnp, dt, v)
              L = (1 / P - 1) / tau
              coupon = Max(rcoupon - L, 0)
              accoupon = accoupon + coupon * tau
              TRNval(v) = TRNval(v) + Eval_Spline(tn) * D
              * coupon * tau
              If accoupon >= TG Then Exit For
          Next j
          TRNval(v) = TRNval(v) + Eval_Spline(tn) * D
      Next v

      HW_TRN = TRNval
End Function
```

Taking $a = 0.1$, $\sigma = 0.01$, number of paths $N = 10,000$, and denomination $D = 1000$, the price of the TRN is equal to 931.07. For more details, please refer to

Ch5.4_Hull_White_MC_Target_Redemption_Notes.

5.3.2 Interest Rate Range Accrual Notes

An interest rate RAN has a similar structure to the RAN of a stock. Consider the following example. There are 10 half-year periods. The coupon rates and ranges of the interest rate RAN are presented in Table 5.7. The coupon amount is calculated by Coupon rate $\times \frac{n}{N}$, where n is the number of days in an interest period that the underlying rate is within the range, and N is the number of calendar days in the interest period. The initial interest period is the period from the issue date ending on the day preceding the first interest payment date. Subsequent interest periods are the periods between two successive interest payment dates, starting on the interest payment date and ending on the day before the next interest payment date.

TABLE 5.7 Specification of the Coupon Rates and Ranges for the Interest Rate RAN

	Coupon rate	Range
Period 1	2.50%	0.00–0.25%
Period 2	3.00%	0.00–0.50%
Period 3	3.50%	0.00–0.75%
Period 4	4.00%	0.00–1.00%
Period 5	4.50%	0.00–1.25%
Period 6	5.00%	0.00–1.50%
Period 7	5.50%	0.00–1.75%
Period 8	6.00%	0.00–2.00%
Period 9	6.50%	0.00–2.25%
Period 10	7.00%	0.00–2.50%

The algorithm for computing the price of this interest rate RAN is as follows.

1. For $j = 0$, set Term/Period length − 1.
2. Initialize Daycount = 0.
3. For $i = 1$ to yN, where $yN = 1/dt$, and dt is the length of time step, set $tn = i \times dt + j \times$ Period length and $tnp = i \times dt + (j + 1) \times$ Period length.
4. Calculate LIBOR L by Equation 5.21.
5. If L is within the range, then Daycount = Daycount + dt.
6. Calculate   Value = Value + Discount function × Coupon rate × D × Daycount/Period length.
7. Loop Steps 1 to 8.
8. Calculate Value = Value + Discount function × D.

The corresponding VBA code is as follows.

```
Function HW_IRRAN(r As Variant, crate As Variant,
  Ranges As Variant, term As Integer, _ pLength As Variant,
  D As Double, dt As Double) As Variant
    Dim N As Long, i As Long, j As Long, v As Long
    Dim yN As Integer
    Dim daycount As Double, tn As Double, tnp As Double
    Dim IRANval() As Double
    Dim L As Double, P As Double, invpLen As Double

    N = UBound(r, 2)
    yN = pLength / dt
    invpLen = 1 / pLength
    ReDim IRANval(1 To N) As Double
    For v = 1 To N
        IRANval(v) = 0
        For j = 0 To term / pLength - 1
```

```
            daycount = 0
            For i = 1 To yN
                tn = i * dt + j * pLength
                tnp = i * dt + (j + 1) * pLength
                P = Bond2(r, tn, tnp, dt, v)
                L = (1 / P - 1) / pLength
                If L >= Ranges(j \ invpLen, 1) And L <=
                Ranges(j \ invpLen, 2) Then
                    daycount = daycount + dt
                End If
            Next i
            IRANval(v) = IRANval(v) + Eval_Spline(tn) * D * _
                crate(j / invpLen) * daycount / pLength
        Next j
        IRANval(v) = IRANval(v) + Eval_Spline(tn) * D
    Next v
    HW_IRRAN = IRANval
End Function
```

With parameters $a = 0.1$, $\sigma = 0.01$, number of paths $N = 10{,}000$ and denomination $D = 1000$, the price of this interest rate RAN is 899.71. For further details, please refer to

Ch5.4_Hull_White_MC_Interest_Rate_RAN.

5.4 PRICING INTEREST RATE PRODUCTS USING THE TRINOMIAL TREE APPROACH

Now that the direct simulation approach has been introduced, we discuss the trinomial tree approach of the Hull–White model. A trinomial tree is a discrete-time approximation of a model; its use involves similar methodology and derivative valuation as those for the binomial tree. Hull and White (1994) proposed a robust two-stage method for constructing a trinomial tree. Recall from Equation 5.12 that

$$dr(t) = (\theta(t) - ar(t))\,dt + \sigma\,dW(t),$$

and from Equation 5.14 that

$$\theta(t) = \frac{\partial}{\partial t} F^M(0, t) + a F^M(0, t) + \frac{\sigma^2}{2a}(1 - e^{-2at}),$$

where $F^M(0, t)$ is the instantaneous market forward rate satisfying

$$F^M(0, T) = -\frac{\partial}{\partial T} \log P^M(0, T).$$

Integrating process $e^{at}r(t)$ yields

$$r(t) = e^{-a(t-s)}r(s) + \int_s^t e^{-a(t-u)}\theta(u)\,du + \sigma \int_s^t e^{-a(t-u)}\,dW(u)$$

$$= e^{-a(t-s)}r(s) + \alpha(t) - e^{-a(t-s)}\alpha(s) + \sigma \int_s^t e^{-a(t-u)}\,dW(u), \quad (5.22)$$

where

$$\alpha(t) = F^M(0, t) + \frac{\sigma^2}{2a^2}(1 - e^{-2at})^2. \quad (5.23)$$

It follows that

$$\mathrm{E}^\mathbb{Q}[r(t)|\mathcal{F}_s] = e^{-a(t-s)}r(s) + \alpha(t) - e^{-a(t-s)}\alpha(s),$$

$$\mathrm{Var}^\mathbb{Q}[r(t)|\mathcal{F}_s] = \frac{\sigma^2}{2a}\left(1 - e^{-2a(t-s)}\right).$$

Define $x(t) = r(t) - \alpha(t)$. Then,

$$x(t) = e^{-a(t-s)}x(s) + \sigma \int_s^t e^{-a(t-u)}\,dW(u),$$

or

$$dx(t) = -ax(t)\,dt + \sigma\,dW(u), \text{ where } x(0) = 0. \quad (5.24)$$

The trinomial tree on $r(t)$ is first constructed by $x(t)$ via Equation 5.24 and then by displacing the result.

The first stage is the construction of the tree for process $x(t)$. Let T be a fixed time horizon such that $0 = t_0 < t_1 < \cdots < t_N = T$. For each $i = 0, 1, \ldots, N-1$, let $\Delta t_i = t_{i+1} - t_i$. For the trinomial tree, index the tree nodes by (i, j), where index i ranges from 0 to N and, at time t_i, index j ranges from $\underline{j}_i < 0$ to $\overline{j}_i > 0$. For process $x(t)$, denote the value of process x on node (i, j) by $x_{i,j}$. Then,

$$M_{i,j} \triangleq \mathrm{E}^\mathbb{Q}[x(t_{i+1})|x(t_i) = x_{i,j}] = x_{i,j}e^{-a\Delta t_i}$$

$$V_i^2 \triangleq \mathrm{Var}^\mathbb{Q}[x(t_{i+1})|x(t_i) = x_{i,j}] = \frac{\sigma^2}{2a}\left(1 - e^{-2a\Delta t_i}\right).$$

Set

$$x_{i,j} = j\Delta x_i, \text{ where } \Delta x_i = \sqrt{3}V_i.$$

Assume that on node (i, j), the process can move to nodes $(i+1, k+1)$, $(i+1, k)$, or $(i+1, k-1)$, where the value of k depends on the current value of j. In other

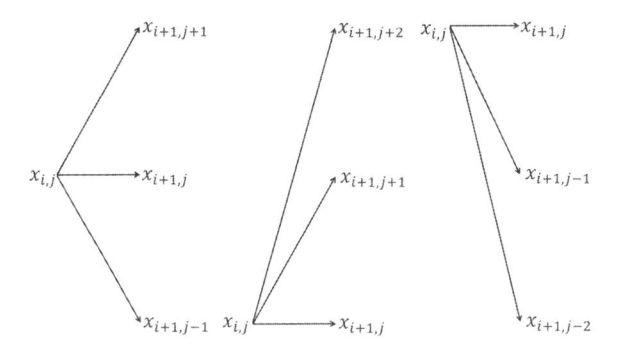

Figure 5.8 Three different kinds of branching for different positions of the trinomial tree.

words, if $\underline{j}_i < j < \bar{j}_i$, then the branching on the left-hand side of Figure 5.8 applies; if $j = \underline{j}_i$, then the branching in the middle of Figure 5.8 applies; and if $j = \bar{j}_i$, then the branching on the right-hand side of Figure 5.8 applies. Figure 5.9 shows an example of a trinomial tree, where $N = 5$, the maximum value of j is 2, and the minimum value of j is -2.

A trinomial tree has upward, middle, and downward probabilities in each step, denoted as p_u, p_m, and p_d in order. The following conditions determine the probability.

$$p_u x_{i+1,k+1} + p_m x_{i+1,k} + p_d x_{i+1,k-1} = M_{i,k}, \text{ (the mean condition)}$$

$$p_u x_{i+1,k+1}^2 + p_m x_{i+1,k}^2 + p_d x_{i+1,k-1}^2 = V_i^2 + M_{i,k}, \text{ (the variance condition)}$$

$$p_u + p_m + p_d = 1. \text{ (the probability condition)}$$

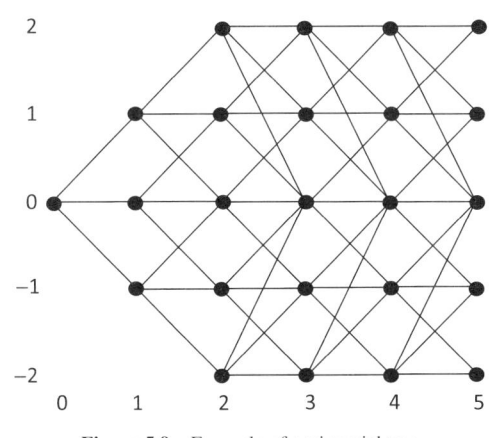

Figure 5.9 Example of a trinomial tree.

Solving the set of equations yields

$$p_u = \frac{1}{6} + \frac{\eta_{j,k}^2}{6V_i^2} + \frac{\eta_{j,k}}{2\sqrt{3}V_i},$$

$$p_m = \frac{2}{3} - \frac{\eta_{j,k}^2}{3V_i^2},$$

$$p_d = \frac{1}{6} + \frac{\eta_{j,k}^2}{6V_i^2} - \frac{\eta_{j,k}}{2\sqrt{3}V_i},$$

where $\eta_{j,k} = M_{i,j} - x_{i+1,k}$ (the dependence on i is omitted to lighten the notations) and $k = \text{round}\,(M_{i,j}/\Delta x_{i+1})$.

The second stage is the displacement of the tree of $x(t)$ to the tree of $r(t)$. An easy way to do so is by means of the explicit formula $r(t) = x(t) + \alpha(t)$, where $\alpha(t)$ is defined in Equation 5.23. However, combining this exact formula with the approximate nature of the tree prevents us from retrieving the correct market discount factor at time 0. For example, as $\alpha(0) = r(0)$, the zero-coupon bond with maturity t_1 calculated in the tree would be $e^{-r(0)t_1}$, which is different from $P^M(0, t_1) = e^{-R(0,t_1)t_1}$, where $R(0, t_1)$ is the continuously compounding rate at time 0 for maturity t_1. Thus, Hull and White (1994a) suggest displacing the tree by discrete values of $\alpha(t)$, denoted by α_i at time t_i. The quantity α_i is calculated as follows. Denote $Q_{i,j}$ as the present value of an instrument paying \$1 if node (i, j) is reached, and zero otherwise. Then the values of α_i and $Q_{i,j}$ are calculated recursively from α_0, where

$$\alpha_0 = -\frac{1}{t_1} \log P^M(0, t_1).$$

As soon as α_i is known, the values of $Q_{i+1,j}$, where $j = \underline{j}_{i+1}, \ldots, \overline{j}_{i+1}$, can be calculated by

$$Q_{i+1,j} = \sum_h Q_{i,h} q(h, j) \exp\left(-(\alpha_i + h\Delta x_i)\Delta t_i\right),$$

where $q(h, j)$ is the probability of moving from node (i, h) to $(i + 1, j)$. The value of α_i is calculated by solving

$$P^M(0, t_{i+1}) = \sum_{j=\underline{j}_i}^{\overline{j}_i} Q_{i,j} \exp\left(-(\alpha_i + j\Delta x_i)\Delta t_i\right),$$

which leads to

$$\alpha_i = -\frac{1}{\Delta t_i} \log \frac{\sum_{j=\underline{j}_i}^{\overline{j}_i} Q_{i,j} \exp(-j\Delta x_i \Delta t_i)}{P(0, t_{i+1})}.$$

To illustrate the foregoing algorithm, consider the first few steps of tree construction. It is known that $Q_{0,0} = 1$, which is the price of a sure payoff of $1 now, and that α_0 is computed from $P^M(0, t_1)$. $Q_{1,1}$, $Q_{1,0}$ and $Q_{1,-1}$ are computed by

$$\begin{cases} Q_{1,1} = Q_{0,0} q(0, 1) \exp(-\alpha_0 \Delta t_0), \\ Q_{1,0} = Q_{0,0} q(0, 0) \exp(-\alpha_0 \Delta t_0), \\ Q_{1,-1} = Q_{0,0} q(0, -1) \exp(-\alpha_0 \Delta t_0). \end{cases}$$

Then, the value of α_1 is determined by solving

$$P^M(0, t_2) = Q_{1,1} \exp(-(\alpha_1 + \Delta x_1)\Delta t_1)$$
$$+ Q_{1,0} \exp(-\alpha_1 \Delta t_1) + Q_{1,-1} \exp(-(\alpha_1 - \Delta x_1)\Delta t_1).$$

Thus, the bond price $P^M(0, t_2)$ is fitted. The next step is to determine the values of $Q_{2,j}$, where $j = -2, \ldots, 2$. In particular, consider node $(2, 1)$. Because $(2, 1)$ can be reached only from $(1, 1)$ and $(1, 0)$,

$$Q_{2,1} = Q_{1,1} q(1, 1) \exp(-(\alpha_1 + \Delta x_1)\Delta t_1) + Q_{1,0} q(0, 1) \exp(-\alpha_1 \Delta t_1).$$

The other $Q_{2,j}$'s are computed similarly. Then, the value of α_2 is determined by solving

$$P^M(0, t_3) = \sum_{j=-2}^{2} Q_{2,j} \exp(-(\alpha_2 + j\Delta x_1)\Delta t_1).$$

Thus, the bond price $P^M(0, t_3)$ is fitted. The procedure is carried out until $i = N - 1$.

In implementing the trinomial tree approach, it is assumed that the Δt_i's are the same. Thus, the rate in the trinomial tree is the Δt-period rate, denoted by R, rather than the instantaneous rate r. However, it should be understood that R also follows the dynamics of r. The unknown parameters a and σ are obtained by calibrating the Hull–White model to interest rate derivatives, such as caps and swaptions, as illustrated in Section 5.2. For more details, please refer to Ch5.5_HW_Tree.

Remark The advantage of the trinomial tree approach over the direct simulation approach is that the former provides an *exact* fit to the initial term structure by choosing the values of α_i for $i = 0, \ldots, N - 1$ without requiring further numerical procedures. In contrast, the direct simulation approach requires information on the entire instantaneous forward rate curve $F^M(0, t)$ to be known, which is computed by interpolating and then differentiating the yield curve or the zero-coupon curve. Such numerical procedures introduce error into the model.

5.4.1 Bond Price

With Δt-period rate R, it can be shown that the price at time t of a zero-coupon bond with maturity T satisfies

$$P(t, T) = \widehat{A}(t, T) \exp(-\widehat{B}(t, T) R(t)),$$

where

$$\log \widehat{A}(t, T) = \log \frac{P(0, T)}{P(0, t)} - \frac{B(t, T)}{B(t, t + \Delta t)} \log \frac{P(0, t + \Delta t)}{P(0, t)}$$

$$- \frac{\sigma^2}{4a}(1 - e^{-2at}) B(t, T)(B(t, T) - B(t, t + \Delta t)),$$

$$\widehat{B}(t, T) = \frac{B(t, T)}{B(t, t + \Delta t)} \Delta t,$$

$$B(t, T) = \frac{1 - e^{-a(T-t)}}{a}.$$

5.4.2 Generalized Hull–White Model: The Tree Approach

The Hull–White model (Eq. 5.12) can be extended to the following generalized form.

$$df(r) = (\theta(t) - af(r)) dt + \sigma \, dW(t). \tag{5.25}$$

If $f(r) = r$, then we have the original Hull–White model. If $f(r) = \log(r)$, then it is the Black–Karasinki model, which restricts the interest rate to a positive value. The trinomial tree approach for the original Hull–White model can be applied to Equation 5.25. Assume that the Δt-period rate R follows the same process as that in Equation 5.25. The first stage is the construction of the tree for process $x(t)$ in Equation 5.24. The second stage is slightly different from the previous one. Define g as the inverse function of f. For example, if $f(r) = \log(r)$, then $g(r) = \exp(r)$. The value of α_0 is given by

$$P^M(0, t_1) = \exp(-g(\alpha_0) t_1),$$

or

$$\alpha_0 = f\left(-\frac{1}{t_1} \log P^M(0, t_1)\right).$$

As soon as α_i is known, the values of $Q_{i+1, j}$, where $j = \underline{j}_{i+1}, \ldots, \overline{j}_{i+1}$, can be calculated by

$$Q_{i+1, j} = \sum_h Q_{i, h} q(h, j) \exp(-g(\alpha_i + h \Delta x_i) \Delta t_i),$$

where $q(h, j)$ is the probability of moving from node (i, h) to node $(i + 1, j)$. The value of α_i is calculated by solving

$$P^M(0, t_{i+1}) = \sum_{j=\underline{j}_i}^{\overline{j}_i} Q_{i,j} \exp\left(-g(\alpha_i + j\Delta x_i)\Delta t_i\right).$$

This equation can also be solved using a numerical procedure such as, for example, the Newton–Raphson method. For further details, please refer to Ch5.5_HW_Tree.

5.4.3 Simulation Using the Trinomial Tree

Building a trinomial tree alone does not immediately provide the solution for the valuation of some path-dependent derivatives or structured products, such as interest rate TRN and RAN. To value such structured products, we can employ Monte Carlo simulation together with the trinomial tree approach. The main idea is that a trinomial tree can be considered as a set of short-rate sample paths, where each path consists of the nodes of different time points. For example, in Figure 5.10, the paths represented by dotted lines are the generated trinomial tree, and those represented by solid lines are the three sample paths of the short rate. Each path is sampled using probabilities p_u, p_m, and p_d corresponding to each current node. For example, for the uppermost path, it is generated by sampling nodes $(1, 1)$, $(2, 2)$, $(3, 1)$, $(4, 2)$, and $(5, 2)$. Starting from the initial node $(0, 0)$, we generate a uniform random variable $U \sim U(0, 1)$. If $U < p_u$, then it moves to $(1, 1)$; if $U < p_m$, then it moves to $(1, 0)$; otherwise it moves to $(1, -1)$. Continuing this sampling process offers a sample path. Other paths are sampled using the same procedure.

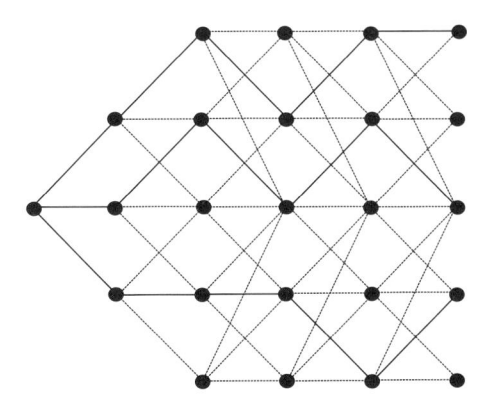

Figure 5.10 Three sample paths simulated from the trinomial tree.

TABLE 5.8 Specification of Coupon Rates and Ranges for the Interest Rate RAN

	Coupon rate	Range
Period 1	2.50%	0.00–0.25%
Period 2	3.00%	0.00–0.50%
Period 3	3.50%	0.00–0.75%
Period 4	4.00%	0.00–1.00%
Period 5	4.50%	0.00–1.25%
Period 6	5.00%	0.00–1.50%
Period 7	5.50%	0.00–1.75%
Period 8	6.00%	0.00–2.00%
Period 9	6.50%	0.00–2.25%
Period 10	7.00%	0.00–2.50%

5.4.4 Pricing Target Redemption Notes

Consider the TRN in the previous section. With $\Delta t = 1$ and the same parameters a and σ, the price of this TRN computed using the trinomial tree with simulation is 929.90. The simulation procedure is similar to that presented in Section 8 except that the sample paths are generated using the tree. For more details, please refer to Ch5.5_Hull_White_MC+Tree_Target_Redemption_Notes. If a smaller Δt is preferred, then the program can be modified in a number of ways, including interpolation of the bond prices and the basic tree.

5.4.5 Pricing Interest Rate Range Accrual Notes

Consider a 10-year non-callable interest rate RAN with semiannual payments, a denomination of 1000 and the 6-month spot LIBOR as the reference rate. The coupon rates and ranges of this interest rate RAN are listed in Table 5.8. With $\Delta t = 0.5$ and the same parameters a and σ as those in the previous section, the price of this note computed using the trinomial tree with simulation is 871.18. For further details, please refer to Ch5.5_Hull_White_MC+Tree_Interest_Rate_RAN.

6

Fixed-Income Derivatives II: LIBOR Market Models

Most fixed-income textbooks start with the concept of bonds and assume a liquid bond market. Although this is the case for the U.S. Treasury bond market, many other interest rate markets have a limited amount of default-free bond trading. The most liquidly traded elementary fixed-income securities in these markets are interest rate swaps (IRS) and forward rate agreements (FRA). A typical example is the London interbank market. The London interbank offered rate (LIBOR) is the benchmark interest rate for liquidly traded IRS and FRA on the offshore U.S. currency interest rate worldwide. Although it would be reasonable to assume that the LIBOR is highly correlated with U.S. Treasury yields, discrepancies between the tax systems, market participants, and credit risk of swap issuers in the two markets make the interest rates quite different from each other. Another pertinent example is the European interbank market, which uses the Euribor as the reference rate for IRS and FRA on interest rates in the eurozone.

As U.S. Treasury yields and the LIBOR are essentially different from each other, the zero-coupon yield curve calibrated to U.S. Treasury bonds is not suitable for the LIBOR market. Instead, we need to construct a yield curve that is based on the market quotes of IRS and FRA. We can do so by transforming the swap rates into synthetic coupon-bearing bonds and then applying the yield curve building procedure discussed in Chapter 5.

As an FRA can be regarded as a particular type of swap contract, we concentrate on IRS and discuss yield curve building on the basis of swap rates. An IRS is a contract in which two parties agree to exchange interest rate cash flows, on the basis of a

---

Handbook of Financial Risk Management: Simulations and Case Studies, First Edition. N.H. Chan and H.Y. Wong.
© 2013 John Wiley & Sons, Inc. Published 2013 by John Wiley & Sons, Inc.

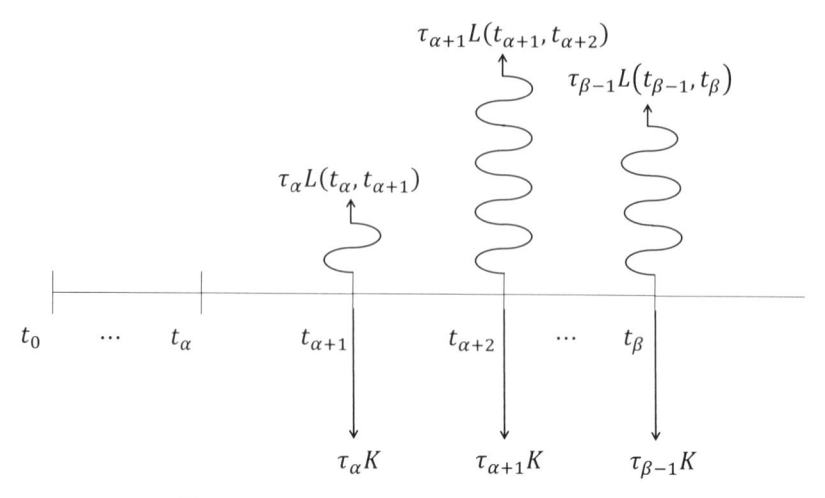

Figure 6.1 Cash flow diagram of an interest rate swap.

specified notional amount (principal) from a fixed rate to a floating rate or vice versa. The party paying the fixed rate is called the payer (while receiving the floating rate), and its counterpart receiving the fixed rate is called the receiver (while paying the floating rate). The position of the payer (receiver) is the holding of a payer (receiver) IRS. An FRA is an IRS with a single transaction time.

Consider a typical payer IRS in which the swap rate is K, with monitoring times $\{t_\alpha, t_{\alpha+1}, \ldots, t_\beta\}$. Figure 6.1 illustrates the cash flows in this IRS. At $t = t_\alpha$ (the first monitoring time specified in the contract), the LIBOR rate for the deposit between t_α and $t_{\alpha+1}$ is realized at t_α and is denoted as $L(t_\alpha, t_{\alpha+1})$. For the notional amount of \$1, the first transaction takes place at $t_{\alpha+1}$ when the payer pays a fixed amount of \$ $\tau_\alpha K$ to the receiver and receives a floating amount of \$ $\tau_\alpha L(t_\alpha, t_{\alpha+1})$, which is realized at t_α but unknown at t_0, where $\tau_\alpha = t_{\alpha+1} - t_\alpha$. At $t_{\alpha+1}$, the realized LIBOR rate for the deposit between $t_{\alpha+1}$ and $t_{\alpha+2}$ is $L(t_{\alpha+1}, t_{\alpha+2})$. The next transaction takes place at $t_{\alpha+2}$ and so on until the last transaction time t_β. Adding \$1 to the cash transactions at t_β to both the upper and lower parts of the cash flow diagram in Figure 6.1 has no effect on the cash flows, but better enables us to explain the pricing. If a principal of \$1 is added to the lower part, then the fixed cash outflows resemble a coupon bond (CB) with coupon rate K. More specifically,

$$\text{Net present value (NPV) of cash outflows} = \sum_{j=\alpha+1}^{\beta} \tau_{j-1} K P(t_0, t_j) + P(t_0, t_\beta)$$

$$= \text{CB}(t_0), \tag{6.1}$$

where $P(t_0, t_j)$ are the synthetic zero-coupon bond prices between t_0 and t_j, and CB stands for a synthetic CB at t_0 with coupon rate K. After adding \$1 to the upper part of the diagram, the upper cash flows form a floating-rate note. This is a scenario in which an investor deposits $1 at t_α and rolls over the deposit at $t_{\alpha+j}$, with the interest rate received at $t_{\alpha+j}$ for all j until t_β. At t_β, the investor gets back the principal of $1 and the final interest. This floating-rate note is certainly worth $1 at t_α because it simply replicates the roll-over strategy of a bank deposit. As the present value of $1 at t_α is $P(t_0, t_\alpha)$,

$$\text{NPV of cash inflows} = P(t_0, t_\alpha). \tag{6.2}$$

The no-arbitrage condition suggests that the NPV of cash outflows = the NPV of cash inflows, which deduces a no-arbitrage swap rate of

$$K = \frac{P(t_0, t_\alpha) - P(t_0, t_\beta)}{\sum_{j=\alpha+1}^{\beta} \tau_{j-1} P(t_0, t_j)}. \tag{6.3}$$

An IRS is often structured in such a way that $t_0 = t_\alpha$, in which case, the NPV of cash inflows in Equation 6.2 is 1, and the CB in Equation 6.1 becomes a (synthetic) par bond. Therefore, swap rate K is the par yield. In other words, a sample of market swap rates is equivalent to a sample of par bonds. All of the par bonds have a value of $1, but they pay different coupon rates that are equivalent to the swap rates. Feeding these synthetic bonds into the regression spline model developed in Chapter 5 generates the yield curve for the LIBOR market, allowing us to then apply the Hull–White model to value interest rate derivatives.

One-factor short-rate models assume the yield curve to be driven by a single Brownian motion, which implies the parallel movement of the entire yield curve over time. This assumption is fine if the interest rate product depends only on a single interest rate, such as the 3-month rate. For products involving the interactions of multiple interest rates, such as the swap rate, however, the model needs to incorporate many possible changes in this curve. In fact, the shape of this curve can change in many different ways, such as taking on an increasing, decreasing or, hump shape. To better capture possible yield curve movements, interest rate models should be generalized to incorporate multiple factors (or Brownian motions). Heath, Jarrow, and Morton (HJM, 1992) introduced a multivariate model for interest rates which, however, is not analytically tractable in many practical situations. To supplement this, LIBOR market models have been developed with all of these practical issues in mind.

6.1 LIBOR MARKET MODELS

The elementary securities in the LIBOR market are FRA and IRS. As noted, an FRA is an IRS with a single transaction time, whereas an IRS can be viewed as the sum of many FRA. Therefore, there are two approaches to model development for the LIBOR market. The first is to directly model the joint stochastic movements of the forward rates. This approach is referred to as a LIBOR market model. The second approach is to directly model the stochastic movements of the swap rates, and it is called a swap market model (Jamshidian, 1997).

The following notations are used throughout this chapter.

- $f_i(t)$: the forward rate observed at time t for the period from t_i to t_{i+1} with the compounding period $\tau_i = t_{i+1} - t_i$.
- τ_i: the compounding period for the ith forward rate, also called the tenor of the ith forward rate.
- $W_k(t)$: the kth $\mathbb{Q}$-standard Brownian motion at time t.
- $\sigma_{ik}(t)$: the instantaneous volatility function at time t of the kth factor of the ith forward rate.
- $\mu_i(t)$: the drift term at time t of the ith forward rate.

Suppose that a (synthetic) zero-coupon bond follows the SDE:

$$\frac{dP(t,T)}{P(t,T)} = r_t\, dt + \sum_{k=1}^{m} \sigma_{p,k}(t,T)\, dW_k(t), \tag{6.4}$$

where r_t is the stochastic instantaneous interest rate, $\sigma_{p,k}(t,T)$ are adapted to $\mathcal{F}_t^W$, the information generated by m-dimensional Brownian motion $W = (W_1, \ldots, W_m)$, such that $\sigma_{p,k}(T,T) = 0$, and m is the number of factors pre-selected in the model. Note that the zero bond price in Equation 6.4 does not necessarily follow a log-normal process because $\sigma_{p,k}(t,T)$ could be a function depending on the bond price itself for each k, for it is adapted to $\mathcal{F}_t^W$.

Recall that the forward rate between t_i and t_{i+1} quoted at t is given by

$$f_i(t) = \frac{1}{\tau_i} \left(\frac{P(t,t_i)}{P(t,t_{i+1})} - 1 \right). \tag{6.5}$$

Applying Itô's lemma to $f_i(t)$ with respect to Equation 6.4, we have

$$\frac{df_i(t)}{f_i(t)} = \sum_{k=1}^{m} \sigma_{ik}(t) \left[dW_k(t) - \sigma_{p,k}(t,t_{i+1})\, dt \right], \tag{6.6}$$

where $i = 1, \ldots, n$ are the number of forward rates in the market, $\{W_k(t) : k = 1, \ldots, m\}$ is a collection of m independent standard Brownian motions and

$$\sigma_{ik}(t) = \frac{1 + \tau_i f_i(t)}{\tau_i f_i(t)} \left[\sigma_{pk}(t,t_i) - \sigma_{pk}(t,t_{i+1}) \right], \text{ for } i = 1, 2, \ldots, n. \tag{6.7}$$

It can be seen from Equation 6.5 that the forward rate is calculated using $P(t,t_{i+1})$ as the reference (numeraire). If $\sigma_{p,k}(t,T_{i+1})$ satisfies the condition in the Girsanov theorem for all i,k, then we are permitted to define a probability measure $\mathbb{Q}^{i+1}$ with respect to the numeraire $P(t, t_{i+1})$, such that

$$\frac{d\mathbb{Q}^{i+1}}{d\mathbb{Q}} = \exp\left[-\frac{1}{2}\int_0^t \sum_{k=1}^m \sigma_{p,k}(s, t_{i+1})^2\, ds + \int_0^t \sum_{k=1}^m \sigma_{p,k}(s, t_{i+1})\, dW_k(s)\right], \quad (6.8)$$

and $\mathbb{Q}^{i+1}$-standard Brownian motions,

$$dW_k^i(t) = dW_k(t) - \sigma_{p,k}(t, t_{i+1})\, dt, \text{ for all } k = 1, 2, \ldots, m.$$

Then, from Equation 6.6, the forward rate has zero drift when $\mathbb{Q}^{i+1}$-standard Brownian motions are used. Hence, $f_i(t)$ is a $\mathbb{Q}^{i+1}$-martingale.

The LIBOR market model proposed by Brace, Gatarek, and Musiela (BGM, 1997) is developed on the basis of Equation 6.6. In their model, the bond volatility functions, $\sigma_{p,k}(t, T), k = 1, 2, \ldots, m$, are chosen in such a way that the forward rate volatility functions in Equation 6.7 are deterministic functions of t, which forces the n forward rates to be log-normal processes driven by m independent Brownian motions. For the monitoring points, $t_0, t_1, \ldots, t_n$, where t_0 is the current time. The forward LIBOR rate for the period between t_i and t_{i+1} follows the SDE Eq. 6.6 in which, as BGM show, the $\mathbb{Q}^{i+1}$-standard Brownian motions are related to the $\mathbb{Q}^i$-standard Brownian motions by the following formula.

$$dW_k^i(t) = dW_k^{i-1}(t) + \frac{\tau_{i-1} f_{i-1}(t)}{1 + \tau_{i-1} f_{i-1}(t)} \sigma_{i-1,k}(t)\, dt, \text{ for all } k = 1, 2, \ldots, m. \quad (6.9)$$

Define

$$\rho_{ij}(t) \triangleq \mathrm{Corr}\left(\sum_{k=1}^m \sigma_{ik}(t)\, dW_k(t), \sum_{k=1}^m \sigma_{jk}(t)\, dW_k(t)\right),$$

$$\sigma_i(t) \triangleq \sqrt{\sum_{k=1}^m \sigma_{ik}^2(t)}.$$

Let

$$b_{ik}(t) = \frac{\sigma_{ik}(t)}{\sigma_i(t)}.$$

It can then be shown that

$$\sum_{k=1}^m b_{ik}(t)^2 = 1,$$

$$\rho_{ij}(t) = \sum_{k=1}^m b_{ik}(t) b_{jk}(t),$$

$$\boldsymbol{\rho}(t) = \boldsymbol{B}(t)\boldsymbol{B}(t)^T,$$

where $\boldsymbol{\rho}(t)$ stands for the matrix $[\rho_{ij}(t)]_{i,j=1,\ldots,n}$ and $\boldsymbol{B}(t)$ stands for the matrix $[b_{ik}(t)]_{i=1,\ldots,n,k=1,\ldots,m}$. With the foregoing modifications, the LIBOR market model in Equation 6.6 can be written as

$$\frac{df_i(t)}{f_i(t)} = \sigma_i(t) \sum_{k=1}^{m} b_{ik}(t) \, dW_k^i(t).$$

By Itô's lemma,

$$d \log f_i(t) = -\frac{\sigma_i(t)^2}{2} dt + \sigma_i(t) \sum_{k=1}^{m} b_{ik}(t) \, dW_k^i(t), \qquad (6.10)$$

or

$$f_i(t) = f_i(0) \exp\left(-\frac{1}{2} \int_0^t \sigma_i(s)^2 \, ds + \int_0^t \sigma_i(s) \sum_{k=1}^{m} b_{ik}(s) \, dW_k^i(s)\right).$$

6.1.1 Pricing Formula for Caplets/Caps

A cap is a derivative on an IRS. Consider the cash flow diagram in Figure 6.1 and a receiver IRS. If the floating LIBOR rate is greater than swap rate K at $t_{\alpha+j}$, then the cap holder will choose to exchange the rates at $t_{\alpha+j+1}$; otherwise, the cap holder has the right to cancel the transaction. A cap can be viewed as a sum of caplets:

$$cap(0, K) = \sum_{i=\alpha+1}^{\beta} caplet_i(0, K).$$

A caplet for periods t_i and t_{i+1} with strike rate K is a call option on LIBOR rate $L(t_i, t_{i+1})$, where the payoff,

$$\tau_i \max\{L(t_i, t_{i+1}) - K, 0\},$$

is determined at expiry date t_i but paid to the caplet holder at payment date t_{i+1}. Similarly, a floor let for periods t_i and t_{i+1} with strike rate K is a put option on LIBOR rate $L(t_i, t_{i+1})$. However, the forward LIBOR rate for the period from t_i to t_{i+1} is equal to the LIBOR rate over the same period at t_i, that is, $f_i(t_i) = L(t_i, t_{i+1})$, by the definitions in these two rates. Hence, the caplet payoff can be alternatively written as

$$\tau_i \max\{f_i(t_i) - K, 0\}.$$

Theorem 6.1 *In the BGM LIBOR market model, the present value of a caplet with reset date t_i, payment date t_{i+1} and strike price K is given by*

$$\text{Caplet}_i(0, K) = \tau_i P(0, t_{i+1})(f_i(0)\Psi(d_1) - K\Psi(d_2)),$$

$$d_1 = \frac{\log \frac{f_i(0)}{K} + \frac{1}{2}v_i^2 t_i}{v_i \sqrt{t_i}},$$

$$d_2 = d_1 - v_i \sqrt{t_i},$$

$$v_i^2 = \frac{1}{t_i} \int_0^{t_i} \sigma_i(t)^2 dt,$$

where v_i is the Black forward rate volatility for forward rate $f_i(t)$, and $P(0, t_{i+1})$ is the current price of a (synthetic) zero-coupon bond maturing at time t_{i+1}.

Proof: As the payment is settled at t_{i+1}, the caplet price is as follows.

$$\text{Caplet}_i(0, K) = \tau_i \mathrm{E}^\mathbb{Q} \left\{ e^{-\int_0^{t_{i+1}} r(s)ds} \max(f_i(t_i) - K, 0) \right\}$$

$$= \tau_i \mathrm{E}^\mathbb{Q} \left\{ \mathrm{E}^\mathbb{Q} \left[e^{-\int_0^{t_{i+1}} r(s)ds} \max(f_i(t_i) - K, 0) \middle| \mathcal{F}_{t_i} \right] \right\}$$

$$= \tau_i \mathrm{E}^\mathbb{Q} \left\{ e^{-\int_0^{t_i} r(s)ds} \mathrm{E}^\mathbb{Q} \left[e^{-\int_{t_i}^{t_{i+1}} r(s)ds} \middle| \mathcal{F}_{t_i} \right] \max(f_i(t_i) - K, 0) \right\}$$

$$= \tau_i \mathrm{E}^\mathbb{Q} \left\{ e^{-\int_0^{t_i} r(s)ds} P(t_i, t_{i+1}) \max(f_i(t_i) - K, 0) \right\}$$

$$= \tau_i \mathrm{E}^\mathbb{Q} \left\{ P(0, t_{i+1}) e^{-\frac{1}{2}\int_0^{t_i} |\sigma_p(s, t_{i+1})|^2 ds + \int_0^{t_i} \sigma_p(s, t_{i+1}) dW(s)} \times \max(f_i(t_i) - K, 0) \right\}.$$

By Girsanov's theorem and Eq. 6.8, we have

$$\text{Caplet}_i(0, K) = \tau_i P(0, t_{i+1}) \mathrm{E}^{\mathbb{Q}^{i+1}} [\max(f_i(t_i) - K, 0)].$$

By Equation 6.10, $f_i(t)$ is a log-normal process with zero drift under $\mathbb{Q}^{i+1}$. Applying the Black–Scholes (BS) formula with a zero interest rate to the last $\mathbb{Q}^{i+1}$-expectation, the result follows.

In Theorem 6.1, the synthetic zero bond can be computed using forward rates as

$$P(0, t_{i+1}) = \prod_{k=0}^{i} \frac{1}{1 + \tau_k f_k(0)}.$$

Similarly, the Black floorlet formula is given by

$$\text{Floorlet} = \tau_i P(0, t_{i+1})\Big(K\Psi(-d_2) - f_i(0)\Psi(-d_1)\Big).$$

6.1.2 Swaption Formula

Consider an IRS for the t_α to t_β period, where a floating rate is exchanged with fixed rate K. At every time t_{j-1}, where $j = \alpha+1, \ldots, \beta$, the floating rate is reset at the prevailing spot LIBOR, $L(t_{j-1}, t_j)$, and payment $\tau_{j-1}L(t_{j-1}, t_j)$ is made at time t_j, when the fixed leg pays $\tau_{j-1}K$.

The cash flow diagram in Figure 6.1 depicts the cash flow to the holder of a payer swaption. The horizontal line is the calendar time, and the arrows are the cash flows to the holder. The arrows pointing downward are the cash flows *paid* by the holder, whereas those pointing upward are the cash flows *received* by the holder. Note that the downward-pointing arrows have the same length, representing the fixed leg paying at rate K, whereas their upward-pointing counterparts have different lengths, representing the floating leg paying at the spot LIBORs reset at different times.

The total value of the floating leg at time $t < t_\alpha$ is

$$\sum_{j=\alpha+1}^{\beta} \tau_{j-1} L(t_{j-1}, t_j) \times P(t, t_j) = \sum_{j=\alpha+1}^{\beta} \left(\frac{1}{P(t_{j-1}, t_j)} - 1\right) P(t, t_j)$$

$$= \sum_{j=\alpha+1}^{\beta} \left(\frac{P(t, t_j)}{P(t_{j-1}, t_j)} - P(t, t_j)\right)$$

$$= \sum_{j=\alpha+1}^{\beta} \left(\frac{P(t, t_{j-1})P(t_{j-1}, t_j)}{P(t_{j-1}, t_j)} - P(t, t_j)\right)$$

$$= \sum_{j=\alpha+1}^{\beta} (P(t, t_{j-1}) - P(t, t_j))$$

$$= P(t, t_\alpha) - P(t, t_\beta).$$

Note that in the fourth line, the no-arbitrage relationship between zero-coupon bond prices applies. The total value of the fixed leg at time t is simply

$$K A_{\alpha,\beta}(t),$$

where

$$A_{\alpha,\beta}(t) = \sum_{j=\alpha+1}^{\beta} \tau_{j-1} P(t, t_j).$$

Thus, the value of the swap at time t is the difference between the floating and fixed legs, which is given by

$$P(t, t_\alpha) - P(t, t_\beta) - K A_{\alpha,\beta}(t).$$

The forward swap rate for the aforementioned IRS at time t, denoted by $S_{\alpha,\beta}(t)$, is the rate K on the fixed leg that renders a swap value equal to zero and is given by

$$S_{\alpha,\beta}(t) = \frac{P(t, t_\alpha) - P(t, t_\beta)}{A_{\alpha,\beta}(t)}$$

$$= \sum_{j=\alpha}^{\alpha-1} w_j(t) f_j(t),$$

where

$$w_j(t) = \frac{\tau_j P(t, t_{j+1})}{A_{\alpha,\beta}(t)}.$$

The forward swap rate becomes the spot swap rate at time t_α.

Now, a European payer swaption is an option to enter into an IRS, paying the fixed leg at rate K and receiving the floating leg. Here, t_α is the expiry date of the swaption and t_β is the maturity date of the IRS. At expiry t_α, the holder of the payer swaption has the right (but no obligation) to decide whether he or she will enter into the IRS. If the IRS has a positive value, then he or she will enter into it; otherwise, he or she will let the swaption expire as worthless. Thus, the payer swaption has the payoff

$$\max\{P(t_\alpha, t_\alpha) - P(t_\alpha, t_\beta) - K A_{\alpha,\beta}(t_\alpha), 0\} = A_{\alpha,\beta}(t_\alpha) \max\{S_{\alpha,\beta}(t_\alpha) - K, 0\}.$$

The price of a European payer swaption is given by

$$\text{PS}(t_\alpha, t_\beta, K) = A_{\alpha,\beta}(0)\Big(S_{\alpha,\beta}(0)\Psi(d_1) - K\Psi(d_2)\Big),$$

$$d_1 = \frac{\log \frac{S_{\alpha,\beta}(0)}{K} + \frac{1}{2} v_{\alpha,\beta}^2 t_\alpha}{v_{\alpha,\beta} \sqrt{t_\alpha}},$$

$$d_2 = d_1 - v_{\alpha,\beta} \sqrt{t_\alpha},$$

where $v_{\alpha,\beta}$ is the Black swap rate volatility for forward swap rate $S_{\alpha,\beta}(t)$. Similarly, a European receiver swaption is an option to enter into an IRS, paying the floating leg and receiving the fixed leg at rate K. At expiry $t\alpha$, the receiver swaption has the payoff

$$\max\{-P(t_\alpha, t_\alpha) + P(t_\alpha, t_\beta) + K A_{\alpha,\beta}(t_\alpha), 0\} = A_{\alpha,\beta}(t_\alpha) \max\{K - S_{\alpha,\beta}(t_\alpha), 0\}.$$

The price of a European receiver swaption is given by

$$\text{RS}(t_\alpha, t_\beta, K) = A_{\alpha,\beta}(0)\Big(K\Psi(-d_2) - S_{\alpha,\beta}(0)\Psi(-d_1)\Big).$$

The Black swap rate volatility can be approximated by either Rebonato's or Hull and White's formula. In Rebonato's formula, $v_{\alpha,\beta}$ is approximated by

$$v_{\alpha,\beta} \approx \frac{1}{S_{\alpha,\beta}(0)\sqrt{t_\alpha}} \sqrt{\sum_{i,j=\alpha}^{\beta-1} w_i(0)w_j(0)f_i(0)f_j(0)\rho_{ij}(0) \int_0^{t_\alpha} \sigma_i(t)\sigma_j(t)\,dt},$$

whereas in Hull and White's, it is approximated by

$$v_{\alpha,\beta} \approx \frac{1}{S_{\alpha,\beta}(0)\sqrt{t_\alpha}} \sqrt{\sum_{i,j=\alpha}^{\beta-1} \hat{w}_i(0)\hat{w}_j(0)f_i(0)f_j(0)\rho_{ij}(0) \int_0^{t_\alpha} \sigma_i(t)\sigma_j(t)\,dt},$$

where

$$\hat{w}_i(t) = w_i(t) + \sum_{j=\alpha}^{\beta-1} f_j(t) \frac{\partial w_j}{\partial f_i}(t),$$

$$\frac{\partial w_j}{\partial f_i}(t) = \frac{\tau_i w_j(t)}{1 + \tau_i f_i(t)} \left(\sum_{k=i}^{\beta-1} w_j(t) - \mathbf{1}_{\{i \leq j\}}\right).$$

The two formulas produce similar prices if the fixed leg dates coincide with the floating leg dates. However, in practice, the fixed period can be longer than the floating period, in which case, Hull and White's formula gives a better approximation. Using the forward structure and parameters specified in Tables 6.1 and 6.2, Table 6.3 shows the performance of the two formulas compared with the simulated prices of several at-the-money (ATM) co-terminal swaptions in a three-factor model (the prices are

TABLE 6.1 Term Structure of the Forward Rate Used in the Test Case

Expiry (years)	Notation	Forward rate
0.00	$f_0(0)$	4.0%
0.25	$f_1(0)$	4.2%
0.50	$f_2(0)$	4.4%
0.75	$f_3(0)$	4.6%
1.00	$f_4(0)$	4.8%
1.25	$f_5(0)$	5.0%
1.50	$f_6(0)$	5.2%
1.75	$f_7(0)$	5.4%
2.00	$f_8(0)$	5.6%

TABLE 6.2 Parameters Used in the Test Case

Parameter	Value
τ	0.25
a	−0.05
b	0.5
c	1.5
d	0.15
h_i	1
β_1	0.1
β_2	0.2

TABLE 6.3 Comparison Between the Performance of Rebonato's and Hull and White's Formulas

Expiry (years)	Maturity (years)	Floating period	Fixed period	Strike (ATM)	Rebonato's formula	Hull and White's formula	Simulated price
0.25	2.25	0.25	2.00	5.115%	39.58	41.30	41.44
0.50	2.25	0.25	1.75	5.191%	51.24	53.16	53.36
0.75	2.25	0.25	1.50	5.265%	55.73	57.50	57.62
1.00	2.25	0.25	1.25	5.337%	55.15	56.57	56.76
1.25	2.25	0.25	1.00	5.406%	50.28	51.27	51.33
1.50	2.25	0.25	0.75	5.473%	41.72	42.28	42.26
1.75	2.25	0.25	0.50	5.538%	30.06	30.27	30.27
2.00	2.25	0.25	0.25	5.600%	15.93	15.93	15.93

given in terms of basis point). Note that we use the volatility function Eq. 6.11 and correlation function Eq. 6.12.

It is easy to see that as the fixed period increases, the pricing error of Rebonato's formula increases significantly, whereas Hull and White's formula performs much better. In fact, the pricing error in the former can be as large as 50% when the fixed period is very long, say 10 years, and the floating period is as short as 3 months. Although, in usual practice, where the fixed period is 6 months and the floating period is 3 months, the two formulas differ very little. However, special care still needs to be taken in calibration when the chosen floating period is much shorter than the fixed period.

6.2 CALIBRATION TO CAPS AND SWAPTIONS

To calibrate the model to caps and swaptions, we must first specify the instantaneous volatility function of the forward rates. Model $\sigma_i(t)$ by

$$\sigma_i(t) = h_i\Big((a + b(t_i - t))e^{-c(t_i - t)} + d\Big), \tag{6.11}$$

where

$$a + d > 0,$$
$$d > 0,$$
$$c > 0,$$
$$a + d \approx \text{Short-maturity implied volatilities},$$
$$d \approx \text{Very long-maturity implied volatilities}.$$

Note that if all h_i's are equal to 1, then the volatility function is time-homogeneous. When $\sigma_i(t)$ takes the form in Equation 6.11, the integration needed to calculate the Black volatilities of the caps and swaptions can be carried out easily. We can verify that the indefinite integral, $\int \sigma_i(t)\sigma_j(t)\,dt$, is given by

$$\int \sigma_i(t)\sigma_j(t)\,dt = \frac{1}{4c^3}\bigg(4ac^2 d\left(e^{c(t-t_i)} + e^{c(t-t_j)}\right) + 4c^3 d^2 t$$
$$- 4bcde^{c(t-t_i)}[c(t-t_i) - 1] - 4bcde^{c(t-t_j)}[c(t-t_j) - 1]$$
$$+ e^{c(2t-t_i-t_j)}\Big(2a^2c^2 + 2abc[1 - c(2t - t_i - t_j)]$$
$$+ b^2\Big[1 + 2c^2(t-t_i)(t-t_j) - c(2t - t_i - t_j)\Big]\Big)\bigg)$$
$$+ \text{Constant terms}.$$

Similar to the instantaneous volatility function, a parametric functional form can be used for the market correlation matrix, such as,

$$\rho_{ij}^{\text{market}} = \beta_1 + (1 - \beta_1)e^{-\beta_2|t_i - t_j|}. \tag{6.12}$$

If heavy correlation-dependent derivatives are required, then other parametric functional forms can be considered. As an extreme, we could even assume $\rho_{ij}^{\text{market}}$ to be piecewise constant, which, however, would mean that the model would have to be calibrated with $\frac{n(n-1)}{2}$ parameters, a possibly difficult task when the number of forward rates n becomes large.

If the volatility function does not deviate significantly from time homogeneity, then the calibration procedure proceeds as follows.

1. Calibrate parameters a, b, c, d, β_1, and β_2 to swaptions and caps by assuming that all h_i's are 1.
2. Decompose market correlation matrix $\rho_{ij}^{\text{market}}$ into b_{ik}'s.
3. Compute the ρ_{ij}'s by $\boldsymbol{\rho} = \boldsymbol{BB}^T$.

4. Re-calibrate parameters a, b, c, and d given ρ_{ij}, to the swaptions and caps.
5. Calibrate the h_i's to the caps and swaptions.

We now discuss the details of each calibration step for an m-factor LIBOR market model with n forward rates.

6.2.0.1 Step 1 Suppose that the market data for N_C caps and N_S swaptions are given. In the first step, find parameters a, b, c, d, β_1, and β_2, such that the model Black volatilities are close to the market Black volatilities of the caps and swaptions. Mathematically, this can be formulated as the following minimization problem.

$$\min_{a,b,c,d,\beta_1,\beta_2} \left(\sum_{i=1}^{N_C} w_i^C (C_i^{\text{market}} - C_i^{\text{model}})^2 + \sum_{i=1}^{N_S} w_i^S (S_i^{\text{market}} - S_i^{\text{model}})^2 \right),$$

where w_i^C is the weight assigned to the ith cap, and C_i^{market} and C_i^{model} are the market and model Black volatilities of the ith cap. Similarly, w_i^S is the weight assigned to the ith swaption, and S_i^{market} and S_i^{model} are its market and model Black volatilities. We test this minimization problem with the DE algorithm using settings identical to those in the previous discussion and with the downhill simplex method (or Nelder–Mead method), and present the results later. For details of the downhill simplex method, see Press, Flannery, Teukolsky, and Vetterling (2007). Iteration stops if the change in the value of the objective function is fractionally smaller than a given tolerance, that is,

$$\frac{|g(x_n) - g(x_0)|}{(|g(x_n)| + |g(x_0)|)/2} < \text{Tolerance},$$

where $g(x_n)$ and $g(x_0)$ are the values of the objective function with highest and lowest costs, respectively.

6.2.0.2 Step 2 After Step 1, we obtain the correlation structure specified by β_1 and β_2. We call that matrix given by Equation 6.12 the market correlation matrix and that calculated by $\boldsymbol{BB}^{\text{T}}$ the model correlation matrix because it is used in the simulation of the m-factor model. For matrix $\boldsymbol{B}$, recall that

$$\sum_{k=1}^{m} b_{ik}^2 = 1,$$

$$\rho_{ij}^{\text{model}} = \sum_{k=1}^{m} b_{ik} b_{jk},$$

$$\rho^{\text{model}} = \boldsymbol{BB}^{\text{T}}.$$

Thus, we need to find $b_{ik}, i = 1, \ldots, n, k = 1, \ldots, m$, such that the objective function

$$\sum_{i,j=1}^{n} \left(\rho_{ij}^{\text{model}} - \rho_{ij}^{\text{market}}\right)^2 \tag{6.13}$$

is minimized subject to the constraint

$$\sum_{k=1}^{m} b_{ik}^2 = 1. \tag{6.14}$$

Instead of directly minimizing Equation 6.13 with the constraint, we transform the problem into an unconstrained one. With the well-known trigonometric relationship

$$\sin^2 \theta + \cos^2 \theta = 1,$$

let

$$b_{i1} = \sin \theta_{i1},$$
$$b_{i2} = \sin \theta_{i2} \cos \theta_{i1},$$
$$\vdots$$
$$b_{ik} = \sin \theta_{ik} \cos \theta_{i(k-1)} \cdots \cos \theta_{i1},$$
$$\vdots$$
$$b_{im} = \sin \theta_{im} \cos \theta_{i(m-1)} \cdots \cos \theta_{i1}.$$

Now, the constraint Eq. 6.14 is satisfied for any choice of θ_{ik}'s, such that the constrained minimization problem Eq. 6.13 becomes an unconstrained minimization problem. For this unconstrained minimization, we use the limited memory Broyden–Fletcher–Goldfarb–Shanno (L-BFGS) multidimensional variable metric method. The BFGS method is a well-known numerical method that approximates Newton's method which seeks a stationary point of a function. The BFGS has proven good performance even for non-smooth optimizations compared with the classical Newton's method (Bonnans, Gilbert, Lemarechal, and Sagastizabal 2006). The L-BFGS, which is a limited-memory version of BFGS that is particularly suited to problems with very large numbers of variables. We choose to use L-BFGS because there are L-BFGS libraries written in C and C#. An alternative implementation uses the DE introduced in previous chapters.

6.2.0.3 Step 3 After calibrating b_{ik}, the model correlation matrix is obtained, which is different from the market correlation matrix. Thus, for Step 3, parameters

a, b, c, and d are recalibrated by the minimization problem

$$\min_{a,b,c,d} \left(\sum_{i=1}^{N_C} w_i^C (C_i^{\text{market}} - C_i^{\text{model}})^2 + \sum_{i=1}^{N_S} w_i^S (S_i^{\text{market}} - S_i^{\text{model}})^2 \right).$$

In this recalibration, we limit the range of a, b, c, and d to keep them close to the original values (e.g., ±0.20). For example, if the calibrated value of a in Step 1 is 0.5, then we set the range of a at 0.3 to 0.7 and recalibrate the model. Recalibration is performed with either the DE algorithm or downhill simplex method. Note that if we have not specified an initial guess for the DE, then it may take much longer to converge and may even end up with a higher value for the objective function if the number of iterations is small. We take the calibrated values obtained in Step 1 to be one member of the initial populations in the DE. The downhill simplex method has a faster convergence rate, and it allows the previously obtained calibrated values to be used as one of the starting vertexes.

6.2.0.4 Step 4
In the final step, we calibrate h_i, for $i = 1, \ldots, n$, to give a better fit to the data. Similar to Steps 1 and 3, we find h_i's, such that

$$\min_{h_1,\ldots,h_n} \left(\sum_{i=1}^{N_C} w_i^C (C_i^{\text{market}} - C_i^{\text{model}})^2 + \sum_{i=1}^{N_S} w_i^S (S_i^{\text{market}} - S_i^{\text{model}})^2 \right).$$

To preserve the time homogeneity of the volatility function, the range of h_i is usually constrained close to 1. Typical constraints for h_i range from around 0.85 to 1.15. However, instead of setting the same lower and upper bounds for all $h'_i s$, we set the range bound for a particular h_i at $[h_i - \delta_1, h_i + \delta_2]$, where h_i is the initial value before calibration. Doing so actually gives us greater flexibility in calibrating the h_i's when the volatility function is not time-homogeneous. When it is time-homogeneous, we simply need to reset all h_i's to 1. For this problem, we again use either the DE algorithm or the downhill simplex method. However, it should be noted that if the number of forward rates is large, for example, $n = 40$, then the number of populations in the DE will be very large. In this case, minimization will be very time-consuming and we may need to decide whether to wait, reduce the size of the population, use parallel computing or employ another minimization algorithm. For this reason, we limit the maximum DE population in the Excel files to 300, and include the downhill simplex method. As before, we also set one of the initial populations in the DE to be the h_i's obtained before, that is, 1.

We now calibrate the model with U.S. swaption and cap quotes obtained from Bloomberg on August 25, 2010. The term structure of the forward rate is shown in Table 6.4, the parameter bounds in Table 6.5 and the swaption and cap quotes in Tables 6.6 and 6.7, respectively. Note that all of the swaptions and the first four caps are ATM, and the market prices are reported in terms of basis points.

Also note that the floating period for the swaptions is a quarter of a year, whereas the fixed period is half of a year. We still use Rebonato's formula to approximate the

TABLE 6.4 Forward Rate Structure

Expiry (years)	Maturity (years)	Notation	Forward rate
0.00	0.25	$f_0(0)$	0.3059%
0.25	0.50	$f_1(0)$	0.4035%
0.50	0.75	$f_2(0)$	0.4660%
0.75	1.00	$f_3(0)$	0.5486%
1.00	1.25	$f_4(0)$	0.6478%
1.25	1.50	$f_5(0)$	0.7858%
1.50	1.75	$f_6(0)$	0.9462%
1.75	2.00	$f_7(0)$	1.1109%
2.00	2.25	$f_8(0)$	1.2700%
2.25	2.50	$f_9(0)$	1.4348%
2.50	2.75	$f_{10}(0)$	1.6091%
2.75	3.00	$f_{11}(0)$	1.7932%
3.00	3.25	$f_{12}(0)$	1.9590%
3.25	3.50	$f_{13}(0)$	2.1104%
3.50	3.75	$f_{14}(0)$	2.2628%
3.75	4.00	$f_{15}(0)$	2.4170%

TABLE 6.5 Parameter Bounds

Parameter	Lower bound	Upper bound
a	−2	2
b	−2	2
c	0	2
d	0	2
β_1	0	1
β_2	0	1

TABLE 6.6 Swaption Quotes

Expiry (years)	Tenor (years)	Fixed payment frequency	Strike	Volatility	Market price
0.25	1	2	0.5167%	86.45%	8.80
0.25	2	2	0.7718%	70.85%	21.51
0.25	3	2	1.0777%	64.08%	40.53
0.5	1	2	0.6123%	86.30%	14.59
0.5	2	2	0.9005%	70.90%	35.25
0.5	3	2	1.2194%	61.15%	61.47
0.75	1	2	0.7325%	81.63%	20.07
0.75	2	2	1.0433%	66.50%	46.63
0.75	3	2	1.3687%	55.38%	76.12
1	1	2	0.8732%	76.80%	25.84
1	2	2	1.1989%	62.13%	57.49
1	3	2	1.5241%	51.65%	90.78
2	1	2	1.5290%	54.93%	45.12
2	2	2	1.8573%	45.45%	90.51
3	1	2	2.1924%	40.68%	57.76

TABLE 6.7 Cap Quotes

Term (years)	Strike	Black volatility	Market price
1	0.4650%	88.01%	8.93
2	0.6912%	80.98%	42.61
3	0.9838%	67.46%	104.50
4	1.2853%	58.57%	193.73
1	1.0000%	85.60%	2.08
2	1.0000%	77.28%	28.94
3	1.0000%	67.25%	103.07
4	1.0000%	62.50%	233.99
1	1.5000%	83.35%	0.69
2	1.5000%	71.35%	15.81
3	1.5000%	61.38%	67.53
4	1.5000%	55.73%	167.27

swaption volatilities to speed up the calibration process. When the result is obtained after calibration, we then use Hull and White's formula. As a first step, we calibrate the model to swaption data using the DE with only 1000 iterations and the downhill simplex method with 10,000 iterations, with tolerance set at 1×10^{-8}. The results are presented in Tables 6.8 and 6.9, respectively. As the calibrated parameters for the two algorithms are similar, we show the calibrated prices for the DE algorithm alone.

If we focus on the calibrated prices, then we may not see any problems. However, if we look at the calibrated β_1, which is 1, then we realize that the correlation between all forward rates is 1, and repeated calibrations give identical results. Increasing the bounds for a, b, c, and d or assigning different weights to the swaptions fails to resolve the problem. To see that the condition that $\beta_2 = 0$ (which implies that $\rho_{ij} = 1$ for all i, j) indeed gives the lowest cost, set $\beta_1 = 0$ and compute the objective function with different values of β_2. The results are presented in Table 6.10.

To resolve this problem, we calibrate β_1 and β_2 using time series of historical forward rates and then calibrate a, b, c, and d to the swaption data. We calibrate the h_i's simultaneously. Note that we cannot calibrate all of the h_i's at once, as doing so would give multiple identical minima. To see this, suppose that the set of parameters $\{a^*, b^*, c^*, d^*, h_i^*, i = 1, \ldots, n\}$ gives a global minimum; then, for any constant

TABLE 6.8 Calibration Results (Parameters)

Parameter	DE	Downhill simplex
a	0.8702	0.8701
b	−0.0001	0.0009
c	0.6076	0.6087
d	0.2434	0.2434
β_1	1.0000	1.0000
β_2	0.0655	0.3116
Stopped at iteration	1000	5157
Computation time (s)	95.1	9.7
Lowest cost	0.0722	0.0722

TABLE 6.9 Calibration Results (Pricing Error)

Expiry (years)	Tenor (years)	Strike	Volatility	Fitted vol.	Vol. error	Error in basis pt.
0.25	1	0.5167%	86.45%	87.71%	1.26%	0.13
0.25	2	0.7718%	70.85%	68.48%	2.37%	0.71
0.25	3	1.0777%	64.08%	55.26%	8.82%	5.54
0.5	1	0.6123%	86.30%	83.20%	3.10%	0.51
0.5	2	0.9005%	70.90%	65.61%	5.29%	2.58
0.5	3	1.2194%	61.15%	53.59%	7.56%	7.51
0.75	1	0.7325%	81.63%	79.25%	2.38%	0.56
0.75	2	1.0433%	66.50%	63.19%	3.31%	2.26
0.75	3	1.3687%	55.38%	52.18%	3.20%	4.33
1	1	0.8732%	76.80%	75.84%	0.96%	0.31
1	2	1.1989%	62.13%	61.09%	1.04%	0.93
1	3	1.5241%	51.65%	50.95%	0.70%	1.20
2	1	1.5290%	54.93%	65.73%	10.80%	8.30
2	2	1.8573%	45.45%	54.65%	9.20%	17.49
3	1	2.1924%	40.68%	58.73%	18.05%	23.83

$\theta > 0$, $\{\theta a^*, \theta b^*, c^*, d^*, \frac{h_i^*}{\theta}, i = 1, \ldots, n\}$ gives the same volatility functions so it is also a global minimum. To resolve this problem, we set $h_1 = 1$ and $h_i = h_{i-1} + \gamma_i$ for $i > 1$. If all γ_i's equal to 0, then all h_i's are equal to 1, which results in time homogeneity. Step 1 now becomes

$$\min_{a,b,c,d,\beta_1,\beta_2,\gamma_i's} \left(\sum_{i=1}^{N_C} w_i^C (C_i^{\text{market}} - C_i^{\text{model}})^2 + \sum_{i=1}^{N_S} w_i^S (S_i^{\text{market}} - S_i^{\text{model}})^2 \right).$$

As the number of γ_i's depends on the number of forward rates, we need to increase the DE population when we calibrate the h_i's simultaneously, which renders the DE time-consuming. Thus, we use the downhill simplex algorithm instead of simultaneous calibration (readers may also try the DE algorithm, as it is included in the Excel file). With this modification, we now calibrate the model to the swaptions again. The parameter bounds are listed in Table 6.11, and the calibration results are presented in Tables 6.12, 6.13 and 6.14.

TABLE 6.10 Lowest Cost with Different β_2 Values

β_2	Lowest cost
0	0.0722
0.1	0.0801
0.2	0.0880
0.4	0.1037
0.6	0.1189
0.8	0.1331
1	0.1464

TABLE 6.11 Parameter Bounds

Parameter	Lower bound	Upper bound
a	-2	2
b	-2	2
c	0	2
d	0	2
β_1	0	1
β_2	0	1
γ_i	-0.25	0.25

From the calibration results for the h_i's, we can clearly see that although the time homogeneity of the volatility function is not violated very much in the first 15 months, it begins to break down after 18 months, which explains the failure of the previous calibration. Note that we also include the calibrated volatility after Steps 2 and 3 in Table 6.14 for the reader's reference. For Step 3, we recalibrate the h_i's simultaneously, as in Step 1. Table 6.14 suggests that the best calibration is obtained after recalibration at Step 3, which is almost a perfect recovery. In this recalibration, it takes 33.6 s to complete 20,000 iterations to attain a cost function as low as 1.49×10^{-5}.

Although the calibrated model now prices swaptions satisfactorily, we still do not know whether it can price other products satisfactorily. We can see from the cap pricing results in Table 6.15 that most of the cap prices are recovered at a satisfactory level.

Before calibrating the model simultaneously to caps and swaptions, we perform further calibration to swaptions with expiry dates up to 10 years (i.e., a total of 39 forward rates, with the last forward rate expiring after 10 years). Figure 6.2 shows how

TABLE 6.12 Calibration Results (γ_i and h_i)

i	Expiry (years)	Maturity (years)	γ_i	h_i
0	0.00	0.25	—	—
1	0.25	0.50	—	1.0000
2	0.50	0.75	0.0164	1.0164
3	0.75	1.00	0.0481	1.0645
4	1.00	1.25	0.0108	1.0753
5	1.25	1.50	-0.0132	1.0620
6	1.50	1.75	-0.1386	0.9234
7	1.75	2.00	-0.0974	0.8260
8	2.00	2.25	-0.1181	0.7080
9	2.25	2.50	-0.0208	0.6872
10	2.50	2.75	-0.0425	0.6447
11	2.75	3.00	-0.0217	0.6230
12	3.00	3.25	0.0023	0.6253
13	3.25	3.50	-0.1107	0.5146
14	3.50	3.75	-0.1495	0.3651
15	3.75	4.00	-0.0429	0.3222

TABLE 6.13 Calibration Results (Parameters)

Parameter	Value
a	−0.4751
b	−0.8455
c	0.6595
d	1.4932
β_1	0.2809
β_2	0.3639
Stopped at iteration	50,000
Computation time (s)	95.1
Lowest cost	0.0011

TABLE 6.14 Calibration Results (Pricing Error)

Expiry (years)	Tenor (years)	Strike	Market volatility	Fitted vol. Step 1	Fitted vol. Step 2	Fitted vol. Step 3	Error in basis pt. Step 3
0.25	1	0.5167%	86.45%	86.32%	89.17%	86.49%	0.00
0.25	2	0.7718%	70.85%	72.90%	74.60%	70.91%	0.02
0.25	3	1.0777%	64.08%	63.69%	64.91%	63.87%	0.13
0.5	1	0.6123%	86.30%	85.89%	88.14%	86.35%	0.01
0.5	2	0.9005%	70.90%	69.08%	70.69%	70.71%	0.09
0.5	3	1.2194%	61.15%	60.52%	61.63%	60.96%	0.19
0.75	1	0.7325%	81.63%	82.34%	83.95%	81.67%	0.01
0.75	2	1.0433%	66.50%	65.43%	67.12%	66.46%	0.03
0.75	3	1.3687%	55.38%	56.01%	57.06%	55.15%	0.31
1	1	0.8732%	76.80%	76.75%	78.22%	76.87%	0.02
1	2	1.1989%	62.13%	62.03%	63.75%	62.08%	0.05
1	3	1.5241%	51.65%	51.57%	52.59%	51.45%	0.35
2	1	1.5290%	54.93%	55.55%	56.89%	54.93%	0.00
2	2	1.8573%	45.45%	45.93%	47.09%	45.75%	0.58
3	1	2.1924%	40.68%	40.29%	41.62%	40.64%	0.05

TABLE 6.15 Cap Pricing Errors

Term (years)	Strike	Market vol.	Fitted vol.	Vol. error	Error in basis pt.
1	0.47%	88.01%	89.89%	1.88%	0.17
2	0.69%	80.98%	83.23%	2.25%	0.88
3	0.98%	67.46%	67.25%	0.21%	0.21
4	1.29%	58.57%	55.16%	3.41%	6.96
1	1.00%	85.60%	89.10%	3.50%	0.24
2	1.00%	77.28%	81.82%	4.54%	1.97
3	1.00%	67.25%	67.12%	0.13%	0.13
4	1.00%	62.50%	57.95%	4.55%	7.80
1	1.50%	83.35%	89.16%	5.81%	0.23
2	1.50%	71.35%	80.32%	8.97%	3.73
3	1.50%	61.38%	64.20%	2.82%	3.34
4	1.50%	55.73%	53.53%	2.20%	4.88

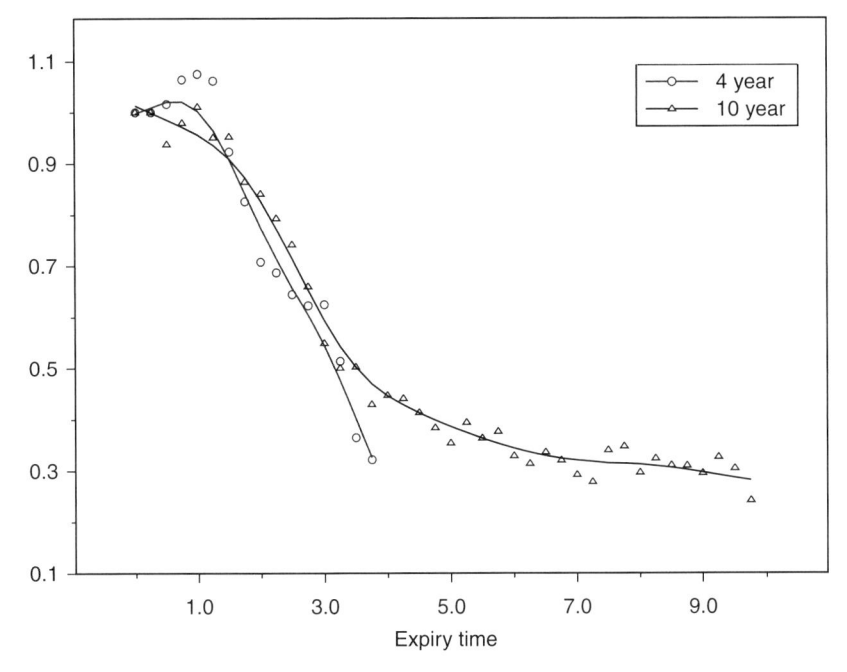

Figure 6.2 h_i against time for 4- and 10-year calibration.

the calibrated h_i's change with time for both the 4- and 10-year calibration. It can be seen that the h_i's obtained from the two calibrations are in agreement, and, although the volatility declines sharply in the first 4 years, it begins to stabilize thereafter and becomes roughly time-homogeneous. Table 6.16 presents the calibrated Black volatility errors for swaptions with different expiry-tenor pairs. The results are again highly satisfactory.

Now, consider the calibration of the model to both caps and swaptions. When we calibrate model parameters a, b, c, d, β_1, and β_2 separately, the problem that $\rho_{ij} = 1$ for all i, j persists, and so we enter the h_i's together in calibration. The calibration

TABLE 6.16 Black Volatility Error in Calibrating Swaptions

Expiry (years)\Tenor (years)	1	2	3	4	5	6	7	8	9
1		0.82%	0.18%	1.34%	1.79%	2.28%	2.53%	2.59%	2.56%	3.13%
2		3.48%	0.13%	0.15%	0.52%	0.07%	0.48%	0.68%	1.14%	—
3		2.13%	0.48%	0.78%	0.69%	0.40%	0.05%	0.25%	—	—
4		0.07%	1.25%	1.13%	0.93%	0.90%	0.52%	—	—	—
5		1.47%	0.87%	0.74%	0.90%	0.85%	—	—	—	—
6		0.26%	0.02%	0.38%	0.48%	—	—	—	—	—
7		0.29%	0.91%	0.89%	—	—	—	—	—	—
8		0.89%	1.26%	—	—	—	—	—	—	—
9		0.16%	—	—	—	—	—	—	—	—

TABLE 6.17 Results of Calibrating γ_i's and h_i's to Caps and Swaptions Simultaneously

i	Expiry (years)	Maturity (years)	γ_i	h_i
0	0.00	0.25	–	–
1	0.25	0.50	–	1.0000
2	0.50	0.75	−0.0813	0.9187
3	0.75	1.00	−0.1032	0.8155
4	1.00	1.25	0.1168	0.9323
5	1.25	1.50	0.0000	0.9324
6	1.50	1.75	−0.1640	0.7684
7	1.75	2.00	−0.2171	0.5513
8	2.00	2.25	0.0245	0.5758
9	2.25	2.50	0.0701	0.6460
10	2.50	2.75	−0.0954	0.5506
11	2.75	3.00	−0.0431	0.5075
12	3.00	3.25	0.0895	0.5970
13	3.25	3.50	−0.1054	0.4916
14	3.50	3.75	−0.1642	0.3274
15	3.75	4.00	−0.0829	0.2445

results with parameter bounds the same as those in Table 6.11 are presented in Tables 6.17, 6.18, 6.19, and 6.20. We can see that the Black volatility of the caps and swaptions is recovered at a satisfactory level. For further details, please refer to Ch6.4_LIBOR_Calibration(Full).xls.

6.2.0.5 More on the Model's Calibration Previously, with n forward rates, we calibrated $n - 1$ free parameters (h_i's), which greatly increased the difficulty when n is large (when, e.g., for a 10-year forward rate term structure, $n = 40$). Instead of allowing each h_i to vary freely, we may also use the functional form to model the h_i's. In the simple case, we can use a linear spline to model them. For example, if we model the h_i's with piecewise linear functions for each year in a 10-year calibration with 40 forward rates, then the number of effective parameters is reduced from $6 + 40 - 1 = 45$ to $6 + 10 = 16$. Tables 6.21 and 6.22 list the volatility errors of calibration using the same set of cap and swaption data and piecewise linear

TABLE 6.18 Results of Simultaneous Calibration to Caps and Swaptions

Parameter	Value
a	−0.1877
b	−0.4020
c	1.1026
d	1.2029
β_1	0.3204
β_2	0.3932
Stopped at iteration	50,000
Computation time (s)	238.2
Lowest cost	0.0074

TABLE 6.19 Swaption Pricing Errors in Simultaneous Cap and Swaption Calibration

Expiry (years)	Tenor (years)	Strike	Market vol.	Fitted vol.	Vol. error	Error in basis pt.
0.25	1	0.5167%	86.45%	86.73%	0.28%	0.03
0.25	2	0.7718%	70.85%	72.22%	1.37%	0.41
0.25	3	1.0777%	64.08%	63.52%	0.56%	0.35
0.5	1	0.6123%	86.30%	86.41%	0.11%	0.02
0.5	2	0.9005%	70.90%	69.25%	1.65%	0.81
0.5	3	1.2194%	61.15%	60.60%	0.55%	0.54
0.75	1	0.7325%	81.63%	82.60%	0.97%	0.23
0.75	2	1.0433%	66.50%	65.47%	1.03%	0.70
0.75	3	1.3687%	55.38%	56.09%	0.71%	0.95
1	1	0.8732%	76.80%	74.30%	2.50%	0.80
1	2	1.1989%	62.13%	62.01%	0.12%	0.11
1	3	1.5241%	51.65%	51.33%	0.32%	0.56
2	1	1.5290%	54.93%	57.00%	2.07%	1.61
2	2	1.8573%	45.45%	47.26%	1.81%	3.48
3	1	2.1924%	40.68%	42.02%	1.34%	1.82

TABLE 6.20 Cap Pricing Errors of Simultaneous Cap and Swaption Calibration

Term (years)	Strike	Market vol.	Fitted vol.	Vol. error	Error in basis pt.
1	0.47%	88.01%	88.25%	0.24%	0.02
2	0.69%	80.98%	79.62%	1.36%	0.53
3	0.98%	67.46%	66.74%	0.72%	0.73
4	1.29%	58.57%	56.11%	2.46%	5.02
1	1.00%	85.60%	85.00%	0.60%	0.04
2	1.00%	77.28%	77.45%	0.17%	0.08
3	1.00%	67.25%	66.63%	0.62%	0.64
4	1.00%	62.50%	58.50%	4.00%	6.87
1	1.50%	83.35%	83.41%	0.06%	0.00
2	1.50%	71.35%	75.41%	4.06%	1.67
3	1.50%	61.38%	64.22%	2.84%	3.36
4	1.50%	55.73%	54.73%	1.00%	2.22

TABLE 6.21 Cap Volatility Errors Using Piecewise Linear Functions

		Black volatility error		
Term (years)	Strike	Original	Linear	Difference
1	0.47%	0.24%	1.63%	1.39%
2	0.69%	1.36%	2.93%	1.57%
3	0.98%	0.72%	0.83%	0.11%
4	1.29%	2.46%	2.55%	0.09%
1	1.00%	0.60%	0.76%	0.16%
2	1.00%	0.17%	0.48%	0.31%
3	1.00%	0.62%	0.72%	0.10%
4	1.00%	4.00%	4.58%	0.58%
1	1.50%	0.06%	2.94%	2.88%
2	1.50%	4.06%	4.14%	0.08%
3	1.50%	2.84%	3.02%	0.18%
4	1.50%	1.00%	0.80%	−0.20%

TABLE 6.22 Swaption Volatility Errors Using Piecewise Linear Functions

| | | | Black volatility error | | |
Expiry (years)	Tenor (years)	Strike	Original	Linear	Difference
0.25	1	0.5167%	0.28%	0.76%	0.48%
0.25	2	0.7718%	1.37%	4.34%	2.97%
0.25	3	1.0777%	0.56%	2.33%	1.77%
0.5	1	0.6123%	0.11%	2.14%	2.03%
0.5	2	0.9005%	1.65%	0.19%	−1.46%
0.5	3	1.2194%	0.55%	2.94%	2.39%
0.75	1	0.7325%	0.97%	1.59%	0.62%
0.75	2	1.0433%	1.03%	0.42%	−0.61%
0.75	3	1.3687%	0.71%	0.64%	−0.07%
1	1	0.8732%	2.50%	1.57%	−0.93%
1	2	1.1989%	0.12%	0.61%	0.49%
1	3	1.5241%	0.32%	0.31%	−0.01%
2	1	1.5290%	2.07%	2.94%	0.87%
2	2	1.8573%	1.81%	2.35%	0.54%
3	1	2.1924%	1.34%	2.46%	1.12%

functions for the h_i's. We also include the Black volatility errors from the previous calibration for comparison. We can see that, although most of the swaptions have larger calibration errors, these errors are still acceptable. Interestingly, there is some improvement in the pricing error of the caps. Also, Figure 6.3 shows that the h_i pattern, which is much smoother than before, shows a clear decreasing trend. This example demonstrates that using simple functional forms to model the h_i's can greatly reduce the number of effective parameters (from $6 + 14 = 20$ to $6 + 4 = 10$) while recovering the volatilities at a satisfactory level.

Actually, the way in which we model the h_i's depends on the data. If time homogeneity is not seriously violated, then calibrating a, b, c, d, β_1, and β_2 alone should be sufficient. For more information, please refer to Jäckel and Rebonato (2003) and Vollrath and Wendland (2009). In these papers, satisfactory calibration results are obtained with the time-homogeneous instantaneous volatility function (i.e., all h_i's are equal to 1).

Finally, the reason that we use caps instead of caplets in the calibrations is that we can obtain quotes for the former directly and easily. To calibrate the cap volatilities, we must first sum up the model prices of the caplets and then compute the implied cap volatility from the model cap price at each iteration, a very slow process when the term length is long. For example, a 10-year cap comprises 39 individual caplets. Newton's method takes three to four iterations, on average, to calculate the model implied cap volatility, and thus the total effort required to find such volatility is almost the same as that required to calculate the prices of $39 \times 4 \times 2 = 312$ caplets ($\times 2$ because we have to calculate both the prices and vegas of the caplets in Newton's method). This process is greatly different from using 39 caplet volatilities as direct inputs, which requires us to compute 39 caplet volatilities alone. Using caplets instead of caps as the input can speed up the calibration significantly.

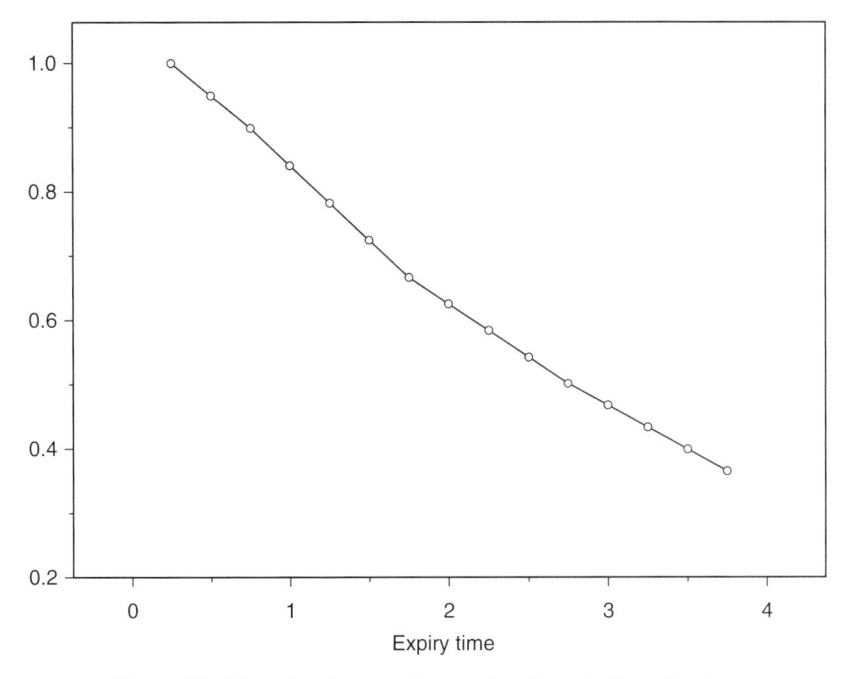

Figure 6.3 h_i's against time over 4 years using piecewise linear functions.

6.3 SIMULATION ACROSS DIFFERENT FORWARD MEASURES

Recall Equation 6.10:

$$d \log f_i(t) = \left(\mu_i(t) - \frac{1}{2}\sigma_i(t)^2\right) dt + \sigma_i(t) \sum_{k=1}^{m} b_{ik}(t) \, dW_k^q(t),$$

where $i = 1, \ldots, n$, and n is the number of forward rates, W^q is the m-dimensional standard Brownian motion under $\mathbb{Q}^{q+1}$, and $\mu_i(t)$ is the drift used to rescale the $\mathbb{Q}^{q+1}$ Brownian motion to $\mathbb{Q}^{i+1}$. To identify μ_i for each forward rate f_i under each forward measure $\mathbb{Q}^{q+1}$, we define forward measure $\mathbb{Q}^{q+1}$, such that $f_q(t)$ is a martingale, and, for every price process $\pi(t)$, $\frac{\pi(t)}{P(t,t_{q+1})}$ is also a martingale. It can be shown that under forward measure $\mathbb{Q}^{q+1}$,

$$\mu_i(t) = \begin{cases} 0, & \text{if } i = q, \\ \sigma_i(t) \sum_{j=q+1}^{i} \dfrac{\rho_{ij}(t)\sigma_j(t) f_j(t)\tau_j}{1 + f_j(t)\tau_j}, & \text{if } i > q, \\ -\sigma_i(t) \sum_{j=i+1}^{q} \dfrac{\rho_{ij}(t)\sigma_j(t) f_j(t)\tau_j}{1 + f_j(t)\tau_j}, & \text{if } i < q, \end{cases}$$

which provides a way of discretizing the dynamics (Eq. 6.6) for simulation. To simulate the forward rate path from time t_p to t_{p+1}, use

$$f_i(t_{p+1}) = f_i(t_p) \exp\left(\left(\mu_i(t_p) - \frac{1}{2}\sigma_i(t_p)^2\right)\Delta t_p + \sigma_i(t_p)\sum_{k=1}^{m} b_{ik}(t_p)\sqrt{\Delta t_p} Z_k\right), \quad (6.15)$$

where $\Delta t_p = t_{p+1} - t_p$ and the Z_k's are independent standard normal random variables.

Let

$$C_{ij}(t_p) = \sigma_i(t_p)\sigma_j(t_p)\rho_{ij}\Delta t_p,$$

$$\widehat{\mu}_i(t_p) = \begin{cases} 0, & \text{if } i = q, \\ \sum_{j=q+1}^{i} \dfrac{f_j(t_p)\tau_j}{1 + f_j(t_p)\tau_j} C_{ij}(t_p), & \text{if } i > q, \\ -\sum_{j=i+1}^{q} \dfrac{f_j(t_p)\tau_j}{1 + f_j(t_p)\tau_j} C_{ij}(t_p), & \text{if } i < q. \end{cases}$$

Then, Equation 6.15 can be rewritten as

$$f_i(t_{p+1}) = f_i(t_p)\exp\left(\left(\widehat{\mu}_i(t_p) - \frac{1}{2}C_{ii}(t_p)\right) + \sqrt{C_{ii}(t_p)}\sum_{k=1}^{m} b_{ik} Z_k\right). \quad (6.16)$$

To improve the simulation of the foregoing discretization scheme, instead of freezing the $\sigma_j(t_p)$'s at t_p, set

$$C_{ij}(t_p) = \int_{t_p}^{t_{p+1}} \sigma_i(s)\sigma_j(s)\rho_{ij}\,ds.$$

This scheme can be shown to be sufficiently accurate in most practical cases. However, if we are not satisfied with the approximation, then the simulation can be further improved by employing the Predictor–Corrector (P–C) method introduced by Hunter, Jäckel, and Joshi (2001). The P–C method is very easy to understand, and proceeds as follows.

1. Evolve the forward rate $f_i(t)$ from $f_i(t_p)$ to $f_i(t_{p+1})$ with Equation 6.16 and compute the drift term μ_i with Equation 6.16.
2. Re-compute the drifts $\widehat{\mu}_i$ with Equation 6.16, but replace the $f_i(t_p)$'s with the values of the evolved forward rates $f_i(t_{p+1})$.
3. Re-evolve the forward rates $f_i(t)$ from $f_i(t_p)$ to $f_i(t_{p+1})$ with Equation 6.16, but this time compute the drift term by the average of μ_i and $\widehat{\mu}_i$.

We have to decide which forward measure to use in the simulation, an important decision because the choice of the forward measure will determine how we discount the price process $\pi(t)$. Recall that the forward measure $\mathbb{Q}^{p+1}$ is defined such that $f_p(t)$ is a martingale and, for every price process $\pi(t)$, $\frac{\pi(t)}{P(t,t_{p+1})}$ should also be a martingale. In simulation and pricing, we use the spot measure as our forward measure at each step. In other words, at $t = t_q$, we use $\mathbb{Q}^{q+1}$ as our forward measure and, for $f_i(t)$, all drifts are calculated as in the case of $i > q$ in Equation 6.16. Under this scheme, it is easy to see that

$$\pi(t_0) = P(t_0, t_1)\mathrm{E}^{\mathbb{Q}^1}[\pi(t_1)|\mathcal{F}_{t_0}],$$

$$\pi(t_0) = P(t_0, t_1)\mathrm{E}^{\mathbb{Q}^1}[P(t_1, t_2)\mathrm{E}^{\mathbb{Q}^2}[\pi(t_2)|\mathcal{F}_{t_1}]|\mathcal{F}_{t_0}].$$

$$\vdots$$

Now, suppose that the payoff of $\pi(t)$ at t_N is denoted by $\pi(t_N)$. Then,

$$\pi(t_0) = P(t_0, t_1)\mathrm{E}^{\mathbb{Q}^1}[\cdots P(t_{N-1}, t_N)\mathrm{E}^{\mathbb{Q}^N}[\pi(t_N)|\mathcal{F}_{t_{N-1}}]\ldots|\mathcal{F}_{t_0}].$$

Note that under forward measure $\mathbb{Q}^{p+1}$, $P(t_p, t_{p+1}) = \frac{1}{1+f_p(t_p)\tau_p}$. Thus, we can compute the value of the price process at t_0 for a particular path by

$$\pi(t_0) = \pi(t_N)\prod_{p=0}^{N-1}\frac{1}{1+f_p(t_p)\tau_p}.$$

The estimated price for N realizations is then given by

$$\pi^{MC}(t_0) = \frac{1}{N}\sum_{k=1}^{N}\pi^k(t_0).$$

Now that we have presented the simulation concept, we provide its complete algorithm. For simplicity, we assume that all forward rates have the same compounding period τ. Denote the number of forward rates in the term structure by n and an arbitrary time point specified by the user by s. To simulate the forward rates with an m-factor LIBOR market model up to time t_s, which is the time at which the sth forward rate is fixed, and assuming we wish to continue the simulation until all forward rates are fixed, we set $s = n$. The algorithm proceeds as follows.

1. Set $p = 0$ and $q = 0$.
2. Generate $Z_k \sim N(0, 1)$, for $k = 1, \ldots, m$.
3. Set $i = q + 1$.
4. Compute $\mu_i(p) = \sum_{j=q+1}^{i}\frac{f_j(p)\tau}{1+f_j(p)\tau}C_{ij}(p)$, where $C_{ij}(p) = \int_{t_p}^{t_{p+1}}\sigma_i(s)\sigma_j(s)\rho_{ij}\,ds$.

5. Set $f_i(p+1) = f_i(p) \exp\left(\left(\mu_i(p) - \frac{1}{2}C_{ii}(p)\right) + \sqrt{C_{ii}(p)} \sum_{k=1}^{m} b_{ik} Z_k\right)$.
6. If $i < n_{fwd}$, then set $i = i + 1$ and go to Step 4.
7. If $p < s - 1$, then set $p = p + 1$, $q = q + 1$ and go to Step 2.

The following algorithm includes the P–C method in the simulation.

1. Set $p = 0$ and $q = 0$.
2. Generate $Z_k \sim \mathcal{N}(0, 1)$, for $k = 1, \ldots, m$.
3. Set $i = q + 1$.
4. Compute $\mu_i^1(p) = \sum_{j=q+1}^{i} \frac{f_j(p)\tau}{1+f_j(p)\tau} C_{ij}(p)$, where $C_{ij}(p) = \int_{t_p}^{t_{p+1}} \sigma_i(s)\sigma_j(s) \rho_{ij}\, ds$.
5. Set $f_i(p+1) = f_i(p) \exp\left(\left(\mu_i^1(p) - \frac{1}{2}C_{ii}(p)\right) + \sqrt{C_{ii}(p)} \sum_{k=1}^{m} b_{ik} Z_k\right)$.
6. If $i < n_{fwd}$, then set $i = i + 1$ and go to Step 4.
7. Set $i = q + 1$ (Re-evolve the forward rate in the P–C method).
8. Compute $\mu_i^2(p) = \sum_{j=q+1}^{i} \frac{f_j(p+1)\tau}{1+f_j(p+1)\tau} C_{ij}(p)$.
9. Set $\mu_i(p) = \frac{\mu_i^1(p) + \mu_i^2(p)}{2}$.
10. Set $f_i(p+1) = f_i(p) \exp\left(\left(\mu_i(p) - \frac{1}{2}C_{ii}(p)\right) + \sqrt{C_{ii}(p)} \sum_{k=1}^{m} b_{ik} Z_k\right)$.
11. If $i < n_{fwd}$, then set $i = i + 1$ and go to Step 8.
12. If $p < s - 1$, then set $p = p + 1$, $q = q + 1$ and go to Step 2.

The VBA code for generating the forward rate paths is as follows.

```
Public Function Libor_Path(n As Long, Optional SimTP As Long
                           = -1, _Optional PC_Method As
                           Boolean = True)
                           As Variant
    Dim i As Long, j As Long, l As Long
    Dim jn As Long, tp As Long
    Dim tMu() As Double, tMu2() As Double
    Dim tmpExp() As Double, tf() As Double
    Dim Zi(1 To 3) As Double
    Dim tmpValue As Double
    Dim f As Variant
    Dim fm As Long

    Call Li_Buffer
    If SimTP = -1 Then SimTP = nFwd
    ReDim f(0 To SimTP, 1 To n, 0 To nFwd) As Double
    ReDim tf(1 To nFwd) As Double
    ReDim tMu(1 To nFwd) As Double, tMu2(1 To nFwd) As Double
    ReDim tmpExp(1 To nFwd) As Double
```

```
For jn = 1 To n
  'Setting the rate at t0
  For i = 0 To nFwd
    f(0, jn, i) = f0(i)
  Next i

  'Generating the path
  fm = 0
  For tp = 0 To SimTP - 1
    Zi(1) = rGauss()
    Zi(2) = rGauss()
    Zi(3) = rGauss()

    'Copy the forward rate if the rate is fixed
    For i = 0 To fm
      f(tp + 1, jn, i) = f(tp, jn, i)
    Next i

    For i = fm + 1 To nFwd
      tMu(i) = 0
      tmpExp(i) = 0

      'the diffusion part
      For l = 1 To 3
        tmpExp(i) = tmpExp(i) + bik(i, l) * Zi(l)
      Next l
      tmpExp(i) = tmpExp(i) * Sqr(Cij(i, i, tp))

      'the drift part
      For j = fm + 1 To i
        tmpValue = f(tp, jn, j) * tau
        tMu(i) = tMu(i) + Cij(i, j, tp) * tmpValue / _
                 (1 + tmpValue)
      Next j

      tmpExp(i) = -0.5 * Cij(i, i, tp) + tmpExp(i)
      'copy to tf(i) for PC method
      tf(i) = f(tp, jn, i) * exp(tMu(i) + tmpExp(i))
      f(tp + 1, jn, i) = tf(i)
    Next i

    If PC_Method = False Then GoTo SkipPC
    'Predictor-Corrector Method
    For i = fm + 1 To nFwd
      tMu2(i) = 0
```

```
            For j = fm + 1 To i
                tmpValue = tf(j) * tau
                tMu2(i) = tMu2(i) + Cij(i, j, tp) * tmpValue /
                          (1 + tmpValue)
            Next j
            f(tp + 1, jn, i) = f(tp, jn, i) *
                               exp(0.5 * (tMu(i) + tMu2(i)) +
                               tmpExp(i))
        Next i
SkipPC:
        fm = fm + 1
    Next tp
  Next jn

  Libor_Path = f
End Function
```

With this function, we generate N forward rate paths with n forward rates until time t_s, and the generated forward rates are then stored in a three-dimensional (3D) array $f(0 \text{ to } s, 1 \text{ to } N, 0 \text{ to } n)$ for later use. After generating these paths, we move on to the pricing of interest rate derivatives. In the following, we employ caplets and swaptions as examples. Suppose that we want to price a caplet with strike price K, reset date t_r and payment date $t_{r+1} = t_r + \tau$. The payoff of this caplet is determined at t_r, and its value at t_{r+1} is

$$\pi(t_{r+1}) = \tau \max\{f_r(t_r) - K, 0\}.$$

In accordance with the previous discussion, the value of this caplet at t_0 is

$$\pi(t_0) = \pi(t_{r+1}) \prod_{p=0}^{r} \frac{1}{1 + f_p(t_p)\tau}$$

$$= \tau \max\{f_r(t_r) - K, 0\} \prod_{p=0}^{r} \frac{1}{1 + f_p(t_p)\tau}.$$

Its price is then estimated by

$$\pi^{MC}(t_0) = \frac{1}{N} \sum_{k=1}^{N} \pi^k(t_0).$$

The corresponding VBA code is as follows.

```
Public Function Caplet_Payoff(f As Variant, K As Double,
reset_time As Long)
  Dim i As Long, j As Long, n As Long
  Dim tmpPayoff As Double
  Dim Payoff() As Double
  n = UBound(f, 2)
  ReDim Payoff(1 To n) As Double

  For j = 1 To n
    tmpPayoff = tau * Max(f(reset_time, j, reset_time)
    - K, 0)
    For i = 0 To reset_time
      tmpPayoff = tmpPayoff / (1 + f(reset_time, j, i) * tau)
    Next i
    Payoff(j) = tmpPayoff
  Next j

  Caplet_Payoff = Payoff
End Function
```

The price of a European swaption can be obtained in a similar fashion, although the procedure is much more tedious. Recall that the payoff at expiry of a European payer swaption written on an IRS for period t_α to t_β with strike price K is given by

$$\pi(t_\alpha) = A_{\alpha,\beta}(t_\alpha) \max\{S_{\alpha,\beta}(t_\alpha) - K, 0\}, \quad (6.17)$$

where

$$A_{\alpha,\beta}(t) = \sum_{j=\alpha+1}^{\beta} \tau_{j-1} P(t, t_j), \quad (6.18)$$

$$S_{\alpha,\beta}(t) = \frac{P(t, t_\alpha) - P(t, t_\beta)}{A_{\alpha,\beta}(t)}. \quad (6.19)$$

To calculate the payoff, we need to compute the prices of the zero-coupon bonds at the swaption expiry date, that is, $P(t_\alpha, t_j)$, for $j = \alpha + 1, \ldots, \beta$, where

$$P(t_\alpha, t_j) = \prod_{p=\alpha}^{j-1} \frac{1}{1 + f_p(t_\alpha)\tau}.$$

They can be computed recursively through

$$P(t_\alpha, t_\alpha) = 1,$$

$$P(t_\alpha, t_j) = \frac{P(t_\alpha, t_{j-1})}{1 + f_{j-1}(t_\alpha)\tau}, \text{ for } j = \alpha + 1, \ldots, \beta.$$

After computing the prices of the zero-coupon bonds, we can compute the payoff of the swaption at expiry t_α, $\pi(t_\alpha)$, through Equations 6.17, 6.18, and 6.19. Then, we discount the payoff by

$$\pi(t_0) = \pi(t_\alpha) \prod_{p=0}^{\alpha-1} \frac{1}{1 + f_p(t_p)\tau}.$$

The price of this swaption is again estimated by

$$\pi^{MC}(t_0) = \frac{1}{N} \sum_{k=1}^{N} \pi^k(t_0).$$

As a remark, we should note that when calculating $P(t_\alpha, t_j)$, for $j = \alpha + 1, \ldots, \beta$, we are standing at t_α, and so the zero-coupon bonds are discounted by the simulated forward rates at t_α, which is different from our discounting of the payoff of the swaption, for which we employ the spot rate at every time point t_p, that is, $f_p(t_p)$. The VBA code for calculating the payoff from the simulated paths is as follows.

```
Public Function Swaption_Payoff(f As Variant, K As Double,
      _expTime As Long, matTime As Long, Optional tp_pmt
       As Long = 1)
 Dim i As Long, j As Long, ni As Long
 Dim nt As Double, n As Long
 Dim SwapVal  As Double
 Dim Payoff As Variant
 n = UBound(f, 2)
 ReDim Payoff(1 To n) As Double

 Dim Zeros_Exp() As Double
 ReDim Zeros_Exp(expTime To matTime) As Double
 Dim fDelta As Double
 fDelta = tau * tp_pmt   'delta(fixed period)

 For ni = 1 To n
   nt = 0
   Zeros_Exp(expTime) = 1
   For i = expTime + 1 To matTime
```

```
    Zeros_Exp(i) = Zeros_Exp(i - 1) / (1 + f(expTime, ni,
        i - 1) * tau)
  Next i

  For j = expTime + tp_pmt To matTime Step tp_pmt
    nt = nt + fDelta * Zeros_Exp(j)
  Next j

  SwapVal = 1 - Zeros_Exp(matTime)
  Payoff(ni) = Max(SwapVal - K * nt, 0)

  For i = 0 To expTime - 1
    Payoff(ni) = Payoff(ni) / (1 + f(expTime, ni, i) * tau)
  Next i
 Next ni

  Swaption_Payoff = Payoff
End Function
```

For further details, please refer to Ch6.4_LIBOR_Simulation.xls.

6.4 BERMUDAN SWAPTIONS IN A THREE-FACTOR MODEL

We now consider the pricing of Bermudan swaptions. A Bermudan swaption is similar to a European swaption, except that the owner is allowed to enter into the swap on a range of dates between today's date and the expiry date. Similar to European swaptions, there are Bermudan payer swaptions and Bermudan receiver swaptions. As the two are essentially identical in terms of pricing, we consider only the Bermudan payer swaption here. This swaption gives the owner the right to enter into a swap in which they receive the fixed leg and pay the floating leg.

Suppose that today is time t_0. A Bermudan swaption written on an IRS maturing at t_β gives the owner the right to enter into a payer swap at any time in $\mathcal{T}_{ex} = \{t_0, \ldots, t_{\beta-1}\}$ (time t_β is excluded because a swap that starts and ends on the same date has zero value). With the foregoing definition, at any time $t_\alpha \in \mathcal{F}_{ex}$, the holder of the contract has the right to receive

$$A_{\alpha,\beta}(t_\alpha) \max\{S_{\alpha,\beta}(t_\alpha) - K, 0\},$$

where

$$A_{\alpha,\beta}(t) = \sum_{j=\alpha+1}^{\beta} \tau_{j-1} P(t, t_j),$$

$$S_{\alpha,\beta}(t) = \frac{P(t, t_\alpha) - P(t, t_\beta)}{A_{\alpha,\beta}(t)}.$$

It is important to realize that the swap always matures at time t_β, which is actually known as a co-terminal Bermudan swaption. There is another type of Bermudan swaption, known as a fixed-maturity Bermudan swaption, in which the swap has a constant length. As they are the same in terms of pricing and modeling, we consider only the co-terminal Bermudan swaption here. Note that this Bermudan swaption has a similar feature to an American option, that is, we need to determine whether to exercise or to wait. Therefore, the pricing of a Bermudan swaption is similar to that of an American option. In the following, we use the algorithm to price the Bermudan swaption in our example. This algorithm is similar to that used in valuing American options.

To value the Bermudan swaption, at each time point, we need to decide whether to enter into the swap or continue to hold the swaption. Denote the vector of forward rates at time t by $f(t)$, the immediate payoff when entering the swap at $t_\alpha \in \mathcal{T}_{ex}$ by $V(t_\alpha, f(t_\alpha))$ and the expected payoff of holding the swaption, that is, the continuation value, by $C(t_\alpha, f(t_\alpha))$. At each entry date t_α, the value of the swaption is

$$\pi(t_\alpha) = \max\{V(t_\alpha, f(t_\alpha)), C(t_\alpha, f(t_\alpha))\}.$$

As we do not know $C(t_\alpha, f(t_\alpha))$, we need to find some weights $\lambda_{l,a}$ such that

$$C(t, f(t)) \approx \widehat{C}(t, f(t)) = \sum_{l=1}^{L} \lambda_{l,a} \phi_l(t, f(t)), \qquad (6.20)$$

for some pre-selected basis function $\phi_l(t, f(t))$. For example, if we choose basis functions of 1, $S_{\alpha,\beta}(t)$, $S_{\alpha,\beta}(t)^2$ and $S_{\alpha,\beta}(t)^3$, then Equation 6.20 becomes

$$\widehat{C}(t, f(t)) = \lambda_{1,a} + \lambda_{2,a} S_{\alpha,\beta}(t) + \lambda_{3,a} S_{\alpha,\beta}(t)^2 + \lambda_{4,a} S_{\alpha,\beta}(t)^3.$$

As the continuation value $C(t_\alpha)$ should be the discounted expectation of the swaption's value at $t_{\alpha+1}$, it can be roughly written as

$$\mathrm{E}[C(t_{\alpha_a})|\mathcal{F}_{t_\alpha}] = P(t_\alpha, t_{\alpha+1})\mathrm{E}[\pi(t_{\alpha+1})|\mathcal{F}_{t_\alpha}],$$

which corresponds to the expectation under the risk-neutral measure, as in the previous case of pricing caplets and European swaptions.

We can then estimate the $\lambda_{l,a}$'s through least squares regression using all of the in-the-money paths. The algorithm for pricing a Bermudan swaption is as follows.

Suppose that the simulated forward rates are stored in a 3D array $f(0 \text{ to } s, 1 \text{ to } n_{ph}, 0 \text{ to } n_{fwd})$, where the ith forward rate at time t_p of the k_{ph}th path is stored in $f(p, k_{ph}, i)$. First, calculate all of the swap rates, the payoffs of entering the swap and the discount factors that will be used later for every $t_\alpha \in \mathcal{T}_{ex}$ for all n_{ph} paths. Doing so may not be very computationally efficient, but it can render the programming easier and more readable.

For simplicity, we denote the price at t_q of the zero-coupon bond maturing at t_p, that is, $P(t_q, t_p)$, as $P(q, p)$. For the k_{ph}th path at time t_α, we need to calculate the prices of the zero-coupon bonds through

$$P(\alpha, \alpha) = 1,$$

$$P(\alpha, p) = \frac{P(\alpha, p-1)}{1 + f(\alpha, k_{ph}, p-1)\tau_{p-1}}, \text{ for } \alpha < p \leq \beta.$$

Note that because all of these $P(\alpha, p)$'s are calculated in the k_{ph}th path, we drop k_{ph} in the notation. For those values that will be stored and used later in least squares regression and pricing, we explicitly include k_{ph} in the notation. Then, we calculate $A_{\alpha,\beta}(t_\alpha)$ by

$$A_{\alpha,\beta}(t_\alpha) = \sum_{j=\alpha+1}^{\beta} \tau_{j-1} P(\alpha, j),$$

and the swap rate used to calculate the payoff at time t_α is given by

$$S(\alpha, k_{ph}) = \frac{1 - P(\alpha, \beta)}{A_{\alpha,\beta}(t_\alpha)}.$$

The corresponding payoff at time t_{α_a} for the k_{ph}th path is

$$V(\alpha, k_{ph}) = A_{\alpha,\beta}(t_\alpha) \max\{S(a, k_{ph}) - K, 0\}.$$

The discount factor for discounting the value of the swaption at the next entry date, $t_{\alpha+1}$, is

$$D(\alpha, k_{ph}) = \frac{1}{1 + f(\alpha, k_{ph}, \alpha)\tau}.$$

We then store $D(\alpha, k_{ph})$, $S(\alpha, k_{ph})$, and $V(\alpha, k_{ph})$ for $\alpha = 0, \ldots, \beta - 1$, $k_{ph} = 1, \ldots, n_{ph}$, so that we can price the Bermudan swaption. The algorithm is as follows.

1. Set $\pi(\beta - 1, k_{ph}) = V(\beta - 1, k_{ph})$ for $k_{ph} = 1, \ldots, n_{ph}$.
2. Set $\alpha = \beta - 2$.
3. Regress $C(S(\alpha)) = D(\alpha)\pi(\alpha + 1)$ on $S(\alpha)$ using every in-the-money path, that is, the k_{ph} corresponding to $V(\alpha, k_{ph}) > 0$, by assuming a cubic conditional function, that is, $\widehat{C}(S) = \lambda_{1,a} + \lambda_{2,a} S + \lambda_{3,a} S^2 + \lambda_{4,a} S^3$.
4. Set $\pi(\alpha, k_{ph}) = V(\alpha, k_{ph})$.
5. Set $\pi(\alpha, k_{ph}) = D(\alpha, k_{ph})\pi(\alpha + 1, k_{ph})$ if $\widehat{C}(S(\alpha, k_{ph})) > V(\alpha, k_{ph})$.
6. If $\alpha > 0$, then set $\alpha = \alpha - 1$ and go to Step 3.

252   FIXED-INCOME DERIVATIVES II: LIBOR MARKET MODELS

7. Set $\pi_0(k_{ph}) = \pi(0, k_{ph}) \prod_{p=0}^{\alpha-1} \frac{1}{1+f(p,k_{ph},p)\tau}$.

8. The price of the Bermudan swaption is given by $\pi_0 = \frac{1}{n_{ph}} \sum_{k_{ph}=1}^{n_{ph}} \pi_0(k_{ph})$.

For further details, please refer to Ch6.4_LIBOR_Bermudan_Swpation.xls.

6.5   EPILOGUE

This chapter contains a lot of information, ranging from the LIBOR market models to different swap-related derivatives. Summarizing the key ideas here would help the readers to grab the bigger picture of the whole framework.

Figure 6.4 is the flowchart of implementing the LIBOR market model. It resembles Figure 5.1. Specifically, there are three sets of observed data in the LIBOR market: swap rates, caps/floors prices, and swaption prices. Based on these market prices, our goal is to value a target interest rate derivative in a consistent manner. The target derivative price is regarded as an unknown (or an output) while observed market prices are inputs.

The left-hand column of Figure 6.4 shows that market swap rates are converted into synthetic bond prices, which are fed into the yield curve building system detailed in Chapter 5. Therefore, the forward rates, $f_i(t), i = 1, \ldots, m$, in the LIBOR market model are calculated from the yield curve.

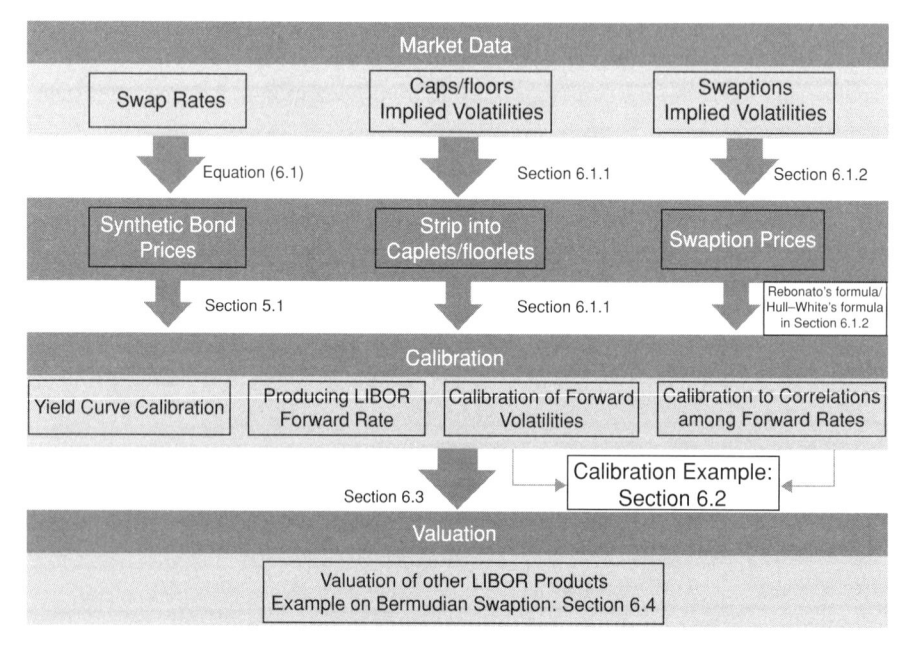

Figure 6.4   Implementation flowchart of LIBOR market models.

The LIBOR market model has coefficient functions, $\sigma(t)$ and $b(t)$, as shown in Equation 6.10. The middle column of Figure 6.4 shows how $\sigma(t)$ is calibrated to market prices of caps and floors. Theorem 2 decomposes a cap (floor) into a sum of caplets (floorlets). Stripped caplet prices are used to filter $\sigma(t)$. A practical way is to assume certain parametric form for $\sigma(t)$ with constant parameters. These constant parameters are calculated by minimizing the sum of differences between the model price of Theorem 2 and the corresponding market cap prices. Figure 6.4 points the readers to the examples in the corresponding sections.

The right-hand column of Figure 6.4 shows that swaption prices are used to calibrate the matrix-valued function $b(t)$. The swaption pricing formula and the Rebonato formula jointly serve this purpose. Section 6.3 demonstrates the entire calibration process.

Once the model is fixed, it can be applied to simulate prices of other interest rate derivatives. Section 6.3 presents the general simulation algorithm and Section 6.4 demonstrates the usage of the simulations in pricing the Bermudian swaption.

7

Credit Derivatives and Counterparty Credit Risk

Credit derivatives are over-txhe-counter (OTC) financial contracts that allow the transfer of credit risk from one market participant to another. Commonly used credit derivatives include credit default swaps (CDSs), credit linked notes, total return swaps and credit spread options, among which CDS is the dominant one. In recent years, the use of such "portfolio credit derivatives" as basket default swaps, collateralized debt obligations (CDOs) and CDOs on CDOs (CDO^2) has grown rapidly. The U.S. subprime mortgage crisis stems in large part from the huge losses suffered by mortgage-backed securities and CDOs backed by subprime mortgages.

It is therefore essential to understand the theory and valuation of credit derivatives. Monte Carlo simulation is an important numerical tool. The valuation of a credit derivative is critically dependent on the so-called default event of trading counterparties and/or reference entities. A default event is an event in which a firm (which can be a trading counterparty or a reference entity) cannot honor its obligation on the payments.

The finance literature discusses two types of default models, namely, structural models and reduced-form models. Structural models assume that the evolution of a firm's economic variables, such as total asset value, determines the time of default and, thus, provides a link between credit quality and the economic and financial conditions of the firm. Merton model (1974), the first default model and structural model, assumes that a firm defaults at the debt repayment time if its asset value falls below the notional amount of its debts. Thus, defaults are endogenously generated by the firm value process. Reduced-form models, in contrast, model a default event by the first jump time of an exogenously given jump process. Thus, defaults are exogenously given.

Handbook of Financial Risk Management: Simulations and Case Studies, First Edition. N.H. Chan and H.Y. Wong.
© 2013 John Wiley & Sons, Inc. Published 2013 by John Wiley & Sons, Inc.

Although default models help us to understand the credit derivatives of a single name reference entity, their extension to multi-name models or the valuation of such portfolio credit derivatives as CDOs is much more challenging. The main problem lies in these models' ability to describe the dependent structures of the default times of different reference entities. As defaults are rare events, the concept of copulas was introduced to model default correlations. Well-known copula approaches include the Gaussian copula and t-copula approaches. Li (2000) introduced the Gaussian copula method to price CODs. Since then, the finance literature adopting the copula approach to credit derivative pricing has grown considerably. However, the aforementioned subprime mortgage crisis offers clear proof that the Gaussian copula is incapable of correctly valuing CDOs. The usefulness of copulas remains rather controversial. Embrechts (2009) offers the view that copulas can be useful in many applications but should be handled with sufficient caution, particularly for high dimensional and extreme value problems. He also suggests a number of important readings regarding copulas. We do not take sides on the issue of whether copulas are really useful in finance, but simply demonstrate the use of Monte Carlo simulation if their application is desired. The valuation of CDO using Gaussian and t-copulas serves as examples.

Prior to introducing the application of simulation to credit risk, we begin with Merton model (1974), which models firm value and default at debt payment time. This model is then extended to incorporate the widely used Vasicek single-factor model (1987, 1991, 2002) to measure the risk of a credit portfolio and to price CDOs. Afterward, we investigate the effect of a Gaussian copula and t-copula on tail dependence, which is crucial to the modeling of default events, and then price an nth-to-default basket default swap. We thus give readers a taste of several credit risk models and their simulation.

An important application of credit risk models in the wake of the subprime mortgage crisis is in calculating the credit value adjustment (CVA) of counterparty risk in the OTC market. The bankruptcy of Lehman Brothers demonstrates the strong likelihood of counterparty default risk on the part of OTC derivative issuers. Although the underlying assets of a derivative may have no credit risk exposure, the issuer can still default, which constitutes the counterparty default risk that OTC derivative holders face. Regulations require institutional OTC investors to report the degree of counterparty risk, and the value of their OTC positions should be adjusted to reflect that risk. It is standard practice for derivative dealers to adjust the reported value of their derivative transactions with a counterparty to reflect the degree of counterparty credit risk. This adjustment is referred to as CVA.

7.1 STRUCTURAL MODELS OF CREDIT RISK

7.1.1 The Merton Model

As noted, Merton model (1974) is both the first default model and the first structural model. Merton (1974) makes use of the Black–Scholes (BS, 1973) option pricing model to value corporate liabilities.

To begin, first suppose that there are N firms and that the asset value of firm i, denoted by $A_i(t)$, for $i = 1, \ldots, N$ follows a geometric Brownian motion (GBM):

$$dA_i(t) = \mu_i A_i(t)\,dt + \sigma_i A_i(t)\,dW_i(t),$$

where σ_i is asset value volatility and $W_i(t)$ is a standard Brownian motion. Note that because the equity of a firm is considered to be a derivative on its assets, it is assumed that the firm asset value process is subject to the risk-neutral probability measure, and so the expected return of this process is the risk-free interest rate r.

Assume that the capital structure of firm i comprises equity and a zero-coupon bond with notional value D_i and maturity T, such that the asset value of this firm is simply the sum of equity and the debt value. At maturity T, if $A_i(T) < D_i$, then the firm defaults, and shareholders receive nothing (and do not pay any liabilities because of the limited liability assumption). If, in contrast, $A_i(T) \geq D_i$, then the firm does not default, and shareholders receive the residual amount $A_i(T) - D_i$. Note that it is implicitly assumed that the firm can default only at time T, not at any time prior to T. The probability that firm i defaults at time T, denoted by $p_{i,T}$, is given by

$$p_{i,T} = \mathbb{P}(A_i(T) < D_i | A_i(0)).$$

By Itô's lemma, the asset value process of firm i can be written as

$$A_i(T) = A_i(0) \exp\left(\left(\mu_i - \frac{\sigma_i^2}{2}\right)T + \sigma_i \sqrt{T} X_{i,T}\right),$$

where

$$X_{i,T} = \frac{W_i(T) - W_i(0)}{\sqrt{T}}$$

is a standard normal random variable. Therefore,

$$p_{i,T} = \Psi(k_{i,T}),$$

where $\Psi(\cdot)$ is the cumulative distribution function of a standard normal random variable and

$$k_{i,T} = -\frac{\log \frac{A_i(0)}{D_i} + \left(\mu_i - \frac{\sigma_i^2}{2}\right)T}{\sigma_i \sqrt{T}}.$$

This is the physical probability that firm i defaults at time T.

The Merton model also links the firm's asset value to its market value of equity. For the case of a single promised payment at time T, if the firm value is higher than the face value of the debt on the maturity date, then equity holders receive the residual value of the firm after paying back the debt; otherwise, they receive nothing because the firm declares bankruptcy and its ownership passes to the debt holders. Equity holders' payoff on the debt maturity date is then given by

$$\max(A(T) - K, 0),$$

which is exactly the payoff function of a European call option. Assuming risk-neutral valuation, the present value of equity is the BS formula on the firm's asset value with strike K.

The Merton model is useful for estimating the default probabilities of public firms whose shares are traded on exchange. Let $\{S(t_0), S(t_1), \ldots, S(t_n)\}$ be a time series of the observed total market value of equity prices. Under the Merton model,

$$S(t_j) = c_{BS}(A(t_j), K, r, \sigma), \qquad (7.1)$$

where c_{BS} is the BS call option pricing formula. Using this pricing formula, we can carry out the following procedure to estimate μ, σ and $\{A(t_0), A(t_1), \ldots, A(t_n)\}$.

1. Set an initial value of $\sigma = \sigma^{(0)}$ and $j = 0$.
2. Solve $A(t_i)$ from Equation 7.1 for $i = 0, 1, \ldots, n$.
3. Set $j = j + 1$, and let $\mu^{(j)}$ be the sample mean of asset returns and $\sigma^{(j)}$ be the sample volatility of asset returns.
4. Repeat Steps 2 and 3 until $|\sigma^{(j+1)} - \sigma^j| < \epsilon$ for some small value ϵ.

Duan, Gauthier, Simonato, and Zaanoun (2004) report that the foregoing estimation is a method of moments that has been implemented by Moody's KMV. In addition, the estimation result is also similar to the maximum likelihood estimation (MLE) proposed by Duan (1994).

Remark

1. The estimation procedure can be applied to any structural credit models that employ different functions to link up a firm's asset value and its market value of equities. We can simply replace Equation 7.1 with another pricing formula associated with equity holders' payoff.
2. Although Moody's KMV employs the foregoing estimation procedure, the firm makes a number of improvements to the Merton model. First, it uses the VK model, which views equity as a perpetual barrier option. Second, after estimation, the KMV approach further calibrates the asset value distribution to the empirical default distribution from a proprietary default database. To obtain these calibrated data, however, one must subscribe to the KMV system.
3. One advantage of Merton model is its simple implementation via BS option pricing theory. However, it relies on the log-normal firm value process, and other disadvantages include the restriction of the default time to debt maturity, the assumption of a constant interest rate and the exclusion of coupon-paying bonds.

7.1.2 First Passage Time Model

The structural credit risk model was first put into commercial use by Moody's KMV, whose model is in the class of first passage time models. To improve the Merton model by allowing firms to default at any time, Black and Cox (1976) incorporate a barrier option approach. When firm value falls below a default barrier, bond holders can force equity holders to declare bankruptcy. This indenture covenant for bond holders avoids further deterioration of the firm's asset value.

In the Black and Cox model, equity holders receive the residual value of the firm if the terminal asset value is higher than the face value and the asset value never falls below the barrier prior to maturity. Suppose that only one zero-coupon corporate bond is issued by the underlying firm. The payoff for equity holders becomes

$$\max(A(T) - K, 0)I_{\{\tau_H > T\}},$$

where I_A is the indicator function for the event A and τ_H is the first passage time:

$$\tau_H = \inf\{t : A(t) < H\}.$$

This is exactly the payoff function of a down-and-out call (DOC) option. When the risk-free interest rate is a constant, there is a closed-form solution to the DOC option:

$$S(t) = DOC(A(t), K, H, r, \sigma) \tag{7.2}$$

$$= A(t)\Psi(b_1) - Ke^{-r(T-t)}\Psi\left(b_1 - \sigma\sqrt{T-t}\right)$$

$$-A\left(\frac{H}{A(t)}\right)^{2\eta}\Psi(b_2) + Ke^{-r(T-t)}\left(\frac{H}{A(t)}\right)^{2\eta-2}\Psi\left(b_2 - \sigma\sqrt{T-t}\right), \tag{7.3}$$

where

$$b_1 = \frac{\log\frac{A(t)}{K} + \left(r + \frac{\sigma^2}{2}\right)(T-t)}{\sigma\sqrt{T-t}},$$

$$b_2 = \frac{\log\frac{H^2}{A(t)K} + \left(r + \frac{\sigma^2}{2}\right)(T-t)}{\sigma\sqrt{T-t}},$$

$$\eta = \frac{r}{\sigma^2} + \frac{1}{2}.$$

If the default barrier level H is specified in advance, then the other parameter values can be estimated using the approach in Section 7.1.1. Moody's KMV specifies the default barrier as the default point, which is the sum of the short-term debts and half of the long-term debts shown in a firm's accounting book. Wong and Choi (2009) discuss MLE incorporating the default barrier, and Forte and Lovreta (2012) propose endogenizing the exogenous default barrier H using the firm's historical equity data.

In first passage time models, the default probability of the ith firm becomes

$$p_{i,T} = \mathbb{P}\left(\tau_{H_i} < T\right), \qquad (7.4)$$

where H_i is the default barrier of the ith firm. If the firm's asset value follows the GBM, then that default probability has a closed-form solution.

$$p_{i,T} = \Psi\left(\frac{\log\frac{H}{A(t)} - \left(\mu - \frac{\sigma^2}{2}\right)(T-t)}{\sigma\sqrt{T-t}}\right)$$

$$+ \left(\frac{A(t)}{H}\right)^{\frac{2\mu}{\sigma^2}-1} \Psi\left(\frac{\log\frac{A(t)}{H} - \left(\mu - \frac{\sigma^2}{2}\right)(T-t)}{\sigma\sqrt{T-t}}\right). \qquad (7.5)$$

Inspired by representation (Eq. 7.4) and risk theory in actuarial science, reduced-form credit risk models directly model the default time τ_H using a survival function that is calibrated to corporate bond yields. The reduced-form model is used with copulas in Section 7.3.3.

There is controversy surrounding the practical use of structural credit risk models in the literature. Eom, Helwege, and Huang (2004) find empirical evidence that all available structural credit risk models seriously underestimate corporate bond yields when the model parameters are estimated using a proxy approach. Ericsson and Reneby (2005) show that incorrect implementation methods, such as the proxy type of estimation, significantly distort the performance of structural credit risk models. Li and Wong (2008) examine several structural models empirically using MLE, and find that the models do not consistently underestimate corporate bond yields and that their pricing errors are much fewer than those using the proxy estimation approach. Jarrow (2010), the major inventor of the reduced-form model, develops a credit market equilibrium theory to argue that structural models should not be used for pricing, hedging, or risk management. Forte and Lovreta (2012) find that, by placing the default barrier at a level that empirically optimizes equity holders' benefit, a structural model can price CDS very accurately, implying that some of these models are useful for pricing and risk management.

7.2 THE VASICEK SINGLE-FACTOR MODEL

To demonstrate the use of simulation in calculating a portfolio of credit risks, we employ the Merton model as an illustrative example. To combine marginal distributions to form a multivariate model, a simple practice in the credit market is to employ the Vasicek single-factor model (1987, 1991, 2002). Consider a portfolio of credit instruments in which the portfolio loses its value if defaults occur and some firms cannot fulfill their contractual obligations. We are interested in the portfolio loss distribution. The techniques introduced in the previous section allow us only to compute the (risk-neutral) probability of the default of an individual firm. However, the loss of a credit portfolio is generally related to the joint default distribution of several firms whose defaults are not independent. The Vasicek model uses the notion of default correlation between two firms.

Recall that the probability that firm i defaults at time T is given by $p_{i,T}$ for $i = 1, \ldots, N$. Practitioners generally prefer the risk-neutral probability of default, which can be calibrated to the market prices of default-free bonds and defaultable bonds. The calibration will be discussed in Section 7.3.3. For the time being, we assume that the risk-neutral probabilities of default for all firms are known and are the same, that is, $p_{1,T} = \cdots = p_{N,T} = p_T$.

To simulate the portfolio loss distribution, it is not sufficient to know the individual probabilities of default. We also need default correlation, which can be defined by introducing a certain kind of correlation structure on the N asset value processes. Assume that the correlation coefficient between each pair of random variables $X_{i,T}$ and $X_{j,T}$ is $\rho_{i,j,T}$. The Vasicek single-factor model specifies that the correlation coefficient between any two firms is constant, denoted by ρ_T, i.e., $\rho_{i,j,T} = \rho_T$ for all i, j. It further assumes that there is a "single" risk factor that drives all of the asset value processes. There are firm-specific risk factors that only affect individual firms. Thus, the random variable $X_{i,T}$ for $i = 1, \ldots, N$ is decomposed as follows.

$$X_{i,T} = \sqrt{\rho_T} Z_T + \sqrt{1 - \rho_T} Z_{i,T},$$

for $i = 1, \ldots, N$, where $Z_T, Z_{1,T}, \ldots, Z_{N,T}$ are independent standard normal random variables. Let $w = \sqrt{\rho_T}$. Then,

$$X_{i,T} = w Z_T + \sqrt{1 - w^2} Z_{i,T},$$

where w is the factor sensitivity. Note that we require that $0 \leq \rho_T \leq 1$.

In other words, each random variable $X_{i,T}$ determines whether or not firm i defaults at time T. It is expressed as the sum of a common risk factor Z_T affecting all firm values and a firm-specific risk factor $Z_{i,T}$ which is independent across firms.

As we are concerned with the probability of default over the same maturity period for all firms, to simplify that notation, we suppress the subscript T in all of the variables; that is, the probability of default for any firm is p, and

$$X_i = w Z + \sqrt{1 - w^2} Z_i,$$

for $i = 1, \ldots, N$, where $Z, Z_1, \ldots, Z_N$ are independent standard normal random variables.

7.2.1 Credit Portfolio Management

We implement the Vasicek single-factor model to simulate the portfolio loss distribution of a credit portfolio.

Consider again the portfolio of N loans that are credit-sensitive, where loan i is for firm i for $i = 1, \ldots, N$. For loan i, we know that the probability that any firm i will default at time T is p, and the loss due to the default of firm i is the product of the loss given default (LGD_i) and the exposure at default (EAD_i). To determine whether firm i has defaulted, we make use of the fact that the firm will default if the log-firm value is lower than some threshold chosen to match p, that is,

$$\Pr(wZ + \sqrt{1 - w^2} Z_i < k) = p.$$

In other words,

$$wZ + \sqrt{1 - w^2} Z_i \leq k = \Psi^{-1}(p).$$

The quantity w incorporates the default correlation between two firms. Consider a standard normal random variable Z. If the standard normal random variable Z_i is such that the foregoing inequality holds, then firm i defaults at maturity T and the loss for loan i is given by $LGD_i \times EAD_i$; otherwise, firm i does not default and the loss for loan i is zero. This procedure is repeated for $i = 1, \ldots, N$, and can be summarized as follows.

1. Input number of simulations (M), number of loans (N), probability of default (p), loss given default (LGD_i, for $i = 1, \ldots, N$), exposure at default (EAD_i, for $i = 1, \ldots, N$) and factor sensitivity (w).
2. Set Portfolio loss $= 0$ and Number of defaults $= 0$.
3. Generate a sequence of independent standard normal random variables $Z, Z_1, \ldots, Z_N$.
4. For $i = 1, \ldots, N$, if $wZ + \sqrt{1 - w^2} Z_i < \Psi^{-1}(p)$, then set Portfolio loss$=$ Portfolio loss $+ LGD_i \times EAD_i$, Number of defaults $=$ Number of defaults $+ 1$, and Default rate $= \frac{1}{N} \times$ Number of defaults.
5. Repeat Steps 2 to 4 M times.
6. Compute the mean and standard deviation of the portfolio loss distribution and the mean default rate.

Ch7.3_Simulate_Portfolio_Loss.xls illustrates the Vasicek one-factor model, that is, Steps 2 to 4 of the foregoing algorithm, and Ch7.3_Simulate_Portfolio_Loss_Distribution simulates the portfolio loss distribution using the following VBA code.

```
Sub Sim_Portfolio_Loss()

Dim M As Long
M = Range("A2")

Dim N As Long
N = Application.Count(Range("A21:A65536"))

Dim i As Long
```

```
Dim j As Long

Dim Default_Threshold() As Double
Dim LGD() As Double
Dim EAD() As Double
Dim w() As Double
Dim Portfolio_Loss()
Dim Z As Double
Dim Sum_Loan_Loss As Double
Dim Number_of_Default As Double
Dim Default_Rate() As Double
Dim Percentage_Loss() As Double

ReDim Default_Threshold(1 To N)
ReDim LGD(1 To N)
ReDim EAD(1 To N)
ReDim w(1 To N)
ReDim Portfolio_Loss(1 To M)
ReDim Default_Rate(1 To M)
ReDim Percentage_Loss(1 To M)

For i = 1 To N
    If Range("B" & 20 + i) > 0 Then
        Default_Threshold(i) = Application.NormSInv(Range
        ("B" & i + 20))
    ElseIf Range("B" & 20 + i) = 0 Then
        Default_Threshold(i) = Application.NormSInv
        (0.000000000000001)
    ElseIf Range("B" & 20 + i) = 1 Then
        Default_Threshold(i) = Application.NormSInv
        (0.999999999999999)
    End If
    LGD(i) = Range("C" & 20 + i)
    EAD(i) = Range("D" & 20 + i)
    w(i) = Range("E" & 20 + i)
Next i

For j = 1 To M
    Z = rGauss()

    Sum_Loan_Loss = 0
    Number_of_Default = 0
    For i = 1 To N
        If w(i) * Z + Sqr((1 - w(i) ^ 2)) * rGauss() <
        Default_Threshold(i) Then
```

```
            Sum_Loan_Loss = Sum_Loan_Loss + LGD(i) * EAD(i)
            Number_of_Default = Number_of_Default + 1
        End If
    Next i
    Portfolio_Loss(j) = Sum_Loan_Loss
    Default_Rate(j) = Number_of_Default / N
    Percentage_Loss(j) = Sum_Loan_Loss / Application.
    WorksheetFunction.Sum(EAD)
Next j

For i = 9 To 13
    Range("B" & i) = Application.WorksheetFunction.Percentile
    (Portfolio_Loss, Range("A" & i))
Next i

Range("A5")  = Application.WorksheetFunction.Average
               (Portfolio_Loss)
Range("A7")  = Application.WorksheetFunction.StDev
               (Portfolio_Loss)
Range("A15") = Application.WorksheetFunction.Average
               (Default_Rate)
Range("A17") = Application.WorksheetFunction.Average
               (Percentage_Loss)

End Sub
```

To illustrate the use of the Vasicek single-factor model in credit portfolio management, we carry out $M = 50{,}000$ simulations using a hypothetical credit portfolio comprising $N = 100$ loans with $LGD_i = 50\%$ and $EAD_i = 100$. We then compute the corresponding summary statistics for different values of default probability p and factor sensitivity w. The results are displayed in Tables 7.1 and 7.2.

Tables 7.1 and 7.2 show the portfolio loss to be positive and the standard deviation of that loss to be much greater than the expected portfolio loss. Therefore, the portfolio

TABLE 7.1 Summary Statistics of Portfolio Loss Distribution for Different Values of Probability of Default p Given Factor Sensitivity $w = 0.3$

	$p = 0.01\%$	$p = 0.1\%$	$p = 1\%$
Mean portfolio loss	0.51	5.05	49.89
SD(Portfolio loss)	5.11	17.00	67.27
90.00th percentile	0.00	0.00	150.00
95.00th percentile	0.00	50.00	200.00
99.00th percentile	0.00	50.00	300.00
99.90th percentile	50.00	150.00	450.00
99.95th percentile	50.00	150.00	550.00
Mean default rate	0.010%	0.101%	0.998%

TABLE 7.2 Summary Statistics of Portfolio Loss Distribution for Different Values of Factor Sensitivity w Given Probability of Default $p = 0.01\%$

	$w = 0.3$	$w = 0.6$	$w = 0.9$
Mean portfolio loss	0.51	0.52	0.51
SD(Portfolio loss)	5.11	6.46	23.27
90.00th percentile	0.00	0.00	0.00
95.00th percentile	0.00	0.00	0.00
99.00th percentile	0.00	0.00	0.00
99.90th percentile	50.00	100.00	100.00
99.95th percentile	50.00	100.00	200.00
Mean default rate	0.010%	0.010%	0.010%

loss distribution has a very long right tail, such that there is positive probability for a very large loss.

It can be seen from Table 7.1 that, other parameters being fixed, increasing the probability of default p increases the mean and standard deviation of portfolio loss, and the default rate because the portfolio loss is the sum of individual loan losses:

$$\text{Portfolio loss} = \sum_{i=1}^{N} LGD_i \times EAD_i \times Y_i,$$

where Y_i is the indicator function of the event that firm i defaults. The expected portfolio loss is given by

$$E[\text{Portfolio loss}] = p \sum_{i=1}^{N} LGD_i \times EAD_i,$$

and so increasing p increases the expected portfolio loss. The variance of portfolio loss is given by

$$\begin{aligned}
&\text{Var(Portfolio loss)}\\
&= \sum_{i=1}^{N} (LGD_i \times EAD_i)^2 \times \text{Var}(Y_i) + 2 \sum_{i=1}^{N} \sum_{j>i} (LGD_i \times EAD_i)\\
&\quad \times (LGD_j \times EAD_j) \text{Cov}(Y_i, Y_j)\\
&= \sum_{i=1}^{N} (LGD_i \times EAD_i)^2 \times (p - p^2)\\
&\quad + 2 \sum_{i=1}^{N} \sum_{j>i} (LGD_i \times EAD_i)(LGD_j \times EAD_j) \left[\mathbb{Q}(Y_i = 1, Y_j = 1) - p^2 \right].
\end{aligned}$$

Because $p \ll 1$, the increase in p outweighs the increase in p^2, thus causing the increase in the variance of portfolio loss. Finally, the mean default rate of the portfolio is given by

$$E^Q[\text{Default rate}] = E^Q\left[\frac{1}{N}\sum_{i=1}^{N} Y_i\right]$$
$$= p.$$

Therefore, an increase in p increases the mean default rate.

It can also be seen from Table 7.2 that, other parameters being fixed, increasing factor sensitivity w increases only the standard deviation of the portfolio loss distribution. The foregoing equations indicate that only the variance of portfolio loss is affected by $Q(Y_i = 1, Y_j = 1)$, which reflects the default correlation.

7.2.2 Pricing Collateralized Debt Obligations

A CDO consists of a portfolio of credit-sensitive instruments, typically loans and bonds, whose credit risk is sold to investors who, in return for an agreed payment, bear the portfolio loss resulting from the default of the instruments. The credit risk of the portfolio underlying the CDO is sold in tranches. A tranche is defined by a lower attachment point and an upper attachment point. The buyer of a tranche with lower attachment point L and upper attachment point U bears all portfolio loss in excess of L percent and up to U percent of the initial portfolio value. To illustrate, Table 7.3 presents a hypothetical CDO tranche structure.

Suppose that the portfolio suffers a loss of 9% of its initial value. The holder of the equity tranche bears the first 3% of the loss, the holder of the first mezzanine tranche bears the next 4%, the holder of the second mezzanine tranche bears the remaining 2%, and the holders of the third mezzanine and senior tranches suffer no loss. CDO tranches thus allow the holder of each tranche to limit their loss exposure to a fixed percentage of the initial portfolio value.

Now, suppose that the CDO originated at time 0. Denote the time variable by t, the CDO's maturity by T, the initial portfolio value by $V(0)$ and the cumulative percentage loss in the initial portfolio value up to time t by $X(t)$. Obviously, $X(t)$ is a random variable that is non-decreasing in t. At time t, the total loss of portfolio value is $X(t)V(0)$. The cumulative loss suffered by the holder of tranche j from time 0 up

TABLE 7.3 Hypothetical CDO Tranche Structure

Tranche number (j)	Tranche name	L_j (%)	U_j (%)
1	Equity	0	3
2	Mezzanine 1	3	7
3	Mezzanine 2	7	10
4	Mezzanine 3	10	15
5	Senior	15	30

to time t is a percentage $X_j(t)$ of the initial portfolio value, which can be expressed as

$$X_j(t) = \min\{X(t), U_j\} - \min\{X(t), L_j\},$$

where L_j and U_j are the lower and upper attachment points of tranche j. Like $X(t)$, $X_j(t)$ is also a random variable that is non-decreasing in t. The losses are paid by the tranche holders during the life of the CDO at fixed time points $t_1, \ldots, t_n$, such that $t_i - t_{i-1} = \delta t$ for $i = 1, \ldots, n$. At each payment date, the tranche holders pay the loss on the portfolio realized since the previous payment date, that is, if t_i is the previous payment date, then the holder of tranche j has to pay at time t_{i+1} the amount

$$(X_j(t_{i+1}) - X_j(t_i))V(0),$$

which is the floating leg of the CDO and represents the cash flows paid by the tranche holder.

At the same time, the tranche holders are compensated for bearing the risk of portfolio loss. The holder of tranche j receives a periodic payment equal to a tranche premium s_j on the outstanding notional amount of tranche j. At time t, the outstanding notional amount of tranche j is its notional amount minus any cumulative loss up to time t, which can be expressed as

$$(U_j - L_j - X_j(t))V(0).$$

Thus, at time t_{i+1}, the periodic payment to the holder of tranche j is

$$s_j(t_{i+1} - t_i)(U_j - L_j - X_j(t_i))V(0),$$

which is the fixed leg of the CDO and represents the cash flows received by the tranche holder. The lower the seniority of the tranche, the greater the expected loss suffered by its holder and, therefore, the higher the premium he or she receives. It should be noted that when $X(t) > U_j$, the loss suffered by the holder of tranche j is $U_j - L_j$ and the outstanding notional amount of tranche j is zero. In this case, all of the payments from and the premium to the holder of tranche j become zero as well.

Pricing a CDO is equivalent to computing the appropriate premium s_j for each tranche j. The premium s_j is fixed in such a way that the NPV of the cash flows received and paid by the tranche's holder is zero. With the assx1umption that the market is arbitrage-free and the term structure of interest rates is deterministic, the following relationship holds.

$$s_j \sum_{i=1}^{n} P(t_0, t_i)(t_i - t_{i-1}) \mathrm{E}[(U_j - L_j - X_j(t_i))V(0)]$$

$$= \sum_{i=1}^{n} P(t_0, t_i) \mathrm{E}[(X_j(t_{i+1}) - X_j(t_i))V(0)],$$

where $P(t_0, t_i)$ is the price at time t_0 of a unit-par zero-coupon bond with maturity t_i. Thus, the premium s_j for tranche j is given by

$$s_j = \frac{\sum_{i=1}^{n} P(t_0, t_i)(E[X_j(t_{i+1})] - E[X_j(t_i)])}{\sum_{i=1}^{n} P(t_0, t_i)(t_i - t_{i-1})(U_j - L_j - E[X_j(t_i)])}. \tag{7.6}$$

The key to CDO pricing is the evaluation of expectation $E[X_j(t_i)]$ for different time points t_i. Theoretically, the computation of this expectation requires knowledge of the distribution of $X(t_i)$ for all $i = 1, \ldots, n$; however, the closed-form formula for the distribution function of $X(t)$ is, in general, extremely difficult to obtain. In many cases, Monte Carlo simulation is the only solution.

To implement Monte Carlo simulation for CDOs, assume that the term structure of interest rates is deterministic, the probability of default is the same for all horizons (i.e., $p_{t_1} = \cdots = p_{t_n} = p$) and the default correlations are the same for all horizons (i.e., $\rho_{t_1} = \cdots = \rho_{t_n} = \rho$). We can summarize the simulation procedure as follows.

1. Input the number of simulations (M), number of loans (N), set of payment dates ($\{t_1, \ldots, t_n\}$), lower attachment points (L_j, for $i = 1, \ldots, K$), upper attachment points (U_j, for $i = 1, \ldots, K$), zero rates ($\{r_1, \ldots, r_n\}$), probability of default (p), loss given exposure (LGD_i, for $i = 1, \ldots, N$), exposure at default (EAD_i, for $i = 1, \ldots, N$) and factor sensitivity (w).
2. Set Portfolio loss $= 0$.
3. At time t_k, set $P(t_0, t_k) = e^{-r_k t_k}$ and generate a sequence of independent standard normal random variables $Z, Z_1, \ldots, Z_N$.
4. For $i = 1, \ldots, N$, if firm i does *not* default and $wZ + \sqrt{1-w^2}Z_i < \Psi^{-1}(p)$, then set Portfolio loss $=$ Portfolio loss $+ LGD_i \times EAD_i$ and record that firm i has defaulted.
5. $X(t_k) = \frac{\text{Portfolio loss}}{\sum_{i=1}^{N} EAD_i}$.
6. For $j = 1, \ldots, K$, $X_j(t_k) = \min\{X(t_k), U_j\} - \min\{X(t_k), L_j\}$.
7. Repeat Steps 3 to 6 for $k = 1, \ldots, n$.
8. Repeat Steps 2 to 7 M times to compute $E[X_j(t_k)]$ for all j and k.
9. For $j = 1, \ldots, K$, compute the premium s_j for tranche j by Equation 7.6.

The Ch7.3_Simulate_CDO_Tranches.xls file covers CDO pricing via Monte Carlo simulation using the following VBA code.

```
Sub Simulate_CDO_Tranches()

Dim M As Long
M = Range("A2")

Dim N As Long
N = Application.Count(Range("A6:A65536"))
```

```
Dim P As Long
P = Application.Count(Range("G2:G65536"))

Dim K As Integer
K = Application.Count(Range("J3:J65536"))

Dim i As Long
Dim j As Long
Dim a As Integer
Dim t As Long

Dim Default_Threshold() As Double
Dim LGD() As Double
Dim EAD() As Double
Dim w() As Double
Dim Z As Double
Dim Portfolio_Loss As Double
Dim Cum_Percentage_Loss() As Double
Dim Sum_EAD As Double
Dim Payment_Date() As Double
Dim Zero_Rate() As Double
Dim Default_Indicator() As Integer
Dim Tranche_Cum_Percentage_Loss() As Double
Dim L() As Double
Dim U() As Double
Dim Premium() As Double
Dim X As Double
Dim Y As Double
ReDim Default_Threshold(1 To N)
ReDim LGD(1 To N)
ReDim EAD(1 To N)
ReDim w(1 To N)
ReDim Cum_Percentage_Loss(1 To M, 0 To P)
ReDim Payment_Date(0 To P)
ReDim Zero_Rate(1 To P)
ReDim Default_Indicator(1 To N)
ReDim Tranche_Cum_Percentage_Loss(1 To K, 0 To P)
ReDim L(1 To K)
ReDim U(1 To K)
ReDim Premium(1 To K)

For a = 1 To K
    L(a) = Range("J" & 2 + a)
    U(a) = Range("K" & 2 + a)
Next a
```

```
' take Payment_Date(0) = 0
For t = 1 To P
    Payment_Date(t) = Range("G" & 1 + t)
    Zero_Rate(t) = Range("H" & 1 + t)
Next t

For i = 1 To N
    If Range("B" & 5 + i) > 0 Then
        Default_Threshold(i) = Application.NormSInv
        (Range("B" & 5 + i))
    ElseIf Range("B" & 5 + i) = 0 Then
        Default_Threshold(i) = Application.NormSInv
        (0.000000000000001)
    ElseIf Range("B" & 5 + i) = 1 Then
        Default_Threshold(i) = Application.NormSInv
        (0.999999999999999)
    End If
    LGD(i) = Range("C" & 5 + i)
    EAD(i) = Range("D" & 5 + i)
    w(i) = Range("E" & 5 + i)
Next i

Sum_EAD = Application.Sum(EAD)

For j = 1 To M

    Portfolio_Loss = 0
    ReDim Default_Indicator(1 To N)

    For t = 1 To P ' proceed in time

        Z = rGauss()

        For i = 1 To N
            If Default_Indicator(i) < 0.5 Then
                If w(i) * Z + Sqr(1 - w(i) ^ 2) * rGauss()
                < Default_Threshold(i) Then
                    Default_Indicator(i) = 1
                    Portfolio_Loss = Portfolio_Loss +
                    LGD(i) * EAD(i)
                End If
            End If

        Next i
```

```
            Cum_Percentage_Loss(j, t) = Portfolio_Loss / Sum_EAD

            For a = 1 To K
                Tranche_Cum_Percentage_Loss(a, t) = Tranche_Cum_
                Percentage_Loss(a, t) + 1 / M * (Application.
                WorksheetFunction.Min(Cum_Percentage_
                Loss(j, t), U(a)) - Application.
                WorksheetFunction.Min(Cum_Percentage_Loss(j, t),
                L(a)))
            Next a
      Next t
Next j

' display the payment times
For t = 0 To P
        Cells(3, 15 + t) = Payment_Date(t)
Next t

' display the tranche number
For a = 1 To K
    Cells(3 + a, 14) = a
Next a

For a = 1 To K

    X = 0
    Y = 0

    For t = 1 To P
        X = X + Exp(-Zero_Rate(t) * Payment_Date(t)) *
        (Tranche_Cum_Percentage_Loss(a, t) - Tranche_Cum_
        Percentage_Loss(a, t - 1))
        Y = Y + Exp(-Zero_Rate(t) * Payment_Date(t)) *
        (Payment_Date(t) - Payment_Date(t - 1)) * (U(a) -
        L(a) - Tranche_Cum_Percentage_Loss(a, t))

    Next t

    Premium(a) = X / Y

    ' display the premium for each tranche
    Range("L" & 2 + a) = Premium(a)

    ' display the cumulative percentage loss for each tranche
```

272 CREDIT DERIVATIVES AND COUNTERPARTY CREDIT RISK

TABLE 7.4 Premium for each Tranche for Different Values of Probability of Default p Given Factor Sensitivity $w = 0.3$

Tranche number (j)	Tranche name	L_j (%)	U_j (%)	$p = 1\%$	$p = 2\%$	$p = 3\%$
1	Equity	0	3	23.8277%	58.8388%	102.0122%
2	Mezzanine 1	3	7	1.1693%	8.0234%	19.2232%
3	Mezzanine 2	7	10	0.0213%	0.7485%	3.7903%
4	Mezzanine 3	10	15	0.0009%	0.0469%	0.4826%
5	Senior	15	30	0.0000%	0.0001%	0.0054%

TABLE 7.5 Premium for each Tranche for Different Values of Factor Sensitivity w with Probability of Default $p = 1\%$

Tranche number (j)	Tranche name	L_j (%)	U_j (%)	$w = 0.3$	$w = 0.6$	$w = 0.9$
1	Equity	0	3	23.8277%	16.2522%	5.7212%
2	Mezzanine 1	3	7	1.1693%	2.7895%	2.6397%
3	Mezzanine 2	7	10	0.0213%	0.8088%	1.7127%
4	Mezzanine 3	10	15	0.0009%	0.2638%	1.1879%
5	Senior	15	30	0.0000%	0.0273%	0.6100%

```
        For t = 0 To P
            Cells(3 + a, 15 + t) = Tranche_Cum_Percentage_Loss
                (a, t)
        Next t

Next a

End Sub
```

To demonstrate the simulation of CDO tranches, we use the hypothetical CDO in Table 7.3 with $M = 50,000$. This CDO consists of $N = 100$ loans with $LGD_i = 50\%$ and $EAD_i = 100$. Its payment dates are 1, 2, 3, and 4 years, and the initial term structure is flat at 5%. We then compute the corresponding premium of each tranche for different values of default probability p (the same applies to all loans) and factor sensitivity w. The results are displayed in Tables 7.4 and 7.5.

It can be seen from Table 7.4 that the premium of each tranche is a positive function of the probability of default p. The impact of default correlation on the tranche premium is slightly more delicate. Table 7.5 shows that a higher default correlation w decreases the premium of an equity tranche because it increases the probability that no default will occur. However, the opposite is true for the second and third mezzanine and senior tranches. The impact on the first mezzanine tranche is not monotonic.

7.3 COPULA APPROACH TO CREDIT DERIVATIVE PRICING

This section begins by introducing the basic concepts of copulas. As previously noted, two commonly used copulas are the Gaussian copula and the t-copula, and our simulation is thus based on these two copulas and shows their effects on the tail dependence between random variables. To apply copula simulation to credit risk, we deduce the valuation representation for an nth-to-default swap and describe the corresponding Monte Carlo simulation, see Abid and Naifar (2007). The numerical results are presented afterward.

7.3.1 Basic Concepts of Copulas

Every joint distribution function for a set of random variables implicitly contains information on both the marginal behavior of individual random variables and their dependence structure. The copula provides a way of isolating the latter information.

Definition 7.1 *An n-dimensional copula, denoted as $C(u_1, \ldots, u_n)$, is a distribution function on $[0, 1]^n$ with standard uniform marginal distributions that exhibits the following properties.*

1. $C(u_1, \ldots, u_n)$ is increasing in each component u_i for $i = 1, \ldots, n$.
2. $C(1, \ldots, 1, u_i, 1, \ldots, 1,) = u_i$ for $i = 1, \ldots, n$ and $0 \leq u_i \leq 1$.
3. For any $(a_1, \ldots, a_n)$, $(b_1, \ldots, b_n)$ in $[0, 1]^n$ with $a_i \leq b_i$,

$$\sum_{i_1=1}^{2} \cdots \sum_{i_n=1}^{2} (-1)^{i_1+\cdots+i_n} C(u_{1i_1}, \ldots, u_{ni_n}) \geq 0,$$

where $u_{i1} = a_i$ and $u_{i2} = b_i$ for $i = 1, \ldots, n$.

We can also write

$$C(u_1, \ldots, u_n) = \Pr(U_1 \leq u_1, \ldots, U_n \leq u_n),$$

where $U_1, \ldots, U_n$ are n uniform random variables.

The first property is clearly required for any multivariate distribution function. The second is a restatement of the uniform marginal distribution functions, and the third ensures that if $U_1, \ldots, U_n$ has a joint distribution function C, then $\Pr(a_1 \leq U_1 \leq b_1, \ldots, a_n \leq U_n \leq b_n) \geq 0$. For illustration, we present the third property for the case that $n = 2$: for any a_1, a_2, b_1, b_2 in $[0, 1]$ with $a_1 \leq a_2$ and $b_1 \leq b_2$, $C(a_2, b_2) - C(a_2, b_1) - C(a_1, b_2) + C(a_1, b_1) \geq 0$.

The importance of copulas in the study of multivariate distribution functions is illustrated by Sklar's theorem, which states that all multivariate distribution functions contain copulas and that copulas may be used in conjunction with univariate distribution functions to construct multivariate distribution functions. Futher details about copula are given in Joe (1997).

Theorem 7.1 *Sklar's Theorem Let F be a joint distribution function with marginal distribution functions $F_1, \ldots, F_n$. Then, there exists a copula $C : [0, 1]^n \to [0, 1]$*

such that, for all $x_1, \ldots, x_n$ in $[-\infty, \infty]$,

$$F(x_1, \ldots, x_n) = C(F_1(x_1), \ldots, F_n(x_n)).$$

If the marginals are continuous, then C is unique; otherwise, C is uniquely determined on $RanF_1 \times \cdots \times RanF_n$, where $RanF_i$ denotes the range of F_i. Conversely, if C is a copula and $F_1, \ldots, F_n$ are univariate distribution functions, then function F defined above is a joint distribution function with marginal distribution functions $F_1, \ldots, F_n$.

Sklar's theorem asserts that a copula essentially combines marginal distributions to form a joint distribution. For continuous distribution functions, the problem of obtaining the joint distribution is reduced to selection of the appropriate copula. Therefore, the critical question is "which copula should we use?" Although there is no definite answer thus far, once the copula is given, simulation can be performed to assist computation.

In the context of credit derivative pricing, copulas allow us to separate the dependence structure between default times into two parts: the specification of the marginal distribution functions of individual default times and the choice of an appropriate copula to describe the dependence structure between default times.

7.3.2 The Gaussian Copula and t-Copula

Although the Gaussian copula and t-copula are the most widely used copulas in the literature, they are not always the most appropriate choices. Choice of the Gaussian copula is substantiated if the individual marginal distribution functions are normal distribution functions and the dependence structure can be fully described by the covariance matrix. The simulation of the Gaussian copula is extremely easy. The t-copula is also convenient to use because it requires the generation of only one additional chi-square random variable (which is illustrated below), and it describes tail dependence better than Gaussian copula.

Let us first consider the Gaussian copula. Let $X_1, \ldots, X_n$ be n standard normal random variables with correlation matrix Σ. Then, the distribution function $C_\Sigma(u_1, \ldots, u_n)$ of the random variables $U_i \triangleq \Psi(X_i)$ for $i = 1, \ldots, n$, is a joint cumulative distribution function of u_is, where Ψ is the univariate standard normal distribution function. The Gaussian copula is written as

$$C_\Sigma^{\text{Gaussian}}(u_1, \ldots, u_n) = \Psi_\Sigma(\Psi^{-1}(u_1), \ldots, \Psi^{-1}(u_n)),$$

where Ψ^{-1} is the inverse of the univariate standard normal distribution function and Ψ_Σ is the joint normal distribution function with correlation matrix Σ. Its simulation takes place as follows.

1. Compute the Cholesky decomposition L of Σ, that is, $\Sigma = LL^T$.
2. Simulate a standard normal random vector $Z = (Z_1, \ldots, Z_n)^T$, where the Z_i's are independent standard normal random variables.

3. $X = LZ$ (such that $X \sim N(\mathbf{0}, \Sigma)$).
4. $U = (\Psi(X_1), \ldots, \Psi(X_n))$ is a random vector from the n-dimensional Gaussian copula $C_\Sigma^{\text{Gaussian}}$.

The VBA code for the Gaussian copula is as follows.

```
Public Function Gaussian_Copula(Correlation_Matrix As
Variant, N As Long) As Variant
' This function generates random numbers from Gaussian copula
' Input:
' Correlation_Matrix: the correlation matrix of the standard
normal random variables
' N: the number of Monte Carlo simulations

Dim M As Long ' the dimension of the multivariate normal
distribution
M = UBound(Correlation_Matrix, 1)

Dim X() As Double ' a vector storing the normal random
variables
ReDim X(1 To M) As Double

Dim Y() As Double ' a matrix storing the random numbers
generated from Gaussian
copula ReDim Y(1 To N, 1 To M) As Double

Dim L As Variant ' the Cholesky decomposition
L = CDecom(Correlation_Matrix)

Dim i As Long ' the running index for simulations
Dim j As Long ' the running index for the dimension of
the multivariate normal distribution

' Monte Carlo simulations
For i = 1 To N
    X = rCGauss(L)
    For j = 1 To M
        Y(i, j) = Application.WorksheetFunction.NormSDist(X(j))
    Next j
Next i

Gaussian_Copula = Y
End Function
```

```
Sub Simulate_Gaussian_Copula()

Dim Correlation_Matrix As Variant ' the correlation matrix
Correlation_Matrix = Range("A2:B3")

Dim M As Long ' the dimension of the multivariate normal
distribution
M = UBound(Correlation_Matrix, 1)

Dim N As Long ' the number of Monte Carlo simulations
N = Range("A6")

Dim Random_Numbers As Variant ' a matrix storing the
random numbers generated from Gaussian copula
Random_Numbers = Gaussian_Copula(Correlation_Matrix, N)

Dim i As Long ' the running index for simulations
Dim j As Long ' the running index for the dimension of the
multivariate normal distribution

For i = 1 To N
    For j = 1 To M
        Cells(8 + i, j) = Random_Numbers(i, j)
    Next j
Next i
End Sub
```

The function *rGauss* can be found in Chapter 1, and *CDecom* and *rCGauss* can be found in Chapter 3. For further details, please refer to Ch7.4_Simulation_of_Gaussian_Copula.xls.

We now consider the *t*-copula. In financial modeling, the main reason for the use of *t*-distribution is that it has fatter tails than the normal distribution and is thus better able to model tail events. The *t*-copula with ν degrees of freedom and correlation matrix Σ is written as

$$C^t_{\nu,\Sigma}(u_1,\ldots,u_n) = t_{\nu,\Sigma}(t_\nu^{-1}(u_1),\ldots,t_\nu^{-1}(u_n)),$$

where t_ν is the univariate standard *t*-distribution function with ν degrees of freedom, and $t_{\nu,\Sigma}$ is the joint *t*-distribution function with ν degrees of freedom and correlation matrix Σ. Its simulation proceeds as follows.

1. Compute the Cholesky decomposition L of Σ, that is, $\Sigma = LL^T$.
2. Simulate a standard normal random vector $Z = (Z_1,\ldots,Z_n)^T$, where the Z_i's are independent standard normal random variables.

3. Simulate a random variable Y (independent of Z) from the chi-square distribution with ν degrees of freedom.
4. $X = LZ\sqrt{\frac{\nu}{Y}}$.
5. $U = (t_\nu(X_1), \ldots, t_\nu(X_n))$ is a random vector from the n-dimensional t-copula $C^t_{\nu,\Sigma}$.

The VBA code for the t-copula is as follows.

```
Public Function t_Copula(Correlation_Matrix As Variant,
DOF As Long, N As Long) As Variant
' This function generates random numbers from t-copula
' Input:
' Correlation_Matrix: the correlation matrix of the standard
normal random variables
' DOF: the degrees of freedom of the t-distribution
' N: the number of Monte Carlo simulations

Dim M As Long ' the dimension of the multivariate normal
distribution
M = UBound(Correlation_Matrix, 1)

Dim L As Variant ' the Cholesky decomposition
L = CDecom(Correlation_Matrix)

Dim X() As Double ' a vector storing the normal random
variables
ReDim X(1 To M) As Double

Dim Y As Double ' a Chi-squared random variable

Dim Z() As Double ' a matrix storing the random numbers
generated from t-copula
ReDim Z(1 To N, 1 To M) As Double

Dim i As Long ' the running index for simulations
Dim j As Long ' the running index for the dimension of the
multivariate normal distribution

' Monte Carlo simulations
For i = 1 To N
    X = rCGauss(L)
    Y = Application.WorksheetFunction.ChiInv(Rnd, DOF)
    For j = 1 To M
        Z(i, j) = Application.WorksheetFunction.T_Dist
        (Sqr(DOF / Y) * X(j), DOF, True)
```

```
    Next j
Next i

t_Copula = Z
End Function
------------------------------------------------------------
Sub Simulate_t_Copula()

Dim Correlation_Matrix As Variant ' the correlation matrix
Correlation_Matrix = Range("A2:B3")

Dim M As Long ' the dimension of the multivariate normal
distribution
M = UBound(Correlation_Matrix, 1)

Dim DOF As Long ' the degrees of freedom of the t-distribution
DOF = Range("A6")

Dim N As Long ' the number of Monte Carlo simulations
N = Range("A9")

Dim Random_Numbers As Variant ' a matrix storing the random
numbers generated from ' t-copula
Random_Numbers = t_Copula(Correlation_Matrix, DOF, N)

Dim i As Long ' the running index for simulations
Dim j As Long ' the running index for the dimension of the
multivariate normal distribution

For i = 1 To N
    For j = 1 To M
        Cells(11 + i, j) = Random_Numbers(i, j)
    Next j
Next i
End Sub
```

For further details, please refer to Ch7.4_Simulation_of_t_Copula.xls.

7.3.3 Modeling Joint Default Times with Copulas

The copula approach can be applied to reduced-form models of Jarrow and Turnbull (1995) and detailed in Duffie (2001) that work directly with the calibrated default time distribution. For each loan i, for $i = 1, \ldots, N$, denote τ_i as the default time, which is a non-negative random variable. Let $F_i(t)$ be the cumulative distribution function of τ_i and $f_i(t)$ be the corresponding probability density function, that is,

$$F_i(t) = \mathbb{Q}(\tau_i \leq t),$$

$$f_i(t) = \frac{d}{dt} F_i(t).$$

The first line is the probability of loan i defaulting before time t.

Define $h_i(t)$ as the hazard rate or intensity process of τ_i, such that it is the probability that loan i will default at time $t + \Delta t$ given that it has survived up to time t. Mathematically,

$$h_i(t) = \frac{f_i(t)}{1 - F_i(t)} = \frac{1}{1 - F_i(t)} \frac{d}{dt} F(t) = \lim_{\Delta t \to 0} \frac{\mathbb{Q}(t < \tau_i \leq t + \Delta t | \tau_i > t)}{\Delta t}$$

or

$$F_i(t) = 1 - \exp\left(-\int_0^t h_i(s)\, ds\right).$$

The survival function, which is the probability that loan i will not default before time t, is defined as

$$S_i(t) = 1 - F_i(t) = \exp\left(-\int_0^t h_i(s)\, ds\right).$$

The default time τ_i is now defined as

$$\tau_i \triangleq \inf\left\{t \geq 0 : \int_0^t h_i(s)\, ds \geq \theta_i\right\},$$

where θ_i is an exponential random variable with parameter 1.

In the context of pricing credit derivatives that are sensitive to default correlation between loans, not only do we need to model the individual default time distributions, $F_i(t)$, but also consider the joint distribution of default times, τ_i:

$$F(t_1, \ldots, t_N) = \mathbb{Q}(\tau_1 \leq t_1, \ldots, \tau_N \leq t_N).$$

The joint survival time distribution is then given by

$$S(t_1, \ldots, t_n) = \mathbb{Q}(\tau_1 > t_1, \ldots, \tau_N > t_N).$$

The choice of a dependence structure between default times drives the prices of basket default swaps. Copula functions allow us to separate the problem of modeling default times into two parts: specification of the marginal distribution functions and the choice of a suitable copula to describe the dependence structure between default

7.3.4 Pricing Basket Default Swaps

The most common type of basket default swap is the first-to-default swap, in which the seller compensates the buyer for any loss of principal and the accrued interest on the first asset in the reference basket to default. In turn, the buyer pays a fixed amount of money to the seller periodically. Similarly, an nth-to-default swap provides protection against the nth default in the underlying pool of credits.

Suppose that the current time is denoted by t_0. Consider an nth-to-default swap that contains N underlying loans and pays a spread $s^{(n)}$ at dates $t_1, \ldots, t_M$. The buyer's periodic payments to the seller until the nth default are denoted by $PL^{(n)}$, the premium leg; the seller's payment to the buyer in case of the default of the underlying credit is denoted by $DL^{(n)}$, the default leg, including any accrued payment, denoted by $AP^{(n)}$. Let Δ denote the year fraction representing the period between payments, for example, $\Delta = 0.25$ for quarterly payments and $\Delta = 1$ for annual payments and so on. $P(t_0, t_j)$ denotes the non-stochastic discount factor for maturity t_j for $j = 1, \ldots, M$. Now, our problem is to determine the fair value of $s^{(n)}$, the fixed periodic payment that the buyer has to pay.

For ease of modeling, we further assume that all loans share the same recovery rate R, the risk-free interest rate r is the same for all maturities, such that $P(t_0, t_j) = e^{-rt_j}$ (alternatively, we could interpolate the zero rates between payment dates, but this would complicate the computation involved), and the correlation matrix for generating the random normal vector is such that the diagonal elements are 1 and the off-diagonal elements are ρ. Moreover, the marginal distributions of the loan default times must be known and, for simplicity, are assumed to share the same constant intensity, that is, $h_i(t) = h$ for $i = 1, \ldots, N$.

Now, the pricing of the nth-to-default swap depends on the time that the nth default occurs. The dependence structure of the default times of different loans is modeled by either a Gaussian copula or t-copula.

The premium legs are paid by the protection buyer until n names have defaulted. Define a counting process $N(t) \triangleq \sum_{j=1}^{N} 1_{\{\tau_j < t\}}$, which counts the number of defaults in the basket before t. The present value of the premium leg of the nth-to-default swap is given by

$$\mathrm{E}[PL^{(n)}] = s^{(n)} \Delta \sum_{i=1}^{M} P(t_0, t_i) \mathrm{E}\left[1_{\{N(t_i) < n\}}\right]. \tag{7.7}$$

In this expression, the expectation is difficult to compute analytically if the τ_j's have had some dependence structure imposed. Thus, it is better to compute the expectation via simulation: for each simulation run, at each time point t_i, if the number of default times that are less than t_i is less than n, then the indicator function should be increased by a magnitude of 1; otherwise, nothing is done.

COPULA APPROACH TO CREDIT DERIVATIVE PRICING   281

The present value of any accrued payment made by the protection seller is given by

$$\mathrm{E}[AP^{(n)}] = s^{(n)} \Delta \sum_{i=1}^{M} \mathrm{E}\left[\frac{\tau_n - t_{i-1}}{t_i - t_{i-1}} P(t_0, \tau_n) 1_{\{t_{i-1} < \tau_n \leq t_i\}}\right]$$

$$= s^{(n)} \sum_{i=1}^{M} \mathrm{E}\left[(\tau_n - t_{i-1}) P(t_0, \tau_n) 1_{\{t_{i-1} < \tau_n \leq t_i\}}\right]. \qquad (7.8)$$

In this expression, we compute the expectation using simulation: for each simulation run, if $\tau_n \in (t_{i-1}, t_i]$, then the present value of the accrued payment should be increased by $(\tau_n - t_{i-1}) P(t_0, \tau_n)$; otherwise, nothing is done.

For the second part of the pricing procedure, if the nth default occurs before maturity t_M, then the protection seller must pay the difference between the par value and the recovery rate of the loan in question. Thus, the present value of the default leg is given by

$$\mathrm{E}[DL^{(n)}] = (1 - R) \mathrm{E}\left[P(t_0, \tau_n) 1_{\{\tau_n \leq t_M\}}\right]. \qquad (7.9)$$

Again, in the foregoing expression, we compute the expectation using simulation: for each simulation run, if $\tau_n \leq t_M$, then the present value of the default premium should be increased by the amount $B(0, \tau_n)$; otherwise, nothing is done.

Now, similar to an interest rate swap (IRS) contract, the fair spread $s^{(n)}$ for the nth-to-default swap is computed by equating the present values of the protection buyer's payoff in Equations 7.7 and 7.8 and the protection seller's payoff in Equation 7.9. As a result,

$$s^{(n)} = \frac{(1 - R) \mathrm{E}\left[P(t_0, \tau_n) 1_{\{\tau_n \leq t_M\}}\right]}{\Delta \sum_{i=1}^{M} P(t_0, t_i) \mathrm{E}\left[1_{\{N(t_i) < n\}}\right] + \sum_{i=1}^{M} \mathrm{E}\left[(\tau_n - t_{i-1}) P(t_0, \tau_n) 1_{\{t_{i-1} < \tau_n \leq t_i\}}\right]}. \qquad (7.10)$$

The algorithm for computing the fair spread $s^{(n)}$ for the nth-to-default swap can be summarized as follows.

1. Simulate an N-dimensional vector of correlated uniform random variables $U = (U_1, \ldots, U_N)$ from a selected copula ($C_\Sigma^{\text{Gaussian}}$ or $C_{\nu, \Sigma}^{\text{t}}$).
2. Compute the default time of loan i by setting $\tau_i = -\frac{1}{h} \log U_i$ for $i = 1, \ldots, N$.
3. Sort the default times so computed and determine the nth default time, which is also denoted by τ_n for convenience.
4. Based on the realization of τ_n, compute $\mathrm{E}[PL^{(n)}]$ by Equation 7.7, $\mathrm{E}[AP^{(n)}]$ by Equation 7.8 and $\mathrm{E}[DL^{(n)}]$ by Equation 7.9.
5. Repeat Steps 1 to 4 for the required number of simulations.
6. Compute $s^{(n)}$ by Equation 7.10.

The VBA code for this algorithm is as follows.

```vba
Sub Basket_Default_Swaps_Spread()

Dim i As Long ' the running index for simulations
Dim j As Long ' the running index for loans
Dim k As Long ' the running index for payment periods
Dim m As Long ' the running index for the number to default

Dim Number_Of_Loans As Long ' the number of loans in the
basket default swap
Number_Of_Loans = Range("E1")

Dim Number_To_Default As Long ' the number to default
'(e.g. 1 for first-to-default swap)

Dim Maturity As Double ' the maturity of the swap
Maturity = Range("E2")

Dim Delta As Double ' payment period
Delta = Range("E3")

Dim Recovery_Rate As Double ' the recovery rate
Recovery_Rate = Range("E4")

Dim Risk_Free_Rate As Double ' the risk-free interest rate
Risk_Free_Rate = Range("E5")

Dim Default_Intensity As Double ' the default intensity
for all loans
Default_Intensity = Range("E6")

Dim rho As Double ' the correlation coefficient between loans
rho = Range("E7")

Dim DOF As Long ' the degrees of freedom of t-Student
distribution
DOF = Range("E8")

Dim Number_Of_MC As Long ' the number of Monte Carlo
simulations
Number_Of_MC = Range("E9")

Dim Number_Of_Payments As Long ' the number of premium
payments
Number_Of_Payments = Maturity / Delta

' construct the correlation matrix
Dim Correlation_Matrix() As Double ' the correlation matrix
for all loans
ReDim Correlation_Matrix(1 To Number_Of_Loans, 1 To Number_
Of_Loans) As Double
```

```
For i = 1 To Number_Of_Loans
    Correlation_Matrix(i, i) = 1
    For j = 1 To (i - 1)
        Correlation_Matrix(i, j) = rho
        Correlation_Matrix(j, i) = rho
    Next j
Next i

' simulate the default times using a specific copula
Dim Random_Numbers As Variant ' a matrix storing the random
numbers generated from copula
Random_Numbers = Gaussian_Copula(Correlation_Matrix,Number_
Of_MC)
'Random_Numbers = t_Student_Copula(Correlation_Matrix, DOF,
Number_Of_MC)

Dim Default_Time() As Double ' a matrix storing the simulated
default times
ReDim Default_Time(1 To Number_Of_MC, 1 To Number_Of_Loans)
As Double

For i = 1 To Number_Of_MC
    For j = 1 To Number_Of_Loans
        Default_Time(i, j) = -Application.WorksheetFunction.Log
        (Random_Numbers(i, j), Exp(1))_
/ Default_Intensity
    Next j
Next i

For m = 1 To Number_Of_Loans

    Number_To_Default = m

    ' the value of premium leg
    Dim Premium_Leg_Payment As Double ' the expected value of
    premium leg payments
    Premium_Leg_Payment = 0

    Dim Indicator_1() As Integer, Indicator_2 As Long

    For k = 1 To Number_Of_Payments

        ' reset the indicators for recursive computations
        ReDim Indicator_1(1 To Number_Of_MC) As Integer

        Indicator_2 = 0

        For i = 1 To Number_Of_MC
            For j = 1 To Number_Of_Loans
                If Default_Time(i, j) < k * Delta Then
                    Indicator_1(i) = Indicator_1(i) + 1
                End If
            Next j

            If Indicator_1(i) < Number_To_Default Then
```

```
                Indicator_2 = Indicator_2 + 1
            End If
        Next i

        Premium_Leg_Payment = Premium_Leg_Payment + Delta_
* Exp(-Risk_Free_Rate * k * Delta) * Indicator_2 / Number_
Of_MC
    Next k

    ' the value of default leg
    Dim Default_Leg_Payment As Double ' the expected value
    of default leg payment
    Default_Leg_Payment = 0

    Dim Sort_Default_Time() As Double ' a matrix storing the
    sorted default times
    ReDim Sort_Default_Time(1 To Number_Of_MC, 1 To Number_
    Of_Loans) As Double

Dim X() As Double ' a vector storing the sorted default
times for each simulation
ReDim X(1 To Number_Of_Loans) As Double

For i = 1 To Number_Of_MC
    For j = 1 To Number_Of_Loans
        X(j) = Default_Time(i, j)
    Next j

    Call Sort(X)

    For j = 1 To Number_Of_Loans
        Sort_Default_Time(i, j) = X(j)
    Next j

    If Sort_Default_Time(i, Number_To_Default) < Maturity Then
        Default_Leg_Payment = Default_Leg_Payment + (1 -
        Recovery_Rate)_* Exp(-Risk_Free_Rate * Sort_Default_
Time(i, Number_To_Default))_/ Number_Of_MC
    End If
  Next i

' the value of accrued premium leg
Dim Accrued_Premium As Double ' the expected value of accrued
premium
Accrued_Premium = 0

For i = 1 To Number_Of_MC
    For k = 1 To Number_Of_Payments
        If Sort_Default_Time(i, Number_To_Default) > (k - 1)
        * Delta Then
            If Sort_Default_Time(i, Number_To_Default)
            <= k * Delta Then
                Accrued_Premium = Accrued_Premium +
```

TABLE 7.6 Fair Spread (in Basis Points) for each n for Different Values of Correlation Coefficient ρ Under the Gaussian Copula

n/ρ	0	0.30	0.60	0.90	0.99	0.9999	0.999999
1	350.8567	274.1034	186.9972	105.7419	64.9789	51.5093	49.4531
2	53.2560	84.3659	83.5521	71.7510	57.5465	51.0162	49.4437
3	5.6398	28.4413	44.0008	54.7973	52.4440	50.6213	49.4379
4	0.2757	9.3991	23.4578	43.4146	48.9299	50.2328	49.2981
5	0	3.1089	12.3381	34.1035	45.9969	49.9097	49.2931
6	0	1.1314	6.5860	25.0512	42.4798	49.6479	49.1527
7	0	0.3559	2.5424	16.0250	37.6418	48.8222	48.9423

```
                (Sort_Default_Time(i, Number_To_Default)_
                - (k - 1) * Delta) * Exp(-Risk_Free_Rate_
                * Sort_Default_Time(i, Number_To_Default))_ /
                Number_Of_MC
            End If
        End If
    Next k
Next i

' the fair spread
Cells(11 + m, 1) = m
Cells(11 + m, 5) = 10000 * Default_Leg_Payment / (Premium_
Leg_Payment
                + Accrued_Premium)
Next m

End Sub
```

For further details, please refer to Ch7.4_Simulate_Basket_Default_Swaps.

We illustrate some of the properties of the fair spreads of nth-to-default swaps with a numerical example. The base case is a 10-named ($N = 10$) basket default swap with a maturity of 7 years ($t_M = 7$), yearly payments ($\Delta = 1$), common recovery rate $R = 0.50$, risk-free rate $r = 3\%$, common correlation coefficient $\rho = 0$, and common default intensity $h = 0.01$. Using 10,000 simulations, we simulate the fair spreads for different ρ and different h under the Gaussian copula in Tables 7.6 and 7.7 and under the t-copula with one degree of freedom in Tables 7.8 and 7.9.

TABLE 7.7 Fair Spread (in Basis Points) for each n for Different Values of Default Intensity h with $\rho = 0.3$ Under the Gaussian Copula

n/h	0.01	0.02	0.03	0.04	0.05
1	350.8567	702.1314	1071.7572	1422.1331	1785.1786
2	53.2560	178.5964	333.3063	501.5467	678.5317
3	5.6398	35.6355	90.7334	170.6078	268.5898
4	0.2757	5.6109	17.6670	46.7268	82.1321
5	0	0.4746	2.1708	7.8541	17.1064
6	0	0.0665	0.3359	0.9438	2.1938
7	0	0	0	0	0.2094

TABLE 7.8 Fair Spread (in Basis Points) for each n for Different Values of Correlation Coefficient ρ Under the t-Copula with one Degree of Freedom

n/ρ	0	0.30	0.60	0.90	0.99	0.9999	0.999999
1	188.6003	151.0042	122.8948	80.4811	57.5275	53.2589	53.0871
2	107.9782	86.6332	80.1569	66.8475	53.0200	52.7921	53.0820
3	54.1441	48.7538	56.0535	57.0880	51.0691	52.6192	53.0784
4	21.6382	29.0083	39.2721	48.6607	49.2208	52.3853	53.0074
5	7.0076	16.3588	27.9897	42.5694	47.0928	52.2848	53.0044
6	1.1642	7.7185	17.0519	35.6854	44.2579	52.0407	53.0012
7	0.2139	1.9818	8.6611	27.1026	40.5154	51.6451	52.9283

TABLE 7.9 Fair Spread (in Basis Points) for each n for Different Values of Default Intensity h Under the t-Copula with one Degree of Freedom

n/h	0.01	0.02	0.03	0.04	0.05
1	188.6003	405.7657	627.7755	894.8479	1167.3732
2	107.9782	216.9198	331.5728	482.4541	637.3077
3	54.1441	112.0211	165.7400	243.4331	322.9564
4	21.6382	50.6389	70.7762	101.9951	137.8195
5	7.0076	17.7783	23.3736	32.5411	45.3576
6	1.1642	2.9417	5.5829	7.0411	8.3710
7	0.2139	0.5858	0.6374	1.0236	1.5769

We can see from Tables 7.6 and 7.7 that (1) for each ρ, $s^{(n)}$ decreases with n; (2) for $n = 1$, $s^{(n)}$ decreases with ρ, for $n = 2, 3$, $s^{(n)}$ first increases and then decreases, and for $n \geq 4$, $s^{(n)}$ increases with ρ; and (3) as $\rho \to 1$, $s^{(n)} \to s$ for all n. The first is obviously true. The second is more delicate. Because ρ represents the default correlation, a higher ρ decreases $s^{(1)}$ because it increases the probability that no default will occur. However, the opposite is true for $s^{(4)}$ to $s^{(7)}$. The impact is not monotonic for $s^{(2)}$ and $s^{(3)}$. The third property is quite reasonable because the limit $\rho \to 1$ means that all of the loans default at the same time, and thus there is no difference between a 1st-to-default swap and an Nth-to-default swap.

Tables 7.8 and 7.9 show that $s^{(n)}$ is an increasing function of h for all n, which is quite reasonable because the protection buyer should pay more to compensate the protection seller for the strong likelihood of default.

7.4 COUNTERPARTY CREDIT RISK

Counterparty credit risk is the risk that the counterparty to a financial contract will default prior to the expiration of the contract and fail to make all of the payments required by the contract (Zhu and Pykhtin, 2007). Only contracts privately negotiated between counterparties (i.e., OTC derivatives and security financing transactions) are subject to such risk. Exchange-traded derivatives are not affected by such risk, because the exchange guarantees the cash flows promised by the derivative to the counterparties.

It has been standard practice for derivative dealers to adjust the reported value of their derivative transactions with a counterparty to reflect the counterparty credit risk. This adjustment is referred to as CVA. The adjusted value of the derivative is the no-default value (i.e., the theoretical price) less the CVA.

A derivatives dealer has one CVA for each counterparty. These CVAs are themselves derivatives and must be managed similarly to other derivatives. They are more complex and more difficult to value than any of the derivative transactions between the dealer and the counterparty because the CVA for the counterparty is contingent upon the net value of the portfolio of derivatives outstanding with that counterparty.

Market variables that affect the no-default value of a dealer's outstanding transactions with a counterparty also affect the dealer's CVA for that counterparty. In addition, CVA is affected by the counterparty's term structure of credit spreads. It therefore gives rise to two types of exposures, namely, potential movements in the underlying market variables and counterparty credit spread.

Transactions between a dealer and a counterparty are typically governed by an International Swaps and Derivatives Association (ISDA) Master Agreement, which specifies that all transactions between the two parties are to be netted and considered as a single transaction in the event of early termination. The circumstances under which one party can send an early termination notice to the other and the procedures that are then used are specified in the ISDA Master Agreement.

Collateralization has become an important feature of the OTC derivative market. An ISDA Master Agreement typically has a credit support annex (CSA) that specifies the rules governing the collateral that both parties must post. In particular, it specifies a variety of items, including the threshold, independent amount, minimum transfer amount (MTA), haircuts that will apply to assets that are posted as collateral, among others. Suppose that the two parties are Party A and Party B, and Party B is required to post collateral. The threshold is the unsecured credit exposure to Party B that Party A is willing to bear. If the value of the derivative portfolio sold to Party A is less than the threshold, then no collateral is required from Party B. If the value is greater than the threshold, then the required collateral is equal to the difference between the value and the threshold. The independent amount plays the same role as the initial margin in a futures contract and can be regarded as a negative threshold. Failure to post the required collateral by Party B is a default event that, unless corrected, leads to the early termination of all outstanding transactions.

The use of CVA is emphasized by the new regulatory framework for banks known as Basel III, which was published by the Basel Committee on Banking Supervision in 2010 and requires the dealer's CVA risk arising from changes in counterparty credit spreads to be identified and included in the calculation of capital market risk. However, the dealer's CVA risk arising from changes in the underlying market variables are not included in this calculation. Therefore, to manage both types of risk, it is necessary to calculate CVA's sensitivity to credit spreads and underlying market variables.

7.4.1 Exposure in Trading Derivatives with a Counterparty

7.4.1.1 Contract-Level Exposure If a counterparty in a derivative contract defaults, then the dealer must close out his or her position with that counterparty. To determine the loss arising from a counterparty's default, it is convenient to assume that the dealer enters into a similar contract with another counterparty to maintain the same market position. Because the dealer's market position is unchanged after replacing the contract, the loss is determined by the contract's replacement cost at the time of default.

If the contract value is negative for the dealer at the time of default, then the dealer closes out the position by paying the defaulting counterparty the market value of the contract and enters into a similar contract with another counterparty and receives the market value of the contract. As a result, the dealer has a net loss of zero.

If the contract value is positive for the dealer at the time of default, then the dealer closes out the position, but receives nothing from the defaulting counterparty and enters into a similar contract with another counterparty and pays the market value of the contract. As a result, the dealer has a net loss equal to the market value of the contract.

Thus, the credit exposure of a dealer that has a single derivative contract with a counterparty is the maximum of the market value of the contract and zero. Denote the value of the derivative contract at time t by $w(t)$. The contract-level exposure is given by

$$E(t) = \max\{w(t), 0\}. \tag{7.11}$$

Because the contract value changes randomly over time as the market moves, only the current ($t = 0$) exposure is known with certainty; future ($t > 0$) exposure is uncertain. Moreover, as the derivative contract can be either an asset or a liability to the dealer, counterparty risk is bilateral between the dealer and the counterparty.

7.4.2 Counterparty-Level Exposure

In general, if there is more than one trade with a defaulting counterparty and counterparty risk is not mitigated in any way, then the maximum loss for the dealer is equal to the sum of the contract-level credit exposure, that is,

$$E(t) = \sum_i \max\{w_i(t), 0\}.$$

However, this exposure can be greatly reduced by means of netting agreements. A netting agreement is a legally binding contract between two counterparties that, in the event of default, allows the aggregation of transactions between the two, that is, transactions with a negative value can be used to offset those with a positive value, and the net positive value alone represents the credit exposure at the time of default. Thus, the total credit exposure created by all transactions in a netting agreement is reduced to the maximum of the net portfolio value and zero, that is,

$$E(t) = \max\left\{\sum_i w_i(t), 0\right\}.$$

7.4.3 Collateral Modeling for Margined Portfolios

Margin agreements are increasingly used by dealers to reduce counterparty credit risk. A margin agreement is a legally binding contract that requires one or both counterparties to post collateral when the non-collateralized exposure exceeds a certain threshold and to post additional collateral if the excess grows larger. If the excess declines, then part of the posted collateral (if there is any) is returned to bring the difference back to the threshold. To reduce the frequency of collateral exchanges, a MTA is specified, which ensures that no collateral transfer occurs unless the required transfer amount exceeds the MTA.

The following time periods are essential for margin agreements.

1. Call period: the period that defines the frequency at which collateral is monitored and called for (typically, 1 day).
2. Cure period: the time interval necessary to close out the counterparty and re-hedge the resulting market risk.
3. Margin period of risk: the time interval from the last exchange of collateral until the defaulting counterparty is closed out and the resulting market risk is re-hedged. It is usually assumed to be the sum of the call and cure periods.

The default unwind date is the time at which the dealer is able to either (a) replace the transactions it has with the counterparty or (b) unwind the hedges it has for those transactions. In practice, the cure period is the time that elapses between the counterparty ceasing to post collateral and the default unwind. It can be further decomposed into two components. The first is the period of time that elapses between the counterparty failing to post collateral (after a margin call) and the dealer declaring an early termination. This is the time during which attempts are made to resolve disputes between the dealer and the counterparty about the value of the portfolio, whether the collateral demand is valid, and so on. The second is the time that elapses between the dealer declaring an early termination and the default unwind date. It depends on market conditions and the nature and size of the portfolio. A total cure period of between 10 and 25 business days is commonly assumed.

Although margin agreements can reduce the counterparty exposure, they pose a challenge in the modeling of collateralized exposure. Here, we outline a common procedure that is used by many dealers to model the effect of a margin call and collateral requirements and show the calculation procedure for collateralized exposure.

As before, denote the value of the derivatives portfolio to the dealer at time t by $w(t)$. If no collateral is posted, then the non-collateralized exposure at time t, as given by Equation 7.11, now denoted by $E_{NC}(t)$, is

$$E_{NC}(t, w(t)) = \max\{w(t), 0\}.$$

Next, suppose that the transactions are collateralized and the amount of collateral that is required at time t is $C(t)$. If early termination occurs as soon as the counterparty fails to post the required collateral, then the collateralized exposure at time t, denoted by $E_C(t)$, is

$$E_C(t, w(t)) = \max\{E_{NC}(t) - C(t), 0\}.$$

In the case of a zero threshold, $C(t) = \max\{w(t), 0\}$. If threshold K is specified in the margin agreement, then

$$C(t, w(t)) = \max\{w(t) - K, 0\}. \tag{7.12}$$

Further, suppose that the length of the cure period is denoted by c. If there is a default unwind at time t, then the collateral available is $C(t-c)$ in Equation 7.12, and the net exposure is

$$E_C(t, w(t)) = \max\{E_{NC}(t, w(t)) - C(t-c, w(t-c)), 0\}. \tag{7.13}$$

7.4.4 Credit Value Adjustment

By definition, CVA is the difference between the default-risk-free portfolio value and the true portfolio value, which takes into account the possibility of a counterparty's default. In other words, CVA is the market value of counterparty credit risk.

Suppose that the current time is $t = 0$ and a dealer has a derivative contract with a counterparty, in which the dealer's collateralized exposure is given by Equation 7.13. If the counterparty defaults at some future time $t > 0$, then the dealer will be able to recover a constant fraction of exposure, which is denoted by R. Denote the default time of the counterparty by τ. The discounted loss to the dealer can be written as

$$L^* = \mathbf{1}_{\{\tau \leq T\}}(1-R)D(\tau)E_C(\tau, w(\tau)),$$

where T is the maturity of the longest transaction in the portfolio, $D(t)$ is the discount factor from time t to time 0, and $\mathbf{1}_{\{\cdot\}}$ is an indicator function that takes a value of one if the argument is true (and zero otherwise).

CVA is the risk-neutral expectation of the discounted loss:

$$\begin{aligned} \text{CVA} &= \mathrm{E}^{\mathbb{Q}}[L^*] \\ &= (1-R)\mathrm{E}^{\mathbb{Q}}\left[\mathbf{1}_{\{\tau \leq T\}} D(\tau) E_C(\tau, w(\tau))\right], \end{aligned} \tag{7.14}$$

where the expectation corresponds to $P^D(t) \triangleq \mathbb{Q}(0 \leq \tau \leq t)$, the unconditional risk-neutral probability of counterparty default between time 0 and time t. The risk-neutral default probability can be obtained from the term structure of CDS data. For the discount factor, it can be assumed that the risk-free interest rate is constant, that is, $D(t) = e^{-rt}$. Equation 7.14 is the foundational valuation formula for CVA.

7.4.5 Independence of Probability of Default and Exposure

Assume that there is no dependence between the probability of default and the dealer's exposure. Denote $V(t) = E^Q\left[D(t)E_C(t)\right]$. Then,

$$\text{CVA} = (1-R)E^Q\left[1_{\{\tau \leq T\}}E^Q\left[D(t)E_C(t,w(t))\Big|\tau = t\right]\right]$$

$$= (1-R)\int_0^T E^Q\left[D(t)E_C(t,w(t))\Big|\tau = t\right]d\mathbb{Q}(t)$$

$$= (1-R)\int_0^T E^Q\left[D(t)E_C(t,w(t))\Big|\tau = t\right]d\mathbb{Q}(t)$$

$$= (1-R)\int_0^T V(t,w(t))d\mathbb{Q}(t). \quad (7.15)$$

The variable $w(t)$ in $E_C(t,w(t))$ is the value of the derivative portfolio contract at time $t > 0$ that the dealer has with a counterparty. It can be computed using the closed-form formula in a simple model such as the BS model. $V(t,w(t))$ is the value of a derivative that pays off $E_C(t,w(t))$ at time $t > 0$. Therefore, CVA is a complex derivative that is contingent upon the portfolio value. As noted earlier, it is much more complex that any derivative traded between the dealer and the counterparty, and thus is computed via Monte Carlo simulation.

To compute CVA using Monte Carlo simulation, partition the interval $[0,T]$ using a set of times t_i for $i = 0,\ldots,n$, where $0 = t_0 < t_1 < \cdots < t_n = T$. Then,

$$\text{CVA} = (1-R)\sum_{i=1}^n V_i(\mathbb{Q}_i - \mathbb{Q}_{i-1}), \quad (7.16)$$

where $\mathbb{Q}_i$ is the unconditional risk-neutral probability of no default occurring between time 0 and time t_i, and $V_i = V(t_i^*)$, where $t_i^* = \frac{1}{2}(t_{i-1} + t_i)$. The $\mathbb{Q}_i$'s are usually calculated from the term structure credit spreads obtained from market data. If s_i is the credit spread for maturity t_i, then an estimate of the average risk-neutral hazard rate between times 0 and t_i is approximately $\frac{s_i}{1-R}$. Then,

$$\mathbb{Q}_i = \mathbb{Q}(\tau \leq t_i)$$
$$= 1 - \mathbb{Q}(\tau > t_i)$$
$$= 1 - \exp\left(-\frac{s_i t_i}{1-R}\right).$$

It follows that the unconditional risk-neutral probability of default between times t_{i-1} and t_i is

$$\mathbb{Q}(t_{i-1} < \tau \leq t_i) = \mathbb{Q}(\tau \leq t_i) - \Pr(\tau \leq t_{i-1})$$
$$= \mathbb{Q}_i - \mathbb{Q}_{i-1}$$
$$= \max\left\{\exp\left(-\frac{s_{i-1}t_{i-1}}{1-R}\right) - \exp\left(-\frac{s_i t_i}{1-R}\right), 0\right\}. \quad (7.17)$$

The maximum function is applied to ensure that the probability distribution function is non-decreasing.

To calculate the V_i's, the market variables affecting the no-default value of a dealer's derivatives with a counterparty are simulated between times 0 and T in a risk-neutral world. One approach is to arrange the simulation such that the value of the dealer's portfolio with the counterparty is calculated at times $t_i^* - c$ and t_i^* for $i = 1, \ldots, n$, which means that on each simulation trial at each time $t_i^* - c$, the collateral is determined by Equation 7.12. Then, at time t_i^*, the value of the dealer's portfolio with the counterparty is determined, and the dealer's net exposure to that counterparty is calculated using Equation 7.13. V_i is estimated as the present value of the average of the calculated net exposures at time t_i^* for $i = 1, \ldots, n$.

Moreover, CVA's sensitivity to a small change, Δs in all of the s_i's (a parallel shift in the term structure of credit spreads) can be obtained through delta–gamma approximation, and is given by

$$\Delta(\text{CVA}) = \sum_{i=1}^{n}\left[t_i \exp\left(-\frac{s_i t_i}{1-R}\right) - t_{i-1}\exp\left(-\frac{s_{i-1}t_{i-1}}{1-R}\right)\right]V_i \Delta s$$
$$+ \frac{1}{2(1-R)}\sum_{i=1}^{n}\left[t_{i-1}^2 \exp\left(-\frac{s_{i-1}t_{i-1}}{1-R}\right) - t_i^2 \exp\left(-\frac{s_i t_i}{1-R}\right)\right]V_i(\Delta s)^2.$$
(7.18)

This equation enables CVA's dependence on counterparty credit spreads to be included in the bank's model for calculating market risk capital. Equations 7.16, 7.17, and 7.18 correspond to the equations used in the Basel III advanced approach to determining capital for CVA risk.

Calculation of CVA's sensitivity to a small parallel shift in the counterparty's term structure of credit spreads is straightforward. However, calculation of the first and second partial derivatives of CVA with respect to the underlying market variables is generally more time-consuming. Consider a market variable w with initial value w_0. It is necessary to calculate the effect on the sampled paths of changing w_0 to $w_0 + \varepsilon$ and $w_0 - \varepsilon$ for a small ε when all random number streams are kept the same. When the variable follows GBM, this is not too difficult because a small percentage change at time zero leads to a same small percentage change at all future times on all simulation trials. (This is true both when volatility is deterministic and when it is stochastic.) For the other variables, such as those following mean reverting processes, the impact of a change at time zero on the change at future times is liable to depend on the path followed by the market variable.

Suppose that V_i^+ and V_i^- are the values calculated for V_i when the initial value of the underlying market variable is $w_0 + \varepsilon$ and $w_0 - \varepsilon$, respectively. From Equation 7.16, it follows that

$$\frac{\partial}{\partial u}\text{CVA} = \frac{1-R}{2\varepsilon}\sum_{i}^{n} p_i(V_i^+ - V_i^-),$$

$$\frac{\partial^2}{\partial u^2}\text{CVA} = \frac{1-R}{\varepsilon^2}\sum_{i}^{n} p_i(V_i^+ + V_i^- - 2V_i).$$

TABLE 7.10 The Impact of Threshold K on a Long Forward Contract Given a Cure Period $c = 15$ days

	$K = -20$	$K = -10$	$K = 0$	$K = 10$	$K = 20$	$K = 30$
CVA	0.0152	0.0145	0.0121	0.0057	0.0020	0.0006
Delta w.r.t. credit spread	1.2023	1.1501	0.9623	0.4479	0.1552	0.0456
Gamma w.r.t. credit spread	0.7724	0.7454	0.6546	0.2455	0.0521	0.0083
Delta w.r.t. stock price	0.0179	0.0256	0.0558	0.0703	0.0285	0.0103

These equations enable the CVA risks relating to the underlying market variables to be assessed and hedged. As already noted, under Basel III, CVA exposure arising from the underlying market variables is not included in the calculation of market risk capital.

Consider the following example.

Example 7.1 *Suppose that the 0.25-year, 0.50-year, 0.75-year, and 1-year credit spreads are 1.25%, that is, $s_i = 1.25\%$ for $i = 1, 2, 3, 4$. Compute the CVA for various values of threshold K and cure period c of a long position in a forward contract on a stock, where the initial stock price is 100, the strike price is 100, the maturity is 1 year, the risk-free rate is 5%, the volatility of the stock price is 0.15 and the recovery rate is 0.4.*

The results are presented in Tables 7.10 and 7.11. Note that the gamma with respect to the stock price is not included because its convergence is not as good as that of the other quantities (CVA, deltas, and gamma with respect to the credit spread).

The VBA code for simulating the CVA of a long forward contract is as follows.

```
Sub Sim_CVA_Long_Forward_Contract()

Dim i As Long   ' a running index
Dim j As Long   ' a running index
Dim Delta_t As Double   ' a symbol for time

Dim Initial_Stock_Price As Double   ' the initial stock price
Initial_Stock_Price = Range("E1")

Dim Maturity As Double   ' the maturity of the forward contract
Maturity = Range("E2")

Dim Strike_Price As Double   ' the strike price of the forward contract
Strike_Price = Range("E3")
```

TABLE 7.11 The Impact of Cure Period c given Threshold $K = 10$

	$c = 5$	$c = 10$	$c = 15$	$c = 20$	$c = 25$	$c = 30$
CVA	0.0031	0.0045	0.0057	0.0069	0.0079	0.0086
Delta w.r.t. credit spread	0.2466	0.3593	0.4479	0.5464	0.6216	0.6832
Gamma w.r.t. credit spread	0.1407	0.2052	0.2455	0.3116	0.3541	0.3978
Delta w.r.t. stock price	0.0384	0.0558	0.0703	0.0882	0.1003	0.1125

```
Dim Risk_Free_Rate As Double ' the risk-free interest rate
Risk_Free_Rate = Range("E4")

Dim Volatility As Double ' the volatility
Volatility = Range("E5")

Dim Recovery_Rate As Double ' the recovery rate
Recovery_Rate = Range("E6")

Dim Threshold As Double ' the threshold
Threshold = Range("E7")

Dim Cure_Period As Double ' the cure period
Cure_Period = Range("E8") / 360

Dim Number_Of_MC As Long ' the number of Monte Carlo
simulations
Number_Of_MC = Range("E9")

Dim Number_Of_Credit_Spread As Long ' the number of credit spreads
Number_Of_Credit_Spread = Application.Count(Range
("A12:A65536"))

Dim Maturity_Of_Credit_Spread() As Double ' the maturities
of credit spreads
ReDim Maturity_Of_Credit_Spread(0 To Number_Of_Credit_Spread)
For i = 1 To Number_Of_Credit_Spread
    Maturity_Of_Credit_Spread(i) = Range("A" & 11 + i)
Next i

Dim Credit_Spread() As Double ' the values of credit spreads
ReDim Credit_Spread(0 To Number_Of_Credit_Spread)
For i = 1 To Number_Of_Credit_Spread
    Credit_Spread(i) = Range("C" & 11 + i)
Next i

Dim Probability_Of_Default() As Double ' the unconditional
probability of default
ReDim Probability_Of_Default(0 To Number_Of_Credit_Spread)
For i = 1 To Number_Of_Credit_Spread
    Probability_Of_Default(i) = (Exp(-Credit_Spread(i - 1)
* Maturity_Of_Credit_Spread(i - 1) _
/ (1 - Recovery_Rate)) - Exp(-Credit_Spread(i) * Maturity_
Of_Credit_Spread(i) _
/ (1 - Recovery_Rate)))
Next i

Dim Time() As Double ' a time variable of stock price paths,
                      including cure period,
                    ' that is, t_0, t_1^*-c, t_1^*, t_2^*-c,
                      t_2^*, ... , t_n^*-c,
                    ' t_n^*
                    ' where t_i^* = 1/2*(t_i-1 + t_i)
```

```
ReDim Time(0 To 2 * Number_Of_Credit_Spread)
For i = 1 To Number_Of_Credit_Spread
    Time(2 * i - 1) = 1 / 2 * (Maturity_Of_Credit_Spread
    (i - 1) + Maturity_Of_Credit_Spread(i))_ - Cure_Period
    Time(2 * i) = 1 / 2 * (Maturity_Of_Credit_Spread(i - 1)
                + Maturity_Of_Credit_Spread(i))
Next i

Dim Stock_Price_Path() As Double  ' the stock price paths
ReDim Stock_Price_Path(1 To Number_Of_MC, 0 To 2 * Number_
Of_Credit_Spread)
For i = 1 To Number_Of_MC
    Stock_Price_Path(i, 0) = Initial_Stock_Price
Next i

Dim Value_Of_Derivative() As Double  ' the value of derivative
for v(t)
ReDim Value_Of_Derivative(1 To Number_Of_MC, 0 To 2 * Number_
Of_Credit_Spread)

Dim Value_Of_Derivative_up() As Double ' the value of
derivative for v^+(t)
ReDim Value_Of_Derivative_up(1 To Number_Of_MC, 0 To 2 *
Number_Of_Credit_Spread)

Dim Value_Of_Derivative_down() As Double ' the value of
derivative for v^-(t)
ReDim Value_Of_Derivative_down(1 To Number_Of_MC, 0 To 2 *
Number_Of_Credit_Spread)

Dim Net_Exposure() As Double ' the net exposure for v(t)
ReDim Net_Exposure(1 To Number_Of_MC)

Dim Net_Exposure_up() As Double ' the net exposure for v^+(t)
ReDim Net_Exposure_up(1 To Number_Of_MC)

Dim Net_Exposure_down() As Double ' the net exposure for v^-(t)
ReDim Net_Exposure_down(1 To Number_Of_MC)

Dim v() As Double ' the value of v(t) for each time point
ReDim v(1 To Number_Of_Credit_Spread)

Dim v_up() As Double ' the value of v^+(t) for each time point
ReDim v_up(1 To Number_Of_Credit_Spread)

Dim v_down() As Double ' the value of v^-(t) for each time point
ReDim v_down(1 To Number_Of_Credit_Spread)

Dim epsilon As Double
epsilon = 0.0001

' simulate the stock price paths on t_0, t_1^*-c, t_1^*,
t_2^*-c, t_2^*, ... , ' t_n^*-c, t_n^*
```

```
For i = 1 To Number_Of_MC
    For j = 1 To 2 * Number_Of_Credit_Spread
        Delta_t = Time(j) - Time(j - 1)
        Stock_Price_Path(i, j) = Stock_Price_Path(i, j - 1)_
 * Exp((Risk_Free_Rate - 1 / 2 * Volatility ^ 2) * Delta_t_
 + Volatility * Sqr(Delta_t) * rGauss())
        Value_Of_Derivative(i, j) = Stock_Price_Path(i, j) -
        Strike_Price_
 * Exp(-Risk_Free_Rate * (Maturity - Time(j)))
        Value_Of_Derivative_up(i, j) = (1 + epsilon) * Stock_
        Price_Path(i, j) - Strike_Price_
 * Exp(-Risk_Free_Rate * (Maturity - Time(j)))
        Value_Of_Derivative_down(i, j) = (1 - epsilon)
        * Stock_Price_Path(i, j) - Strike_Price_
 * Exp(-Risk_Free_Rate * (Maturity - Time(j)))
    Next j
Next i

' compute the value of v(t), v^+(t) and v^-(t) at time t_j^*
For j = 1 To Number_Of_Credit_Spread
    For i = 1 To Number_Of_MC
        Net_Exposure(i) = Exp(-Risk_Free_Rate * Time(2 * j))_
 * Max(Max(Value_Of_Derivative(i, 2 * j) - Threshold, 0)_
 - Max(Value_Of_Derivative(i, 2 * j - 1) - Threshold, 0), 0)
        Net_Exposure_up(i) = Exp(-Risk_Free_Rate * Time(2 * j))
        * Max(_
Max(Value_Of_Derivative_up(i, 2 * j) - Threshold, 0)_
 - Max(Value_Of_Derivative_up(i, 2 * j - 1) -
 Threshold, 0), 0)
        Net_Exposure_down(i) = Exp(-Risk_Free_Rate *
        Time(2 * j)) * Max(_
Max(Value_Of_Derivative_down(i, 2 * j) - Threshold, 0)_
 - Max(Value_Of_Derivative_down(i, 2 * j - 1) -
 Threshold, 0), 0)
    Next i

    v(j) = Average(Net_Exposure)
    v_up(j) = Average(Net_Exposure_up)
    v_down(j) = Average(Net_Exposure_down)

Next j

Dim CVA As Double    ' the CVA
Dim Delta_CVA_Spread As Double   ' the delta of CVA with respect
                                   to a parallel shift in
                                 ' the term structure of credit spreads
Dim Gamma_CVA_Spread As Double   ' the gamma of CVA with respect
                                   to a parallel shift in
                                 ' the term structure of credit spreads
Dim Delta_CVA_Price As Double    ' the delta of CVA with respect
                                   to a 0.01&VERBATIMpercent; change in
                                 ' stock price
Dim Gamma_CVA_Price As Double    ' the gamma of CVA with respect
                                   to a 0.01&VERBATIMpercent; change in
                                 ' stock price
```

```
' compute the CVA and its delta and gamma with respect to
 spread and stock price
For j = 1 To Number_Of_Credit_Spread
    CVA = CVA + (1 - Recovery_Rate) * Probability_Of_
    Default(j) * v(j)
    Delta_CVA_Spread = Delta_CVA_Spread + (Maturity_Of_
    Credit_Spread(j)_
 * Exp(-Credit_Spread(j) * Maturity_Of_Credit_Spread(j) /
 (1 - Recovery_Rate))_
 - Maturity_Of_Credit_Spread(j - 1)_
 * Exp(-Credit_Spread(j - 1) * Maturity_Of_Credit_Spread
   (j - 1)
 / (1 - Recovery_Rate)))
 * v(j)
    Gamma_CVA_Spread = Delta_CVA_Spread + 1 / (2 * (1 -
    Recovery_Rate))_
 * (Maturity_Of_Credit_Spread(j - 1) ^ 2_
 * Exp(-Credit_Spread(j - 1) * Maturity_Of_Credit_Spread(j -
 1) / (1 - Recovery_Rate))_
 - Maturity_Of_Credit_Spread(j) ^ 2_
 * Exp(-Credit_Spread(j) * Maturity_Of_Credit_Spread(j) /
 (1 - Recovery_Rate))) * v(j)
    Delta_CVA_Price = Delta_CVA_Price + (1 - Recovery_Rate) /
 (2 * epsilon)_
 * Probability_Of_Default(j) * (v_up(j) - v_down(j))
    Gamma_CVA_Price = Gamma_CVA_Price + (1 - Recovery_Rate) /
 (epsilon ^ 2)_
 * Probability_Of_Default(j) * (v_up(j) + v_down(j) - 2 * v(j))
Next j

Range("F" & 12) = CVA
Range("F" & 15) = Delta_CVA_Spread
Range("F" & 18) = Gamma_CVA_Spread
Range("F" & 21) = Delta_CVA_Price
Range("F" & 24) = Gamma_CVA_Price
End Sub
```

For more details, please refer to Ch7.5_Simulate_CVA_Long_Forward_Contract.

Now, using the same set of parameters, we repeat the foregoing computation for a short position in a forward contract on a stock. The results are presented in Tables 7.12 and 7.13. For the VBA code and other details, please refer to Ch7.5_Simulate_CVA_Short_Forward_Contract.

TABLE 7.12 The Impact of Threshold K on a Short Forward Contract Given a Cure Period $c = 15$ days

	$K = -20$	$K = -10$	$K = 0$	$K = 10$	$K = 20$	$K = 30$
CVA	0.0140	0.0115	0.0052	0.0011	0.0002	0.00001
Delta w.r.t. credit spread	1.1102	0.9088	0.4089	0.0899	0.0126	0.0009
Gamma w.r.t. credit spread	0.7517	0.6298	0.2361	0.0298	0.0007	−0.0004
Delta w.r.t. stock price	−0.0035	−0.0346	−0.0582	−0.0156	−0.0031	−0.0003

TABLE 7.13 The Impact of Cure Period c on a Short Forward Contract Given Threshold $K = 10$

	$c = 5$	$c = 10$	$c = 15$	$c = 20$	$c = 25$	$c = 30$
CVA	0.0007	0.0009	0.0011	0.0014	0.0016	0.0017
Delta w.r.t. credit spread	0.0516	0.0721	0.0899	0.1091	0.1230	0.1351
Gamma w.r.t. credit spread	0.0163	0.0222	0.0298	0.0331	0.0417	0.0422
Delta w.r.t. stock price	−0.0080	−0.0120	−0.0156	−0.0187	−0.0216	−0.0247

7.4.6 Modeling Right-Way and Wrong-Way Risks

It must be emphasized that the expectation of the net exposure at time t in Equation 7.14 is conditional on the counterparty defaulting at time t. Such conditionality is material when there is significant dependence between the counterparty's probability of default and the dealer's exposure to the counterparty. This dependence is known as right-way risk or wrong-way risk.

The risk is described as wrong-way risk if the probability of default by the counterparty tends to be high (low) and the dealer's exposure to the counterparty is high (low). An example is a dealer who enters into a swap with an oil producer in which the former receives a fixed and pays a floating crude oil price, because a lower oil price simultaneously increases the oil producer's probability of default and increases the value of the swap to the dealer. Another example is that of a dealer who buys credit protection on an underlying reference entity whose credit quality is positively correlated with that of the counterparty to the trade. As the credit quality of the reference name worsens, so does that of the reference name, thereby increasing the value of the credit protection purchased by the dealer.

In contrast, the risk is considered a right-way risk if the probability of default by the counterparty tends to be high (low) and the dealer's exposure to the counterparty is low (high). One example is that of a dealer who enters into a swap with an oil producer, in which the dealer pays a fixed and receives a floating crude oil price. Another example is that of a dealer selling credit protection on a reference name whose credit quality is positively correlated with that of the counterparty.

Hence, a subjective judgment on the degree of wrong- or right-way risk in transactions with a counterparty requires good knowledge of the counterparty's business, particularly knowledge of the nature of the risks facing the business and of the transactions the counterparty has entered into with other dealers.

To model right-way/wrong-way risk, a hazard rate function, $h(t)$, which is a function of the variable or variables that may affect the dealer's exposure to the counterparty, is introduced to parameterize the probability of default by the counterparty. The hazard rate function is defined such that

$$\mathbb{Q}(t < \tau \leq t + dt | \tau > t) = h(t)\, dt.$$

It can be shown that

$$\mathbb{Q}(\tau > t) = \exp\left(-\int_0^t h(s)\, ds\right),$$

which is the probability that there will be no default between time 0 and time t. If the hazard rate function is constant, then it is simply $\exp(-ht)$. If it is determined by a stochastic variable $x(t)$, then it can be written as $h(t, x(t))$, and

$$\mathbb{Q}(\tau > t|\{x(s) : 0 \le s \le t\}) = \exp\left(-\int_0^t h(s, x(s))\,ds\right).$$

The probability of no default between time 0 and time t is the default's expected value. Hence, if the hazard rate function depends in a certain sense on a stochastic variable x that affects the dealer's exposure, then the probability of default by the counterparty can be related to x in such a way that right-way/wrong-way risk is incorporated into the CVA calculation.

Hence, the next step is to assume a relationship between the hazard rate function of the counterparty and the stochastic variable x that affects the dealer's exposure to that counterparty. A straightforward approach is to set x equal to w, the value of the dealer's exposure to the counterparty. If there is no relationship between the hazard rate function and w, then there is no right-way/wrong-way risk, whereas a positive relationship represents wrong-way risk and a negative relationship right-way risk. More specifically, the following functional form of the hazard rate function is used.

$$h(t, w(t)) = \exp(a(t) + bw(t)),$$

where $a(t)$ is a deterministic function of t, and b is a constant parameter. Equation 7.14 still applies with more technicality.

The problem of the intensity of the counterparty default time being correlated with the underlying market variable can be resolved using techniques from credit derivative pricing.

Under the risk-neutral measure, consider two filtrations, $\{\mathcal{F}_t\}_{t=0}^T$ and $\{\mathcal{G}_t\}_{t=0}^T$. Let $\mathcal{F}_t = \sigma(\{w(s) : 0 \le s \le t\})$ for any $t \in [0, T]$ be the σ-field generated by the path of the underlying market variable w up to time t in a default-free market. For example, the underlying market variable can be the price of a stock by which the value of a forward contract on the same stock is determined. It is assumed that w undergoes GBM under the risk-neutral measure. Let $\mathcal{G}_t = \sigma(\{1_{\{\tau<s\}} : 0 \le s \le t\})$ for any $t \in [0, T]$ be the σ-field generated by an event of counterparty default before time T, where τ is the default time. Now, $\mathcal{F}_t$ contains information on the default-free market, whereas $\mathcal{G}_t$ contains information on the default. A crucial assumption is that the intensity of τ is correlated with $w(t)$. Define $\mathcal{H}_t = \mathcal{F}_t \vee \mathcal{G}_t$ for any $t \in [0, T]$.

The following "filtration switching formula," which can be found in of Brigo and Mercurio (2007, p. 777), suffices for our purpose and is stated here without proof. Under general measurability conditions for the payoff and, for $t < T$, we have

$$E^\mathbb{Q}\left[1_{\{\tau>T\}}\text{Payoff}\big|\mathcal{H}_t\right] = \frac{1_{\{\tau>t\}}}{\mathbb{Q}(\tau > t|\mathcal{F}_t)} E^\mathbb{Q}\left[1_{\{\tau>T\}}\text{Payoff}\big|\mathcal{F}_t\right].$$

It must be emphasized that the intensity function of default time τ, h, need not be independent of the underlying market variable w. Indeed, intensity function h can be correlated with w. In our case, $h(t, w(t)) = \exp(a(t) + bw(t))$. Hence, the conditional probability of counterparty default after time t is given by

$$\mathbb{Q}(\tau > t | \mathcal{F}(t)) = \exp\left(-\int_0^t h(u, w(u))\, du\right).$$

It also holds that

$$\mathbb{E}^{\mathbb{Q}}\left[\exp\left(-\int_0^t h(u, w(u))\, du\right)\right] = \exp\left(-\frac{s(t)t}{1-R}\right), \tag{7.19}$$

where $s(t)$ is the credit spread with maturity t.

Consider the CVA value at time t:

$$\text{CVA}(t) = 1_{\{\tau > t\}}(1 - R)\mathbb{E}^{\mathbb{Q}}\left[1_{\{\tau \leq T\}} D(t, \tau) E_C(\tau, w(\tau)) \Big| \mathcal{H}_t\right]$$

$$= \frac{1_{\{\tau > t\}}}{\mathbb{Q}(\tau > t | \mathcal{F}_t)}(1 - R)\mathbb{E}^{\mathbb{Q}}\left[1_{\{\tau \leq T\}} D(t, \tau) E_C(\tau, w(\tau)) \Big| \mathcal{F}_t\right]$$

(using the filtration switching formula)

$$= \frac{1_{\{\tau > t\}}}{\mathbb{Q}(\tau > t | \mathcal{F}_t)}(1 - R)\mathbb{E}^{\mathbb{Q}}\left[\int_t^\infty 1_{\{s \leq T\}} D(t, s) E_C(s, w(s)) 1_{\{\tau \in (s, s+ds]\}} \Big| \mathcal{F}_t\right]$$

$$= \frac{1_{\{\tau > t\}}}{\Pr(\tau > t | \mathcal{F}_t)}(1 - R)\mathbb{E}^{\mathbb{Q}}\left[\int_t^T D(t, s) E_C(s, w(s)) 1_{\{\tau \in (s, s+ds]\}} \Big| \mathcal{F}_t\right]$$

$$= \frac{1_{\{\tau > t\}}}{\mathbb{Q}(\tau > t | \mathcal{F}_t)}(1 - R)\mathbb{E}^{\mathbb{Q}}\left[\mathbb{E}^{\mathbb{Q}}\left[\int_t^T D(t, s) E_C(s, w(s)) 1_{\{\tau \in (s, s+ds]\}} \Big| \mathcal{F}_T\right] \Big| \mathcal{F}_t\right]$$

$$= \frac{1_{\{\tau > t\}}}{\mathbb{Q}(\tau > t | \mathcal{F}_t)}(1 - R)\mathbb{E}^{\mathbb{Q}}\left[\int_t^T D(t, s) E_C(s, w(s)) \mathbb{E}^{\mathbb{Q}}\left[1_{\{\tau \in (s, s+ds]\}} \Big| \mathcal{F}_T\right] \Big| \mathcal{F}_t\right]$$

$$= \frac{1_{\{\tau > t\}}}{\mathbb{Q}(\tau > t | \mathcal{F}_t)}(1 - R)\mathbb{E}^{\mathbb{Q}}\left[\int_t^T D(t, s) E_C(s, w(s)) \mathbb{Q}(\tau \in (s, s+ds] | \mathcal{F}_T) \Big| \mathcal{F}_t\right]$$

$$= \frac{1_{\{\tau > t\}}}{\mathbb{Q}(\tau > t | \mathcal{F}_t)}(1 - R)\mathbb{E}^{\mathbb{Q}}\left[\int_t^T D(t, s) E_C(s, w(s)) \frac{d}{ds}\mathbb{Q}(\tau \leq s | \mathcal{F}_T) \Big| \mathcal{F}_t\right]$$

$$= \frac{1_{\{\tau > t\}}}{\exp\left(-\int_0^t h(u, w(u))du\right)}$$

$$\times (1 - R)\mathbb{E}^{\mathbb{Q}}\left[\int_t^T D(t, s) E_C(s, w(s)) \exp\left(-\int_0^s h(u, w(u))du\right) h(s, w(s))\, ds \Big| \mathcal{F}_t\right]$$

$$= 1_{\{\tau > t\}}(1 - R)\mathbb{E}^{\mathbb{Q}}$$

$$\times \left[\int_t^T D(t, s) E_C(s, w(s)) \exp\left(-\int_t^s h(u, w(u))du\right) h(s, w(s))\, ds \Big| \mathcal{F}_t\right].$$

Similar computations can be found in Brigo and Mercurio (2007, p. 791). Taking $t = 0$ yields

$$\text{CVA} = (1-R)\text{E}^Q \left[\int_0^T D(0,s) E_C(s, w(s)) \exp\left(-\int_0^s h(u, w(u)) du\right) h(s, w(s)) ds \right]. \tag{7.20}$$

The discrete-time version of Equation 7.19 is

$$\text{E}^Q\left[\exp\left(-\sum_{j=1}^k h(t_j^*, w(t_j^*)) \Delta t_j\right) \right] = \exp\left(-\frac{s_k t_k}{1-R}\right), \tag{7.21}$$

where s_k is the credit spread of maturity t_k. For Equation 7.20, it is

$$\text{CVA} = (1-R)\text{E}^Q$$
$$\times \left[\sum_{k=1}^n D(0, t_k^*) E_C(t_k^*, w(t_k^*)) \exp\left(-\sum_{j=1}^k h(t_j^*, w(t_j^*)) \Delta t_j\right) h(t_k^*, w(t_k^*)) \Delta t_k \right], \tag{7.22}$$

where $0 = t_0 < t_1 < \cdots < t_n = T$, $t_k^* = \frac{1}{2}(t_{k-1} + t_k)$ and $\Delta t_k = t_k^* - t_{k-1}^*$.

To perform Monte Carlo simulation, let $w_{i,k}$, $E_{Ci,k}$, and $h_{i,k}$ be the simulated values of $w(t)$, $E_C(t, w(t))$, and $h(t, w(t))$, respectively, in the ith simulation trial at time t_k^*, and let a_k be the value of $a(t)$ at time t_k^*. Given the simulated paths $\{w_{i,k}, k = 0, \ldots, n\}_{i=1,\ldots,m}$, Equation 7.21 is replaced by

$$\frac{1}{m} \sum_{i=1}^m \exp\left(-\sum_{j=1}^k \exp(a_j + bw_{i,j}) \Delta t_j\right) = \exp\left(-\frac{s_k t_k}{1-R}\right),$$

for $k = 1, \ldots, n$, and Equation 7.22 is replaced by

$$\text{CVA} = \frac{1-R}{m} \sum_{k=1}^n D(0, t_k^*) \left(\sum_{i=1}^m E_{Ci,k} \exp\left(-\sum_{j=1}^k h_{i,j} \Delta t_j\right) h_{i,k} \Delta t_k \right).$$

8

Value-at-Risk and Related Risk Measures

In the financial markets, risk scenario analysis is usually conducted to measure and test a particular risk measure. A widely adopted risk measure is the Value-at-Risk (VaR) measure. In broad terms, VaR is the potential loss in monetary value that could be suffered within a given time period with no more than a given probability. For example, if the 1-month 95% VaR of a portfolio is $5 million, then there is only a 0.05% probability that the loss within 1 month will exceed $5 million.

VaR applies not only to equities and derivatives, but also to portfolios comprising financial instruments. Regulators use VaR as a benchmark risk measure and require financial institutions to maintain a certain amount of capital as a reserve against financial crisis. VaR applications can be classified into three types: information reporting (passive), controlling risk (defensive), and managing risk (active).

This chapter first introduces VaR as a risk measure, and then discusses the VaR calculation of a portfolio using parametric VaR, delta-normal approximation, delta–gamma approximation, historical simulation, and Monte Carlo simulation. For the Monte Carlo simulation, the use of Gibbs sampling to generate random variables is demonstrated. This chapter also introduces several VaR-related risk measures, namely, conditional VaR, marginal VaR, incremental VaR, and component VaR. It concludes with a discussion of VaR backtesting and the credit conversion factor.

Handbook of Financial Risk Management: Simulations and Case Studies, First Edition. N.H. Chan and H.Y. Wong.
© 2013 John Wiley & Sons, Inc. Published 2013 by John Wiley & Sons, Inc.

8.1 VALUE-AT-RISK

Definition 8.1 *VaR summarizes the worst possible portfolio loss over a target horizon under normal market conditions at a given level of confidence.*

This definition defines VaR in terms of the absolute dollar loss (absolute VaR), although it can also be defined in terms of the dollar loss relative to the mean (relative VaR), as follows.

$$\text{Absolute VaR} = -\text{Rev}^*,$$
$$\text{Relative VaR} = \text{Absolute VaR} + \text{Mean Revenue},$$

where Rev* is the cut-off revenue conditioned on the confidence level and horizon chosen. VaR can also be represented in terms of the rate of return (the return) on the portfolio. The return can be regarded as the revenue divided by the initial value of the portfolio. If we denote the cut-off return by R^*, the initial portfolio value by Π_0, and the mean rate of return by μ, then

$$\text{Absolute VaR} = -R^*\Pi_0,$$
$$\text{Absolute VaR in return} = -R^*,$$
$$\text{Relative VaR} = -R^*\Pi_0 + \mu\Pi_0,$$
$$\text{Relative VaR in return} = -R^* + \mu.$$

Because VaR measures the worst possible loss, it is usually reported as a positive number. If a negative VaR is reported, for example, −$2 million, then this means that the probability of earning more than $2 million is very high.

Definition 8.2 *A risk measure constitutes mapping from a set of random variables to the set of real numbers representing different risk levels.*

According to this definition, the Greeks, standard deviation, and VaR are all risk measures. However, VaR is a downside risk measure, whereas standard deviation penalizes both positive and negative returns. Unlike the Greeks, VaR also provides a way to measure the total risk of a portfolio.

VaR assumes that the portfolio constituents do not change over the horizon and that the current portfolio is marked-to-market (MTM). Statistically speaking, VaR describes the specified *quantile* or *percentile* of the projected distribution of profits and losses over the target horizon. Denote R_t by the return of a portfolio for a horizon t. Then the $c\%$ confidence VaR of the portfolio is measured through the expression

$$\Pr(R_t < -\text{VaR}) = (1-c)\% := \alpha.$$

Hence, VaR is the negative of the αth percentile of the probability distribution. The larger the VaR, the higher the portfolio risk. An advantage of VaR is that it allows the user to specify the confidence level so as to reflect his or her individual risk-aversion. The more risk-averse the user is, the higher the confidence level that will be selected. For further detail, please refer to Jorion (2007).

VaR is indispensable for market risk analysis because it produces a number that splits possible future asset returns into two scenarios: risky and non-risky. Returns that are less than the negative of VaR belong to the class of risky scenarios. Decision-makers can test their policies by examining the associated consequences under the risky scenario. For instance, a bank may check whether it retains enough money to compensate for a risky or otherwise terrible situation.

8.2 PARAMETRIC VaR

Parametric VaR focuses on the random process that describes the behavior of the asset (portfolio) return; that is, it allows us to make assumption about the probability density function (pdf) of the return. A conventional way to measure VaR is to assume that portfolio returns follow a normal distribution. VaR obtained in this way is called normal VaR. A typical model is

$$R_t = \mu_t + \sigma_t Z, Z \sim \mathcal{N}(0, 1).$$

In such a parametric model,

$$\text{Absolute VaR}_\alpha(t) = -z_\alpha \sigma_t - \mu_t, \qquad (8.1)$$

$$\text{Relative VaR}_\alpha(t) = -z_\alpha \sigma_t, \qquad (8.2)$$

where z_α is the α-quantile of the standard normal distribution, μ_t is the drift, and σ_t is the standard deviation of return R_t over horizon t.

Although Equations 8.1 and 8.2 can be proved mathematically, we verify them here via simulation. This simulation exercise not only demonstrates the idea of model verification, but also shows how VaR is simulated in general. The algorithm is as follows.

1. Generate independent standard normal random variables $Z_j \sim \mathcal{N}(0, 1)$ for $j = 1, 2, \ldots, n$.
2. Set $R_j = \mu + \sigma Z_j$.
3. Rank $\{R_1, R_2, \ldots, R_n\}$ in ascending order as $\{R_1^*, R_2^*, \ldots, R_n^*\}$.
4. Set Absolute VaR $= -R_k^*$, where $k = \text{int}(\alpha \times n)$.

Example 8.1 *Suppose that $\mu = 0.001$, $\sigma = 0.13$, $\alpha = 5\%$, and $n = 10{,}000$. Then the 95% VaR corresponds to the 500th smallest return generated from the simulation. The simulation results show that the absolute VaR $= 0.2133$, which is close to the true value of 0.2128 obtained by Equation 8.1. The VBA code is as follows.*

```
Dim i&, mean#, sigma#, alpha#, n&
Dim rev() As Double
mean = Cells(1, 2)
sigma = Cells(2, 2)
alpha = 1 - Cells(3, 2)
n = Cells(4, 2)
ReDim rev(1 To n)
For i = 1 To n
rev(i) = mean + sigma * rGauss()
Next i
Cells(6, 2) = -(Percentile(rev, alpha))
Cells(8, 2) = Cells(6, 2) + mean
```

For further details, please refer to Ch8.3_Simulate_Return_VaR.xls.

Remark The user-defined function *Percentile* includes the user-defined function *Sort*.

The foregoing model can be extended to the two following situations.

1. The portfolio contains two correlated assets.
2. Z follows a *t*-distribution or a heavy-tailed distribution, which may fit the data better.

8.2.1 Two-Asset Case

The following example illustrates how to calculate the VaR of a two-asset portfolio whose returns follow a bivariate normal distribution. Generalizing the idea to n assets is straightforward.

Example 8.2 *Consider two stocks, S_1 and S_2, whose returns, R_1 and R_2, have a bivariate normal distribution with a correlation of $\rho = 0.4$. Assuming that $\mu_1 = 0.06$, $\sigma_1 = 0.3$, $\mu_2 = 0.08$, and $\sigma_2 = 0.4$, the investment in S_1 is \$1 million and that in S_2 is \$2 million, calculate the 1-year 95% VaR.*

Because R_1 and R_2 have a bivariate normal distribution, $R_1 + R_2$ is normally distributed. Portfolio return R_p is $R_p = w_1 R_1 + w_2 R_2$, which implies that

$$\mu_p = w_1 \mu_1 + w_2 \mu_2,$$
$$\sigma_p^2 = w_1^2 \sigma_1^2 + w_2^2 \sigma_2^2 + 2 w_1 w_2 \rho \sigma_1 \sigma_2,$$
$$R_p \sim \mathcal{N}(\mu_p, \sigma_p^2),$$

where w_1 and w_2 are the weights of the stocks in the portfolio. Therefore, we can calculate the required VaR using the same method by regarding the entire portfolio as one stock. The calculation (see Ch8.3_Two_Assets_Case.xls) results are summarized in Table 8.1.

TABLE 8.1 Absolute and Relative VaRs (in Terms of Dollar and Return) of a Two-Asset Portfolio with Correlated Normal Returns

	95% VaR
Absolute VaR in dollar	$1,359,402
Relative VaR in dollar	$1,579,402
Absolute VaR in return	0.45313
Relative VaR in return	0.52647

Remark If the two stocks are perfectly correlated ($\rho = 1$), then the VaR of the portfolio is equal to the sum of the individual VaRs of each stock. If they are not perfectly correlated, then the portfolio VaR is smaller as the portfolio variance is smaller, assuming that both w_1 and w_2 are positive, which shows the benefits of diversification.

If the asset returns do not follow a multivariate normal distribution, then a conventional way of simulating VaR is to use the copula approach, such as the Gaussian copula or t-copula approach discussed in Chapter 7.3. The simulation algorithm is similar to those in that chapter except that VaR requires us to record the quantile of the distribution. In the following section, we consider a heavy-tailed distribution for a single asset. The multiple asset case requires specification of a copula function.

8.2.2 Heavy-Tailed Distribution

In reality, the returns of market prices do not follow a normal distribution, but rather a heavy-tailed distribution. Assume that

$$R = \mu + \sigma Z, \text{ where } Z \text{ follows a heavy-tailed distribution,} \qquad (8.3)$$

which means that the two tails of the empirical density decay less rapidly than the normal density. As the closed-form solution for the VaR of a heavy-tailed distribution is not readily available, a realistic method is to generate random variables according to such a distribution.

8.2.2.1 Generalized Error Distribution A commonly used type of heavy-tailed distribution is generalized error distribution (GED). The pdf of a GED with parameter ξ is given by

$$f(z) = \frac{\xi \exp\left(-\frac{1}{2}|z/\lambda|^\xi\right)}{\lambda 2^{1+1/\xi} \Gamma(1/\xi)},$$

$$\lambda = \left(\frac{2^{-2/\xi} \Gamma(1/\xi)}{\Gamma(3/\xi)}\right)^{1/2},$$

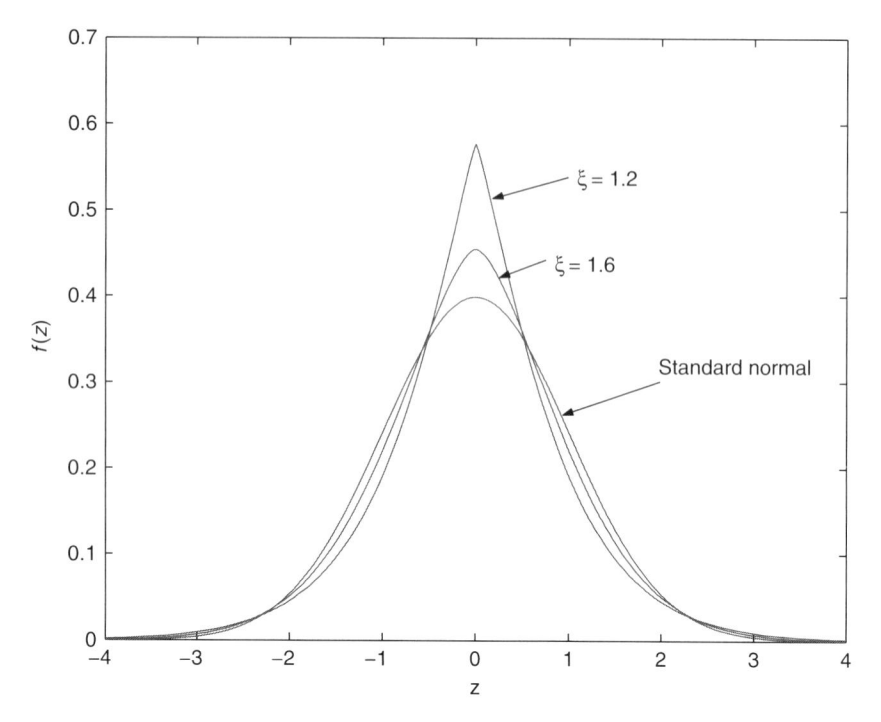

Figure 8.1 The pdfs of GED (with $\xi = 1.2, 1.6$) and standard normal distribution.

where $\Gamma(\cdot)$ denotes the gamma function. Figure 8.1 plots the whole pdf of a GED with different parameters ξ and Figure 8.2 zooms in on the left tail of the density function. It can be seen that the smaller the ξ is, the heavier the left tail of the density function. In fact, the GED becomes normal when $\xi = 2$, has heavier than normal tails when $\xi < 2$, and has thinner than normal tails when $\xi > 2$.

The key to VaR simulation is to generate random variables for the desired distribution. Here, we apply the acceptance-rejection method using the exponential distribution because it shares the same domain as the target distribution (we first generate the positive GED) and its tail is heavier than that of the target distribution. The algorithm goes as follows.

1. Generate $Y \sim \text{Exp}(1)$.
2. Generate $U \sim U(0, 1)$.
3. If $U \leq \frac{2f(Y)e^Y}{a}$, then $Z = Y$; otherwise, go to Step 1.
4. Generate $V \sim U(0, 1)$. If $V < 1/2$, then $Z = -Y$.
5. Repeat Steps 1 to 4 for n times to obtain $\{Z_1, Z_2, \ldots, Z_n\}$.
6. Set $R_i = \mu + \sigma Z_i$.
7. Sort the returns in ascending order as $\{R_1^*, R_2^*, \ldots, R_n^*\}$.
8. Set VaR $= -R_k^*$, where $k = \text{int}(\alpha \times n)$.

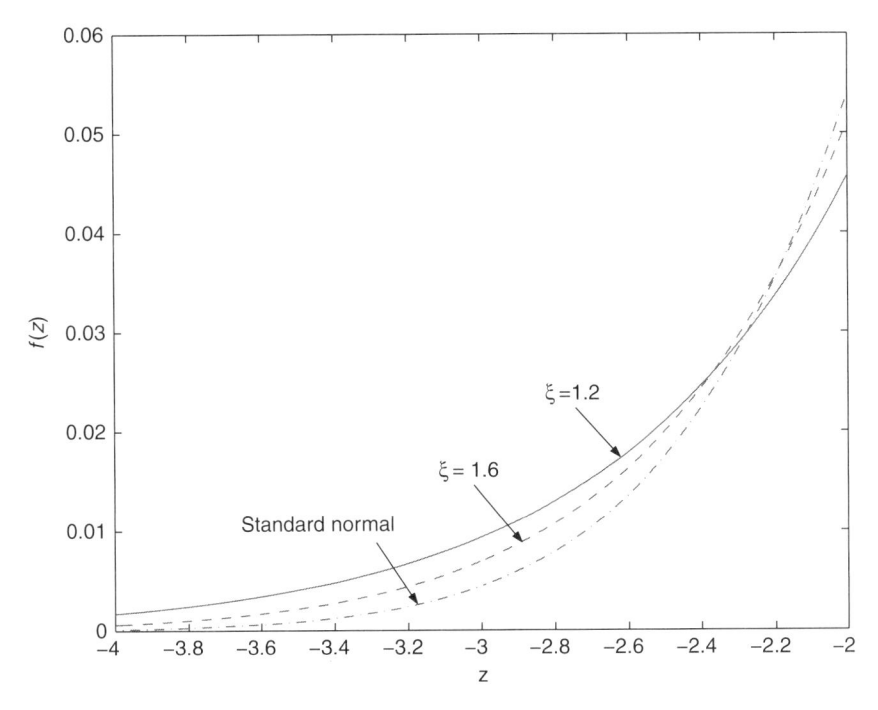

Figure 8.2 The left tails of GED (with $\xi = 1.2, 1.6$) and standard normal distribution.

Remarks

1. In Step 3, a is a constant not less than $\max_y\{2f(y)e^y\}$.
2. As the exponential distribution is defined with a domain of positive real numbers, Steps 1 to 3 of the algorithm generate a positive GED. Then Step 4 is required to convert this positive GED into a GED random variable.

Example 8.3 *Suppose that Z in Equation 8.3 follows a GED with $\xi = 1.21$. Calculate the 95% and 99% VaRs using the foregoing algorithm with $\mu = 0.05$, $\sigma = 0.3$, and an initial portfolio value of $1 million.*

To implement the acceptance-rejection method, we first identify the constant a that bounds the function $2f(y)e^y$ for all y. As obtaining the constant a with differentiation is cumbersome, we adopt a graphical approach, with result presented in Figure 8.3.

From this graph, we can see that the function is bounded above by 1.2. Therefore, we select 1.2 as a. For more details, please refer to Ch8.3_Simulate_GED_VaR.xls. The results are summarized in Table 8.2.

310 VALUE-AT-RISK AND RELATED RISK MEASURES

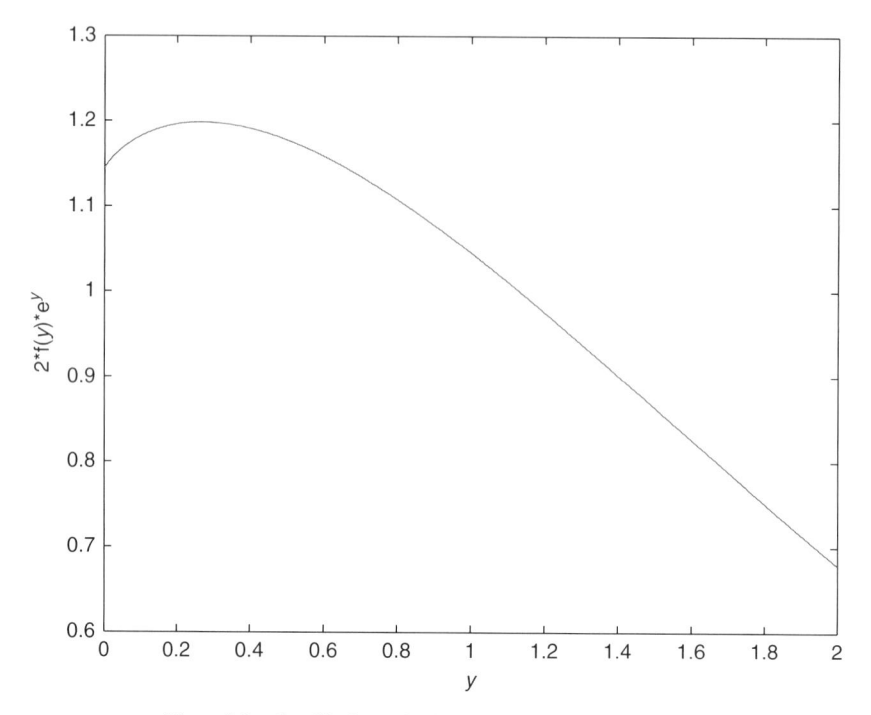

Figure 8.3 Graphic determination of the maximum of $2f(y)e^y$.

The VBA code for simulating GED-VAR is as follows.

```
Dim Y#, U#
Dim mu#, sigma#, v#, a#, confidence1#, confidence2#
Dim i&, n&
Dim R() As Double, Z() As Double

v = Cells(3, 2)
a = Cells(4, 2)
n = Cells(5, 2)
mu = Cells(1, 2)
sigma = Cells(2, 2)
```

TABLE 8.2 Calculation of Absolute and Relative VaRs (in Dollar and Return Terms) Using GED with $\xi = 1.21$

	95% VaR	99% VaR
Absolute VaR in dollar	$283,571	$506,374
Relative VaR in dollar	$330,950	$553,752
Absolute VaR in return	0.28357	0.50637
Relative VaR in return	0.33095	0.55375

```
confidence1 = Cells(6, 2)
confidence2 = Cells(7, 2)

ReDim R(1 To n)
ReDim Z(1 To n)

For i = 1 To n
Do
Y = -Application.Ln(Rnd())
U = Rnd()
If (U <= 2 * GEDpdf(v, Y) * Exp(Y) / a) Then
Z(i) = Y
End If
Loop Until (U <= 2 * GEDpdf(v, Y) * Exp(Y) / a)
U = Rnd()
If U < 0.5 Then
Z(i) = -Y
End If
R(i) = mu + sigma * Z(i)
Next i

Cells(11, 2) = -Percentile(R, 1 - confidence1)
Cells(11, 3) = -Percentile(R, 1 - confidence2)
Cells(12, 2) = Cells(11, 2) + Average(R)
Cells(12, 3) = Cells(11, 3) + Average(R)
Cells(15, 2) = Cells(11, 2) * Cells(8, 2)
Cells(15, 3) = Cells(11, 3) * Cells(8, 2)
Cells(16, 2) = Cells(12, 2) * Cells(8, 2)
Cells(16, 3) = Cells(12, 3) * Cells(8, 2)
```

8.2.2.2 *t*-Distribution Instead of GED, we can also employ a *t*-distribution to model the return. A *t*-distribution with mean zero has the following pdf.

$$f_\nu(x) = \frac{\Gamma((\nu+1)/2)}{\sqrt{\nu\pi}\,\Gamma(\nu/2)} \left(1 + \frac{x^2}{\nu}\right)^{-(\nu+1)/2}, \quad -\infty < x < \infty,$$

where $\Gamma(\cdot)$ denotes the gamma function and ν represents the degrees of freedom and controls the heaviness of the tails. The smaller the ν, the heavier the tail will be. When $\nu \to \infty$, f_ν becomes the density of the normal distribution. The multivariate version of the *t*-distribution enables us to model the returns of a number of assets.

8.2.3 Holding Period Adjustment

If we are given information on one particular holding period, but desire VaR information on a different holding period, then we require a holding period adjustment. Imagine that we are still dealing with normally distributed daily returns, but are interested in a longer horizon period, say 20 days (one business month). Assume that the daily returns are uncorrelated and identically distributed. Then,

$$\mu_{\text{monthly}} = 20\mu_{\text{daily}},$$
$$\sigma^2_{\text{monthly}} = 20\sigma^2_{\text{daily}},$$
$$\sigma_{\text{monthly}} = \sqrt{20}\sigma_{\text{daily}}.$$

Further, the relative 1-month VaR is

$$\begin{aligned}\text{Relative VaR}_{\text{monthly}} &= -z_a \sigma_{\text{monthly}} \Pi_0 \\ &= -z_a(\sigma_{\text{daily}}\sqrt{20})\Pi_0 \\ &= \sqrt{20}\text{VaR}_{\text{daily}},\end{aligned}$$

and the absolute 1-month VaR is

$$\begin{aligned}\text{Absolute VaR}_{\text{monthly}} &= -z_a \sigma_{\text{monthly}} W + \mu_{\text{monthly}} \Pi_0 \\ &= -z_a(\sigma_{\text{daily}}\sqrt{20})W + 20\mu_{\text{daily}} \Pi_0 \\ &\approx \sqrt{20}\text{VaR}_{\text{daily}} (\text{since } \mu_{daily} \text{ is generally small}).\end{aligned}$$

In general, we assume that

$$N\text{-day VaR} = 1\text{-day VaR} \times \sqrt{N}.$$

This formula is exact when the returns are independent normal random variables with mean zero. For other cases, it is only an approximation. However, we can still check via simulation whether the formula does indeed provide a good approximation. For instance, we could use the GED to simulate the daily VaR and then project it to a holding horizon of 10 days employing the square-root rule. The Basel Accords require banks to report the 99% 10-day VaR.

8.2.4 Portfolio VaR

Consider a portfolio of n risky assets, whose returns jointly follow a multivariate normal distribution with mean vector μ and variance-covariate matrix Σ. The portfolio value at time t is

$$\Pi(t) = \sum_{j=1}^{n} \alpha_j S_j(t),$$

where S_j is the value of the jth asset in the portfolio. The portfolio is said to be self-financing if there are no cash withdrawals from or injections to the portfolio. In turn, the portfolio return is driven solely by the returns of its individual constituent assets such that

$$\frac{d\Pi}{\Pi} = \sum_{j=1}^{n} w_j \frac{dS_j}{S_j},$$

where

$$w_j = \alpha_j \frac{S_j(t)}{\Pi(t)} \quad \text{and} \quad \sum_{j=1}^{n} w_j = 1.$$

Let $R_j = dS_j/S_j$ be the return of the jth asset and $\mathbf{R}$ be the vector collecting the returns of these n assets. Then we have $\mathbf{R} \sim \mathcal{N}(\mu, \Sigma)$. Using matrix-vector notation, let $\mathbf{w}' = (w_1, \ldots, w_n)$, the portfolio return, R_p, is

$$R_p = \mathbf{w}'\mathbf{R}.$$

The variance of this portfolio return can be derived as $\text{Var}(R_p) = \mathbf{w}'\Sigma\mathbf{w}$ such that its relative VaR is reduced to $\text{VaR}_p = -z_\alpha \sqrt{\mathbf{w}'\Sigma\mathbf{w}}\sqrt{T}$, including the holding period adjustment. The variance–covariance matrix can be decomposed into the product of three matrices:

$$\begin{pmatrix} \sigma_1 & \cdots & 0 \\ \vdots & \cdots & \vdots \\ 0 & \cdots & \sigma_n \end{pmatrix} \begin{pmatrix} 1 & \rho_{12}, & \cdots & \rho_{1n} \\ \rho_{21} & & \cdots & \rho_{2n} \\ \vdots & \vdots & \vdots & \vdots \\ \rho_{n1} & \cdots & & 1 \end{pmatrix} \begin{pmatrix} \sigma_1 & \cdots & 0 \\ \vdots & \cdots & \vdots \\ 0 & \cdots & \sigma_n \end{pmatrix},$$

where the middle matrix is the correlation coefficient matrix denoted as $\mathbf{C}$. Then the formula of the portfolio relative VaR in revenue terms can be simplified as

$$\text{VaR}_p = \sqrt{\mathbf{VaR}' \cdot \mathbf{C} \cdot \mathbf{VaR}}, \tag{8.4}$$

where $\mathbf{VaR}$ is the vector of the VaRs of individual assets. In many practical situations, although the marginal distributions of individual asset returns do not follow a normal distribution, Equation 8.4 can still be applied to the portfolio VaR of these assets as short-hand calculation. In fact, the genuine joint distribution of risky assets is very difficult to model and estimate. The short-hand portfolio VaR formula serves as a proxy for daily reporting and signals the significant risks contained in the portfolio.

8.3 DELTA-NORMAL APPROXIMATION

In delta-normal approximation, we assume that a change in portfolio value is approximately linearly related to changes in the underlying risk factors. For a portfolio of stocks and stock options, the risk factor is simply the underlying stocks; for a portfolio of bonds, the risk factor is the yield. As indicated by its name, delta-normal approximation makes use of the assumption that changes in the underlying risk factors are multivariate normally distributed and uses the partial derivative (the Greek) Δ to measure the sensitivity of portfolio value changes to these risk factors. It constitutes local valuation because the portfolio is valued once at the initial position. It is also a linear model and constitutes an analytical method because a closed-form solution is available.

8.3.1 Option VaR

The delta of an option is the option's partial derivative with respect to the underlying asset value S. For a call option,

$$\Delta = \frac{\partial c}{\partial S} = \Psi(d_1).$$

Consider the Taylor expansion on the call option pricing formula:

$$dc = \frac{\partial c}{\partial S} dS + \frac{1}{2} \frac{\partial c}{\partial S} dS^2 + \ldots.$$

If we ignore all terms higher than the first order, then the approximation is

$$dc \simeq \Delta \, dS.$$

Delta-normal approximation assumes the Δ to remain unchanged during a short period of time and the return of the underlying asset to follow a normal distribution, that is, $dS/S \sim \mathcal{N}(\mu, \sigma^2)$. This assumption implies that

$$\text{Var}(dc) = \Delta^2 \text{Var}(dS).$$

In addition, the variance of the underlying asset is further approximated as $\text{Var}(dS) = \sigma^2 S^2$. Hence, the relative VaR for the option is given by

$$\text{VaR} = -|\Delta| z_\alpha \sigma S.$$

In practice, the relative VaR is usually employed to report the risk of a financial institution. In such a situation, the delta-normal approximation of an option position is given by

$$\text{VaR}_{\text{option}} = |\Delta| \text{VaR}_S, \tag{8.5}$$

where VaR_S is the VaR for holding the underlying asset for the same horizon as the option is held. In this formula, the term $-z_a \sigma S$ is essentially the relative VaR of holding S if its return follows a normal distribution.

Although market practitioners admit that asset returns are not normally distributed, Equation 8.5 still applies, and VaR_S must be computed using a distribution fitted to the empirical data. For example, the VaR_S of the underlying asset is estimated using a GARCH model and then substituted into Equation 8.5, where Δ is computed using the Black–Scholes (BS) formula with market-implied volatility. This approach is remarkably efficient in practice because BS Δ has a direct quote from the systems of data providers.

The value of a general structured product can be a function of multiple assets. In this case, consider the Taylor expansion in the multivariable calculus:

$$dc = \sum_{j=1}^{n} \frac{\partial c}{\partial S_j} dS_j + \frac{1}{2} \sum_{i,j} \frac{\partial^2 c}{\partial S_i \partial S_j} dS_i dS_j + \dots.$$

Ignoring terms higher than the first order yields the approximation

$$dc \simeq \sum_{j=1}^{n} \frac{\partial c}{\partial S_j} dS_j.$$

Therefore, delta-normal approximation views the option on multiple assets as a portfolio of the underlying assets. Combining Equations 8.4 and 8.5 gives us the following short-hand formula.

$$\text{VaR}_{\text{option}} = \sqrt{\textbf{VaR}' \cdot \textbf{D} \cdot \textbf{C} \cdot \textbf{D} \cdot \textbf{VaR}}, \quad (8.6)$$

where $\textbf{D}$ is a diagonal matrix collecting the deltas with respect to individual assets:

$$\textbf{D} = \begin{pmatrix} \frac{\partial c}{\partial S_1} & 0 & \cdots & 0 \\ \vdots & \vdots & & \vdots \\ 0 & \cdots & 0 & \frac{\partial c}{\partial S_n} \end{pmatrix}.$$

Delta-normal approximation of multi-asset options is also useful for single-asset options when volatility is regarded as a risk factor. In such a situation, the first-order Taylor expansion is

$$dc \simeq \frac{\partial c}{\partial S} dS + \frac{\partial c}{\partial \sigma} d\sigma,$$

where the differential with respect to σ is known as the vega in the market, that is,

$$\text{vega} = \frac{\partial c}{\partial \sigma}.$$

The variance of the change in option price has the following delta-normal approximation.

$$\text{Var}(dc) \simeq \left(\frac{\partial c}{\partial S}\right)^2 \text{Var}_S + \left(\frac{\partial c}{\partial \sigma}\right)^2 \text{Var}_\sigma + 2\rho \left(\frac{\partial c}{\partial S}\right)\left(\frac{\partial c}{\partial \sigma}\right)\sqrt{\text{Var}_S \text{Var}_\sigma},$$

where Var_S is the variance of the change in asset price and Var_σ is the variance of the change in volatility. Both the Δ and vega have market quotes for standard call and put options. However, these sensitivity measures should be computed for other types of derivatives and structured products. Further details about Greek simulation are given in the next chapter.

A "hybrid" approach to option VaR captures the effect of the implied volatility surface through delta-normal approximation. For instance, we can use the historical volatility to estimate Var_S and calibrate ρ and Var_σ to market option prices using the Heston model, which was introduced in Chapter 4. For a short holding period of δt, a possible approximation is

$$\text{Var}_\sigma = \epsilon^2 V(0) \delta t,$$

where $V(0)$ is the calibrated instantaneous variance of the asset return. Note that ρ and ϵ are obtained within the calibration. Please refer to Chapter 4.2 for further details. The delta-normal approximation for the Heston option VaR is given by

$$\text{VaR}_{\text{option}} = \sqrt{\Delta^2 \text{VaR}_S^2 + 2\rho \Delta \, \text{vega} \, \text{VaR}_S \text{VaR}_\sigma + \text{vega}^2 \text{VaR}_\sigma^2},$$

where

$$\text{VaR}_\sigma = -z_\alpha \epsilon \sqrt{V(0)} \sqrt{\delta t}.$$

8.3.2 Fixed-Income VaR

Analysis of a fixed-income portfolio is similar to options analysis. The results of empirical studies using principal components analysis (PCA) on bond yields suggest that the parallel movement component explains more than 60% of the variations in the yield curve. The parallel movement of a yield curve is often employed as the underlying stochastic variable for simplification. For example, we can use the one-factor short-rate model introduced in Chapter 5 or directly measure the volatility of the yield-to-maturity of the fixed-income security. Suppose that we adopt the latter approach. The price-yield relationship is then given by

$$dV = (-D^* V) dy,$$

where D^* is the *modified duration*, dy is the daily MTM change in the yield, and V is the value function of the fixed-income security. Here, we assume the change in yield to be normally distributed with variance σ^2. Therefore, the relative VaR is approximated as

$$\text{VaR} = -|D^*V|z_a\sigma.$$

Again, we can apply a short-hand formula for relative VaR:

$$\text{VaR}_{FP} = |D^*V|\text{VaR}_y, \qquad (8.7)$$

where VaR_{FP} is the VaR of the fixed-income portfolio and VaR_y is the VaR of the yield.

In general situations, a fixed-income security is likely to be affected by the multiple interest rate factor driving the yield curve movement. Therefore, it is practical to use the LIBOR market model presented in Chapter 6 to model the yield curve movement. Then a short-hand VaR formula can be obtained by combining Equations 8.7 and 8.4 to produce a formula similar to Equation 8.6, where diagonal matrix $\mathbf{D}$ uses durations rather than deltas.

Remark Delta-normal approximation is easy to implement and is computationally fast. However, it is inadequate for nonlinear instruments, and its normality assumption is questionable.

8.4 DELTA–GAMMA APPROXIMATION

When a portfolio contains options, using delta–gamma approximation to calculate the VaR sometimes confers greater accuracy. Recall that the gamma (Γ) of a portfolio is defined as the second partial derivative of the portfolio value with respect to the asset price:

$$\Gamma = \frac{\partial^2 \Pi}{\partial S^2}.$$

Equivalently, it is the partial derivative of Δ with respect to the asset price:

$$\Gamma = \frac{\partial \Delta}{\partial S}.$$

8.4.1 Option VaR

To obtain a more accurate result, we reconsider the Taylor expansion. This time, however, we ignore terms higher than the second order. Then,

$$dC = \Delta\, dS + \frac{1}{2}\Gamma\,(dS)^2.$$

Using the rate of return, $R = \frac{dS}{S}$, this becomes

$$dV = S\Delta R + \frac{1}{2}S^2 \Gamma R^2.$$

If $R \sim \mathcal{N}(0, \sigma^2)$, then R^2 is a chi-squared random variable. The delta–gamma approximation ignores this fact, but regards $R^2 = R_2$ as another *normal* random variable. It is clear that $E[R_2] = E[R^2] = \sigma^2$, $\text{cov}(R, R_2) = E[R^3] = 0$, and $\text{Var}(R^2) = E[R^4] - (\sigma^2)^2 = 2\sigma^4$. Assuming a portfolio of two uncorrelated assets, R and R_2, the portfolio variance is given by

$$S^2 \Delta^2 \sigma^2 + \frac{1}{2} S^4 \Gamma^2 \sigma^4.$$

Hence, the delta–gamma approximation of the relative VaR of an option is given by

$$\text{VaR}_{\text{option}} = -z_\alpha \sqrt{S^2 \Delta^2 \sigma^2 + \frac{1}{2} S^4 \Gamma^2 \sigma^4} = \sqrt{\Delta^2 \text{VaR}_S^2 - \frac{1}{2}\Gamma^2 \text{VaR}_S^4/z_\alpha}. \quad (8.8)$$

It is clear that delta–gamma approximation produces a higher VaR than delta-normal approximation. Similar to previous cases, the VaR of the underlying asset can be estimated with another distribution that is fit to the empirical data. The option VaR can then be estimated by plugging the estimated VaR$_S$ into Equation 8.8. For standard options, the Δ and Γ can be quoted directly from the data provider, and so Equation 8.8 offers a convenient way of calculating VaR on a daily basis.

For the case of n underlying assets, we have

$$dV = \sum_{i=1}^{n} \Delta_i \, dS_i + \frac{1}{2} \sum_{i=1}^{n} \sum_{j=1}^{n} \Gamma_{ij} \, dS_i \, dS_j, \quad (8.9)$$

where Γ_{ij} is the cross-gamma:

$$\Gamma_{ij} = \frac{\partial^2 V}{\partial S_i \partial S_j}.$$

Further assumptions would need to be imposed on the cross-term $dS_i \, dS_j$ for $i \neq j$ to produce a short-hand user-friendly formula, but we are unaware of a standard way of doing this.

8.4.2 Fixed-Income VaR

For a fixed-income portfolio, the price-yield relationship is

$$dV \approx -(D^* V) \, dy + \frac{1}{2} CV \, (dy)^2,$$

where C is the convexity. Using Equation 8.8, we have

$$\text{VaR}_{\text{option}} = \sqrt{(D^*V)^2 \text{VaR}_y^2 - \frac{1}{2}(CV)^2 \text{VaR}_y^4/z_\alpha}.$$

However, computation involving multiple interest rate factors will most likely encounter the problems associated with Equation 8.9. Thus, fixed-income risk managers generally prefer to employ delta-normal approximation for complex fixed-income derivatives.

Remark For complicated derivatives, valuation may rely on simulation, but the corresponding Greeks, such as Δ and Γ, cannot be accurately estimated with simulation, particularly in the case of multiple risk factors. To manage and report risks, financial institutions are required to compute the Greeks in a very efficient manner. The next chapter details several methods of Greek computation and readers who are interested in the practical use of Greek-approximation approaches to VaR will find it useful.

8.5 VaR SIMULATION METHODS

In parametric VaR, we first model the portfolio return and then calculate the VaR by an analytic method or simulation. In this section, we focus the simulation methods used to calculate the VaR of a portfolio. The two most common methods are historical simulation and Monte Carlo simulation, both of which are full-valuation methods that measure risk by fully repricing the portfolio over a range of scenarios. Monte Carlo simulation in this section specifies the stochastic process for the assets or risk factors involved, which is more general than specifying the distribution of the portfolio return.

8.5.1 Historical Simulation

Historical simulation is a non-parametric approach to VaR prediction based on historical data. It does not assume any distribution for the asset return and, in practice, is relatively easy to implement. It is sometime confused that the term "historical simulation" used in the financial market does not involve simulation in the statistical sense. It simply means to rank historical returns and then to read the empirical VaR from the given data set. However, the way of determining VaR in historical simulation helps better understanding the Monte Carlo simulation to VaR in the subsequent subsection.

In the simplest case, historical simulation assumes that the asset returns are independent and identically distributed (i.i.d.). Consider a portfolio of N assets, where the market prices of each asset over a period of $T+1$ days are given. Then we calculate the daily change in asset prices by

$$\Delta S_t^i = S_t^i - S_{t-1}^i \quad \text{for} \quad t = 1, \ldots, T \quad \text{and} \quad i = 1, \ldots, N.$$

We have now created T scenarios:

$$\{\Delta S_t^1, \ldots, \Delta S_t^N\} \quad \text{for} \quad t = 1, \ldots, T.$$

Denote the current portfolio value by

$$V_0 = V(S_T^1, \ldots, S_T^N).$$

Then we have T hypothetical portfolio values, $V_1, \ldots, V_T$, where

$$V_k = V(S_T^1 + \Delta S_k^1, \ldots, S_T^N + \Delta S_k^N) \quad \text{for} \quad k = 1, \ldots, T.$$

The revenue and return for the kth scenario are calculated by

$$\text{Rev}_k = V_k - V_0,$$
$$R_k = \frac{V_k - V_0}{V_0}.$$

The VaR is then obtained from the hypothetical return distribution. The general procedure is as follows.

1. Read the N asset prices.
2. Calculate the change in price of each asset ΔS_t^i for $t = 1, \ldots, T$ and $i = 1, \ldots, N$.
3. Calculate the hypothetical portfolio values V_k for $k = 1, \ldots, T$.
4. Calculate the revenue of portfolios Rev_k for $k = 1, \ldots, T$.
5. Rank $\{\text{Rev}_1, \text{Rev}_2, \ldots, \text{Rev}_T\}$ in ascending order as $\{\text{Rev}_1^*, \text{Rev}_2^*, \ldots, \text{Rev}_T^*\}$.
6. Set Absolute VaR $= -\text{Rev}_k^*$, where $k = \text{int}(\alpha \times T)$.

Example 8.4 *Calculate via historical simulation the 1-day 95% and 99% VaRs of a portfolio containing four stocks, namely, HSBC HOLDINGS, CHEUNG KONG, HANG SENG BANK, and BANK OF EAST ASIA, using data from the most recent 501 trading days if there are 10,000 stocks for each company in the portfolio.*

In this example, today's date is taken as July 8, 2011, and the data are collected from July 6, 2009, to July 8, 2011. The calculation results are summarized in Table 8.3

TABLE 8.3 Calculation of Absolute and Relative VaRs (in Dollar and Return Terms) Using Historical Simulation

	95% VaR	99% VaR
Absolute VaR in dollar	$59,400	$84,300
Relative VaR in dollar	$61,075.2	$85,975.2
Absolute VaR in return	0.01692	0.02401
Relative VaR in return	0.01740	0.02449

and the VBA code is as follows.

```
Dim i&, j&
Dim stock(1 To 4, 1 To 501) As Double
Dim change(1 To 4, 1 To 500) As Double
Dim Rev(1 To 500) As Double
Dim nostock(1 To 4) As Double
Dim confidence1#, confidence2#, V0#

For i = 1 To 4
nostock(i) = Cells(1 + i, 8)
Next i
confidence1 = Cells(6, 8)
confidence2 = Cells(6, 9)
For i = 1 To 4
For j = 1 To 501
stock(i, j) = Cells(j + 1, i + 1)
Next j
Next i

For i = 1 To 4
For j = 1 To 500
change(i, j) = stock(i, j) - stock(i, j + 1)
Next j
Next i

For j = 1 To 500
For i = 1 To 4
Rev(j) = Rev(j) + change(i, j) * nostock(i)
Next i
Next j

For i = 1 To 4
V0 = V0 + nostock(i) * stock(i, 1)
Next i
Cells(8, 8) = V0

Cells(11, 8) = -Percentile(Rev, 1 - confidence1)
Cells(12, 8) = Cells(11, 8) + Average(Rev)
Cells(13, 8) = Cells(11, 8) / Cells(8, 8)
Cells(14, 8) = Cells(12, 8) / Cells(8, 8)
Cells(11, 9) = -Percentile(Rev, 1 - confidence2)
Cells(12, 9) = Cells(11, 9) + Average(Rev)
Cells(13, 9) = Cells(11, 9) / Cells(8, 8)
Cells(14, 9) = Cells(12, 9) / Cells(8, 8)
```

For further details, please refer to Ch8.6_Historical_Simulation.xls.

8.5.1.1 Bootstrapping
An alternative way to perform historical simulation is to regard the historical data as the realized values of an unknown distribution. We would then sample a value from the distribution by randomly replacing a historical datum with a replacement. This method assigns an equal probability to each realization. After repeating the process, we obtain the VaR from the resulting portfolio revenue distribution. This method is known as bootstrapping in statistics.

8.5.2 Advantages and Disadvantages

The advantages of the historical approach are as follows.

1. The method is relatively simple to implement if historical daily MTM data are available. The same data can be stored to estimate VaR.
2. It deals directly with the choice of horizon for VaR measurement. For example, to obtain a monthly VaR, we can reconstruct the historical monthly returns over, say, 5 years.
3. It does not depend on the probability distribution, and also accounts for the fat tails in the historical data.
4. It allows correlation between assets.

The disadvantages of historical approach are as follows.

1. The approach assumes the asset returns to be i.i.d., which is usually untrue.
2. It requires a sufficient history of price changes. For example, to obtain 1000 independent returns for a 10-day move, we need 4 years of continuous data. In the case of monthly returns, 1000 independent monthly returns require more than 80 years of data.
3. Only one sample path is used, which creates difficulties for scenario analysis.
4. The approach is very slow to incorporate structural breaks, which can be more easily handled with an analytical method such as RiskMetrics.
5. It may be unsuitable for the analysis of derivative risk. Derivative products have very short lives in the market, say 3 months. Therefore, we may wish to make use of the underlying asset prices. However, incorporating the prices of underlying assets can be tricky because the historical approach does not incorporate a parametric model that relates these prices to derivative prices.
6. The method places the same weight on all observations, including old data points.
7. It may produce a large error in estimating VaR. For example, a 99% daily VaR estimated over 100 days produces only one observation in the tail, which necessarily leads to an imprecise VaR measure. Thus, very long sample paths are required to obtain meaningful results.
8. It becomes cumbersome for large portfolios with complicated structures, although, in practice, users adopt such simplifications as interest rate

payoff grouping into bands, which increase the speed of computation considerably. However, if too many simplifications are imposed, then the benefit of distribution-free valuation may be jeopardized.

8.5.3 Monte Carlo Simulation

Monte Carlo simulation was originally developed to value derivatives, although its use can be extended to VaR calculation and confidence interval construction. It constitutes a parametric method because it assumes certain stochastic processes for the underlying assets. The parameters in stochastic processes can be estimated from historical data or calibrated from current market data. Finally, asset paths are simulated and used to generate a distribution of portfolio values.

The general procedure involved in calculating the VaR of a portfolio is as follows.

1. Select appropriate stochastic processes for the assets and other market variables in the portfolio.
2. Simulate T paths for the random variables involved, either by means of discrete approximation or one-shoot simulation.
3. Calculate the portfolio value using a closed-from solution or simulation.
4. Calculate the portfolio revenue $\{\text{Rev}_1, \text{Rev}_2, \ldots, \text{Rev}_T\}$.
5. Rank $\{\text{Rev}_1, \text{Rev}_2, \ldots, \text{Rev}_T\}$ in ascending order as $\{\text{Rev}_1^*, \text{Rev}_2^*, \ldots, \text{Rev}_T^*\}$.
6. Set Absolute VaR $= -\text{Rev}_k^*$, where $k = \text{int}(\alpha \times T)$.

For simplicity, we consider one stock first. Assume that the stock price follows the dynamics

$$dS(t) = \mu S(t)\,dt + \sigma S(t)\,dW(t).$$

By Itô's lemma,

$$S(T) = S(0) \exp\left(\left(\mu - \frac{1}{\sigma^2}\right)T + \sigma\sqrt{T}Z\right),$$

where Z is a standard normal random variable. By generating n standard normal random variables, $Z_1, \ldots, Z_n$, and estimating parameters μ and σ, we have n terminal stock prices. After calculating the revenue and ranking the data in ascending order, we select the revenue that corresponds to the required quantile as the VaR.

Example 8.5 *Suppose that the stock price follows lognormal dynamics. Perform simulation to calculate the 10- and 20-day 95% VaR, where $\mu = 0.08$ and $\sigma = 40\%$. Assume that there are 252 trading days in the year.*

The calculation results are summarized in Table 8.4.

TABLE 8.4 Monte Carlo Simulation of Absolute and Relative VaRs (in Dollar and Return Terms) of One Stock

	10-Day	20-Day	20-Day (Holding period adjustment)	10-Day (Normal VaR)
Absolute VaR in dollar	12.331	16.880	17.439	12.789
Relative VaR in dollar	12.558	17.592	17.760	13.107
Absolute VaR in return	0.12331	0.16880	0.17439	0.12789
Relative VaR in return	0.12558	0.17592	0.17760	0.13107

The corresponding VBA code is as follows.

```
Dim A As BS_PathType
Dim S, i&, j&
Dim confidence#, target#
Dim ST() As Variant
Dim rev() As Variant

A.S0 = Cells(1, 2)
A.q = Cells(2, 2)
A.sigma = Cells(3, 2)
A.rf = Cells(4, 2)
A.t = Cells(5, 2)
A.m = Cells(7, 2)
A.n = Cells(8, 2)
A.dt = A.t / A.m

confidence = Cells(9, 2)

ReDim ST(1 To A.n)
ReDim rev(1 To A.n)

S = BS_Path(A)
For i = 1 To A.n
    ST(i) = S(A.m, i)
    rev(i) = ST(i) - A.S0
Next i
Cells(12, 2) = -Percentile(rev, 1 - confidence)
Cells(13, 2) = -Percentile(rev, 1 - confidence)
   + Average(rev)
Cells(14, 2) = Cells(12, 2) / A.S0
Cells(15, 2) = Cells(13, 2) / A.S0

A.t = Cells(5, 3)
S = BS_Path(A)
```

TABLE 8.5 Monte Carlo Simulation of Absolute and Relative VaRs (in Dollar Terms) of the Forward Contract

	10-Day	20-Day	20-Day (Holding period adjustment)
Absolute VaR in dollar	12.411	17.235	17.551
Relative VaR in dollar	12.564	17.512	17.768

```
For i = 1 To A.n
    ST(i) = S(A.m, i)
    rev(i) = ST(i) - A.S0
Next i
Cells(12, 3) = -Percentile(rev, 1 - confidence)
Cells(13, 3) = -Percentile(rev, 1 - confidence)
  + Average(rev)
Cells(14, 3) = Cells(12, 3) / A.S0
Cells(15, 3) = Cells(13, 3) / A.S0
```

For more details, please refer to Ch8.6_MC_Simulation_Stock.xls.

The following example illustrates the use of Monte Carlo simulation to calculate the VaR of a derivative.

Example 8.6 *Suppose that we long a 6-month forward contract and that the underlying asset is the same stock as that considered in the previous example. Calculate the 10- and 20-day 95% VaR.*

Recall that the value at time t of a forward contract with maturity T in the long position is

$$f(t, T) = S(t)e^{-q(T-t)} - Ke^{-r(T-t)},$$

where K is the delivery price, r is the risk-free rate, and q is the dividend yield. At contract initiation, $f(0, T) = 0$ and $K = S(0)e^{(r-q)(T)}$, where $T = 0.5$. We now employ simulation to find the distribution of the forward value by generating 50,000 stock prices after 10 days. The results are summarized in Table 8.5, which is followed by the corresponding VBA code.

```
Dim a As BS_PathType
Dim r#
Dim S As Variant
Dim i&, j&, confidence#, target#
Dim T#, ttm#, K#, begintime#
Dim ST() As Double
Dim rev() As Double
```

326   VALUE-AT-RISK AND RELATED RISK MEASURES

```
begintime = Cells(8, 2)
T = Cells(7, 2) 'time to maturity
r = Cells(2, 2)
a.S0 = Cells(1, 2)
a.q = Cells(3, 2)
a.sigma = Cells(4, 2)
a.rf = Cells(5, 2)
a.T = Cells(6, 2) 'target horizon
a.m = Cells(9, 2)
a.n = Cells(10, 2)
a.dt = a.T / a.m
confidence = Cells(11, 2)

K = a.S0 * Exp((r - a.q) * (T - begintime))

ReDim ST(1 To a.n)
ReDim rev(1 To a.n)

ttm = T - a.T
S = BS_Path(a)
For i = 1 To a.n
    ST(i) = S(a.m, i)
    rev(i) = fvalue(ST(i), K, a.q, r, ttm)
Next i
Cells(14, 2) = -Percentile(rev, 1 - confidence)
Cells(15, 2) = -Percentile(rev, 1 - confidence)
  + Average(rev)

a.T = Cells(6, 3)
ttm = T - a.T
S = BS_Path(a)
For i = 1 To a.n
    ST(i) = S(a.m, i)
    rev(i) = fvalue(ST(i), K, a.q, r, ttm)
Next i
Cells(14, 3) = -Percentile(rev, 1 - confidence)
Cells(15, 3) = -Percentile(rev, 1 - confidence)
  + Average(rev)
```

For further details, please refer to Ch8.6_MC_Simulation_Forward.xls.

Remark   *fvalue* is a user-defined function employed to calculate the value of a forward contract.

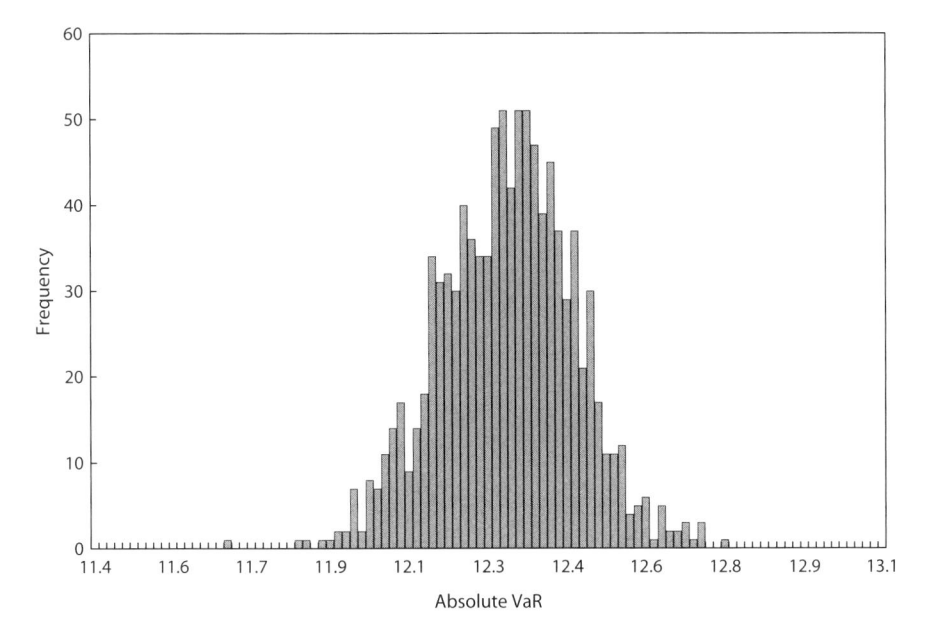

Figure 8.4 Distribution of Absolute VaR.

Using Monte Carlo simulation, we can also generate a VaR distribution by repeating the simulation process. For the one-stock example, we need to repeat the calculation 1000 times. The results are shown in Figure 8.4.

8.5.4 Gibbs Sampling and Multivariate Normal Distribution

In this section, we demonstrate the use of simulation to calculate the VaR of a portfolio comprising more than one asset. As described in Chapter 3, by using Cholesky decomposition, we can create a vector of multivariate normal variables that can be used to obtain the terminal asset prices. Here, we demonstrate the use of Gibbs sampling to generate these variables.

Gibbs sampling is one of the most commonly used Markov Chain Monte Carlo (MCMC) methods. It is simple, intuitive, easy to implement, and designed to handle multidimensional problems. The basic limit theorem of the Markov chain serves as the theoretical building block by which it is guaranteed that draws from Gibbs sampling agree with the posterior asymptotically. We first demonstrate the mechanism of Gibbs sampling.

Gibbs sampling offers a way to reduce a multidimensional problem to an iteration of low dimensional problems. More specifically, let $x = (x_1, \ldots, x_n)$ be the data set, where each data item follows the same distribution and has r parameters, $\theta = (\theta_1, \theta_2, \ldots, \theta_r)$. For each $i = 1, \ldots, r$, specify the one-dimensional conditional conjugate prior $p(\theta_j)$ and construct the conditional posterior by means of Baye's theorem. Then iterate the Gibbs procedure as follows.

Set an initial parameter vector $(\theta_2^0, \ldots, \theta_r^0)$. Update the parameters using the following procedure.

- Sample $\theta_1^1 \sim p(\theta_1 | \theta_2^0, \ldots, \theta_r^0, x)$.
- Sample $\theta_2^1 \sim p(\theta_2 | \theta_1^1, \theta_3^0, \ldots, \theta_r^0, x)$.
- $\vdots$
- Sample $\theta_r^1 \sim p(\theta_r | \theta_1^1, \theta_2^1, \ldots, \theta_{r-1}^1, x)$.

This completes one Gibbs iteration and the parameters are updated to $(\theta_1^1, \ldots, \theta_r^1)$. Using these new parameters as our starting values, we repeat the iteration and obtain a new set of parameters $(\theta_1^2, \ldots, \theta_r^2)$. Repeating the iteration M times gives us a sequence of parameter vectors, $\theta^{(1)}, \ldots, \theta^{(M)}$, where $\theta^{(i)} = (\theta_1^i, \ldots, \theta_r^i)$, for $i = 1, \ldots, M$. By the basic limit theorem of the Markov chain, see Asmussen and Glynn (1987), the limiting distribution of Markov chain $\theta^{(M)}$ converges to the joint posterior $p(\theta_1, \theta_1, \ldots, \theta_r | x)$ when M is sufficiently large. M refers to the burn-in period. After simulating $\theta^{(M+1)}, \theta^{(M+2)}, \ldots, \theta^{(M+n)}$ from the Gibbs sampling, Bayesian inference can be conducted easily. For example, to compute the posterior mean, we evaluate

$$\widetilde{\theta}_i = \frac{1}{n} \sum_{i=1}^n \theta_i^{(M+i)}.$$

To acquire a better understanding of Gibbs sampling, consider the following example.

Example 8.7 *Generate the following bivariate normal random variables through Gibbs sampling.*

$$X = \begin{pmatrix} X_1 \\ X_2 \end{pmatrix} \sim \mathcal{N}\left(\begin{pmatrix} 0 \\ 0 \end{pmatrix}, \begin{pmatrix} 1 & \rho \\ \rho & 1 \end{pmatrix}\right).$$

We first find the conditional density functions of $X_1 | X_2$ and $X_2 | X_1$, that is, $f(x_1 | x_2)$ and $f(x_2 | x_1)$.

$$\begin{aligned}
f(x_1 | x_2) &= \frac{f(x_1, x_2)}{f(x_2)} \\
&= \frac{\frac{1}{2\pi\sqrt{1-\rho^2}} \exp\left(-\frac{x_1^2 - 2\rho x_1 x_2 + x_2^2}{2(1-\rho^2)}\right)}{\frac{1}{\sqrt{2\pi}} \exp\left(\frac{-x_2^2}{2}\right)} \\
&\propto \exp\left(-\frac{x_1^2 - 2\rho x_1 x_2 + x_2^2}{2(1-\rho^2)}\right) \exp\left(\frac{x_2^2}{2}\right)
\end{aligned}$$

$$\propto \exp\left(-\frac{x_1^2 - 2\rho x_1 x_2 + \rho^2 x_2^2}{2(1-\rho^2)}\right)$$

$$\propto \exp\left(-\frac{(x_1 - \rho x_2)^2}{2(1-\rho^2)}\right).$$

Observe that $X_1|x_2 \sim \mathcal{N}(\rho x_2, 1-\rho^2)$ and, similarly, $X_2|x_1 \sim \mathcal{N}(\rho x_1, 1-\rho^2)$. Then, the Gibbs sampling proceeds as follows.

1. Initialize x_2^0 and parameter ρ.
2. Set $i = 1$.
3. Generate $x_1^i \sim \mathcal{N}(\rho x_2^{i-1}, 1-\rho^2)$.
4. Generate $x_2^i \sim \mathcal{N}(\rho x_1^i, 1-\rho^2)$.
5. Set $i = i+1$ and repeat Steps 3 and 4 n times.
6. The sequence $(x_1^1, x_2^1), (x_1^2, x_2^2), \ldots, (x_1^n, x_2^n)$ forms n pairs of bivariate normal random variables.

The VBA code is as follows.

```
Dim x() As Double, y() As Double
Dim rho#, sigma As Double
N = 50000
rho = 0.5
sigma = 1 - rho ^ 2
ReDim x(0 To N)
ReDim y(0 To N)
y(0) = 0

For i = 1 To N
    x(i) = rho * y(i - 1) + Sqr(sigma) * rGauss()
    y(i) = rho * x(i) + Sqr(sigma) * rGauss()
Next i
```

Example 8.8 *Consider a portfolio comprising two stocks that satisfy*

$$dS_i(t) = \mu_i S_i(t)\,dt + \sigma_i S_i(t)\,dW_i(t), \text{ for } i = 1, 2,$$

$$E[dW_1(t)\,dW_2(t)] = \rho\,dt,$$

where $S_1(0) = 50$, $S_2(0) = 60$, $\mu_1 = 0.08$, $\mu_2 = 0.1$, $\sigma_1 = 0.35$, $\sigma_2 = 0.4$, and $\rho = 0.3$. Calculate the 10-day 95% VaR of a portfolio comprising 10,000 units of stock 1 and 10,000 units of stock 2.

330   VALUE-AT-RISK AND RELATED RISK MEASURES

TABLE 8.6 Monte Carlo Simulation of the Absolute and Relative VaRs (in Dollar and Return Terms) of a Two-Stock Portfolio Using Gibbs Sampling

	10-Day VaR
Absolute VaR in dollar	103,340
Relative VaR in dollar	107,150
Absolute VaR in return	0.09395
Relative VaR in return	0.09741

By Itô's lemma,

$$S_i(T) = S_i(0) \exp\left(\left(\mu_i - \frac{\sigma_i^2}{2}\right)T + \sigma_i\sqrt{T}X_i\right), \text{ for } i = 1, 2,$$

where

$$\begin{pmatrix} X_1 \\ X_2 \end{pmatrix} \sim \mathcal{N}\left(\begin{pmatrix} 0 \\ 0 \end{pmatrix}, \begin{pmatrix} 1 & \rho \\ \rho & 1 \end{pmatrix}\right).$$

The results of Example 25 allow simulation of the bivariate normal random variables (X_1, X_2) from which $S_1(T)$ and $S_2(T)$ are calculated accordingly. The results are summarized in Table 8.6.

The VBA code is as follows.

```
Dim x(), y() As Double
Dim rho#, variance#
Dim i&, T#, n#, confidence#, P0#
Dim S01#, q1#, sigma1#, mean1#, no1#
Dim S02#, q2#, sigma2#, mean2#, no2#
Dim ST1() As Double
Dim ST2() As Double
Dim rev() As Double

no1 = Cells(2, 2)
no2 = Cells(2, 3)
S01 = Cells(3, 2)
S02 = Cells(3, 3)
q1 = Cells(4, 2)
q2 = Cells(4, 3)
sigma1 = Cells(5, 2)
sigma2 = Cells(5, 3)
mean1 = Cells(6, 2)
mean2 = Cells(6, 3)
T = Cells(7, 2)
```

```
n = Cells(8, 2)
rho = Cells(9, 2)
confidence = Cells(10, 2)

variance = 1 - rho ^ 2
ReDim x(0 To n)
ReDim y(0 To n)
ReDim ST1(1 To n)
ReDim ST2(1 To n)
ReDim rev(1 To n)
y(0) = 0
If rho <> 1 Then
For i = 1 To n
x(i) = rho * y(i - 1) + Sqr(variance) * rGauss()
y(i) = rho * x(i) + Sqr(variance) * rGauss()
Next i
Else
For i = 1 To n
x(i) = rGauss()
y(i) = x(i)
Next i
End If

P0 = no1 * S01 + no2 * S02
For i = 1 To n
ST1(i) = S01 * Exp((mean1 - sigma1 ^ 2 / 2) * T + sigma1
   * Sqr(T) * x(i))
ST2(i) = S02 * Exp((mean2 - sigma2 ^ 2 / 2) * T + sigma2
   * Sqr(T) * y(i))
rev(i) = no1 * ST1(i) + no2 * ST2(i) - P0
Next i

Cells(13, 2) = -Percentile(rev, 1 - confidence)
Cells(14, 2) = -Percentile(rev, 1 - confidence)
   + Average(rev)
Cells(15, 2) = Cells(13, 2) / P0
Cells(16, 2) = Cells(14, 2) / P0
```

8.5.5 Advantages and Disadvantages

The advantages of Monte Carlo simulation are as follows.

1. The method is by far the most powerful for computing VaR because of its flexibility. It incorporates different volatility models, interest rate models, fat tails, and extreme scenarios.

2. It also incorporates the passage of time, which creates structural changes in the portfolio, including the time decay of options, the daily settlement of fixed, floating, or contractually specified cash flows, and the effect of prespecified trading or hedging strategies. These features are particularly important when the horizon lengthens, and are thus of particular importance in credit risk management.

The disadvantages of Monte Carlo simulation include the following.

1. The computational time required to calculate VaR is lengthy, particularly when the portfolio is large and contains exotic derivatives, whose valuation also requires the use of simulation.
2. The method suffers from model risk, which means that if the stochastic processes assumed for the assets are insufficiently realistic, then the VaR calculation may contain a large degree of uncertainties.

8.6 VaR-RELATED RISK MEASURES

Although VaR is a popular risk measure widely used by market practitioners, it has a number of limitations, in light of which several alternative risk measures have been proposed. The most popular of these is the coherent risk measure proposed by Artzner, Delbaen, Eber, and Heath (1999). Weaknesses of VaR are also detailed in McNeil, Frey, and Embrechts (2005).

Definition 8.3 *A risk measure ρ is coherent if it satisfies the four following axioms.*
(i) Monotonicity

$$\text{If } W_1 \leq W_2, \text{ then } \rho(W_1) \geq \rho(W_2),$$

which means that if portfolio W_2 has a higher return than portfolio W_1 in all scenarios, then the risk of W_1 should be larger than that of W_2.
(ii) Sub-additivity

$$\rho(W_1 + W_2) \leq \rho(W_1) + \rho(W_2),$$

which shows that merging portfolios together cannot have greater risk than adding the partial risks separately. This is the idea behind portfolio diversification.
(iii) Positive homogeneity

$$\rho(\alpha W) = \alpha \rho(W).$$

In other words, increasing the size of a portfolio should increase its risk by the same factor.

(iv) Translation invariance

$$\rho(W + a) = \rho(W) - a.$$

In other words, adding an amount of cash to the portfolio should reduce its risk by the same amount, as it acts as insurance.

One of the aforementioned limitations of VaR is that it is not a coherent risk measure because it fails to satisfy the sub-additivity property. Portfolio diversification is thus discouraged when VaR is used. In this section, we introduce some of the coherent risk measures that serve as alternatives to VaR.

8.6.1 Conditional Value-at-Risk

VaR has the advantage of simple implementation. For portfolios with a low probability of extremely large losses, VaR fails to represent the amount of risk suffered beyond the VaR value. In addition, as just stated, VaR is not a coherent risk measure. As an alternatives, a coherent risk measure, conditional Value-at-Risk (CVaR), is introduced. CVaR is also called expected shortfall (ES) or expected tail loss (ETL) and is defined as follows.

Definition 8.4 *CVaR at the $\alpha\%$ level is the expected loss of a portfolio with value X_t at time t in the worst $\alpha\%$ of cases.*

For example, 10-day CVaR$_{10\%}$ represents the average losses over a 10-day period provided that the loss is in the 10% left tail. This quantity helps us summarize the expected loss that might be suffered beyond a given confidence level.

Suppose that we have n sorted realizations, $x_1, \ldots, x_n$, of random variable X and that $\alpha\%$ of the case is equal to $[n\alpha]$, which is the maximum integer that is no greater than $n\alpha$. The simplest non-parametric estimate for CVaR is given by

$$\text{CVaR}_\alpha = -\frac{1}{[n\alpha]} \sum_{i=1}^{[n\alpha]} x_i. \tag{8.10}$$

A more formal definition of CVaR can be stated as follows.

Definition 8.5 *Suppose that X is the value of a portfolio with horizon T and confidence level $(1 - \alpha\%)$. Then, CVaR is defined as*

$$\begin{aligned} \text{CVaR}_\alpha &= -\frac{1}{\alpha} \int_0^\alpha \text{VaR}_\alpha(X) \, d\alpha \\ &= -\frac{1}{\alpha} \left(E[X 1_{\{X \leq x_\alpha\}}] - x_\alpha (\Pr(X \leq x_\alpha) - \alpha) \right), \end{aligned}$$

where x_α is the $\alpha\%$ left tail of the distribution.

For a continuous distribution function of the portfolio, CVaR can be defined as follows.

$$CVaR_\alpha = E[-X_t | X_t < -VaR_\alpha]$$
$$= VaR_\alpha + E[\max\{-VaR_\alpha - X_t, 0\} | X_t < -VaR_\alpha].$$

The methods used to calculate CVaR are the same as those used for VaR. They include the parametric, historical simulation and Monte Carlo simulation approaches. We illustrate only the Monte Carlo simulation approach here.

With n simulated values $x_t^i, i = 1, \ldots, n$, $CVaR_\alpha$ is estimated by

$$\widehat{CVaR}_\alpha = \widehat{VaR}_\alpha + \frac{1}{n\alpha} \sum_{i=1}^{n} \max\{-\widehat{VaR}_\alpha - x_t^i, 0\}. \tag{8.11}$$

The procedure used to calculate CVaR is as follows.

1. Generate n final values of portfolio $x_1, \ldots, x_n$.
2. Rank the x_i's such that x_1 is the smallest and x_n is the largest.
3. Set $VaR_\alpha = -x_{n\alpha}$ and $CVaR_\alpha = -\frac{1}{[n\alpha]} \sum_{i=1}^{[n\alpha]} x_i$ or $CVaR_\alpha = VaR_\alpha + \frac{1}{n\alpha} \sum_{i=1}^{n} \max\{-VaR_\alpha - x_i, 0\}$.

Example 8.9 *Find the $CVaR_{5\%}$ for a stock return following a normal distribution with $\mu = 0.01$ and $\sigma = 0.3$ and assume that the initial portfolio value is $1 million.*

After calculation, the absolute VaR is 476,983, and the CVaR generated by Equations 8.10 and 8.11 is the same, that is, 601,212. The corresponding VBA code is as follows.

```
For i = 1 To n
    valuef(i) = value0 * (mean + sigma * rGauss())
Next i

'Calculation of VaR
VaR = -Percentile(valuef, alpha)

'sort R()
Call Sort(valuef)

'CVaR under equation(1)
cutoff = n * alpha
es = 0
For i = 1 To cutoff
es = es + valuef(i)
```

```
Next i
CVaR1 = -es / cutoff

'CVaR under equation(2)
tmp = 0
For i = 1 To n
    tmp = tmp + Max(-Cells(8, 2) - valuef(i), 0)
Next i
CVaR2 = VaR + tmp / cutoff
```

8.6.2 CVaR Distribution

Similar to VaR, we can use the CVaR distribution as a risk measure.

Example 8.10 *Find the distribution of $CVaR_{5\%}$ for the stock return in Example 8.9.*

The results are illustrated in Figure 8.5.

8.6.3 Marginal, Incremental, and Component VaRs

In the case of portfolio selection, marginal, incremental, and component VaRs are used to measure the impact of changing positions on portfolio risk. Only a brief

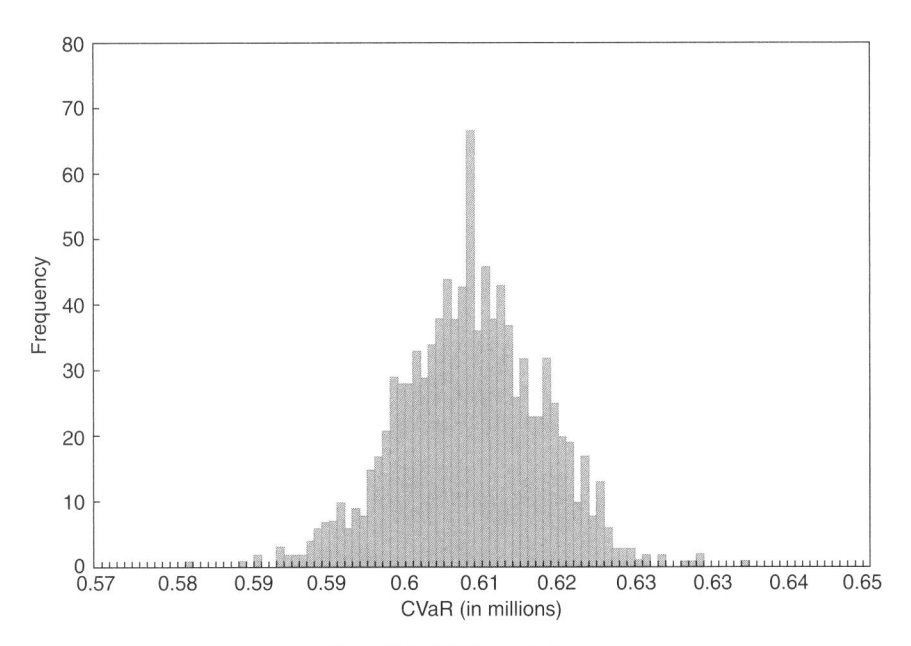

Figure 8.5 CVaR distribution.

introduction to these VaR tools is given here. For more thorough coverage, please refer to other books specializing in these topics, for example, Jorion (2007).

Definition 8.6 *Marginal VaR is the change in portfolio VaR resulting from an additional dollar of exposure to a given component i.*

The expression for marginal VaR is

$$\Delta \text{VaR}_i = z_\alpha \frac{\text{Cov}(R_i, R_p)}{\sigma_p} = z_\alpha \beta_i \sigma_p = \frac{\text{VaR}_p}{W} \beta_i.$$

Marginal VaR is often used in portfolio management. For example, if an investor wants to change his or her position to reduce the portfolio VaR, then he or she can rank the marginal VaRs of all components and choose that with the largest ΔVaR to achieve the greatest reduction in VaR.

Incremental VaR is a viable means of measuring the impact of changing positions on portfolio risk.

Definition 8.7 *Incremental VaR is the change in portfolio VaR owing to a new position A.*

$$\text{Incremental VaR} = \text{VaR}_{p+A} - \text{VaR}_p.$$

It is time-consuming to evaluate incremental VaR, particularly for large portfolios. An approximation by Taylor series expansion of VaR_{p+A} is thus proposed:

$$\text{Incremental VaR} \approx \Delta \text{VaR} \times A.$$

This approximation requires only one valuation because ΔVaR can be obtained through initial VaR_p computation and is thus much faster. To investigate the contribution of an individual component of the portfolio risk, we can employ component VaR.

Definition 8.8 *Component VaR is the decomposition of portfolio VaR to determine how much it would change if a given component was deleted.*

$$\text{Component VaR}_i = \Delta \text{VaR}_i w_i W = \text{VaR}_p \beta_i w_i,$$
$$\text{Component VaR}_i + \cdots + \text{Component VaR}_N = \text{VaR}_p.$$

Component VaR can also be expressed as individual VaR multiplied by the correlation coefficient between component i and the portfolio.

8.6.4 VaR and CVaR in Local Volatility Models

We now demonstrate the estimation of the VaR and CVaR of shorting a plain vanilla European call option using importance sampling under a local volatility model with initial stock price S_0, strike price K, risk-free rate r, time-to-maturity T, number of steps m, and number of paths n. Suppose that at each step i, for $i = 1, \ldots, m$, instead of generating a standard normal random variable Z_i with density

$$f(z) = \frac{1}{\sqrt{2\pi}} \exp\left(-\frac{z^2}{2}\right),$$

we generate a normal variable Y_i with mean μ, variance 1, and density

$$g(y) = \frac{1}{\sqrt{2\pi}} \exp\left(-\frac{(y-\mu)^2}{2}\right).$$

Define

$$h(y) = \frac{f(y)}{g(y)} = \exp\left(\frac{\mu^2 - 2\mu y}{2}\right),$$

$$L(y_1, \ldots, y_m) = \prod_{i=1}^{m} h(y_i),$$

where L is the likelihood ratio function. Denote

$$P_j = \max\{S_T^j - K, 0\},$$

$$L_j = L(y_1^j, \ldots, y_m^j).$$

Here, P_j is the payoff of a call option at maturity with respect to the jth simulated path, and y_i^j is the normal random variable used in simulating the ith step of the jth path, which implies L_j is the likelihood ratio for the jth simulated path. Then the price P of the foregoing call option is estimated by

$$P = \frac{e^{-rt}}{n} \sum_{j=1}^{n} P_j L_j.$$

To calculate the α-VaR of shorting this call option, we denote the profit and loss of the jth simulated path by

$$X_T^j = P - P_j.$$

Here, we find a value VaR_α such that

$$\alpha = \frac{1}{n} \sum_{j=1}^{n} 1_{\{X_T^j \leq -\text{VaR}_\alpha\}} L_j. \tag{8.12}$$

To estimate $\widehat{\text{VaR}}_\alpha$ using Equation 8.12, we implement the following steps.

1. Sort the X_T^j such that $X_T^{(1)}$ is the smallest and $X_T^{(n)}$ the largest.
2. Set $k = 1, \theta = 0$.
3. Set $\theta = \theta + L_{(k)}$.
4. If $\theta \geq n\alpha$, then set $\text{VaR}_\alpha = -X_T^k$; otherwise, continue with Step 5.
5. Set $k = k + 1$ and return to Step 3.

For Step 4, instead of calculating $\widehat{\text{VaR}}_\alpha$ with the payoff having a θ larger than $n\alpha$, we can also estimate VaR_α by interpolating the two payoffs when θ is smaller and larger than $n\alpha$, although the difference between the estimates of these two methods is minor. The revised steps are as follows.

1. Sort the X_T^j such that $X_T^{(1)}$ is the smallest and $X_T^{(n)}$ the largest.
2. Set $k = 1, \theta = 0$.
3. Set $\theta = \theta + L_{(k)}$.
4. If $\theta \geq n\alpha$, then set $\text{VaR}_\alpha = -\frac{aX_T^{(k-1)} + bX_T^{(k)}}{a+b}$, where $a = \theta - n\alpha$ and $b = L_{(k)} - a$; otherwise, continue with Step 5.
5. Set $k = k + 1$ and return to Step 3.

In calculating α-CVaR in importance sampling, similar to Equation 8.10, we can compute it by

$$\widehat{\text{CVaR}}_\alpha = \widehat{\text{VaR}}_\alpha + \frac{1}{n\alpha} \sum_{j=1}^{n} \max\{-\widehat{\text{VaR}}_\alpha - X_T^j, 0\} L_j.$$

With $S_0 = 50, r = 5\%, q = 0\%, n = 10,000, dt = 1/360$, and the local volatility function specified in Equation 4.4, we repeat the simulation 50 times to calculate the VaR and CVaR of European call options with different strikes. We first consider an ATM call option with $K = 50$, and the results are presented in Table 8.7.

It can be seen that although normal simulation and importance sampling produce a similar call option price, VaR, and CVaR, the standard deviation of the simulated values is much smaller for the latter, which suggests the efficacy of this approach. We can also see from these results that whether we employ interpolation to calculate VaR is irrelevant because the two methods give nearly identical results.

For in-the-money (with $K = 40$) and out-of-the-money (with $K = 60$) call options, the performance of importance sampling is similar to that in the ATM

TABLE 8.7 Performance of Importance Sampling for an ATM Call Option

Normal simulation	Mean	Standard deviation
Price	6.05916	0.082873
95% VaR	15.2651	0.175508
95% CVaR	19.0993	0.213756
Importance sampling	Mean	Standard deviation
Price	6.06607	0.028360
95% VaR	15.2691	0.099851
95% VaR (with interpolation)	15.2708	0.100082
95% CVaR	19.1328	0.105419

case, and the results are presented in Tables 8.8 and 8.9, respectively. Note that we calculate VaR and CVaR by shorting the call option, and thus the in-the-money call gives the highest VaR and CVaR and the out-of-the-money call the lowest. For further details, please refer to Ch8.7_Conditional_VaR_Local_Volatility.xls.

8.7 VaR BACK-TESTING

The Basel Accords permit banks to use their own internal rating-based approaches to calculate their capital reserves, although that for market risk should be greater than 8% of the estimated economic capital, where the economic capital is three times the 10-day 99% VaR for an approved method. Overestimating VaR is fine with the regulator, but is disadvantageous to the bank because an excessive capital reserve reduces investment capital. However, underestimating VaR is not premitted by the regulator, and thus banks should calculate their reserve capital using a standardized approach. As a bank has no control over its capital reserve, the VaR method has important implications for its investment strategy.

In this chapter, we have introduced many different ways to calculate the approximations of VaR. To ensure that a VaR approach works well, back-testing is essential and is a central feature of the Basel Accords. Back-testing is a formal statistical technique that verifies whether actual losses are in line with projected losses. VaR

TABLE 8.8 Performance of Importance Sampling for an In-the-Money Call Option

Normal simulation	Mean	Standard deviation
Price	13.07589	0.108326
95% VaR	18.29677	0.194798
95% CVaR	22.14008	0.214461
Importance sampling	Mean	Standard deviation
Price	13.01518	0.056723
95% VaR	18.34482	0.137871
95% VaR (with interpolation)	18.34592	0.137954
95% CVaR	22.21663	0.143620

TABLE 8.9 Performance of Importance Sampling for an Out-of-the-Money Call Option

Normal simulation	Mean	Standard deviation
Price	1.817794	0.050934
95% VaR	9.581228	0.195291
95% CVaR	13.46969	0.228505
Importance sampling	Mean	Standard deviation
Price	1.808660	0.015583
95% VaR	9.551457	0.087970
95% VaR (with interpolation)	9.552682	0.088029
95% CVaR	13.40637	0.095607

back-testing involves systematic comparison of the history of VaR forecasts with their associated portfolio returns.

8.7.1 Back-Testing of VaR Models

Model back-testing systematically compares historical VaR measures with subsequent returns. Because VaR is reported at a specified confidence level, say, 95%, we would expect only 5% of observations to exceed the predicted VaR level. As this percentage may deviate from 5% if the variation in observations is great, we have to decide whether "to accept" or "to reject" the model, which consititutes typical statistical hypothesis testing.

The simplest method for checking the validity of a VaR model is to calculate the failure rate, that is, the number of times that the VaR is exceeded in a given sample. Suppose that there are T trading days in a year and that the bank requires the VaR to be based on a $(1 - \alpha)$ confidence level (say $\alpha = 0.05$). Let N be the number of failure days in a year. Then, the failure rate is $\frac{N}{T}$, and the expected failure rate is $E[\frac{N}{T}] = \alpha$. Now, we have to deal with the following hypothesis testing problem.

$$H_0 : E[\frac{N}{T}] = \alpha \text{ against } H_1 : E[\frac{N}{T}] \neq \alpha.$$

The setup of this test can be tackled with Bernoulli trials. Let X_j be a Bernoulli random variable for $j = 1, \ldots, T$, that is,

$$X_j = \begin{cases} 1, & \text{for a failure day with probability } \alpha, \\ 0, & \text{for not a failure day with probability } 1 - \alpha. \end{cases}$$

Therefore, $N = \sum_{j=1}^{T} X_j$ follows a Binomial distribution with mean $E[N] = \alpha T$ and variance $\text{Var}(N) = \alpha(1-\alpha)T$. By the Central Limit Theorem, the Binomial distribution can be approximated by a normal distribution:

$$Z = \frac{N - \alpha T}{\sqrt{\alpha(1-\alpha)T}} \xrightarrow{\mathcal{L}} \mathcal{N}(0, 1) \text{ as } T \to \infty.$$

Hypothesis testing then becomes

$$H_0 : E[Z] = 0 \text{ against } H_1 : E[Z] \neq 0.$$

Using the Central Limit Theorem with a large sample size, Kupiec (1995) developed a method that approximates the 95% confidence regions for such a test using likelihood ratio statistics. These regions are defined by the tail points of the log-likelihood ratio:

$$\text{LR} = -2\log\left[(1-\alpha)^{(T-N)}\alpha^N\right] + 2\log\left[\left(1-\frac{N}{T}\right)^{(T-N)}\left(\frac{N}{T}\right)^N\right] \sim \chi_1^2,$$

that is, the log-likelihood ratio follows a chi-squared distribution with one degree of freedom. We reject the model if LR > 3.84 with a 5% type-I error.

For example, a company wants to test for a VaR model with returns in the past 255 (T) trading days (approximately 1 year). The company would like to determine the rejection region based on the number of days (N) that the model fails to forecast the 99% VaR ($\alpha = 1\%$). Suppose further that the company can tolerate a type-I error of 5% ($p = 5\%$). Using the back-testing formula, we have

$$\text{LR} = -2\log\left[0.99^{(255-N)}0.01^N\right] + 2\log\left[\left(1-\frac{N}{255}\right)^{(255-N)}\left(\frac{N}{255}\right)^N\right] > 3.84.$$

Solving the above inequality numerically, we obtain $N < 7$, where N is an integer. It means that the model is not rejected with a 5% type-I error if the number of failures in a year is less than 7 days. This information then provides a guideline for selecting a model with 99% VaR for 255 trading days.

One simple way to apply this result is to convert it into a tabular form as follows. If we want to reject a $c\%$ VaR model ($\alpha = 1 - c\%$) with a 5% ($p = 5\%$) type-I error, then the following Table 8.10 extracted from Jorion (2007) can be used to construct the desired critical region.

TABLE 8.10 Critical Regions for VaR

α	Confidence intervals for $p = 0.05$		
	$T = 255$	$T = 510$	$T = 1000$
0.01	$N < 7$	$1 < N < 11$	$4 < N < 17$
0.025	$2 < N < 12$	$6 < N < 21$	$15 < N < 36$
0.05	$6 < N < 21$	$16 < N < 36$	$37 < N < 65$
0.075	$11 < N < 28$	$27 < N < 51$	$59 < N < 92$
0.10	$16 < N < 36$	$38 < N < 65$	$81 < N < 120$

9

The Greeks

This chapter describes several applications of Greeks and their calculation in different situations, including direct differentiation, the binomial tree, finite difference approximation, pathwise derivative estimation, adjoint simulation, and the likelihood ratio method. These methods may not be suitable for all types of options. For example, the pathwise derivative method cannot be used to compute the Greeks of a digital option. As an application example, we demonstrate the use of adjoint simulation in the LIBOR market model.

Let $V(t, S, K, r, q, \sigma, T)$ be the value function of an option, where the current underlying asset price is S, volatility is σ, the dividend yield is q, the strike price is K, the time-to-expiration is $T - t$, and the risk-free interest rate is r. As the strike price is fixed, we have six first-order derivatives of the option price with respect to each of these variables. When calculating Greeks, we assume that everything remains fixed except for the underlying variable under consideration. The following is a list of some common Greeks.

- Delta: The rate of change of an option price with respect to the change in the underlying asset price:

$$\Delta = \frac{\partial V}{\partial S}.$$

Handbook of Financial Risk Management: Simulations and Case Studies, First Edition. N.H. Chan and H.Y. Wong.
© 2013 John Wiley & Sons, Inc. Published 2013 by John Wiley & Sons, Inc.

344 THE GREEKS

- Vega: The rate of change of an option price with respect to the change of the underlying asset's volatility:

$$\nu = \frac{\partial V}{\partial \sigma}.$$

- Theta: The rate of change of an option price with respect to time, which is also called the time decay of the option:

$$\Theta = \frac{\partial V}{\partial t}.$$

- Rho: The rate of change of an option price with respect to the risk-free interest rate:

$$\rho = \frac{\partial V}{\partial r}.$$

- Gamma: The rate of change of delta with respect to the underlying asset price, which is also called curvature, as it measures the curvature of the option price curve against the underlying asset price:

$$\Gamma = \frac{\partial^2 V}{\partial S^2}.$$

For an exotic option, there can be multiple deltas or other Greeks. As an example, consider a crack spread option in the commodity market whose payoff function is $\max\{S_2(T) - S_1(T) - K, 0\}$, where $S_i(T)$ is the price at the expiration time T for underlying assets $i = 1$ and $i = 2$. This option has two deltas, one for each of the underlying assets:

$$\Delta_1 = \frac{\partial V}{\partial S_1} \text{ and } \Delta_2 = \frac{\partial V}{\partial S_2}.$$

To allow general discussion, we also provide definitions for several uncommon Greeks, all of which (except Psi) are higher-order derivatives of the option price with respect to the common variables. They are given in Table 9.1.

The Greek of a portfolio is simply the sum of such Greeks of individual instruments constituting the portfolio. Let Π be the portfolio value, V_i be the value of the ith instrument, and w_i be the unit of holding in the ith instrument, for $i = 1, \ldots, n$. Then,

$$\Pi = \sum_{i=1}^{n} w_i V_i.$$

TABLE 9.1 Some Uncommon Greeks

Name	Definition
Psi	$\dfrac{\partial V}{\partial q}$
Speed	$\dfrac{\partial^3 V}{\partial S^3}$
Vanna	$\dfrac{\partial^2 V}{\partial S \partial \sigma}$
Vomma	$\dfrac{\partial^2 V}{\partial \sigma^2}$

Thus,

$$\frac{\partial \Pi}{\partial \theta} = \sum_{i=1}^{n} w_i \frac{\partial V_i}{\partial \theta},$$

where θ is any of the common variables.

Greeks are useful in risk management, the most obvious being hedging. Delta hedging is a hedging strategy that aims to eliminate the delta of a portfolio. After application of the delta hedging strategy, the portfolio is called a delta-neutral portfolio. In this way, a small change in an asset price will not cause a large change in the overall portfolio value. However, option deltas change over time such that the hedger must frequently rebalance the portfolio to ensure it remains delta-neutral. A long position in a call option has a positive delta, whereas a short position has a negative delta. The opposite is true for a put option. The delta of a stock is 1. Therefore, a portfolio can be delta-hedged by buying or short-selling the stock dynamically. Although this strategy sounds reasonable in theory, the transaction costs associated with buying and selling the underlying asset could ruin the dynamic hedging portfolio.

Option elasticity, Ω, measures the percentage change in the option price relative to that in the stock price. It is also referred to as effective gearing.

$$\Omega = \frac{\frac{\partial V}{V}}{\frac{\partial S}{S}} = \frac{S}{V} \Delta.$$

The ratio $\frac{S}{V}$ is called simple gearing.

A gamma-neutral strategy aims to eliminate the change in delta in order to reduce the frequency of portfolio rebalancing. A large gamma implies that the delta will change significantly when the stock price changes. In other words, delta hedging will be less effective if the portfolio has a large gamma. As a result, a trader may need to make the portfolio gamma-neutral. In practice, a trader first makes a derivative position gamma-neutral by using derivatives in the market and then delta-neutral by using the underlying asset. A delta–gamma neutral portfolio helps the trader market the profit and loss of a derivative portfolio.

TABLE 9.2 Closed-Form Greeks of European Call Options in the BS Model

Greeks	Call (long position)
Delta	$e^{-q(T-t)}\Psi(d_1)$
Gamma	$\dfrac{e^{-q(T-t)}\psi(d_1)}{S\sigma\sqrt{T-t}}$
Theta	$Sqe^{-q(T-t)}\Psi(d_1) - rKe^{-r(T-t)}\Psi(d_2) - \dfrac{\sigma Se^{-q(T-t)}\psi(d_1)}{2\sqrt{T-t}}$
Vega	$S\sqrt{T-t}\,e^{-q(T-t)}\psi(d_1)$
Rho	$K(T-t)e^{-r(T-t)}\Psi(d_2)$

In the VaR discussion in Chapter 8, we noted that Greeks, such as the delta, gamma, and vega, are possible candidates for improving VaR computation for a derivative position. This chapter concentrates on simulating Greeks in high-dimensional problems.

9.1 BLACK–SCHOLES GREEKS

The closed-form solutions for the Greeks of European call and put options under the Black–Scholes (BS) model are summarized in Tables 9.2 and 9.3. Note that the gamma and vega are the same for call and put options. The Greeks in a short position are the negative of the same Greeks in a long position.

Here, $\psi(\cdot)$ and $\Psi(\cdot)$ are the pdf and cdf of the normal distribution, respectively.

In the following, we derive the remaining common Greeks of a European call option in the BS model. Recall that if the underlying asset of a stock follows the GBM under risk-neutral measure

$$\frac{dS(t)}{S(t)} = (r-q)\,dt + \sigma\,dW(t),$$

then the call and put option prices are given by

$$c(S, K, t, r, q, \sigma, T) = Se^{-q(T-t)}\Psi(d_1) - Ke^{-r(T-t)}\Psi(d_2),$$

$$p(S, K, t, r, q, \sigma, T) = Ke^{-r(T-t)}\Psi(-d_2) - Se^{-q(T-t)}\Psi(-d_1),$$

TABLE 9.3 Closed-Form Greeks of European Put Options in the BS Model

Greeks	Put (long position)
Delta	$e^{-q(T-t)}(\Psi(d_1) - 1)$
Gamma	$\dfrac{e^{-q(T-t)}\psi(d_1)}{S\sigma\sqrt{T-t}}$
Theta	$-Sqe^{-q(T-t)}\Psi(-d_1) + rKe^{-r(T-t)}\Psi(-d_2) - \dfrac{\sigma Se^{-q(T-t)}\psi(d_1)}{2\sqrt{T-t}}$
Vega	$S\sqrt{T-t}\,e^{-q(T-t)}\psi(d_1)$
Rho	$-K(T-t)e^{-r(T-t)}\Psi(-d_2)$

with

$$d_1 = \frac{\log \frac{S}{K} + \left(r - q + \frac{\sigma^2}{2}\right)(T-t)}{\sigma\sqrt{T-t}},$$

$$d_2 = d_1 - \sigma\sqrt{T-t},$$

where S is the current stock price, K is the strike price, t is the current time, r is the risk-free interest rate, q is the dividend yield, σ is the volatility and T is the maturity. The following relationship is useful.

$$Se^{-q(T-t)}\psi(d_1) = K\psi(d_2)e^{-r(T-t)}.$$

To see it, consider

$$\psi(d_1) = \psi(d_2 + \sigma\sqrt{T-t})$$

$$= \frac{1}{\sqrt{2\pi}} \exp\left(-\frac{d_2^2}{2} - d_2\sigma\sqrt{T-t} - \frac{\sigma^2(T-t)}{2}\right)$$

$$= \psi(d_2) \exp\left(-d_2\sigma\sqrt{T-t} - \frac{\sigma^2(T-t)}{2}\right)$$

$$= \psi(d_2) \exp\left(-\log\left(\frac{S}{K}\right) - (r-q)(T-t)\right)$$

$$= \frac{K}{S}\psi(d_2)e^{-(r-q)(T-t)}.$$

In addition,

$$d_1 - d_2 = \sigma\sqrt{T-t}$$

and

$$\frac{\partial d_1}{\partial S} = \frac{\partial d_2}{\partial S} = \frac{1}{S\sigma\sqrt{T-t}}.$$

The delta of the call is computed as

$$\frac{\partial c}{\partial S} = e^{-q(T-t)}\Psi(d_1) + Se^{-q(T-t)}\frac{\partial \Psi(d_1)}{\partial S} - Ke^{-r(T-t)}\frac{\partial \Psi(d_2)}{\partial S}$$

$$= e^{-q(T-t)}\Psi(d_1) + Se^{-q(T-t)}\psi(d_1)\frac{\partial d_1}{\partial S} - Ke^{-r(T-t)}\psi(d_2)\frac{\partial d_2}{\partial S}$$

$$= e^{-q(T-t)}\Psi(d_1) + \frac{\partial d_1}{\partial S}\left(S\psi(d_1)e^{-q(T-t)} - K\psi(d_2)e^{-r(T-t)}\right)$$

$$= e^{-q(T-t)}\Psi(d_1).$$

Hence, the gamma of the call is

$$\frac{\partial^2 c}{\partial S^2} = \frac{\partial}{\partial S}(e^{-q(T-t)}\Psi(d_1))$$

$$= e^{-q(T-t)}\psi(d_1)\frac{\partial d_1}{\partial S}$$

$$= \frac{e^{-q(T-t)}\psi(d_1)}{S\sigma\sqrt{T-t}}.$$

The call theta is then deduced from the BS equation. To derive the call vega, consider

$$\frac{\partial c}{\partial \sigma} = Se^{-q(T-t)}\psi(d_1)\frac{\partial d_1}{\partial \sigma} - Ke^{-r(T-t)}\psi(d_2)\frac{\partial d_2}{\partial \sigma}$$

$$= Se^{-q(T-t)}\psi(d_1)\left(\frac{\partial d_1}{\partial \sigma} - \frac{\partial d_2}{\partial \sigma}\right)$$

$$= S\sqrt{T-t}\, e^{-q(T-t)}\psi(d_1).$$

Similarly, the rho of a call is calculated as

$$\frac{\partial c}{\partial r} = Se^{-q(T-t)}\psi(d_1)\frac{\partial d_1}{\partial r} + Ke^{-r(T-t)}\Psi(d_2) - Ke^{-r(T-t)}\psi(d_2)\frac{\partial d_2}{\partial r}$$

$$= Se^{-q(T-t)}\left(\frac{\partial d_1}{\partial r} - \frac{\partial d_2}{\partial r}\right) + Ke^{-r(T-t)}\Psi(d_2)$$

$$= K(T-t)e^{-r(T-t)}\Psi(d_2).$$

9.2 GREEKS IN A BINOMIAL TREE

A binomial tree or binomial option pricing model is a discrete-time model that is useful for pricing American and other exotic options. In this section, we briefly introduce how the common Greeks are obtained in a binomial tree.

Consider a stock that pays dividends at rate q where S is the initial stock price. In each period, the stock goes up by a factor u to S_u or down by a factor d to S_d. The corresponding option prices are c_u and c_d, and c_0 is the option price when stock price does not move. If the stock price goes up in one period and down in the next one, then define that stock price as S_{ud} and the corresponding option price to be c_{ud}.

1. *Delta* The delta is essentially the number of shares of the stock that must be bought to replicate the option. Recall that to replicate the option, we must buy Δ shares of the stock and invest B dollars in a risk-free bond, with all dividends reinvested to buy additional shares. To replicate the value of the option after

one period, we require that

$$\Delta e^{q\delta t} S_u + B e^{r\delta t} = c_u,$$
$$\Delta e^{q\delta t} S_d + B e^{r\delta t} = c_d.$$

Solving the equations, we have

$$\Delta = e^{-q\delta t} \frac{c_u - c_d}{S_u - S_d}$$
$$= e^{-q\delta t} \frac{\text{change in option price}}{\text{change in stock price}}.$$

As δt tends to zero, we have

$$\Delta = \frac{\partial c}{\partial S}.$$

2. *Gamma* Note that we cannot compute the gamma at time 0. Its estimate at time δt is given by

$$\Gamma(S_{\delta t}, \delta t) = \frac{\Delta(S_u) - \Delta(S_d)}{S_u - S_d}.$$

3. *Theta* If $u = \frac{1}{d}$, then we can estimate the theta by

$$\Theta = \frac{c_{ud} - c_0}{2\delta t}.$$

Otherwise, we can employ delta–gamma–theta approximation:

$$dc = \Delta\, dS + \Theta\, dt + \frac{1}{2}\Gamma\, (dS)^2.$$

Rearranging terms, we have

$$\Theta = \frac{1}{2\delta t}\left(c_{ud} - c_0 - \Delta(S_{ud} - S) - \frac{1}{2}\Gamma(S_{ud} - S)^2\right).$$

4. *Rho* Rho calculation cannot be performed with a single tree. We have to construct another tree with a small change in the interest rate to obtain a new option price, holding all else the same. The rho estimate is

$$\rho = \frac{c_0^* - c_0}{\delta r},$$

where c_0^* is calculated using the new interest rate $r + \delta r$.

5. *Vega* The calculation of the vega is very similar to that of the rho. The vega estimate is

$$\sigma = \frac{c_0^* - c_0}{\delta\sigma},$$

where c_0^* is calculated using the new volatility $\sigma + \delta\sigma$.

9.3 FINITE DIFFERENCE APPROXIMATION

In addition to closed-form solutions, finite difference approximation can also be used. Although it is the simplest method of calculating the Greeks of options, it produces biased estimates.

To begin with, we define a "big O" and "little o" as follows.

Definition 9.1 *(Big O) We say that*

$$f(x) = O(g(x)) \quad (x \to \infty)$$

if and only if there exists a positive real number M and a real number x_0 such that

$$|f(x)| \leq M |g(x)|$$

for all $x > x_0$.

Definition 9.2 *(Little o) We say that*

$$f(x) = o(g(x)) \quad (x \to x_0)$$

if

$$\lim_{x \to x_0} \frac{f(x)}{g(x)} = 0.$$

If $x_0 = 0$, then we say informally that $f(x)$ goes to zero at a faster speed than $g(x)$ as x goes to zero.

To approximate the first-order derivatives, we can use the forward difference, backward difference, or central finite difference schemes. To approximate the second-order derivatives, we must use the second-order central difference scheme. These methods can be derived from Taylor series expansion.

Suppose that we are interested in finding the derivative of $\alpha(\theta)$ with respect to θ, where $\alpha(\theta) = E[Y(\theta)]$; $\alpha(\theta)$ is the option price, θ is the stock price, and $Y(\theta)$ is the discounted payoff function. As we assume that the other parameters do not change, we write $\alpha(\theta) = E[Y(\theta)]$.

Consider the function $\alpha(\theta)$. By Taylor series expansion,

$$\alpha(\theta + h) = \alpha(\theta) + h\alpha'(\theta) + \frac{h^2}{2}\alpha''(\theta) + o(h^2),$$

provided that α is twice-differentiable at θ. Rearranging the foregoing expression, we have

$$\alpha'(\theta) = \frac{\alpha(\theta + h) - \alpha(\theta)}{h} - \frac{h}{2}\alpha''(\theta) - o(h).$$

Therefore, we can approximate $\alpha'(\theta)$ by

$$\alpha'(\theta) = \frac{\alpha(\theta + h) - \alpha(\theta)}{h}$$

$$= \frac{E[Y(\theta + h)] - E[Y(\theta)]}{h}.$$

This scheme is called the forward difference scheme. The forward difference estimator is given by

$$\Delta_F = \frac{\overline{Y}_n(\theta + h) - \overline{Y}_n(\theta)}{h}.$$

The bias of the forward difference estimator is

$$\text{Bias}(\Delta_F) = E[\Delta_F] - \alpha'(\theta)$$

$$= \frac{\alpha(\theta + h) - \alpha(\theta)}{h} - \left(\frac{\alpha(\theta + h) - \alpha(\theta)}{h} - \frac{h}{2}\alpha''(\theta) - o(h)\right)$$

$$= \frac{h}{2}\alpha''(\theta) + o(h).$$

Now, consider the central finite difference scheme. Again, by Taylor series expansion, we have

$$\alpha(\theta + h) = \alpha(\theta) + h\alpha'(\theta) + \frac{h^2}{2}\alpha''(\theta) + \frac{h^3}{6}\alpha'''(\theta) + o(h^3),$$

$$\alpha(\theta - h) = \alpha(\theta) - h\alpha'(\theta) + \frac{h^2}{2}\alpha''(\theta) - \frac{h^3}{6}\alpha'''(\theta) + o(h^3),$$

given that α'' is also differentiable at θ. Subtracting these equations, we have

$$\alpha'(\theta) = \frac{\alpha(\theta + h) - \alpha(\theta - h)}{2h} - \frac{h^2}{6}\alpha'''(\theta) - o(h^2).$$

Similar to the forward difference estimator, we have the following central difference estimator.

$$\Delta_C = \frac{\overline{Y}_n(\theta + h) - \overline{Y}_n(\theta - h)}{2h}.$$

The bias of the central difference estimator is

$$\text{Bias}(\Delta_C) = E[\Delta_C] - \alpha'(\theta)$$

$$= \frac{\alpha(\theta + h) - \alpha(\theta - h)}{2h} - \left(\frac{\alpha(\theta + h) - \alpha(\theta - h)}{2h} - \frac{h^2}{6}\alpha'''(\theta) - o(h^2)\right)$$

$$= \frac{h^2}{6}\alpha'''(\theta) + o(h^2).$$

It can be seen that the central difference estimator has a smaller bias than the forward difference estimator. However, the former requires the computation of both $\overline{Y}_n(\theta + h)$ and $\overline{Y}_n(\theta - h)$, whereas the latter requires $\overline{Y}_n(\theta + h)$ alone (as $\overline{Y}_n(\theta)$ is calculated in the pricing process). In other words, the computational cost is doubled for the central difference estimator.

For second-order derivatives, we employ the second-order central difference scheme. The second-order central difference estimator can also be derived from Taylor series expansion, giving us

$$\Delta_{sc} = \frac{\overline{Y}_n(\theta + h) - 2\overline{Y}_n(\theta) + \overline{Y}_n(\theta - h)}{h^2}.$$

We use this estimator to estimate the gamma of a call.

Example 9.1 *Suppose that $S(0) = 50$, $r = 0.02$, $\sigma = 40\%$, $q = 0$, $\tau = T - t = 1$, and $K = 48$. Calculate the delta and gamma of a European call option using a closed-form solution, the forward difference estimator (for the delta only), and the central difference estimator, and compare the results.*

The algorithm used to calculate the forward difference estimator for the delta is as follows.

1. Set $i = 1$.
2. Generate a standard normal random variable Z_i.
3. Compute the call option price by

$$c(S_0) = e^{-rT} \max\left\{S(0)\exp\left(\left(r - q - \frac{\sigma^2}{2}\right)T + \sigma\sqrt{T}Z_i\right) - K, 0\right\}.$$

TABLE 9.4 Finite Difference Estimates

	Closed-form	Forward difference	Central difference
Delta	0.637601487	0.63712429	0.637032697
Variance	–	9.86124E–06	9.87708E–06
Bias of Delta	–	–4.771970E–04	–5.687900E–04
Gamma	0.018748488	–	0.018318607
Variance	–	–	–0.000429881
Bias of Gamma	–	–	1.83351E–05

4. Set $S(0) = S(0) + h$, where h is a small number, say 0.01. Use the same normal random variables to calculate the call price $c(S(0) + h)$, as in Step 3.
5. Set $i = i + 1$ and repeat Steps 2 to 4 until $i = n$.
6. Delta $= \dfrac{\bar{c}_n(S(0) + h) - \bar{c}_n(S(0))}{h}$.
7. Repeat the foregoing steps m times to obtain the mean and variance of the estimate.
8. Bias = Mean of estimate − Closed-form solution.

The calculation results are summarized in Table 9.4. The variance is calculated using 100 estimates, and each estimate is calculated using $n = 50,000$. The VBA code is as follows.

```
Dim mnormal() As Double
Dim i&, n&, h#, j&
Dim call1() As Double, call2() As Double, call3() As Double
Dim S0#, r#, q#, sigma#, K#, T#
Dim deltaF(1 To 100) As Double, deltaC(1 To 100) As Double,
 gammaC(1 To 100) As Double
Dim c1#, c2#, c3#

n = Cells(1, 2)
h = Cells(2, 2)
S0 = Cells(4, 2)
r = Cells(5, 2)
q = Cells(6, 2)
sigma = Cells(7, 2)
K = Cells(8, 2)
T = Cells(9, 2)

ReDim mnormal(1 To n)
ReDim call1(1 To n)
ReDim call2(1 To n)
ReDim call3(1 To n)
```

354   THE GREEKS

```
For j = 1 To 100
For i = 1 To n
mnormal(i) = rGauss()
call1(i) = Exp(-r * T) * Max(S0 * Exp((r - q -
   sigma ^ 2 / 2) * T + _sigma * Sqr(T) * mnormal(i)) - K, 0)
call2(i) = Exp(-r * T) * Max((S0 + h) * Exp((r - q -
   sigma ^ 2 / 2) * T + _sigma * Sqr(T) * mnormal(i)) - K, 0)
call3(i) = Exp(-r * T) * Max((S0 - h) * Exp((r - q -
   sigma ^ 2 / 2) * T + _sigma * Sqr(T) * mnormal(i)) - K, 0)
Next i

c1 = Average(call1)
c2 = Average(call2)
c3 = Average(call3)

deltaF(j) = (c2 - c1) / h
deltaC(j) = (c2 - c3) / (2 * h)
gammaC(j) = (c2 - 2 * c1 + c3) / (h ^ 2)
Next j

Cells(2, 7) = deltaF(1)
Cells(3, 7) = Application.Var(deltaF)
Cells(4, 7) = Average(deltaF) - Cells(2, 6)

Cells(2, 8) = deltaC(1)
Cells(3, 8) = Application.Var(deltaC)
Cells(4, 8) = Average(deltaC) - Cells(2, 6)

Cells(5, 8) = gammaC(1)
Cells(6, 8) = Application.Var(gammaC)
Cells(7, 8) = Average(gammaC) - Cells(5, 6)
```

For further details, please refer to Ch9.4_Finite_Difference.xls.

It is tempting to reduce h so as to reduce the bias. However, doing so will increase the variance of the estimate. Take the forward difference estimator as an example:

$$\text{Var}(\Delta_F) = \frac{1}{h^2} \text{Var}\left(\overline{Y}_n(\theta + h) - \overline{Y}_n(\theta)\right).$$

From this equation, we can see that decreasing h increases the variance of the estimator, which is also affected by the dependence between $\overline{Y}_n(\theta + h)$ and $\overline{Y}_n(\theta)$. For simplicity, assume that the pairs $(Y(\theta), Y(\theta + h))$ and $(Y_i(\theta), Y_i(\theta + h))$ are i.i.d.

for $i = 1, 2, \ldots, n$. Then,

$$\text{Var}(\Delta_F) = \frac{1}{nh^2}\text{Var}(Y(\theta+h) - Y(\theta)).$$

There are three scenarios for the order of $\text{Var}(Y(\theta+h) - Y(\theta))$, as follows.

Scenario 1. $\text{Var}(Y(\theta+h) - Y(\theta)) = O(1)$. This scenario occurs when $Y(\theta+h)$ and $Y(\theta)$ are simulated independently, that is, using independent random numbers. In fact,

$$\text{Var}(Y(\theta+h) - Y(\theta)) = \text{Var}(Y(\theta+h)) + \text{Var}(Y(\theta)) \to 2\text{Var}(Y(\theta)).$$

Scenario 2. $\text{Var}(Y(\theta+h) - Y(\theta)) = O(h)$. This scenario occurs when $Y(\theta+h)$ and $Y(\theta)$ are simulated using common random numbers.

Scenario 3. $\text{Var}(Y(\theta+h) - Y(\theta)) = O(h^2)$. For this scenario to hold, not only do we require that $Y(\theta+h)$ and $Y(\theta)$ be simulated using common random numbers, but also that, for (almost) all values of the random numbers, the output $Y(\cdot)$ is continuous in the input θ.

It is for this reason that we use common random numbers to estimate the Greeks, that is, so as to reduce the variance and increase the convergence rate. For more details about the relationship between h and n, please refer to Glasserman (2004).

9.4 LIKELIHOOD RATIO METHOD

The pathwise method involves differentiation of the payoff function, which may be discontinuous, and thus is not applicable to exotic options, such as barrier and digital options. An alternative solution is the likelihood ratio method, which does not require the continuity of the payoff function, but involves differentiation of the PDF.

Suppose that we have a discounted payoff Y, which can be expressed as a function $f(X_1, \ldots, X_m)$. The X_i's can be any values of the underlying asset that determine the payoff function. The likelihood ratio method relies on the PDF g_θ of X, which in turn depends on the parameter of interest θ. Then the expected value of the discounted payoff is

$$E_{g_\theta}[Y] = E[f(X_1, \ldots, X_m)] = \int_{\mathbb{R}^m} f(x)g(x)\,dx.$$

Interchanging the order differentiation and expectation, we have

$$\frac{d}{d\theta}E_{g_\theta}[Y] = \int_{\mathbb{R}^m} f(x)\frac{dg(x)}{d\theta}\,dx.$$

Multiplying the integrand by $\frac{g(x)}{g(x)}$, we have

$$\frac{d}{d\theta} \mathrm{E}_{g_\theta}[Y] = \int_{\mathbb{R}^m} f(x) \frac{\dot{g}(x)}{g(x)} g(x) \, dx$$

$$= \mathrm{E}_{g_\theta} \left[f(X) \frac{\dot{g}(X)}{g(X)} \right],$$

where $\dot{g} = \frac{dg}{d\theta}$. Here, E_{g_θ} denotes the expectation computed with respect to g_θ. The likelihood ratio method estimator is $f(X) \frac{\dot{g}(X)}{g(X)}$, which is unbiased. The expression $\frac{\dot{g}(x)}{g(x)}$ is called the score function, and the random variable $\frac{\dot{g}(X)}{g(X)}$ is called the score.

Note that the form of the estimator does not depend on the payoff function, and thus the payoff function is irrelevant in the likelihood ratio method. If the underlying path for two payoff functions are the same, then, once the score function is calculated, the estimate can be obtained easily by multiplying the payoff function by the score.

Example 9.2 *Estimate the delta and vega of a vanilla call option under the BS model using the likelihood ratio method, where $S(0) = 50$, $K = 60$, $r = 0.01$, $q = 0$, $\sigma = 0.3$, and $T = 0.5$.*

In the BS model, the stock price is log-normally distributed. The density of $S(T)$ is given by

$$g(x) = \frac{1}{x\sigma\sqrt{T}} \psi(h(x)),$$

where $h(x) = \frac{\log \frac{x}{S(0)} - (r - \frac{\sigma^2}{2})T}{\sigma\sqrt{T}}$. The score function is calculated as

$$\frac{1}{g(x)} \frac{dg(x)}{dS(0)} = \frac{\log \frac{x}{S(0)} - (r - \frac{\sigma^2}{2})T}{S(0)\sigma^2 T}.$$

The unbiased estimator of the delta is given by

$$e^{-rT} \max\{S(T) - K, 0\} \frac{\log \frac{S(T)}{S(0)} - (r - \frac{\sigma^2}{2})T}{S(0)\sigma^2 T} = e^{-rT} \max\{S(T) - K, 0\} \frac{Z}{S(0)\sigma\sqrt{T}},$$

where $S(T) = S(0) \exp\left((r - \frac{\sigma^2}{2})T + \sigma\sqrt{T}Z \right)$. The score function for the vega is

$$\frac{1}{g(x)} \frac{dg(x)}{d\sigma} = -\frac{1}{\sigma} - h(x) \frac{\log \frac{S(0)}{x} + (r + \frac{\sigma^2}{2})T}{\sigma^2 \sqrt{T}}.$$

LIKELIHOOD RATIO METHOD

TABLE 9.5 Delta and Vega Estimation Using the Likelihood Ratio Method

	Closed-form	Likelihood ratio method estimator
Delta	0.232745274	0.232063993
Variance	–	1.67959E−05
Bias of Delta	–	0.000212538
Vega	10.80685572	10.73423919
Variance	–	0.093406855
Bias of Vega	–	0.026576296

The unbiased estimator of the vega is given by

$$e^{-rT}\max\{S(T)-K,0\}\left(-\frac{1}{\sigma}-h(S(T))\frac{\log\frac{S(0)}{S(T)}+(r+\frac{\sigma^2}{2})T}{\sigma^2\sqrt{T}}\right)$$

$$=e^{-rT}\max\{S(T)-K,0\}\left(\frac{Z^2-1}{\sigma}-Z\sqrt{T}\right),$$

where $S(T) = S(0)\exp((r-\frac{\sigma^2}{2})T+\sigma\sqrt{T}Z)$.

The calculation results are summarized in Table 9.5. The variance is calculated using 100 estimates, and each estimate is calculated using $n = 50,000$. The delta and vega values obtained by the likelihood ratio method are close to those obtained by the closed-form solutions.

The corresponding VBA code is as follows.

```
Dim S0#, ST#, K#, r#, q#, T#, sigma#, Z#, n&
Dim i As Long, j As Long
Dim delta() As Double
Dim vdelta() As Double
Dim vega() As Double
Dim vvega() As Double

S0 = Cells(1, 2)
K = Cells(2, 2)
r = Cells(3, 2)
q = Cells(4, 2)
sigma = Cells(5, 2)
T = Cells(6, 2)
n = Cells(7, 2)

ReDim delta(1 To n) As Double
ReDim vdelta(1 To 100) As Double
ReDim vega(1 To n) As Double
ReDim vvega(1 To 100) As Double
```

358 THE GREEKS

```
For j = 1 To 100

For i = 1 To n
Z = rGauss()

ST = S0 * Exp((r - q - (sigma ^ 2) / 2) * T + sigma *
        Sqr(T) * Z)
delta(i) = Exp(-(r - q) * T) * Max(ST - K, 0) * Z / S0 /
        sigma / Sqr(T)
vega(i) = Exp(-(r - q) * T) * Max(ST - K, 0) * ((Z ^ 2 - 1) /
        sigma - Z * Sqr(T))
Next i

vdelta(j) = Average(delta)
vvega(j) = Average(vega)

Next j

Cells(10, 2) = vdelta(1)
Cells(11, 2) = Application.Var(vdelta)
Cells(10, 5) = vvega(1)
Cells(11, 5) = Application.Var(vvega)
Cells(12, 2) = Average(vdelta) - Cells(9, 2)
Cells(12, 5) = Average(vvega) - Cells(9, 5)
```

For further details, please refer to Ch9.5_Likelihood_Ratio_Method_Vanilla.xls.

Note that this method can be used to estimate the delta of a digital option, which is not possible using the pathwise method. Such estimation is achieved by replacing the payoff function with the indicator function $\mathbf{1}_{\{S(T) > K\}}$.

Example 9.3 *A forward start option is an option that starts at some future time T_1 and matures at time T_2. The payoff function of a forward start option is $\max\{S(T_2) - S(T_1), 0\}$. Estimate the path-dependent vega of a forward start option using the likelihood ratio method, where $S(0) = 50$, $r = 0.01$, $q = 0$, $\sigma = 0.3$, $T_1 = 0.2$, and $T_2 = 0.5$.*

The density of the path is

$$g(x_1, x_2) = g_1(x_1|S(0)) g_2(x_2|x_1)$$
$$= \frac{1}{x_1 \sigma \sqrt{T_1}} \psi(h_1(x_1|x_0)) \frac{1}{x_2 \sigma \sqrt{T_2 - T_1}} \psi(h_2(x_2|x_1)),$$

where $h_i(x_i|x_{i-1}) = \dfrac{\log \frac{x_i}{x_{i-1}} - (r - \frac{\sigma^2}{2})\tau_i}{\sigma\sqrt{\tau_i}}$. Then the score function is given by

$$\dfrac{\partial \log g(S(T_1), S(T_2))}{\partial \sigma} = \sum_{i=1}^{2} \dfrac{\partial \log g(S(T_i)|S(T_{i-1}))}{\partial \sigma}$$

$$= -\sum_{i=1}^{2}\left(\dfrac{1}{\sigma} + h_i(S_i|S_{i-1})\dfrac{\log \frac{S_{i-1}}{S_i} + (r + \frac{\sigma^2}{2})\tau_i}{\sigma^2\sqrt{\tau_i}}\right).$$

The unbiased estimator of the vega is equal to

$$e^{-rT}\max\{S(T_2) - S(T_1), 0\}\left(\dfrac{Z_1^2 - 1}{\sigma} - Z_1\sqrt{T_1} + \dfrac{Z_2^2 - 1}{\sigma} - Z_2\sqrt{T_2 - T_1}\right),$$

where $S(T_1) = S(0)\exp((r - \frac{\sigma^2}{2})T_1 + \sigma\sqrt{T_1}Z_1)$ and $S(T_2) = S(T_1)\exp((r - \frac{\sigma^2}{2})(T_2 - T_1) + \sigma\sqrt{T_2 - T_1}Z_2)$. After calculation, the vega is 10.62672, with the variance of the estimate being 0.13308 using 100 estimates, where each estimate is calculated using $n = 50,000$. The corresponding VBA code is as follows.

```
Dim S0#, ST1#, ST2#, r#, q#, T1#, T2#, sigma#, Z1#, Z2#, n&
Dim i&, j&, score#
Dim vega() As Double
Dim vvega() As Double

S0 = Cells(1, 2)
r = Cells(2, 2)
q = Cells(3, 2)
sigma = Cells(4, 2)
T1 = Cells(5, 2)
T2 = Cells(6, 2)
n = Cells(7, 2)

ReDim vega(1 To n) As Double
ReDim vvega(1 To 100) As Double

For j = 1 To 100
For i = 1 To n
Z1 = rGauss()
Z2 = rGauss()
ST1 = S0 * Exp((r - q - (sigma ^ 2) / 2) * T1 + sigma *
    Sqr(T1) * Z1)
ST2 = ST1 * Exp((r - q - (sigma ^ 2) / 2) * (T2 - T1) +
    sigma * Sqr(T2 - T1) * Z2)
```

```
score = ((Z1 ^ 2 - 1) / sigma - Z1 * Sqr(T1) + (Z2 ^ 2 - 1) /
        sigma - Z2 * Sqr(T2 - T1))
vega(i) = Exp(-(r - q) * T) * Max(ST2 - ST1, 0) * score
Next i

vvega(j) = Average(vega)
Next j

Cells(9, 2) = vvega(1)
Cells(10, 2) = Application.Var(vvega)
```

For futher details, please refer to Ch9.5_Likelihood_Ratio_Method_Path_Vega.xls.

The pathwise method cannot be extended further to the estimation of higher-order derivatives. However, the likelihood ratio method can be used to obtain higher-order derivatives provided that the PDF is differentiable at a higher order. For example, the estimator of the gamma is given by $f(X)\frac{\ddot{g}(X)}{g(X)}$, where $\ddot{g} = \frac{d^2 g}{dS(0)^2}$.

The likelihood ratio method has two limitations, however. First, it requires knowledge of the PDF. Second, it generally produces greater variance than the pathwise method, a consequence of the failure of interchange between differentiation and expectation. In practice, when estimating second- or higher-order derivatives, a mixed estimator employing both the pathwise and likelihood ratio methods is used to reduce the variance.

9.5 PATHWISE DERIVATIVE ESTIMATES

Better and faster estimation of derivatives can often be accomplished if more information about the model dynamics in a Monte Carlo simulation is known. Pathwise differentiation is one of the methods used in this regard. The key idea behind the pathwise method is to differentiate the evolution of the underlying asset or the parameters along the paths. Compared to the finite difference method, more model analysis and computational skills are required. However, such additional effort is justified by the concomitant improvement in the quality of the calculated Greeks.

The pathwise method encompasses the forward method and the adjoint method. The difference between the two lies in the direction of the differentiation. In this section, we focus primarily on the adjoint method, as it is computationally more efficient than its forward counterpart.

9.5.1 Application to European Options

We begin our discussion by reviewing the one-dimensional diffusion process that satisfies the Itô's process:

$$dS(t) = a(S(t), t)\, dt + b(S(t), t)\, dW(t),$$

where $S(t)$ is the asset price process, $W(t)$ is a one-dimensional standard Brownian motion, $a(\cdot)$ is the drift term, and $b(\cdot)$ is the diffusion term.

In Monte Carlo simulation, the evolution of process $S(t)$ is often approximated by Euler discretization. We write $S(n)$ for the approximation at time nh, and it evolves according to

$$S(n+1) = S(n) + a(S(n))h + b(S(n))Z(n+1)\sqrt{h}, \quad (9.1)$$

where $S(0) = S_0$ and $Z(1), Z(2), \ldots$ are i.i.d. standard normal random variables. If the normal random variables are fixed, then Equation 9.1 can be written as a functional transformation:

$$S(n+1) = F_n(S(n)), \quad (9.2)$$

where F_n is a transformation.

Consider a financial derivative with a discounted payoff function $g(S(T))$ that depends on the terminal asset price, where $N = T/h$. To estimate its delta, consider the partial derivative

$$\frac{\partial}{\partial S(0)} E[g(S(T))].$$

The pathwise method estimates the delta by

$$\frac{\partial}{\partial S(0)} g(S(T)), \quad (9.3)$$

which is the sensitivity of the discounted payoff along the path. Suppose that the differentiation and expectation can be interchanged, and the delta can be estimated by

$$\frac{\partial}{\partial S(0)} E[g(S(T))] = E\left[\frac{\partial}{\partial S(0)} g(S(T))\right].$$

Applying the chain rule to Equation 9.1, we obtain the following pathwise derivative

$$\frac{\partial}{\partial S(0)} g(S(N)) = \frac{\partial g(S(N))}{\partial S(N)} \frac{\partial S(N)}{\partial S(N-1)} \cdots \frac{\partial S(2)}{\partial S(1)} \frac{\partial S(1)}{\partial S(0)}. \quad (9.4)$$

Suppose that process $S(t)$ follows the BS dynamics, with constant drift r and diffusion coefficient σ. Equation 9.1 becomes

$$S(n+1) = S(n) + rS(n)h + \sigma S(n)Z(n+1)\sqrt{h}.$$

Consider the case for a European call option. The discounted payoff function $g(S(T))$ is given by $e^{-rT} \max\{S(T) - K, 0\}$, where r is the risk-free rate, T is the time to maturity, and K is the strike price. The corresponding partial derivatives are as follows.

$$\frac{\partial g(S(N))}{\partial S(N)} = \begin{cases} e^{-rT}, & \text{if } S(N) > K, \\ 0, & \text{otherwise,} \end{cases}$$

$$\frac{\partial S(n+1)}{\partial S(n)} = 1 + rh + \sigma\sqrt{h}Z(n+1) = \frac{S(n+1)}{S(n)}. \tag{9.5}$$

With this information, Equation 9.4 can be written as

$$\frac{\partial}{\partial S(0)} g(S(N)) = \frac{\partial g(S(N))}{\partial S(N)} \frac{\partial S(N)}{\partial S(N-1)} \cdots \frac{\partial S(2)}{\partial S(1)} \frac{\partial S(1)}{\partial S(0)}$$

$$= \begin{cases} e^{-rT} \frac{S(N)}{S(N-1)} \cdots \frac{S(N-1)}{S(N-2)} \frac{S(1)}{S(0)}, & \text{if } S(N) > K, \\ 0, & \text{otherwise,} \end{cases}$$

$$= \begin{cases} e^{-rT} \frac{S(N)}{S(0)}, & \text{if } S(N) > K, \\ 0, & \text{otherwise.} \end{cases} \tag{9.6}$$

Using these equations, we can construct the following simulation algorithm.

1. Generate an asset price path $\{S(0), \ldots, S(N)\}$.
2. Calculate the differentiated payoff function by Equation 9.5.
3. Compute the delta stepwise backward by Equation 9.6.
4. Repeat Steps 1 to 3 M times, and average the estimate.

Now, suppose that we want to calculate other pathwise Greeks using the adjoint method. Let θ denote parameter F_n in Equation 9.2. θ can be the volatility of an individual asset, the risk-free rate, or the lifetime of the derivative. The pathwise estimate of the sensitivity to θ is

$$\frac{\partial g}{\partial \theta} = \frac{\partial g}{\partial S(N)} \frac{\partial S(N)}{\partial \theta}.$$

Let $\Theta(n)$ be $\frac{\partial S(n)}{\partial \theta}$. Then,

$$\Theta(n+1) = \frac{\partial F_n}{\partial S(n)}(S(n), \theta)\Theta(n) + \frac{\partial F_n}{\partial \theta}(S(n), \theta)$$

$$= D(n)\Theta(n) + B(n).$$

If $\theta = \sigma$, then we can calculate the vega of the derivatives, where

$$\frac{\partial F_n}{\partial S(n)}(S(n), \sigma) = \frac{S(n+1)}{S(n)}$$

and
$$\frac{\partial F_n}{\partial \sigma}(S(n), \sigma) = S(n)\sqrt{h}Z(n+1).$$

The sensitivity to $\theta = \sigma$ is given by

$$\begin{aligned}
\frac{\partial g}{\partial \sigma} &= \frac{\partial g}{\partial S(N)} \Theta(N) \\
&= \frac{\partial g}{\partial S(N)} (B(N-1) + D(N-1)B(N-2) + \cdots \\
&\quad + D(N-1)D(N-2)\ldots D(1)B(0)) \\
&= \frac{\partial g}{\partial S(N)} \left(S(N-1)\sqrt{h}Z(N) + \frac{S(N)}{S(N-1)} S(N-2)\sqrt{h}Z(N-1) + \cdots \right. \\
&\quad \left. + \frac{S(N)}{S(N-1)} \frac{S(N-1)}{S(N-2)} \ldots S(0)\sqrt{h}Z(1) \right) \\
&= \frac{\partial g}{\partial S(N)} \left(S(N-1)\sqrt{h}Z(N) + \frac{S(N)}{S(N-1)} S(N-2)\sqrt{h}Z(N-1) + \cdots \right. \\
&\quad \left. + \frac{S(N)}{S(1)} S(0)\sqrt{h}Z(1) \right).
\end{aligned}$$

These equations give us the following simulation algorithm.

1. Generate an asset price path $\{S(0), \ldots, S(N)\}$.
2. Calculate the differentiated payoff function by Equation 9.5.
3. Compute $\Theta(N)$ stepwise backward by the aforementioned equation.
4. Calculate the corresponding estimate of the vega.
5. Repeat Steps 1 to 4 M times, and average the estimate.

The corresponding VBA code is as follows.

```
Public Sub EC_Adj_Greek(A As BS_PathType, K As Double, _
  ByRef Value As Variant, ByRef Delta As Variant, ByRef Vega
  As Variant)
Dim i As Long, j As Long

ReDim S(1 To A.n, 0 To A.m) As Double
ReDim S_b(1 To A.n, 0 To A.m) As Double
ReDim S_b_v(1 To A.n, 0 To A.m) As Double
ReDim z(1 To A.m) As Double
ReDim Value(1 To A.n) As Double
ReDim Delta(1 To A.n) As Double
ReDim Vega(1 To A.n) As Double
```

```
For i = 1 To A.n
  S(i, 0) = A.S0
  For j = 1 To A.m
    z(j) = rGauss()
    S(i, j) = S(i, j - 1) * (1 + A.rf * A.dt + A.sigma *
             Sqr(A.dt) * z(j))
  Next j
  Value(i) = Exp(-A.rf * A.T) * Max(S(i, A.m) - K, 0)
  S_b(i, A.m) = 0
  S_b_v(i, A.m) = 0
  If Value(i) > 0 Then
    S_b(i, A.m) = Exp(-A.rf * A.T)
    S_b_v(i, A.m) = Exp(-A.rf * A.T)

    For j = A.m - 1 To 0 Step -1
      S_b(i, j) = S_b(i, j + 1) * S(i, j + 1) / S(i, j)
      S_b_v(i, j) = S(i, j) * Sqr(A.dt) * z(j + 1) *
                    S(i, A.m) / S(i, j + 1)

      If j <> A.m - 1 Then
        S_b_v(i, j) = S_b_v(i, j) + S_b_v(i, j + 1)
      End If
    Next j
  End If
  Delta(i) = S_b(i, 1)
  Vega(i) = S_b_v(i, 1) * S_b_v(i, A.m)
Next i
End Sub
```

If we assume $S(0) = 10$, $K = 12$, $T = 1$, $r = 5\%$, and $\sigma = 40\%$ and generate 50,000 paths, then the exact price from the BS model is 1.08059, the exact delta is 0.447965, and the exact vega is 3.95544. The results using different simulation methods are presented in Table 9.6, which shows that the likelihood ratio method is the fastest method, but produces the largest variance in estimation. The finite difference method

TABLE 9.6 Comparison of the Greeks of a European Call Option Calculated by Different Methods

	Likelihood ratio	Finite difference	Adjoint method (stepwise)	Adjoint method (one-shoot)
Value	1.075269457	1.069390328	1.095131811	1.067705506
Delta	0.4422509	0.448835501	0.450734632	0.44613116
sd(Delta)	1.406276012	0.712750935	0.714223855	0.712890081
Vega	3.796132405	3.942509866	3.973986098	3.913102811
sd(Vega)	25.71505033	9.527871248	9.428493464	9.597380255
Time (s)	0.1875	6.203125	5.0078125	0.2265625

produces a fairly accurate estimation, but its speed is the slowest. Finally, the estimation of adjoint method with one-shoot simulation is as accurate as that of the finite difference method, and its speed is the same as that of the likelihood method. For more details, please refer to Ch9.6_Adjoint_European_Option.xls.

9.5.2 Application to Multi-Asset Derivatives

We now consider a multi-asset call option with the following discounted payoff function g.

$$g(S(T)) = e^{-rT} \max \left\{ \sum_{i=1}^{n} w_i S_i(T) - K, 0 \right\},$$

where $S_i(T)$ is the terminal value of the ith asset and w_i is the corresponding weight. The process $S_i(t)$ follows the multidimensional stochastic differential equation,

$$dS_i(t) = r S_i(t) \, dt + \sigma_i S_i(t) \, dW_i(t),$$

for $i = 1, 2, \ldots, n$, where the W_i's are correlated Wiener processes.

Using the analysis in the previous section, we calculate the partial derivatives with respect to the individual asset prices. Let $B = \sum_{i=1}^{n} w_i S_i(T)$ and

$$\frac{\partial g}{\partial S_i(0)} = \begin{cases} e^{-rT} w_i \frac{S_i(T)}{S_i(0)}, & \text{if } B > K, \\ 0, & \text{otherwise.} \end{cases} \quad (9.7)$$

If we calculate the sensitivity to r, then we have to compute

$$\frac{\partial g}{\partial r} = \begin{cases} -T e^{-rT} (B - K), & \text{if } B > K, \\ 0, & \text{otherwise.} \end{cases} \quad (9.8)$$

The simulation algorithm is as follows.

1. Generate a multi-asset path for $S(0)$ to $S(N)$.
2. Calculate the payoff of the derivative.
3. Calculate the differentiated payoff function by Equations 9.7 and 9.8.
4. Delta $= \frac{\partial g}{\partial S_i(0)}$ and rho $= \frac{\partial g}{\partial r}$.
5. Repeat Steps 1 to 4 M times, and average the estimates.

The corresponding VBA code is as follows.

```
Public Sub BasketOption_Adj_Greek(A() As BS_PathType, VCmatrix
  As Variant, K As Double, _W() As Double, ByRef value As
  Variant, ByRef delta As Variant, ByRef rho As Variant)

Dim i As Long, j As Long, m As Long
```

366 THE GREEKS

```
Dim B As Double, B_b As Double
Dim l As Variant
m = UBound(VCmatrix, 1)

ReDim ST(1 To m) As Double
ReDim z(1 To A(1).n) As Double

ReDim value(1 To A(1).n) As Double
ReDim delta(1 To m, 1 To A(1).n) As Double
ReDim rho(1 To A(1).n) As Double
l = CDecom(VCmatrix)

For i = 1 To A(1).n
  z = rCGauss(l)
  For j = 1 To m
    ST(j) = A(j).S0 * Exp((A(j).rf - 1 / 2 * A(j).sigma ^ 2) * _
       A(j).T + A(j).sigma * Sqr(A(j).T) * z(j))
  Next j

  B = 0
  For j = 1 To m
    B = B + W(j) * ST(j)
  Next j

  value(i) = Exp(-A(1).rf * A(1).T) * Max(B - K, 0)
  B_b = 0
  rho(i) = 0
  If value(i) > 0 Then
    B_b = Exp(-A(1).rf * A(1).T)
    rho(i) = -A(1).T * value(i)
  End If

  For j = 1 To m
    delta(j, i) = W(j) * B_b * ST(j) / A(j).S0
  Next j
Next i
End Sub
```

Consider the example of a basket option with four underlying assets with initial price $S_1(0) = 1.3$, $S_2(0) = 1$, $S_3(0) = 1.2$, $S_4(0) = 1.5$, $w_1 = 0.1$, $w_2 = 0.3$, $w_3 = 0.5$, $w_4 = 0.1$, $K = 1$, $T = 1$, and $r = 5\%$, and generate 50,000 paths. The delta and rho results produced using the adjoint and finite difference methods are presented in Table 9.7. When the option is based on more underlying assets, the difference in computational speed between the two methods becomes more

TABLE 9.7 Comparison of the Greeks of a European Call Option Calculated Using the Adjoint and Finite Difference Methods

	Adjoint method	Finite difference
Value	0.195921838	0.196188286
DeltaS1	0.088683732	0.088859997
DeltaS2	0.268484838	0.26838605
DeltaS3	0.452728308	0.453596083
DeltaS4	0.090740029	0.09080874
Rho	−0.195921838	−0.196178477
Time (s)	0.828125	1.5625

significant for higher dimensional cases. The adjoint and finite difference methods provide similar estimations, although the former is much faster, taking about half the computational time needed for the latter. For more details, please refer to Ch9.6_Adjoint_Basket_Option.xls.

9.5.3 Application to Interest Rate Derivatives in LIBOR Market Model

Recall the m-factor LIBOR market model, the forward rate dynamics of which are described by the following SDE.

$$\frac{df_i(t)}{f_i(t)} = \mu_i(t)\,dt + \sum_{k=1}^{m} \sigma_{ik}(t)\,dW_k(t),$$

where $i = 1, \ldots, m$ and $W_k(t)$ for $k = 1, \ldots, m$ are independent standard Brownian motions, and

$$\mu_i(t) = \sum_{j=\eta(t)}^{i} \frac{\sigma_{ij}\tau_j f_j(t)}{1 + \tau_j f_j(t)},$$

$\eta(t)$ denotes the index of the next nearest maturity date after time t, $T_{\eta(t)-1} \le t < T_{\eta(t)}$ and $\tau_i = T_{i+1} - T_i$.

Consider again the general setting of Equation 9.4, and write $\frac{\partial g}{\partial f(0)}$ for the row vector of the derivatives of $g(f(N))$ with respect to the elements of $f(0)$, where $f(0) = (f_1(0), \ldots, f_m(0))$:

$$\frac{\partial g}{\partial f(0)} = \frac{\partial g}{\partial f(N)} \frac{\partial f(N)}{\partial f(N-1)} \cdots \frac{\partial f(2)}{\partial f(1)} \frac{\partial f(1)}{\partial f(0)}$$

$$= \frac{\partial g}{\partial f(N)} D(N-1)D(N-2)\ldots D(0)\Delta(0)$$

$$\equiv V(0)^T \Delta(0),$$

where $\mathbf{\Delta}(n)$ is an $m \times m$ matrix with $\Delta_{ij}(n) = \frac{\partial f_i(n)}{\partial f_j(0)}$, and $\mathbf{D}(n)$ is an $m \times m$ matrix with

$$D_{ik}(n) = \delta_{ik} + \frac{\partial \mu_i}{\partial f_k} \tau_i + \sum_{l=1}^{d} \frac{\partial \sigma_{il}}{\partial f_k} dW_l,$$

δ_{ik} is 1 if $i = k$ and 0 otherwise. $V(0)$ can be calculated recursively by

$$V(n) = \mathbf{D}(n)^T V(n+1), \text{ where } V(N) = \left(\frac{\partial g}{\partial f(N)}\right)^T. \tag{9.9}$$

Consider a simple example of a caplet for the interval $[T_m, T_{m+1})$ with strike price K. Its discounted payoff is

$$\left(\prod_{i=0}^{m} \frac{1}{1 + \tau_i f_i(T_i)}\right) \tau_m \max\{f_m(T_m) - K, 0\}.$$

The contract-dependent derivatives for this caplet are calculated as

$$\frac{\partial g(f(T_m))}{\partial f_j(T_j)} = \tau_m \prod_{i=0}^{m} \frac{1}{1 + \tau_i f_i(T_i)} \left(1_{\{f_m(T_m) > K\}} - (f_m(T_m) - K)^+ \frac{\tau_j}{1 + \tau_j f_j(T_j)}\right), \tag{9.10}$$

where $1_{\{\cdot\}}$ is the indicator function. Note that $V_i(n) = V_i(n+1)$ for $i < \eta(nh)$, whereas, for $i \geq \eta(nh)$,

$$V_i(n) = \frac{f_i(n+1)V_i(n+1)}{f_i(n)} + \frac{\tau_i h}{(1 + \tau_i f_i(n))^2} \sum_{j=i}^{m} f_j(n+1)V_j(n+1)\sigma_{ij}. \tag{9.11}$$

The simulation algorithm proceeds as follows.

1. Generate a forward rate path $\{f(0), \ldots, f(N)\}$.
2. Initialize $V(N)$ according to Equation 9.10.
3. Calculate $V_i(n)$ backward according to Equation 9.11 for $n = 0, 1, \ldots, N-1$.
4. Calculate the corresponding delta with respect to the individual forward rate by Equation 9.9.
5. Repeat Steps 1 to 4 M times, and average the estimates.

The corresponding VBA code is as follows.

```
Public Sub Caplet_delta_adjoint(f As Variant, Strike As
  Double, Re As Long, _ByRef Value As Variant, ByRef v_b
  As Variant)
Dim i As Long, j As Long, k As Long, w As Long
Dim S As Double
Dim nSim As Long, nPath As Long

nSim = UBound(f, 1)
nPath = UBound(f, 2)
ReDim Value(1 To nPath) As Double
ReDim v(0 To nSim, 1 To nPath, 0 To nFwd) As Double
ReDim v_b(1 To nPath, 0 To nFwd) As Double

For j = 1 To nPath
  Value(j) = tau * Max(f(Re, j, Re) - Strike, 0)
  For i = 0 To Re
    If f(Re, j, Re) > Strike Then
      If i = Re Then
        v(Re, j, Re) = (1 + tau * Strike) / (1 + tau *
        f(Re, j, Re)) * tau
      Else
        v(Re, j, i) = -tau ^ 2 * (f(Re, j, Re) - Strike) _
        / (1 + tau * f(Re, j, Re))
      End If
    Else
      v(Re, j, Re) = 0
    End If
    Value(j) = Value(j) / (1 + f(Re, j, i) * tau)
    For k = 0 To i
      v(Re, j, i) = v(Re, j, i) / (1 + tau * f(Re, j, k))
    Next k
  Next i

  For i = 0 To nFwd
    For w = Re - 1 To 0 Step -1
      If i >= w And i <> 0 Then
        S = 0
        For k = i To nFwd
          S = S + f(w + 1, j, k) * v(w + 1, j, k) *
             Cij(i, k, w)
        Next k
        v(w, j, i) = f(w + 1, j, i) / f(w, j, i) *
```

```
            v(w + 1, j, i) + _tau / (1 + tau *
            f(w, j, i)) ^ 2 * S
        Else
            v(w, j, i) = v(w + 1, j, i)
        End If
    Next w
  Next i
Next j

For j = 1 To nPath
  For k = 0 To nFwd
    v_b(j, k) = v(0, j, k)
  Next k
Next j
End Sub
```

For further details, please refer to Ch9.6_Adjoint_LIBOR_Simulation_Caplet.xls.

In general, computing the exact derivatives of the payoff function with respect to the terminal interest rate is not an easy task particularly in the case of exotic interest rate derivatives, such as interest rate range accrual notes and callable swaptions. In practice, we have to apply the finite difference method to bypass the calculation of exact differentiation, but by doing so we face the extra finite difference error.

To illustrate the difficulty, consider a cap with eight tenors, each of which is 0.25 years. The strike price of the cap is 3%. The VBA code using the finite difference rather than the exact differentiated payoff is as follows.

```
For j = 1 To nPath
 Value(j) = tau * Max(f(Re, j, Re) - Strike, 0)
 For i = 0 To Re
   Value(j) = Value(j) / (1 + f(Re, j, i) * tau)
 Next i

 For i = 0 To Re
   If f(Re, j, Re) > Strike Then
     If i = Re Then
       Value_h(j) = Value(j) * (Max((f(Re, j, Re) + h) -
         Strike, 0) * _(1 + f(Re, j, i) * tau)) /
         (Max(f(Re, j, Re) - Strike, 0) _ * (1 + (f(Re, j, i) +
         h) * tau))
     Else
       Value_h(j) = Value(j) * (1 + f(Re, j, i) * tau) _
         / (1 + (f(Re, j, i) + h) * tau)
     End If
       v(Re, j, i) = (Value_h(j) - Value(j)) / h
```

TABLE 9.8 Delta Comparison of a Cap Calculated Using Exact Differentiation and the Finite Difference Method

	Exact differentiation	Finite difference approximation
$f_0(0)$	−0.00937839	−0.00872843
$f_1(0)$	0.235526592	0.228843513
$f_2(0)$	0.232990617	0.221264612
$f_3(0)$	0.229441883	0.212970823
$f_4(0)$	0.226454488	0.204999233
$f_5(0)$	0.224218084	0.197635372
$f_6(0)$	0.22245076	0.190627645
$f_7(0)$	0.220802498	0.183897312
$f_8(0)$	0.219548602	0.177411106

```
Else
   v(Re, j, Re) = 0
End If
Value(j) = Value(j) / (1 + f(Re, j, i) * tau)
For k = 0 To i
   v(Re, j, i) = v(Re, j, i) / (1 + tau * f(Re, j, k))
Next k
Next i
' The remaining part is the same as above
```

For further details, please refer to Ch9.6_Adjoint_LIBOR_Simulation_Caplet_Finite_Difference.xls.

The differences in the results are highlighted in Table 9.8, which shows that the estimated values obtained using finite difference approximation are generally smaller than those obtained using exact differentiation, particularly those for the forward rates of longer terms.

For the case of a European swaption, we only need to introduce minor modifications to the payoff function. Recall that the payoff of a European swaption is

$$\pi(t_\alpha) = A_{\alpha,\beta}(t_\alpha) \max\{S_{\alpha,\beta}(t_\alpha) - K, 0\},$$

where

$$A_{\alpha,\beta}(t) = \sum_{j=\alpha+1}^{\beta} \tau_{j-1} P(t, t_j),$$

$$S_{\alpha,\beta}(t_\alpha) = \frac{1 - P(t_\alpha, t_\beta)}{A_{\alpha,\beta}(t_\alpha)},$$

$$P(t_\alpha, t_k) = \prod_{p=\alpha}^{k-1} \frac{1}{1 + f_p(t_\alpha)\tau}.$$

We then compute the discounted payoff at time t_0:

$$\pi(t_0) = \pi(t_\alpha) \prod_{p=0}^{\alpha-1} \frac{1}{1 + f_p(t_p)\tau}.$$

The derivative of the discounted payoff function is given by

$$\prod_{p=0}^{\alpha-1} \frac{1}{1 + f_p(t_N)} \left(\frac{\mathbf{1}_{\{j \geq \alpha, S_{\alpha,\beta}(t_\alpha) \geq K\}} \tau_j - \tau_j (S_{\alpha,\beta}(t_\alpha) - K)^+ A_{\alpha,\beta}(t_\alpha)}{1 + f_j(t_\beta)} \right). \quad (9.12)$$

The following is the VBA code representing the initialization.

```
For i = 0 To matTime - 1
  If payoff(ni) > 0 Then
    If i >= expTime Then
      v(matTime - 1, ni, i) = tau * (1 - (SwapVal -
        Strike * nt)) _ / (1 + tau * f(matTime - 1, ni, i))
    Else
      v(matTime - 1, ni, i) = -tau * (SwapVal -
        Strike * nt) _ / (1 + tau * f(matTime - 1, ni, i))
    End If
  Else
    v(matTime - 1, ni, i) = 0
  End If

  payoff(ni) = payoff(ni) / (1 + f(expTime, ni, i) * tau)
  For k = 0 To expTime - 1
    v(matTime - 1, ni, i) = v(matTime - 1, ni, i) _
      / (1 + tau * f(matTime - 1, ni, k))
  Next k
Next i
```

For more details, please refer to Ch9.6_Adjoint_LIBOR_Simulation_Swaption.xls.

For Bermudan swaptions, the general framework can also be used. As Bermudan swaptions have similar features to American options, we need to determine the optimal exercise time. We can employ the Longstaff and Schwartz algorithm to determine the optimal exercise date and then work with the derivatives of the net present value of the remaining coupons at the exercise date in the adjoint simulation.

Calculation of the delta of a Bermudan swaption is performed using the following algorithm.

1. Generate M forward rate paths under the spot measure.
2. For each path, use the Longstaff–Schwartz algorithm to determine the optimal exercise time $T_r(\omega)$.
3. For each path, initialize $V(N)$ according to Equation 9.12.
4. For n from $M - 2$ to $r(\omega)$, calculate $V(m)$ backward from $m = n + 1$ to $m = n$ by the recursive Equation 9.11.
5. Compute $V(m)$ backward from $m = r(\omega)$ to $m = 0$ by the recursive Equation 9.11.
6. Calculate the corresponding delta with respect to the individual forward rate by Equation 9.9.
7. Average the results over all M paths.

The VBA code for the initialization is as follows.

```
For i = 0 To matTime - 1
  If payoff(ni) > 0 Then
    If i >= strTime + r(ni) Then      'Note r(ni) is the
        exercise time
      v(matTime - 1, ni, i) = tau * (1 - nt
        * (bS(r(ni), ni) - Strike)) _ / (1 + tau
        * f(matTime - 1, ni, i))
      'bS(r(ni),ni) is the swap rate at r(ni)
    Else
      v(matTime - 1, ni, i) = -tau * nt * (bS(r(ni), ni)
        - Strike) _ / (1 + tau * f(matTime - 1, ni, i))
    End If
  Else
      v(matTime - 1, ni, i) = 0
  End If

  For k = 0 To strTime + r(ni)
    v(matTime - 1, ni, i) = v(matTime - 1, ni, i) _
      / (1 + tau * f(matTime - 1, ni, k))
  Next k
Next i
```

For further details, please refer to Ch9.6_Adjoint_LIBOR_Simulation_Bermudan_Swaption.xls.

9.5.4 Problem with the Adjoint Method

The pathwise method provides a fast and accurate approach to computing the Greeks of derivatives. However, it breaks down if the payoff function of the derivative

374 THE GREEKS

is not differentiable, as in the case of a digital option. A first-order differentiable payoff function is not sufficient. We cannot compute the second-order Greeks unless the payoff function is second-order differentiable. The practicality of the adjoint method is also highly dependent on the nature of the payoff function. To circumvent this difficulty, we can apply the likelihood ratio method or Malliavin calculus. The payoff function can also be approximated by a continuous and differentiated form for analysis, and the "vibrato" Monte Carlo method introduced in the next section is another viable solution to the problem.

9.6 GREEK CALCULATION WITH DISCONTINUOUS PAYOFFS

In most cases, the payoff functions of derivatives are discontinuous and not differentiable. A simple case is the digital call option. There is a jump at the strike price in the payoff function at maturity, and this jump causes discontinuity and non-differentiability for the payoff function. The payoff of a digital option is

$$f(S(T)) = \begin{cases} 1, & \text{if } S(T) > K, \\ 0, & \text{otherwise.} \end{cases}$$

In this case, we can apply the "vibrato" Monte Carlo method, which can easily deal with a discontinuous payoff function. Also, the generalization to multidimensional cases is straightforward.

9.6.1 Functional Approximation for Digital Options

Recall the case of a digital option. Because the payoff function $f(S(T))$ takes the form of a heaviside step function, it can be approximated by

$$f(S(T)) \approx \frac{1}{2} + \frac{1}{2}\tanh\left(\frac{1}{2}u(S(T) - K)\right) = \frac{1}{1 + e^{-u(S(T)-K)}}, \quad (9.13)$$

where u is the shape parameter of the approximation and K is the strike price of the digital option. A larger u means a sharper transition at K. Differentiating the approximated payoff function $f(S(T))$ with respect to the terminal asset price $S(T)$, we have

$$\frac{\partial f(S(T))}{\partial S(T)} \approx \frac{ue^{-u(S(T)-K)}}{(1 + e^{-u(S(T)-K)})^2}.$$

Suppose that the asset price process $S(T)$ follows the GBM such that $S(T)$ can be written as

$$S(T) = S(0)\exp\left(\left(r - \frac{\sigma^2}{2}\right)T + \sigma\sqrt{T}Z\right),$$

GREEK CALCULATION WITH DISCONTINUOUS PAYOFFS 375

where r is the risk-free rate, σ is the volatility, T is the time to maturity, and Z is a standard normal random variable. Using the analysis in the adjoint method, we can show that

$$\text{Delta} = \frac{\partial f(S(T))}{\partial S(0)} = \frac{\partial f(S(T))}{\partial S(T)} \frac{\partial S(T)}{\partial S(0)} = \frac{ue^{-u(S(T)-K)}}{(1+e^{-u(S(T)-K)})^2} \frac{S(T)}{S(0)}, \quad (9.14)$$

$$\text{Vega} = \frac{\partial f(S(T))}{\partial \sigma} = \frac{\partial f(S(T))}{\partial S(T)} \frac{\partial S(T)}{\partial \sigma} = \frac{ue^{-u(S(T)-K)}}{(1+e^{-u(S(T)-K)})^2} \left(-\sigma T + \sqrt{T}Z\right). \quad (9.15)$$

We compute the delta and vega using the foregoing equations, and the procedure is as follows.

1. Generate a one-shoot asset path from $S(0)$ to $S(T)$.
2. Compute the payoff by the approximated functional form in Equation 9.13.
3. Compute the delta and vega by Equations 9.14 and 9.15.
4. Repeat Steps 1 to 3 M times, and average the estimates.

The VBA code is as follows.

```
Public Sub Digital_Adj_Greek_Fd(A As BS_PathType, K As Double,
 ByRef Value As Variant, _ByRef Delta As Variant, ByRef Vega
 As Variant, Optional u As Double = 1)
Dim i As Long, j As Long, z As Double
ReDim S(1 To A.n) As Double
ReDim Value(1 To A.n) As Double
ReDim Delta(1 To A.n) As Double
ReDim Vega(1 To A.n) As Double
  For i = 1 To A.n
    z = rGauss()
    S(i) = A.S0 * Exp((A.rf - 1 / 2 * A.sigma ^ 2) * A.T +
      A.sigma * Sqr(A.T) * z)
    Value(i) = 1 / (1 + Exp(-u * (S(i) - K))) * Exp(-A.rf
      * A.T)
    Delta(i) = u * Exp(-u * (S(i) - K)) / (1 + Exp(-u
      * (S(i) - K))) ^ 2 _ * S(i) / A.S0 * Exp(-A.rf * A.T)
    Vega(i) = u * Exp(-u * (S(i) - K)) / (1 + Exp(-u
      * (S(i) - K))) ^ 2 _ * S(i) * (-A.sigma * A.T + Sqr(A.T)
      * z) * Exp(-A.rf * A.T)
  Next i
End Sub
```

9.6.2 Vibrato Method for Digital Options

"Vibrato" means a "rapid slight variation in pitch in singing or playing a musical instrument." Giles (2009) illustrated its analogy to Monte Carlo simulation: a path in Monte Carlo simulation produces an output value that has a sharp probability distribution.

The vibrato Monte Carlo method can thus be viewed as a hybrid of the likelihood ratio method and adjoint simulation. We illustrate the method for a digital option with a discontinuous payoff function.

Consider a path simulation for a stochastic process for the first $N-1$ steps. On the final step, we consider the full distribution of possible values for ΔW_N instead of just one realization. Doing so produces a normal distribution for S_N at time T, conditional on the value of S_{N-1} at time $T-h$. The pdf is

$$p_S(S_N) = \frac{1}{\sqrt{2\pi\sigma_W^2}} \exp\left(-\frac{(S_N - \mu_W)^2}{2\sigma_W^2}\right),$$

where

$$\mu_W = S_{N-1} + a(S_{N-1}, T-h)h \qquad (9.16)$$

$$\sigma_W = b(S_{N-1}, T-h)\sqrt{h}, \qquad (9.17)$$

and $a(S, t)$ and $b(S, t)$ are the drift and diffusion terms of the stochastic differential equation of process $S(t)$.

The main idea behind vibrato Monte Carlo simulation is simple: it adopts the conditional expectation approach. We compute the conditional normal distribution $p_S(S_N|W)$, given the set of Wiener increments $W = \{\Delta W_1, \Delta W_2, \ldots, \Delta W_{N-1}\}$. Then,

$$S_N(W, Z) = \mu_W + \sigma_W Z,$$

where Z is a standard normal random variable. The expected payoff can then be written as

$$V = E_W[E_Z[f(S_N)|W]] = \int \left(\int f(S_N) p_S(S_N|W) \, dS_N\right) p_W(W) \, dW.$$

In computing the sensitivity to parameter θ, the first step is to apply the pathwise sensitivity approach to obtain $\frac{\partial \mu_W}{\partial \theta}$ and $\frac{\partial \sigma_W}{\partial \theta}$. Then we apply the likelihood ratio method to the inner expectation to obtain

$$\frac{\partial V}{\partial \theta} = E_W\left[\frac{\partial}{\partial \theta} E_Z[f(S_N)|W]\right] = E_W\left[E_Z\left[f(S_N) \frac{\partial \log p_S}{\partial \theta}\bigg|W\right]\right], \qquad (9.18)$$

and

$$\frac{\partial \log p_S}{\partial \theta} = \frac{\partial \log p_S}{\partial \mu_W}\frac{\partial \mu_W}{\partial \theta} + \frac{\partial \log p_S}{\partial \sigma_W}\frac{\partial \sigma_W}{\partial \theta}. \tag{9.19}$$

Note that

$$\log p_s = -\log \sigma_W - \frac{(S_N - \mu_W)^2}{2\sigma_W^2} - \frac{1}{2}\log 2\pi.$$

Equation 9.19 becomes

$$\frac{\partial \log p_S}{\partial \theta} = \frac{Z}{\sigma_W}\frac{\partial \mu_W}{\partial \theta} + \frac{Z^2 - 1}{\sigma_W}\frac{\partial \sigma_W}{\partial \theta}.$$

To increase simulation accuracy, observe

$$E_Z\left[f(S_N)\frac{\partial \log p_S}{\partial \theta}\bigg|W\right] = \frac{\partial \mu_W}{\partial \theta}E_Z\left[f(S_N)\frac{\partial \log p_S}{\partial \mu_W}\bigg|W\right]$$
$$+ \frac{\partial \sigma_W}{\partial \theta}E_Z\left[f(S_N)\frac{\partial \log p_S}{\partial \sigma_W}\bigg|W\right].$$

Transform the first expectation on the right-hand side into

$$E_Z\left[f(S_N)\frac{\partial \log p_S}{\partial \mu_W}\bigg|W\right] = E_Z\left[\frac{Z}{\sigma_W}f(\mu_W + \sigma_W Z)\right]$$
$$= E_Z\left[\frac{Z}{2\sigma_W}(f(\mu_W + \sigma_W Z) - f(\mu_W - \sigma_W Z))\right].$$

Similarly, using the result that $E_Z[Z^2 - 1] = 0$, we have

$$E_Z\left[f(S_N)\frac{\partial \log p_S}{\partial \sigma_W}\bigg|W\right] = E_Z\left[\frac{Z^2 - 1}{\sigma_W}f(\mu_W + \sigma_W Z)\right]$$
$$= E_Z\left[\frac{Z^2 - 1}{2\sigma_W}(f(\mu_W + \sigma_W Z) - 2f(\mu_W) + f(\mu_W - \sigma_W Z))\right].$$

Combining the two foregoing derivations, Y_θ becomes

$$Y_\theta = \frac{\partial \mu_W}{\partial \theta}Y_\mu + \frac{\partial \sigma_W}{\partial \theta}Y_\sigma, \tag{9.20}$$

where

$$Y_\mu = \frac{Z}{2\sigma_W}(f(\mu_W + \sigma_W Z) - f(\mu_W - \sigma_W Z))$$

378 THE GREEKS

and

$$Y_\sigma = \frac{Z^2 - 1}{2\sigma_W} (f(\mu_W + \sigma_W Z) - 2f(\mu_W) + f(\mu_W - \sigma_W Z)).$$

The following algorithm is used to compute the delta of a digital call option with strike price K.

1. Generate an asset path for $\{S(0), \ldots, S(N-1)\}$.
2. Generate $S(N)$ from $S(N-1)$ in one step.
3. Calculate μ and σ by Equations 9.16 and 9.17.
4. Calculate the delta by Equation 9.18.
5. Repeat Steps 1 to 4 M times, and average the estimate.

To achieve accurate simulation, we modify Step 4 by using Equation 9.20. The corresponding VBA code is as follows.

```
Public Sub Digital_Adj_Greek(A As BS_PathType, K As Double,
 ByRef Value As Variant, _ByRef Delta As Variant, ByRef Vega
 As Variant, Optional Efficient As Boolean = False)
Dim i As Long, h As Double, W As Double, z As Double
Dim mu As Double, sig As Double, Y_mu As Double, Y_sig As
    Double
Dim fh As Double, f As Double, fd As Double
Dim S_N_minus As Double, T_N_minus As Double
ReDim S(1 To A.n) As Double
ReDim Value(1 To A.n) As Double
ReDim Delta(1 To A.n) As Double
ReDim Vega(1 To A.n) As Double

h = 0.01
T_N_minus = A.T - h
For i = 1 To A.n
  W = rGauss()
  S_N_minus = A.S0 * Exp((A.rf - 1 / 2 * A.sigma ^ 2) * A.T
    + _A.sigma * Sqr(T_N_minus) * W)
  z = rGauss()
  S(i) = S_N_minus * Exp((A.rf - 1 / 2 * A.sigma ^ 2) * h + _
    A.sigma * Sqr(h) * z)
  mu = S_N_minus * (1 + A.rf * h)
  sig = S_N_minus * A.sigma * Sqr(h)
  Value(i) = 0
  Delta(i) = 0
  Vega(i) = 0
```

GREEK CALCULATION WITH DISCONTINUOUS PAYOFFS

```
    If Efficient = False Then
      If S(i) > K Then
        Value(i) = Exp(-A.rf * A.T)
        Delta(i) = Exp(-A.rf * A.T) * (z / sig * mu / A.S0 +
                   (z ^ 2 - 1) / A.S0)
        Vega(i) = Exp(-A.rf * A.T) * (z / sig * mu * (-A.sigma
          * A.T + Sqr(A.T) * W) + _(z ^ 2 - 1) * ((-A.sigma * A.T
          + Sqr(A.T) * W) + sig / A.sigma))
      End If
    Else
      Value(i) = 0
      If S(i) > K Then
        Value(i) = Exp(-A.rf * A.T)
      End If

      fh = 0
      If mu + sig * z > K Then fh = Exp(-A.rf * A.T)
      f = 0
      If mu > K Then f = Exp(-A.rf * A.T)
      fd = 0
      If mu - sig * z > K Then fd = Exp(-A.rf * A.T)
      Y_mu = z / 2 / sig * (fh - fd)
      Y_sig = (z ^ 2 - 1) / 2 / sig * (fh - 2 * f + fd)

      Delta(i) = mu / A.S0 * Y_mu + sig / A.S0 * Y_sig
      Vega(i) = mu * (-A.sigma * A.T + Sqr(A.T) * W) * Y_mu + _
        (sig * (-A.sigma * A.T + Sqr(A.T) * W) + sig / A.sigma)
        * Y_sig
    End If

Next i
End Sub
```

Table 9.9 illustrates the estimation of the delta and vega of a digital option with $S_0 = 10$, $K = 12$, $T = 1$, $r = 0.05$, and $\sigma = 0.4$ with 1,000,000 sample paths. We can see that the use of functional approximation and vibrato Monte Carlo simulation with variance reduction produces accurate estimations, but note that functional approximation produces error in mimicking the original function. For futher details, please refer to Ch9.7_Digital_Option.xls.

9.6.3 Multivariate Generalization

The vibrato method can easily be generalized to multiple assets with multivariate random variables. If μ_W is a column vector and then Σ_W is the variance-covariance

TABLE 9.9 Comparison of the Greeks of a Digital Option Calculated Using Different Methods

	Functional approximation	Vibrato MC	Vibrato MC (variance reduction)	Finite difference
Value	0.283486406	0.282671141	0.282205038	0.282404796
Delta	0.082405209	0.081597283	0.081830986	0.083898435
sd(Delta)	0.267619182	1.312399494	0.385493992	2.82376257
Vega	0.104526637	0.091732555	0.105778604	0.103398638
sd(Vega)	0.373565919	12.09929708	0.623442127	3.134469856
Time (s)	4.37890625	4.33984375	5.359375	3.71875

matrix, then S_W can be written as

$$S_N(W, Z) = \mu_W + C_W Z,$$

where Z is a vector of independent standard normal random variables and C_W is the matrix from Cholesky decomposition, such that $\Sigma_W = C_W C_W^T$. The joint pdf of S is given by

$$\log p_S = -\frac{1}{2}\log|\Sigma_W| - \frac{1}{2}(S_N - \mu_W)^T \Sigma_W^{-1}(S_N - \mu_W) - \frac{1}{2}d\log 2\pi,$$

where d is the dimension of Z. Differentiating the foregoing equation, we obtain

$$\frac{\partial \log p_S}{\partial \mu_W} = \Sigma_W^{-1}(S_N - \mu_W)$$

$$= C_W^{-T} Z,$$

where $C_W^{-T} = ((C_W)^{-1})^T$, and

$$\frac{\partial \log p_S}{\partial \Sigma_W} = -\frac{1}{2}\Sigma_W^{-1} + \frac{1}{2}\Sigma_W^{-1}(S_N - \mu_W)(S_N - \mu_W)^T \Sigma_W^{-1}$$

$$= \frac{1}{2}C_W^{-T}(ZZ^T - I)C_W^{-1}.$$

For a given W,

$$E_Z\left[f(S_N)\frac{\partial \log p_S}{\partial \theta}\bigg|W\right] = \left(\frac{\partial \mu_W}{\partial \theta}\right)^T E_Z\left[f(S_N)\frac{\partial \log p_S}{\partial \mu_W}\bigg|W\right]$$

$$+ \text{tr}\left(\frac{\partial \Sigma_W}{\partial \theta} E_Z\left[f(S_N)\frac{\partial \log p_S}{\partial \Sigma_W}\bigg|W\right]\right),$$

where $\text{tr}(\cdot)$ is the trace of a square matrix.

Appendix

Treasury & Structured Products – Equity
Fixed Coupon Equity-Linked Note on HSBC Holdings PLC

Indicative terms & conditions
11 Sep 2008

Please note that the Notes are not principal protected and the Notes may be redeemed by delivery of shares which may be worth substantially less than the principal amount of the Notes. Also, if an investor elects to redeem the Notes or the Notes are otherwise early redeemed prior to the Maturity Date, they may not receive 100% of the amount invested.

Issuer	
Issuer's rating	AA / Aa1 (S&P /Moody's)
Aggregate Principal Amount	HKD 50,000,000.
Denomination	HKD 100,000.
Integral multiples of Notes for transfer	Minimum transfer of 5 Note and 1 Note thereafter
Trade Date	Thu 11 Sep 2008
Strike Date	Thu 11 Sep 2008, which shall be deemed to be a Valuation Date and subject to the "Rights of the Issuer in the event of a Disrupted Day or Disruption Event" provisions.
Issue Date	Thu 25 Sep 2008
Maturity Date	The later of : (i) Thu 26 Mar 2009 and (ii) 3 Business Days after the Final Valuation Date.
Issue Price	100% of par
Share	Hsbc Holdings Plc (RIC: 0005.HK)
Exchange	Stock Exchange of Hong Kong
Related Exchange	All Relevant Stock Exchanges
Initial Price	HKD 122.9 (being the price of the Share as of the Valuation Time on the Strike Date)
Strike Price	HKD 112.4535 (91.5% of Initial Price)
Barrier Price	HKD 0 (0% of Initial Price)
Trigger Price	HKD 121.671 (99% of Initial Price)

Coupon:

Coupon Amounts	On each Coupon Payment Date$_t$, the Issuer shall pay to the Noteholder in respect of each Note an amount in HKD equal to: Denomination * Coupon Rate$_t$ Where "t" represents a number from 1 to 3 and each iteration of "t" represents an Observation Period and the corresponding Coupon Payment Date and Coupon Rate
Coupon Rate$_t$	Subject to the Trigger Event provisions below, means: (i) in respect of the first Coupon Payment Date$_1$: Coupon Rate$_1$ = 1.3333% (ii) in respect of subsequent Coupon Payment Dates$_t$ (where t = a number from 2 to 3): Coupon Rate$_t$ = $1.3333\% * \dfrac{n_t}{N_t}$

Figure A.1   Term sheet for the CRAN, page 1.

APPENDIX 383

Treasury & Structured Products – Equity
Fixed Coupon Equity-Linked Note on HSBC Holdings PLC

Where:

"n_t" means, in respect of Coupon Payment Date$_t$, the number of Valuation Dates during the Observation Period corresponding to such Coupon Payment Date$_t$ in respect of which the closing price of the Share as of the Valuation Time on a Valuation Date is at or above the Barrier Price.

"N_t" means, in respect of Coupon Payment Date$_t$, the number of days in the Observation Period corresponding to such Coupon Payment Date$_t$ that is both (i) a Scheduled Trading Day and (ii) a Business Day. The expected number of N_t in the relevant Observation Period is specified in the "Observation Period" provision below.

For the avoidance of doubt, the Period Start Dates and Period End Dates (each as defined below) of an Observation Period shall not be adjusted notwithstanding the postponement of a Valuation Date following the occurrence of a Disrupted Day for the purpose of determining "n_t."

Observation Period$_t$

In respect of a Coupon Payment Date, each Observation Period from the relevant Period Start Date to the relevant Period End Date (both dates inclusive), without adjustment, as set out in the table below.

For the purpose of determining Coupon Rate$_t$ (where t = a number from 2 to 3), the first Observation Period shall not be applicable.

t	(From and including) Period Start Date	(To and including) Period End Date	Expected N	Coupon Payment Dates
1	Not applicable	Fri 21-Nov-2008	Not applicable	Wed 26-Nov-2008
2	Mon 24-Nov-2008	Wed 21-Jan-2009	40	Thu 29-Jan-2009
3	Thu 22-Jan-2009	Mon 23-Mar-09 (The "Final Valuation Date")	40	Thu 26-Mar-09 (The "Maturity Date")

Valuation Date Means, in respect of an Observation Period, each Scheduled Trading Day during such period.

Valuation Time Means, in respect of a date, the Scheduled Closing Time on the Exchange on such date.

Coupon Payment Dates$_t$ As set out in the table in the "Observation Period" provision.

Provided that if a scheduled Valuation Date is postponed in accordance with the terms of the Base Prospectus dated **28 March 2008**, as amended and/or supplemented (the "Base Prospectus") relating to the Issuer's Structured Securities Programme (the "Programme") following the occurrence of a Disrupted Day, the relevant Coupon Payment Date shall be adjusted to 3 Business Days after the Valuation Date.

Trigger Event provisions:

Trigger Event A Trigger Event is deemed to have occurred if the price of the Share as of the Valuation Time on any Period End Date other than the Final Valuation Date is at or above the Trigger Price. For the purpose of this Trigger Event provision, a Period End Date is deemed to be a Valuation Date and subject to postponement on the occurrence of a Disrupted Day in accordance with the terms of the Base Prospectus.

In such case, the Determination Agent shall promptly notify the Noteholders of the occurrence of a Trigger Event and the Notes will be redeemed early in full by the Issuer on the Trigger Event Settlement Date at the Trigger Event Settlement Amount.

Figure A.2 Term sheet for the equity-linked notes, page 2.

Treasury & Structured Products – Equity
Fixed Coupon Equity-Linked Note on HSBC Holdings PLC

	Following the payment of the Trigger Event Settlement Amount, the Issuer shall have no further obligations under the Notes.
	For the avoidance of doubt, the failure by the Determination Agent in notifying the Noteholders of the occurrence of a Trigger Event shall not however prejudice or invalidate the occurrence or effect of such event.
Trigger Event Settlement Date	The Coupon Payment Date corresponding to the Period End Date in respect of which a Trigger Event is deemed to have occurred.
Trigger Event Settlement Amount	In respect of each Note, an amount in HKD equal to: Denomination * 100% + the Relevant Coupon Amount
	"**Relevant Coupon Amount**" means the Coupon Amount which would have been paid by the Issuer on the Coupon Payment Date corresponding to the Period End Date in respect of which a Trigger Event is deemed to have occurred but for the occurrence of the Trigger Event.

Redemption at Maturity:

Redemption Amount	At maturity, the Issuer shall redeem each Note as follows:
	(i) **Cash Settlement:** if the Final Price of the Share is at or above the Strike Price, the Issuer shall redeem each Note by the payment of the Redemption Amount on the Maturity Date determined as: Denomination * 100% ; or
	(ii) **Physical Settlement:** if the Final Price of the Share is below the Strike Price, the Issuer shall redeem the Notes by the delivery of the Reference Assets on the Physical Delivery Date.
Final Price	Means the closing price of the Share as of the Valuation Time on the Final Valuation Date.
Reference Assets	Such number of Shares determined as follows: $$\text{Denomination} * \frac{1}{K}$$ "K" means the Strike Price. No fraction of Shares will be delivered and a Noteholder will be entitled to receive an amount in cash calculated on the basis of the Final Price as determined by the Determination Agent, rounded down to the nearest whole unit of currency in lieu of such fraction.
Redemption Expenses and Taxes	As provided in the Base Prospectus save that stamp duty payable in connection with the transfer of the Reference Assets shall be borne equally by the Issuer and the Noteholder.

General Terms:

Business Days	London and Hong Kong
Business Day Convention	Following
Settlement Type	Cash, and if applicable, physical
Listing	None
Clearing	Euroclear / Clearstream, Luxembourg
Determination Agent	
Secondary Market Transactions	Under normal market conditions, ▮ may purchase the Notes in the secondary market and, upon request by a Noteholder, will, within a reasonable time, provide secondary market prices during the term of the Notes. Such prices may be subject to change by the time of the transaction. The minimum transaction size for a secondary market

Figure A.3 Term sheet for the equity-linked notes, page 3.

Treasury & Structured Products – Equity
Fixed Coupon Equity-Linked Note on HSBC Holdings PLC

	transaction is 5 Note. Notes cannot be partially sold.
Market Disruption Events:	A Market Disruption Event shall have occurred if any of the following occurs: (i) Trading Disruption; (ii) Exchange Disruption; or (iii) Early Closure.
Early Redemptions	On the occurrence of an Issuer Tax Event and/or Change in Law and/or Hedging Disruption and/or Increased Cost of Hedging, the Issuer may redeem the Notes in whole and not in part on the Early Redemption Date by giving a Special Redemption Notice to the Noteholders at the Early Redemption Amount which shall be an amount determined by the Determination Agent acting in a reasonable manner.
Early Redemption Date	The third Business Day after the Special Redemption Notice is given by or on behalf of the Issuer to the Noteholders.
Selling Restrictions	Applicable, as set out in the Base Prospectus. **SUBJECT TO CERTAIN EXCEPTIONS, AS DETAILED IN "PURCHASE AND SALE" IN THE BASE PROSPECTUS, THE NOTES MAY NOT BE OFFERED OR SOLD WITHIN THE UNITED STATES OR TO, OR FOR THE ACCOUNT OR BENEFIT OF, US PERSONS (AS DEFINED IN REGULATIONS UNDER THE US SECURITIES ACT OF 1933).**
Documentation	The proposed Notes would be issued by the Issuer under the Programme. The full terms and conditions of the Notes will be set out in the Final Terms, to be dated the Issue Date of the Notes, relating to the Notes, and in the Base Prospectus. A copy of the Base Prospectus should be obtained from the Issuer if the investor does not already have a copy.
Governing Law	English

Risk Warning : It is not an offer to the public. The contents of this document have not been reviewed by any regulatory authority in Hong Kong. You are advised to exercise caution in relation to the offer. If you are in any doubt about any of the contents of this document, you should obtain independent professional advice.

Figure A.4 Term sheet for the equity-linked notes, page 4.

Treasury & Structured Products – Equity
Fixed Coupon Equity-Linked Note on HSBC Holdings PLC

Risk Disclosure Statements

The followings are the standard risk disclosure statements of ▮▮▮▮▮▮ ("the Bank") covering equity-linked instruments/equity-linked notes/equity-linked certificates ("Equity-linked Product"). You are advised to read and fully understand all the relevant risk disclosure statements herein and to obtain independent legal advice, if necessary.

General Disclosure : Users of the information contained in this Term Sheet are advised to make their own independent judgment or obtain advice from their professional advisers with respect to the information, legal implications and any other matters contained herein.
Any notice or other communication from ▮▮▮▮▮▮ (the "Bank") to you shall be deemed to be received (a) if given or made by post, the following Business Day after the date of despatch; and (b) if given or made by fax or email, when despatched, regardless of whether you have actually received it.
The Bank shall have no payment obligation to you under this Term Sheet unless and until it has been paid by the Issuer, the payment agent or the calculation agent (as the case may be).
The Bank shall have no obligation to make payment and/or give notice to the investors on Hong Kong non-business days. If any day within any specified notice period falls on a Hong Kong non-business day or if any corresponding notice from the Issuer, the payment agent or the calculation agent (as the case may be) is received by the Bank outside its normal office hours, the length of such notice period will be abridged accordingly. Thus, the Bank may give notice to the investors after the relevant notified event or incident has taken place.
The Bank may (but is not obliged to) give notice to the investors by phone. If such phone notice is given to the investors, it shall be deemed to be valid and effective and will be followed by a written notice sent out by personal delivery, post, fax or email. Any failure or delay in delivery of the written notice will not affect the validity and effectiveness of the phone notice.

Investment Suitability : The risk of loss in investing the Equity-linked Product can be substantial. Investor should therefore firstly, study and understand the structure of the Equity-linked Product before he/she places an order and secondly, carefully consider whether the Equity-linked Product is suitable in light of his/her financial position and investment objectives. If the investor provides irrevocable instructions to the Issuer he/she does so at his/her risk and has not relied on the Bank's advice and recommendation.

Credit Risk : Investors of the Equity-linked Product are exposed to the credit risk of the Issuer, whose Moody's and Standard & Poor's ratings (if applicable) are set out respectively in the Term Sheet attached herewith. The aforesaid ratings reflect the independent opinion of the relevant rating agencies as to the safety of payments of principal and interest. These ratings are not a guarantee of credit quality. These ratings do not take into consideration any risks associated with fluctuations in the market value of the Equity-linked Product, or where factors other than the Issuer's credit quality determine the level of principal and interest payments.

Currency Risk : The profit or loss in the Equity-linked Product will be affected by fluctuations in currency exchange rates where there is a need to convert from the currency denomination of the Equity-linked Product to another denomination. Any fall in the currency denomination of the Equity-linked Product will reduce the amount the investor may receive when a conversion is made.

Hedging Risk : The market price of the underlying share may depend upon the hedging transactions of the Issuer or any of its affiliates which in turn will depend upon market conditions at the time of such hedging. The market may be affected by such hedging.

Potential Conflict of Interest : The Issuer or any of its affiliates may from time to time engage in transaction involving the security or securities underlying the Equity-linked Product for their proprietary accounts and for other accounts under their management. Such trading may influence the value of the underlying stock or stocks and therefore the value of the Equity-linked Product.

Liquidity Risk : The investor shall not be entitled to withdraw all or part of the Equity-linked Product during the tenor without the Bank's prior consent (which, if granted, may be subject to such conditions and terms as the Bank may require). The Bank may at its absolute discretion refuse to give such consent, or impose such conditions as the Bank may determine for the conversion or withdrawal of the Equity-linked Product at the investor's request, such conditions to include (without limitation) the deduction of such breakage costs as the Bank shall determine conclusively acting in good faith. Such breakage costs shall include the costs, expenses, liabilities or losses incurred or suffered by the Bank as a consequence of breaking its hedge, or funding from other sources in respect of the Equity-linked Product. Therefore, the total amount repaid on an early withdrawal of the Equity-linked Product at the investor's request may be less than the Principal Amount.

Figure A.5   Term sheet for the equity-linked notes, page 5.

APPENDIX 387

Treasury & Structured Products – Equity
Fixed Coupon Equity-Linked Note on HSBC Holdings PLC

Secondary Market : Equity-linked Products are not a trading instrument. There will be no a liquid secondary market for the Equity-linked Products. On request the Issuer may but is not obliged to purchase the Equity-linked Product from the holder at a price determined by the Issuer by reference to current market conditions. Prior to maturity, the value of an option is influenced by various factors including, but not limited to: volatility, interest rates, dividends and time remaining to maturity.

Corporate Actions : Other risks may impact on the value of an Equity-linked Product, for example corporate actions in relation to the underlying stock(s) may occur and have a dilutive effect on the value of the underlying stocks. In certain circumstances the Issuer has discretion as to the adjustments that it makes, if any, following corporate events.

Risks of Investing In Equity-linked Product : The price of the underlying stock may go down as well as up. For customers investing in Equity-linked Products, their end-investment may therefore be the underlying stock. There is an inherent risk that losses may be incurred rather than profits made as a result of buying and selling stocks. Stocks may even be valueless. Equity-linked Product is suitable only for those investors who can afford the risks involved and are conversant in the stock market in which the underlying stock is traded. Investors should also consider whether the investment strategy or Equity-linked Product is suitable for them in light of their own financial position and investment objectives.

The contents of this document have not been reviewed by any regulatory authority in Hong Kong. You are advised to exercise caution in relation to the offer. If you are in any doubt about any of the contents of this document, you should obtain independent professional advice.

Figure A.6 Term sheet for the equity-linked notes, page 6.

Treasury & Structured Products – Equity
Fixed Coupon Equity-Linked Note on HSBC Holdings PLC

The Product is for yield enhancement purpose.

REQUESTED BY			ISSUER REFERENCE		
Notional Amount / Number of Certificates	:		Handling AO	:	
			Principal AO	:	
Customer Investment Objective	:	☐ Yield Enhancement ☐ Hedging ☐ Cost Reduction I / We understand that my / our Investment Objective is same as / different from* that of Product Objective and I / We fully understand all the inherent risk(s).			
Customer Signature	:		Customer Name	:	
Trade Date and Time	:		Checked by	:	
Settlement Account #	:		Cus Reg #	:	
Securities Account #	:		HKMA R.I. Registration #	:	
Date and Time Phone Confirmed with Customer	:		Location of Tape Recording:	:	
Bank Use Only					
Customer Risk Rating	:	G B C RA E	Product Risk Rating	:	H M L VL
Customer Investment Risk Questionnaire (CIRQ) signed	:	YES NO N/A	Verified by	:	
Elderly Declaration Signed	:	YES NO N/A	Verified by	:	
Declaration of Deviation Signed	:	YES NO N/A	Verified by	:	
W8- Ben Signed	:	YES NO N/A	Verified by	:	
Professional Investor (PI)	:	YES NO N/A	Verified by	:	
HF	:	Y W: Approved by _____			

Please delete as appropriate.

Figure A.7 Term sheet for the equity-linked notes, page 7.

Treasury & Structured Products – Equity

2-Year HKD 34.00% (annualized basis) Periodic Daily Knock Out Variable Maturity Range Accrual Equity-Linked Notes (redemption linked to the ordinary/H-shares of China Communications Construction Co Ltd-H and Datang Intl Power Gen Co-H)

Indicative terms & conditions
6 Sep 2007

Issuer:	
Issuer Credit Rating (long term):	AA+ Standard & Poor's /Aa2 Moody's. For the avoidance of doubt, this is the long term credit rating of the Issuer and the Note are not rated.
Instrument:	Structured Notes
Structure:	2-Year HKD 34.00% (annualized basis) Periodic Daily Knock Out Variable Maturity Range Accrual Equity-Linked Notes with 5.6667% Fixed Coupon after the first 2 months and Variable Coupon payable 2 mos thereafter, subject to Mandatory Early Redemption Provision.
Trade Date:	September 6, 2007
Settlement Date:	September 20, 2007
Scheduled Fixing Date:	September 21, 2009
Maturity Date:	Scheduled Fixing Date, provided that in respect of each Share, if such date is not a Scheduled Trading Day then the next following Scheduled Trading Day, subject to the provisions under "Effects of Disrupted Day"
Redemption Date:	Maturity Date + 5 Business Days if cash settlement (which is currently expected to be September 28, 2009.) Maturity Date + 5 Scheduled Trading Days if physical settlement (which is currently expected to be September 28, 2009)
Issue size:	HKD 14,000,000
Denomination of Notes:	HKD 50,000
Minimum Transfer Amount:	HKD 500,000
Issue Price:	100%

Basket: A basket composed of Shares as indicated below:

Issuer of Shares (with Reuters Code)	Initial Price (S_o)	Conversion Price# and Lower Range Band# $(X_n = 80.00\% \times S_o)$	Callable Price# $(92.00\% \times S_o)$	Number of Shares per Note if physical delivery at Maturity (N_I)
China Communications Construction Co Ltd-H (1800.HK)	HKD 18.02	HKD 14.416	HKD 16.5784	HKD50,000 / X_n
Datang Intl Power Gen Co-H (0991.HK)	HKD 7.8	HKD 6.24	HKD 7.176	HKD50,000 / X_n

rounded to the nearest HKD0.0001, HKD0.00005 being rounded upward

Figure A.8 Term sheet for the multi-asset structured notes, page 1.

Treasury & Structured Products – Equity

2-Year HKD 34.00% (annualized basis) Periodic Daily Knock Out Variable Maturity Range Accrual Equity-Linked Notes (redemption linked to the ordinary/H-shares of **China Communications Construction Co Ltd-H and Datang Intl Power Gen Co-H**)

Exchange:	The Stock Exchange of Hong Kong Limited
Related Exchange:	In respect of a Share means the principal exchange (if any) on which options or futures contracts relating to the Share are traded or quoted, as determined by the Calculation Agent.
Periodic Coupon Determination Dates:	On each 2-month anniversary of the Settlement Date up to and including the Scheduled Fixing Date, which are expected to be November 20, 2007; January 21, 2008; March 20, 2008; May 20, 2008; July 21, 2008; September 22, 2008; November 20, 2008; January 20, 2009; March 20, 2009; May 20, 2009; July 20, 2009; and September 21, 2009 provided that if any such date is not a Scheduled Trading Day then the next following Scheduled Trading Day, subject to the provisions under "Effects of Disrupted Day."
Periodic Coupon Payment Dates:	5 Business Days after each Periodic Coupon Determination Date, provided that if Mandatory Early Redemption has occurred and the Mandatory Early Redemption Date is earlier than such Periodic Coupon Determination Date, 5 Business Days after such Mandatory Early Redemption Date.
Periodic Coupon:	On each Periodic Coupon Payment Date, a coupon (calculated to 4 decimal places, with 0.00005 being rounded upwards) in HKD will be payable by the Issuer in accordance with the provisions below:

Figure A.9 Term sheet for the multi-asset structured notes, page 2.

Treasury & Structured Products – Equity

2-Year HKD 34.00% (annualized basis) Periodic Daily Knock Out Variable Maturity Range Accrual Equity-Linked Notes (redemption linked to the ordinary/H-shares of **China Communications Construction Co Ltd-H and Datang Intl Power Gen Co-H**)

Coupon Details:

Coupon Period and Type	Start Date (Sdt_x)	End Date (Edt_x)	Coupon*
1st Periodic Fixed Coupon	September 21, 2007	November 20, 2007	5.6667% × Denomination of the Notes, with no adjustment.
2nd Periodic Variable Coupon	November 21, 2007	January 21, 2008	Coupon(x)
3rd Periodic Variable Coupon	January 22, 2008	March 20, 2008	Coupon(x)
4th Periodic Variable Coupon	March 21, 2008	May 20, 2008	Coupon(x)
5th Periodic Variable Coupon	May 21, 2008	July 21, 2008	Coupon(x)
6th Periodic Variable Coupon	July 22, 2008	September 22, 2008	Coupon(x)
7th Periodic Variable Coupon	September 23, 2008	November 20, 2008	Coupon(x)
8th Periodic Variable Coupon	November 21, 2008	January 20, 2009	Coupon(x)
9th Periodic Variable Coupon	January 21, 2009	March 20, 2009	Coupon(x)
10th Periodic Variable Coupon	March 21, 2009	May 20, 2009	Coupon(x)
11th Periodic Variable Coupon	May 21, 2009	July 20, 2009	Coupon(x)
12th Periodic Variable Coupon	July 21, 2009	September 21, 2009	Coupon(x)

* Coupon will be calculated as follow:
Coupon(x) = Accrual Factor x (n_x/N_x) x Denomination of Notes
Where: Accrual Factor = 5.6667%, and
 x = 2nd to 12th
n_x = the number of Exchange Business Days in the xth Periodic Variable Coupon period (from Start Date (Sdt_x) to the earlier of (i) End Date (Edt) and (ii) the Mandatory Early Redemption Date (if any), both inclusive) on which the Closing Price of all the Shares in the Basket are greater than or equal to the respective Lower Range Band
N_x = the number of Exchange Business Days in the xth Periodic Variable Coupon period (from Start Date (Sdt_x) to End Date (Edt_x), both inclusive)

Observation Date:	Each Scheduled Trading Day during the period from and including the first Periodic Fixed Coupon End Date to but excluding the Maturity Date, subject to the provisions under "Effects of Disrupted Day."
Mandatory Early Redemption Provision:	If the Closing Price of the Laggard Share on an Observation Date is at or above its Callable Price, a Mandatory Early Redemption Event is deemed to have occurred on the Scheduled Observation Date relating to such Observation Date (the "Mandatory Early Redemption Date") and each Note will be mandatorily early redeemed on the 5th Business Day after the last occurring Observation Date in respect of the Scheduled Observation Date (the "Mandatory Early Redemption Payment Date") at HKD 50,000 (the "Mandatory Early Redemption Amount"), together with payment of the Periodic Coupon (if any).

Figure A.10 Term sheet for the multi-asset structured notes, page 3.

Treasury & Structured Products – Equity

2-Year HKD 34.00% (annualized basis) Periodic Daily Knock Out Variable Maturity Range Accrual Equity-Linked Notes (redemption linked to the ordinary/H-shares of **China Communications Construction Co Ltd-H and Datang Intl Power Gen Co-H**)

Redemption at Maturity: Depending on the Closing Prices of the Shares in the Basket on the Maturity Date, each ELN shall be redeemed according to either (1) or (2) below:

(1) If Snl is quoted at or above its Xnl on the Maturity Date, each ELN will give a return of HKD 50,000.

(2) If Snl is quoted below Xnl on the Maturity Date, each ELN will be converted into the Nl number of Laggard Shares.

Where

- Snl is the Closing Price of the Laggard Share on the Maturity Date.

  $Laggard$ Share means, in respect of a Mandatory Early Redemption Date or the Maturity Date (as the case may be), the Share with the lowest value of $\frac{S_n}{S_o}$ by comparison of $\frac{S_n}{S_o}$ of all the Shares comprising the Basket on such Mandatory Early Redemption Date or the Maturity Date (as the case may be), provided that if more than one Share has such lowest value, the Calculation Agent shall in its sole discretion determine which of such Shares shall be the Laggard Share for such Mandatory Early Redemption Date or the Maturity Date (as the case may be).

- Xnl is the Conversion Price of the Laggard Share.
- S_n is the Closing Price of a Share comprising the Basket on a Mandatory Early Redemption Date or the Maturity Date (as the case may be)
- S_o is the Initial Price of a Share on Trade Date.

"Closing Price" means, in respect of a Share and a Scheduled Trading Day, the official closing price of such Share as published by the relevant Exchange for that day, subject to the provisions under "Effects of Disrupted Day", or if such price is not published for whatever reason other than as a result of the occurrence of Disrupted Day, the value of a Share as of the actual closing time of the relevant Exchange on that Scheduled Trading Day in the good faith estimation of the Calculation Agent.

Investors should note that, where the Notes are to be physically redeemed, the number of Laggard Shares to be delivered will be rounded down to the nearest whole number of Laggard Shares (on a

Figure A.11   Term sheet for the multi-asset structured notes, page 4.

Treasury & Structured Products – Equity

2-Year HKD 34.00% (annualized basis) Periodic Daily Knock Out Variable Maturity Range Accrual Equity-Linked Notes (redemption linked to the ordinary/H-shares of **China Communications Construction Co Ltd-H and Datang Intl Power Gen Co-H)**

	per Note basis), and the *cash amount* in respect of the amount rounded off will be paid to the Holder, being the quantity of Laggard Shares rounded off times the Closing Price of the Laggard Shares as of the Maturity Date converted into the prevailing exchange rate, as determined by the Calculation Agent.
	Notwithstanding (2) above, please also note that the Issuer is entitled to cash settle all or any of the Laggard Shares as more particularly set out in the terms and conditions of the Global Security.
Settlement:	Cash settlement in HKD or physical delivery of Underlying Shares through CCASS
Scheduled Trading Day:	In respect of a Share, a day on which each relevant Exchange and each relevant Related Exchange are scheduled to be open for their respective regular trading sessions.
Scheduled Closing Time:	means, in respect of an Exchange or Related Exchange and a Scheduled Trading Day, the scheduled weekday closing time of such Exchange or Related Exchange on such Scheduled Trading Day, without regard to after hours or any other trading outside of the regular trading session hours.
Exchange Business Day:	Any Scheduled Trading Day on which each Exchange and each Related Exchange are open for trading during their respective regular trading sessions, notwithstanding any such Exchange or Related Exchange closing prior to its Scheduled Closing Time PROVIDED THAT for the purposes of determining the Periodic Variable Coupons the definition of "Exchange Business Day" shall be modified to exclude a day on which it is a Disrupted Day.
Business Day:	A day (excluding a Saturday and Sunday) on which banks and foreign exchange markets are open for business in Hong Kong.
Adjustments and Extraordinary Events:	If the Calculation Agent determines that an event has occurred which has a diluting, concentrative or any other effect on the Shares, then following each such event, the Calculation Agent shall determine any corresponding adjustments to the conditions (including, without limitation, adjusting the Initial Price, Conversion Price, Callable Price, and Lower Range Band, replacing a Share with another share and/or other securities and/or assets, Nl number of Shares per Note if physical delivery at maturity, the Periodic Variable Coupon, or the Redemption Amount or Mandatory Early Redemption Amount), which in the sole

Figure A.12 Term sheet for the multi-asset structured notes, page 5.

Treasury & Structured Products – Equity

2-Year HKD 34.00% (annualized basis) Periodic Daily Knock Out Variable Maturity Range Accrual Equity-Linked Notes (redemption linked to the ordinary/H-shares of **China Communications Construction Co Ltd-H and Datang Intl Power Gen Co-H**)

	discretion of the Calculation Agent is appropriate to account for the diluting, concentrative or other effect of the relevant event and which adjustments shall be effective as of the date determined by the Issuer.
Disrupted Day:	means in respect of a Share, a Scheduled Trading Day on which the relevant Exchange or Related Exchange fails to open for trading during its regular trading session or on which there is, during 1 h prior to the actual closing time of the relevant Exchange or Related Exchange, material trading or exchange disruption or there is an early closure of the relevant Exchange or Related Exchange with less than 1 h (which shall exclude, where relevant, any time period when the Exchange or Related Exchange is closed between the end of the morning trading session and the start of the afternoon trading session) notice (till the actual time of closure or the deadline for inputting orders to execute trades at the closing time of the relevant Exchange or Related Exchange), all as set out in the 2002 ISDA Equity Derivatives Definitions.
Effects of Disrupted Day:	If the Maturity Date, an Observation Date or a Periodic Coupon Determination Date is a Disrupted Day for a Share, then the Maturity Date, such Observation Date or such Periodic Coupon Determination Date shall be the first succeeding Scheduled Trading Day which is not a Disrupted Day, unless each of the 8 Scheduled Trading Days immediately following the day originally scheduled to be the Maturity Date, such Observation Date or such Periodic Coupon Determination Date is a Disrupted Day, in which case that 8th Scheduled Trading Day shall be the Maturity Date, such Observation Date or such Periodic Coupon Determination Date, notwithstanding the fact that it is a Disrupted Day, and the Calculation Agent shall determine the Closing Price of the affected Share as of that based on its good faith estimate of the value of that Share as of the closing time of the relevant Exchange on that 8th Scheduled Trading Day. For the avoidance of doubt, (a) for the purposes of determining the Laggard Share as of the Maturity Date or an Observation Date (as the case may be), the Closing Price of the unaffected Share shall be determined on the Scheduled Maturity Date or the Scheduled Observation Date relating to such Observation Date (as the case may be) and the Closing Price of the affected Share shall be determined on the Maturity Date or such Observation Date (as the case may be) as postponed in accordance with the provisions under this paragraph "Effects of Disrupted Day"; and (b) the Redemption Date is determined by reference to the last occurring Maturity Date and in the event that no Mandatory Early Redemption Event occurs, in respect of a Scheduled Periodic Coupon Determination Date, the Periodic Coupon Payment Date is determined

Figure A.13 Term sheet for the multi-asset structured notes, page 6.

APPENDIX   *395*

Treasury & Structured Products – Equity

2-Year HKD 34.00% (annualized basis) Periodic Daily Knock Out Variable Maturity Range Accrual Equity-Linked Notes (redemption linked to the ordinary/H-shares of **China Communications Construction Co Ltd-H and Datang Intl Power Gen Co-H**)

	by reference to the last occurring Periodic Coupon Determination Date. The Mandatory Early Redemption Payment Date is determined by reference to the last occurring Observation Date in respect of the Mandatory Early Redemption Date.
Scheduled Maturity Date:	any original date that, but for the occurrence of an event causing a Disrupted Day, would have been a Maturity Date.
Scheduled Observation Date:	Means any original date that, but for the occurrence of an event causing a Disrupted Day, would have been an Observation Date.
Scheduled Periodic Coupon Determination Date:	any original date that, but for the occurrence of an event causing a Disrupted Day, would have been a Periodic Coupon Determination Date.
Limited Recourse Provisions:	The parties acknowledge and agree that to the extent the Issuer (or its affiliates) enter into securities or futures or derivatives transaction(s) ("Hedge Transactions") with any party in the local jurisdiction, including, without limitation, an entity affiliated, related to or controlled by the Issuer ("Hedge Counterparty") to hedge these Notes and the Hedge Counterparty for such transactions fails or delays for any reason (including a default by the local exchange or clearinghouse) to make any payment, delivery, or distribution with respect to a Hedge Transaction, then the Issuer's obligation to pay any amounts due hereunder shall be reduced and/or delayed accordingly.
Clearing Systems:	Euroclear and Clearstream
Listing:	None
Form:	The Notes will be issued as registered notes in permanent global form, with the ▮▮▮ representing the Notes deposited with a common depositary of the Clearing Systems. Copies of the form of the Global Security containing the Terms and Conditions of the Notes are available on request from UBS AG, Hong Kong Branch.
Further Issue:	The Issuer may, from time to time without the consent of the Holder, issue further securities having the same terms and conditions as the Notes so as to form a single series and be fungible with the Notes.
Market Making:	The Notes are not listed, traded, or publicly quoted on any stock

Figure A.14 Term sheet for the multi-asset structured notes, page 7.

Treasury & Structured Products – Equity

2-Year HKD 34.00% (annualized basis) Periodic Daily Knock Out Variable Maturity Range Accrual Equity-Linked Notes (redemption linked to the ordinary/H-shares of **China Communications Construction Co Ltd-H and Datang Intl Power Gen Co-H**)

exchange or quotation system. The Issuer or its affiliates may from time to time, whether upon request or otherwise, offer to purchase Notes from existing holders or to sell Notes, at such price and in such quantity as determined in the absolute discretion of the offeror. The Issuer or its affiliates are under no obligation to make such offer to sell or purchase, and if made, may be withdrawn at any time without notice. Any offer to sell or purchase by the Issuer or its affiliates or actual sales and purchases made pursuant to the offers do not assure the existence or continuance of a liquid secondary market for the Notes, and the Issuer or its affiliates may discontinue such activities at any time.

Governing Law:	English law
Calculation Agent:	

Figure A.15 Term sheet for the multi-asset structured notes, page 8.

Treasury & Structured Products – Equity

2-Year HKD 34.00% (annualized basis) Periodic Daily Knock Out Variable Maturity Range Accrual Equity-Linked Notes (redemption linked to the ordinary/H-shares of **China Communications Construction Co Ltd-H and Datang Intl Power Gen Co-H**)

Risk Disclosure Statements

The followings are the standard risk disclosure statements of ▮▮▮▮▮▮▮▮▮▮ ("the Bank") covering equity-linked instruments/equity-linked notes/equity-linked certificates ("Equity-linked Product"). You are advised to read and fully understand all the relevant risk disclosure statements herein and to obtain independent legal advice, if necessary.

General Disclosure	:	Users of the information contained in this Term Sheet are advised to make their own independent judgment or obtain advice from their professional advisers with respect to the information, legal implications and any other matters contained herein.
		Any notice or other communication from ▮▮▮▮▮▮▮▮▮▮ (the "Bank") to you shall be deemed to be received (a) if given or made by post, the following Business Day after the date of despatch; and (b) if given or made by fax or email, when despatched, regardless of whether you have actually received it.
		The Bank shall have no payment obligation to you under this Term Sheet unless and until it has been paid by the Issuer, the payment agent, or the calculation agent (as the case may be).
		The Bank shall have no obligation to make payment and/or give notice to the investors on Hong Kong non-business days. If any day within any specified notice period falls on a Hong Kong non-business day or if any corresponding notice from the Issuer, the payment agent or the calculation agent (as the case may be) is received by the Bank outside its normal office hours, the length of such notice period will be abridged accordingly. Thus, the Bank may give notice to the investors after the relevant notified event or incident has taken place.
		The Bank may (but is not obliged to) give notice to the investors by phone. If such phone notice is given to the investors, it shall be deemed to be valid and effective and will be followed by a written notice sent out by personal delivery, post, fax, or email. Any failure or delay in delivery of the written notice will not affect the validity and effectiveness of the phone notice.
Investment Suitability	:	The risk of loss in investing the Equity-linked Product can be substantial. Investor should therefore firstly, study and understand the structure of the Equity-linked Product before he/she places an order and secondly, carefully consider whether the Equity-linked Product is suitable in light of his/her financial position and investment objectives. If the investor provides irrevocable instructions to the Issuer he/she does so at his/her risk and has not relied on the Bank's advice and recommendation.
Credit Risk	:	Investors of the Equity-linked Product are exposed to the credit risk of the Issuer, whose Moody's and Standard & Poor's ratings (if applicable) are set out respectively in the Term Sheet attached herewith. The aforesaid ratings reflect the independent opinion of the relevant rating agencies as to the safety of payments of principal and interest. These ratings are not a guarantee of credit quality. These ratings do not take into consideration any risks associated with fluctuations in the market value of the Equity-linked Product, or where factors other than the Issuer's credit quality determine the level of principal and interest payments.
Currency Risk	:	The profit or loss in the Equity-linked Product will be affected by fluctuations in currency exchange rates where there is a need to convert from the currency denomination of the Equity-linked Product to another denomination. Any fall in the currency denomination of the Equity-linked Product will reduce the amount the investor may receive when a conversion is made.
Hedging Risk	:	The market price of the underlying share may depend upon the hedging transactions of the Issuer or any of its affiliates which in turn will depend upon market conditions at the time of such hedging. The market may be affected by such hedging.
Potential Conflict of Interest	:	The Issuer or any of its affiliates may from time to time engage in transaction involving the security or securities underlying the Equity-linked Product for their proprietary accounts and for other accounts under their management. Such trading may influence the value of the underlying stock or stocks and therefore the value of the Equity-linked Product.
Liquidity Risk	:	The investor shall not be entitled to withdraw all or part of the Equity-linked Product during the tenor without the Bank's prior consent (which, if granted, may be subject to such conditions and terms as the Bank may require). The Bank may at its absolute discretion refuse to give such consent, or impose such conditions as the Bank may determine for the conversion or withdrawal of the Equity-linked Product at the investor's request, such conditions to include (without limitation) the deduction of such breakage costs as the Bank shall determine conclusively acting in good faith. Such breakage costs shall include the costs, expenses, liabilities, or losses incurred or suffered by the Bank as a consequence of breaking its hedge, or funding from other sources in respect of the Equity-linked Product. Therefore, the total amount repaid on an early withdrawal of the Equity-linked Product at the investor's request may be less than the

The information contained herein is provided to you by ▮▮▮▮▮▮▮▮▮▮ for discussion purposes only and may be amended, superseded or replaced in its entirety by subsequent proposals or communications. The issuance of and details contained in this document, which is not for public circulation, does not constitute an offer or solicitation for, or advice that you should enter into, the purchase or sale of any security, commodity or other investment product or investment agreement, or any other contract or agreement whatsoever. Any information contained herein is confidential and proprietary in nature and must not be disclosed to any third party without the prior written consent of ▮▮▮▮▮▮▮▮▮▮. The information may contain information obtained from sources which ▮▮▮▮▮▮▮▮▮▮ Limited believes to be reliable, but ▮▮▮▮▮▮▮▮▮▮ has not independently verified such information. ▮▮▮▮▮▮▮▮▮▮ makes no representation or warranty (express or implied) of any nature, nor does ▮▮▮▮▮▮▮▮▮▮ accept any responsibility or liability of any kind, with respect to the accuracy or completeness of the information and ▮▮▮▮▮▮▮▮▮▮ accepts no responsibility for any errors, omissions or misstatements however caused. Use of the information contained herein is entirely at your own risk. Any opinion contained herein (if any) constitutes ▮▮▮▮▮▮▮▮▮▮ judgment as of the date indicated and is subject to change without notice. The information does not purport to identify or but it to somebody all of the risks (direct or indirect) which may be associated with the transaction(s) (if any) stated in the above information. Neither ▮▮▮▮▮▮▮▮▮▮ nor any of its affiliates is advising you in respect hereof; accordingly you should seek such advice and assistance before acting on the information, as you deem necessary from your professional advisers. Please note that the above prices or levels are for indicative purposes only and may vary in accordance with changes in market conditions. No liability is accepted whatsoever for any direct, indirect or consequential loss arising from the use of this document, the distribution of which may be restricted by law in certain jurisdictions. ▮▮▮▮▮▮▮▮▮▮ or connected companies, their clients and employees, may have a position or engage in the transaction(s) contained in the information. Brokerage or fees may be earned by the affiliates of ▮▮▮▮▮▮▮▮▮▮ in respect of any business transacted by them in all or any of the securities or investments referred to in this document. ▮▮▮▮▮▮▮▮▮▮ is not acting as a fiduciary for or an adviser to you in any matter in respect of the information.

Figure A.16 Term sheet for the multi-asset structured notes, page 9.

Treasury & Structured Products – Equity

2-Year HKD 34.00% (annualized basis) Periodic Daily Knock Out Variable Maturity Range Accrual Equity-Linked Notes (redemption linked to the ordinary/H-shares of **China Communications Construction Co Ltd-H and Datang Intl Power Gen Co-H**)

	:	Principal Amount.
Secondary Market	:	Equity-linked Products are not a trading instrument. There will not be a liquid secondary market for the Equity-linked Products. On request the Issuer may but is not obliged to purchase the Equity-linked Product from the holder at a price determined by the Issuer by reference to current market conditions. Prior to maturity, the value of an option is influenced by various factors including, but not limited to: volatility, interest rates, dividends, and time remaining to maturity.
Corporate Actions	:	Other risks may impact on the value of an Equity-linked Product, for example, corporate actions in relation to the underlying stock(s) may occur and have a dilutive effect on the value of the underlying stocks. In certain circumstances the Issuer has discretion as to the adjustments that it makes, if any, following corporate events.
Risks of Investing in Equity-linked Product	:	The price of the underlying stock may go down as well as up. For customers investing in Equity-linked Products, their end-investment may therefore be the underlying stock. There is an inherent risk that losses may be incurred rather than profits made as a result of buying and selling stocks. Stocks may even be valueless. Equity-linked Product is suitable only for those investors who can afford the risks involved and are conversant in the stock market in which the underlying stock is traded. Investors should also consider whether the investment strategy or Equity-linked Product is suitable for them in light of their own financial position and investment objectives.
		The contents of this document have not been reviewed by any regulatory authority in Hong Kong. You are advised to exercise caution in relation to the offer. If you are in any doubt about any of the contents of this document, you should obtain independent professional advice.

Figure A.17 Term sheet for the multi-asset structured notes, page 10.

APPENDIX *399*

Treasury & Structured Products – Equity

2-Year HKD 34.00% (annualized basis) Periodic Daily Knock Out Variable Maturity Range Accrual Equity-Linked Notes (redemption linked to the ordinary/H-shares of **China Communications Construction Co Ltd-H and Datang Intl Power Gen Co-H**)

REQUESTED BY			ISSUER REFERENCE		
Notional Amount / Number of Certificates	:		Handling AO	:	
Customer Signature	:		Principal AO	:	
Customer Name	:		Professional Investor	:	YES NO
Trade Date and Time	:		Checked by	:	
Settlement Account #	:		Cus Reg #	:	
Securities Account #	:		HKMA R.I. Registration #	:	
Date and Time Phone Confirmed with Customer	:		Location of Tape Recording:	:	
Customer Risk Rating	:	G B C RA E	Product Risk Rating	:	H M L VL
Cus Investment Risk Questionnaire Signed	:	YES NO N/A	Verified by	:	
Elderly Declaration Signed:	:	YES NO N/A	Verified by	:	
Declaration of Deviation Signed	:	YES NO N/A	Verified by	:	
W8- Ben Signed	:	YES NO N/A	Verified by	:	

Figure A.18 Term sheet for the multi-asset structured notes, page 11.

References

Abid F, Naifar N. Copula based simulation procedures for pricing basket credit derivatives. MPRA Working Paper (2007).

Andersen L. Simple and efficient simulation of the Heston stochastic volatility model. Journal of Computational Finance 2008;11:1–42.

Artzner P, Delbaen F, Eber JM, Heath D. Coherent measures of risk, Mathematical Finance 1999;9:203–228.

Asmussen S, Glynn PW. *Stochastic Simulation: Algorithm and Analysis*. New York: Springer; 1987.

Bjork T. *Arbitrage Theory in Continuous Time*. London: Oxford Finance Series; 2009.

Bollerslev T. Generalized autoregressive conditional heteroskedasticity. Journal of Econometrics 1986;31:307–327.

Bonnans J, Gilbert JC, Lemarechal C, Sagastizabal CA. *Numerical Optimization: Theoretical and Practical Aspects*. Berlin: Springer-Verlag; 2006.

Black F, Cox JC. Valuing corporate securities: Some effects of bond indenture provisions. The Journal of Finance 1976;31:351–367.

Black F, Scholes M. The pricing of options and corporate liabilities. Journal of Political Economy 1973;81:637–659.

Brace A, Gatarek D, Musiela M. The market model of interest rate dynamics. Mathematical Finance 1997;7:127–154.

Brigo D, Mercurio F. *Interest Rate Models: Theory and Practice*. New York: Springer; 2007.

Carr P, Madan D. Option valuation using the fast Fourier transform, Journal of Computational Finance 1999;2:61–73.

Chan NH. *Time Series: Applications to Finance with R and S-Plus*. 2nd ed. New York: Wiley; 2010.

Chan NH, Wong HY. *Simulation Techniques in Financial Risk Management*. New York: Wiley; 2006.

Derman E, Kani I. Riding on a Smile. Risk 1994;7:139–145.

Duan JC. Maximum likelihood estimation using price data of the derivative contract. Mathematical Finance 1994;4:155–167.

Duan JC. The GARCH option pricing model. Mathematical Finance 1995;5:13–32.

Duan JC, Gauthier G, Simonato JG, Zaanoun S. Estimating Merton's model by maximum likelihood with survivorship consideration, http://dx.doi.org/10.2139/ssrn.557088 (2004).

Duan JC, Simonato JG. Empirical martingale simulation for asset prices. Management Science 1998;44:1218–1233.

Duffie D. *Dynamic Asset Pricing Theory*. 3rd ed. Princeton, New Jersey: Princeton University Press; 2001.

Dupire B. Pricing with a smile. Risk 1994;7:18–20.

Durrett R. *Probability: Theory and Examples*. 2nd ed. Boston: Duxbury; 1996.

Embrechts P. Copulas: A personal view. Journal of Risk and Insurance 2009;76:639–650.

Engle R. Autoregressive conditional heteroscedasticity with estimates of the variance of United Kingdom inflation. Econometrica 1982;50:987–1007.

Eom YH, Helwege J, Huang JZ. Structural models of corporate bond pricing: An empirical analysis. Review of Financial Studies 2004;17:499–544.

Ericsson J, Reneby J. Estimating structural bond pricing models. The Journal of Business 2005;78:707–735.

Fang F, Oosterlee CW. A novel pricing method for European options based on Fourier-cosine series expansions. SIAM Journal on Scientific Computing 2008;31:826–848.

Forte S, Lovreta L. Endogenizing exogenous default barrier models: The MM algorithm. Journal of Banking and Finance 2012;36:1639–1652.

Glasserman P. *Monte Carlo Methods in Financial Engineering*. New York: Spring-Verlag; 2004.

Giles MB. Vibrato Monte Carlo sensitivities. Monte Carlo and Quasi-Monte Carlo methods 2008 Part 3:2009; 369–382.

Heath D, Jarrow R, Morton A. Bond pricing and the term structure of interest rates. Econometrica 1992;60:77–106.

Heston SL. A closed-form solution for options with stochastic volatility with applications to bond and currency options. The Review of Financial Studies 1993;6:327–343.

Ho T, Lee S. Term structure movements and pricing interest rate contingent claims. Journal of Finance 1986;41:1011–1029.

Hull J. *Options, Futures and Other Derivatives*. 6th ed. New Jersey: Pearson Education Press; 2006.

Hull J, White A. Pricing interest-rate derivative securities. The Review of Financial Studies 1990;3:573–592.

Hull J, White A. Numerical procedures for implementing term structure models I: Single-factor models. Journal of Derivatives 1994a;2:7–16.

Hull J, White A. Numerical procedures for implementing term structure models II: Multi-Factor models. Journal of Derivatives 1994b;2:37–48.

Hull J, White A. CVA and wrong way risk. *Working Paper*, Toronto, Canada: University of Toronto; 2012.

Hunter C, Jäckel P, Joshi M. Getting the drift. Risk 2001;14:81–84.

Jamshidian F. Libor and swap market model and measures. Finance and Stochastics 1997;1:293–330.

Jäckel P, Rebonato R. Linking caplet and swaption volatilities in a BGM/J framework: Approximate solutions and empirical evidence. Journal of Computational Finance 2003;6:41–59.

Jacod J, Protter P. *Discretization of Processes*, Heidelberg: Springer-Verlag; 2011.

Jarrow RA. *Financial Derivatives Pricing: Selected Works of Robert Jarrow*. Singapore: World Scientific Press; 2008.

Jarrow RA. The economics of credit default swaps (CDS). Johnson School Research Paper Series No. 31-2010. SSRN: http://ssrn.com/abstract=1646373 (2010).

Jarrow RA. Problems with using CDS to Infer default probabilities. Journal of Fixed Income 2012;21:6–12.

Jarrow RA, Turnbull SM. Pricing derivatives on financial securities subject to credit risk. Journal of Finance 1995;50:53–85.

Joe H. *Multivariate Models and Dependence Concepts*. New York: Chapman and Hall; 1997.

Jorion P. *Value-at-Risk: The New Benchmark for Managing Financial Risk*, The McGraw-Hill Companies; 2007.

Karatzas I, Shreve S. *Brownian Motion and Stochastic Calculus*. New York: Springer-Verlag; 1991.

Kloeden P, Platen E. *Numerical Solution of Stochastic Differential Equations*, 2nd Ed. New York: Springer-Verlag; 2010.

Kupiec P. Techniques for verifying the accuracy of risk management models. Journal of Derivatives 1995;3:73–84.

Li D. On default correlation: A copula function approach. Journal of Fixed Income 2000;9: 43–54.

Li KL, Wong HY. Structural models of corporate bond pricing with maximum likelihood estimation. Journal of Empirical Finance 2008;15:751–777.

Longstaff F, Schwartz ES. Valuing American options by simulation: A simple least-squares approach. Review of Financial Studies 2001;14:113–147.

Lord R, Koekkoek R, van Dijk D. A comparison of biased simulation schemes for stochastic volatility models. Tinbergen Institute Discussion Paper No. 06-04614. http://ssrn.com/abstract=903116 (2008).

McNeil AJ, Frey R, Embrechts P. *Quantitative Risk Management: Concepts, Techniques and Tools*. Princeton, New Jersey: Princeton University Press; 2005.

Merton R. On the pricing of corporate debt: The risk structure of interest rates. The Journal of Finance 1974;29:449–470.

Merton R. Option pricing when underlying stock returns are discontinuous. Journal of Financial Economics 1976;3:125–144.

Mikosch T. *Elementary Stochastic Calculus with Finance in View*. Singapore: World Scientific Press; 1998.

Milstein GN. *Numerical Integration of Stochastic Differential Equations*. Dordrecht: Kluwer; 1995.

Moreno M, Navas JF. On the robustness of least-squares Monte Carlo (LSM) for pricing American derivatives. Review of Derivatives Research 2003;6:107–128.

Needleman PD, Roff TA. Asset shares and their use in the financial management of a with-profits fund. British Actuarial Journal 1995;1:603–688.

Oksendal B. *Stochastic Differential Equations: An Introduction with Applications*, 6th Edition. Berlin: Springer; 2003.

Press WH, Flannery BP, Teukolsky SA, Vetterling WT. *Numerical Recipes: The Art of Scientific Computing*. 3rd ed. New York: Cambridge University Press; 2007.

Rudin W. *Real and Complex Analysis*. 3rd ed. New York: McGraw-Hill; 1987.

Stentoft L. Assessing the least squares Monte-Carlo approach to American option valuation. Review of Derivatives Research 2004;7:129–168.

Shreve S. *Stochastic Calculus for Finance I: The Binomial Asset Pricing Model*. New York: Springer Finance; 2004.

Vasicek O. An equilibrium characterization of the term structure. Journal of Financial Economics 1977;5:177–188.

Vasicek O. Probability of loss on loan portfolio, KMV Corporation (1987).

Vasicek O. Limiting loan loss distribution, KMV Corporation (1991).

Vasicek O. Loan portfolio value. Risk 2002;15:160–162.

Vasicek O, Fong HF. Term structure modeling using exponential splines. The Journal of Finance 1982;37:339–348.

Vollrath I, Wendland J. Calibration of interest rate and option models using differential evolution, SSRN: http://ssrn.com/abstract=1367502 (2009).

Wong HY, Choi TW. Estimating default barriers from market information. Quantitative Finance 2009;9:187–196.

Zhu S, Pykhtin M. A guide to modeling counter-party credit risk. GARP Risk Review, June–July (2007).

Author Index

Abid, 273, 401
Andersen, 144, 145, 401
Artzner, 332, 401
Asmussen, 328, 401

Bjork, 34, 401
Black, 33, 41, 256, 259, 401
Bollerslev, 161, 401
Bonnans, 230, 401
Brace, 221, 401
Brigo, 299, 401

Carr, 136, 401
Chan, 34, 55, 156, 402
Choi, 259, 404
Cox, 259, 401

Delbaen, 332, 401
Derman, 126, 402
Dijkvan Dijk, 403
Duan, 87, 161, 258, 402
Duffie, 278, 402
Dupire, 123, 402
Durrett, 48, 402

Eber, 332, 401
Embrechts, 256, 332, 402, 403
Engle, 34, 402
Eom, 260, 402
Ericsson, 260, 402

Fang, 140, 402
Flannery, 229, 404
Fong, 187, 404
Forte, 259, 260, 402
Frey, 332, 403

Gatarek, 221, 401
Gauthier, 258, 402
Gilbert, 230, 401
Giles, 376, 402
Glasserman, 355, 402
Glynn, 328, 401

Heath, 219, 332, 401, 402
Helwege, 260, 402
Heston, 136, 402
Ho, 195, 402
Huang, 260, 402

Handbook of Financial Risk Management: Simulations and Case Studies, First Edition. N.H. Chan and H.Y. Wong.
© 2013 John Wiley & Sons, Inc. Published 2013 by John Wiley & Sons, Inc.

Hull, 195, 209, 212, 402, 403
Hunter, 242, 403

Jäckel, 240, 242, 403
Jacod, 43, 403
Jamshidian, 219, 403
Jarrow, 219, 260, 278, 402, 403
Joe, 273, 403
Jorion, 305, 336, 341, 403
Joshi, 242, 403

Kani, 126, 402
Karatzas, 34, 403
Kloeden, 43, 403
Koekkoek, 144, 403
Kupiec, 341, 403

Lee, 195, 402
Lemarechal, 230, 401
Li, 256, 260, 403
Longstaff, 80, 372, 403
Lord, 144, 403
Lovreta, 259, 260, 402

Madan, 136, 401
McNeil, 332, 403
Mercurio, 299, 401
Merton, 166, 255, 256, 403
Mikosch, 34, 404
Milstein, 43, 404
Moreno, 80, 404
Morton, 219, 402
Musiela, 221, 401

Naifar, 273, 401
Navas, 80, 404
Needleman, 106, 404

Oksendal, 48, 404
Oosterlee, 140, 402

Platen, 43, 403
Press, 229, 404
Protter, 43, 403
Pykhtin, 286

Rebonato, 240, 403
Reneby, 260, 402
Roff, 106, 404
Rudin, 48, 404

Sagastizabal, 230, 401
Scholes, 33, 41, 256, 401
Schwartz, 80, 372, 403
Shreve, 34, 403, 404
Simonato, 87, 258, 402
Stentoft, 80, 404

Teukolsky, 229, 404
Turnbull, 278, 403

van Dijk, 144
Vasicek, 187, 195, 256, 404
Vetterling, 229, 404
Vollrath, 139, 240, 404

Wendland, 139, 240, 404
White, 195, 209, 212, 402, 403
Wong, 34, 55, 259, 260, 402–404

Zaanoun, 258, 402
Zhu, 286

Subject Index

Absolute VaR, 304
American option, 79
Antithetic variables, 56
Arrays and matrices, 13
   dynamic array, 13
   multidimensional array, 13
   one-dimensional array, 13
   two-dimensional array, 13
Arrow-Debreu price, 132
Asset path simulation functions, 30
At-the-money (ATM) straddle, 152

Back-testing, 339
Basket default swap, 280
Bayesian framework, 171
   Bayes' Theorem, 172
   conjugate prior, 171
   Gibbs sampling, 173
   posterior, 171
Bermudan swaption, 249, 372
   co-terminal Bermudan swaption, 250
   fixed-maturity Bermudan swaption, 250
BGM model, 221

Binomial tree, 348
Black formula, 201
Black forward rate volatility, 223
Black-Scholes equation, 43
Black-Scholes formula, 48
Black swap rate volatility, 225
Bootstrapping, 321
Brownian motion, 36
   exponential martingale, 36
   Markov property, 36
   martingale property, 36
   multidimensional Brownian motion, 38
   quadratic variation, 36

Calibration, 55
Call period, 289
Callable equity-linked note, 163
Caplet, 222
Cholesky decomposition, 109, 144, 146, 380
CIR process, 41
Clamped cubic spline, 180
Clean price, 183

Coherent risk measure, 332
  component VaR, 336
  conditional value-at-risk (CVaR), 333
  incremental VaR, 336
  marginal VaR, 336
  monotonicity, 332
  positive homogeneity, 332
  sub-additivity, 332
  translation invariance, 333
Collateralized debt obligation (CDO), 266
  lower attachment point, 266
  upper attachment point, 266
Collateralized exposure, 289
Component VaR, 336
Conditional statements, 14
  if-then-else statement, 14
    multi-lined form, 14
    single-lined form, 14
  select-case statement, 15
Conditional value-at-risk (CVaR), 333
Const statement, 10
Contract-level exposure, 287
Control variates, 58
Copula, 273
  t-copula, 276
  dependence structure, 273
  Gaussian copula, 274
  marginal behavior, 273
  Sklar's theorem, 273
Counterparty credit risk, 286
Counterparty-level exposure, 288
  call period, 289
  collaterallized exposure, 289
  contract-level exposure, 287
  cure period, 289
  default unwind date, 289
  margin agreement, 289
  margin period of risk, 289
  netting agreement, 288
  non-collaterallized exposure, 289
Credit derivatives
  basket default swap, 280
  collateralized debt obligation (CDO), 266
  default correlation, 261
  first-to-default swap, 280
  Merton model, 256
  Vasicek single-factor model, 260

Credit value adjustment (CVA), 290
  right-way risk, 298
  sensitivity to credit spreads, 292
  sensitivity to underlying market variables, 292
  term structure of credit spreads, 291
  unconditional risk-neutral probability of default, 291
  wrong-way risk, 298
Cubic spline discount function, 185
Cubic spline interpolation, 179
Cure period, 289
Currency-translated options, 116

Dampened Fourier transform, 136
Data input and output, 14
Declaration of Constants, 10
Declaration of Variables, 8
  date data type, 9
  numeric data type, 9
    Boolean, 9
    byte, 9
    decimal, 9
    double, 9
    integer, 9
    long, 9
    single, 9
  string data type, 9
  variant data type, 9
    empty, 9
    error code, 9
    null, 9
Default correlation, 261
Default leg, 280
Default unwind date, 289
Delta hedging, 345
Delta–gamma approximation, 317
Delta-normal approximation, 314
Differential evolution (DE), 139
Digital call option, 374
Dirty price, 183
Discontinuous payoffs, 374
Discounted loss, 290
Downhill Simplex, 139

Early redemption request, 94
Empirical martingale correction, 149
Empirical martingale simulation (EMS), 87

SUBJECT INDEX   409

Equity linked note (ELN), 72
Euler discretization, 361
Euler scheme, 42, 144
Exposure at default, 262
Extended Vasicek model, 195

Factor sensitivity, 261
Fast Fourier transform, 137
Filtration switching formula, 299
Finite difference approximation, 350
    central difference estimator, 352
    central difference scheme, 351
    forward difference estimator, 351
    forward difference scheme, 351
First passage time, 259
First-to-default swap, 280
Floorlet, 222, 224
Fokker-Plank equation, 124
Forward measure, 241
Forward rate, 192
Forward rate curve, 192
Forward swap rate, 225
Fourier inversion operator, 137
Function procedure, 19
FX accumulator, 95
    CITIC Pacific Limited, 95
    sensitivity analysis, 103
    valuation, 97
    with target redemption, 100
    with target redemption and barrier rate, 101
    without knock-out feature, 99

Gamma neutral, 345
GARCH option pricing model, 156
    bumping, 162
    estimation, 157
    generalized autoregressive conditional, heteroskedastic (GARCH), 156
    Ljung-Box test, 159
    locally risk-neutral valuation relationship (LRNVR), 161
    long-run average variance, 157
    maximum likelihood estimation (MLE), 157
    mean reversion level, 157
    risk-neutral process, 161
    standardized residuals, 159
    stationarity, 157
    variance targeting, 159
    volatility clustering, 157
Gaussian copula, 274
Generalized error distribution, 307
Geometric Brownian motion (GBM), 73
Girsanov's theorem, 48
Greeks
    binomial tree, 348
    closed-form solutions, 346
    delta, 343
    delta hedging, 345
    discontinuous payoffs, 374
    finite difference approximation, 350
    gamma, 344
    gamma neutral, 345
    Greeks of a portfolio, 344
    likelihood ratio method, 355
    lption elasticity, 345
    pathwise derivative estimates, 360
    psi, 345
    rho, 344
    speed, 345
    theta, 344
    vanna, 345
    Vega, 344
    Vomma, 345

Hazard rate, 279
Heston model, 136
    calibration, 139
    correlation between the stock and variance, 141
    implementation, 138
    initial variance, 141
    long-term average variance, 141
    mean-reverting speed, 141
    parameter bounds, 141
    parameter constraint, 141
    quadratic-exponential discretization scheme, 143
    volatility of variance, 141
Historical simulation, 319
Historical volatility, 51
Holding period adjustment, 312
Hull and White's formula, 226
Hull–White model, 194
    calibration, 197
    mean-reverting speed, 195
    volatility, 195

Implied binomial tree, 130
Implied volatility, 51
Importance sampling, 65
Incremental VaR, 336
Intensity process, 279
Interest rate range accrual note, 207
Interest rate swap, 224
inverse Fourier transform, 137, 166
Itô's process, 39
   discretization methods, 41
      Euler scheme, 42
      Milstein scheme, 42
   Ito's lemma, 40
   SDE, 39
   stochastic differential equation, 39

Jump-diffusion model
   Bayesian framework, 171
   Gibbs sampling, 173
   simulation, 167

Kolmogorov equation, 124

Levenberg-Marquardt, 139
LIBOR market model, 219
   Black forward rate volatility, 223
   Black swap rate volatility, 225
   caplet, 222
   floorlet, 222
   forward measure, 241
   Hull and White's formula, 226
   predictor-corrector method, 242
   Rebonato's formula, 226
Life insurance contract, 105
   bonus payment, 106
   expected future life, 107
   linear smoothing scheme, 106
   mortality table, 107
   reserve, 106
   smoothing mechanism, 106
Likelihood ratio method, 355
   likelihood ratio method estimator, 356
   score, 356
   score function, 356
Ljung-Box test, 159
Local volatility model, 122
   estimation, 123
   implied binomial tree, 130
   simulation, 123

Loops, 16
   Do loop, 16
      Do Until loop, 17
      Do While loop, 17
   For-Next loop, 16
Loss given default, 262
Lower attachment point, 266

Malliavin calculus, 374
Margin agreement, 289
Margin period of risk, 289
Marginal VaR, 336
Mark to market (MTM), 53
Martingale, 34
   continuous martingale, 35
   discrete martingale, 35
Memoryless property, 168
Merton model, 256
   probability of default, 257
Milstein scheme, 42
Moody's KMV, 258
Multi-asset instruments, 108
   Cholesky decomposition, 109
   multi-asset range accrual equity linked note, 112
   multidimensional geometric Brownian motion, 108
   multivariate normal random vector, 109
Multi-asset range accrual equity linked note, 112
Multivariable declaration, 10
Multidimensional geometric Brownian motion, 108
Multiple linear regression, 23

Natural cubic spline, 180
Nelson-Siegel model, 182
Netting agreement, 288
Non-collateralized exposure, 289

Operators, 11
   assignment operators, 11
      equal sign, 11
   comparative operators, 11
      equal to, 11
      greater than, 11
      greater than or equal to, 11
      less than, 11
      less than or equal to, 11
      not equal to, 11

Logical operators, 11
  And, 11
  Eqv, 11
  Imp, 11
  Not, 11
  Or, 11
  Xor, 11
Mathematical operators, 11
  addition, 11
  division, 11
  exponentiation, 11
  multiplication, 11
  subtraction, 11
Option elasticity, 345
Outstanding notional amount, 267
Over-the-counter OTC, 89

Parametric VaR, 305
  heavy-tailed distribution, 307
    t-distribution, 311
    generalized error distribution, 307
  holding period adjustment, 312
  multiple assets, 306
  normal VaR, 305
Pathwise derivative estimates, 360
Payer swaption, 225
Portfolio loss distribution, 261
Portfolio Replication, 72
Predictor-corrector method, 242
Premium leg, 280
Probability of default, 257
Proxy approach, 260
Pseudo-random, 25

Random number generation, 25
  acceptance-rejection method, 26
  Box-Muller transform, 27
  inverse transform, 25
  randomize, 25
  rnd, 25
Range accrual note (RAN), 89
  European, 89
Rebonato's formula, 226
Receiver swaption, 225
Regression spline, 192
Relative VaR, 304

Right-way risk, 298
Risk measure, 304
Risk-neutral probability, 35
Risk-neutral valuation, 258
Risk reversal (RR), 152

Short rate, 195
Sklar's theorem, 273
Stratified sampling, 61
Sub procedure, 19
Survival function, 279
Swap market model, 219
Swaption formula, 224

t-copula, 276
t-distribution, 311
Target redemption note, 206
Term structure of credit spreads, 291
Tranche, 266
Tranche premium, 267

UDTs, 28
Unconditional risk-neutral probability of default, 291
Upper attachment point, 266
User-defined data types, 11

Value at Risk, VaR, 54, 304
  absolute VaR, 304
  bootstrapping, 321
  historical simulation, 319
  Monte Carlo simulation, 323
  parametric VaR, 305
  percentile, 304
  quantile, 304
  relative VaR, 304
  risk measure, 304
Value-at-Risk
  Gibbs sampling, 327
Variance reduction techniques, 55
  antithetic variables, 56
  control variates, 58
  importance sampling, 65
  stratified sampling, 61
Vasicek, 260
Vasicek single-factor model, 260
  exposure at default, 262
  factor sensitivity, 261
  loss given default, 262
  portfolio loss distribution, 261

VBA, 1
VBA Built-in Functions, 22
  Abs, 23
  Atn, 23
  Cos, 23
  Exp, 23
  Int, 23
  Log, 23
  MInverse, 25
  MMult, 25
  Sgn, 23
  Sin, 23
  Sqr, 23
  Tan, 23
  Transpose, 25
  UBound, 25
  Round, 23
VBA
  command button, 5
  comment, 5
  macro, 2
  macro recorder, 3
  module, 2
  project, 2
Visual Basic Editor, 2
Visual Basic for Application, 1

Vega-weighted butterfly, 152
Vibrato Monte Carlo simulation, 376
Volatility, 50
Volatility clustering, 53
Volatility smile, 52
Volatility surface, 52
Volatility
  historical volatility, 51
  implied volatility, 51
  volatility clustering, 53
  volatility smile, 52
  volatility surface, 52

Wrong-way risk, 298

Yield curve, 179
  clamped cubic spline, 180
  clean price, 183
  cubic spline discount function, 185
  cubic spline interpolation, 179
  dirty price, 183
  natural cubic spline, 180
  Nelson-Siegel model, 182
  zero rate, 179

Zero rate, 179

Wiley Handbooks in
FINANCIAL ENGINEERING AND ECONOMETRICS

Advisory Editor
Ruey S. Tsay
The University of Chicago Booth School of Business, USA

The dynamic and interaction between financial markets around the world have changed dramatically under economic globalization. In addition, advances in communication and data collection have changed the way information is processed and used. In this new era, financial instruments have become increasingly sophisticated and their impacts are far-reaching. The recent financial (credit) crisis is a vivid example of the new challenges we face and continue to face in this information age. Analytical skills and ability to extract useful information from mass data, to comprehend the complexity of financial instruments, and to assess the financial risk involved become a necessity for economists, financial managers, and risk management professionals. To master such skills and ability, knowledge from computer science, economics, finance, mathematics and statistics is essential. As such, financial engineering is cross-disciplinary, and its theory and applications advance rapidly.

The goal of this Handbook Series is to provide a one-stop source for students, researchers, and practitioners to learn the knowledge and analytical skills they need to face today's challenges in financial markets. The Series intends to introduce systematically recent developments in different areas of financial engineering and econometrics. The coverage will be broad and thorough with balance in theory and applications. Each volume will be edited by leading researchers and practitioners in the area and covers state-of-the-art methods and theory of the selected topic.

Published Wiley Handbooks in Financial Engineering and Econometrics

Bauwens, Hafner, and Laurent · *Handbook of Volatility Models and Their Applications*
Chan and Wong · *Handbook of Financial Risk Management: Simulations and Case Studies*
James, Marsh, and Sarno · *Handbook of Exchange Rates*
Viens, Mariani, and Florescu · *Handbook of Modeling High-Frequency Data in Finance*

Forthcoming Wiley Handbooks in Financial Engineering and Econometrics

Bali and Engle · *Handbook of Asset Pricing*
Brandimarte · *Handbook of Monte Carlo Simulation*
Chacko · *Handbook of Credit and Interest Rate Derivatives*
Cruz, Peters, and Shevchenko · *Handbook of Operational Risk*

Florescu, Mariani, Stanley, and Viens · *Handbook of High-Frequency Trading and Modeling in Finance*

Jacquier · *Handbook of Econometric Methods for Finance: Bayesian and Classical Perspecitves*

Szylar · *Handbook of Market Risk*